SF: THE JAPANESE SCIENCE FICTION FILM ENCYCLOPEDIA

日本のSF映画百科事典

by J.L. Carrozza

C000102990

Additional articles by Patrick Galvan, Kevin Derendorf, John LeMay and Tyler E. Martin

SPECIAL THANKS

Keith Aiken   Sean Barry   Kiefer Beelman   Simon Broad   Kyle Byrd   Michael Callari
Nancy Carrozza   Jim Cironella   Ryan Clark   Francois Coloumbe   Kevin Derendorf   Norman England
Warwick Paul Evans   Ian Friedman   Stuart Galbraith IV   Patrick Galvan   Camilo Garcia   Ed Godziszewski
Cody Himes   Edward Holland   Brett Homenick   Ted Johnson   David Kalat   Matti Keskiivari
Nathaniel Knight   John LeMay   Robert Lindsey   Scott David Lister   Patrick Macias   Andrew Mallard
Tyler E. Martin   Tom Mes   David Milner   Chris Morrill   Justin Mullis   Sydney Perkins
Richard Pusateri   Kevin Pyrtle   Michael Quade   August Ragone   Anthony Romero   Steve Ryfle
Paulie Senkowsky   Takao Yoshiba

DEDICATED TO

Nick Adams (1931-1968)   Eiji Tsuburaya (1901-1970)   Hajime Tsuburaya (1931-1973)
Motoyoshi Oda (1910-1973)   Ikio Sawamura (1905-1975)   Tetsuo Kinjo (1938-1976)
Hiroshi Inagaki (1905-1980)   Teizo Toshimitsu (1909-1982)   Takashi Shimura (1905-1982
Ryosaku Takayama (1917-1982)   Shin Kishida (1939-1982)   Akihiko Hirata (1927-1984)
Jun Tazaki (1913-1985)   Takeshi Kimura (1912-1987)   Eitaro Ozawa (1909-1988)
Shinichi Sekizawa (1920-1992)   Ishiro Honda (1911-1993)   Raymond Burr (1917-1993)
Takeo Murata (1910-1994)   Hajime Sato (1929-1995)   Noboru Tsuburaya (1935-1995)
Taro Okamoto (1911-1996)   Frankie Sakai (1929-1996)   Toru Kawai (died 1996)
Ko Nishimura (1923-1997)   Toshio Mifune (1920-1997)   Tomoyuki Tanaka (1910-1997)
Sachio Sakai (1925-1998)   Shotaro Ishinomori (1938-1998)   Akira Kurosawa (1910-1998)
Momoko Kochi (1932-1998)   Akira Watanabe (1908-1999)   Masaru Sato (1928-1999)
Masao Fukazawa (1921-2000)   Jun Fukuda (1923-2000)   Toru Narita (1929-2002)
Kinji Fukasaku (1930-2003)   Hideyo Amamoto (1926-2003)   Noriaki Yuasa (1933-2004)
Soji Ushio (1921-2004)   Tatsuya Mihashi (1923-2004)   Kihachi Okamoto (1924-2005)
Sadamasa Arikawa (1925-2005)   Hisaya Ito (1924-2005)   Koji Hashimoto (1936-2005)
Yu Fujiki (1931-2005)   Akira Ifukube (1914-2006)   Tetsuro Tanba (1922-2006)
Akio Jissoji (1931-2006)   Guy Mariner Tucker (died 2006)   Senkichi Taniguchi (1912-2007)
Tokimaro Karasawa (1935-2007)   Koichi Takano (1935-2008)   Fumio Tanaka (1941-2009)
Tadao Nakamaru (1933-2009)   Yoshifumi Tajima (1918-2009)   Shue Matsubayashi (1920-2009)
Keiju Kobayashi (1923-2010)   Ryo Ikebe (1918-2010)   Sakyo Komatsu (1931-2011)
Mototaka Tomioka (1924-2011)   Yasuyuki Inoue (1922-2012)   Emi Ito (1941-2012)
Susumu Ishikawa (1933-2012)   Yonesaburo Tsukiji (1923-2012)   Kojiro Hongo (1938-2013)
Goro Naya (1929-2013)   Teruo Aragaki (1937-2014)   Anna Nakagawa (1965-2014)
William Ross (1923-2014)   Koichi Kawakita (1942-2014)   Riichiro Manabe (1924-2015)
Hiroshi Koizumi (1926-2015)   Niisan Takahashi (1926-2015)   Noriyoshi Ohrai (1935-2015)
Yoshiyuki Kuroda (1928-2015)   Yumi Ito (1941-2016)   Yumi Shirakawa (1931-2016)
Kensho Yamashita (1944-2016)   Yoshio Tsuchiya (1927-2017)   Yoshimitsu Banno (1931-2017)
Haruo Nakajima (1929-2017)   Riki Hashimoto (1933-2017)   Yosuke Natsuki (1936-2018)
Yuriko Hoshi (1943-2018)   Ren Osugi (1951-2018)   Tadao Takashima (1931-2019)
Nobuo Yajima (1928-2019)   Shozo Uehara (1937-2020)   Nobuhiko Obayashi (1938-2020)
Eizo Kaimai (1929-2020)   Shigeo Kato (1925-2020)   Ted Newsom (1952-2020)
Haruma Miura (1990-2020)   Ben Goto (1929-2020)   Tsugunobu Kotani (1935-2020)
Kunie Tanaka (1932-2021)   Minoru Nakano (1931-2021)

INTRODUCTION

序論

"We the Japanese are in a better position than people of any other nation to make a film such as this."
-The Last War (1961), English Export Trailer

SF is a loaned term used in Japanese advertising. Short for "science fiction", it categorizes films, novels and animated works with sci-fi elements. In **SF**, you will learn about Japan's science fiction film tradition and history from *Godzilla* to *Space Battleship Yamato*. This book contains in-depth analyses for dozens of Japanese sci-fi films along with articles providing background information. It should appeal to both casual fans looking to learn more and obsessed initiates alike.

There's a phrase often said in Japan: *shoganai*, translating to "Can't be helped". The word is quintessential to understanding the collective attitude of the Japanese. It exemplifies a mindset that to Americans seems almost fatalistic.

Japan is a small, rocky archipelago without much tenable farmland. It was settled in prehistory by shipwrecked mainland Asians who fought and then interbred with an indigenous people called the Ainu. Pummeled by earthquakes and typhoons, it contains over tenfold the volcanoes of Hawaii. The Japanese people are survivors, living through one disaster and misfortune after another. In the first half of the 20th century, the Japanese survived cataclysmic earthquakes including the great Kanto quake of 1923 and saw their colonialist ambitions punished with a devastating loss in World War II. Japan became the first and to date only country to have nuclear weapons used against it. The Japanese were then forced to renounce their Imperial pride and occupied by the United States. Today, post-war Japan neighbors former adversaries like China, Korea and Russia. Stripped of their military might after the Pacific War, the Japanese are still dependent on their former American occupiers for protection.

This is where *shoganai* comes in. It is the collective acceptance that sometimes disaster and misfortune befall and nothing can be done but make the best of it. This can be seen in Japan's reverence to its Shinto roots. In Shinto, everyone and everything is part of a natural order that isn't always fortuitous to humans. This mindset is also informed by Zen Buddhism, which teaches one to accept the circumstance of the present moment without judgement. Americans, by contrast, are taught that they are the heroes of their own narrative and should always fight for a more favorable outcome. This is one of the main marked differences between East and West and Japan and the U.S.

This attitude of *shoganai* is nowhere more prevalent than in Japanese science fiction. Before World War II, science fiction was rare in Japan and seen as a children's genre.

There were a handful of pictures with slight science fiction elements made pre-war. Few survive as much of Japan's pre-war cinematic history was destroyed by the war to come. Post-war, influenced by novels and films brought in by American occupiers, science fiction became popular with *manga* works by Osamu Tezuka. One of Japan's first notable science fiction films is its most famous: 1954's *Godzilla*. Made shortly after the occupation's end and playing on Japan's post-war traumas, this influential film from Toho would kick off a boom in special effects driven science fiction features. In the coming decades, Japan's silver screen was clobbered by every form of assailant in its sci-fi works. These films would play out one apocalyptic scenario after another. They included sundry pantomime monsters, alien invasions, nuclear war, viral pandemics and even the sinking of the entire country beneath the waves. These sci-fi disasters are treated with a sense of fatalistic awe. Military might, exalted by Hollywood films, is depicted with futility in Japanese science fiction. Cinematic catastrophes like Godzilla humble its audience, reminding them that they are a part of the natural order and humanity's hubris brings on tragedy. Or, as Blue Oyster Cult would say, *"History shows again and again how nature points out the folly of man"*. In feudal Japan, many chalked up the frequent natural disasters to monster Shinto gods that brought about cataclysm and "world renewal" or *yonaoshi*. *Kaiju* are but the modern, cinematic descendants of the old Shinto *yonaoshi* gods.

The 21st century has brought little respite for the Japanese. On March 11, 2011, Japan would be hit by a magnitude 9.1 'quake that triggered near-apocalyptic destruction. This would include the Fukushima Daiichi nuclear plant disaster, the worst since Chernobyl. As a result, Japan's latest Godzilla incarnation, *Shin Godzilla*, shifted its focus from the zeitgeist of the original to the 3/11 earthquake, updating the mythology for a modern era. The country has now exited the *Heisei* period and entered the *Reiwa* era with the unprecedented abdication of Emperor Akihito. Japan comes into this period faced with another cataclysm: the COVID-19 coronavirus pandemic which originated in nearby Wuhan, China. Like Godzilla, though science may halt its rampage, COVID-19 will remind the Japanese and humanity alike that they aren't above the natural order. Japanese science fiction does offer hope, however, in the form of its science. Science's double-edged sword causes these tragedies and yet often poses the solution. In both *Godzilla* and *Shin Godzilla*, science saves the day as Godzilla is defeated by a chemical compound.

Now is a better time than ever to revisit a selection spanning over six decades of the best and most important films from Ishiro Honda and Eiji Tsuburaya to Hideaki Anno and Shinji Higuchi. This is the history of a distinctive genre. A genre long maligned and misunderstood by Western critics and moviegoers alike. The average American sees Japanese science fiction as "campy" with poor scripts, special effects and acting. There is far deeper subtext in many of these films than meets the eye. They are also filled with some of Japan's greatest actors and actresses. Many also worked for esteemed filmmakers like Akira Kurosawa, Yasujiro Ozu, Mikio Naruse and Masaki Kobayashi. Additionally, *tokusatsu*, the traditional art of Japanese cinematic special effects. is misinterpreted by those used to the Western aesthetic. In Hollywood, special effects are designed to be as photo-realistic as can be achieved. In Japan, they have a little more fun. *Tokusatsu* is a pantomime art form with roots in the colorful fakery of *kabuki* stage dramas and *bunraku* puppetry. This has even caused creative conflicts when Hollywood and Japanese film crews worked together. Everything you see, often smashed or blown up, is crafted with love and care. The men and women who build these miniatures and monster suits are true artisans. They are like modern day samurai sword makers or Renaissance sculptors. These films have even predicted the future in haunting ways. The apocalyptic images from 1973's *Submersion of Japan* and its 2006 remake could almost be mistaken for news footage from the March 11th tsunami. There's a scene in 1974's *Prophecies of Nostradamus* where the Fukushima planet explodes during an earthquake. The early act in *Virus* showing the film's pandemic emerging in Europe as "the Italian flu" is beyond unsettling now. The Japanese are a people who have had a better taste of the apocalypse than nearly any other. Today, perhaps their warnings are worth heeding.

Despite Hollywood's general ambivalence toward these films, there are some notable champions. Tim Burton is a huge *kaiju* film fan. He put an entire Godzilla sequence in his debut *Pee Wee's Big Adventure* and there's a Gamera-style turtle monster in 2012's *Frankenweenie*. He has visited the sets in Japan several times, including on *Godzilla vs. Mothra* (1992). Quentin Tarantino also adores these films, putting multiple nods to them in *Kill Bill*. The film even uses miniatures built by Toshio Miike, left over from the-then newest Godzilla

entries. At his New Beverly Cinema, he has shown prints of his favorite kaiju films many times. Guillermo Del Toro is also a lover of the *tokusatsu* genre. His *Pacific Rim* (2013) was a full-on big budget homage, even calling its monsters *kaiju*. George Lucas is said to be a fan and you can see influence in the mechanical designs of *Star Wars*. Even Martin Scorsese, beloved by film critics, was gleeful to meet Ishiro Honda on the set of Kurosawa's *Dreams*. *South Park*'s Trey Parker is yet another high profile fan, with his dream project called *Giant Monsters Attack Japan*. Other notable fans include actor Nicolas Cage, *Halloween*'s John Carpenter, *Phantasm*'s Don Coscarelli, *Nekromantic*'s Jörg Buttgereit, *Repo Man*'s Alex Cox, *Gremlins*' Joe Dante and musicians like Gene Simmons and Glenn Danzig.

I've long held a fascination with these movies since my parents brought home a rented VHS copy of *Godzilla: King of the Monsters!* As I watched its monochrome visuals flicker on the screen, I was transfixed by the images of Godzilla's victims, maimed and radiation burned, on futons. To my five year old mind, it left an early impression that the world isn't always a merciful place. I will be dissecting these films in comprehensive detail and also writing from a filmmaker's perspective, analyzing the cinematic technique from superficial to complex. My hope is that you, the reader, enjoy reading about and watching these films as much as I enjoyed sharing my decades long passion for them.

NOTE: *This book covers only live action and theatrically released Japanese science fiction films. I considered including a handful of animated films but sci-fi anime is such a* distinctive medium in of itself that it requires its own volume to do justice. Special effects television shows are also excluded. This is because there is such an immense variety of them that they would also need a volume of their own to properly analyze and document. Lastly, the alternate versions analyzed are mainly Anglophone focused as this book's audience is English speaking and covering every single foreign language version is too great a task.

Another thing worth noting is that this book covers a select few of what I consider to be the most notable Japanese science fiction films. Others are attached to the main entries as supplemental capsule reviews. This book would have taken much, much longer to write if every single Japanese science fiction film was covered in-depth so a selective approach had to be used.

SHOWA

昭和

December 25th, 1926 to January 7th, 1989

The *Showa* period is possibly the most eventful in Japan's long history. It started with the rise of militarism, then continued through conquest, war and historic defeat. Afterwards, a reconstruction effort by the U.S. paved the way for a decades-long postwar economic miracle. *Showa* began with the ascension of Hirohito to the Chrysanthemum Throne. This was after the death of Yoshihito, his sickly and politically ineffectual father, at only 47. Yoshihito's death ended the *Taisho* era and with it democratic ideals that were popping up as Japan continued to modernize. During Hirohito's reign, a form of fascist militarism gained immense political power in Japan. This led to a colonialistic military strategy. Northern Manchuria was soon annexed and Japan subsequently invaded mainland China and much of Asia. With worldwide conflict brewing, Japan chose the side of Adolf Hitler's Axis. Desiring Hawaii as part of their empire, the Japanese made the mistake of provoking America at Pearl Harbor, drawing the U.S. into World War II. At the Battle of Midway, Japan's Imperial pride suffered an historic defeat. As the years went on, the situation on the Pacific Theater's front became increasingly dire for Japan. The Japanese saw a horrific loss at the Stalingrad of the Pacific: Okinawa. Okinawa made the Empire's brass and likely Hirohito himself realize the war was unwinnable. It also made American military high ups rethink their planned "Operation Downfall". That was to have been a full-scale invasion of the Japanese mainland. America, fearing Soviet intervention, now chose to act fast. It decisively ended the war with a terrifying new weapon: the atomic bomb. After the wholesale nuclear destruction of Hiroshima and Nagasaki, Hirohito opted to surrender to save his people from further destruction.

The immediate post-war years were chaotic and humbling for many Japanese, but the U.S. helped Japan rebuild its economy. By the Korean War, Japan became an American tributary state of sorts. It provided the U.S. with a useful economic and military hub in mostly communist Asia. After the Occupation, Japan began to prosper in the 1950s and '60s. When Tokyo hosted the 1964 Olympics, many Japanese felt like the post-war economic miracle was here to stay. The winds of the Cold War, however, became icier as the years went on. Nearby China tested a nuclear weapon right as the Olympics were being held in Japan. Vietnam was soon invaded by the United States. Japan, a small archipelago with many urban centers and military targets, had much to lose from all-out nuclear war. Having been the only country to have survived nuclear warfare, Japan now led the world in advocating for peace. The 1970s oil shocks especially hurt Japan's economy as the country's petroleum supplies are entirely imported. However, like the U.S., Japan became an economic powerhouse in the 1980s. The Japanese even resumed economic ties with post-Cultural Revolution China. Hirohito finally died in January of 1989 and was succeeded by his son Akihito, ushering in the *Heisei* era.

EIJI TSUBURAYA
The Wizard

円谷英二

7/10/1901-1/25/1970

"He has a firm grasp of special effects: the cameras, the film...He could bring out the best in everything. He was always investigating means of expression only possible in film..."
-Ishiro Honda, *Toho Special Effects Outtake Collection* (1986)

The father of Japanese special effects, Eiji Tsuburaya is a figure of innumerable influence in popular culture. A Renaissance Man of sorts, he was a visionary akin to Walt Disney. Like Disney, his legacy is vast and enduring. Tsuburaya was integral to the creation of Japan's two most iconic pop properties: Godzilla and Ultraman. Over the course of his half century career, he refined Japanese special effects into an artisanal technique like Japan's sword making or the sculpture of the Italian Renaissance. Tsuburaya was well versed in the science of his work as well. The special effects director

often composed detailed mathematical calculations to help him execute his sequences. Yet Tsuburaya was also story conscious and allowed the directors he worked with to edit out any special effects scenes that didn't serve the narrative.

He was born Eiichi Tsuburaya in 1901. His mother passed away when he was only three, so he was mainly raised by his grandmother and young uncle Ichiro. As a boy, he excelled in school and became interested in aviation. He would often build model planes out of wood and was considered a child prodigy of sorts. In 1911, he had his first cinematic experience, seeing documentary footage of a volcanic eruption. This spurred a love of the moving picture for the young Tsuburaya. He was especially fascinated by the technical aspect of it. This fascination inspired him to try and build his own film projector.

After graduating primary school, his interest in aviation blossomed. He enrolled in the Nippon Flying School under Seitaro Taimai. Taimai died in a plane crash a few years later. The school closed and Tsuburaya was accepted into the Tokyo Engineering School. While studying and working for a toy manufacturer, by chance he was approached by Yoshiro Edamasa, a film director. Edamasa offered him the position as a cameraman. The 18 year old Tsuburaya relished the opportunity. His early film career was interrupted by conscription into the military but Tsuburaya was honorably discharged after six months. He returned to Tokyo after the great Kanto earthquake and worked at the silent era studio Kokukatsu. In 1926, he was recruited by cinematographer Kohei Sugiyama to assist him on shooting Teinosuke Kinugasa's *A Page of Madness* (1926). An early silent masterpiece, the film's haunting and atmospheric images are no doubt Tsuburaya's partial contribution. He became a respected and innovative cinematographer for Shochiku studios.

In 1930, he married a woman named Masano Araki. They had their first son, Hajime, in 1931. Tsuburaya shot numerous films around this time and invented his own camera crane. He became known for atmospheric images and use of smoke on set. This got him the nickname *"Smoke Tsuburaya"*. In 1933, his career took a turn when he saw Merian C. Cooper and Ernest Schoedsack's monster masterwork *King Kong*. He was floored and even purchased a 35mm print. He studied and analyzed it frame by frame, learning Willis O'Brien's stop motion techniques through simple close observation.

Tsuburaya was hired at Nikkatsu to help them develop better shooting techniques. He quit after clashing with the brass. Afterwards, film producer and entrepreneur Yoshio Osawa recruited Tsuburaya for his fledgling film company, J.O. Studios. Tsuburaya devised a better version of his crane made of metal and was appointed chief cinematographer. He developed a reputation as one of the best DPs in Imperial Japan. One project in particular, 1935's *Princess Kaguya* directed by Nobuo Aoyagi and Yoshitsugu Tanaka, was notable. This early stop motion adaptation of the folktale *The Tale of the Bamboo Cutter* was Tsuburaya's first film to use extensive miniatures and visual effects. Sadly, it is lost. Much of Japan's pre-war cinematic history went up in flames during America's fire-bombings of Tokyo. Many other prints were destroyed by the army to harvest its metal in the war to come.

In 1937, industrialist Ichizo Kobayashi acquired J.O. Studios and merged it with PCL Film Company and other studios. This was the birth of Toho Company Ltd. One of Toho's heads, Iwao Mori, brought Tsuburaya into the fold. Mori gave him an entire "Special Arts Department" division of his own. He was to help advance the company in the development and filming of visual effects techniques. Tsuburaya was apprehensive as he was now esteemed as a cinematographer. Yet he always had a particular passion for the technical trickery of filmmaking. He accepted and began work on various propaganda films. One of these was called *The New Earth* and was a co-production between Imperial Japan and Nazi Germany. In 1939, he had a second son with Masano, Noboru. He was also recruited by the Imperial air force, commissioned to work as a combat photographer and make flight training pieces. This would benefit his special effects work at Toho tremendously. His first major film as FX director was *Naval Bomber Squadron* (1940), directed by Sotoji Kimura. It was Tsuburaya's first official credit for special effects.

After the bombing of Pearl Harbor, Toho commissioned a propaganda film celebrating it. *The War at Sea From Hawaii to Malay* (1942), directed by Kajiro Yamamoto, was the first film to gain Tsuburaya notoriety. Its main set piece was a stunning recreation of the Pearl Harbor attack. This film was the highest grossing in Japanese cinema history up to that time. It was also one of his first films where he worked with art director Akira Watanabe. This was followed by films like *Colonel Kato's Falcon Squadron* (1944), though by this time the tide was turning against Japan in the Pacific Theater. Around this time, Tsuburaya's wife Masano gave birth to a third son, Akira. The Tsuburaya family also converted to Catholicism.

The war ended unfavorably for Japan and the country was occupied. Tsuburaya found himself targeted by MacArthur's occupation forces. To them, his special effects work on *The War at Sea From Hawaii to Malay* was just too realistic. For him to have created such detailed miniatures of a U.S. naval base and its warships, he had to have been a spy. He was thus blacklisted from Toho. Tsuburaya and his son Hajime worked freelance for the next several years. They took work when they could get it such as on Daiei's *The Rainbow Man* and *The Invisible Man Appears* (both 1949). After the American occupiers departed in 1952, he returned to Toho. One of the first major projects upon his return was a semi-remake of *The War at Sea: Eagle of the Pacific* (1953). This project paired him with a director whom he would work with many times hence: Ishiro Honda.

In 1954, after working on Honda's *Farewell Rabaul*, Tsuburaya was brought on board a project that would put him on the map internationally. This was *Project G*, soon to be known as *Godzilla* and also directed by Honda. Tsuburaya had largely put the project into motion two years prior with a monster film proposal he submitted to producer Tomoyuki Tanaka. Lacking the time and resources to do stop motion animation, he pioneered the use of a stuntman in a monster suit filmed on miniature sets. After this, Tsuburaya became Toho's premiere special effects guru and his career took off. *Godzilla Raids Again* and *Half Human* followed in 1955. Then came, in color, *Madame White Snake* and *Rodan* (both 1956). For *The Mysterians* in 1957, Tsuburaya worked in Cinemascope and color, upping his game with optical printing. *The H-Man, Varan* (both 1958) and *Submarine I-57 Will Not Surrender* (1959) followed. Tsuburaya and his team even created many of Toho's classic logos using rotating sheets of glass to simulate its spinning sun rays.

It is said stop motion master Ray Harryhausen on the other side of the Pacific was not fond of Tsuburaya's work. By most accounts, he saw him as a bitter rival. It's been rumored that Harryhausen still had lingering anti-Japanese sentiment left over from the war. There was also jealousy that Tsuburaya could produce films quicker. Tsuburaya's dream project was a film featuring a giant octopus. Incidentally, Harryhausen did visual effects for a film with that concept called *It Came From Beneath the Sea* in 1955.

With *The Three Treasures* and *Battle in Outer Space* (both 1959), Tsuburaya further improved his optical printing techniques. A color semi-remake of *The War at Sea* and *Eagle of the Pacific*, *Storm Over the Pacific* (1960), followed. Afterwards came lavish work on *Mothra*, *The Last War* (both 1961), *Gorath* and *King Kong vs. Godzilla* (both 1962). 1963 was a particularly busy year for Tsuburaya. He worked on *Attack Squadron, Siege of Fort Bismark, Matango, Samurai Pirate* and *Atragon*. Around this time, he acquired an Oxberry 1200 optical printer. This state of the art compositing device was in use at only one other studio: Disney. Unlike Harryhausen, producer and luminary George Pal was quite impressed with Tsuburaya's work. The two had a friendly meeting at least once.

In 1963, he began development of a television series which started off titled *Woo* and then *Unbalance*. Eventually it became *Ultra Q*. *Ultra Q* would finally hit airwaves in early 1966 under the banner of Tsuburaya's own company: Tsuburaya Pro. At the same time, Tsuburaya kept up his work at Toho for the next several years. He worked on *Whirlwind, Mothra vs. Godzilla,*

Dogora and *Ghidorah the Three-Headed Monster* in 1964. During 1965 he did several films including *Retreat From Kiska, Frankenstein Conquers the World* and *Invasion of Astro-Monster*. Frank Sinatra even recruited him for his U.S./Japanese co-production *None But the Brave*. In 1966, his company began work on another TV series that would become quite iconic: *Ultraman*. This show featured a silver-skinned superhero from space battling weekly monsters. It became wildly popular around the world.

His schedule going back and forth between Toho and Tsuburaya Pro became overly hectic. After *The War of the Gargantuas*, he left his cameraman and assistant, Sadamasa Arikawa, in charge of FX work on some films including the subsequent Godzilla entries. He directed the FX for *King Kong Escapes* in 1967 and *Admiral Yamamoto* in 1968. This was all while supervising another Ultra franchise show, *Ultraseven*. His swan-song of sorts was *Battle of the Japan Sea* in 1969. Directed by Seiji Maruyama, this was a lavish film about the Imperial Navy's victory in the Russo-Japanese War. He soon became ill and was unable to work on the newest Godzilla film, *All Monsters Attack*. The film was still credited to him out of respect, however. In January 1970, he passed away from a heart attack in his sleep before he could start work on Honda's *Space Amoeba*. As one of his technicians, Minoru Nakano, wept over his coffin, his loss was felt strongly throughout the Japanese film industry. Toho would never relive its glory days when Tsuburaya was head of the FX unit. Yet the legacy that Tsuburaya has left is profound and resonates a half century after his death. Like Walt Disney's, it is still felt to this day as

Godzilla and Ultraman films and TV shows continue to be produced.

<u>Selected Filmography</u>

A Page of Madness (1926) [assistant cinematographer]

Princess Kaguya (1935) [director of photography]

The New Earth (1937) [special effects]

The Abe Clan (1939) [special effects]

The Burning Sky (1939) [special effects]

Naval Bomber Squadron (1940) [special effects director]

The War at Sea From Hawaii to Malay (1942) [special effects director]

Decisive Battle in the Skies (1943) [special effects director]

Colonel Kato's Falcon Squadron (1944) [special effects director]

Rainbow Man (1949) [special effects]

The Invisible Man Appears (1949) [special effects]

The Man Who Came to Port (1952) [special effects]

Eagle of the Pacific (1953) [special effects director]

Farewell Rabaul (1954) [special effects director]

Godzilla (1954) [special effects director]

The Invisible Avenger (1954) [director of photography, special effects]

Godzilla Raids Again (1955) [special effects director]

Half Human (1955) [special effects]

Madame White Snake (1956) [special effects]

Rodan (1956) [special effects director]

The Mysterians (1957) [special effects director]

The H-Man (1958) [special effects director]

Varan (1958) [special effects director]

Monkey Sun (1959) [special effects]

Submarine 1-57 Will Not Surrender (1959) [special effects director]

The Three Treasures (1959) [special effects director]

Battle in Outer Space (1959) [special effects director]

Secret of the Telegian (1960) [special effects]

Storm Over the Pacific (1960) [special effects director]

The Human Vapor (1960) [special effects director]

Mothra (1961) [special effects director]

The Last War (1961) [special effects director]

Gorath (1962) [special effects director]

KIng Kong vs. Godzilla (1962) [special effects director]

Chushingura (1962) [special effects]

Attack Squadron (1963) [special effects director]

Siege of Fort Bismark (1963) [special effects director]

Matango (1963) [special effects director]

Samurai Pirate (1963) [special effects director]

Atragon (1963) [special effects director]

Whirlwind (1964) [special effects]

Mothra vs. Godzilla (1964) [special effects director]

Dogora (1964) [special effects director]

Ghidorah, the Three-Headed Monster (1964) [special effects director]

None But the Brave (1965) [special effects]

Retreat From Kiska (1965) [special effects director]

Frankenstein Conquers the World (1965) [special effects director]

Crazy Adventure (1965) [special effects director]

Invasion of Astro-Monster (1965) [special effects director]

"Ultra Q" (1966, TV) [producer]

Zero Fighter (1966) [special effects director]

The War of the Gargantuas (1966) [special effects director

"Ultraman" (1966-67, TV) [producer]

Ebirah, Horror of the Deep (1966) [special effects director/supervisor]

King Kong Escapes (1967) [special effects director]

"Ultraseven" (1967-68) [producer]

Son of Godzilla (1967) [special effects supervisor]

Destroy All Monsters (1968) [special effects supervisor]

Admiral Yamamoto (1968) [special effects director]

Latitude Zero (1969) [special effects director]

Battle of the Japan Sea (1969) [special effects director]

All Monsters Attack (1969) [special effects director, honorary]

Gojira "Godzilla"
Toho, 11/3/1954 (*Showa 29*), 10 reels (2,663 meters), 96:14, 35mm, Academy (1.37:1), black and white, monaural sound

Crew
Executive Producer: Iwao Mori
Producer: Tomoyuki Tanaka
Director: Ishiro Honda
Special Effects Director: Eiji Tsuburaya
Screenplay: Takeo Murata, Ishiro Honda, Shigeru Kayama (original story)
Director of Photography: Masao Taimi
Editor: Kazuji Taira
Music: Akira Ifukube
Production Design: Takeo Kita
Art Director: Satoru Chuko
Sound Recording: Hisashi Shimonaga
Sound Effects: Ichiro Minawa
Lighting: Choshiro Ishii
Assistant Director: Koji Kajita
Production Manager: Teruo Maki
2nd AD: Susumu Takebayashi
SFX Cinematography: Sadamasa Arikawa
SFX Lighting: Kuichiro Kishida
SFX Art Director: Akira Watanabe
Composites: Hiroshi Mukoyama

Suit Modeler: Teizo Toshimitsu
Suit Builders: Kanju Yagi, Yasuei Yagi, Eizo Kaimai, Fuminori Ohashi
Miniatures: Yoshio Irie
Still Photographer: Kazukiyo Tanaka

Cast
Akira Takarada *(Hideto Ogata)*
Momoko Kochi *(Emiko Yamane)*
Akihiko Hirata *(Dr. Daisuke Serizawa)*
Takashi Shimura *(Dr. Kyohei Yamane)*
Fuyuki Murakami *(Professor Tanabe)*
Sachio Sakai *(Reporter Hagiwara)*
Toranosuke Ogawa *(Shipping Company President)*
Ren Yamamoto *(Masaji)*
Hiroshi Hayashi *(Diet Chairman)*
Toyoaki Suzuki *(Shinkichi)*
Seijiro Onda *(Representative Oyama)*
Tsuruko Mano *(Shinkichi's Mother)*

Takeo Oikawa *(Chief of Emergency Headquarters)*
Kokuten Kodo *(Old Fisherman)*
Kin Sugai *(Ozawa)*
Shizuko Higashi *(Angry Representative at Diet)*
Tadashi Okabe *(Tanabe's Assistant)*
Ren Imaizumi *(Radio Operator)*
Junpei Natsuki *(Power Station Engineer)*
Saburo Iketani *(News Reporter)*
Yasuhisa Tsutumi *(Soldier)*
Haruo Nakajima *(Godzilla)*
Katsumi Tezuka *(Godzilla)*

Alternate Titles
Godzilla, King of the Monsters! (US)
Godzilla, uhyrernes konge (Denmark)
哥吉拉的誕生 **[Birth of Godzilla]** (Greater China)
Japón bajo el terror del monstruo **[Japan Under the Terror of a Monster]** (Spain)
Godzilla, rey de los monstruos (Mexico)

O Monstro do Oceano Pacífico **[Monster of the Pacific Ocean]** (Portugal)
Godzilla, O Monstro do Mar **[Godzilla, the Sea Monster]** (Brazil)

Гκοτζίλα: Το Τέρας του Αιώνος **[Godzilla: Monster of the Century]** (Greece)
Godzilla: Król potworów (Poland)

Godzilla - monstret från havet (Sweden)
Годзилла (Russia)

"Godzilla is the son of the atomic bomb. He is a nightmare created out of the darkness of the human soul. He is the sacred beast of the apocalypse."
-Tomoyuki Tanaka

Many film scholars have difficulty admitting this, but *Seven Samurai* is not the most famous Japanese movie. The original *Godzilla* is. As beloved as Akira Kurosawa's masterwork is, you can go anywhere in the developed world and ask any person about Godzilla. This is powerful pop culture iconography akin to American creations like *Superman* and *Star Wars*. Opening to harsh reviews in both Japan and the Western world, the original *Godzilla* has stood the test of time. It remains hauntingly relevant; a classic cross between the B-movie populism of Hollywood science fiction works and a deeper subtext. On the surface *Godzilla* is a genre picture about a giant, dinosaurian beast destroying a city. Yet its then-topical themes and documentary-style depiction of a nuclear spawned monster's hellish rampage are more in line with the arthouse than drive-in.

PLOT

The salvage ship *Eiko Maru* is destroyed by a blinding flash of light. A young sailor named Ogata (Akira Takarada) is called into work as the *Eiko Maru* is reported missing by the Nankai Salvage Shipping Company. They dispatch the *Bingo Maru*,

a rescue vessel, but it too meets the same fate. A reporter, Hagiwara (Sachio Sakai), arrives at nearby Odo, an island hamlet off the coast of Honshu. The fishing community there has a belief in a monster deity called Godzilla whom they hold responsible for the shipwrecks. An unnaturally violent storm pummels the island and results in a high loss of property and life. One of the islanders, Shinkichi (Toyoaki Suzuki), loses his brother Masaji (Ren Yamamoto) and mother to a seemingly living creature. After Odo Islanders arrive in Tokyo begging for aid, the Japanese government begins an investigation. They send noted paleontologist Dr. Yamane (Takashi Shimura) to the island to gather data. In the destroyed village, Yamane finds a giant radioactive footprint containing a trilobite. a prehistoric crustacean thought to be extinct.

Yamane's investigation is interrupted by the village alarm bell. The monster in question soon appears: sticking its head over a hill as the terrified villagers huddle in shock. Yamane returns to Tokyo and gives a presentation of his findings for government officials. He christens the monster Godzilla after the Odo Island legend. He also reveals the creature is radioactive, baptized in the fire of hydrogen bomb testing. The Self Defense Force dispatches a fleet to destroy the monster with depth charges. This upsets Yamane who wants Godzilla to be left alive for study. Meanwhile, Yamane's daughter Emiko (Momoko Kochi) has fallen in love with Ogata. She has decided to break off her engagement to her fiance, the scarred, brooding scientist Daisuke Serizawa (Akihiko Hirata). Serizawa gives Emiko a demonstration of his new research. Emiko screams as she witnesses an aquarium of fish destroyed in an instant.

Godzilla soon comes ashore in Tokyo's Shinagawa district. It proves impervious to artillery shells and destroys a train. In response, the Self Defense Force erects a barrier of electrical towers as a line of defense against the monster. Godzilla returns the following night and makes quick work of the electric towers. It cuts a swath of fiery destruction through Tokyo, destroying many buildings and human lives. The creature is driven off by a squadron of jets, but the destruction is catastrophic. The hospitals overflow with the maimed, many suffering from radiation sickness from being exposed to the monster. Emiko, working as a field nurse, is unhinged by the suffering she sees and reveals Serizawa's secret to Ogata. Serizawa has invented a compound called the Oxygen Destroyer that liquefies oxygen molecules. Could it be used to kill Godzilla?

BACKGROUND

Japanese studio Toho was planning a co-production with Indonesia's Perfini called *In Glory's Shadow*. It was to be a lavish color war film directed by Senkichi Taniguchi and starring Ryo Ikebe. The visas for the cast and crew wound up denied by the Indonesian government. The Indonesian Foreign Minister disagreed with the film's message and still harbored bitterness towards the Japanese. Toho were thus left scrambling for a replacement project to fill their release slate. It should be noted that in *Godzilla*, the first ship destroyed was named the *"Eiko Maru"*. This could be a production in-joke to that project, *"Eiko"* meaning "Glory" in Japanese.

It is said producer Tomoyuki Tanaka, on the flight back from Jakarta, looked out at the vast sea and wondered what might be lurking beneath the waves. The truth is that Eiji Tsuburaya had been pitching a monster project to Tanaka for several years and he likely decided such a film could be a suitable replacement. *King Kong* (1933) had been re-released in Japan and did excellent business so Tanaka felt a monster movie could be profitable. Toho's president, Iwao Mori (1899-1979), who was convicted as a Class B war criminal by the Allies for making propaganda films, agreed. Tanaka got to work devising a concept similar to the previous year's Hollywood production *The Beast From 20,000 Fathoms*. He brought in Shigeru Kayama, a famous science fiction novelist, to write the treatment. Eiji Tsuburaya was also brought on board to direct the effects sequences. He was already known for his elaborate miniature work on World War II propaganda pieces such as *The War At Sea From Hawaii To Malay* (1942). Iwao Mori wanted *In Glory's* potential director Taniguchi to helm the film but he passed on the project. Instead, Tanaka brought Ishiro Honda on board. Honda was fresh off directing two brooding war dramas, *Eagle of the Pacific* and *Farewell Rabaul*, where he worked with Tsuburaya. Mori, once Honda's film school instructor, approved this decision.

The picture was christened *Project G*. The monster's name Gojira, as is commonly known, comes from "gorilla" and *"kujira"* (whale). Urban myths that the creature was named after a hulking crewman who worked at Toho are almost certainly false. *Manga* artist Kazuyoshi Abe did an early design for the monster with a mushroom cloud-like head, but this design was rejected. Eventually a dinosaurian monster was developed, designed by Tsuburaya's art director Akira Watanabe and modeled by Teizo Toshimitsu (1909-1982). Tanaka announced the film in July of 1954 to much ballyhoo. Yet the design and nature of Godzilla was kept secret for months. A radio drama based on the film aired weekly up to the release and helped stoke anticipation as well.

Director Honda and screenwriter Takeo Murata fleshed out a screenplay from Kayama's treatment. Honda and Murata would consult with Tsuburaya and Tanaka while writing the script to make sure their vision for scenes was executable and affordable. Despite their iconic association with each other, Honda and Tsuburaya were never personal friends. In their years of working together, they seldom socialized outside the Toho backlot. An amusing anecdote goes that at one point during pre-production, Honda, Tsuburaya and assistant director Koji Kajita (1923-2013) stood on the roof of the Matsukaya Department Store. They were planning Godzilla's destructive rampage, mentioning where fires would break out and what buildings would be destroyed. The authorities overheard this conversation and found it alarming. The trio were made to show identification proving they worked for Toho.

PRINCIPAL PHOTOGRAPHY

Shooting for *Godzilla* began in August of 1954. Conceptually Honda and Tsuburaya worked closely, but at Toho, *tokusatsu* (special effects) films were always shot with two units. One unit was managed by the main director who would shoot the actor-driven drama scenes. The other was run by the special effects director with a separate crew who shot the films' trick photography. The director and special effects director would have to coordinate closely to make sure their footage matched and edited together cohesively. Director Honda, however, had final say in the editing process.

The scenes at fictional Odo Island were shot early on at Ijikacho in Mie Prefecture. The area was brutally hot and Honda developed a severe sunburn while filming. The extras in these scenes were locals and Honda had difficulty directing them. They did not understand that the monster was going to be added in post-production. The sequence atop the hill where Godzilla makes its first appearance was particularly grueling to film. It took an hour and a half by boat to reach the locale and another hour to climb the summit. Actors and crew often passed out during filming and communication was difficult due to the terrain. At one point, the camera magazine was left behind at the hotel and an assistant had to go all the way back down the hill to get it back. Honda and company would film for twenty days in Mie before returning to Tokyo to shoot mostly on Toho's lot. There were a handful of sequences filmed that were deleted or unused in the final edit, particularly for the Odo Island sequences. These include Ogata and Emiko seeing Godzilla's tail in the ocean while walking along the beach of Odo. Footage was also shot by Tsuburaya's unit of Godzilla first appearing with a cow in its mouth. Like *King Kong*'s "spider pit" sequence, these no longer exist, though some stills have survived.

Masao Taimai (1908-1997) shot *Godzilla*. Unlike later DP Hajime Koizumi who became a permanent fixture of Honda's team, this was Taimi's only film with Honda. He was better known for his work on Mikio Naruse's films, most notably *Late Chrysanthemums, Floating Clouds* and *When a Woman Ascends the Stairs*. He insisted on bringing his lighting crew from his Naruse pictures on board. His images, shot on old school nitrate film, are atmospheric and rich. One of the most difficult scenes to shoot was the underwater footage for the film's climax. These shots were done at Gokasho Bay, also in Mie Prefecture. A pair of divers were hired as stand-ins for actors Takarada and Hirata. These scenes used a waterproof camera type created for Honda's debut *The Blue Pearl*. Yuzuru Aizawa, Taimi's assistant, was charged with shooting the underwater segments. He nearly drowned on his first day after a crew member forgot to turn on his suit's oxygen. Aizawa would act as DP twenty years later for *Godzilla vs. Megalon* and *Godzilla vs. Mechagodzilla*.

ACTORS

Criticized for having "bad acting" on both sides of the Pacific, *Godzilla* is quite well performed. *Ikiru* and *Seven Samurai*'s Takashi Shimura (1905-1982) leads the cast as Yamane. Shimura, of course, needs no introduction as one of *Showa* Japan's premiere thespians. Akira Takarada as Ogata and Akihiko Hirata as Serizawa shine as well. Both young actors would become favorites of Ishiro Honda and frequent fixtures in his movies. This was the first real leading role for Takarada, only 20 years old at the time. He was both nervous and excited to work with Takashi Shimura and to take on a pivotal role in a high concept production for Toho. Shimura would become a mentor figure to Takarada, teaching him much about the craft. Hirata (1927-1984) was born Ahikiko Onoda to a wealthy family in Japanese occupied Seoul, Korea. He was a graduate of a prestigious military academy and a political science major at Tokyo University. His family was unamused by his decision to enter the film industry, spurned by his older brother Yoshiki. At first, he was interested in working behind the camera but took a liking to acting, aided no doubt by his handsome looks. Taking the stage name Hirata, his debut was in 1953's *The Last Embrace* by Masahiro Makino. He became something of the *"Japanese Gregory Peck"*. Tragically, he died at only 56 of lung cancer in 1984, playing a final role in that year's *Bye Bye Jupiter*. Hirata was planning to play Dr. Hayashida in *The Return of Godzilla* before he died.

Momoko Kochi (1932-1998) plays Emiko Yamane. She was born Momoko Okochi, the daughter of painter Nobuhiro Okochi. Kochi was accepted into Toho's New Face program in the same class as Akira Takarada and Kenji Sahara. Her debut was in 1953's *A Woman's Heart Released*. Though Kochi also appeared in Honda's *Half Human* (1955) and *The Mysterians* (1957), she declined to appear in any of the Godzilla sequels. She did not like that people on the street would point to her and say "Godzilla". Eventually she left Toho to pursue more serious stage acting. Before she died, Kochi did reprise the role of Emiko in *Godzilla vs. Destoroyah* (1995). Sachio Sakai plays journalist Hagiwara and was one of Honda's favorite character actors. Sakai (1925-1998) worked with Honda as late as 1970's *Space Amoeba*. His debut was in Akira Kurosawa's *One Wonderful Sunday* (1947) and he would appear in several more Kurosawa movies including *Seven Samurai* and *Yojimbo* (1961). He was also a fixture of Toho's popular Young Guy series with Yuzo

Kayama. His final role was in Kurosawa's *Rhapsody in August* (1991). Fuyuki Murakami (1911-2007) was another one of Honda's preferred character actors. Born in Yamaguchi, for Honda he often played scientists and politicians. Most notably, he later played Dr. Sano who created *The Human Vapor* in the 1960 film of the same name. For all the film's thespians, trying to act while envisioning a giant monster looming over them was a mind-boggling endeavor.

SFX

Eiji Tsuburaya, obsessed with *King Kong*, estimated how long it would take to animate Godzilla with stop motion animation. His calculation of seven years drew laughter from Toho's brass. Nonetheless, as a nod to Willis O' Brien, Tsuburaya would insert a handful of stop motion shots into the movie. Tsuburaya pioneered a high frame rate shooting style which was then slowed down to 24 frames per second. This would give the miniatures and monster suits the illusion of immense weight. Working from extensive photographs of downtown Tokyo, a team of 40 carpenters led by Yoshio Irie spent a whole month building a miniature Tokyo at 1/25th scale. Over 500 miniature buildings were made for *Godzilla*. Portions of the tiny streets were made with sawdust, so they would crumble as Godzilla's feet trampled them. Models that weren't destroyed in some scenes were refurbished and reused in others. Wafer crackers were even used to build some of the smaller buildings, as they looked convincing when blown up. Thousands of pounds of gelatin, mixed with water, created convincing ocean water, soon a Toho FX tradition. The electrical towers melted by Godzilla were built from wax and hot air was blown on them. This would become another trademark of Tsuburaya's FX unit, often used for melting tanks in subsequent films. An auxiliary third "C" unit run by Hiroshi Mukoyama assisted Tsuburaya's main team. They created the film's impressive composites using mattes, background plates and double exposures. Choosing effective camera angles was difficult for the creative team and required a lot of ingenuity. In total, 263 of *Godzilla*'s 868 cuts were special effects shots. By Toho's brass, Tsuburaya's unit were considered a group of eccentric misfits until the success of this film. They would go on to shoot for an extra three weeks once Honda's unit wrapped.

Godzilla was played by stuntmen Katsumi Tezuka and Haruo Nakajima. Nakajima suffered tortures of the damned inside the heavy suit. It was so stiflingly hot under the studio lights that he would often faint if a take ran long. Nakajima was chosen based on his martial arts training and experience in *jidai-geki* (period piece) films. He had to move fast per Tsuburaya's shooting style, which in a heavy monster suit was excruciating. Tsuburaya screened Nakajima his print of *King Kong* as inspiration. In addition, Nakajima visited the local zoo to study how animals moved, especially bears. The Godzilla suit was built out of natural rubber with an armature made of bamboo and mesh wire, its construction headed by brothers Kanju and Yasuei Yagi. It would take

two entire months to construct the first suit, which wound up weighing over 220 pounds. Nakajima was unable to move in it and so another, lighter suit had to be built, this time taking only two weeks to finish. The first suit wound up cut in half; its bottom used for certain close-ups of Godzilla's feet stomping buildings. The main suit had to be cleaned and repaired constantly throughout production. It was frequently damaged by stunts and the inside was lined with cotton which absorbed sweat. A cup of sweat would be drained from the suit after each day of filming. For some shots of Godzilla expelling its heat ray, propane was used and Nakajima's face had to be shielded. Other "heat ray" shots were done using hand drawn animation courtesy of Mukoyama's unit. Nonetheless, Nakajima was a trooper and would return to sweat inside a myriad of monster suits in the decades to come. A smaller hand puppet was also employed for certain close-up shots, such as Godzilla biting the radio tower.

MUSIC

The film opens in a spartan but effective fashion. Haunting footfalls are heard against a black screen before the monster's iconic roar cuts through the sound mix. This unmistakable sound effect was made by a glove rubbing on the strings of a contrabass then played backwards. The driving main theme by monster maestro Akira Ifukube then begins to blare on the soundtrack. While scoring *Godzilla*, Ifukube was not allowed to see any of the special effects footage as Tsuburaya wasn't comfortable screening his unfinished work. It did not help that Mori and Tanaka were skeptical when viewing dailies of the monster footage. Yet when the score was finished and synced with the movie, the brass responded far more favorably. Like John Williams with *Jaws* and *Star Wars*, some even felt Ifukube had single-handedly saved the film.

REAL WORLD

Godzilla is evocative from its first scene, immediately stirring up unsettling memories in the mind of its audience. The opening is a nod to the *Dai-go Fukuryu Maru* (Lucky Dragon No. 5) incident, a political hot button issue involving the United States. At the time, the U.S. was testing hydrogen bombs at the Marshall Islands, ironically captured from Imperial Japanese control a decade prior. In early 1954, the tuna vessel Lucky Dragon strayed too close to America's Castle Bravo atomic test site. Seeing a mysterious flash of light like in the movie, the fishermen encountered the dusty fallout and developed radiation sickness, with the radioman dying. Some of their contaminated catches even reached the market. Press called the incident the *"third atomic bombing of Japan"*. The Castle Bravo atomic test in later films would become Godzilla's origin story. Kayama's original treatment directly referenced the Lucky Dragon No. 5 incident, opening with it returning to Japan. Honda rewrote this into the destruction of the *Eiko Maru* as he felt it was too on the nose.

In later films the military hardware became more outlandish and science fiction based. In *Godzilla*, the military weapons used by the Self Defense Force against the monster are completely realistic. The tanks are mainly M24 Chaffees. Mounted with a 75mm M6 cannon, these mobile fortresses came into use by the U.S. army during the end of World War II. They first saw action in December 1944's Battle of the Bulge and were more streamlined than their Sherman tank counterparts. They were used against the Japanese themselves in Iwo Jima and Okinawa. Their smaller size helped them navigate through Okinawa's narrow roads. Along with the Sherman, they were phased out from use before the Vietnam War. In the Self Defense Force, they would be supplanted by the Type 61 Tanks. The cannons used to attack Godzilla are 155mm Howitzer M1s. These cannons, first introduced by the U.S. in World War II, would also see use in Korea and early Vietnam. In the later years of the Vietnam war, they were supplanted by the M198 which is still in use to this day. Howitzer M1s are still used by the armies of many less wealthy countries, however. The jets that battle Godzilla are F-86 Sabres, a favorite of Tsuburaya's unit. Those aircraft were developed by the United States Air Force in 1949 and were used in the Korean War. They were retired by the USAF and SDF by the mid '60s. Bolivia, however, continued to use them until 1994.

THEMES AND MOTIFS

By Hollywood standards, the characters are not given a lot of development in Honda and Murata's script. Yet they serve their purpose in the film's narrative efficiently. They are quintessentially Japanese archetypes, torn between righteous duty and their inner passions. Serizawa's character is the best written among them: a tormented man bearing the scars of war and driven to a uniquely Japanese sacrifice for the greater good. He was a character science-loving Honda had a strong empathy for.

As *Godzilla* gets going, the references to Japan's wartime trauma take on more gravity. There's a scene midpoint that shows a Nagasaki survivor lamenting at having to go back into the shelters. Once Godzilla begins its rampage through Tokyo, there are numerous unsettling scenes invoking the war. People are burned by Godzilla's ray in the streets and a mother, cuddling her two children, tells them that they'll be with their dead father soon. The aftermath of Godzilla's destruction is where the film most channels Japan's war scars. The high contrast monochrome images depict smoldering rubble and the victims of Godzilla's wrath suffering on futons in overcrowded hospitals. They are impossible to distance from similar documentary images of the bombings of Hiroshima and Nagasaki. Ifukube's arresting choral *"Prayer For Peace"*, filmed with hundreds of student extras from a Tokyo girls' academy, only makes this message more poignant. Akira Kurosawa would himself soon direct a film themed around the existential horror of nuclear weapons: *I Live In Fear* (1955).

There's dark irony in the fact that Godzilla is only destroyed by a weapon with as much terrible destructive potential as it. Serizawa's Oxygen Destroyer is easily equivalent in terrible power to the atomic bomb. Yet its origins are unclear. One scene has Sachio Sakai's reporter Hagiwara mention a "German colleague" of Serizawa to which the clearly uncomfortable scientist vehemently denies knowing. It's a minor detail, but important enough to be included. Could this be a subtle hint that the Oxygen Destroyer is "Axis tech" derived from Nazi and Imperial Japanese research? If true, it's an ironic twist that the American H-bomb spawned Godzilla is only brought down by an equally horrifying weapon created by Nazi Germany and Imperial Japan's own dark science.

Ultimately, *Godzilla* is a film about Japan's collective trauma. Almost five decades later, director Shusuke Kaneko would explore this theme more directly with 2001's *Godzilla, Mothra and King Ghidorah: Giant Monsters All-Out Attack*. Godzilla is *shoganai* incarnate. The creature is akin to a Shinto *yonaoshi* god who seeks to humble humanity, particularly the Japanese, into realizing their place in the natural order. In his 2019 book *Agents of World Renewal: The Rise of Yonaoshi Gods* in Japan, author Takashi Miura explains that in feudal Japan, the peasants believed that the frequent local disasters were due to monstrous gods. Gods that brought about cataclysms, social change and "world renewal" (*yonaoshi*). Cinematic *kaiju* like Godzilla are the modern equivalent. They are a force of realignment, showing up when, ala Icarus, we fly too close to the sun. These monsters are like the Kanto earthquake, the atomic bombings of Hiroshima and Nagasaki, the Lucky Dragon incident, the 3/11 quake and now, perhaps, the COVID-19 pandemic.

RELEASE AND LEGACY

At the end of *Godzilla*, Dr. Yamane exclaims *"If we continue testing nuclear weapons, another Godzilla may appear, somewhere in the world, again"*. He wasn't wrong. *Godzilla* was completed on October 25, 1954. Toho arranged a Shinto ceremony for its success at the box office and the film was screened for the staff and Toho's brass. On its first day of release, *Godzilla* would break records for ticket sales. Toho's executives and the shooting staff celebrated and the beer, sake and liquor flowed. Naturally Toho couldn't resist the allure of a sequel. *Godzilla Raids Again*, ala 1933's *Son of Kong*, was rushed into production as a quickie follow-up. After that, Godzilla wouldn't be back until 1962's *King Kong vs. Godzilla*. Thankfully for Japan, the second Godzilla would wind up a more neutral force.

ALTERNATE VERSIONS

In 1955, Toho sold the film's U.S. rights to producer Joseph E. Levine (1905-1987). Levine created the most famous alternate version of the film: *Godzilla, King of the Monsters!* released stateside on April 27, 1956. Embassy Pictures handled the distribution on the East Coast and TransWorld on the West. Some states got it in a double bill with *Prehistoric Women* and others with Jerry Warren's *Man Beast*. Director Terry Morse (1906-1984) shot new scenes for this version, filmed quickly in Los Angeles. Actor Raymond Burr would play an American reporter covering the carnage in Japan.

Burr (1917-1993) was one of Hollywood's most fascinating players. He often appeared as villains in film noirs. His most notable role was in Alfred Hitchcock's *Rear Window* (1954). Afterwards, Burr was best known for his long running roles as TV's *Perry Mason* (1957-1966) and *Ironside* (1967-1975). He was a closeted gay man who kept a secret domestic partnership with actor Robert Benevides. Anecdotally, Burr often went on dates with actress Natalie Wood as cover. He was known for his kindness as a generous philanthropist in later years. Burr would return years later to reprise the role of Steve Martin in *Godzilla 1985,* the U.S. version of *The Return of Godzilla* (1984).

Japanese-American actor Frank Iwanaga (1922-1963) plays Martin's translator. Overall, *Godzilla: King of the Monsters!*, running around 80:40, is a very passable re-edit of the movie but vastly inferior to its Japanese counterpart. Burr gives a compelling performance but it is still the Japanese characters who drive the plot. The use of doubles to show Burr's character Steve Martin interacting with the Japanese actors is done passably. The Japanese footage is reduced to an hour or so of material. Most references to Hiroshima and Nagasaki and implications that America is responsible for creating the monster are removed. *Godzilla: King of the Monsters!* is missing most, but not all, of the political commentary of Honda's original.

Much of the film is left un-dubbed with Burr providing a narration track. When the film does employ dubbing it's quite crude. According to actor James Hong who provided the voices of Ogata and Serizawa, it was done without the use of loops and the technical sloppiness really shows. There's even an instance where Yamane says a line of dialogue without his lips moving. There are sound design improvements, anguished screams are added to certain destruction scenes such as the train and police car segments. While this version of the film holds up well to Hollywood's atomic monster B-movies of the '50s, it's neutered of its distinctiveness. Surprisingly, *Godzilla: King of the Monsters!* would be reverse-exported back to Japan with subtitles in 1957. In Japanese theaters, scenes involving Martin's translator were said to elicit laughter from audiences. It was cropped to anamorphic TohoScope in a process. called "TohoPanScope", to be used on *Varan* the following year.

James Hong (1929-) is a very noteworthy Chinese-American actor with over 600 film and television credits. Born in Minnesota, after these early dubbing roles, he appeared in major parts on *The New Adventures of Charlie Chan* (1957-58) and *Hawaii Five-O* (1968-1980). Later notable roles include in Roman Polanski's *Chinatown* (1974), Ridley Scott's *Blade Runner* (1982), John Carpenter's *Big Trouble in Little China* (1986) and the comedy *Balls of Fury* (2007). He has continued to do voice work over the years and can be heard in Disney's *Mulan*

and the *Kung Fu Panda* franchise among many other animated works.

Some international versions of *Godzilla* (the German one especially) were patterned after the Japanese original. Most, however, were based on *King of the Monsters!* In 1957, the Fillipino film company People's Pictures released a version called *Tokyo 1960*. It appears to be a similar re-edit to *King of the Monsters!* using mainly Tsuburaya's FX footage with Filipino actors edited in. This version may, however, be completely lost.

In 1977, Italian filmmaker Luigi Cozzi (1947-, *Starcrash*) would create his own version of *King of the Monsters!* Affectionately called "Cozzilla" by fans, this is a drastically re-edited and Italian dubbed version using a rudimentary colorization that tints the footage with a kaleidoscopic effect. With added synth music by Fabio Frizzi (*Zombi 2*) and very '70s sound design, it adds a lengthy Hiroshima-themed prologue. Copious footage of the atomic bombings and real life scenes of wartime destruction are spliced into the movie to make Godzilla's rampage more violent. It was also to pad the run time as Cozzi was under obligation to make the film over 90 minutes. Kamikaze footage is used during the jet fighters' attack on Godzilla. A lengthy montage of Hiroshima and Nagasaki footage is also edited into the aftermath of Godzilla's rampage. This gives *Cozzilla* a feel like a Godzilla movie filtered through an Italian *mondo* sensibility. Some destruction scenes are shown in slow motion. Shots from *The Beast From 20,000 Fathoms* and *Godzilla*

Raids Again are also added. Running around 96 minutes, this version is worth seeing primarily as a curiosity, though it does boast a nightmarish and unique tone. It was technically the first colorization of a black and white film ever created.

AMERICAN HOME VIDEO HISTORY

In 1983, *Godzilla, King of the Monsters!* was released to U.S. home video by Vestron, licensed from Henry Saperstein's UPA, on VHS, Betamax and laserdisc. Paramount Home Video would later re-release the film to VHS and LD in 1992. Goodtimes Home Video also released it around 1995. Simitar would buy the rights in 1998, releasing it to DVD for the first time. Classic Media then acquired the rights and released *King of the Monsters!* to DVD in 2002. In 2004, the Japanese version had a small but successful theatrical run in American repertory theaters. Classic Media released a set containing the Japanese original and *King of the Monsters!* to region 1 DVD in 2006. They later followed it up with a re-pressing and then a lackluster upscaled Blu-ray release. In 2014, Criterion released a superb Blu-ray with beautiful 2K scans of both versions of the movie. This disc was repackaged for their 2019 *Godzilla: The Showa Era* boxed set.

Further Viewing:

(1955)

ゴジラの逆襲
Toho, *Director*: Motoyoshi Oda

After the original *Godzilla* was a hit, Toho's brass ordered Tomoyuki Tanaka to "make another one". Ishiro Honda, however, was occupied with other assignments. Instead "B-list" director Motoyoshi Oda (1910-1973, *Ghost Man, The Invisible Avenger)* was hired. The sequel was rushed into theaters a mere five months after the first, with parallels to *Son of Kong*. The problem with *Godzilla Raids Again* is that Oda's direction is among the most pedestrian in a Japanese programmer. Shigeaki Hidaka's script is also terrible with a poor structure. It violates the basic three act plot and not in a way that works. *Godzilla Raids Again* places Godzilla and Anguirus' Osaka battle in the film's center rather than climax. The rest of the film is devoted to the dull human plot.

The saving grace is the special effects work from Eiji Tsuburaya's unit. Hiccups aside, it is nearly on par with his work in the original with especially moody miniature photography. Unlike in future entries, photographed in slow motion where the monsters lumber as they battle, Godzilla and Anguirus' battle is a ferocious brawl. The monsters move with lighting speed, more in line with real animals. This was caused by an error from cameraman Koichi Takano who accidentally undercranked the camera. Yet Tsuburaya liked the effect so continued filming it that way.

The U.S. version was re-titled *Gigantis, the Fire Monster* and released in 1959 on a double bill with *Teenagers From Outer Space*. Besides irritatingly renaming Godzilla, it cuts the film down and punctuates the monotony with a narration track by Keye Luke. It's an Ed Woodsian experience filled with stock footage taken from the anti-Japanese propaganda film *Know Your Enemy: Japan*. The scene where Yamane returns to give his presentation to the Osaka authorities, is quite hilarious. It's a barrage of comically pseudoscientific nonsense, patched with stock shots from films like *One Million B.C.* and *Unknown Island*. Overall, *Godzilla Raids Again* is among the weaker films in the *Showa* series.

(1955)
獣人雪男
Toho, *Director*: Ishiro Honda

Honda's next monster film after *Godzilla* is a fairly routine abominable snowman flick. It's far superior to say, *The Snow Creature* (1954) and on par with Hammer's *The Abominable Snowman* (1957). It features several *Godzilla* cast members including Takarada, Momoko Kochi and Sachio Sakai. It's not Honda at top form, but there are beautiful sequences and the alpine locales lend to the atmosphere. The best bits of the film depict the monster snowman with King Kong-like pathos. The snowman is well executed; the suit was both created and acted in by Fuminori Ohashi. It's a far better primate costume than Toho's later

iterations of Kong. Ohashi (1915-1989) had created one of Japan's first monster ape suits in *King Kong Appears in Edo* (1938). He later helped create the iconic prosthetics for Hollywood's *Planet of the Apes*.

Sadly, *Half Human*'s depiction of *burakumin* people living in the Japan alps is grotesque. The *burakumin* are a marginalized group in Japan akin to India's *dalits*. Prejudice against them is a tragic leftover of strict feudal hierarchies. Upon release, *Half Human* was not particularly controversial. Since then however, advocacy for *burakumin* has grown and most Japanese film and TV studios have shied away from the issue. Toho has thus relegated the film to the vaults ala *Song of the South*. Like 1974's *Prophecies of Nostradamus*, the only way to view the uncut Japanese version is by squinting at a VHS-sourced bootleg with time code.

Half Human was released in the U.S. in 1957. Distributor DCA took a similar approach to *Godzilla, King of the Monsters!* The Japanese footage was reduced to around an hour of runtime and sequences with John Carradine were added. One sequence features Carradine examining the dead baby snowman's corpse and uses the actual suit, sent to Hollywood for filming. These scenes were directed by Kenneth G. Crane. Vastly inferior to its Japanese counterpart, it was released on a double bill with Crane's own *Monster From Green Hell*. Crane would later co-direct the far more interesting U.S./Japanese co-production *The Manster* (1959).

ISHIRO HONDA
The Pacifist

本多猪四郎

5/7/1911-2/28/1993

"His war experience was hard, yet he had a warm heart for mankind. His mind was full of hope that no one would have as sad a war experience as his."
-Akira Kurosawa, *Monsters Are Attacking Tokyo* by Stuart Galbraith (1998)

A luminary of Japanese science fiction, Honda was known for his gentle nature and interest in scientific studies. The latter was what inspired him to accept the job of directing *Godzilla* in 1954. Born in mountainous Yamagata Prefecture, he was the youngest son of Hokan Honda, a Buddhist monk. Ishiro Honda had a long standing love of science as a youth, encouraged by his physician brother Takamoto. As a teenager he became interested in films, often sneaking to the theater to see silent movies against his parents' wishes. At the time, silent films were shown in Japan with live commentary from a narrator called a *benshi*. This enraptured young Honda. He was accepted into Nihon University's film program in 1931. One of Honda's teachers there was Iwao Mori who was working on founding a film production company. Mori offered Honda a job at PCL (Photographic Chemical Laboratories) where he became an assistant director. His mentor was Kajiro Yamamoto whom he learned a great deal from before being drafted into the army.

Honda enlisted in the infantry under commanding officer Yasuhide Kurihara. At the time, military service in Imperial Japan was only compulsory for 18 months. In 1936, Kurihara led a military coup against the government to be infamously known as the February 29th Incident. Honda, due to his association with Kurihara, was sent to Manchuria despite having nearly finished his service. Until the end of World War II, he would serve several tours in China. At one point, he was almost killed by a mortar shell. Between tours, he returned to Japan and worked as an assistant director. He was an AD on the acclaimed *Humanity and Paper Balloons* (1937). On the set of Kajiro Yamamoto's *A Husband's Chastity* that same year, he met another young AD named Akira Kurosawa. The two developed a deep friendship, spending all their off-set waking hours talking about art and cinema. The up-and-coming Honda, Kurosawa and Senkichi Taniguchi were known as the *"Three Crows"*. Honda recalled seeing Kajiro Yamamoto's *Horse*, co-directed by an uncredited Kurosawa, while stationed in Wuhan in 1941. As he watched the film, Honda immediately recognized his friend's aesthetic style.

Around this time, Honda would also meet a young assistant editor named Kimi Yamazaki. Ishiro Honda would soon marry her in March 1939, against the will of her conservative father. The couple had two children: Takako, born in 1939, and Ryuji, born in 1944. The years 1940-41 were a dark period in Honda's life where he was assigned to run a "comfort station" or army brothel in China. He recalled feeling great pity for the women forced to work there. Despite all his wartime hardships, Honda still dreamt of directing. His hope that one day he could return home and make films again kept him going. At one point during a battle, he remembers seeing a single flower growing in the Chinese countryside. He wondered why the Japanese and Chinese had to kill each other in such a beautiful place. During his final deployment in 1945, Honda was captured by the Chinese and spent months as a prisoner-of-war. He returned to his wife Kimi and children Takako and Ryuji in early 1946, visiting the bombed out ruins of Hiroshima on his way to Tokyo. This had a profound impact on Honda. He also brought the mortar which almost killed him back to Japan. Keeping it on his desk for the rest of his life, it would serve as a stark reminder of his war experience and near brush with death.

Upon his return to Japan, Honda resumed work as an assistant director. He worked on projects for directors like Yamamoto, Senkichi Taniguchi and Motoyoshi Oda. Honda did second unit photography on Akira Kurosawa's *Stray Dog*, helping to create the film's gritty post-war atmosphere. He directed educational shorts in the meantime for a subsidiary of Toho to prove his mettle. His former teacher Iwao Mori was keen to let him direct. Sadly multiple projects planned to be his directorial debut were shelved. This included a drama called *Newspaper Kid* and a war film entitled

Kamikaze Special Attack Corps. Honda finally got his chance with 1951's *The Blue Pearl*, a docudrama of sorts about pearl divers. He followed that up with films like *The Skin of the South* (1952) and the war dramas *Eagle of the Pacific* (1953) and *Farewell Rabaul* (1954). All were early collaborations with FX wizard Eiji Tsuburaya. In 1954, after director Senkichi Taniguchi refused it, producer Tomoyuki Tanaka chose him to direct Toho's new monster film. Teaming him again with Tsuburaya, the project would be known as *Godzilla* and become Honda's most famous film.

Godzilla would put Honda on the map at Toho and his directing career blossomed. He directed films in many genres. Yet he was best known for his science fiction pictures which were exported internationally. This included most of the sequels to *Godzilla* in the 1960s. In the United States, his friend Kurosawa's work played with subtitles to sophisticated arthouse crowds in major cities. By contrast, Honda's films had a more populist appeal, widely shown in drive-ins across the country. While Tsuburaya gave these films their distinctive monster spectacle, Honda gave them their subtext and science. Kurosawa was keen on Honda directing his *MacBeth* adaptation *Throne of Blood* (1957). Toho, however, wanted Kurosawa to direct it himself due to its large budget. After Tsuburaya's death, Honda directed *Space Amoeba* in 1970 before shifting his focus to television. His friendship with Akira Kurosawa was strained by frustration with the fellow director's suicide attempt, which he felt was dramatic and petulant. The two soon rekindled, however. On the small screen he helmed episodes of *Mirrorman*

(1971), *Return of Ultraman* (1971) and *Zone Fighter* (1973). Honda left the Godzilla series in the hands of protege Yoshimitsu Banno. Tanaka, however, was not pleased with Banno's directorial debut *Godzilla vs. Hedorah*. After Toho decided not to give its 1975 Godzilla production to Banno, Honda stepped in out of necessity. *Terror of Mechagodzilla* would be his final film.

Not long afterwards, Honda was out golfing with Kurosawa. Kurosawa asked the now retired Honda to act as a creative assistant on his upcoming *Kagemusha* (1980). Honda would spend the last decades of his life helping Kurosawa on these later works with *Ran* (1985) and *Dreams* (1990) to follow. His fingerprints are particularly noticeable on *Dreams*. He acted as an advisor for "*The Tunnel*" segment, said to be based on one of Honda's dreams. He passed away in 1993, his photo appearing in Nobuhiko Obayashi's *Samurai Kids* that same year. Honda left behind a film legacy that will continue to be enjoyed by young and old alike in the years to come.

Selected Filmography *(as director)*

Humanity and Paper Balloons (1937) [assistant director]
Stray Dog (1949) [assistant and second unit director]
The Blue Pearl (1951)
The Skin of the South (1952)
The Man Who Came to Port (1952)
Eagle of the Pacific (1953)
Farewell Rabaul (1954)
Godzilla (1954)
Lovetide (1955)
Mother and Son (1955)
Half Human (1955)
Night School (1956)
Rodan (1956)
The Mysterians (1957)
The H-Man (1958)

Varan (1958)
Battle in Outer Space (1959)
The Human Vapor (1960)
Mothra (1961)
The Man in Red (1961)
Gorath (1962)
King Kong vs. Godzilla (1962)
Matango (1963)
Atragon (1963)
Mothra vs. Godzilla (1964)
Dogora (1964)
Ghidorah, the Three Headed Monster (1964)
Frankenstein Conquers the World (1965)
Invasion of Astro-Monster (1965)
The War of the Gargantuas (1966)
Come Marry Me (1966)
King Kong Escapes (1967)

Destroy All Monsters (1968)
Latitude Zero (1969)
All Monsters Attack (1969)
Space Amoeba (1970)
The Return of Ultraman *[episodes 1, 2, 7, 9, 51]* (1971-72, TV)
Mirrorman *[episodes 1 and 2]* (1971-72, TV)
Zone Fighter *[episodes 3, 4, 12, 13, 18, 19, 23, 24]* (1973, TV)
Terror of Mechagodzilla (1975)
Kagemusha (1980) [assistant director]
Ran (1985) [assistant director]
Dreams (1990) [assistant director and creative consultant]

宇宙人 東京に現わる

Uchujin Tokyo ni arawaru "An Alien Appears in Tokyo"
Daiei, 1/29/1956 (*Showa 31*), 13 Reels (2,389 meters), 86:39, 35mm, Academy (1.37:1), Eastman color, monaural sound

Crew

Producer: Masaichi Nagata
Planning: Fujio Nakadai
Director: Koji Shima
Screenplay: Hideo Oguni, Gentaro Nakajima (story)
Director of Photography: Kimio Watanabe
Music: Seitaro Omori
Editor: Toyo Suzuki
Production Design: Shigeo Mano
Lighting: Kuichi Kubota
Color Film Consultant: Toru Matoba
Designs: Taro Okamoto
Production Manager: Keiichi Sakaso
Special Effects: Toru Motaba, Yonesaburo Tsukiji
Still Photographer: Tadao Miyazaki

Cast

Toyomi Karita *(Hikari Aozora/Ginko)*
Keizo Kawasaki *(Dr. Toru Isobe)*
Bin Yagisawa *(Pairan #2)*
Bontaro Miake *(Dr. Yoshio Komura)*
Shozo Nanbu *(Dr. Naotaro Isobe)*
Frank Kumagai *(Observatory Scientist)*
Kanji Kawahara *(Dr. Takashima)*
Fumiko Okumura *(Madam Ohana)*
Meiko Nagai *(Taeko Komura)*
Toshiyuki Obara *(Kenichi Amano)*
Isao Yamagata *(Dr. Eisuke Matsuda)*
Kiyoko Hirai *(Kiyoko Matsuda)*
Akira Natsuki *(Pairan #3)*
Sachiko Meguro *(Tokuko Isobe)*
Shiko Saito *(Mystery Man)*
Tetsuya Watanabe *(Sankichi)*
Seiji Izumi *(Drunk)*
Kenichi Tani *(Bouncer)*
Ko Sugita *(Reporter)*
Yuzo Hayakawa *(Policeman)*
Shunji Tsuda *(Pairan #4)*
Yasuko Hanamura *(Geisha)*
Gai Harada *(Sailor)*

Alternate Titles

The Mysterious Satellite (UK)
Die Außerirdischen erscheinen in Tokio (Germany)
Le Satellite mystérieux (France)
Asalto a la tierra **[Assault On Earth]** (Spain)
O Alerta do Espaço (Brazil)

"There's a starman
Waiting in the sky
He'd like to come and meet us
But he thinks he'd blow our minds."
-David Bowie, *"Starman"*, *The Rise and Fall of Ziggy Stardust and the Spiders From Mars* (1972)

Warning From Space is an underappreciated gem of a film. Made by Toho's biggest rival, Daiei, it is the first color Japanese *tokusatsu* movie. *Warning From Space* is a lavishly produced work well directed by Koji Shima. It's a smart science fiction story with an engaging script by Kurosawa scribe Hideo Oguni. The film evokes Robert Wise's *The Day The Earth Stood Still* and the George Pal production *When Worlds Collide* (both 1951).

PLOT

In Tokyo, UFO sightings are increasing. At a restaurant, reporter Kenichi Amano (Toshiyuki Obara) hounds scientist Dr. Komura (Bontaro Miake) for a theory. Komura, however, refuses to speculate without evidence. At the observatory, Komura's assistant Dr. Toru Isobe (Keizo Kawasaki) sees a UFO flying towards Tokyo on the telescope. This causes radio interference. As Komura and Toru discuss this sighting, the "saucer" is seen up close and falls into Tokyo Bay. Soon, "monsters" resembling giant starfish begin to be seen in the Tokyo area. Dr. Komura's daughter Taeko (Meiko Nagai) sees the "monster". The creature then appears during a stage show of Hibari Misora-like idol Hikari Aozora (Toyomi Karita).

The saucer leaves Tokyo Bay. Returning to a satellite orbiting the Earth, the alien consults with more of its kind. Initial attempts to make contact with humans have been a failure. Using the likeness of Hikari Aozora, they transmute the first alien into her doppleganger. Toru and Taeko are out boating when they see a young woman floating in the water. This mysterious girl (also Toyomi Karita) is a dead ringer for Hikari Aozora and seems to have amnesia. Nicknamed Ginko, she displays unusual superhuman abilities. Toru's father Dr. Isobe (Shozo Nanbu) finds that she has no pattern on her fingerprints. Ginko reveals to Drs. Komura, Isobe and Matsuda that she is, in fact, an alien. She comes from a planet called Paira, unknown to humanity because it orbits parallel to the sun. Paira has decided to make contact with Earth because both planets face destruction. Runaway Planet R is on a collision course with both Earth and Paira.

BACKGROUND

It's a shame that *Warning From Space* is not more esteemed, even among fans of *tokusatsu* films. Its intelligent script, based on a novel by Gentaro Nakajima, is by Hideo Oguni. Oguni (1904-1996) was one of Japan's most talented screenwriters. Along with Shinobu Hashimoto, he was a favorite of Akira Kurosawa. He wrote or co-wrote *Ikiru, Seven Samurai, Throne of Blood, The Hidden Fortress, The Bad Sleep Well, High and Low* and *Ran*. With Oguni on hand, *Warning From Space* is unusually well structured and narratively engaging. It is said the famous Japanese folktale *The Tale of the Bamboo Cutter* was influential on the story. Also influential on *Warning* was George Pal's production *When Worlds Collide* (1951), directed by Rudolf Mate. That film was based on a 1933 novel by Philip Wylie and Edwin Balmer. It introduced the concept of armageddon via collision by a rogue planetoid. An asteroid now being known to have caused extinction of the dinosaurs, this would become a popular sci-fi trope. Ishiro Honda and Eiji Tsuburaya themselves would visit it in *Gorath* (1962). In Hollywood, it would form the basis for films as varied as *Meteor* (1979), *Deep Impact*, Michael Bay's *Armageddon* (both 1998) and even Lars Von Trier's *Melancholia* (2011).

PRINCIPAL PHOTOGRAPHY

Warning From Space is also compellingly directed by Koji Shima. Shima (1901-1986) began his career as an actor in the silent era. He started directing in 1939 and specialized in dramas. After the war, he mainly directed for Shin Toho and Daiei. At the end of his career, he went to Hong Kong and made a quartet of films for Shaw Brothers. *Warning From Space* is beautifully shot by Kimio Watanabe in almost dream-like Eastman color tones. While Shochiku made the first Japanese color film *Carmen Comes Home*, it was Daiei who revolutionized color in Japanese cinema. Teinosuke Kinugasa's *Gate of Hell* (1953) showed the world the potential of Eastman color and was an international success. With *Warning From Space* they beat their rivals at Toho again, creating the first color Japanese special effects film. Toho was quick to follow with Shiro Toyoda's *Madame White Snake* and Ishiro Honda's *Rodan* later that year. In contrast to Toho's more set-bound films, there's a lot of location photography in *Warning From Space*. With its luminous images of temples, old Tokyo and the countryside, it has a rustic Japaneseness Toho's films lacked. Yet the film's production values are quite solid. It's a shame Daiei did not make more lavish science-fiction pictures in this period.

Warning From Space's distinctive aliens were designed by Japanese surrealist Taro Okamoto. Okamoto (1911-1996) was something of Japan's own Picasso. He was a painter, sculptor and even writer. Educated at the Pantheon-Sorbonne in Paris, his art career blossomed after the war. His most iconic sculpture is the *"Tower of the Sun"*, commissioned and built for Osaka's Expo '70. The tower itself is featured in quite a few films from *Gamera vs. Jiger* (1970) to Hirokazu Kore-eda's *I Wish* (2011) and inspired a Shonen Knife song. There are now two museums dedicated to Okamoto. One is in his former studio in Aoyama Ward, Tokyo and the other in his hometown in Kawasaki. The aliens are not convincingly executed per say. Yet they are effective, looking like Japanese theater with the satellite's expressionistic set.

ACTORS

Warning From Space stars a number of Daiei contract players. The most famous was Shozu Nanbu (1898-198?) who played Dr. Isobe. Nanbu was born Masatsugu Oshiumi in 1898 in Oita Prefecture. Nanbu served in the Imperial Army in World War I where he fought in the Siberian Intervention. After leaving the army, Nanbu entered college and became an actor, joining Nikkatsu. His debut was in the 1926 silent film *Nichiren*. Nanbu quit Nikkatsu after experiencing friction with president Sadayori Nakatani. Afterwards, he appeared on stage and joined the fledgling studio Shinko Kinema. It was integrated into Daiei in 1942. Towards the end of his life in 1977, he received a government honor for achievements. The year of Nanbu's death is unknown, but likely sometime in the 1980s.

Keizo Kawasaki (1933-2015) would go on to become a popular actor at Daiei. Born in Kawasaki, Kanagawa, he debuted with *I've Never Seen Such a Wife* in 1954. After *Warning From Space*, his star was elevated by his leading role in *Sorrowful Train* (1957). Following the bankruptcy of Daiei he became active on television where he began to host the popular *New Afternoon Show*. Isao Yamagata (1915-1996) plays Dr. Matsuda. Yamagata was born in the U.K. as his father, Iwao Yamagata, was a circus performer who had been living in Europe. As a youth, he lost a lung to tuberculosis. Yamagata graduated acting school in 1935 and joined Toho after compulsory military service. After the war, he turned heads with a performance as Wataru, the husband of Machiko Kyo's tragic Kesa in Teinosuke Kinugasa's *Gate of Hell* (1953). He also appeared in Akira Kurosawa's *Seven Samurai* (1954), Kenji Mizoguchi's *Princess Yang Kwei Fei* and Mikio Naruse's *Floating Clouds* (both 1955). For tokusatsu fans, he later played a memorable role on episode 14 of *Ultraman Ace* (1972). Yamagata received the coveted *Order of the Sacred Treasures* from the Japanese government in 1988.

SFX

The miniature and special effects work by Toru Matoba and Yonesaburo Tsukiji is spirited. It is only slightly less polished than the work Eiji Tsuburaya was doing for Toho. The images of coastal flooding, the glowing planet approaching Earth and the satellite hovering in space are nearly equal to Toho quality. Matoba (1920-1992), graduated from the prestigious Tokyo University of the Arts in 1938. Answering a newspaper ad for photography students, he joined the technical department of Nikkatsu. By 1941, he was drafted into the Japanese Imperial Army where he served in the Chinese front during the war. Returning to Japan in 1946, Matoba helped establish the special effects division at Daiei. The rogue Planet R was mainly a matte painting drawn by Matoba and his crew. Matoba would go on to provide the special effects work on such Daiei films as *The Invisible Man vs. the Human Fly* (1957), the 70mm religious epic *Buddha* (1961) and Tokuza Tanaka's Nihon *Moby Dick: The Whale God* (1962). He was then hired, along with Keiji Kawakama, by Tsuburaya Pro. He directed the special effects units on numerous episodes of *Ultra Q, Ultraman, Kaiju Booska* (all 1966), *Ultraseven* (1967) and *Operation: Mystery* (1968). After Tsuburaya's death, Matoba went freelance and worked on P-Production's *Spectreman* (1972).

THEMES AND MOTIFS

Stories of benevolent aliens are rarer in science fiction than hostile alien invaders. Physicist Stephen Hawking believed that intelligent alien life is unlikely to have benevolent intentions towards humanity. Yet the opposite scenario makes for an intriguing narrative. What if, rather than to conquer

Earth, space creatures visited to help us? Bringing us a higher state of consciousness rather than apocalyptic destruction? This is a novel, philosophical concept for what many regard as a Japanese B-movie. Similar themes were delved into with Robert Wise's 1951 *The Day the Earth Stood Still.* It's clear *Day* was an influence on *Warning From Space.* Such tropes would be explored more frequently in many iconic works. These range from Gene Roddenberry's *Star Trek* franchise to Stanley Kubrick's *2001: A Space Odyssey* (1968) to Stephen Spielberg's *Close Encounters of the Third Kind* (1977) and *E.T.* (1982). Kubrick himself was said to have a particular fondness for *Warning From Space.* *Warning From Space* may have even been influential on Tsuburaya's Ultraman franchise. *Ultraman* also concerns a benevolent alien race and the trope of an alien assuming human form is used. David Bowie's song *"Starman"* off his album *Ziggy Stardust* also iconically tackles the theme of a benevolent alien visitor. The concept of a *"starman"* being both literally and figuratively similar, one might wonder if perhaps Bowie caught *Warning From Space* on late night television in a drug-fueled haze. More recently, Denis Villenueve's *Arrival* (2016) explores such themes. Like *Warning,* *Arrival* deals with a visit by benevolent aliens who are met with suspicion by humans. In both films, the creatures come to make a mutually beneficial exchange with humanity.

RELEASE AND LEGACY

While Daiei would move away from science fiction and *tokusatsu* productions for the next few years, this was far from their last. In the mid 1960s, they would become the house of giant flying terrapin Gamera and rampaging stone idol Majin. A Pairan alien would make a cameo years later in Daicon Film's *Daicon IV Opening Animation.* In the meantime, *Warning From Space* is an underrated and clever little film that cries out for rediscovery.

ALTERNATE VERSIONS

Daiei had some degree of difficulty selling the film internationally. This was likely due to its more Japanese tone and intellectual themes. It was not distributed in the U.S. until 1964, released to television by Four Star International. The American edit is similar to the Japanese save for a few minor but significant differences. Running 87:50, it's a rare U.S. version longer in runtime than its Japanese counterpart. So the film would play better on American airwaves, there's more editorial emphasis on the aliens. Extra material bookends this version. An added opening with footage re-edited from a later scene is put in. The aliens have a more foreboding conversation that hints at desire for conquest. Only one small, minute long sequence is deleted from the U.S. version showing Taeko having dinner with Dr. Matsuda and his wife. The other change is at the film's end, featuring Ginko transforming back into a Pairan. This is the transmutation scene from earlier in the film, played in reverse. The Japanese version, which introduces the aliens gradually, is more effective at building tension. Re-filmed

English language newspapers are also added, supplanting the Japanese ones.

The English dubbing was done at Titra Sound Studios (later Titan Productions) in New York City. These dub tracks contain faux Asian accents some may find problematic. Yet they put more time and effort into the writing and lipsync than the cheaply done Tokyo and Hong Kong export tracks. Those tended to be recorded in a night or two. By contrast, Titra/Titan's dubs tended to take three days to two weeks to record. In their own words: *"If it doesn't look bubbed, if it doesn't sound bubbed, it was dubbed by Titan"*. Dubbing cast includes Lucy Martin, Jack Curtis, Bret Morrison and Larry Robinson. The dub's script is credited to Jay H. Cipes and Edward Palmer. Jack Curtis (1926-1970) besides being a very prolific voice actor, also made *The Flesh Eaters* (1964). *The Flesh Eaters* is an imaginative horror flick with early gore and a similar "castaways-on-an-island" setting to Honda's *Matango*. Curtis wrote, directed, shot and edited it. Tragically, Jack Curtis died of pneumonia at only 44. Bret Morrison (1912-1978) was best known for playing iconic comic book character *The Shadow* on its radio drama. He occupied the role for over 10 years in the 1940s and '50s. Later on, he would narrate the original trailer for *Night of the Living Dead* (1968).

AMERICAN HOME VIDEO HISTORY

Warning From Space was available on VHS through mail order companies like Sinister Cinema, Video Yesteryear and Something Weird Video in the U.S., telecined from 16mm prints. As the U.S. version now holds public domain status, it was released on DVD by Alpha Video around 2005. *Warning From Space* was released on Blu-ray from Arrow in October 2020 in a superior transfer of the Japanese version.

Further Viewing:

(1949)
透明人間現わる
Daiei, *Director*: Nobuo Adachi

The Invisible Man Appears is not a particularly good film but an important one. It is the first major and surviving live action Japanese science fiction film. *The Invisible Man Appears* presents a loose, post-war Japanese adaptation of H.G. Wells' literary classic. It is directed by Nobuo Adachi (*Claw of Iron*), a filmmaker with a short-lived, mostly horror-based career. *The Invisible Man Appears* also features an early post-war effects job by Eiji Tsuburaya. Tsuburaya was currently in exile from Toho as he had been targeted by MacArthur's Occupation forces for his role in Imperial propaganda films like *The War at Sea From Hawaii to Malay* (1942). Daiei offered him the chance to head their special effects department, but Tsuburaya chose to remain freelance for now. He was allowed to return to Toho in 1952 once the U.S. Occupiers departed. A few years later, he worked on his most famous film: 1954's *Godzilla*.

The Invisible Man Appears is a convoluted and confusing picture but not totally without merit. Originally titled *The Transparent Devil*, the production values are quite good for a film made in a Japan still recuperating from the Pacific War. There are plenty of dream-like monochrome images to be seen, along with lighting evocative of film noir. The titular Invisible Man boasts a bandage wrapped-face just like Claude Rains in Universal's iconic 1933 adaptation. Close ups of the villain's leering eyes invoke Bela Lugosi in *White Zombie* (1932). Best of all are Tsuburaya's subtle practical FX and inventive visual trickery, easily on par with anything in Universal's *Invisible Man* films. Particularly impressive is a scene early on featuring an invisible cat. Also intriguing are later scenes showing the Invisible Man sitting in a chair smoking a cigarette, driving a police moped and firing a pistol.

This would be far from the last Invisible Man picture produced in Japan. Toho next made *The Invisible Avenger* on the heels of *Godzilla* in 1954. This film, directed by Motoyoshi Oda (*Godzilla Raids Again*) featured actor Seizaburo Kawazu in the title role. He performs in a circus and uses clown makeup to hide his invisibility. Next was *The Invisible Man vs. the Human Fly* (1957), produced at Daiei and directed by Mitsuo Murayama. Tsuburaya did not take part in this production as he was contracted to Toho. Ishiro Honda's *The Human Vapor* (1960) also boasts some Wellsian *Invisible Man*

tropes. Both *The Invisible Man Appears* and *The Invisible Man vs. the Human Fly* can now be had on Blu-ray via Arrow.

SUPER GIANT
(1957-59)
スーパージャイアンツ
Shin Toho, *Directors*: **Teruo Ishii, Akira Mitsuwa, Chogi Akasaka**

Shin Toho, an offshoot of Toho caused by union disputes, created one of the very first Japanese superheroes: Super Giant. Played by Ken Utsui (1931-2014), the name was a portmanteau of DC's Superman and the baseball team the Yomiuri Giants. The nine short films that resulted were shown serial-style in Japan from 1957 to '59. When they came to the U.S., they were repackaged into four English dubbed compilation features: *Atomic Rulers, Invaders From Space, Attack From Space* and *Evil Brain From Outer Space*. Super Giant himself was renamed "Starman".

These films are a hard sell for modern audiences but are interesting to say the least. They're not particularly good, but there's a charming ridiculousness. In addition, these mini-movies boast a breathless atmosphere akin to the Hollywood serials of old. They have the same off the wall pacing, goofy but eclectic costume and production design and gravity defying stunt silliness. The *Super Giant* films recall *Flash Gordon, Buck Rogers* and *King of the Rocketmen* a lot more than *Godzilla*. The first three "Starman" compilation films at least have somewhat cohesive plots. Each is edited from the Teruo Ishii-directed two part entries. The final film, *Evil Brain From Outer Space,* is a Jerry Warren-style hodgepodge of footage from the final three stand-alone entries. These are all weaved together into an incoherent narrative that is almost dream-like. The eight and ninth episodes were shot in the 'scope ratio so the cropped footage is intercut with the "Academy ratio" footage of episode seven.

The first six *Super Giant* installments were early works of director Teruo Ishii. After the bankruptcy of Shin Toho in 1961, Ishii (1924-2005) moved to Toei. It was there that he redefined the screen madness Toei would be known for. He made such *ero-guro* (erotic-grotesque) works as *The Joy of Torture* (1968), *Horrors of Malformed Men* (1969), *Blind Woman's Curse* (1970) and *Bohachi Bushido* (1973). The child-oriented *Super Giant* films are far from that, though *Invaders From Space* has slight elements of the Edogawa Rampo-like grotesquery that

would one day be Ishii's trademark. Teruo Ishii wound up quitting the series and leaving the last three episodes in the hands of other directors. This was because a child, pretending to be Super Giant and wearing a blanket as a cape, jumped off his family's porch. The child badly injured himself on the street below and Ishii was unsettled. Actor Ken Utsui was said to hate the character, tight pants and stuffed crotch in all. He disliked playing Super Giant to such a degree that he refused to be interviewed about it up until his death. The *Super Giant* films are certainly more influential than commonly believed. Rival studio Toei produced their own superhero series, *Moonlight Mask,* in TV and serialized film form only a year after Super Giant's debut. Toei followed *Moonlight Mask* with *Planet Prince,* which became its own two part theatrical serial. The two episodes were edited together into a direct-to-TV feature film in the U.S. entitled *Prince of Space.*

EARLY COLOR FILMS IN JAPAN
日本の初期のカラー映画

by Patrick Galvan

Patrick Galvan is a freelance writer specializing in Japanese cinema. His work has been published on Toho Kingdom and SyFy Wire.

The proliferation of color film in Japan was decades in the making. As early as the 1900s, camera-armed businessmen were experimenting with additive hues for black and white movies. They manually colored scenes frame by frame. Shots of cherry blossoms exploded with pink and gloomy

night scenes became drenched in shades of orange. In the 1910s, the short-lived film studio Tenkatsu adopted a British projection technique called Kinemacolor. Black and white footage was projected through alternating filters of red and green to create the tacky illusion of color. While the novelty factor was exciting, these pseudo-color films didn't sell enough to make up for their expensive techniques. With fewer Hollywood films imported in the years leading to World War II, the Japanese had less opportunity to study Western photographic developments. *Gone With the Wind*, for instance, was not released in Japan until 1952. Consequently, Japanese studios defaulted to black and white for the next few decades, awaiting a film stock designed to shoot color images.

Interest resuscitated in 1946 with the release of Motoyoshi Oda's *Eleven Girl Students*. An occupation-era film whose title sequence was the first public demonstration of Fujicolor, Oda's movie paved the way for further experimentation. Over the next four years, the Japanese utilized Fujicolor in shooting newsreels, select scenes of feature-length movies and *kabuki* performances. The perception of color as a technique for limited use persisted though. In 1951, Shochiku produced Keisuke Kinoshita's *Carmen Comes Home*, now remembered as Japan's first full-color movie. Kinoshita worked with two different cameras on this production: one shooting in Fujicolor, the other in traditional black and white. Two versions of the movie were released. Despite *Carmen Comes Home*'s significance, it was the black and white version that played in most Shochiku theaters when the film was new. The studio had only printed eleven copies of the color version.

Historically, 1953 was a significant year for Japanese color films. This was when most of the major studios tried to capitalize on the trend, encouraged by the recent success of imports from Hollywood. Two years after *Carmen Comes Home* and one year after its black and white sequel, *Carmen's Innocent Love*, Shochiku took another stab at Fujicolor with *Natsuko's Adventure* directed by Nobuo Nakamura. Toho followed suit with Kajiro Yamamoto's *Girls in Flowers*. Toei also tested a new brand of Japanese film stock in making Kunio Watanabe's *The Sun*. Nikkatsu, often last to catch up on the latest fads, was a few years away from their first Konicolor release. Yet it wasn't until Daiei imported Eastman stock from the West that a color Japanese film found widespread succession.

With opulent costumes and photographed on Eastman color stock, Teinosuke Kinugasa's *Gate of Hell* (1953) promptly went overseas. Its lush color cinematography won praise in the New York Times; *"In color of a richness and harmony that matches that of any film we ve ever seen"*. It also snatched the Palme d'Or at the 1954 Cannes Film Festival and took home the Best Foreign Language Film prize at the 1955 Academy Awards. Beloved Danish filmmaker Carl Theodor Dreyer even applauded the film. The timing was perfect. Akira Kurosawa's *Rashomon* (1950) and Kenji Mizoguchi's *Ugetsu* (1953) had won numerous awards and Japanese cinema was at last making waves internationally. Tantalized by *Gate of Hell*'s success, the major studios set out to prepare "export-worthy" films in the lushest manner they could afford.

This was most evident at Toho. They invested $500,000, the second highest budget for a Japanese movie at that time, into Hiroshi Inagaki's *Musashi Miyamoto*. Inagaki's crew constructed huge sets, cast hundreds of extras and followed Daiei's example of shooting in Eastman color. All of this required a longer production schedule: six months for a 93 minute film. While *Musashi Miyamoto* was getting attention at the Academy Awards, the studio searched for another international hit. They joined forces with Hong Kong's Shaw Brothers, producing Shiro Toyoda's *Madame White Snake* (1956). Based on a Chinese legend, it was a lavish supernatural fantasy that climaxes with an Eiji Tsuburaya typhoon. This same legend would be re-adapted into *The Tale of the White Serpent* (1958), the first feature length anime. Daiei, however, had been first in getting a color *tokusatsu* film to the public. The sci-fi spectacular *Warning from Space* had premiered a few months before *Madame White Snake*. Toho was determined to catch up and surpass them. Having pioneered the kaiju eiga sub-genre, it was only a matter of time before Tsuburaya and director Ishiro Honda pointed color cameras at city-wide mass destruction. While *Madame White Snake* failed to strike international gold, Honda and Tsuburaya's *Rodan* performed well at home and spectacularly abroad.

1957 was a pivotal year for Japanese special effects cinema. Anamorphic widescreen films were finally taking off thanks to renovated theaters now equipped to show their elongated images. It was in this year that Toho added 'scope to their itinerary. They debuted their version of Cinemascope with *On Wings of Love*, the latest color musical starring idol Hibari Misora. The film ended up becoming the studio's biggest moneymaker that year. Yet there was another TohoScope film released in 1957 that is now more iconic. *The Mysterians* was an ambitious alien invasion spectacular that would revolutionize *tokusatsu* and implement genre tropes followed for generations to come.

Rodan

Sora no Daikaiju Radon "Rodan: Monster of the Sky
Toho, 12/26/1956 (*Showa 31*), 9 Reels (2,253 meters), 82:08, 35mm, Academy (1.37:1), Eastman color, monaural sound

Crew
Producer: Tomoyuki Tanaka
Director: Ishiro Honda
Special Effects Director: Eiji Tsuburaya

Screenplay: Takeo Murata, Takeshi Kimura, Ken Kuronuma *(original story)*
Director of Photography: Isamu Ashida
Music: Akira Ifukube

Assistant Director: Jun Fukuda
Production Design: Tatsuo Hoku
Editor: Koichi Iwashita
Sound Recording: Masanobu Miyazaki

Sound Effects: Ichiro Minawa
Lighting: Shigeru Mori
Production Manager: Teruo Maki
SFX Art Director: Akira Watanabe
SFX Lighting: Masao Shirota
Optical Compositing: Hiroshi Mukoyama
SFX Production Manager: Yasuaki Sakamoto
Still Photographer: Jiro Tsuchiya

Cast
Kenji Sahara *(Shigeru Kawamura)*
Yumi Shirakawa *(Kiyo)*
Akihiko Hirata *(Professor Kyuchiro Kashiwagi)*
Yoshifumi Tajima *(Iseki)*
Fuminito Matsuo *(Hayama)*
Akio Kusama *(Suda)*
Minosuke Yamada *(Osaki)*
Akio Kobori *(Police Chief Nishimura)*
Fuyuki Murakami *(Professor Minami)*
Kiyoshi Takagi *(Dr. Minakami)*
Hideo Mihara *(Commander of the Air Defense Force)*
Mitsuo Tsuda *(Air Defense Force Officer Takeuchi)*
Ichiro Chiba *(Chief of Police)*
Junichiro Mukai *(Defense Corp Leader)*
Jiro Kumagai *(Policeman Tashiro)*
Ren Imaizumi *(Sunagawa)*
Saburo Kadowaki *(Sunagawa's Colleague)*
Junnosuke Suda *(Coroner)*
Mitsuo Matsumoto *(Professor Isogawa)*

Kiyomi Mizunoya *(Yuzo's Wife)*
Takeo Kawasaki *(Foreman Tsune)*
Kanta Kisaragi *(Miner Suteyan)*
Ichiro Nakatani *(Miner Senkichi)*
Kenji Sakaikita *(Miner Tahei)*
Rinsaku Ogata *(Miner Goro)*
Jiro Suzukawa *(Miner Yuzo)*
Yasuhiro Shigenobu *(Miner Sabu)*
Saeko Kuroiwa *(Nurse)*
Seiji Onaka *(Young Man)*
Yasuko Nakada *(Young Woman)*
Koji Uno *(Reporter)*
Tadashi Okabe *(Reporter)*
Tsuruko Mano *(Osumi)*
Tsurue Ichimanji *(Haru)*
Katsumi Tezuka *(Hotel Manager)*
Haruo Nakajima *(Rodan/Meganulon)*
Toshiko Nakano *(Kiyo's Neighbor)*
Shoichi Hirose *(Pilot/Meganulon)*
Keichiro Katsumoto *(Coal Miner)*
Yutaka Oka *(Pilot Kitahara)*
Kazuo Hinata
Akira Yamada *(Radioman)*
Shigemi Sunagawa *(Pilot)*
Bontaro Taira *(Coal MIner)*
Masaki Tachibana *(Policeman)*
Shin Yoshida
Yasuhisa Tsutumi *(Pilot Imamura)*
Hideo Unagami *(Coal Miner)*
Takashi Narita
Koji Suzuki

Haruya Sakamoto
Yasumasa Onishi
Kamayuki Tsubono *(Crime Lab Policeman)*
Masao Sengoku
Kazuo Fukuda
Hideo Shibuya
Haruo Suzuki
Masao Ibarata
Koji Iwamoto
Kenzo Echigo
Minoru Ono
Masayoshi Kawabe
Tokio Okawa
Mike Daneen *(American Radioman)*

Alternate Titles
Rodan, the Flying Monster (Alternate U.S. title)
Bloodthirsty Hawk (Alternate)
Rodan il mostro alato **[Rodan the Winged Monster]** (Italy)
Rodan, Los hijos del volcán **[Rodan, Sons of the Volcano]** (Spain)
Rodan! O Monstro do Espaço **[Rodan! The Monster From Space]** (Brazil)
Ροντάν, ο δράκος του Qiu Shu **[Rodan, the Dragon of Qiu Shu]** (Greece)
Skräck över Japan **[Horror Over Japan]** (Sweden)
Rodan, tuntematon vihollinen **[Rodan, An Unknown Enemy]** (Finland)
Radon, az égi szörny **[Rodan the Celestial Monster]** (Hungary)
Rodan - ptak śmierci **[Rodan: Bird of Death]** (Poland)
Радон (Russia)

"It was as if something human were dying. As the flames consumed them in a fiery holocaust, their last agony wails ended in a mournful cry. We stood there standing with a strange fascination."
-Shigeru (Kenji Sahara, voice of Keye Luke), U.S. version (1957)

Rodan was Japan's first color *kaiju* flick. Overall, it lacks the novelty of Ishiro Honda and Eiji Tsuburaya's classic *Godzilla* or *Mothra* (1961). Nonetheless, it's a stellar monster movie, if fairly routine. It follows many tropes of *Godzilla* while throwing some curveballs. Horror-themed early scenes give way to impressive destruction sequences where Tsuburaya's unit takes center stage.

PLOT

In the Kyushu coal mining community of Kitamatsu, trouble is afoot. Two miners go missing. The miners, Goro (Rinsaku Ogata) and Yuzo (Jiro Suzukawa), had a physical altercation earlier in the day which draws suspicion. Shigeru Kawamura (Kenji Sahara), a safety engineer at the mine, investigates and finds Yuzo's corpse. An autopsy is conducted and the cause of death is determined to be laceration with a sharp weapon. This makes the village further suspect Goro as the murderer.

An investigating policeman and two miners are killed next. That night, Shigeru and his fiancee Kiyo (Yumi Shirakawa), Goro's sister, encounter the culprit: a giant, insect-like monster. The police force pursues the monster and it kills two policemen before disappearing underground. Shigeru, along with a detachment of police and Self Defense Force soldiers, pursue it into the mines.

They find Goro's lacerated body and are attacked by the creature. Shigeru kills the monster by crushing it with mine carts. Another giant insect appears and Shigeru is soon trapped underground in a cave in. Scientist Professor Kashiwagi (Akihiko Hirata) claims that the insects are *Meganuron*, larvae of prehistoric dragonflies. An earthquake soon hits and it is feared Mount Aso may be nearing an eruption. Shigeru is found by the authorities near the volcano, with his memory completely gone.

Meanwhile, an unidentified flying object is noticed flying at a supersonic speed in the nearby skies. A pursuing pilot and his jet are swiftly destroyed. The UFO is also sighted in China, Okinawa and over the Philippines. A newlywed couple next vanishes near Mt. Aso, leaving their camera behind. The film is developed and the last picture shows what appears to be a gigantic wing. Professor Kashiwagi surmises that the wing could belong to a *Pteranodon*. Shigeru, meanwhile, is shown by Kiyo eggs laid by her pet birds. As one of the eggs hatches, Shigeru regains his memory. He flashes back to being trapped underground and witnessing a gigantic egg hatch, out of which came a monster *Pteranodon*. The newborn *Pteranodon* then devours the *Meganuron* as food.

Sure enough, the authorities and Shigeru find a fragment of the gigantic egg in the cavern. Kashiwagi confirms that the egg is indeed that of a *Pteranodon*. The UFO is this creature, likely awoken by atomic tests. The monster is christened Rodan. Rodan soon emerges from its underground lair and does battle with the Air Defense Force. Rodan next flies to the city of Fukuoka which it completely destroys. Another Rodan, its mate, joins in on the destruction.

BACKGROUND

Rodan was Toho's third giant monster film and the first in color. Genre writer Ken Kuronuma was tapped to draft the story. Like *Godzilla* and the Lucky Dragon incident, *Rodan* drew influence from a then recent news headline. On January 7th, 1948, a young Kentucky National Guard pilot named Thomas Mantell was ordered to pursue an unidentified flying object in his P-51 Mustang jet. He never returned. Occuring only six months after the infamous Roswell UFO incident, it birthed numerous conspiracy theories. Such incidents only increased the popularity of alien invaders and UFO tropes in sci-fi.

The concept of a winged, flying monster was likely a carryover from Hideo Unagami's 1955 script *Bride of Godzilla*. The treatment had been scrapped, likely for being too expensive. Akira Watanabe's early designs for Rodan were much closer to the *Archeopteryx*, which appeared in Unagami's script. Eventually, a more *Pteranodon*-like design

was created. The script was the first monster picture written by the brooding genre scribe Takeshi Kimura. Early drafts featured only one Rodan. The creature was also to do battle with U.S. forces over Okinawa which was to have injured the beast. The latter was likely removed as the U.S. presence in Okinawa was and still is a hot button issue in Japan. Just as Ishiro Honda almost directed *Throne of Blood*, Akira Kurosawa was possibly keen on directing the picture. It's said he was turned down by Tanaka because of his known perfectionism and the high cost of his films as a result. Kurosawa, however, was allowed to contribute to the script. Several ideas, including the film being set during the summer, came from him.

PRINCIPAL PHOTOGRAPHY

Ishiro Honda was enlisted to direct instead and this was his first color film. Honda's unit dominates the film's first half. DP Isamu Ashida's Eastman color images are luminous and the Southern Japanese locales are scenic. Some location scenes were filmed at the Nittetsu Mining Company's coal mine in Nagasaki Prefecture. The extras for these scenes were made up of miners employed there.

Early sequences with the human-scaled *Meganuron* monsters have a horror film flair. This looks forward to later Honda films like *The H-Man* (1958) and *Frankenstein Conquers the World* (1965). These scenes are also quite reminiscent of 1954's *Them!*, directed by Gordon Douglas. They would be influential on future films. The early

"Shokiras" scenes in *The Return of Godzilla* (1984) are quite reminiscent of them. The "Aggregate Destoroyah" segments in *Godzilla vs. Destoroyah* (1995) also invoke these sequences. Shusuke Kaneko paid particular homage to them in the Soldier Legion scenes in *Gamera 2: Attack of Legion* (1996). The main *Meganuron* suit was a whopping 15 feet long and were played by three actors with Haruo Nakajima at the lead. It is one of the best and most effective pantomime horse-style suits from the *Showa* era. The sound design for the creatures is oddly unnerving for a Toho film.

ACTORS

Newcomers Kenji Sahara and Yumi Shirakawa play young lovers for the first time. Both would soon become genre stalwarts. Shirakawa (1936-2016) was born Akiko Yamazaki. She began her career appearing in advertisements for Morinaga Chocolate at 19. Shirakawa was soon recommended to Toho and first appeared in *Rodan*. She would go on to appear in several more science fiction themed films. Her stunning beauty got her the nickname *"The Grace Kelly of Japan"*. She was said to be ashamed of her science fiction appearances and refused to be interviewed. Her husband was actor Hideaki Nitani. Yoshifumi Tajima also plays one of his first roles for director Honda. Tajima (1918-2009), from Kobe, would soon become a favorite character actor of Honda's. He played bit parts for Kurosawa and Inagaki but showed a lot of range when given juicier roles. His standout is greedy entrepreneur

Kumayama in Honda's *Mothra vs. Godzilla* (1964).

SFX

Rodan can be a formulaic picture but it boasts impressive special effects and miniature work from Tsuburaya and company. *Rodan* is a little slow to get going with the titular monsters not appearing until almost an hour in. It's a middling Ishiro Honda picture but a stupendous Eiji Tsuburaya one. Tsuburaya's effects unit takes impressive command of the film's final act. The sequence where Shigeru witnesses Rodan hatching in a grotty underground cavern is a particular highlight. It feels like Honda and Tsuburaya in perfect creative synergy. A hand puppet was used to portray the baby monster in this sequence. The *Meganuron* being devoured by the hatchling Rodan is a nightmarish little moment. There's a certain existential horror to it that almost invokes H.P. Lovecraft. It was apparently suggested by none other than Akira Kurosawa and his genius shows.

In *Rodan*'s final third, it is a thrilling film. There are stunning optical compositions. A shot of Rodan emerging from its lair in front of horrified onlookers is among Tsuburaya's finest. As with *Godzilla*, the main suit was made by Teizo Toshimitsu and Kanju and Yasuei Yagi. A variety of flying Rodan props were also constructed in various sizes and scales for the aerial sequences. The replicas of the F-86 Saber jets were constructed by Yoshio Irie, also at varying scales. For the largest ones, Irie was allowed access to designs and mechanical parts from the U.S. Air Force at nearby Yokota base. Suit actor Haruo Nakajima was nearly killed playing Rodan. Throughout the film he was suspended above set in the suit with cables. While shooting the monster rising from the sea before wrecking the Saikai Bridge, the cables snapped and Nakajima fell 20 feet into the water. Luckily the physics of the suit largely broke his fall. The Saikai Bridge itself had just been built only a year prior in 1955. The model, built at 1/20th scale, had been painted red. When Tsuburaya's crew realized that the bridge was actually silver, they frantically repainted it overnight. Amusingly, Saikai Bridge became much more popular as a tourist destination after the release of *Rodan*.

Rodan's rampage through Kyushu's Fukuoka is one of Tsuburaya's best-executed monster sequences. It's on par with *Godzilla*'s Tokyo scenes but in broad daylight and Eastman color. Early Eastman stock was slow (not light sensitive) and *Rodan* was shot in the peak of summer. As a result, the lighting set-ups required were massive and brutally hot. Most of Tsuburaya's scenes thus had to be shot at night. The elaborate miniature work is quite remarkable. Realistic and impressive shots of tiles flying off rooftops were inspired by a crewman's childhood memories of a typhoon. These tiles were made from cardboard so they would blow off easily. Rodan's gusts were created with a modified airplane engine. An interior shot of the military brass running as the building they're in is destroyed was accomplished by reflecting the actors with a mirror placed inside a model building. Shinji Higuchi and his team would pay homage to

the shot by using the same technique in 1996's *Gamera 2: Attack of Legion*.

For *Rodan*'s final 10 minutes, Tsuburaya's unit ferociously lets loose on the pyrotechnics. The repeated firing of missiles and subsequent explosions are a little repetitive. These shots involved the heaviest and most sophisticated pyrotechnics Tsuburaya had used yet. They were extremely dangerous for the crew to stage. The ending is quite poignant, as the two Rodans are immolated in a fiery volcanic eruption. For this last scene, an enormous, over 30 foot Mount Aso model was built. Tsuburaya's team used molten iron as realistic lava and puppets were used for the dying Rodans. A happy accident occured when, due to the intense heat, one of the wires on the puppets snapped. The operator's reaction gave the effect that the monster was trying to save itself. Tsuburaya ordered Sadamasa Arikawa, who was about to stop the camera, to keep rolling. There's a pathos to this sequence where the viewer feels genuine pity for the Rodans. This impressive ending somewhat sets *Rodan* apart.

MUSIC

Akira Ifukube contributes another classic score. Eerie, guttural tones create the main theme. The most memorable piece of music in the film is *"Get Rodan"*, a stirring military march that plays throughout the air battle scenes. The piece would later be reused in 1991's *Godzilla vs. King Ghidorah*.

THEMES AND MOTIFS

Takeo Murata and Takeshi Kimura's script largely dispenses with the allegorical themes of *Godzilla* for a straight-up no-nonsense monster thriller. The anti-nuclear themes of *Godzilla* are not totally abandoned, however. Atomic weapons are mentioned as a possible reason for the monsters' appearance. Regardless, *Rodan*'s execution is far more resplendent and creative than its Hollywood counterparts thanks to Eiji Tsuburaya's contributions. It is overall another classic Honda and Tsuburaya collaboration worth seeing.

RELEASE AND LEGACY

Though not as successful as *Godzilla*, *Rodan* did good business. In the narration for the U.S. version by Keye Luke, Shigeru says *"May not other and even more terrible monsters even now be stirring in the darkness?"*. Tomoyuki Tanaka was keen to produce more science fiction and monster pictures. Rodan itself would be back opposite Godzilla and Mothra in 1964's *Ghidorah, the Three-Headed Monster* and became a staple of the Godzilla series. The creature last appeared in 2019's *Godzilla: King of the Monsters*. The *Meganuron* would also return one day, forming the basis for the foe Megaguiras in 2000's *Godzilla vs. Megaguirus*.

ALTERNATE VERSIONS

For U.S. release, *Rodan* was acquired by movie moguls the King Brothers, who later produced 1961's *Gorgo* in the UK. *Rodan*

was released on August 6, 1957 via Distributors Corporation of America (DCA). It wound up being not only the highest grossing Japanese film to date but also broke records for a science fiction picture. This was thanks in part to the King Brothers pouring a lot of money into a large scale TV advertising blitz in metro areas.

While the changes to the U.S. version are more minor compared to *Godzilla: King of the Monsters!*, they are significant. Running around 72:11, around fifteen minutes of the film are trimmed and the picture is heavily reedited and re-shuffled. An opening segment with narration by Art Gilmore composed of American atomic test footage is added. Sequences trimmed include a shortening of Goro fighting with Yuzo and the Meganuron's onscreen introduction is cut down. The scene where the two honeymooners are killed by Rodan is made far shorter and a scene of Professor Kashiwagi identifying the monster as a Pteranodon is truncated. The second Rodan is given more screen time in the U.S. version. In the Japanese version, its appearance is a surprise at the end of the Fukuoka sequence. The U.S. version makes it clear Rodan has a mate when it first emerges from Mt. Aso. The creature also emerges with provocation by the air force whereas in the Japanese version, the creature emerges unprovoked. A scene where a helicopter investigates the Rodans' lair is rearranged to before Rodan's attack on Fukuoka (changed to Sasebo in this version) instead of afterward. The U.S. version also replaces much of Ifukube's score with library music by composers Paul Sawtell and Bert

Shefter. The editing is credited to Robert S. Eisen and the sound effects to Anthony Carreras. The U.S. version of *Rodan* makes some improvements but overall, the Japanese version is more recommended.

One of the biggest changes the U.S. *Rodan* makes is adding a narration track to the film, the writing credited to David Duncan. The voice of Shigeru, who also narrates, is by Keye Luke. George Takei, one day to become famous on *Star Trek*, provided the voice of Professor Kashiwagi. Paul Frees did many additional voices. According to Takei, the voice cast consisted of only four people, most of whom dubbed up to nine roles (!). This dub was recorded at MGM Studios in Culver City, California. Luke and Takei would also both contribute voices to the similarly re-edited U.S. version of *Godzilla Raids Again*, called *Gigantis, the Fire Monster*.

Keye Luke (1904-1991) is best known in popular culture for his role as the elderly shopkeeper in Joe Dante's *Gremlins* (1984) and as Master Po on *Kung Fu* (1972-75). Luke was one of the most distinctive, versatile and prolific early Asian American actors in Hollywood. He was born in Guangzhou, China. He struggled as an artist before making his screen debut in 1934. He would go on to play Charlie Chan's son in several entries of the iconic series. Luke was also the first Kato in the original *The Green Hornet* serials starting in 1940. Later on, he appeared in *The Chairman* (1969), opposite Gregory Peck. One of his last roles was in Woody Allen's *Alice* (1990).

AMERICAN HOME VIDEO HISTORY

The U.S. version of *Rodan* was first released to American VHS, Betamax and laserdisc in 1983 by Vestron. The next VHS release was by Video Treasures in 1989. UPA next licensed the film to Paramount Home Video in 1992 and it was released to VHS and laserdisc. It was next released to DVD in 2002 by Classic Media. *Rodan* was then-reissued by Classic Media in 2008 in a double disc set with *The War of the Gargantuas*. This set contained both the Japanese and U.S. versions. Sadly, the U.S. version was still sourced from the same master first used by Vestron. In 2017, *Rodan* was next acquired by Janus Films. While they have not yet released it to physical media, it is available for streaming on the Criterion Channel.

Further Viewing:

(1958)

大怪獣バラン

Toho, *Director:* Ishiro Honda

Originally a U.S./Japanese co-production intended for television, *Varan* is not a particularly interesting nor high quality *kaiju eiga* effort. It is possibly Ishiro Honda and Eiji Tsuburaya's single weakest collaboration. As a standard monster-on-the-loose movie, however, it entertains. *Varan* was intended to be a four part TV mini series produced with ABC's film subsidiary AB-PT. *Varan* was thus shot with a lower budget than the average Toho *tokusatsu* effort and in black and white full frame. AB-PT soon pulled out, leaving Toho holding the bag with the film largely shot. As a result, the picture was released to Japanese theaters instead. By this time, Toho was releasing their films in a signature anamorphic widescreen process, TohoScope. *Varan*'s footage was thus cropped to 'scope using a process similar to Hollywood's "Superscope". The practice of shooting 'scope films with spherical lenses on full frame film was later perfected as Super 35. It became industry standard on both sides of the Pacific. Most of the Millennium Godzilla films would be shot in this process.

That *Varan* started out made for television and became a theatrical film is part of its problem. The movie was made directly in the wake of the superb *The Mysterians* (1957) and *The H-Man* (1958). If *Varan* had been a television oddity not compared to the Honda/Tsuburaya team's theatrical films it would have been more successful. Tsuburaya's effects end is decent though pales in comparison to his work on *Godzilla*, *Rodan* and *The Mysterians*. Varan, later to cameo in 1968's *Destroy All Monsters*, is one of the least interesting of Toho's monster menagerie. It boasts an especially handsome suit, however, courtesy of monster maker pro Teizo Toshimitsu and apprentice Keizo Murase. Varan's ability to glide using membranes under its arms like a flying squirrel somewhat set it apart. The footage is marred mainly by a technical issue with the monster's back flopping around and an overabundance of stock shots from *Godzilla*. This was a harbinger of things to come as the Toho FX unit's penchant for recycling

footage from earlier movies became a near trademark. *Varan* is most notable as the film that got suit actor demigod Haruo Nakajima the worst injury of his entire career. While filming the movie's explosive pyrotechnic climax, he sustained a nasty burn requiring hospital treatment. *Varan* also boasts a superb score from Akira Ifukube that is, oddly, one of his very finest. Many themes that would become iconic parts of his repertoire in later movies are introduced. Some tracks would later come to be associated with Godzilla and Rodan, along with a military march later used in *Battle in Outer Space* and recycled over a half century later in *Shin Godzilla*.

The Japanese version of *Varan* is an unremarkable if mildly entertaining film. By contrast, the U.S. version, called *Varan the Unbelievable* and not released until 1962, makes it look like a masterpiece. It is a shoddy bastardization that is among the worst Westernizations of a *tokusatsu* film. Ifukube's majestic score is mostly gone save for some of the ceremonial chanting. Very little of the dramatic end is left intact. Honda's sequences are all but replaced with dull scenes featuring B-player Myron Healy as a jerky American navalman. Tsuruko Kobayashi plays his Japanese wife whom he treats as a verbal punching bag. The plot now revolves around the U.S. Navy waking up Varan by conducting chemical experiments in a saltwater lake on a fictional island. The SFX footage is jumbled around, underused and printed very badly in most versions. Varan's flying scenes, oddly enough, are removed from the picture. This Jerry Warren-like mess is for the most part a completely different film. It was double-billed with another Americanized foreign sci-fi film, namely the East German *First Spaceship on Venus*.

AKIRA IFUKUBE
The Primitivist

伊福部昭

5.31.1914-2.8.2006

"There are two types of composers. Like Stravinsky, some always are aware of the instrument that will be playing a given melody. However, other composers do work out the orchestration only after they have finished composing. I'm like Stravinsky. I always write music with specific instruments in mind."
-Akira Ifukube (1992)

In their own ways, Tomoyuki Tanaka, Ishiro Honda, and Eiji Tsuburaya created the SF genre and made it what it is. But as clearly as the visual, structural, and thematic elements stand out as key to defining these films, so too does the sound, and for that, we have Akira Ifukube to thank.

Born in 1914 in Kushiro, Hokkaido, Akira Ifukube was the seventh and final child of Toshizo and Kiwa Ifukube. Growing up in rural Hokkaido, young Akira was introduced to and subsequently became fascinated with the culture of the Ainu, the indigenous people of northern Japan. The ancient customs of the Ainu, which hinged on a deep-seated love for nature, greatly impressed the young boy. The primitive qualities of their music, combined with the influence of his musically inclined brother Isao and the wealth of Japanese folk music he was exposed to at the same time, inspired him to become a musician. Toshizo, a career public servant who fully embodied the stern Meiji-Era ethic, felt that music was an unworthy pursuit for his son; nonetheless, it

would become the focus of the boy's life and future career.

Ifukube entered Hokkaido Imperial University in 1932, where he studied forestry. Music, however, was never far from his thoughts, and, having become an accomplished violinist, he quickly became concertmaster of the school's orchestra. As his passion for music swelled, Ifukube also began to craft original compositions.

Upon graduation, Ifukube went to work as a forestry officer in the remote region of Akkeshi, where he worked in total isolation, often for weeks at a time. Surrounded by the untouched natural world he so loved, the burgeoning composer continued his musical pursuits, and in 1935, his *Japanese Rhapsody* was entered into a competition in Paris, where it took first place. This further cemented the young man's future as a composer.

With the outbreak of war, Japan's imperial government sought to promote their agenda through the arts, and Ifukube, by now studying wood acoustics in Sapporo, was commissioned to write a number of commemorative pieces in addition to being brought on board as a government researcher due to his expertise. Although somewhat reticent at first, he obliged, as this spoke to his increasingly nationalist leanings. (Around this time, Ifukube met and married Ai Yuzaki, a ballet dancer with whom he worked on the extravagant composition *Etenraku*.) In August 1945, Ifukube fell gravely ill with radiation sickness, a result of his experiments with x-rays. Though he recovered, this experience would prove hauntingly relevant in the years to come.

After the war's end, work proved hard to come by. His college friend, Fumio Hayasaka, who had begun working in film (and would soon partner with Akira Kurosawa for some of the latter's most celebrated works), invited Ifukube to join him in this endeavor. In 1947, producer Tomoyuki Tanaka reached out, and in short order he received his first assignment, Senkichi Taniguchi's *Snow Trail*. Ifukube quickly became a highly sought-after film composer, and in 1954, an especially big opportunity came knocking.

The concept of *Godzilla*, involving as it did the primal forces of nature wreaking vengeance on mankind, resonated deeply with the composer, as did the explicit thematic element of radiation, which carried special personal significance for him. Moreover, his very direct and often barbaric compositional style, which uniquely blended such varied influences as the musical traditions of the Ainu and Russian composers like Stravinsky, was a perfect match for the subject matter; the horror,

tension, and tragedy of the picture are all amplified exponentially by the maestro's keen sensibilities. He also famously used his musical expertise in another way, devising the unorthodox technique of pulling a contrabass string with gloves coated in pine tar, the sound of which became the basis for the monster's iconic roar. Thus began the most famous association of Akira Ifukube's career.

The value of Ifukube's contributions to SF film cannot be overstated. The larger-than-life spectacle of tokusatsu cinema cries out for an aggressive bombast which the composer's distinct sound more than meets, creating a wonderful sonic complement to these magnificent scenes of grandeur and destruction. What is more, although their respective worldviews might not have meshed well, he got on famously with director Ishiro Honda, and it seems they were of the same mind as to the value and purpose of giant monsters in film. While Eiji Tsuburaya was keen on having the creatures engage in comical hijinks, Honda was adamantly opposed to humanizing these fearsome beasts in such a way. When King Kong fusses with his singed fur or Godzilla dances a victory jig, Ifukube's music keeps straight and true, and one gets the sense that he is scoring these scenes as Honda would have preferred them.

Throughout his career, Ifukube contributed to nearly 300 motion pictures in various genres, such as Kon Ichikawa's *The Burmese Harp* (1956), Hiroshi Inagaki's *Chushingura* (1962), and the *Zatoichi* series (1962-1973). As the years passed, Ifukube eventually began to drift away from film scores, but remained dedicated to classical composition as well as teaching; his students remember him as an eccentric personality, an engaging instructor, and a true gentleman. In the 1990s, he was coaxed out of retirement to work on several of the Heisei-Era Godzilla films, elevating them to a level that could not have been achieved without his help. He finally retired from film scoring after 1995's *Godzilla vs. Destroyer*, though he continued to produce a number of chamber works. Akira Ifukube passed away in February 2006, leaving behind a singularly grand legacy.

Tyler E. Martin

Selected Filmography
(*as music composer*)

Snow Trail (1947)
The Quiet Duel (1949)
The Rainbow Man (1949)
The Tale of Genji (1952)
Children of Hiroshima (1952)
Anatahan (1953)
Godzilla (1954)
Human Torpedo Kaiten (1955)
The Burmese Harp (1956)
The Will O' the Wisp (1956)
Rodan (1956)
Yagyu Secret Scrolls (1957)
The Mysterians (1957)
Varan (1958)
The Three Treasures (1959)
Battle in Outer Space (1959)
Daredevil in the Castle (1961)
Buddha (1961)
The Tale of Zatoichi (1962)
The Whale God (1962)
King Kong vs. Godzilla (1962)
The Great Wall (1962)
Chushingura (1962)
The New Tale of Zatoichi (1963)

The Little Prince and the Eight-Headed Dragon (1963)
Zatoichi the Fugitive (1963)
Zatoichi on the Road (1963)
Atragon (1963)
Mothra vs. Godzilla (1964)
Dogora (1964)
Fight, Zatoichi, Fight (1964)
Ghidorah, the Three-Headed Monster (1964)
Whirlwind (1964)
Zatoichi's Revenge (1965)
Frankenstein Conquers the World (1965)
Invasion of Astro-Monster (1965)
Zatoichi and the Chess Expert (1965)
Majin (1966)
Adventure of Taklamakan (1966)
Zatoichi's Vengeance (1966)
The War of the Gargantuas (1966)
Return of Majin (1966)
Majin Strikes Again (1966)

King Kong Escapes (1967)
Zatoichi Challenged (1967)
Ghost Story of the Snow Woman (1968)
Destroy All Monsters (1968)
Latitude Zero (1969)
Zatoichi Meets Yojimbo (1970)
Space Amoeba (1970)
The Will to Conquer (1970)
Godzilla vs. Gigan (1972)
[stock music]
Zatoichi's Conspiracy (1973)
The Human Revolution (1973)
Terror of Mechagodzilla (1975)
Godzilla vs. King Ghidorah (1991)
Godzilla vs. Mothra (1992)
Godzilla vs. Mechagodzilla II (1993)
Godzilla vs. Destoroyah (1995)

THE MYSTERIANS

地球防衛軍

Chikyu Boeigun "The Earth Defense Force"
Toho, 12/28/1957 (*Showa 32*), 11 Reels (2,424 meters), 87:36, 35mm, TohoScope (2.35:1 anamorphic), Eastman color, Perspecta stereo (3 track)

Crew

Producer: Tomoyuki Tanaka
Director: Ishiro Honda
Special Effects Director: Eiji Tsuburaya
Screenplay: Takeshi Kimura, Shigeru Kayama (*treatment*), Jojiro Okami (*story*)
Director of Photography: Hajime Koizumi
Music: Akira Ifukube
Assistant Director: Koji Kajita
Production Design: Teruaki Abe
Editor: Koichi Iwashita
Sound Recording: Masanobu Miyazaki
Sound Effects: Ichiro Minawa
Lighting: Kuichiro Kishida
Production Manager: Yasuaki Sakamoto
SFX Cinematography: Sadamasa Arikawa, Shuzaburo Araki
SFX Art Director: Akira Watanabe
SFX Lighting: Masao Shirota
Optical Compositing: Hiroshi Mukoyama
Mechanical Designs: Shigeru Komatsuzaki
Still Photographer: Jiro Tsuchiya

Cast

Kenji Sahara (*Joji Atsumi*)
Akihiko Hirata (*Ryoichi Shiraishi*)
Yumi Shirakawa (*Etsuko Shiraishi*)
Momoko Kochi (*Hiroko Iwomoto*)
Takashi Shimura (*Dr. Tanjiro Adachi*)
Fuyuki Murakami (*Dr. Nobu Kawanami*)
Rikie Sanjo (*Mrs. Shiraishi*)
Ren Imaizumi (*Assistant Hayami*)
Tetsu Nakamura (*Dr. Koda*)
Soji Ubukata (*Dr. Noda*)
Yutaka Sada (*Police Captain Miyamoto*)
Akio Kusama (*Police Chief Togawa*)
Shin Otomo (*Policeman Kawada*)
Rinsaku Ogata (*Policeman Ogata*)
Minosuke Yamada (*Secretary of Defense Hamamoto*)
Susumu Fujita (*Commander Morita*)
Takuzo Kumagai (*Col. Ito*)
Hideo Mihara (*Commander Emoto*)
Hisaya Ito (*Captain Seki*)
Tadao Nakamaru (*Lt. Yamamoto*)
Harold Conway (*Dr. DeGracia*)
George Furness (*Dr. Svenson*)
Henry Okawa (*Foreign Affairs Minister*)
Haruya Koto (*Villager Senzo*)
Yoshio Tsuchiya (*Mysterian Leader*)
Haruo Nakajima (*Mogera*)
Katsumi Tezuka (*Mysterian*)

Alternate Titles

Weltraum-Bestien [**Space Monsters**] (Germany/Austria)
I misteriani (Italy)
Los Misterianos (Spain)
Los bárbaros invaden la Tierra [**Barbarians Invade Earth**] (Argentina)
Prisonnières des Martiens [**Prisoners of the Martians**] (France)
Monstros do Espaço (Portugal)
Os Bárbaros Invadem a Terra (Brazil)
Εισβολή από τη Σελήνη [**Invasion From the Moon**] (Greece)
De ukjente [**The Unknown**] (Norway)
Tajemniczy przybysze [**The Mysterious Newcomers**] (Poland)
Jorden anfalles [**Attack on Earth**] (Sweden)

"I would like to wipe away the notion of East vs. West and convey a simple, universal aspiration for peace: the coming together of all humankind as one to create a peaceful society."
-Ishiro Honda, from *Ishiro Honda: A Life in Film, from Godzilla to Kurosawa* (2017) by Steve Ryfle and Ed Godziszewski

After *Godzilla* and *Rodan*, the Honda and Tsuburaya team would create another classic science fiction picture. Toho's first alien invasion flick is breathtaking. It represents the best of their early special effects film cycle. *The Mysterians* holds its own against similar Hollywood productions like *The War of the Worlds* (1952) or *Earth vs. the Flying Saucers* (1956). It combines phantasmagoric visuals by Eiji Tsuburaya with humanist subtexts from director Honda. Its influence was vast, stretching to Leiji Matsumoto and possibly George Lucas.

PLOT

At an *Obon* festival near Mount Fuji, scientist Ryoichi Shiraishi (Akihiko Hirata) is acting strange. He refuses to dance with his former fiancee Hiroko (Momoko Kochi). As his colleague Joji Atsumi (Kenji Sahara) confronts him, a forest fire breaks out. The fire is unusual in that the trees appear to be burning from the roots. Shiraishi has become obsessed with studying the planet Mysteroid. Mysteroid is a planetoid on the dark side of the moon Shiraishi claims to have discovered. This confounds Dr. Adachi (Takashi Shimura). As Adachi looks over his incomplete thesis, landslides break out in the village where Shiraishi is staying.

The military and a group of scientists, Joji included, investigate the destroyed village. The ground there becomes so hot that tires burn and Joji finds high degrees of radioactivity. A giant robot then emerges from a nearby hill and begins a path of destruction. Joji and Shiraishi's sister Etsuko (Yumi Shirakawa) evacuate as the police force does battle with the robot. The Self Defense Force manages to disable it by blowing up a bridge as the mechanical monster crosses it. Joji and Etsuko see unidentified flying objects leaving the scene.

Joji addresses the Diet, stating that the fire, landslides and robot are all likely the same cause. Later, Dr. Adachi notices UFOs flying from behind the moon at his observatory. Adachi is now convinced Shiraishi's findings on Mysteroid must be correct. The next day, Adachi, Joji and a group of scientists and military personnel are exploring the region of Mt. Fuji where Shiraishi claims the Mysteroid aliens reside. A gigantic dome appears from the ground. An alien voice asks to negotiate with five scientists, including Adachi and Joji. The Mysterians introduce themselves. Their leader (Yoshio Tsuchiya) explains that Mysteroid engaged in nuclear war thousands of years ago. For them to survive, the radiation sickend Mysterians must migrate to Earth. For terms, the

Mysterians ask for three kilometers of land. They also ask to marry five Earth women to produce superior offspring. Two of these women are Etsuko and Hiroko, outraging Joji.

Japan's government declines the Mysterians' terms and resists them. The Self Defense Force attacks the Mysterian dome. It is impervious to all tank, cannon and jet fire and decimates the military's forces. Dr. Adachi calls for international unity and cooperation between America and the Soviet Union. The nations of the world come together and form the Earth Defense Force to counter the invaders.

BACKGROUND

The Mysterians was Toho's first alien invasion film and special effects film in the Cinemascope format. Studying Hollywood's anamorphic lenses, Toho debuted their own version, TohoScope, in 1957. Toho films would come to be known for their dynamic use of widescreen. By this time, director Ishiro Honda and special effects director Eiji Tsuburaya were called the "Golden Duo". Riding high on the success of *Godzilla* and *Rodan*, producer Tomoyuki Tanaka was eager to make an alien invasion flick. The original treatment was written in novella form by Jojiro Okami. Okami (1918-2003) was an engineer and aviator who had a knack for writing harder science fiction. *Dogora* (1964) was his one *kaiju* concept. Shigeru Kayama rewrote it into a treatment for the screen. He added the giant robot monster

Mogera and other elements at Tanaka's request.

PRINCIPAL PHOTOGRAPHY

Unlike Daiei's *Warning From Space, The Mysterians* would go for classical hostile aliens. Yet Honda creates a story of international brotherhood all the same. He wanted to show humanity putting aside its differences and uniting against a common threat. The influence of George Pal is quite noticeable. *The Mysterians'* images bring to mind Pal's adaptation of Welles' *The War of the Worlds* (1952), directed by Byron Haskin. Yet *The Mysterians* is a more mature and complex film.

ACTORS

The Mysterians boasts an all-star cast headed by Kenji Sahara and Yumi Shirakawa. Akihiko Hirata, Momoko Kochi and Takashi Shimura are back from *Godzilla*, each playing similar characters. Actor Susumu Fujita plays the military's top brass. Fujita (1912-1991) was a Kurosawa veteran, starring in his debut *Sanshiro Sugata* (1943). He became a heartthrob during the war for his role in the propaganda film *Colonel Kato's Falcon Squadron* (1944). He supported the union disputes that led to the founding of Shin Toho but returned to Toho in 1957. For Honda, he often played stern authority figures. Hisaya Ito (1924-2005) and Tadao Nakamaru also make early appearances in this film as soldiers. A stand-out in the film is Yoshio Tsuchiya as the Mysterian leader. Tsuchiya (1927-2017) was born in Koshu in

Yamanashi Prefecture. Educated as a medical student, he was one of Toho's finest thespians. Appearing as tragic peasant Rikichi in Kurosawa's *Seven Samurai*, he relished darker roles. One of his greatest would be the titular *The Human Vapor* in Honda's 1960 film of the same name. He had loved *Godzilla* and was eager to make a film with Honda. The studio was against casting Tsuchiya as they did not want his face obscured. Tsuchiya fought for the role and Tanaka relented. He invented an alien language which he spoke on set. Tsuchiya would go on to play a very similar role in *Invasion of Astro-Monster* (1965). The Mysterian uniforms themselves, their ranks differentiated by color, were designed by Komatsuzaki. The helmets, likely based on the *Daruma* doll, were made of plexiglass. The actors' skin was irritated by the glass fragments.

This would also be one of Honda's first films to use Western actors. George Furness (1896-1985) was a military lawyer. He had acted as a defense attorney for Japanese military officials accused of war crimes in the Tokyo Trial. He got naval admiral Soemu Toyoda acquitted. As gratitude, Toyoda used his influence to get Furness roles in Japanese films. Harold Conway (1911-1996) was an American financial advisor living in Japan who took on small roles, often as diplomats. He would go on to appear in *Battle in Outer Space* (1959), *The Last War*, *Mothra* (both 1961) and *King Kong vs. Godzilla* (1962).

SFX

Eiji Tsuburaya's effects work is in many ways even more lavish than *The War of the Worlds'*. Here, he takes the *tokusatsu* craft to an even higher level than *Godzilla* or *Rodan*. Aided by the novelty of the 'scope ratio, his images are dynamic and painterly. Fittingly, *The Mysterians* was the first film where Tsuburaya had his name displayed right before director Ishiro Honda in the credits. *The Mysterians* is filled with jaw dropping composite shots. These were done through color separation on the film's internegatives. Mattes were cut out and directly superimposed onto the film through multiple exposure. A Mitchell projector was used for rear projection shots.

Designer Shigeru Komatsuzaki (1915-2001) was brought in to create the film's alien and futuristic craft. He was a brilliant designer skilled in retro-futurism. Komatsuzaki's lavish illustrations would grace model kit boxes in the years to come. His art is particularly associated with Gerry Anderson's *Thunderbirds* franchise. *The Mysterians'* extensive miniature work and retro-futuristic designs certainly bring Anderson to mind.

The mechanical monster Mogera was the first giant robot in Japanese cinema. Designed by Akira Watanabe, it was likely added to cash in on Mitsuteru Yokoyama's then popular manga *Tetsujin No. 28*. Better known as *Gigantor*, it had just started running a year prior. A giant robot had also appeared in writer Hideo Unagami's scrapped 1955 *Bride of Godzilla* script. Mogera was first conceived as a living mole-like creature. A rough maquette was modeled by Teizo Toshimitsu, who also built the head of the suit. The suit was created in multiple pieces that had to be put on Haruo Nakajima one at a time. A moving mechanical puppet was also constructed and planned for use in some shots. However, it proved too difficult to engineer and was scrapped midway through building. The Sengawa river, right outside Toho's backlot, was used to build the miniature bridge that would be booby-trapped to destroy the robot.

The miniatures are beautifully built. A motorized model for the Mysterians' satellite was constructed, the camera placed on a mechanical rail in front of it. The Mysterian dome was one of the first *tokusatsu* miniatures to be made from plastic. Commercial plastic, at this point, was new but found to be cheaper than glass. Shots of melting tanks were done by blowing hot air on wax models. Shooting the Marker-light Gyro's launch and ascension into the sky was difficult. The studio's ceiling was far too low so the "money shot" had to be done outdoors. It would require numerous takes as the outdoor breeze proved a problem. The breeze caused the miniature to sway in an unrealistic fashion. It was held still with piano wire suspended from a bridge.

The Mysterians also features elaborate use of superimposed ray beams. Some were hand-animated, one of the first gigs for Sadao Iizuka (1934-), who would become the Tsuburaya unit's resident optical animator. The Marker-light FAHPs' beams were created

from an oxygen cylinder's gas emptied in a water tank. This was then turned sideways and superimposed onto the footage. There are also top notch landslide and flood scenes to be used as stock footage for years to come. The special effects footage is impressively shot by Sadamasa Arikawa and Shuzaburo Araki. Arikawa (1925-2005) was Tsuburaya's premiere DP. His experience as an airman during the war gave him a dynamic eye. He would go on to shoot Tsuburaya's FX footage for years. Finally, he would be outright promoted to special effects director with 1967's *Son of Godzilla*.

MUSIC

As usual, Akira Ifukube composed a rousing score. His battle theme for the "Earth Defense Force" is a driving *leitmotif*. The aliens themselves have more sinister tones, signifying their true malevolent intentions for humanity. *The Mysterians* was also the first *tokusatsu* film mixed in stereophonic sound. The process used was Perspecta. With low frequency tones, it panned a mono soundtrack to three speakers.

REAL WORLD

The flying ships and Marker-lights, designed by Komatuzaki, began Tsuburaya's penchant for outlandish weaponry. Nonetheless, the Self Defense Force lent their full support to the production. They even sent Honda 600 soldiers as extras. The military sequences in *The Mysterians* are particularly impressive as a result. The soldiers using flamethrowers on

Mogera are real soldiers using real flamethrowers.

Chaffee and Sherman tanks can be seen prominently. The M4 Sherman was a larger tank than the Chaffee. It could fire heavier duty rounds with a 104mm Howitzer mount. Replacing the M3 Lee, it was created to compete with Germany's tanks. In North Africa, it helped the British win a decisive victory over Rommel's tank corps in the Second Battle of El Alamein. Whereas the M24 Chaffee was used more in the Pacific Theater, Shermans were the tank of choice in Europe. They were then used in Korea before being retired in the U.S. in the late '50s. Middle Eastern countries continued to use them, however, until the early '80s.

The MGR-1 Honest John missile launcher also appears in *The Mysterians*. In *Rodan*, it had helped bury the monsters in Mount Aso. These missile launchers were developed during the Cold War. Capable of launching miniature nuclear weapons, they were prominent in the U.S. military's Cold War era arsenal. They were phased out in the '70s with the development of the MGM-52 Lance system. The F-104 Starfighter jet, developed by Lockheed, can also be glimpsed. This is rare as Eiji Tsuburaya tended not to feature them, preferring the F-86 Sabre. The other Japanese studios by contrast used Starfighters liberally in their monster movies. Developed in the 1950s, they had a more "space age" design, hence their name. When *The Mysterians* was released the Starfighter still had not been introduced into combat. Throughout the Cold War, they were the pride of the U.S. Air Force until they began to be phased out in the late '70s. After *The Mysterians*, Honda would not get the same level of support from the JSDF again. Honda's frequent assistant Koji Kajita was often sent to deal directly with the SDF brass. Kajita often felt guilty that the Defense Force were seldom victorious in these films. Tsuburaya began to lean more on miniature recreations and stock footage in the films to come.

THEMES AND MOTIFS

Like *Godzilla* being a monster on the loose film that holds far more subtext, *The Mysterians* is only a classic alien invasion flick on surface level. It's more morally complex than comparable American fare like 1956's *Earth vs. the Flying Saucers*. Despite its hostile aliens, it's an optimistic film. In *The Mysterians*, the aliens "wake up" humanity in a different way. Unlike American sci-fi films which could be jingoistic, in *The Mysterians* humanity puts its Cold War differences aside. A united front forms a coalition to battle the aliens. This even includes enemies such as the Soviet Union and Mao's China. Honda's egalitarian vision was daring for its time. It was also timely, as Japan had entered the United Nations a year prior to the film's release. *The Mysterians*, in fact, caught the attention of the FBI when it was released in the United States. In now declassified memos shared with J. Edgar Hoover, it was accused of communist sympathy and promoting a "One World" government.

Hirata's character Ryoichi Shiraishi is the film's most interesting. Shirashi is a similar character to Hirata's prior Daisuke Serizawa. Both are young scientists brought to terrible discoveries by their inquiries. Both must also sacrifice their lives for the sake of humanity. Honda was fond of exploring the moral dilemmas of science. Like Serizawa, Shiraishi struggles between being a good scientist and a human being, with his humanity winning out. There's a moral grayness to *The Mysterians* that is unusual for a film of this type. One could argue that the Mysterians themselves aren't the villains humanity makes them out to be and are just trying to save their dying race. The Self Defense Force does, after all, attack them immediately. Yet towards the end of the film they have taken more than the three kilometers of land and five women they asked for, suggesting they were planning to conquer humanity. Similar tropes are revisited in *Invasion of Astro-Monster*. There is darker subtext in the film as well as overarching social commentary from its screenwriter Takeshi Kimura. The radiation poisoned Mysterians represent what humanity could become if it doesn't unite. At the end of the film, several Mysterians lay dying with their hideous visages unmasked. One can't help but feel pity for them. As Shimura's Dr. Adachi says *"We must try not to make the Mysterians' mistakes."*

RELEASE AND LEGACY

The Mysterians did good business at the Japanese box office. It proved timely and influential. Only two months before its release, the Russians launched Sputnik into Earth's orbit. The Mysterians' pistols wound up sold in Japanese toy stores and were quite popular. Space-themed media was now at peak in popularity and Tanaka was eager to make another space film. *The Mysterians* was followed by the loose sequel *Battle in Outer Space* (1959), also directed by Honda and Tsuburaya. *The Mysterians'* Marker-light FAHP cannons would influence the iconic Masers in 1966's *The War of the Gargantuas*. Komatsuzaki's *Alpha* and *Beta* space battleships would also prove quite influential. Toho would feature similar giant submarines in *Atragon* and *Latitude Zero*, along with a large spaceship in *Destroy All Monsters*. The Super-Xs in *The Return of Godzilla, Godzilla vs. Biollante* and *Godzilla vs. Destoroyah* also carry on this tradition.

The Mysterians' influence would even stretch into anime. Anime luminaries Leiji Matsumoto and Yoshinobu Nishizaki were likely influenced by *The Mysterians'* giant spaceships and themes of international cooperation for their iconic *Space Battleship Yamato*. Along with *Battle in Outer Space*, the images of miniature spacecraft exchanging rays bring to mind another popular franchise: *Star Wars*. It's unclear if George Lucas was directly influenced, but he had a known liking for Japanese fantasy films. Mogera itself would return in *Godzilla vs. Space Godzilla* (1994). *Space Godzilla's* special effects director, Koichi Kawakita, was a huge fan of *The Mysterians*. He saw the film in junior high and credited it for making him want to work for Toho. His dream project was a modern remake of *The*

Mysterians. Sadly such a project never materialized before his death in 2014.

ALTERNATE VERSIONS

The Mysterians was released to American theaters on May 15th, 1959 on a double bill with *Watusi*. It was originally acquired by RKO Radio Pictures, but they went bankrupt. The release was thus handled by MGM. The U.S. version is similar to the Japanese with some notable exceptions.

Running 85:08, the main differences are that the credits are pushed to the end rather than opening along with a few trimmed scenes. The first two battles have minor tidbits deleted. In the final sequence, there's a deleted scene showing another Mogera re-emerging from the ground, then destroyed by a falling Marker-light. Dialog where Joji explains that humanity is launching a satellite to monitor the Mysterians is also cut. The last shot showing this satellite is not used, substituted instead by blue and black title cards saying "A Toho Production" and "The End".

The English dub is credited to Peter Riethof and Carlos Montalban. Recorded in New York City and well performed, it sounds like a proto-Titra dub. Riethof (1905-1994) was an Austrian-born businessman who ran a dubbing studio in New York. He dubbed a wide variety of European films from Fellini's *La Strada* (1954) to Paul Naschy's *Assignment Terror* (1970). He also did the little heard dub of Kurosawa's *Yojimbo* (1961). Carlos Montalban (1904-1991) was a character actor and voice artist born in Mexico. He played mainly bit parts but his most notable role was in *The Harder They Fall* (1956). His younger brother was Ricardo Montalban, known for playing Khan Noonian Singh on *Star Trek*.

The Mysterians was re-released in Toho's final March 1978 Champion Matsuri festival. This was likely to cash-in on the Japanese release of *Star Wars*. The Champion cut of *The Mysterians* runs 70:39. Unlike many of the other Champion edits, it was not edited on the negatives. The first minute of the film's opening scene showing the *Obon* festival has been shorn. Also cut is Shirashi warning the firefighters not to attempt fighting the forest fire. Dr. Adachi's introductory scene is trimmed. Also truncated is some of the investigation into the destroyed village before Mogera appears, mainly a bit where Joji and the authorities notice that the fish in the river are all dead. The opening of the police scene after Mogera's first appearance is removed. Also cut is the bit with Etsuko in the tub as Mogera attacks. The second half of a meeting at the Diet after Mogera is destroyed is removed. A military montage before a TV broadcast is cut. A segment showing a helicopter conducting surveillance on the Mysterian Dome is taken out. A JSDF meeting after the first attack on The Mysterian dome is completely removed. The opening of another meeting where Commander Morita is shown the blueprints for the Alpha is deleted. Newspaper headlines and a U.N. conference at the Diet are also cut. The most major cut scene introduces Drs. Svenson and DeGracia and shows the

Defense council talking to Shirashi on the television. Another U.N. meeting is severely truncated. The rest of the picture is largely untouched with even some bits cut from the U.S. version, such as the second Mogera cameo, still intact.

AMERICAN HOME VIDEO HISTORY

The Mysterians did not get a widespread VHS or laserdisc release in the U.S. It was released by smaller companies VCI and Star Classics in the 1980s. Its next release would not be until 2005 when Media Blasters put the film on DVD. The Japanese version was used but Toho would not allow the use of the Riethof dub. To get an English option on the disc, Media Blasters commissioned a new dub from Bang Zoom! Entertainment. The new dub, directed by Eric P. Sherman and written by Clark Cheng is terrible. It features crisp anime dubber voices that feel mismatched with a film from 1957. The Media Blasters DVD is now long out of print and *The Mysterians* has not been released to U.S. home video since.

Further Viewing:

(1959)
宇宙大戦争
Toho, *Director*: Ishiro Honda

Toho's follow-up to *The Mysterians* is a loose semi-sequel where humanity unites again to stop an even nastier gaggle of aliens. *Battle in Outer Space* is far more Eiji Tsuburaya's film

than Ishiro Honda's. The plot is thin and the characters undeveloped. Yet Tsuburaya commands the special effects sequences. Honda does, however, provide a strong pro-science and egalitarian subtext. A montage showing collective humanity preparing for war against the aliens is quintessential Honda. Yoshio Tsuchiya plays one of the film's most interesting roles; a dark turn as the alien possessed Iwomura. *Battle in Outer Space* has an even stronger George Pal vibe than *The Mysterians,* evoking both *Destination: Moon* and *The War of the Worlds.* Shigeru Komatsuzaki once again created the film's striking retro-futuristic mechanical designs.

Not every shot is perfect, but Tsuburaya creates one stunning composition after another. The lunar battle sequence is gorgeously unreal. This was one of set painter Fuchimu Shimakura's very first jobs and his painted backdrops are striking. *Battle in Outer Space*'s final act is where the film comes alive, set to Akira Ifukube's exhilarating score. The score's final medley would be effectively re-used in *Shin Godzilla* decades later. A sequence where Tokyo is destroyed by an anti-gravity beam is eye-popping. This scene was created with soft paraffin buildings placed under powerful electric fans. The masterful special effects work more than earns Tsuburaya his title as the *"God of tokusatsu"*.

Battle in Outer Space is also more influential than given credit. Its DNA can be seen in a wide variety of films. This includes future Honda works like *Invasion of Astro-Monster* and *Destroy All Monsters* along with

Matsumoto and Nishizaki's *Space Battleship Yamato* franchise. Images of interstellar spacecraft exchanging rays and alien bases covertly destroyed were likely influential on *Star Wars*. Roland Emmerich's *Independence Day* (1996), as well, follows *Battle in Outer Space*'s tropes closely.

SF ON HOME VIDEO

ホームビデオのSF

"Why would we want to do that? Fans are going to buy it anyway."

It is said that special effects director Koichi Kawakita begged Toho's brass for a proper restoration of *The Mysterians*, his favorite film. Their answer was that they didn't need to do one as *tokusatsu* fans would buy the film no matter what. This is sadly indicative of the attitude studios on both sides of the Pacific have taken towards Japanese science fiction films on video. Subpar transfers have long been the norm and such practices still persist to this day. Toho's rules towards its American distributors have also gotten stricter; now including suppression of the U.S. versions. It's a situation not too different from the fate of the original edits of *Star Wars*. As in that case, fan editors are taking matters into their own hands to preserve certain films and versions in higher quality.

Like many corporations, Toho has always valued profits over proper film preservation. To save money in the 1970s, Toho edited the Champion Matsuri versions of several Godzilla entries on the films' negatives. This has led to preservation issues for decades. The worst affected was *King Kong vs. Godzilla*. For nearly 30 years, many scenes in the film were only available in laserdisc quality as original elements were thought lost. Eventually, Toho rediscovered these scenes and did a 4K remaster of *King Kong vs. Godzilla*. They did not allow this transfer to be used in the Criterion Blu-ray set, however.

Compared to the crisp digital scans available today, the early VHS and laserdisc period was a stone age for film-to-video transfers. Japanese science fiction films and most genre/cult films in general never had a reputation for looking good on U.S. home video. For decades, American transfers tended to be panned and scanned for TV viewing. 2.35:1 "scope" ratio films, which comprised much of *Showa* Japanese cinema, suffered particularly badly. Over half the shot composition tended to be lost. This practice thankfully ended with the death of 4:3 television sets. In the 1980s, most transfers were mastered on ¾" tape. The better ones, such as New World's VHS and laserdisc releases of *Godzilla vs. Gigan* and *Godzilla vs. Mechagodzilla*, came from 35mm materials. The worst were crudely done telecines of faded 16mm prints left over from the television era. Japanese transfers tended to be better and unlike in the U.S., letterbox format was the norm. Many collectors imported Japanese laserdiscs of American films unavailable in widescreen domestically. In the U.S, laserdisc never caught on. Being the size of an LP, they were bulky, required large and expensive players and were costlier than VHS. As a result they stayed a niche format only for hardcore cinemaphiles and collectors. In Japan, laserdiscs were more popular. This was partially because they were priced only slightly higher than their VHS counterparts. The first stateside widescreen release of a Japanese sci-fi film was the VHS and laserdisc of *Godzilla vs. Biollante*, put out around 1993.

The arrival of digital imaging technology was a boon for home video and film restoration alike. Films could now be transferred to a digital format, resulting in less quality loss on video. Japanese genre films were slow to be released on DVD. Yet by the late '90s they began to trickle onto the format as companies cashed in on Tristar's 1998 *Godzilla*. Simitar released the U.S. versions of *Mothra vs. Godzilla*, *Invasion of Astro-Monster* and *All Monsters Attack* to both VHS and DVD in widescreen format. ADV Films released the letterboxed export version of *Destroy All Monsters* for the first time to both formats as well. ADV's *Gamera: Guardian of the Universe* and *Gunhed* tapes were letterboxed too. *Gappa, the Triphibian Monster* was also released in widescreen by Media Blasters. In 1999, Neptune Media released *Gamera, the Giant Monster* in its original Japanese version. It was notable as one of the first ever subtitled releases of a Japanese monster film. While most other releases were still panned and scanned, these were a good step in the right direction. Japanese science fiction films were starting to look better on home video.

With digital technology came far superior film to video transfer methods. In 1993, the first digital restoration was undertaken of Disney's *Snow White and the Seven Dwarves*, made with Kodak's Cineon system. The old school telecines evolved into digital film scanners. The difference is subtle to the layman but significant. Telecines transfer film to video in real time. Scanners scan a film's frames into a computer at high resolution. With the advent of computer technology, commercial films, starting with *Oh Brother Where Art Thou* and *The Lord of the Rings: The Fellowship of the Ring*, were scanned directly to and mastered in a digital format. This allowed for better integration of computer generated elements and more freedom with color grading than could be done chemically. 2003's *Godzilla: Tokyo SOS* was the first Godzilla movie mastered on a digital intermediate.

In 2004 to '05, Sony acquired a handful of Godzilla entries and released them to DVD. These releases were far from perfect. They contained video generated English credits, subtitles based on the export dubs and few special features. Yet they were special in one major way: they were mastered from new, high quality HD scans. Visually, these were the best these films had looked on home video, looking far better than Toho's own lackluster telecined DVD transfers. The colors were vivid and life-like and the dynamic range was superb with deep blacks. In 2014, ADV's successor Kraken Releasing distributed *Ebirah, Horror of the Deep*, *Godzilla vs. Hedorah* and *Godzilla vs. Gigan* to Blu-ray in these transfers. They still look far superior to Toho's own HD masters. Sony's razor sharp scan of

Godzilla, Mothra and King Ghidorah: Giant Monsters All-Out Attack still looks better upscaled from DVD than its HD Toho counterpart. Sony's 2K scan of *Mothra* is also night and day compared to Toho's lackluster version on Blu-ray. Ditto with Universal's for *King Kong vs. Godzilla* and *King Kong Escapes*. Once, U.S. videophiles imported Japanese laserdiscs of American films. Now, almost ironically, *tokusatsu otaku* reverse import better looking American Blu-ray releases of Japanese films to Japan.

In the mid 2000s with some ballyhoo, Toho remastered all the Godzilla entries in HD themselves. These transfers were disappointing with dull blacks and muted color. They were made in HiVision on a Cintel C-Reality at Togen Tokyo Laboratory. The Cintel is a digital telecine that was already outdated by the mid 2000s. In Hollywood, digital telecines have fallen out of use except to create quick dailies. In 2014 Criterion was allowed to do a quality scan of *Godzilla '54* in 2K. But a mix of Toho's policies and budgetary restrictions led to these outdated HiVision transfers being used on Criterion's 2019 *Godzilla: The Showa Era* set. The *Showa* Godzilla series being made part of the Criterion Collection is certainly exciting for the respectability of the franchise. Yet most of the films in this set don't look nearly as good as they should and are below Criterion's usual quality standards. To make matters worse, few of the U.S. versions and only a handful of the English dubs are included due to Toho's restrictions.

Since the mid 2010s, thrifty Japanese studios like Toho, Kadokawa and Toei have started to issue better transfers. Toho created 4K versions of *Godzilla* and *King Kong vs. Godzilla* which have aired on Japanese television. Kadokawa also did beautiful 4K remasters of the '90s Gamera trilogy. In 2017, Toho released *Frankenstein Conquers the World* and *Matango* to Blu-ray. These transfers were different, clearly made on Togen's far better Arriscan film scanner. Versions of the Champion Matsuri re-edits captured from Japanese HDTV have also been making the rounds. These look far better than Toho's HiVision transfers, showing off colors one didn't even know existed in these films. Kadokawa was more permissive than Toho when working with UK-based company Arrow for their recent Gamera boxed set. They provided better materials, allowed Arrow freedom in touching them up and permitted all U.S. versions and English dubs to be included. The 2020 Gamera Arrow boxed set is everything the Criterion Godzilla set is not. Toho does have plans to undertake more 4K restorations of Godzilla entries. Yet only time will tell if these better scans will ever reach American shores. In the meantime, it's a shame that outdated and subpar telecines are the highest quality versions available of many Japanese sci-fi films. As the physical media market shrinks in favor of streaming, it's possible that the 2019 Criterion Godzilla set could be the final release of those films on stateside home video. This is regretful as these marvelous films deserve to be viewed in the highest possible quality. In the meantime, fan editors have been undertaking Herculean tasks to unofficially preserve many films and English versions in better quality. Some have even arranged professional scans of film prints bought on eBay.

THE H-MAN

美女と液体人間

Bijo to Ekitai Ningen "Beauty and the Liquid Men"
Toho, 6/24/1958 (*Showa 33*), 9 Reels (2,360 meters), 86:04, 35mm, TohoScope (2.35:1 anamorphic), Eastman color, Perspecta stereo (3 track)

Crew

Producer: Tomoyuki Tanaka
Director: Ishiro Honda
Special Effects Director: Eiji Tsuburaya
Screenplay: Takeshi Kimura, Hideo Unagami (story)
Director of Photography: Hajime Koizumi
Music: Masaru Sato
Assistant Director: Koji Kajita
Production Design: Takeo Kita
Editor: Kazuji Taira
Sound Recordist: Choshichiro Mikami
Sound Effects: Masanobu Miyazaki
Lighting: Tsuruzo Nishikawa
Production Manager: Teruo Maki
SFX Cinematography: Sadamasa Arikawa, Shuzaburo Araki
SFX Art Director: Akira Watanabe
SFX Lighting: Masao Shigeta
SFX Opticals: Hiroshi Mukoyama
Modeling: Eizo Kaimai, Keizo Murase
Still Photographer: Matsuo Yoshizaki

Cast

Yumi Shirakawa (*Chikako Arai*)
Kenji Sahara (*Dr, Masada*)
Akihiko Hirata (*Inspector Tominaga*)
Eitaro Ozawa (*Police Chief Miyashita*)
Koreya Senda (*Dr. Maki*)
Makoto Sato (*Uchida*)
Hisaya Ito (*Misaki*)
Machiko Kitagawa (*Hanae*)
Yoshio Tsuchiya (*Detective Taguchi*)
Naomi Shiraishi (*Lab Assistant Mineko*)
Ko Mishima (*Kishi*)
Yoshifumi Tajima (*Detective Sakata*)
Tetsu Nakamura (*Mr. Chin*)
Haruya Kato (*Matchan*)
Ayumi Sonoda (*Emi*)
Kan Hayashi (*Executive Police Officer*)
Minosuke Yamada (*Chief Inspector Kusuda*)
Jun Fujio (*Nishiyama*)
Ren Yamamoto (*Saeki*)
Akira Sera (*Horita*)
Tadao Nakamaru (*Detective Seki*)
Yosuke Natsuki (*Man*)
Yoshiko Ieda (*Woman*)
Yasuhiro Shigenobu (*Yasukichi*)
Akira Yamada (*Wakasugi*)

Nadao Kirino (*Shimazaki*)
Yutaka Sada (*Taxi Driver*)
Shin Otomo (*Hamano*)
Soji Ubukata (*Police Officer*)
Mitsuo Suda (*Police Officer*)
Yutaka Nakayama (*An-chan*)
Kamayuki Tsubono (*Detective Ogawa*)
Shigeo Kato (*Matsu-chan*)
Yutaka Oka (*Self Defense Force Search Party Leader*)
Shoichi Hirose (*Fireman*)
Takuzo Kumagai (*Self Defense Force Officer*)
Akio Kusama (*Police Officer*)
Shiro Tsuchiya (*Police Officer*)
Katsumi Tezuka (*Fishing Boat Captain*)
Haruo Nakajima (*Fisherman*)
Senkichi Omura (*Fisherman*)

Alternate Titles

Das Grauen schleicht durch Tokio [**The Horror That Stalks Tokyo**] (Germany)
L'homme H (France)
El Hombre H (Spain/Mexico)
Uomini H (Italy)
O Monstro da Bomba H [**Monster of the H-Bomb**] (Brazil)
Fasans monster (Sweden)
H-Manden, det flydende uhyre (Denmark)

Vetyihminen **[Hydrogen Man]**
(Finland)

Водородный человек
(Russia)

> *"If Earth were covered in radioactive fallout and humanity faced extinction, the next dominant species could be the H-Man..."*
> -Dr. Maki (Koreya Senda)

An early horror-themed *tokusatsu* film, *The H-Man* is another of Ishiro Honda and Eiji Tsuburaya's premiere 1950s works. Honda combines police procedural, gangster intrigue, a vivid view of Tokyo nightlife and horror and sci-fi elements. Tsuburaya's FX are all the while inventive, dynamic and grotesque. It was released the same year as Jack Harris and Irvin Yeaworth's *The Blob*. Yet *The H-Man* is superior in production value and visual effects.

PLOT

In Tokyo on a rainy night, two gangsters make a drug deal. One of them, Misaki (Hisaya Ito) is attacked by something and fires his pistol. As the other gangster drives away, the police find that Misaki has completely vanished. All that remains are his clothes, some personal items and the bag of heroin he was smuggling. The police, led by Inspector Tominaga (Akihiko Hirata), are flummoxed. Police Chief Miyashita (Eitaro Ozawa) and Detectives Taguchi (Yoshio Tsuchiya) and Sakata (Yoshifumi Tajima) go to Misaki's apartment to arrest him. They find only his girlfriend Chikako (Yumi Shirakawa). Chikako claims she hasn't seen him for five days. She is brought in for a statement.

Taguchi and Sakata next scope out the nightclub where Chikako works as a cabaret singer. During her performance, a man named Masada (Kenji Sahara) shows Chikako a note asking about Misaki. Masada is arrested and brought to the police station. Tominaga identifies Masada as an assistant biochemistry professor. Masada explains that he was trying to contact Chikako as he suspects Misaki dissolved from radiation exposure. Tominaga scoffs at his theory and warns him not to get involved.

The police begin surveillance of Chikako's apartment. At night, a gangster named Nishiyama (Jun Fujio) breaks in and accosts Chikako, demanding to know where Misaki is. While escaping, he encounters something which he fires at. Chikako then faints as she hears him scream. The police find only his clothes and the gun. Chikako is once again questioned by both the police and Masada, but she can be of little help. Masada takes the police to a hospital where radiation poisoned fishermen claim to have seen similar phenomena. While returning to Japan, they encountered a derelict ship. Investigating, they found nothing but discarded clothing on board. One of the fishermen was then attacked by a blob-like liquid mass which seemed to dissolve him, leaving only his clothes. Another fisherman was liquified by a humanoid-shaped mass and a third dissolved as well. As the two surviving fishermen escaped, they saw several of these "liquid people" walking on the abandoned boat's deck.

The police run a sting on the drug buyers in Chikako's club. An arrested suspect fires his gun, alerting the waiter. The waiter helps the ringleader, Uchida (Makoto Sato), leave the club. As they make their escape, the liquid monster appears. Uchida fires at it with no effect. It liquifies the waiter, along with one of the dancers (Ayumi Shinoda). The monster next attacks Chikako but officers Taguchi and Sakata shoot at it. The creature liquifies Sakata. Dr. Maki (Koreya Senda) explains that atomic testing in the Pacific has spawned a new form of liquid-based life. Dubbed "H-Man", this life form has made its way to Tokyo from the drifting *Ryujin Maru*. Maki tells the police and military that the only way to kill the H-Men are through electrocution or immolation. Masada informs Tominaga that Uchida is alive as his clothes weren't radioactive. Uchida soon reappears and kidnaps Chikako. The police and military decide to fill Tokyo's sewers with gasoline and ignite it with flamethrowers. As the city evacuates and the military begins preparations, Uchida takes Chikako into the sewer to retrieve a bag of heroin he stashed there.

PRINCIPAL PHOTOGRAPHY

The H-Man is based on a story by Hideo Unagami, who had written the unmade Godzilla script *Bride of Godzilla* a few years prior. *The H-Man* has a darker and more lurid tone than much of director Ishiro Honda's other work. Though *Half Human* and *Rodan* had horrific elements, *The H-Man* is his first legitimate horror film. Takeshi Kimura's script mixes together police drama, noirish *yakuza* film intrigue and sci-fi/horror tropes. The film's highlight is the unsettling flashback where the fishermen encounter the derelict *Ryujin Maru*. It is a masterfully directed sequence combining the aesthetic of Japan's native ghost stories with modern atomic terror. It features expressionistic lighting by Tsuruzo Nishikawa who mostly gaffed samurai pictures. This and other horrific set pieces elevate the picture.

The H-Man's police procedure and criminal intrigue is effectively handled. You could almost remove the monsters and still have a good Japanese pseudo-noir picture. The colorful Cinemascope visuals are attractively realized by Honda's favorite DP Hajime Koizumi and gaffer Nishikawa. The nightclub scenes present a vivid and gritty view of post-war Tokyo nightlife. There's an energetically directed on location car chase sequence. The sewer scenes, shot on sets leftover from Kurosawa's *Drunken Angel*, are highly atmospheric. The noir aspects, coupled with nightmarish horror elements, make *The H-Man* feel novel. It is the closest thing Honda ever directed to an exploitation flick which the more lascivious Japanese title plays up. Honda would later make a straight-up crime potboiler, *The Man in Red,* in 1961. He would also once more meld monsters and gangsters in 1964's *Dogora.*

ACTORS

Like Honda's later *kaijin* (human-sized monster) films such as *The Human Vapor* and *Matango,* there is more emphasis on the actors than in the *kaiju* pictures. Kenji Sahara, Yumi Shirakawa and Akihiko Hirata return from *Rodan* and *The Mysterians.* Hirata is cast against type as a stern police inspector. Shirakawa is the "Beauty" hinted at in the Japanese title and especially lovely in this film. The noirish scenes where she croons English songs (her singing voice dubbed by Martha Miyake) are a highlight. Her lack of agency as a gangster's moll turned damsel in distress is problematic but typical of a '50s genre film. Esteemed character actor Eitaro Ozawa is on hand as the police chief. Ozawa (1909-1988) was a favorite of Kenji Mizoguchi in particular and was versatile, acting in over 200 films. For genre films, he later appeared in *Gorath* (1962), *Blood Type: Blue* (1978) and *The Return of Godzilla* (1984).

Yoshio Tsuchiya plays a supporting role, as does Yoshifumi Tajima. Makoto Sato also plays an early role as gangster antagonist Uchida. Sato (1934-2012) was a short but distinctive actor who often played either *yakuza* or soldiers for a wide assortment of directors. Koreya Senda appears in the film as well. He occasionally played Takashi Shimura-like roles in Honda's films. In reality, Senda (1904-1994), born Keio Ito, was an esteemed actor who started off as an avant garde stage player and left wing political activist. Arrested during World War II for leftist sympathies, he founded the Haiyuza Theater Company with Eijiro Tono, Eitaro Ozawa and others. Actor Jerry Ito (*Mothra*) was his nephew and Anna Nakagawa, who appeared in 1991's *Godzilla vs. King Ghidorah,* was his granddaughter.

SFX

As with *The Human Vapor* and *Matango,* there is less distinction between Honda's scenes and Tsuburaya's FX work. Tsuburaya's special and visual effects are grotesque and inventive. He had plenty of experience with human-sized *kaijin* in films like *Rainbow Man* (1949) and *The Invisible Avenger* (1954). The liquid effects were made from a seaweed solution used in cosmetics. Shots of the monsters dripping down walls were achieved with a rotating set and bolted down camera. Other shots were achieved by dripping the seaweed mixture and printing it in reverse. The unsettling sequences of the creatures dissolving their victims were done by deflating balloon dummies. *The H-Man* also features some particularly impressive miniature work. By the climax, Tsuburaya takes command with his penchant for phantasmagorical spectacle. The final images, of Tokyo's sewers and bay alight with orange-green conflagration, are hauntingly beautiful.

MUSIC

Masaru Sato's score is unusual but effective. It features an almost Ifukube-like main theme, noirish jazz songs for the club and an experimental feel for the horror scenes. Sato (1928-1999) had already composed music for such genre films as *Godzilla Raids Again* and *Half Human*. A native of Hokkaido, he was a student of Fumio Hayasaka. Hayasaka was Kurosawa's composer of choice, creating the scores for such films as *Rashomon* and *Seven Samurai*. Hayasaka died when Kurosawa's *I Live in Fear* was in production. Sato was put in his mentor's shoes and asked by Toho and Kurosawa to finish the score. Sato soon became Kurosawa's favorite composer; scoring most of his subsequent films. Kihachi Okamoto also liked working with him. His music for *Yojimbo* is particularly noteworthy and quintessential to his style. In contrast to Akira Ifukube or Yuji Koseki, Sato was entirely a film composer and did no classical work. Sato would return to the genre for several more films. These include Jun Fukuda's *Ebirah, Horror of the Deep* (1966), *Son of Godzilla* (1967) and *Godzilla vs. Mechagodzilla* (1974) along with Shiro Moritani's *Submersion of Japan* (1973) and Okamoto's *Blood Type: Blue* (1978).

THEMES AND MOTIFS

The H-Man has strong science fiction elements in addition to its horrific tropes, however. Like *Godzilla*, it's a story of the double-edged sword of scientific advancement. The misuse of science, as in *Godzilla*, creates a new, atomic age form of

life. Yet it's scientists who sound the alarm and save the day. Dr. Maki's final plea is almost identical to Yamane's at the end of Godzilla. "*So long as we continue to test nuclear weapons, there may be more H-Men*".

Even more so than *Godzilla*, *The H-Man's* premise is a pointed reference to the *Dai-go Fukuryu Maru* (Lucky Dragon No. 5) incident. Honda had a macabre fascination with it. Kaneto Shindo, later to direct *Onibaba*, would incidentally bring a docudrama adaptation to the screen for Toho the following year. *The H-Man* was, incidentally, released the same year as Jack Harris and Irvin Yeaworth's *The Blob*. Tsuburaya's work bests the special effects in that film by a considerable margin. Besides their liquid monsters, *The H-Man* and *The Blob* have little in common and the former is a better made, smarter movie.

RELEASE AND LEGACY

The H-Man opened to harsh reviews but did decent business thanks to its exploitation elements. Toho would go on to make more *kaijin* films, first *The Secret of the Telegian* (1960), directed by up and coming program director Jun Fukuda. *The Human Vapor* by Honda followed, also in 1960 and melding crime and science fiction. After the financial failure of 1963's *Matango*, Toho opted to focus on giant monsters instead.

ALTERNATE VERSIONS

The H-Man was sold to Columbia Pictures. It was released in the U.S. on May 28th, 1959 on a double bill with the British horror flick *The Woman Eater*. The U.S. version has around eight minutes of cuts, running 78:57. The credit sequence has identical Sato musical cues but is altered. Rather than shots of the derelict *Ryujin Maru*, the credits appear over a static shot of one of the H-Men. Additionally, U.S. prints were color timed differently, making the H-Men blue instead of Japanese prints' green. The edits amount to around eight minutes of material, mostly a few of the film's police procedural sequences. Some of the dissolving scenes, especially of Tajima's Sakata, are shortened to be less graphic.

The English dub was recorded in Los Angeles and features the voice of prolific Paul Frees as Tominaga, Uchida and Dr. Maki. Frees (1920-1986), was best known for his work in cartoons beyond count, particularly as Boris in *Rocky and Bullwinkle*. He did voices for everyone from Disney to independent horror filmmakers. At Disney World and Disneyland, you can hear his distinctive pipes on the classic *Pirates of the Caribbean* and *Haunted Mansion* rides. He did a lot of work for Rankin-Bass as well, including Burgermeister Meisterburger in *Santa Claus is Comin' to Town* (1970). His most notable Japanese genre film dubbing role was Hideyo Amamoto's Dr. Who in the U.S. version of *King Kong Escapes* (1967).

AMERICAN HOME VIDEO HISTORY

The H-Man was released on VHS by Columbia in 1988. It wouldn't be re-released to U.S. home video until 2008, when it was released by Sony in a three DVD *"Icons of Sci-Fi"* set. Containing both the Japanese and American versions, it was bundled with Honda's *Battle in Outer Space* and *Mothra*. In 2020, the film was sub-licensed from Sony by Mill Creek and released to Blu-ray, again paired with *Battle in Outer Space*.

Further Viewing:

(1957)
透明人間と蝿男
Daiei, *Director*: Mitsuo Murayama

Invisible Man vs. the Human Fly is the most interesting Japanese take on H.G. Wells' classic literary character. Previous renditions included Daiei's *The Invisible Man Appears* (1949) and Toho's *The Invisible Avenger* (1954). Both featured special effects work by Eiji Tsuburaya. After an opening, energetically directed by Murayama, it becomes something of a police procedural. This is until the titular human fly (Shizuo Chujo) and his benefactor (Ichiro Izawa) appear. They can make themselves tiny and escape after committing murders via a solution developed by the wartime Japanese military. Like in Honda's films, scientists play a major part. A young researcher named Tsukioka (Ryuji Shinagawa) becomes invisible to combat them.

There are some seedy nightclub scenes almost shockingly risque for the 1950s. These would have inevitably been censored stateside. The final third, where the ensemble cast is picked off one by one until a Holmesian finale, is confusingly plotted. Yet the visual effects, supervised by Toru Matoba, are imaginative and impressive. A memorable moment features the human fly crawling on the voluptuous body of a scantily clad dancer (Ikuko Mori). Mori (1933-) would go on to play the long-necked *rokurokubi* in *100 Monsters* and *Spook Warfare* (both 1968). One has to wonder how influential *Invisible Man vs. the Human Fly* was on Toho's "transformed human" films soon to come. Like *The H-Man*, the film alternates between noirish pot boiler and sci-fi with a horror touch.

THE SECRET OF THE TELEGIAN

(1960)
電送人間
Toho, *Director*: Jun Fukuda

The Secret of the Telegian was Toho's next "transformed human" *kaijin* flick. Only the second film by director Jun Fukuda, it's a minor Toho genre piece. It is overall forgettable but peppered with interesting moments. The film stars Tadao Nakamaru as Sudo, a bitter Imperial army veteran who transforms himself into a human television signal. He then takes murderous revenge on his comrades who left him for dead. The opening, featuring a murder in a funhouse, is effective and bring horror director Nobuo Nakagawa's work to mind. The most

interesting subtext of *The Secret of the Telegian* revolves around Japan's wartime misdeeds coming back to haunt it. Sudo's former comrades who killed and robbed him are now wealthy businessmen. They run a grotesque Imperial Army-themed nightclub featuring gold-painted dancers that glorifies Japan's past militarism. Their sins come back to terrorize them in the form of Sudo, now able to project himself electronically thanks to research by an Imperial military scientist.

The Secret of the Telegian boasts a stylishness looking forward to director Fukuda's crime thrillers. The film is well shot by Kazuo Yamada. Its horror and action sequences are energetically directed and boast a more kinetic editing style than Honda's films. Sadly, outside of these scenes, *The Secret of the Telegian* is a clunky and dull police procedural. Actress Yumi Shirakawa is all but wasted. Fukuda would get better at engaging potboiler-style storytelling. The contributions of Tsuburaya's FX unit are subtle though the optical work is impressive. His unit's work only stands out with shots of a miniature volcano featured in the climax. Starting with a tiny role in *Godzilla Raids Again*, Tadao Nakamaru (1933-2009) was a prolific Toho actor. He appeared in numerous contemporary and samurai films. Here he masters an unsettlingly cold sociopathic stare. He would go on to play a similar role as real life Imperial Army official Jiro Shizaki in Kihachi Okamoto's *Japan's Longest Day* (1967). Later, he also appeared in *Submersion of Japan* (1973) and *Terror of Mechagodzilla* (1975). *The Secret of the Telegian* was released directly to American television by Herts-Lion who also put out *Carnival of Souls* (1962). The export dubbing kept, its TV prints, interestingly, were in black and white. The film is better in color but the black and white version gives the picture a noirish vibe that oddly benefits it.

THE HUMAN VAPOR
(1960)
ガス人間第一号
Toho, *Director*: Ishiro Honda

The Human Vapor is, like *Matango*, another unusually character driven film where Ishiro Honda's unit dominates. It features one of Yoshio Tsuchiya's greatest roles. He plays Mizuno, an airforce pilot turned librarian who volunteers for a scientific experiment. This gives him the ability to transform into a gaseous state. He uses his newfound power to commit robberies to woo Fujichiyo (Kaoru Yachigusa), a beautiful *No* dancer he's infatuated with. Mizuno puts the money he's stolen into financing her comeback. The police force, led by Detective Okamoto (Tatsuya Mihashi), use the recital to set a trap for him. Like *The H-Man* and *The Secret of the Telegian*, it blends science fiction with police procedural. The film opens as a standard heist thriller with Tatsuya Mihashi's detective in pursuit of the disappearing bank robber. At the midpoint, Tsuchiya takes the stage along with Tsuburaya's impressive optical effects.

Scripted by Takeshi Kimura, *The Human Vapor* is one of Honda's bleakest films alongside *Matango*. Far removed from Honda's optimistic space films, it's a tragedy about human frailty. *The Human Vapor* is both visually striking and is well carried by Tsuchiya and Yachigusa in particular. The finale is stunning. It's a suspenseful and well directed final reel ending in betrayal and conflagration. Honda was inspired by the classical Japanese narrative of doomed romance leading to double suicide (*shinju*). *The Human Vapor* was heavily altered in Brenco's U.S. version. The film is reshuffled and starts off with Mizuno giving his interview to the reporters. It is now told from Mizuno's perspective, with James Hong dubbing his voice and narrating the film. The music is overhauled. Paul Sawtell's score from *The Fly* replaces much of Kunio Miyauchi's offbeat chords. In an amusing change, the traditional *No* chants are swapped out for *kabuki* music during Fujichiyo's dances. In Japan, *The Human Vapor* is now considered one of Ishiro Honda's standout films.

KENJI SAHARA
The Debonair

佐原健二
5/14/1932-

"I have the same attitude toward acting in television and in movies. For me, the only difference is the size of the screen..."
- Kenji Sahara (1997)

Kenji Sahara is one of the most prolific and notable Toho actors; a handsome man with strong screen presence and surprising range. He was born Masayoshi Kato in Kawasaki City, Kanagawa, the eldest of six. His father was the director of a medical school and wanted him to become a lawyer. His break came in 1953 when he entered the *"Mr. Heibon"* contest while in law school. He won second prize, giving him the opportunity to join Toho's "New Face" program. He was in the same class as Akira Takarada and Momoko Kochi. First taking the stage name of Tadashi Ishihara, he played a small role in Ishiro Honda's *Farewell Rabaul*. He next had a cameo in the original *Godzilla* in the pleasure boat sequence. Taking the name Kenji Sahara and making his starring debut in *Rodan*, he became another favorite actor of Honda's. Next he headlined *The Mysterians* (1957) and *The H-Man* (1958).

Sahara started off playing boyish heroes before playing varied roles in the 1960s. These included darker parts like low class sailor Koyama in *Matango* (1963) and greedy investor Torahata in *Mothra vs. Godzilla* (1964). He played scientists, military officials, villains and was also active on television. Sahara even appeared in Frank Sinatra's *None But the Brave* (1965). He was handpicked by Eiji Tsuburaya to headline Tsuburaya Pro's first show, *Ultra Q* (1966). A black and white *kaiju Outer Limits* of sorts, he played Cessna pilot Jun Manjoume. He also played a supporting guest role on *Ultraseven* (1967-68). Though no longer a young heartthrob, he continued playing character roles even in the leaner years of the '70s. Sahara was a mainstay on the television show *Western Police*.

He returned in more recent years to play authority figures in many of Toho's Godzilla films in the '90s and 2000s. Sahara has appeared in 13 Godzilla entries, more than any other player. In Jet Li's Hong Kong production *Hitman* (1998), he plays a Japanese gangster who reminisces about his WWII war crimes, a far cry from his boyish early roles. His most recent film was a cameo in *Homecoming* (2011), by Ultra franchise director Toshihiro Iijima. Sahara still occasionally appears on television. He is said to love golfing as a hobby and spends much of his free time on the course.

Selected Filmography (as actor)

Farewell Rabaul (1954)
Godzilla (1954)
Rodan (1956)
The Mysterians (1957)
The H-Man (1958)
Mothra (1961)
Gorath (1962)
King Kong vs. Godzilla (1962)
Matango (1963)

Atragon (1963)
Mothra vs. Godzilla (1964)
Ghidorah, the Three-Headed Monster (1964)
Frankenstein Conquers the World (1965)
None but the Brave (1965)
"Ultra Q" (1966, TV)

The War of the Gargantuas (1966)
"Ultraseven" (1967-68)
Son of Godzilla (1967)
Destroy All Monsters (1968)
All Monsters Attack (1969)
Space Amoeba (1970)
"Return of Ultraman" (1971-72, TV)

The Human Revolution (1973)
Godzilla vs. Mechagodzilla (1974)
"Submersion of Japan" (1974, TV)
Terror of Mechagodzilla (1975)

"Western Police" (1979-82, TV)
"Ultraman 80" (1980, TV)
Godzilla vs. King Ghidorah (1991)
Godzilla vs. Mechagodzilla II (1993)
Godzilla vs. Space Godzilla (1994)

Hitman (1998)
"Sonic X" (2004, TV)
"Ultraman Nexus" (2004-05, TV)
Godzilla: Final Wars (2004)
Superior Ultraman 8 Brothers (2008)
Homecoming (2011)

MOTHRA

モスラ

Mosura "Mothra"
Toho, 7/30/1961 (*Showa 36*), 7 Reels (2,752 meters), 100:51, 35mm, TohoScope (2.35:1 anamorphic), Eastman color, Perspecta stereo (4 track)

Crew
Producer: Tomoyuki Tanaka
Director: Ishiro Honda
Special Effects Director: Eiji Tsuburaya
Screenplay: Shinichi Sekizawa, Shinichiro Nakamura (story), Takehiko Fukunaga (story), Yoshie Hotta (story)
Director of Photography: Hajime Koizumi
Music: Yuji Koseki
Assistant Director: Samaji Nonagase
Production Design: Teruaki Abe, Takeo Kita
Editor: Kazuji Taira
Lighting: Toshio Takashima
Sound Recording: Shoichi Fujinawa
Sound Effects: Masanobu Miyazaki
Choreography: Yoji Ken
Production Manager: Shin Morita
SFX Cinematography: Sadamasa Arikawa

SFX Art Director: Akira Watanabe
SFX Lighting: Kuichiro Kishida
SFX Composites: Hiroshi Mukoyama
Assistant SFX Art Director: Yasuyuki Inoue
Modeling: Teizo Toshimitsu
SFX Production Manager: Nuki Narita
Still Photographer: Kazukiyo Tanaka

Cast
Frankie Sakai (*Zenichiro Fukuda*)
Hiroshi Koizumi (*Shinichi Chujo*)
Kyoko Kagawa (*Michi Hanamura*)
Yumi Ito (*Twin Fairy*)
Emi Ito (*Twin Fairy*)
Jerry Ito (*Clark Nelson*)
Ken Uehara (*Dr. Harada*)
Takashi Shimura (*Editor Amano*)

Masamitsu Tayama (*Shinji Chujo*)
Seizaburo Kawazu (*Secretary of Defense*)
Tetsu Nakamura (*Nelson's Assistant*)
Hisaya Ito (*Defense Force Commander*)
Kenji Sahara (*Helicopter Pilot*)
Akihiko Hirata (*Director of National Nuclear Center*)
Obel Wyatt (*Professor Rahk*)
Yoshio Kosugi (*Captain of Genyo Maru*)
Ren Yamamoto (*Genyo Maru Navigator*)
Haruya Kato (*Sailor Murata*)
Yutaka Nakayama (*Radioman Homma*)
Koji Iwamoto (*Genyo Maru Helmsman*)
Goro Sakurai (*Rescue Task Force Member*)
Junnosuke Suda
Akira Kichijoji
Toshiko Nakano

Harold Conway (*Rolisican Ambassador*)
Kenzo Echigo (*Helicopter Co-Pilot*)
Ko Mishima (*Captain Hayakaze*)
Tadashi Okabe (*Doctor Hayaze*)
Kohei Furukawa (*Geiger Operator*)
Hideyo Shibuya (*Journalist*)
Masaki Tachibana (*Journalist*)
Toshihiko Furuta (*Reporter*)
Osman Yusuf (*Nelson's Henchman*)
Akira Wakamatsu (*Nelson's Henchman*)
Toshio Miura (*Nelson's Henchman*)
Hiroshi Takagi (*Nelson's Henchman*)
Junpei Natsuki (*Rest House Owner*)
Teruko Mita (*Rest House Owner's Wife*)
Shoichi Hirose (*Dam Worker*)
Shigeo Kato (*Dam Watchman*)
Tsurue Ichimanji (*Chujo's Aunt*)

Terumi Oka (*Theater Guide*)
Mitsuo Tsuda (*Captain of Orion Maru*)
Keisuke Matsuyama (*Orion Navigator*)
Yu Sekita (*Orion Helmsman*)
Yutaka Oka (*Captain of Transport*)
Akira Yamada (*Island Worshipper*)
Mitsuo Matsumoto (*Japanese Expedition Member*)
Yoshio Katsube (*Japanese Expedition Member*)
Hiroyuki Satake (*Japanese Expedition Member*)
Ko Hayami (*Japanese Expedition Member*)
Kazuo Imai (*Japanese Expedition Member*)
Koji Uno (*Policeman*)
Yukihiko Gondo (*Policeman*)
Yasuhisa Tsutsumi (*Woodcutter*)
Yoshifumi Tajima (*Military Advisor*)
Robert Dunham (*New Kirk City Police Chief*)

Ed Keane (*New Kirk City Mayor*)
Wataru Omae
Yoshiyuki Uemura
Takeo Nagashima (*Island Dancer*)
Kazuo Nichikata
Rinsaku Ogata
Ryoji Shimizu
Ryuichi Hosokawa
Toku Ihara
Tatsuo Sakai
Nanako Yamada
Haruo NaKajima (*Mothra Larva*)
Katsumi Tezuka (*Mothra Larva*)

Alternate Titles
Mothra la indestructible
[Mothra, the Indestructible]
(Mexico)
Mothra bedroht die Welt
[Mothra Threatens the World]
(Germany)
Mothra, a Deusa Selvagem
[Mothra, the Wild Goddess]
(Brazil)

"Who is MOTHRA?! What is MOTHRA?! Why does all the world fear MOTHRA?!"
-U.S. Teaser Trailer (1962)

Mothra is one of Ishiro Honda and Eiji Tsuburaya's finest monster films alongside *Godzilla*. Produced in Toho's heyday, it boasts a distinctive, fantastical tone. *Mothra* also features lavish, near Hollywood tier production values. Honda and the film's writers delve into interesting subtexts. These include environmentalism, indigenous issues and the dark side of Western capitalism. At the same time, Tsuburaya impresses with one stunning destruction sequence after another.

PLOT

As a typhoon rolls in, the steamer *Genyo Maru* is caught in it. The survivors are shipwrecked on Infant Island which had atomic bombs tested on it by the nation of Rolisica. A rescue party finds the four men in good health and unaffected by radiation sickness. This puzzles scientists as the men claim the natives gave them a juice to drink. Reporter Zenichiro Fukuda

(Frankie Sakai) and his photographer Michi Hanamura (Kyoko Kagawa) infiltrate the hospital examining the men.

Rolisica puts together a joint Rolisican/Japanese expedition to Infant Island. It is led by Dr. Rahk (Obel Wyatt) and Dr. Harada (Ken Uehara). Secretly, the true benefactor of this expedition is a mysterious man named Clark Nelson (Jerry Ito). Nelson raises the ire of the press by refusing to allow reporters to come along. Fukuda, however, sneaks onto the ship by disguising himself as a cabin boy. Anthropologist Shinichi Chujo (Hiroshi Koizumi) is appalled when Nelson insists all data be reviewed by him.

The expedition soon reaches Infant Island and explores a vast radioactive jungle. Chujo is attacked by a bloodsucking plant but saved by what appears to be two twin girls less than a foot in height. The next day, the expedition encounters the two "Twin Fairies". Nelson attempts to kidnap them. He lets them go over the protest of the other expedition members. The expedition returns to Japan and the existence of the Twin Fairies is concealed from the public.

Nelson, however, sneaks back to Infant Island. He steals the Fairies as his henchmen massacre the natives. Returning to Japan, Nelson turns the Twin Fairies into a stage act and profiteers off them. The Fairies and the surviving natives sing to the island's god, Mothra. A mysterious giant egg suddenly rises from the catacombs. The egg hatches and an enormous caterpillar emerges from it. The larval Mothra destroys a cruise liner at sea as it swims to Japan. Mothra is then attacked by the Defense Force. The creature survives a napalm bombardment and continues to make a beeline for the Twin Fairies.

Nelson's act is soon cancelled and Mothra makes landfall and destroys Kurobe Dam. Fukuda saves an infant from a collapsing bridge as Mothra makes its way to Tokyo. Chujo's brother Shinji (Masamitsu Tayama) tries to rescue the Fairies but is subdued by Nelson's men. The Rolisican government orders Nelson to return the Fairies. Nelson and his men have already skipped town, however. Mothra flattens Yokota air base and heads for downtown Tokyo. In the chaos, Nelson flees to Rolisica with the Fairies. Mothra, meanwhile, destroys Tokyo Tower and builds a cocoon around it. The Rolisican government agrees to help Japan destroy Mothra. They send their "Atomic Heat Ray Guns" to Japan which fire a nuclear-powered death ray. The next morning, the Heat Ray Guns commence fire on the cocooned Mothra. The cocoon is burned to a husk. Hiding on his ranch, Nelson and his cohorts celebrate Mothra's death. Yet as the Fairies sing to Mothra, the creature emerges in winged form from the smoldering cocoon.

BACKGROUND

By 1960, producer Tomoyuki Tanaka was eager to make another monster movie. Toho's last such film had been the fairly disastrous *Varan* (1958), though a recreation of the mythical beast *Yamata no Orochi* appeared in 1959's *The Three Treasures*. Tanaka wanted a different kind of monster film this time around: a feminine beast with elements of magical realism. To this aim, he hired writer Shinichiro Nakamura to come up with a concept. Nakamura was a dramatic scribe who had adapted Yukio Mishima's *The Sound of Waves* into a screenplay. He was far removed from sci-fi authors like Shigeru Kayama or Jojiro Okami. Nakamura collaborated with two other writer friends: Takehiko Fukunaga and Yoshie Hotta. Each writer would come up with one act of the story. The original story, *The Glowing Fairies and Mothra*, was serialized prior to the release of the film. While it had the movie's basic elements, it was significantly different. Nakamura and company's story was far longer and contained many bulky subplots. There were four, larger fairies instead of two. The Christian-influenced mythology of Infant Island was also delved into. Screenwriter Shinichi Sekizawa was hired to turn the long-winded story into a concise script. Inspired by the original *King Kong*, he simplified the story's beats into a more adventurous form.

PRINCIPAL PHOTOGRAPHY

Mothra had one of Toho's biggest budgets for a monster film and there's a lavishness to it reminiscent of old Hollywood films. The production values are some of the best Honda and Tsuburaya ever achieved. Hajime Koizumi's images are luminous and *Mothra* has a fantastical tone. The production design of the Infant Island sequences is especially impressive. It is said Honda drew aesthetic influence from an unexpected place: Michael Powell and Emeric Pressburger's *The Red Shoes* (1948).

There was an alternate ending shot. Columbia bought the rights to the film before shooting began. Their contract stipulated that the ending take place in an American-style city to give *Mothra* more marketability overseas. The original story had an epic finale in Rolisica's capital of New Kirk City. The bean counters at Toho, however, wanted a less expensive ending. They petitioned Columbia to allow for a finale set in Japan. In this ending. Nelson and his men kidnap Chujo's brother Shinji and flee into the volcanic mountains of Kyushu. Engaging in a shoot-out with police, Nelson is finally blown into a volcano by Mothra. In many ways, it was a more satisfying end for Nelson than what appeared in the final cut. Toho, not wanting to delay principal photography, started shooting the film while waiting for approval from Columbia. The alternate ending was one of the first scenes shot. Columbia declined Toho's request shortly after and the footage was never developed. This ending will forever be a lost relic ala *King Kong*'s "spider pit" scene, with scant glimpses available on the film's poster and in publicity shots. Honda's end of Rolisica sequences, containing just about every Western expat who resided in Tokyo, are the weakest link of the film, stagebound on obvious sets.

ACTORS

Mothra's cast is eclectic; a mix of consummate Japanese players and amateur foreigners. Frankie Sakai (1929-1996) plays tenacious reporter Zenichiro "Zen-Chan" Fukuda. He was a beloved triple threat: a comedian, jazz musician and actor. Born Masatoshi Sakai in the South Japanese city of Kagoshima, he was the descendent of samurai. His uncle was Gokuro Soga, one of Japan's first comic actors. His name "Frankie" was christened when he was performing at an American military cabaret during the Occupation. In 1954 he formed the jazz band "Frankie Sakai and the City Slickers". While performing he met comic actor Junzaburo Ban who got him into show business. His big breakout role was in the acclaimed TV drama and later movie *I Wanna Be a Shellfish* (1959). He was also known for frequent roles in Toho's *Company President* and *Train Station* comedy films. Sakai was something of an activist and lobbied for a strong actors' union. He also hosted a string of quiz and variety shows. Later on in his career, Sakai appeared in James Clavell's *Shogun* (1980). A passion of his was *ukiyo-e* printer Sharaku and one of his final projects was a biopic directed by Masahiro Shinoda. Kyoko Kagawa plays Zen's trusty photographer Michie Hamamura. Kagawa (1931-) was an esteemed actress who appeared in films by Kurosawa, Ozu, Mizoguchi and Naruse. At 17, she joined Shin Toho. She first turned

heads in Mikio Naruse's *Mother* (1952) and in the role of an Okinawan girl pressed into the role of army nurse in 1953's *Tower of the Lilies*. Soon she appeared in Yasujiro Ozu's beloved *Tokyo Story* (1953). She was a favorite actress of Kurosawa's, acting in *The Lower Depths* (1957), *The Bad Sleep Well* (1960), *High and Low* (1963) and *Red Beard* (1965). She married and moved to New York City for a while but returned to Japan soon after. Still active to this day, more recently she was in Masayuki Suo's *Shall We Dance* (1996).

Hiroshi Koizumi (1926-2015) plays one of his first scientist roles for director Honda. Koizumi was not new to the genre, however. He previously appeared in *Godzilla Raids Again* (1955). Koizumi was born in Kamakura, Kanagawa, the son of Shotaro Koizumi, a politician. He studied economics at Keio University but got into broadcasting after he graduated. His radio performances showed a great deal of talent. Koizumi was encouraged to apply at Toho's New Face program. Making the cut, his first film was 1952's *Youth Conference,* directed by Toshio Sugie. In 1956, Koizumi played the main character's suitor in the romantic comedy *Sazae-San (Miss Sazae).* He became especially beloved for this role which he reprised in sequels a dozen more times. For Honda, Koizumi became a favorite: appearing in five more of his films in a row. His acting career died down but Koizumi became the host of a popular quiz show. He returned to the kaiju genre occasionally, playing smaller roles in *Godzilla vs. Mechagodzilla* (1974), *The Return of Godzilla* (1984) and *Godzilla: Tokyo S.O.S.* (2003). In the latter, he reprised

Mothra's role of Chujo. Koizumi's older brother Junsaku was an equally famous painter.

Jerry Ito plays the vile Nelson with lip-smacking albom. Ito (1927-2007) was born Gerald Tamekichi Ito in New York City. He was the second son of dancer and choreographer Michio Ito and an American woman. He grew up in California and after his parents divorced, his father was accused of spying for Japan by the FBI. Michio Ito fled back to his home country to avoid trial. To save young Jerry from internment, his American family took him to New York where he finished high school before being drafted into the U.S. Navy. Jerry wound up serving in the Occupation forces in Japan. During this time, he searched for his father whom he had lost contact with during the war. After several months, he finally reunited with him and met his Japanese family for the first time. Returning to the United States, Jerry Ito studied drama in New York. After two years of studies, he appeared on Broadway for the first time. Ito did a short stint in the Korean War where he avoided being sent to the front-lines and instead helped put on musical shows at Fort Dix and West Point. He returned to Broadway where he appeared in a stage version of *Tea House of the August Moon*. In the mid 1950s, Jerry Ito returned to Japan to visit his family. One of his uncles was actor Koreya Senda and another was production designer Kisaku Ito. His two uncles got him into Japanese show business and Ito remained in Tokyo. In addition to *Mothra*, Ito also appeared in the same year's *The Last War* and the 1959 US/Japanese co-production *The Manster*. He also appeared on the Tsuburaya TV show *Mighty Jack* (1968) and its follow-up. His final onscreen role was in Kinji Fukasaku's *Message From Space* (1978). He moved back to California later in life. Ito suffered a stroke but was gradually recovering before cancer took him.

Other notable actors in *Mothra* include Ken Uehara and Tetsu Nakamura. Uehara (1909-1991) was born the son of an army colonel. After graduating from university, he joined Shochiku and became a popular actor there. His career was interrupted by a short stint fighting in China. Uehara's unit was overwhelmed by the amount of fan mail he received. After the war he quit Shochiku. He appeared in films for Daiei and Toho including Naruse's *Late Chrysanthemums* (1954). Eventually, he contracted with Toho. There he focused on character acting as he began to suffer from Meniere's Disease. His son was Yuzo Kayama, adored for his role in Toho's *Young Guy* series. Uehara appeared in Nobuhiko Obayashi's *The Little Girl Who Conquered Time* (1983) in his later years. Tetsu Nakamura (1908-1992) was born Satoshi Nakamura in British Columbia, Canada. As a youth, he trained to be a singer at the Britannia Secondary School. Nakamura eventually emigrated to Japan in the early 1940s. There he began to pursue acting and was contracted to Toho in 1942. Postwar, his fluent English made him an asset on international co-productions where he often acted as interpreter. He also appeared in a memorable role in *The Manster*. Later, he appeared in *Red Sun* (1971) opposite Toshio

Mifune, Charles Bronson and Alain Delon. A later role was in the U.S./Japanese co-production *The Last Dinosaur* (1977).

Tanaka had only one choice in mind for the Twin Fairies. That was popular chanteuse duo Emi (1941-2012) and Yumi Ito (1941-2017), better known as The Peanuts. Being identical twins, they were discovered in a nightclub by a talent scout. The Peanuts had debuted in Japan's music scene only a few years prior to *Mothra* and were now top of the charts. Tanaka was able to procure them in spite of their busy schedule. They were indeed a massive asset in selling the film. Ishiro Honda loved working with them and thought they were very professional. Speaking in unison was easy for them as they were used to singing together. When filming their scenes, Honda found it nearly impossible to tell them apart. For sequences where the tiny Fairies interact with the regular-sized actors, dolls were used as on-set stand-ins. Their lines were played on a tape recorder to the actors. *Mothra* wound up being very good for The Peanuts' career and international notability. They would go on to make guest appearances on *The Ed Sullivan Show* and *The Danny Kaye Show* in the states.

Mothra contains more Western actors than the average Toho production. Generally, *gaijin* in Japanese films were played by an eclectic group of expats. These were mainly businesspeople and military men working or stationed in Tokyo. Only with *Frankenstein Conquers the World* did Toho start to bring professional, Hollywood actors to Japan.

There are several interesting figures in *Mothra*. The first is Osman "Johnny" Yusuf. Yusuf (1920-1982) was a Turkish national whose parents emigrated to Japan during the *Taisho* era. He started off playing American villains in films produced by the Imperial government. After the defeat, Yusuf continued playing bit parts in Japanese films, especially for Toho. He ran an agency called Kokusai that specialized in obtaining Western actors for Japanese productions. Yusuf was also, for lack of a better word, a glorified pimp who specialized in obtaining Western women for wealthy Japanese businessmen. He can be glimpsed in film after film, often appearing in crowd scenes. Another memorable role Yusuf played was as a mafia goon in *The Street Fighter* (1974) with Sonny Chiba. After playing one final role as a military tribunal member in Toshio Masuda's *The Imperial Japanese Empire* (1982), he died. His younger brother, Omar Yusuf, was a Japan-based professional wrestler. Robert Dunham (1931-2001) was another such figure. A native New Englander from Maine and Massachusetts, he studied art history before enlisting in the Marines. There he was stationed in Japan. Dunham decided to stay in Japan after discharge. He played a notable role in Kinji Fukasaku's *Greed in Broad Daylight* (1961). Dunham later appeared in *Dogora* (1964), *The Green Slime* (1968), *Godzilla vs. Megalon* (1973) and *ESPY* (1974). He spoke Japanese almost fluently and was one of the few foreign actors in Japan who could recite Japanese lines. He also dabbled in filmmaking, producing a 45 minute short called *Time Travelers* (1966) that was shown on television. Dunham did a lot of English dubbing work for William Ross' Frontier Enterprises as well. In 1975, Dunham returned to the U.S. however where he lived out the rest of days with his family as a freelance writer.

SFX

Eiji Tsuburaya's special effects sequences are beautifully executed, boasting one impressive image after another. As Tsuburaya began work on *Mothra*, he was hit hard by the death of his colleague Shuzaburo Araki (1913-1961). Araki was Tsuburaya's brother-in-law. He had been a combat photographer for the Imperial Army at the Chinese front. Araki had long helped Tsuburaya and Sadamasa Arikawa with miniature and optical photography. Yukio Manoda thus took over the optical shooting arm of Tsuburaya's unit.

Tsuburaya was given more money to work with than usual and it shows. The composites are among the very finest in Tsuburaya's career. Three different versions of Mothra's larval form were constructed. These included a smaller, mechanical puppet. The attack on Mothra by the Defense Force at sea was one of the first monster sequences shot in Toho's "Big Pool". It was built in 1960 to stage the attack on Pearl Harbor in Shue Matsubayashi's *Storm Over the Pacific*. The "Big Pool" covered a whopping 86,000 square feet. It would be integral to the water sequences for Toho's monster and war films in the coming decades. It was used one last time in 2004's *Godzilla: Final Wars* before being paved over. The destruction of Kurobe

dam is an impressive scene. The dam was recreated at 1/50th scale. Eiji Tsuburaya was planning to destroy and flood the miniature with water pumped from four tanks. Assistant art director Yasuyuki Inoue thought that four water tanks wouldn't be enough. The water used needed to burst the miniature dam and make the deluge look realistic. He was adamant on sixteen tanks. Toho only had eight such tanks on their backlot. Undaunted, the brilliant Inoue built four more for twelve in total. Tsuburaya was at first irritated with Inoue. He was frustrated that Inoue's rigging of the tanks made camera placement difficult. It took multiple takes to destroy the miniature, but Tsuburaya was impressed with the results.

For shots where the larva smashes buildings, a gigantic, almost 40 foot long suit was built. This suit was crafted by Teizo Toshimitsu with help from apprentice Keizo Murase and built by the Yagi brothers. It was performed pantomime horse style with eight people in total, headed by Haruo Nakajima and Katsumi Tezuka. The back of the costume was manned by younger members of the special effects staff. Murase did a lot of work on the costume to make it look more "lived in". This included adding a barnacle to its face along with a vinyl coating so it looked slimy. Tsuburaya was quite happy with these touches. Larval Mothra's attack on Tokyo is one of the very best effects sequences Tsuburaya's unit ever produced. The miniature work is stunning and, thanks to the giant suit, was built at a larger than usual scale. Some of it was constructed as big as 1/20th and made from photographs

Tsuburaya's FX crew took around town, a tradition since *Godzilla*.

The original story called for Mothra to cocoon itself on the Diet Building, Japan's House of Parliament. Tsuburaya and company perhaps found this redundant as Godzilla had already trampled it in 1954. They opted to go with the recently built Tokyo Tower instead. A nod to this would appear in 1992's *Godzilla vs. Mothra*, however. Tsuburaya's staff petitioned to use the original Tokyo Tower blueprints but the local government declined. Instead, the staff made their own miniature blueprints through photos. These blueprints came in handy for future films like *Ghidorah, the Three-Headed Monster* (1964) and *King Kong Escapes* (1967). Rumor has it they may have even been stolen by Daiei and used for *Gamera the Giant Monster* (1965). Mothra's cocoon silk was made from a liquid polystyrene, a recipe used on future films for decades. The Atomic Heat Ray Cannons were designed by Akira Watanabe and built by Inoue. Part of the miniature was recycled to make the A-Cycle Light Ray in *Invasion of Astro-Monster* (1965). It was also influential on the Maser Cannon in *The War of the Gargantuas* (1966). As with the larval Mothra, three versions of the adult imago Mothra prop were made. The largest and most elaborate had glowing eyes from small light bulbs. The props were suspended from a moving rig with piano wire. The wires were attached to the center of the wings, which gave them a more realistic flapping motion.

MUSIC

Mothra features a novel score by Yuji Koseki. Koseki (1909-1989) was chosen after Akira Ifukube turned down the opportunity to compose the music. Koseki's score gives *Mothra* a different and more whimsical feel. Koseki was born in Fukushima Prefecture to a wealthy family. He grew up around music; his father was one of the few *Taisho*-era Japanese to own a gramophone and collect records. Koseki studied business in college but self-taught himself music composition as a hobby. This hobby paid off as he became the first Japanese composer to gain success overseas. At only 20, Koseki performed at the British branch of the International Society for Contemporary Music. In 1931, he was signed with Nippon Columbia. Koseki became a successful composer with a penchant for populist work. During the war, he composed Imperial army and naval marches. Koseki also scored the early *anime* propaganda film *Momotaro: Sacred Sailors* (1945). Post-war, he created the iconic theme for the baseball team the Yomiuri Giants among other achievements. In *Mothra*, it was decided to have the Peanuts sing Mothra's iconic theme song in Bahasa Indonesian for a more exotic flair. The song was translated by an Indonesian foreign exchange student studying at Tokyo University. It became one of the most iconic and popular *kaiju* film melodies and was reused numerous times in the Godzilla series.

THEMES AND MOTIFS

Like *Godzilla*, *Mothra* also has deeper themes than meets the eye. Nakamura, Fukunaga and Hotta's original story was less subtle in its political overtones. There was an anti-discrimination message and jabs at America and Japan's controversial 1960 AMPO security treaty. While Sekizawa toned these themes down, there are still strong hints. Rolisica, its name a portmanteau of Russia and America, is a biting parody of a Western nation. It's much akin to the portrayal of Russia and America as the "Alliance" and "Federation" in the same year's *The Last War*. The Rolisicans, responsible for conducting atomic tests on Infant Island, are quick to defend Nelson's property rights despite moral conundrums. They are also swift to deploy an atomic weapon on Japanese soil, blatantly violating Japan's non-nuclear principles. The sociopathic Clark Nelson is a grotesque personification of Western imperialism. A darker take on *King Kong*'s Carl Denham, he is a quintessential "ugly American". There is subtext in *Mothra* about indigeneous peoples' rights, capitalism and even environmentalism. Nelson, as if standing in for "manifest destiny", massacres the natives of Infant Island before exploiting the Fairies for capitalist gain. His appalling greed brings about the wrath of nature through Mothra, who takes on the classic role of Shinto *yonaoshi* god.

RELEASE AND LEGACY

Mothra performed well at the Japanese box office. It was the 10th highest grossing film that year. The success of *Mothra* convinced Tanaka to revive the Godzilla series after a seven year hiatus. *King Kong vs. Godzilla* followed soon after in 1962. Along with a cameo in the comedy *Cheers! Mr. Awamori* in late 1961, Mothra would, of course, return. In 1964's *Mothra vs. Godzilla*, it would become one of Godzilla's most popular foes. Variations of the creature would appear in nine more entries up to the recent *Godzilla: King of the Monsters* (2019). Mothra would also get its own standalone film series starting with *Rebirth of Mothra* (1996).

ALTERNATE VERSIONS

Mothra was pre-sold to Columbia as it was, more or less, a U.S./Japanese co-production. With a big ad blitz, it was released to American theaters on May 10th, 1962. In some regions, it was shown on a double bill with *The Three Stooges in Orbit*. The U.S. version runs 90:11, though its ten minutes of cuts are surprisingly subtle. The American credits oddly forget to list Frankie Sakai, Kyoko Kagawa or Hiroshi Koizumi in the cast. The scenes where the expedition explores the jungles of Infant Island are trimmed. The most notable edit is much of a Peanuts musical number before larval Mothra destroys the luxury liner. There's a military preparation scene that is cut before the nautical air raid on larval Mothra. A brief dialog exchange between the two dam workers is cut before Mothra's attack. Some slight trimming was done to Mothra's attack on downtown Tokyo. Minor dialog and scene cuts were made to the New Kirk City finale along with the removal of some religious imagery. *Mothra* got unusually good stateside reviews for a Japanese monster film. Even *The New York Times* sang its praises, albeit faintly.

The English dubbing for *Mothra* was done at Titra in New York. The dub was directed by Lee Kressel with a script by Robert Myerson. Dubbing cast includes Bernard Grant (Fukuda), Bret Morrison (Dr. Harada) and Peter Fernandez. Bernard "Bernie" Grant (1920-2004) was a television and voice actor. Grant was best known for appearing on the long running soap opera *Guiding Light.* He did a lot of work for Titra/Titan and his voice can be heard in many of the Toho films they dubbed. He was also a frequent voice in Spaghetti Westerns including Sergio Leone's seminal *The Good, the Bad and the Ugly* (1966). He often voiced actor Gian Maria Volonte in particular.

In December 1974, Toho reissued *Mothra* for their winter Champion Matsuri festival. This version, reedited by Honda himself, runs a scant 62 minutes. The "Champion" *Mothra* opens with a montage of destruction scenes from later in the film. The music over the ensuing credits is replaced with the native chant from midway. Numerous drama scenes are cut. What others remain are often reduced. Chujo's introductory scene and the expedition departure sequence are removed. The scenes on Infant Island are severely truncated. Chujo being attacked by the vampire plant and saved by the Fairies is cut. In this version, the expedition encounters the Fairies quite early on. Chujo and Fukuda discussing the language of Infant Island is intercut with Nelson kidnapping the Fairies. Nelson massacring the Infant Islanders is not shown, likely per the Festival's child audience. The film also cuts straight from the egg's hatching to the cruise liner's destruction. Chujo's brother Shinji's attempt to rescue the girls is cut down and Fukuda's tussle with Nelson's thugs is edited out. Mothra's attack on Yokota air base is trimmed down. The New Kirk City finale feels a little more intact and some religious imagery removed from the U.S. version is left in. The final bit showing Mothra and the Fairies returning to Infant Island is cut, however. This recut version is recommended only as a curiosity.

AMERICAN HOME VIDEO HISTORY

Mothra was first released on VHS and Betamax by Columbia in 1984. It was then sublicensed by Goodtimes Home Video in 1988. It was later reissued on VHS by Columbia itself in 1993. The version on the Columbia tape isn't the exact American version and is something of a reconstruction with sync problems and some footage from the Japanese version left in. *Mothra* was released to region 1 DVD in 2008, alongside *The H-Man* and *Battle in Outer Space*, in a three disc *"Icons of Sci-Fi"* set from Sony. This contained both the U.S. and Japanese versions. In 2019 it was sublicensed by Mill Creek and released to Blu-ray.

Further Viewing:

KING KONG vs GODZILLA

(1962)
キングコング対ゴジラ

Toho, *Director:* **Ishiro Honda**

King Kong vs. Godzilla is a film with a genesis almost as legendary as the movie itself. It was not the first Japanese film to capitalize on the Kong phenomenon. The Shochiku comedy *Wasei King Kong* (1933) featured a vaudeville actor dressing up as the monster. In 1938, a two part silent *jidai-geki* called *King Kong Appears in Edo* was released. Directed by Soya Kumagai, the monster ape was human-sized but called "King Kong" as cash-in. Sadly both are now lost films ala *King Kong*'s own spider-pit sequence. Much of Japan's pre-war cinematic history was destroyed by Allied fire-bombings and the Imperial military's destruction of film prints for their metal.

By the 1950s, stop motion pioneer Willis O'Brien (1886-1962) had fallen on hard times. Though he won an Oscar for 1949's *Mighty Joe Young*, he struggled to find work and get projects off the ground. One of these projects was *King Kong vs. Prometheus*, pitting Kong against a Frankenstein-like creature. He partnered with a producer named John Beck. Beck hired screenwriter George Worthing Yates to turn O'Brien's treatment into a full script. What happened next is the stuff of much debated cinema legend. Beck, unable to find any interested buyers in Hollywood, took the script to Japan. Toho jumped at the chance to make a King Kong movie on the heels of *Mothra*. When they purchased the script, however, it was rewritten from scratch by Shinichi Sekizawa. Tanaka and company also jettisoned the story's Frankenstein Monster: "Ginko". In its place, they substituted their own monster king, Godzilla. Toho would, however, entertain ambitions of making a Frankenstein movie as well. These would be realized in 1965's *Frankenstein Conquers the World*. To date, Beck is a controversial figure among tokusatsu and stop motion enthusiasts alike. Did he "betray" O'Brien as the stop motion crowd tends to think or was he being a pragmatic producer? Regardless, Merian C. Cooper, director of the original *King Kong*, was not pleased. He unsuccessfully tried to sue Beck, Universal and Toho to stop the release stateside. O'Brien tragically died only a few months after *King Kong vs. Godzilla* was released in Japan.

King Kong vs. Godzilla is far from the best Honda/Tsuburaya collaboration. Hampered by uneven effects work and a genuinely awful Kong suit, the film delights in silliness. Toho began to notice that child audiences appreciated these films with *Mothra*'s success. *King Kong vs. Godzilla* is notable as being one of the very first *kaiju* films made with children in mind. The goofy scenes of Godzilla and King Kong throwing boulders at each other are a beginning of the end for the brooding, subtext-riddled aesthetic of films like the 1954 *Godzilla*. Yet the Japanese version has a comic self-awareness. Honda understands the inherent ridiculousness of the film's base concept. With such understanding, he creates a cunning satire that is almost proto-ironic. Honda mocks post-war consumerism and the newfangled television media cycle while channeling Toho's popular *Company President* series. Comic actor Ichiro Arishima (1916-1987) appeared in many such films. He plays an amusing turn as greedy but lovable Mr. Tako with Chaplin-like timing. Seen through the lens of subtle parody, *King Kong vs. Godzilla* is a blast. Tsuburaya's FX end has some beautiful composite shots. The highlight is an impressively staged sequence where a giant octopus attacks Kong's island village. Tsuburaya had long wanted to make a giant octopus movie, so he took the scene to heart. It's a practical effects tour-de-force combining Honda's footage, miniatures, two octopus

puppets, stop motion animation and numerous live cephalopods. Prodded around miniatures with cigarettes and blasts of hot air, these octopi were eaten by the crew after filming. Akira Ifukube's score is also one of his very best, boasting rousing motifs he would recycle for decades to come.

The U.S. version of *King Kong vs. Godzilla* is not recommended. It is one of the most heavily altered films of its type. Containing dull new sequences directed by Thomas Montgomery, it misses the point of Honda's far superior cut. Beck's cut of *King Kong vs. Godzilla* makes the dire mistake of playing much of the film's goofiness straight. Additionally, Ifukube's majestic score is replaced by music from past Universal productions, including *The Creature From the Black Lagoon*. The Japanese version is overall a far more rewarding experience.

TOMOYUKI TANAKA
The Money Man

田中友幸
4/26/1910-4/2/1997

"He should be considered a legend in his time."
-Henry G. Saperstein, *Monsters Are Attacking Tokyo* by Stuart Galbraith (1998)

One day to become Toho's CEO, Tomoyuki "Yuko" Tanaka was a pivotal architect of Godzilla's pop cultural phenomenon. He was also an advocate for Akira Kurosawa, producing many of his best films. Tomoyuki Tanaka was born in Osaka to a military family. He attended college at the Kansai University of Economics, graduating in

1935. From there, he started producing stage plays. He joined Taisho Studios as an associate film producer. Taisho soon merged with Toho.

The producer is a figure misunderstood outside the industry. If the director brings a film project its creative vision, the producer tempers it with realism. They keep the director and their team on budget and time. Tanaka, with his education in economics, showed a knack for this as he was mentored by his senior Iwao Mori. Tanaka's first film as full-fledged producer was *Three of the North* (1945). It was, incidentally, the last film released in Imperial Japan. In theaters on August 5th, Hiroshima was bombed only a day later.

After the war Tanaka continued his producing career. He left Toho for a time when the union disputes took place in 1947. Unlike others who migrated to Shin Toho, Tanaka took over a small company called the Film Arts Association. He returned to Toho in 1952 when his mentor Iwao Mori was allowed to return per the end of the U.S. Occupation. 1954 would be the year Tanaka rose to prominence as one of Japan's most successful producers. An Indonesian-Japanese co-production he was producing, *In Glory's Shadow*, had to be cancelled. The Indonesian government bowed to local anti-Japanese sentiment and pulled their support. Toho was left with an empty slot in their release slate and Tanaka in a precarious position. It is said that he looked out the window of his plane back to Tokyo and imagined a creature living under the sea. That was when it hit him: a monster movie could be highly profitable. At that time, *King Kong* had done well in re-release at Japanese theaters. Toho's resident special effects wizard Eiji Tsuburaya jumped at the chance to make a monster movie. Soon, with Iwao Mori's approval and Ishiro Honda on board as director, *Project-G* was launched. This film became better known as *Godzilla*.

Godzilla was a tremendous success. It revolutionized Japanese special effects filmmaking and made the bean counters at Toho very happy. Tanaka soon became Toho's go-to producer for their pulpier films. This was in contrast to their other major producer Sanezumi Fujimoto, who specialized in comedies and love stories. Through the 1950s and '60s, Tanaka produced monster and science fiction films, war films and samurai epics. He produced all of Kurosawa's 1960s films from *The Bad Sleep Well* on. He also oversaw nearly every film Eiji Tsuburaya worked on as special effects director. He was a pivotal force behind Expo '70 in Osaka and was promoted to Toho's board of directors in 1971.

In the 1970s came economic uncertainty and oil shocks. The Japanese film industry thus fell into a creative and financial rut. The Godzilla series, even, stopped being profitable to produce and in 1975 was put in hibernation. Tanaka, however, persevered. He produced some of Japan's biggest hits, including the blockbuster disaster epic *Submersion of Japan* (1973). He soon became president of Toho and in 1980 he helped Kurosawa bring *Kagemusha* to the screen. *Kagemusha* was Tanaka's only production nominated for Best Foreign Film at the Academy Awards. Tanaka, also a Mitsubishi shareholder, continued to run Toho in varying capacities, bringing hit after hit to the screen. In the 1990s, Tanaka took a more supervisory approach, leaving the younger Shogo Tomiyama in charge of the Godzilla series. He died in early 1997 of a stroke. His widow was Chieko Nakakita (1926-2005), an actress who played a small role in *Ebirah, Horror of the Deep*.

Selected Filmography (*as producer*)

Three of the North (1945)
The Man Who Came to Port (1952)
Adolescence (1952)
Farewell Rabaul (1954)
Godzilla (1954)
Godzilla Raids Again (1955)
Half Human (1955)
Madam White Snake (1956)
Rodan (1956)
A Man in the Storm (1957)
The Mysterians (1957)
The H-Man (1958)
Varan (1958)
Submarine I-57 Will Not Surrender (1959)
Monkey Sun (1959)
Battle in Outer Space (1959)
The Three Treasures (1959)
Secret of the Telegian (1960)
The Human Vapor (1960)
Storm Over the Pacific (1960)
The Bad Sleep Well (1960)
The Man in Red (1961)
The Merciless Trap (1961)
Daredevil in the Castle (1961)
Mothra (1961)
Yojimbo (1961)
The Last War (1961)
Gorath (1962)
King Kong vs. Godzilla (1962)
Chushingura (1962)
Sanjuro (1962)
Attack Squadron (1963)
Siege of Fort Bismark (1963)
Matango (1963)
High & Low (1963)
Atragon (1963)
Whirlwind (1964)
Mothra vs. Godzilla (1964)
Dogora (1964)

Ghidorah, the Three-Headed Monster (1964)
Samurai Assassin (1965)
Red Beard (1965)
Retreat From Kiska (1965)
Frankenstein Conquers the World (1965)
Fort Graveyard (1965)
Key of Keys (1965)
Ironfinger (1965)
Crazy Adventure (1965)
Invasion of Astro-Monster (1965)
Adventure of Taklamakan (1966)
The War of the Gargantuas (1966)
Ebirah. Horror of the Deep (1966)
The Age of Assassins (1967)
The Killing Bottle (1967)
Samurai Rebellion (1967)
King Kong Escapes (1967)
Japan's Longest Day (1967)
Son of Godzilla (1967)
Kill! (1968)
Destroy All Monsters (1968)
Admiral Yamamoto (1968)
Samurai Banners (1969)
Latitude Zero (1969)
Battle of the Japan Sea (1969)
Portrait of Hell (1969)
All Monsters Attack (1969)
The Vampire Doll (1970)
Terror in the Streets (1970)
Space Amoeba (1970)
Godzilla vs. Hedorah (1971)
Godzilla vs. Gigan (1972)
Horror of the Wolf (1973)
Godzilla vs. Megalon (1973)
The Human Revolution (1973)

Submersion of Japan (1973)
Godzilla vs. Mechagodzilla (1974)
Prophecies of Nostradamus (1974)
ESPY (1974)
Terror of Mechagodzilla (1975)
Conflagration (1975)
Continuing Human Revolution (1976)
Zero Pilot (1976)
The Alaska Story (1977)
The War in Space (1977)
Kagemusha (1980)
Deathquake (1980)
Imperial Navy (1981)
The Makioka Sisters (1983) [executive producer]
Bye Bye Jupiter (1984) [executive producer]
Zero (1984) [executive producer]
The Return of Godzilla (1984) [executive producer]
Princess From the Moon (1987) [executive producer]
Gunhed (1989) [executive producer]
Godzilla vs. Biollante (1989) [executive producer]
Godzilla vs. King Ghidorah (1991) [executive producer]
Godzilla vs. Mothra (1992) [executive producer]
Godzilla vs. Mechagodzilla II (1993) [executive producer]
Yamato Takeru (1994) [executive producer]
Godzilla vs. Space Godzilla (1994) [executive producer]
Godzilla vs. Destoroyah (1995) [executive producer]

THE LAST WAR

世界大戦争

Sekai Daisenso "The Great World War"
Toho, 10/8/1961 (*Showa 36*), 6 Reels (3,012 meters), 109:57, 35mm, TohoScope (2.35:1 anamorphic), Eastman color, Perspecta stereo (4 track)

Crew

Producers: Tomoyuki Tanaka, Sanezumi Fujimoto
Director: Shue Matsubayashi
Special Effects Director: Eiji Tsuburaya
Screenplay: Toshio Yasumi, Takeshi Kimura, Shinobu Hashimoto (original script)
Director of Photography: Rokuro Nishigaki
Music: Ikuma Dan
Assistant Director: Yasuyoshi Tajitsu
Production Design: Takeo Kita, Teruaki Abe
Editor: Koichi Iwashita
Sound Recordist: Fumio Yanoguchi
Sound Effects: Hisashi Shimonaga
Lighting: Hiromitsu Mori
Production Manager: Boku Morimoto
SFX Cinematography: Sadamasa Arikawa, Yoshiyuki Tokumasa
SFX Art Director: Akira Watanabe
SFX Opticals: Takao Saiwai
SFX Lighting: Kuichiro Kishida
SFX Composites: Hiroshi Mukoyama
SFX Production Manager: Nuki Narita
Still Photographer: Kazukiyo Tanaka

Cast

Frankie Sakai *(Mokichi Tamura)*
Nobuko Otowa *(Oyoshi Tamura)*
Yuriko Hoshi *(Saeko Tamura)*
Akira Takarada *(Takano)*
Chishu Ryu *(Ebara)*
Yuko Tominaga *(Harue Tamura)*
Koji Abe *(Ichiro Tamura)*
Yumi Shirakawa *(Sanae)*
Jerry Ito *(Watkins)*
Chieko Nakakita *(Oharu)*
Naoko Sakabe *(Suzue)*
Shigeki Ishida *(Arimura)*
Masao Oda *(Potato Seller)*
Kozo Nomura *(Ishibashi)*
Teruko Mita *(Imoto)*
Eijiro Tono *(Captain of Kasagi Maru)*
Yuki Shimizu *(Trading Company Clerk)*
Kyoko Mori *(Shipping Company Clerk)*
Toshiko Nakano *(Neighbor)*
Tsurue Ichimanji *(Neighbor)*
So Yamamura *(Prime Minister)*
Ken Uehara *(Foreign Minister)*
Seizaburo Kawazu *(Secretary of Defense)*
Nobuo Nakamura *(Chief Cabinet Secretary)*
Minoru Takada *(JSDF Commander)*
Ed Keane *(Alliance Commander)*
Harold Conway *(Federation Commander)*
Hank Brown *(Federation Lieutenant)*
Bernard Vallé *(Alliance Officer)*
Howard Larson *(Federation Staff)*
Cump Cubens *(Alliance Engineer)*
Yutaka Sada
Nadao Kirino
Koji Uno
Seiji Yoshida
Toshihiko Furuta
Takuzo Kumagai
Soji Ubukata
Shiro Tsuchiya
Keiichiro Katsumoto
Naoya Kusakawa
Wataru Omae
Yoshio Katsube
Masaki Shinohara
Yutaka Oka
Koji Uruki
Asami Hodaka
Clifford Harrington
Robert Dunham
Daniel Jones
Ben Greenhough
Mike Snape
Roy Lessard
Hans Horneff
Osman Yusuf

Alternate Titles

Todesstrahlen aus dem Weltall
[Death Rays From Space]
(Germany)

La dernière guerre de l'apocalypse **[The Last War of the Apocalypse]** (France)

La ultima guerra (Spain)
L'ultima guerra (Italy)
La guerra final (Mexico)

> *"Mankind must put an end to war, or war will put an end to mankind."*
> -John F. Kennedy (1961)

Alongside *On the Beach* and BBC's *Threads*, *The Last War* is one of the greatest speculative films about thermonuclear war. Directed with a mournful fatalism by naval war drama specialist Shue Matsubayashi, it features spectacular scenes of inventive atomic destruction by Eiji Tsuburaya. *The Last War* is also a heartbreaking drama, meditating on the true human cost of war. The picture shuttles towards its devastating finale with tragic inevitability. It was released only a year before the Cuban Missile Crisis almost brought its speculations to reality.

PLOT

Since the end of World War II, Tokyo has risen from the ashes to become one of the world's major economic hubs. A working man, Mokichi Tamura (Frankie Sakai) drives a limousine for foreign diplomats to support his family while investing his money in the stock market. Yet trouble is brewing on the world stage. Countries are split into two factions: the capitalist Federation and the communist Alliance. The Alliance captures and boards a submarine belonging to the Federation. Mokichi's teenage daughter Saeko (Yuriko Hoshi), meanwhile, has fallen in love with Takano (Akira Takarada), a sailor.

A military plane is next shot down near Africa. This further exacerbates relations between the Federation and Alliance. Takano comes ashore after the *Kasagi Maru* docks, first going to see Ebara (Chishu Ryu), his ship's cook who just had surgery. Unable to serve on their last voyage, Ebara has been helping his daughter Sanae (Yumi Shirakawa) run her pre-school. Ebara tells Takano that the children have helped him learn to enjoy life more in his old age. Takano stops in to see Saeko next and the two embrace. They plan to get married in spite of both the tensions gripping the world and Mokichi's disapproval. As the Federation and Alliance continue war games and ready their missiles, Takano and Saeko discuss asking for Mokichi's consent. Mokichi overhears the conversation and the two ask for his approval. He hesitates, but his wife Oyoshi (Nobuko Otowa) talks him into giving his blessing.

At the same time, The Prime Minister (So Yamamura) campaigns for peace in spite of suffering from a kidney ailment. As Takano and Saeko make plans for marriage, a Federation nuclear missile base has a close call. Oyoshi and Mokichi plant tulips in their yard as the 38th parallel reaches critical mass and both sides open fire. The Prime Minister and his cabinet race against time to try and mediate. They find out a nuclear warhead was used on the battlefield. This ruins plans for a peace summit and makes the likelihood of nuclear exchange far greater.

Takano and Saeko spend a final day together as he prepares to disembark on the *Kasagi Maru*. At the North Pole, meanwhile, both sides begin shooting again and nuclear weapons are deployed in the battle. Takano and Saeko marry in secret as the Japanese government implores the Alliance and Federation to come to another ceasefire. Saeko tearfully waves goodbye to Takano as his ship vanishes from view on the coastline, unsure if she'll ever see him again. War appears inevitable and Tokyo erupts into panic as people try to flee the city. The Tamuras face their doom with quiet resignation, eating a lavish New Year's meal. The first of the missiles launch and World War III begins. As the Tamuras mournfully await their fate, the missiles strike Tokyo.

BACKGROUND

Toho's president Iwao Mori, likely influenced by United Artists' production of *On the Beach*, long had interest in making a nuclear war film. In 1960, rival company Toei beat Toho to it with *World War III Breaks Out* (aka *The Final War*). Mori quickly greenlit production on a similar film to be called *World War III: The Day of Tokyo's End*. With a screenplay written by Shinobu Hashimoto, the film was to be directed by Kurosawa apprentice Hiromichi Horikawa.

Toho decided to put the brakes on the project after it was decided the script was too similar to Toei's film. A different screenplay by Toshio Yasumi and Takeshi Kimura was commissioned. With Horikawa now unavailable, Shue Matsubayashi was brought on board as director. Matsubayashi was mainly known for his *Company President* series of comedies. Yet he had more than shown that he could handle special effects laden films with *Submarine I-57 Will Not Surrender* (1959) and *Storm Over the Pacific* (1960).

PRINCIPAL PHOTOGRAPHY

Director Matsubayashi was hesitant to take on the project at first but gradually became morbidly fascinated with its concepts. Like Stanley Kramer's *On the Beach*, there is a sense of slow burning impending doom throughout *The Last War* tinged with tragic inevitability. *The Last War* opens with an overture, uncharacteristic of most Japanese films. This was because Matsubayashi wanted to put his audience in a meditative state. It then follows with a similar montage of post-war Tokyo's economic miracle as the later *Submersion of Japan*. By the early 1960s, Tokyo was already preparing for the 1964 Olympics which was a boon for its economy. Matsubayashi was encouraged by Japan's post-war recovery but also anxious that it was too good to be true.

ACTORS

Frankie Sakai was only 32 at the time of production despite convincingly playing a middle aged man. His comic actor roots allowed him to bring a tragic humanism to the character of Mokichi. The 18 year old Yuriko Hoshi gives one of her finest, most empathetic performances. Born Yuriko Shimizu, at only 15, Hoshi (1943-2018) joined the prestigious *Takarazuka Revue* theater troupe. There she was quickly discovered and recruited by Toho. She was one of Toho's most popular actresses with a mix of beauty and everywoman accessibility. Hoshi was known for appearing in several early entries in Toho's beloved *Young Guy* series with Yuzo Kayama. In 1964, she starred in two Godzilla entries, *Mothra vs. Godzilla* and *Ghidorah, the Three Headed Monster*. Decades later, she returned to the series in 2000's *Godzilla vs. Megaguiras*. Hoshi was active up to her death. Her final film, *First Love*, was released in 2019 after her passing. Nobuko Otowa plays the sickly Oyoshi. Otowa (1924-1994) was the mistress and eventual wife of director Kaneto Shindo. She also began her career with *Takarazuka* and became a star at Daiei in 1950. She appeared in Shindo's early films *Story of a Beloved Wife* (1951) and *Children of Hiroshima* (1952). Otowa ended her contract at Daiei and went freelance so she could take part in Shindo's independent productions. She appeared in many of his subsequent films, including *The Naked Island* (1962), *Onibaba* (1964) and *Kuroneko* (1968). Her final film was Shindo's *The Last Note*, released after her death in 1995. For that film she posthumously won the Japanese Academy Award for Best Supporting Actress. It was a bittersweet bookend to an illustrious career.

Chishu Ryu (1904-1994) needs no introduction, having played the lead role in Yasujiro Ozu's *Tokyo Story* (1953). Alongside Mifune and Nakadai, he was one of Japan's greatest *Showa*-era thespians. His scenes in *The Last War* are especially powerful and heartrending. So Yamamura, who plays the Prime Minister, is another notable actor. Yamamura (1910-2000) played the role of the Prime Minister of Japan in more films than any other actor. Born in Nara as Hirosada Koga, he was a stage actor during the war. He then became a film actor in 1946's *As Long As There is Life*. Having played almost 200 roles, Yamamura was a rare Japanese actor to have something of a Hollywood career. He appeared in John Houston's *The Barbarian and the Geisha* (1958) opposite John Wayne. He also starred as Admiral Yamamoto in Fox's *Tora! Tora! Tora!*. In 1986, he played tycoon Mr. Sakamoto in Ron Howard's *Gung Ho*, opposite Michael Keaton.

SFX

The Last War truly comes to life in its final reel whereupon Eiji Tsuburaya's FX unit takes center stage. Matsubayashi respected Tsuburaya to the point that he gave him little direction. Certain images: a squadron of bombers flying low, an ICBM fired from a submarine in the Arctic, not to mention Tokyo's fiery destruction, are Tsuburaya's very finest. Much of the military hardware in *The Last War*, executed via stunning miniatures, is not taken from life but futuristic and outlandish. For shots of the world's landmarks being destroyed, blasts of compressed air were blown at miniatures hung upside down. These facsimile cities were made from wafer crackers. Mice would often nibble on these miniatures much to the annoyance of Tsuburaya's crew.

Tokyo's spectacular atomic decimation is one of Tsuburaya's most iconic FX scenes. Due to the intense heat and fire hazards, it was filmed off Toho's backlot at a nearby steel mill. Tsuburaya's teams crafted the miniatures from charcoal so as to produce an eerie glow like immolated concrete. Ala *Rodan*, molten lead and iron was poured onto the miniatures for the effect of lava-like melting buildings flowing through the ruins of Tokyo. The mushroom cloud was done with a soon to be classic Tsuburaya technique. Paint was poured into a water tank and the resulting image was flipped vertically. This technique would be used again by Tsuburaya's team for underwater eruptions in *Atragon* (1963) and *Latitude Zero* (1969). Interestingly, the same technique would also be used for the mushroom clouds in ABC's *The Day After* (1983) and less effectively at that. A sign of its quality is that *The Last War* became one of the Toho FX unit's favorite works to pilfer for stock footage. Films to re-use its shots included *Atragon, Frankenstein Conquers the World* (1965), *Destroy All Monsters* (1968), *Godzilla vs. Gigan* (1972), *Prophecies of Nostradamus* (1974) and *The War in Space* (1977). Shots were even used as recently as 1995's *Godzilla vs. Destoroyah*.

MUSIC

Ikuma Dan's score is stellar, building emotion effectively. It features a haunting ending theme and use of the famous children's folk song *"New Years Day"*. In Buddhist fashion, Dan and director Matsubayashi chose to use the children's song *"New Years' Day"* in the film because in Eastern culture the new year represents both the beginning and the end in a cycle of rebirth. The original cues for the film's ending were to be far more bleak, a version of the foreboding opening credits theme. The overture's music wound up used instead for a more melancholy and bittersweet tone. Dan (1924-2004) was one of Japan's most accomplished composers. Born to a wealthy family, he attended Tokyo Music Academy during the war. His film music was but a drop in the pail of his achievements. He was the creator of numerous symphonies and operas. Dan had a love for Chinese culture and sought to improve relations between China and Japan. He died during a visit to Suzhou.

THEMES AND MOTIFS

Director Matsubayashi, an unusual man who was both a Buddhist monk and proud ex-Imperial navalman, takes an intriguing approach. The film's tone is informed by the Buddhist concept that all things are "transient". In an interview in Stuart Galbraith's *Monsters Are Attacking Tokyo*, he said *"When the bombs hit Tokyo, every living thing dies and everything that has any shape changes and becomes something else. This is the kind of Japanese philosophy which we have inherited throughout our history- that everything changes and does not last forever."*

Like both the original *Godzilla* and *Submersion of Japan*, *The Last War* is one of Japan's greatest films focusing on its collective existential dread. Director Matsubayashi tried to balance both a God's eye view of the situation with a child's perspective to show the inherent ridiculousness and futility of nuclear warfare. During the Cold War, Japan was in a particularly vulnerable position, stripped of its military autonomy. Close neighbors China, Russia and North Korea were communist enemies with bitter grudges against Japan for its colonialist misdeeds. Japan was and still is dependent on the United States for military protection. *The Last War* is about Japan's collective anxiety over its place in the Cold War. Japan remains, to this day, the only country to have had nuclear weapons used against it. It is the only culture to have, for all intents and purposes, survived nuclear warfare. A small country with lots of U.S. military base targets, it had and still has a lot to lose from nuclear war. Indeed, Matsubyashi was frustrated that the Cold War's dynamics reduced Japan to the role of a helpless child. He stressed his intent in *Monsters Are Attacking Tokyo*: "*America and the Soviet Union were in the midst of the Cold War. The world was terrified about the possibility of World War III. It was a very dangerous time and very tense at military bases. What would happen if a war was triggered accidentally?*"

The film's fictionalized depiction of NATO and the Warsaw Pact as the "Federation" and "Alliance" makes this clear. They are shown as two monolithic groups of war-like, English speaking Westerners whose only apparent difference is the color of their uniforms. Many Japanese viewed America and the Soviet Union as two Western countries playing a high stakes game of three-dimensional chess with apocalyptic weapons. The 38th parallel, where war begins in both *World War III Breaks Out* and *The Last War,* would become home to the Demilitarized Zone after the Korean War. The Japanese still watch this diplomatic hotspot with anxiety. It is to this day a political powder keg and a nuclear armed North Korea has the potential to destroy Tokyo. As of the writing, North Korea recently blew up its liaison office with the South in the Demilitarized Zone. *The Last War*'s themes are still quite relevant. Matsubayashi's depiction of the United Nations is in stark contrast to Ishiro Honda's. Whereas Honda depicts it as humanity's salvation in films like *Battle in Outer Space* and *Gorath*, in *The Last War,* the U.N. is ineffectual at taming international tensions.

Like the BBC's *Threads*, there is a heartbreaking emphasis on the human element. *The Last War* spares the viewer the grisly, petulant aftermath *Threads* graphically indulges in. Yet both intimately follow families whose lives are cut short by thermonuclear war. The Tamuras represent the sort of average post-war Japanese family. The film takes on a haunting air as the viewer realizes their lives are destined to be upended by the ruthlessness of a few. There's a tear-jerking scene emphasizing this where Mokichi, a Japanese everyman of sorts played by comedic actor Frankie Sakai, laments his family's fate from the porch of his Tokyo home. He becomes horrified at the realization that he will never see his children grow up. Matsubayashi and writers Takeshi Kimura and Toshio Yasumi chose to make Mokichi the protagonist as they felt an everyman-like character would connect with post-war audiences. The doomed romance between Akira Takarada's sailor Takano and Yuriko Hoshi's ingenue Saeko is handled with similar somber fatalism. To this day, *The Last War* is one of Akira Takarada's favorite films he appeared in. Matsubayashi took particular emphasis in showing the Tamuras' last moments, as if they were trying to resist the inevitable. His war dramas from *Storm Over the Pacific* to 1981's *Imperial Navy* have a similar fatalism as they depict their own tragic inevitability. The inevitability of a country doomed to be defeated by larger powers. But in *The Last War*, it isn't Japan who "loses the war" but humanity.

RELEASE AND LEGACY

The Last War wound up a huge box office success for Toho, their second highest grossing film of 1961. Indeed, it proved relevant. In October 1962, the events it forecast almost came true. Following the failed U.S. Bay of Pigs Invasion of 1961, the Soviets placed ballistic missiles in Cuba. This sparked off the Cuban Missile Crisis, a political showdown between the United States and Russia. It lasted 13 days and nearly resulted in nuclear confrontation. It intensified when an air force major, Rudolf Anderson, was killed, his U-2 jet shot down by the Cubans. At one point, a nuclear torpedo was almost launched from a Soviet submarine, B-59, after it was hit with American depth charges. This launch would have likely sparked off World War III. It was stopped only by the disagreement of a cool-headed officer on board, Vasily Arkhipov. The Cold War ended, but *The Last War* has not lost its relevance. Global turmoil is rising once more and we no longer have leaders of John F. Kennedy's calibre. Shue Matsubayashi himself was not optimistic about the post-Cold War political situation. He believed modern Japan to be ideologically confused. *The Last War* ends with a message imploring humanity to *"stand hand in hand to stop this from happening"*. It's a little on the nose but a message worth heeding.

ALTERNATE VERSIONS

An export version of *The Last War* exists but is unavailable. Proof of its existence lies in that an English dubbed version is listed in Toho's 1960s sales pamphlets. An export trailer featuring the voice of William "Bill" Ross is also available on the Japanese DVD. Ross (1923-2014) was an expat living in Japan from Ohio. He founded Frontier Enterprises, a Tokyo-based dubbing outlet that dubbed hundreds of films into English. Ross wound up in Tokyo after fighting in the Korean War. In 1959, he was given a gig by actor So Yamamura to help dub a Japanese film into English for a Philipine distributor. Ross was so good at it that the Japanese ADR director, who barely spoke English, let Ross take over. Thus Ross began a long career of dubbing mostly Japanese films into English. At first his outlet was called Eikosa but in 1964 became Frontier. For a while, Frontier was Toho's preferred dubbing studio. In addition to dubbing, William Ross often played on screen roles in Japanese films. Pictures he appeared in include *Emperor Meiji and the Russo-Japanese War* (1957), *The War in Space* (1977), *The Last Dinosaur* (1977) and *Zero* (1984). In the latter he amusingly played General MacArthur. He had a good relationship with director Kinji Fukasaku and appeared in his films *The Green Slime* (1968), *Graveyard of Honor* (1975) *Message From Space* (1978) and *Virus* (1980).

The Last War was purchased by Brenco around 1964. It was intended to be released theatrically after *The Human Vapor* and *Gorath*. The poor performance of those two films, followed by Brenco going bankrupt, led to the release being delayed for years. Heritage Enterprises acquired Brenco's library and in 1967 it was released to stateside television. Like Brenco's versions of *The Human Vapor* and *Gorath*, their cut of *The Last War* is drastically altered. Running 79:23, it's far shorter and is narratively restructured. The film now revolves around Takano as the main character and opens with the *Kasagi Maru*'s decision to return to Tokyo. The rest of the film is presented as Takano's flashback, narrated by Marvin Miller who provides the voices of most male characters. The film has a good deal of material cut. Scenes deleted include those involving Jerry Ito's character Watkins along with Mokichi's work at the Tokyo Press Club and mentions of investing in the stock market. The Prime Minister's health problems and a conversation among Alliance missile base staffers over whether peaceful coexistence is possible are also cut. Expository narration from Takano is added and there are significant music differences. The biggest is *"New Year's Day"* replaced by the grating *"It's A Small World"*. In lieu of the title card at the end of the film is a segment of a speech that John F. Kennedy made at the United Nations. This is one improvement as it is less on the nose than its Japanese counterpart.

Marvin Miller (1913-1985) is worth mentioning. He was best known for voicing Robby the Robot in *Forbidden Planet* (1956) and *The Invisible Boy* (1957). He also narrated Disney's *Sleeping Beauty* (1959). Like Paul Frees, whom he appeared opposite to on the TV show *The Millionaire*, he was a versatile and prolific voice actor. He would dub Akira Takarada's voice again in the U.S. version of *Invasion of Astro-Monster* (1965).

AMERICAN HOME VIDEO HISTORY

The Last War's sole U.S. home video release was to VHS in 1985 by Video Gems. It has not been released since.

Further Viewing:

I LIVE IN FEAR

(1955)
生きものの記録
Toho, *Director*: Akira Kurosawa

While not an outright science fiction picture, *I Live in Fear* makes for sobering viewing alongside a film like *The Last War*. It is a riveting psychodrama delving into the same existential horrors of the atomic age. A wittily written film, *I Live in Fear* is one part in-depth character study, another Rod Serling-like morality play.

I Live in Fear opens in dramatic chaos with elderly industrialist Kichi Nakajima (Toshiro Mifune) engaged in a legal battle with his own family. Nakajima has become convinced World War III is nigh and desperately wants to move his family to Brazil to avoid the nuclear fallout. His grown-up children, led by his scheming son Jiro (Minoru Chiaki), object. They are trying desperately to get him declared mentally incompetant. A dentist turned juror in the case, Dr. Harada (Takashi Shimura), begins to take pity on Nakajima's and realize that perhaps his anxieties aren't so unreasonable.

I Live in Fear starts as a riveting courtroom drama capturing the social grotesquery of an ugly family feud. Early on, Mifune's Nakajima comes off as an almost cartoony villain, spewing apocalyptic fury like a scientist in a Toho disaster film. As *I Live in Fear* goes on, however, you begin to forget the character is the 35 year old Mifune under heavy makeup. Akira Kurosawa's direction and Mifune's electrifying performance begin to humanize him. His family, who give new meaning to the term "nuclear family", treacherously scheme to get their cut of this mentally ill man's fortune. Nakajima's characterization reveals moments of humanity; he shows his illegitimate children surprising tenderness. He becomes

empathetic as the viewer begins to better understand his fear. Certain moments are heartbreaking, such as Nakajima "ducking and covering" at a flash of lightning. By the film's heartrending and devastating final scene, he becomes a pathetic wraith of a man; his soul poisoned by fear the same way the mushroom cloud's radiation poisons the body. *I Live in Fear* is aided by Kurosawa's premiere DP Asakazu Nakai's painterly monochrome compositions. The film is capped in a stunning climactic shot, silhouetted against the sun streaming through a psych-ward's window. A weaker director or writer would have veered the film into outright sci-fi; ending the film in a nuclear holocaust and Nakajima being proven right. Akira Kurosawa instead chooses to focus entirely on the bomb's subtle, existential dread and its effect on the human soul. Like the genius he was, Kurosawa creates a film that serves as both a compelling character study *and* a commentary and indictment of Japan's Cold War situation. Kevin Rafferty's *The Atomic Cafe* (1982) also makes for good viewing alongside *I Live in Fear* when it comes to understanding the genuine existential horror of the Cold War's height.

WORLD WAR III BREAKS OUT
(1960)
第三次世界大戦 四十一時間の恐怖
Toei, *Director*: Shigeaki Hidaka

Toei's black and white rival film that beat *The Last War* to theaters, *World War III Breaks Out* and *The Last War* are interesting films to contrast. They are similar to *Fail Safe* and *Dr. Strangelove* or *The Day After* and *Threads*. Like both pairs of films, they were produced around the same time and revolve around similar subject material. Yet they take markedly different approaches. *World War III Breaks Out*, in typical Toei fashion, is a more nihilistic film. In *The Last War*, the characters accept their end with honor and humility. In *World War III*, there's more focus on the acute social degradation that takes place as the end inches closer. As it becomes clear that the world is doomed, people become uglier and the ensemble cast devolves into savagery. *World War III Breaks Out* also delves into a more gruesome aftermath. In the end, Argentina is one of the few countries left on the map and must try to rebuild the world. The cast is headed by heartthrob Tatsuo Umemiya (1938-2019). Having played the titular role in Toei's *Planet Prince* (1959), he would go on to play a lot of *yakuza* roles. *World War III Breaks Out* is

directed by Shigeaki Hidaka, who wrote the screenplay for *Godzilla Raids Again*.

Portions of the explosive finale were reused for New Toei's 1961 superhero programmer *Iron Sharp* (aka *Invasion of the Neptune Men*). These special effects scenes were created by Toei's own specialist, Nobuo Yajima, who went on to have a long career. Yajima (1928-2019) would work on *Terror Beneath the Sea* (1966), supervise many of Toei's television franchises and *Message From Space* (1978). *World War III Breaks Out* was released stateside as *The Final War*. For years it was an ever elusive holy grail for Japanese cinema collectors, unavailable on video in Japan or America. Toei aired the film in the early 2010s, putting it back in circulation. The U.S. version, however, still hasn't turned up. Anecdotes from those who saw it on television in the '60s say it had footage of *Iron Sharp*'s saucer attack spliced into it.

SHUE MATSUBAYASHI
The Navalman

松林宗恵

7/7/1920-8/5/2009

"I am the only Imperial navy officer to have become a director. Many of my colleagues died during the war; as a movie director, I wanted my five (war) films to serve as a memorial to my comrades. All of them."
-Shue Matsubayashi, *Monsters Are Attacking Tokyo* (1998) by Stuart Galbrath IV

Shue Matsubayashi was another one of Toho's powerhouse directors. He was known for, almost eclectically, *salaryman* comedies and spectacular war dramas. Matsubayashi was similar to his colleague

Ishiro Honda yet markedly different. In contrast to Honda's pacifism, Matsubayashi was proud of his service to the Japanese Imperial Navy. Yet there's a fatalism to his best films indicative of his devout Buddhist beliefs. In his works, all things are tenuous and impermanent, Japan's Empire included. His war epics are more self conscious than the propaganda produced during the Imperial years. Their characters tend to realize that they are fighting for a doomed cause when it's too late.

Shue Matsubayashi was born in Shimane Prefecture to parents Shuken and Hisato Matsubayashi. His father was a Buddhist minister and he had eight siblings. His family later moved to the village of Ibara near Hiroshima where he spent his formative years. Matsubayashi became interested in films as his father's temple had a small hall used to screen movies. At 18, he entered Ryukoku University, a Buddhist monastery and college in Kyoto. After graduating, however, he chose to pursue filmmaking after seeing a documentary entitled *Dharma's Country*. He attended graduate studies at Nihon University's College of Arts. He began to work as an assistant director at Toho, hoping to make films reflecting Buddhist values. Before long, he was drafted into the Imperial Navy during World War II. He was promoted to ensign and fought in the South China Sea aboard the *Akishima Maru* stationed near Amoy Island. Matsubayashi grew a beard, determined to shave it off when Japan won the war. Japan lost and he continued to wear his beard for much of his life.

After the war, he was recuperating back home. His colleague Kon Ichikawa sent him a letter saying *"Hurry back to Tokyo! We can make movies again"*. Matsubyashi returned to Toho and resumed his work as AD. Soon afterward, Toho's union strikes took place. Disgruntled former employees left the company and founded a new studio,

Shin Toho. Matsubayashi went to Shin Toho, following his mentors Kunio Watanabe and Torajiro Saito. It was at Shin Toho, in 1952, that he directed his first film, the romantic comedy *Tokyo Dimples*.

Matsubayashi's next notable film as director was a war flick entitled *Human Torpedo Kaiten* (1955). He soon went back to Toho. There he directed the third entry, *Third Generation Company President*, in their tentpole *Shacho (Company President)* series of comedies. These films starred beloved comedian Hisaya Morishige as the title character. They were sitcoms themed around post-war Japanese office life. The real-life salarymen of Japan adored these films. The *Shacho* films helped them cope with the stress of their workaholic lives through humor. Like Honda with the Godzilla series, Matsubayashi became a fixture of the *Shacho* movies. He directed 22 of the 42 entries, his last in 1970.

Matsubayashi also directed more internationally known films where he collaborated with Eiji Tsuburaya. His first at Toho was *Submarine I-57 Will Not Surrender* (1959). This was followed by a soft remake of *The War at Sea From Hawaii to Malay: Storm Over the Pacific* (1960). This film depicts Pearl Harbor in living Eastman color but ends in fatalism with Japan's disastrous defeat at Midway. In 1961, Matsubayashi directed the haunting nuclear war drama *The Last War*. This powerful anti-war film embodied Japan's collective anxiety over brewing Cold War tensions. Unlike many of his films, *Storm Over the Pacific* and *The Last War* were even distributed in the U.S, the former as *I Bombed Pearl Harbor*.

More war dramas such as *Attack Squadron* (1963) followed, along with *jidai-geki* and salaryman comedies. He switched to directing for television in the 1970s, even doing a pair of episodes for Tsuburaya's *Return of Ultraman*. His magnum opus of sorts was 1981's *Imperial Navy*. Though oversaturated with stock footage, the film is a two and a half hour tribute to his *alma mater*. Teruyoshi Nakano and his FX crew built a meticulous miniature version of the iconic naval battleship *Yamato*. When it came time to fire its cannons, Matsubayashi insisted on being at the special effects unit to watch it. His final two films were *Golf Before Dawn* in 1987 and Tsuburaya Pro's *Winners* (1992). He retired shortly after that and died in 2009.

Selected Filmography (*as director*)

Tokyo Dimples (1952)
Human Torpedo Kaiten (1955)
Blue Mountains (1957)
Third Generation Company President (1958)
Pacific Company President (1959)
Submarine 1-57 Will Not Surrender (1959)
Storm Over the Pacific (1960)
Company President On the Road (1961)
The Last War (1961)

Office Workers of Shimizu Port (1962)
Attack Squadron (1963)
Company President Travelogue (1963)
The Company President's Honor (1964)
Ninja Company President (1965)
Company President's Line Statement (1966)
Tenamon Goes To Tokaido Road (1966)
Company President: Thousand and One Nights (1967)

Tenamon and Ghosts (1967)
The Company President's Prosperity (1968)
Devil Company President (1969)
Company President's ABCs (1970)
The Return of Ultraman *[episodes 49, 50]* (1971-72, TV)
Love in the Air (1976)
Imperial Navy (1981)
Golf Before Dawn (1987)
Winners (1992)

Yosei Gorasu "Gorath the Ominous Star"
Toho, 3/21/1962 (*Showa 37*), 7 Reels (2,413 meters), 88:04, 35mm, TohoScope (2.35:1 anamorphic), Eastman color, Perspecta stereo (4 Track)

Crew
Producer: Tomoyuki Tanaka
Director: Ishiro Honda
Special Effects Director: Eiji Tsuburaya

Screenplay: Takeshi Kimura, Jojiro Okami (story)
Director of Photography: Hajime Koizumi, Sadamasa Arikawa

Music: Kan Ishii
Assistant Director: Koji Kajita
Production Design: Takeo Kita, Teruaki Abe
Editor: Reiko Kaneko

Sound Recordist: Toshiya Ban
Sound Effects: Hisashi Shimonaga
Lighting: Toshio Takashima
Production Manager: Yasuaki Sakamoto
SFX Cinematography: Sadamasa Arikawa, Mototaka Tomioka
SFX Art Director: Akira Watanabe
SFX Opticals: Takao Saiwai, Yukio Manoda
SFX Lighting: Kuichiro Kishida
SFX Composites: Hiroshi Mukoyama
SFX Production Manager: Nuki Narita
Still Photographer: Kazukiyo Tanaka

Cast

Ryo Ikebe *(Dr. Tazawa)*
Ken Uehara *(Dr. Kono)*
Yumi Shirakawa *(Tomoko Sonoda)*
Akira Kubo *(Tatsuma Kanai)*
Kumi Mizuno *(Takiko Nomura)*
Hiroshi Tachikawa *(Wakabayashi)*
Akihiko Hirata *(Endo, Captain of Otori)*
Kenji Sahara *(Vice Captain of Otori)*
Jun Tazaki *(Captain Raizo Sonoda)*
Takashi Shimura *(Kensuke Sonoda)*

Seizaburo Kawazu *(Tada, Minister of Finance)*
Ko Mishima *(Sanada, Engineer)*
Sachio Sakai *(Physician)*
Takamaru Sasaki *(Prime Minister Seki)*
Ko Nishimura *(Murata, Minister of Space)*
Eitaro Ozawa *(Kinami, Minister of Justice)*
Masaya Nihei *(Ito, Otori Astronaut)*
Kozo Nomura *(Otori Observer)*
Keiko Sata *(Prime Minister's Secretary)*
Hideyo Amamoto *(Drunk)*
George Furness *(Hooverman)*
Ross Benette *(Gibson)*
Junichiro Mukai *(Space Base Security Guard)*
Nadao Kirino *(Manabe)*
Fumio Sakashita *(Hayao Sonoda)*
Ikio Sawamura *(Taxi Driver)*
Toshihiko Furuta *(Otori Observer)*
Yoshiyuki Uemura *(Otori' Mathematician)*
Rinsaku Ogata *(Otori Engineer)*
Masayoshi Kawabe *(Otori Observer)*
Yasushi Matsubara *(Otori Radio Operator)*
Tadashi Okabe *(Otori Mathematician)*
Koji Uno *(Reporter)*
Yukihiko Gondo *(Otori Pilot)*

Kenichiro Maruyama *(Otori Engineer)*
Yasuhiko Saijo *(Otori Radio Operator)*
Katsumi Tezuka *(Otori Radio Operator)*
Akira Yamada *(Hayabusa Engineer)*
Hiroshi Takagi *(Hayabusa Engineer)*
Toshitsugu Suzuki *(Hayabusa Pilot)*
Wataru Omae *(Hayabusa Mathematician)*
Ichiro Shoji *(Hayabusa Observer)*
Yasuo Araki *(Hayabusa Observer)*
Hideo Shibuya *(Reporter)*
Kazuo Imai *(Hayabusa Radio Operator)*
Takuya Yuki *(Hayabusa Mathematician)*
Koji Ishikawa *(Hayabusa Pilot)*
Yusuke Suzuki *(Hayabusa Fuel Check)*
Takuzo Kumagai *(Government Personnel)*
Saburo Iketani *(News Anchor)*
Han Horneff *(Dr. König)*
Haruo Nakajima *(Maguma)*

Alternate Titles
Ufos zerstören die Erde **[UFOs Destroy the Earth]** (Germany)
Le choc des planètes **[Collision of the Planets]** (France)

"Let us forever cherish this victory humanity has won with a desire for eternal peace and cooperation."
-Newscaster (Saburo Iketani)

Before certain conglomerates made space opera trilogies mainstream, Ishiro Honda did his own "original space opera trilogy". *Gorath* is its third and final film, expanding upon themes introduced in *The Mysterians* and *Battle in Outer Space*. *Gorath* is an imperfect but splendid science fiction epic. It features Honda's most earnest humanist themes and Tsuburaya's finest miniature work. *Gorath* is marred only by a few superfluous elements including a *kaiju* added through studio interference. Its impact possibly stretched to Stanley Kubrick's *2001: A Space Odyssey*.

PLOT

In fall of 1979, the Japanese space research vessel the JX-1 *Hayabusa* is launched from Mount Fuji. Commanded by Dr. Sonoda (Jun Tazaki), its mission is to investigate gravitational changes near Saturn. The crew hears news of a mysterious white dwarf star entering the solar system named "Gorath". Sonoda and crew decide to investigate the rogue star further to make sure it's no threat to Earth's gravity. Caught in Gorath's ferocious gravitational pull, The *Hayabusa* is destroyed. Sonoda and all aboard are killed, but they get their data back to Earth. Gorath's gravity is 6,000 times that of the Earth and it's making a beeline straight for it.

During Christmas, news of the Hayabusa's destruction is received on Earth. Sonoda's daughter Tomoko (Yumi Shirakawa) mourns her father's death. Scientists Dr. Tazawa (Ryo Ikebe) and Dr. Kono (Ken Uehara), having analyzed the data, raise the alarm to the Prime Minister (Takamaru Sasaki) and his cabinet. Gorath is due to collide with Earth in only two years. At a space academy, young cadet Kanai (Akira Kubo) and friends prepare for an upcoming mission in the the JX-2

Otori. Dr. Kono and Dr. Tazawa go before the United Nations. They unveil a plan to use rocket thrusters placed on the South Pole and generate enough energy to change Earth's orbit. This will potentially move the planet out of Gorath's way. The U.N. agrees to back this plan.

As the military contemplates destroying Gorath, the *Otori* is launched for a reconnaissance mission to gather data on the star. The *Otori* starts its survey of Gorath as construction begins on the Antarctic base. The operation at the South Pole commences in earnest with international cooperation. A massive cave-in causes delays, losing critical time. The *Otori*, meanwhile, makes contact with Gorath. Kanai mans a capsule close to the star to gather data. The capsule is caught in Gorath's pull and almost destroyed, but a recovery mission succeeds in saving Kanai. Kanai has lost his memory completely, but he's collected an unsettling bit of data. Gorath's mass is growing as it absorbs planets and debris in its wake.

BACKGROUND

Based on another concept by Jojiro Okami, *Gorath* started development shortly after *Battle in Outer Space*. It took three years to bring to the screen. *Gorath* invokes the works of George Pal more than any other Honda/Tsuburaya film, especially *When Worlds Collide*. The concept of a rogue planetoid on a collision course with Earth had been explored once before in Japanese sci-fi with Daiei's *Warning From Space*. It is unknown if *Warning* was an influence on *Gorath*, but the studios were ferociously competitive. They watched each others' production slates closely. Like *Warning From Space*, *Gorath* features mass destruction caused by the rogue star's gravitational pull. Yet Honda's vision is novel. In *Warning*, it takes the intervention of space aliens to put a stop to its rogue planet's advance. In *Gorath* it is humanity's scientific inquiry that saves the day.

At first, the story was to be darker with an outcome akin to *When Worlds Collide*. Gorath was to destroy Earth and only a small fraction of humanity makes it off the planet. During scripting, Honda and his assistant Koji Kajita spent almost a month at Tokyo University's astronomy department. They often did scientific research during pre-production of Honda's sci-fi films. Honda and Kajita consulted with astrophysics professor Takeo Hatanaka and his assistant Genichiro Horii over whether the story was scientifically sound. It was determined that, per Newton's laws, with enough force it could be possible to change Earth's orbit. Hatanaka and Horii had one major issue with the script: a climactic sequence where the moon is swallowed up by Gorath before it misses Earth. If Gorath, an object with over six thousand times the gravity of Earth, was close enough to destroy the moon, it would be too late to escape its pull. Honda considered removing it, but Tomoyuki Tanaka wanted the scene kept in. The mathematical formulas on the blackboard when Ryo Ikebe's Tazawa addresses the U.N. were devised by Horii

himself. They determine how much of a force is necessary to alter Earth's orbit to evade Gorath's gravity.

PRINCIPAL PHOTOGRAPHY

A lavish production like *Mothra*, the film revels in retro-futurism. Almost every image looks like it could be the cover of a pulp magazine. Yet *Gorath*'s concepts are based on relative science fact. It is the closest thing Ishiro Honda ever directed to a hard science fiction film. When *Gorath* comes alive, it is a tautly made film that puts *When Worlds Collide* to shame. Honda builds feelings of tension and impending doom before an exhilarating finale. *Gorath*'s main flaws are some mildly superfluous elements. The first is a pair of musical numbers featuring a song, *"We Are Space Pilots"*, belted by the cadets. These sequences contribute little to the plot and eat up running time.

ACTORS

Gorath features an all star cast that dominates the picture. In the lead is Ryo Ikebe, who had also been in *Battle in Outer Space*. Ikebe (1918-2010) was one of Honda's favorite actors, having starred in his directorial debut *The Blue Pearl* (1951). Ikebe, a Tokyo native, set out to become a director. Unfortunately, when he joined Toho, World War II was under way. Due to low film output there were no vacant positions for assistant directors. Ikebe thus became an actor and wowed audiences with his role in *Fighting Fish* (1941). After a few more roles, Ikebe was drafted into the army. He was quickly made an officer because of his college education and fought in Shandong, China before being sent to Indonesia. Ikebe was captured by the Australians and not released until June 1946. Upon returning to Japan, his career was further stalled by the union disputes at Toho that lead to the formation of Shin Toho. He finally became a popular actor in the late '40s and due to his military experience often played officers, including for Honda in *Farewell Rabaul* (1954).

Genre stalwarts like Yumi Shirakawa, Kenji Sahara and Akihiko Hirata all appear. This is also one of Honda's first collaborations with Akira Kubo and Kumi Mizuno. Ko Nishimura appears in the film as the aptly titled "Minister of Space". Nishimura (1923-1997), also known as Akira Nishimura, was a memorable character actor. Gaunt with an almost silent film star appearance, fittingly, genre fans know him best for Shochiku's *The Living Skeleton* (1968). He was an airman during the war who got into stage acting. His roles were vast and included parts in Kon Ichikawa's *The Burmese Harp* (1956), Kurosawa's *The Bad Sleep Well* (1960) and several Zatoichi entries. Masanari Nihei also appears in a supporting part. Nihei (1940-) later played the comic relief role of Ide on Tsuburaya's signature show *Ultraman* (1966-67). He was also in Kurosawa's *Dodes'kaden* (1970).

SFX

Eiji Tsuburaya's miniature work is among the greatest in his career. Its execution is inventive, creative and realistic. Tsuburaya was given one of the biggest budgets in his career. Gorath itself was built from fire-proof acrylic cloth with a powerful lighting mechanism placed inside it. For miniature shots of the frozen Antarctic, styrofoam was used to create icebergs, a then newly invented material. The scenes showing the propulsion were done with burning propane tanks, a whopping 200 cylinders worth. Filming those shots made the set brutally hot. The miniatures for the spaceships *Hayabusa* and *Otori* were designed by Akira Watanabe and built by Yasuyuki Inoue. They were around three feet tall and equipped with propane ports. The *mecha* designs are sleek and the space shots have stunning composites. The urban flooding sequences at the end of *Gorath* are among the most impressive work Tsuburaya's team accomplished. For shots at the end of the picture showing submerged cities, Tsuburaya and company placed miniatures in the nearby Arakawa river. As the miniatures were mainly made of wood and lightweight, they would often float away, much to the crew's annoyance. The Osaka Castle model seen submerged was a leftover from Tsuburaya's work on the previous year's *Daredevil in the Castle*.

Gorath features a gratuitous giant monster added at the behest of Tomoyuki Tanaka. A prehistoric walrus named "Maguma", the suit was constructed by Teizo Toshimitsu and the Yagi Brothers with assistance from Keizo Murase. A small puppet version, built by Eizo Kaimai, was used for shots of the creature's death. Honda was vehemently opposed to the monster's inclusion. While it's a lavish FX scene from Tsuburaya's team, it stops the picture in its tracks. Honda would later say that *Gorath* was his favorite film he directed, *"except for that monster"*. Maguma's suit would be re-used on episode 27 of *Ultra Q* as Todola.

THEMES AND MOTIFS

Gorath is one of director Honda's most hopeful and pro-science works. The script by Takeshi Kimura is unusually optimistic for a writer known for his pessimism. *Gorath* represents Honda and Kimura's idealistic hope for humanity; a vision of our highest potential. A film like *Matango*, by contrast, presents their anxieties over the frailty of the human condition. *Gorath* continues and further expands on the "brotherhood of man" themes present in *The Mysterians* and *Battle in Outer Space*. Whereas in those films it takes the invasion of aliens to unite humanity, in *Gorath* the human race comes together over a more existential threat.

RELEASE AND LEGACY

Gorath, despite its relative obscurity, is more influential than given credit. The first act of Toei's international co-production *The Green Slime* (1968) concerns an asteroid headed for Earth. As Akira Watanabe was special effects director, it's likely *Gorath* was a significant influence. Another, better known 1968 space film, Stanley Kubrick's *2001: A Space Odyssey*, has surprising aesthetic similarities. Both films depict sprawling, George Pal-influenced space station infrastructure. Station V in *2001,* itself given a callback in *Star Wars,* even features a docking bay with a

rectangular door akin to the *Otori*. It is known that Stanley Kubrick obsessively watched as many space movies as he could, especially foreign ones, during *2001*'s pre-production. A nod to *Gorath* would later appear in *Godzilla: Final Wars* (2004). In Hollywood, the concept of Earth being threatened by a foreign body such as an asteroid, meteor or star remains a very popular trope. Lars Von Trier's *Melancholia* makes for interesting viewing alongside a film like *Gorath*. In sharp contrast to *Gorath*'s optimistic faith in science, it presents a grim, hopeless vision of the same situation.

ALTERNATE VERSIONS

An export version dubbed in Tokyo was likely created as an international trailer, featuring the voice of William Ross, is available on the Japanese DVD. This version doesn't seem to have been released to home video and may not be extant.

Gorath came to the U.S. from Brenco on May 15th, 1964, double-billed with their other Toho release, *The Human Vapor*. The run was short and mainly limited to Southern California. The films did not perform well despite unusually good reviews from critics who praised the special effects work. This scuttled plans for a theatrical release of *The Last War,* which Brenco also had the rights to.

The U.S. version is *Gorath* is heavily altered and an editorial mess. It ran around 82 minutes in theaters and the TV version was cut down further, to 77 minutes. The early scenes in the film are haphazardly assembled. Yumi Shirakawa's Tomoko and Kumi Mizuno's Takiko are no longer reacting to the *Hayabusa*'s launch, but rather "gravitational changes". Explanation bits, narrated by William Conrad, are edited in with all the precision of a butter knife. The sound design is significantly altered, with electronic beeping added to the spaceship scenes. Gorath itself has an irritating electronic hum looped over its shots. The crew of the *Hayabusa* yelling "banzai" was cut, perhaps due to its association with World War II *kamikaze*. After the *Hayabusa* is destroyed, a news flash montage from *The Last War* is cut into the film.

The rest of this version is more palatable, closer resembling the Japanese version with notable exceptions. A lot of dialogue and debate scenes, especially at the U.N., are reduced in length. There are a few improvements, such as editing out the musical numbers and much of the Maguma sequence. Anecdotally, test screening versions contained the monster but it was cut after previewing poorly. This is likely as other scenes mentioning the monster are intact and the editing around it is sloppy. A dead giveaway is that some prints even contain reaction shots from the monster scene edited almost nonsensically. The moon is destroyed by Gorath right before it passes Earth, whereas in the Japanese version it happens earlier. It adds to a sense of climactic tension, but its placement in the Japanese version builds more foreboding dread. The final moments of the movie are re-scored with cues from Ikuma Dan's *The Last War* soundtrack.

Amusingly, the music is miscredited to Kunio Miyauchi in the end credits.

Despite the sloppily assembled nature of the U.S. version, the dubbing is quite competent. It was done in Los Angeles and written by John Meredyth Lucas, with a dubbing cast that included Paul Frees, Virginia Gregg, William Eidleson and Vic Perrin.

AMERICAN HOME VIDEO HISTORY

Gorath was released on VHS in the 1980s by Prism. Since then, it has not been released stateside in any format. MGM holds the rights to *Gorath* and their materials are reported to be in poor shape. MGM and Toho are allegedly unable or unwilling to work together on a release.

Further Viewing:
DOGORA
(1964)
宇宙大怪獣ドゴラ
Toho, *Director*: Ishiro Honda

Also based on a story by Jojiro Okami, *Dogora* is not a top tier Toho monster flick. It is however a highly interesting one. Originally, it was to be called *Space Mons*. *Space Mons* was a far more ambitious project meant to cross Toho's space opera films with its *kaiju* cycle. The story was eventually simplified and the budget cut. *Dogora* features a jellyfish-like mutant space cell that eats diamonds and coal. Like *The H-Man* it throws a gaggle of cartoony gangsters into the mix, albeit less effectively. Gorgeous future bond girl Akiko Wakabayashi shows up as a gangster's moll. Robert Dunham's international investigator Mark Jackson is a fervent Japanophile long before Millennial anime buffs made it cringeworthy. The production suffered from budget cuts. It's not Ishiro Honda in top form but the direction is passabe. There's a darkly comedic quality that tends to be lost on Western audiences. *Dogora*'s black humor plays far better in Japanese than in the almost surreal Hong Kong English dub job.

While Honda's side is not his best work, Eiji Tsuburaya's footage is strong and inventive. He puts his Oxberry printer to work with one amazing composite after another. The monster's mid-film attack on Kitakyushu is a downright stunning sequence. It is a tour-de-force combining optical printing, miniature work, a water puppet for the monster and even cel animation impressively created by the Tsuburaya unit's resident animator Sadao Iizuka (1934-). It's made even better by a particularly resplendent Ifukube soundtrack. In the U.S., panned and scanned, badly processed 16mm TV prints were the bane of the film's existence. *Dogora*, despite its flaws, deserves a reappraisal for its uniqueness and brilliant FX work. The creature would recently cameo in *Godzilla: Planet of the Monsters* (2017).

HARUO NAKAJIMA
The Trooper

中島春雄

1/1/1929-8/7/2017

"Inside the Godzilla suit, it was very dark, lonely and isolated. Usually the person who wears the suit becomes anxious and nervous. During the summertime it's very hot, it can become hell in there. But Mr. Nakajima always persevered. He acted in the suit underwater, he was buried underground, he withstood pyrotechnic explosions- and through it he was always Godzilla."
-Teruyoshi Nakano, *Monsters Are Attacking Tokyo* (1998) by Stuart Galbraith

The first man who acted inside the iconic Godzilla suit, Nakajima was a dedicated stuntman. He sweated inside a variety of cumbersome monster skins under searing tungsten lights. Nakajima suffered chafing, near drowning, painful falls and severe burns. Yet he was a trooper who never complained and kept coming back to smash Tsuburaya's miniature cities again and again. Haruo Nakajima was born the third son of five brothers in Sakata, Yamagata in early 1929. His father was a butcher and at a young age he developed a love of athletics and swimming. Unbeknownst to him, his athleticism would come to be useful later in life.

When Nakajima was a teenager the Pacific War broke out. In 1943, he was enlisted in the Imperial Navy's aerial training program.

He wanted to fly but dreaded being sent to his death as a *tokko (kamikaze)*. The war ended and he was lucky enough to escape such a fate. At the age of 16 he returned home. After the war, he first assisted his father in his butcher business and then drove a transport for the U.S. Occupation forces at Misawa Air Base. At the age of 18 he found his calling when he saw a newspaper ad for an actor training program. From here, Nakajima entered the film industry. His first onscreen role was an extra in Akira Kurosawa's *Stray Dog* (1949). Sadly his shots wound up on the cutting room floor.

In 1950, he formally joined Toho and continued work as an extra. From here, Nakajima began to work as a stuntman or "doppelganger actor" as the industry called it. In 1953, director Ishiro Honda needed an actor to be set on fire for a stunt in his war movie *Eagle of the Pacific*. Only the fearless Nakajima volunteered. His reputation as a stunt person was solidified and his can-do attitude impressed Honda. He also played one of the bandits in Kurosawa's masterwork *Seven Samurai* (1954). Honda and special effects director Eiji Tsuburaya soon needed a stuntman to portray the title monster in their new film, *Godzilla*. Nakajima acted inside the heavy monster suit, enduring great hardship and injury. Yet he persevered. Nakajima was back to smash miniatures again for the sequel: *Godzilla Raids Again* (1955).

Throughout the 1950s and '60s, Nakajima acted in a colorful myriad of giant monster suits. These included Rodan, Varan, larval Mothra, Matango, Baragon, Gaira and King Kong. Of course, he also reprised the role of Godzilla numerous times along with portraying a medley of monsters on Tsuburaya's TV shows. He put up with injuries, discomforts and harsh working conditions that would be of questionable legality today. Nakajima, when not suit acting, trained in Judo to keep up his endurance and stay fit. He also enjoyed scuba diving as a hobby.

With the collapse of Japan's studio system in 1971, Nakajima's exclusive contract to Toho was cancelled. He portrayed Godzilla twice more, however, in *Godzilla vs. Hedorah* and *Godzilla vs. Gigan*. During this time, Toho employed him at their bowling alley and then a *mahjong* shop. One of his last on screen roles was in 1973's *Submersion of Japan*. In the mid 1990s to his death, Nakajima became a fixture of the convention circuit. Sadly, by the 2010s his health was declining. He was invited to an early screening of Legendary's *Godzilla* (2014) at Yokota Air Base. Haruo Nakajima died of pneumonia in August of 2017. Survived by his daughter Sonoe, he was honored in the memorial ceremony at the 90th Academy Awards in 2018.

Selected Filmography (as actor)

Sword For Hire (1952)
Eagle of the Pacific (1953)
Seven Samurai (1954)
Farewell Rabaul (1954)
Godzilla (1954)

The Invisible Avenger (1954)
Godzilla Raids Again (1955)
Rodan (1956)
The Mysterians (1957)
Varan (1958)

Mothra (1961)
Gorath (1962)
King Kong vs. Godzilla (1962)
Matango (1963)
Mothra vs. Godzilla (1964)

Ghidorah, the Three-Headed Monster (1964)
Frankenstein Conquers the World (1965)
Invasion of Astro-Monster (1965)

The War of the Gargantuas (1966)
Ebirah, Horror of the Deep (1966)
King Kong Escapes (1967)
Son of Godzilla (1967)
Destroy All Monsters (1968)

Latitude Zero (1969)
All Monsters Attack (1969)
Space Amoeba (1970)
Godzilla vs. Hedorah (1971)
Godzilla vs. Gigan (1972)
Submersion of Japan (1973)

MATANGO

マタンゴ

Matango
Toho, 8/11/1963 (*Showa 38*), 6 Reels (2,447 meters), 89:25, 35mm, TohoScope (2.35:1 anamorphic), Eastman color, monaural sound

Crew
Producer: Tomoyuki Tanaka
Director: Ishiro Honda
Special Effects Director: Eiji Tsuburaya
Screenplay: Takeshi Kimura, Shinichi Hoshi (story), Masami Fukushima (story), William Hope Hodgson (short story *Voice in the Night*)
Directors of Photography: Hajime Koizumi
Music: Sadao Bekku
Assistant Director: Koji Kajita
Production Design: Shigekazu Ikuno
Editor: Reiko Kaneko
Sound Recordist: Fumio Yanoguchi
Sound Effects: Hisashi Shimonaga, Minoru Kaneyama
Lighting: Shoshichi Kojima
Production Manager: Shigeru Nakamura
Conceptual Artist: Shigeru Komatsuzaki
Assistant SFX Director: Teruyoshi Nakano

SFX Cinematography: Sadamasa Arikawa, Mototaka Tomioka
SFX Art Director: Akira Watanabe
SFX Lighting: Kuichiro Kishida
SFX Optical Photography: Yukio Manoda, Yoshiyuki Tokumasa
Modeling: Teizo Toshimitsu
SFX Production Manager: Tadashi Koike
Still Photographer: Kazukiyo Tanaka

Cast
Akira Kubo (*Kenji Murai*)
Kumi Mizuno (*Mami Sekiguchi*)
Hiroshi Koizumi (*Naoyuki Sakuta*)
Kenji Sahara (*Senzo Koyama*)
Hiroshi Tachikawa (*Etsuro Yoshida*)
Yoshio Tsuchiya (*Masafumi Kasai*)
Miki Yashiro (*Akiko Soma*)
Hideyo Amamoto (*Skulking Transitional Matango*)

Haruo Nakajima (*Hero Matango*)
Katsumi Tezuka (*Policeman*)
Takuzo Kumagai (*Doctor*)
Akio Kusama (*Policeman*)
Yutaka Oka (*Doctor*)
Keisuke Yamada (*Doctor*)
Kazuo HInata (*Policeman*)
Tokio Okawa (*Matango*)
Koji Uruki (*Matango*)
Masaki Shinohara (*Matango*)
Kuniyoshi Kashima (*Transitional Matango*)
Toku Ihara (*Transitional Matango*)
Mitsuko Hayashi (*Nurse*)
Tsurue Ichimanji (*Nurse*)

Alternate Titles
Matango: Fungus of Terror (U.K)
Attack of the Mushroom People (U.S.)
Matango il mostro **[The Monster Matango]** (Italy)
Matango, a Ilha da Morte **[Matango: Island of Death]** (Brazil)
Atak ludzi-grzybów (Poland)

"Under trying conditions, humans become selfish and cruel."
-Kenji Murai (Akira Kubo)

Another of Ishiro Honda's finest films, *Matango* is a hallucinogenic sci-fi/horror hybrid. It is perhaps Toho's finest 1960s genre production. Akin to a childhood nightmare, it compares well with the works of Mario Bava or Terence Fisher in atmospheric dread. *Matango*'s bleak *Lord of the Flies*-like narrative is compelling while Eiji Tsuburaya's FX work is inventive as always.

PLOT

A former university professor named Kenji Murai (Akira Kubo) is committed to a mental institution. He tells his story to the hospital's staff. He, along with six others, set sail in a yacht for what was meant to be a short boating trip. These include wealthy businessman and boat owner Kasai (Yoshio Tsuchiya), mystery novelist Yoshida (Hiroshi Tachikawa), starlet Mami (Kumi Mizuno) and Murai's student, Akiko (Miki Yashiro). The boat's skipper is Sakuta (Hiroshi Koizumi) along with boatswain Koyama (Kenji Sahara). As the weather becomes choppy, Sakuta warns Kasai to turn the boat around but he refuses. The yacht is hit by a violent storm and its mast is broken, leaving it adrift in the Pacific Ocean.

After drifting for days, the boat makes landfall on a deserted island. The castaways find water and a giant, abandoned ship on the shore. The ship is covered wall to wall in a repulsive fungus.

The castaways find a store of canned food on board, along with a rifle and captain's log. They clean the inside of the derelict vessel and take shelter there. The ship appears to have been researching the effects of an atomic explosion. Also growing on this island is a mysterious breed of mushroom called "Matango". With food on the island scarce, the castaways consider eating the mushrooms. Murai notes that according to the logbook the mushrooms seem to damage humans' nerve tissue. Sakuta forbids the castaways from eating the mushrooms for now.

One night, a ghostly humanoid comes aboard the ship. After frightening the group, the figure seems to vanish but leaves footprints behind. An incensed Koyama pressures the group to work together to find food. Unable to cope, Yoshida finally succumbs and eats the mushrooms. The castaways' social order soon breaks down.

BACKGROUND

Director Ishiro Honda had long wanted to make a darker picture; a film mocking the materialism being seen in modern Japan. By this time, post-war Japan had recovered economically. The war seemed only a faint memory, particularly to the young. Like *Godzilla*, part of *Matango*'s genesis came from news headlines. Honda had heard a story about a group of wealthy youths. They had taken a parents' yacht and sailed it too far into the Pacific. Lost at sea, they wound up needing rescue. Reports of ships vanishing in the Bermuda Triangle also got Honda's imagination going.

Tomoyuki Tanaka and Honda soon turned to a short story published in 1907. Written by British author William Hope Hodgson, it was entitled *The Voice in the Night*. Hodgson (1877-1918) had spent years at sea. He had a particular affinity for maritime horror stories. Hodgson was tragically killed on the battlefield in World War I. *Voice in the Night* had already been adapted into a 1958 episode of the American anthology series *Suspicion*. The episode was directed by Arthur Hiller and starred Barbara Rush, James Donald, Patrick Macnee and James Coburn. The concept of castaways stranded on an island and transformed into fungus came from *Voice in the Night*. Like Hodgson's novel, the yacht in *Matango* is called the "Albatross". Beloved science fiction writer Masami Fukushima created a loose adaptation for Tanaka with help from Shinichi Hoshi. Takeshi Kimura penned the final screenplay. He let his penchant for misanthropy and darker subtext run. *Matango* was also one of his favorite genre films he wrote up until his death.

PRINCIPAL PHOTOGRAPHY

Matango is like a childhood fever dream. To call it a Japanese *Gilligan's Island* on psilocybin would be no understatement. The film's bad trip kicks in with hallucinogenic intensity in its second half. Ishiro Honda and actors Akira Kubo, Kumi Mizuno and Kenji Sahara also considered *Matango* a favorite of

the films they worked on. Most of *Matango*'s location shooting was done on Oshima and Hachijo-Jima islands. The more outlandish indoor sets were filmed on Toho's Tokyo backlot. Honda was a bit insecure about the editing between its island locales and interior sets. Regardless, it's fairly seamless. Before shooting began, Honda took the cast aside. He told them that it was a dark picture and to take their roles seriously. Indeed, unlike most of Honda and Tsuburaya's *kaiju* films, the human actors do not play second fiddle to the monsters. *Matango* is actor and character focused.

The shoot was grueling. At Oshima, the actors and crew had to contend with poisonous snakes and centipedes. Yet Toho's sets tended to have an open and friendly atmosphere. Arguments amongst the cast and crew were almost nonexistent. Honda was less of a perfectionist and method director than Akira Kurosawa. He gave the actors freedom to perform their own interpretations of the characters. For early scenes inside the derelict ship, Honda instructed the performers to pretend the sets smelled awful. Unlike Honda's other films, *Matango* was largely shot in sequence to help the actors keep momentum. In the early storm scenes on the yacht, giant drums of water were dumped on the cast again and again. Kenji Sahara and Yoshio Tsuchiya both thought the on-set mushrooms looked ridiculous. They were sold, however, when they saw the finished picture. The final scene shot was the hospital wraparound with Akira Kubo.

ACTORS

Matango is indeed well acted with the characters' intense hunger feeling palpable. Akira Kubo leads the film. Kubo (1936-) became one of Honda's favorite leading men. He later appeared in *Invasion of Astro-Monster* (1965), *Destroy All Monsters* (1968) and *Space Amoeba* (1970). Born Yasuyoshi Yamauchi, he started acting in elementary school. He was discovered by a theater troupe after the war. Eventually, director Seiji Maruyama caught one of his plays. At 15 he was cast in his first film, *Adolescence* (1952), directed by Maruyama. Tomoyuki Tanaka convinced him to use the stage name "Akira Kubo", named after his character in *Adolescence*. Kubo went on to appear in numerous films. He played the Malcolm role in Kurosawa's *Macbeth*-based *Throne of Blood* (1957). At his career's peak, he appeared in a dozen films a year. Kubo was Tsuburaya's first choice for the role of human alter-ego Hayata in his TV show *Ultraman*. Worried he wouldn't be able to balance appearing in a television show with his film career, Kubo turned the role down. The part went to Susumu Kurobe and Kubo now regrets this decision. In 1995, he appeared as a ship's captain in *Gamera: Guardian of the Universe* for Shusuke Kaneko. More recently, he played the Prime Minister in Hiroto Yokokawa's independent *The Great Buddha Arrival* (2019). Kubo recalls that he was once approached by an American G.I. stationed in Japan who recognized him from *Matango*.

The other actors shine as well. Consummate Yoshio Tsuchiya gives a powerful turn as businessman Kasai. He starts off a rich and pompous blowhard and as the going gets tough becomes a pathetic wraith. Kumi Mizuno is particularly memorable as Kasai's mistress Mami. Betraying the man she used for his wealth, she ends up personifying the allure of the Matango itself and becoming a succubus-like creature. The special effects crew wanted to disfigure her with keloid-style bumps like the male characters but Honda disagreed. Honda opted to make her more beautiful instead which he believed was scarier. Kenji Sahara, against type, plays low class sailor Koyama, a base but honest man. Sahara had played fairly wholesome roles up until this point. He was gleeful to play a "dirty" character. He worked out hard before the shoot and built his muscle tone. He also had his dentist mess up his teeth. Hiroshi Koizumi also appears against type. For Honda he mainly played intellectuals, but his Sakuta is a world weary working class man. Hiroshi Tachikawa is chilling as Yoshida, a pretentious novelist whose behavior turns sociopathic. Tachikawa (1931-) was a more minor but notable player at Toho. He had appeared in *Gorath* for Honda the year prior and for Kurosawa he also appeared in *Throne of Blood*. Actress Miki Yashiro (1943-) plays the virginal Akiko. She joined Toho after graduating high school but left after 1964, probably to start a domestic life.

SFX

For *Matango*'s shoot, the distinction between the live action and SFX units was less clear than on the *kaiju* pictures. Many scenes were more or less co-directed by Honda and Eiji

Tsuburaya. Fresh off *Siege of Fort Bismark*, Tsuburaya creates phantasmagorical and atmospheric images rivaling European horror maestros like Mario Bava, Terence Fisher and Jacques Tourneur. Tsuburaya's crew was allowed to be more experimental than usual on *Matango*. They worked hard to elevate the film beyond its B-picture status. *Matango* was one of the first Toho films to use front projection rather than rear projection. Front projection involved a projector placed closer to the camera. With nearer projection and better screens made of road sign material, the result was more bright and crisp. The first scenes on the yacht were filmed on a soundstage. Footage of the ocean was front projected behind them and the result is stellar for 1963. This was also one of Tsuburaya's first films to use his Oxberry optical printer which had just been purchased. The Oxberry could composite up to six layers of film. This printer is used to make some fanciful composites. The yacht and derelict ship had elaborate miniatures built. The miniature yacht was quite large and actually sailable, its scenes shot in Toho's "Big Pool". The glowing Tokyo cityscape outside of the psych ward Kubo's character is confined to is also a miniature set built by Tsuburaya's team.

Shigeru Komatsuzaki did much of the film's conceptual designs. He came up with the visual motif for the monsters themselves. Besides bringing radiation burns and atomic clouds to mind, they resemble forest *yokai*. The film's sets are fantastic. Art director Shigekazu Ikuno and SFX art director Akira Watanabe kept in good communication. The derelict ship's walls were made to look fungus encrusted with rubber glue spiked with acetone. For later scenes, this mixture was diluted and used to make spores. An unsung hero of the classic Tsuburaya unit was the *tokusatsu* set backdrop painter Fuchimu Shimakura (1940-). Called the *"Master of Clouds"*, he painted the backgrounds in numerous films and particularly specialized in clouds and mountains. In *Matango*, his work is particularly noticeable. Teizo Toshimitsu modeled and built the on-set mushrooms as well as the prosthetics and monster suits. The prosthetics were latex which Toshimitsu was beginning to favor. He was proud of his work on Hideyo Amamoto's "Skulking Transitional Matango". Amamoto had to have lunch at Toho's cafeteria in full makeup, giving the staff quite a fright.

The shots where the mushrooms bloom and grow from the ground were a difficult technical feat. Tsuburaya's team considered using spun sugar ala cotton candy. In the end, they found the best results with a liquid nylon solution. This mixture was poured into cans and produced mushroom-like shapes. Smaller mushrooms were made with soft drink Bireley's cans. Medium sized mushrooms came from corned beef cans and giant ones from paint cans. The expansion only took several seconds and had to be shot quickly at a very high frame rate. The edible mushrooms consumed by the actors on set were mochi rice pastry. The mochi was made by a local confectionary shop. It was then crafted into mushrooms by the special effects crew. The staff added flavors to the mochi as a playful prank on the actors. They were delicious enough that the crew would steal some for dessert after lunch.

MUSIC

Sadao Bekku's haunting score is almost experimental and enhances the film's moody psychedelia. Bekku (1922-2012) was born in Tokyo. Musically trained in Paris, he was influenced by both classical music and jazz. Bekku was less prolific in film composition than Akira Ifukube or Masaru Sato. He wrote far fewer film scores than non-film compositions. Bekku's second best known score is likely for *International Secret Police: Key of Keys* (1965) which became Woody Allen's *What's Up Tiger Lily*.

THEMES AND MOTIFS

Matango is a misanthropic and unsettling film. Invoking Sartre's *No Exit* and Golding's *Lord of the Flies*, it's more disturbing than its subject matter suggests. The film's cast of characters represent a good cross section of Japanese society. They range from a wealthy tycoon and a singer to a shy college student and tough working class sailors. In *Matango*, we witness a microcosmic breakdown of society. As circumstances toughen, their social order fragments. As this happens, the characters' darker impulses, held back by social norms, take hold. Kimura's script brings to mind the famous quote from *No Exit*: *"Hell is other people"*.

Typical of Ishiro Honda, there's inference that the Matango threat itself may have been spawned by nuclear testing. This is hinted at by the fact that the derelict ship was studying nuclear contamination. It can also be seen in the keloid scar-like makeup of the transitional creatures. The fully transformed Matango monsters, played by actors in suits ala *kaiju*, have mushroom cloud-like heads. Note that an early, rejected design of the first Godzilla had similar features. Films like *The H-Man* and *Matango* make one wish Honda had directed more horror pictures.

RELEASE AND LEGACY

Matango did poor business in Japan and was critically skewered. Honda was disheartened but unsurprised. In his own words it was not a *"typical Japanese mainstream movie"*. This would be Honda's final horror film. Regardless, *Matango* developed strong cult status over the years on both sides of the Pacific. Shinji Higuchi is a particular fan of the film. He paid homage to it in an episode he storyboarded for Hideaki Anno's *anime Nadia: Secret of Blue Water* in 1991. More recently, a 2011 episode of *Naruto: Shippuden* paid tribute to the film. Additionally, Steven Soderbergh *(Sex, Lies, and Videotape, Ocean's 11)* wanted to direct a Hollywood remake. He was apparently unable to procure the rights from Toho and so plans were scuttled.

ALTERNATE VERSIONS

Toho commissioned an export version of *Matango* editorially identical to the Japanese version. The English dubbing was recorded in Hong Kong by a firm called Axis International, run by a man named Theodore

"Ted" Thomas. Dubbing cast includes Thomas as Sakuta, John Wallace as Koyama and Lynn Wilson (suspected) as Akiko. For a Hong Kong job, it isn't bad, but it lacks the depth and nuance of the Japanese performances. It devolves the film into more of a campy B-movie than is necessary.

Thomas (1929-) is an English expat still living in Hong Kong to this day. His voice is unmistakable to anyone familiar with dubbed Asian cinema. He was employed by Radio Television Hong Kong (RTHK) as an announcer while running his dubbing hustle on the side. He later dubbed Toshiaki Nishizawa's Kubota in *Godzilla vs. Gigan* and Robert Dunham's Emperor Antonio in *Godzilla vs. Megalon*. Yet his Japanese film dubs were a drop in the bucket compared to the mind-blowing amount of Chinese martial arts films he voiced. Throughout the 1960s and '70s, he dubbed thousands of films into English. He had a good relationship with Run Run Shaw, who preferred using Thomas' firm to dub Shaw Brothers films. Ted Thomas played a significant onscreen role in the Shaws' King Kong cash-in *The Mighty Peking Man* as a British military official. Ironically, his voice is dubbed by another actor.

Matango was bought by American International Pictures and given the hokey title *Attack of the Mushroom People*. It was released directly to stateside television in 1965. Unusually for AIP, the export dubbing was kept intact and not redone by Titra/Titan. The cuts are minor and amount to under 30 seconds of dialogue.

AMERICAN HOME VIDEO HISTORY

A 16mm telecine of *Attack of the Mushroom People* was released on VHS by Something Weird Video in the '90s. Later, Media Blasters released *Matango* to DVD in 2005. This DVD included both the Japanese audio and export dub along with some behind the scenes material ported from the Japanese release. The DVD is out of print and *Matango* has not been released on U.S. home video since. The dubbed version is available to stream on Amazon Prime, however.

Further Viewing:

SPACE AMOEBA

(1970)
ゲゾラ・ガニメ・カメーバ 決戦! 南海の大怪獣
Toho, *Director*: **Ishiro Honda**

Ishiro Honda's other monsters-on-an-island film, *Space Amoeba* is mediocre but fun. Also known as *Yog, Monster From Space*, it began development in 1966 as *The Space Monsters*. Originally a co-production with UPA, Toho wound up producing it on their own with a smaller budget. Eiji Tsuburaya was long attached to the project. He was due to take a supervisory role over Sadamasa Arikawa like with *Son of Godzilla* and *Destroy All Monsters*. Tsuburaya died only two days after *Space Amoeba* started principal photography. Therein lies *Space Amoeba*'s main problem, it's a classic Tsuburaya film without Tsuburaya.

Space Amoeba starts off with the popular trope of cosmic gunk attaching itself to a space probe. The probe crash lands near a tropical island. The space gunk possesses a squid, a stone crab and a matamata turtle. It transforms the animals into a trio of giant monsters as a resort company plans to turn the island into a tourist trap. *Space Amoeba* is noteworthy because it was something of a last hurrah for Toho's old guard. Yet Tsuburaya's absence is both noticeable and significant. Competently helmed by Honda, *Space Amoeba* is lacking Tsuburaya's ingenuity. In general, it seems uninspired with a formulaic story and goofy monsters. Sadamasa Arikawa's special effects sequences have decent miniature work but are unremarkable. The monsters are especially silly and generic. Only Gezora, a pantomime giant squid played by Haruo Nakajima, is of much character. Teizo Toshimitsu built it, while Nobuyuki Yasumaru handled the giant crab Gamine and turtle Kamoebas. Classic Toho contact players like Akira Kubo, Kenji Sahara and Yoshio Tsuchiya seem almost bored. Even Ifukube's score is weirdly pedestrian by his standards.

It was a slightly troubled production. To Honda's frustration, the budget was slashed, ending plans to shoot the film in Guam like *Son of Godzilla*. Neither Takeshi Kimura nor Shinichi Sekizawa worked on the screenplay. Instead, Ei Ogawa (*The Vampire Doll*) penned a dry and formulaic script. *Space Amoeba*'s screenplay is like a parade of "been there done that" to the point that it feels almost satirical. The tropes are tired and the characters are pastiches of stereotypical *kaiju eiga* protagonists. The special effects crew, now solely under Arikawa, did not have the bargaining power that Tsuburaya exercised at Toho. As a result, they weren't given the time to properly finish the FX scenes. Arikawa was very keen on including an onscreen tribute to Eiji Tsuburaya in the film but Toho would not allow it. In protest, Arikawa resigned from Toho's FX division and went freelance. This was also Ishiro Honda's last film at Toho for five years. During that time, he directed for television, helming episodes of *Mirrorman*, *Return of Ultraman* and *Zone Fighter*. *Space Amoeba*, however, isn't all bad. It's the final collaboration between much of the classic Toho talent and Honda's last monster movie produced under the studio system. In that regard, it still has a lot of charm.

TAKESHI KIMURA
The Cynic

木村武

2/4/1911-5/3/1987

"Kimura was very good at writing about social and political problems. When it came to stories about human traits in particular situations, it had to be Kimura.."
-Ishiro Honda, from *Ishiro Honda: A Life in Film, From Godzilla to Kurosawa* (2017) by Steve Ryfle and Ed Godziszewski

To write their genre films, producer Tomoyuki Tanaka and director Ishiro Honda liked to employ two writers. The first was Shinichi Sekizawa. Sekizawa saw writing science fiction as "fun". He liked to write films with an optimistic, fantastical tone. The other was Takeshi Kimura. A brooding and reclusive figure to the point that no photographs of him are known to exist, his scripts were darker. Kimura's screenplays tended to have somber subtexts and tragic elements. Takeshi Kimura was born in 1911 in Osaka. As a youth, he joined the Japanese Communist Party and attended Kansai University. Dropping out of school, Kimura's communist sympathies got him imprisoned as a dissident through World War II. After the war, Kimura was released and became the chairman of the JCP's Saga Prefecture branch.

Eventually, Kimura grew bitter towards political activism. He got in a disagreement with JCP head Kyuichi Tokuda over the use of Molotov cocktails and quit. Kimura started writing screen and stage plays. Fellow writer Toshio Yasumi took him under his wing, helping Kimura break into the industry. His first major scripting job was *Red Light Base* (1953) directed by Senkichi Tanguchi. This film, produced in the wake of the American Occupation, wound up being controversial due to an unflattering portrayal of American G.I.s. Kimura's next script was the pacifistic war drama *Farewell Rabaul* (1954) helmed by Ishiro Honda. After co-writing *Rodan* and writing *The Mysterians* and *The H-Man* for

Honda, he began to specialize in science fiction scripts.

In the 1960s, Kimura's notable works included the character-driven *The Human Vapor* (1960), the apocalyptic tragedy *The Last War* (1961) and the space epic *Gorath* (1962). His signature screenplay was for Honda's *Matango*. The story's misanthropic overtones summed up Kimura's mindset. In 1965, Kimura started writing scripts under the pseudonym *"Kaoru Mabuchi"*. Losing interest in writing monster movies, he took on the role of a writer for hire. His scripts became barebones but he continued, writing films like *Frankenstein Conquers the World*, *The War of the Gargantuas*, *King Kong Escapes* and *Destroy All Monsters*.

His final script credit was for *Godzilla vs. Hedorah*, co-written with Yoshimitsu Banno. His morose sensibilities can be felt in the finished product as it is the first Godzilla film to present pollution as an existential threat akin to nuclear weapons. His last contribution to Toho was a treatment called *Godzilla vs. the Space Monsters*. It formed the basis for *Godzilla vs. Gigan* and, very loosely, *Godzilla vs. Megalon*. Kimura then disappeared from the limelight. He was not friendly with anyone at Toho save for, to some degree, Toshio Yasumi. Years later, in 1987, Yasumi received a strange phone call. He heard a voice gasping for air and trying to speak but unable to. The call was traced to Kimura's Tokyo apartment. Kimura was found dead from a throat obstruction. It was a hauntingly tragic end for a writer who specialized in tragedies.

Selected Filmography
(as screenwriter)
Red Light Base (1953)
Farewell Rabaul (1954)
Rodan (1956)
The Mysterians (1957)
The H-Man (1958)
Submarine 1-57 Will Not Surrender (1959)
The Human Vapor (1960)
Daredevil in the Castle (1961)
The Last War (1961)
Gorath (1962)

Matango (1963)
Samurai Pirate (1963)
Whirlwind (1964)
Frankenstein Conquers the World (1965) [as Kaoru Mabuchi]
Adventure of Taklamakan (1966) [as Kaoru Mabuchi]
The War of the Gargantuas (1966) [as Kaoru Mabuchi]

King Kong Escapes (1967) [as Kaoru Mabuchi]
Destroy All Monsters (1968) [as Kaoru Mabuchi]
Godzilla vs. Hedorah (1971) [as Kaoru Mabuchi]
Godzilla vs. Gigan (1972) [story *'Godzilla vs. the Space Monsters'*]

ATRAGON

Kaitei Gunkan "The Undersea Warship"
Toho, 12/22/1963 (*Showa 38*), 7 Reels (2,589 meters), 94:32, 35mm, TohoScope (2.35:1 anamorphic), Eastman color, monaural sound

Crew
Producer: Tomoyuki Tanaka
Director: Ishiro Honda
Special Effects Director: Eiji Tsuburaya
Screenplay: Shinichi Sekizawa, Shigeru Komatsuzaki (story *"The Undersea Kingdom"*), Shunro Oshikawa (novel)
Director of Photography: Hajime Koizumi
Music: Akira Ifukube
Assistant Director: Koji Kajita
Production Design: Takeo Kita
Editor: Ryohei Fujii
Sound Recordist: Masao Uehara
Sound Effects: Minoru Kaneyama

Sound Editor: Hisashi Shimonaga
Lighting: Shoshichi Kojima
Production Manager: Shigeru Nakamura
Conceptual Artist: Shigeru Komatsuzaki
Assistant SFX Director: Teruyoshi Nakano
SFX Cinematography: Sadamasa Arikawa, Mototaka Tomioka
SFX Art Director: Akira Watanabe
SFX Lighting: Kuichiro Kishida
SFX Optical Photography: Yukio Manoda, Yoshiyuki Tokumasa

SFX Continuity: Hiroshi Mukoyama
SFX Production Manager: Tadashi Koike
Still Photographer: Jiro Tsuchiya

Cast
Tadao Takashima (*Susumu Hatanaka*)
Yoko Fujiyama (*Makoto Jinguji*)
Hiroshi Koizumi (*Detective Ito*)
Ken Uehara (*Admiral Kusumi*)
Yu Fujiki (*Yoshito Nishibe*)
Kenji Sahara (*Uoto Uno*)
Jun Tazaki (*Captain Hachiro Jinguji*)

Akihiko Hirata (Mu Agent No. 23)
Hideyo Amamato (High Priest of Mu)
Tetsuko Kobayashi (Empress of Mu)
Yoshifumi Tajima (Lt. Amano)
Michiro Minami (Lt. Fujinaka)
Haruya Sakamoto (Sergeant Yamada)
Akemi Kita (Rimako, Model)
Sadako Amemiya (Momoko)
Minoru Takada (Defense Minister)
Susumu Fujita (Defense Commander)
Misuo Tsuda (Defense Agency)
Shin Otomo (Defense Official)
Hisaya Ito (Shindo)
Nadao Kirino (Kidnapped Engineer)
Ikio Sawamura (Taxi Driver)
Koji Uno (Shipping Employee)
Tetsu Nakamura (Cargo Ship Captain)

Yutaka Nakayama (Cargo Ship Crew)
Hiroshi Hasegawa
Rinsaku Ogata
Hideo Otsuka
Yutaka Oka (Man on Bus)
Yukihiko Gondo (Military Official)
Shoichi Hirose (Mu Henchman)
Katsumi Tezuka (Mu Henchman)
Takuzo Kumagai
Yasuzo Ogawa (Mu Henchman)
Jiro Tsuchiya
Wataru Omae (Policeman)
Toshio Miura
Masayoshi Kawabe
Hiroshi Akitsu
Hideo Shibuya
Keisuke Yamada
Shinjiro Hirota
Keisuke Yamaji
Kuniyoshi Kashima

Haruo Nakajima (Mu Agent Double)

Alternate Titles
Atoragon (alternate English export title)
Ataragon (France)
U 2000 - Tauchfahrt des Grauens [U 2000: Undersea Horror] (Germany)
Agente 04 del imperio sumergido [Agent 04 of the Sunken Empire] (Spain)
Atoragon, el supersubmarino atómico [Atragon: The Atomic Supersubmarine] (Mexico)
Άτραγκον, οι σούπερμεν των θαλασσών [Atragon, Supermen of the Seas] (Greece)
Аторагон: Летающая суперсубмарина [Atragon: The Flying Supersub] (Russia)

"It seems I have been wearing rusty armor. It's time for me to take it off."
-Captain Hachiro Jinguji (Jun Tazaki)

Atragon is another top tier science fiction opus from Ishiro Honda and company. It is unusually character driven for a Toho special effects film. *Atragon* is quintessential in understanding director Honda's pacifist mindset. It features surprising subtext on Japanese nationalism and the dark specter of the Pacific War. Eiji Tsuburaya impresses with eye-popping composites and some of his best miniature work.

PLOT

Shindo (Hisaya Ito), an engineer, is kidnapped in a taxi cab. While on a night shoot, photographers Susumu Hatanaka (Tadao Takashima) and Yoshito Nishibe (Yu Fujiki) witness a steaming figure rising from the water. The taxi then plunges into the sea, confounding the photographers. The car is pulled from the ocean the next morning and no bodies are found. As Susumu and Yoshito give statements to Detective Ito (Hiroshi Koizumi), they see a young woman, Makoto (Yoko Fujiyama).

Interested in recruiting her as a model, they start trailing her. A mysterious man is also following her.

Makoto is the daughter of supposedly deceased Imperial navalman Hachiro Jinguji. Her uncle is his former superior, Admiral Kusumi (Ken Uehara). Kusumi is visited by an odd reporter, Uno (Kenji Sahara). Uno claims that he's heard Jinguji, who disappeared with his crew in submarine I-403, is still alive and building a powerful warship. Kusumi and Makoto are then abducted by a taxi driver who takes them to the shore. The driver (Akihiko Hirata) pulls a pistol, claiming himself to be Agent No. 23 of the Mu Empire and intending to take them to Mu. The two photographers, in hot pursuit of Makoto, manage to disarm him. Agent 23 flees into the ocean as Kusumi fires upon the man.

At the police office, a package purporting to be from the agent arrives. It is a documentary film that reveals the Mu Empire's existence to the world. The Mu Empire, thousands of years ago, was the ultimate world superpower with the rest of the world as its colonies. Mu then sank beneath the waves but the survivors rebuilt their society under the bottom of the sea. They even constructed their own "sun" that powers the entire Empire. The agent demands humanity surrender and submit as a colony of Mu once more. They mention that they captured Jinguji's submarine sans its crew and warn humanity not to let him build another one.

The United Nations scoffs at the film, believing it to be an elaborate prank. After a cargo ship is destroyed by the Muans at sea, they take the threat seriously. The U.N. dispatches the American submarine *Red Satan* after the Muans. The sub is unable to destroy Mu's warships and is crushed by deep sea water pressure while diving after one.

The man who has been following Makoto is captured on suspicion of being a Mu agent. He reveals himself to be Amano (Yoshifumi Tajima), a naval officer who serves under Jinguji. He reveals Captain Jinguji is alive. Amano refuses to divulge his location, but offers to take Kusumi to him. Kusumi, Makoto, Susumu, Yoshito, Detective Ito and Uno accompany Amano to a remote Pacific island. Here Jinguji and his officers reside, having chosen not to surrender at the end of the Pacific War.

The company is greeted by Jinguji (Jun Tazaki) and his men. They are headquartered above a giant underground docking bay where the new submarine, the *Goten-go*, is being built. Kusumi urges Jinguji to use the *Goten-go* to defend humanity against the Mu Empire. Jinguji refuses, stating that it is only to be used in the interest in restoring the Japanese Empire. The *Goten-go*'s test run is successful and the ship is shown to travel underwater and through the air. Jinguji and his crew toast at the test's success. The reporter Uno reveals himself to be a Mu agent. He kidnaps both Susumu and

Makoto and detonates a bomb in Jinguji's headquarters.

Susumu and Makoto are taken before the Empress of Mu (Tetsuko Kobayashi) and her High Priest (Hideyo Amamoto). The Empress orders them fed to Manda, a gigantic sea serpent worshipped by the Muans as a god. The *Goten-go* is unharmed by the explosion and Jinguji and his men begin operations to relaunch it. The Mu Empire, meanwhile, begins its attack, killing fleeing civilians on Oshima Island. The Muans next threaten attacks on Tokyo and New York City. Jinguji launches his submarine and tells Kusumi that he has decided to come to the world's aid.

BACKGROUND

In spite of its lavish production values, *Atragon* was a hectic production. In September of 1963, Toho decided to produce a special effects film for their New Years' holiday slot. As inspiration, they turned to *Meiji*-era writer Shunro Oshikawa (1876-1914) and his 1899 novel *The Undersea Warship*. *Atragon* would be a very loose adaptation of Oshikawa's book. *The Undersea Warship* is a militaristic tome inspired by Jules Verne and Japan's then-recent naval victory against China. The Russians, soon to battle the Japanese on the high seas, were the book's antagonists. One element from the story was used: the concept of a patriotic renegade captain building a super-submarine in seclusion. The context, however, would be quite different in screenwriter Shinichi Sekizawa's script.

Sekizawa drew influence from English occult writer James Churchward (1851-1936) and his writings on the Mu Empire. In the late 19th to early 20th century, Mu was believed to be an Atlantis-like supercontinent that perished by sinking into the ocean. Sekizawa drew more plot elements from a novel written by artist Shigeru Komatsuzaki: *The Undersea Kingdom*.

PRINCIPAL PHOTOGRAPHY

The shoot began later in September after rushed but extensive storyboard meetings between directors Ishiro Honda and Eiji Tsuburaya. The two worked hand-in-hand on *Atragon*. They thought that the special effects sequences should especially compliment the story. Much of the film was shot on location as a cost cutting measure, though about 15 sets were built. Honda preferred shooting on location as he felt the actors gave better, more realistic performances. Several scenes were lensed on Oshima Island. Sequences of Jinguji's island hideout tend to cut back and forth from footage shot on Oshima to jungle sets. The largest scene on Oshima was where the Mu Empire attacks fleeing residents near Mount Mihara. The sequence used a large number of locals. It contains a realistic wide shot of an exploding miniature boat composed against authentic extras.

The design motif for the Mu Empire, its architecture and wardrobe was based on Easter Island folklore. The Mu sets were made to appear expansive with wide lenses, matte paintings and depth perspective. Many foreign extras were cast in the Mu sequences as Honda wanted to depict it as a multiethnic society. The dance numbers, though a weak link, were performed by students from Tokyo dancing schools. Honda was unhappy with the Mu scenes, however. He wanted to show the Muans' towns and living areas but didn't have the time or budget. Honda's live action shoot was finished well ahead of schedule in under 35 days. Regardless of its rushed nature and budget cuts, *Atragon*'s production values are top tier. Only some stock footage, mostly from 1961's *Mothra*, betrays any sign of cut corners.

ACTORS

By this time, there was a camaraderie between Honda's usual troupe of actors. They were starting to very much enjoy appearing in these films. Tadao Takashima heads *Atragon*'s cast. Takashima (1930-2019) was well known for his *kaiju* film roles. He also appeared in *King Kong vs. Godzilla, Frankenstein Conquers the World, Son of Godzilla* and later on: *Godzilla vs. Mechagodzilla II*. Takashima was born in what is now Kobe, the first born son of a wealthy landowner. As a child he loved to swim and soon developed an interest in jazz. In high school and university he joined a jazz band. At the age of 21, he joined Shin Toho as an actor. His debut was in *Love's Cheerleader* (1952). Takashima was multi-talented: he could sing, play jazz and portray both dramatic and comedic roles in film, television and stage. He moved to Toho in 1958 and also acted in movies from *Takarazuka Revue*'s film production arm. He married Hanayo Sumi (1932-), a former actress at *Takarazuka*.

Their first son, Michio, was tragically murdered by the couple's teenage maid. Takashima and Sumi had two more sons, Masahiro and Masanobu. Both the Takashima brothers would go on to appear in Godzilla entries themselves. From this point, Takashima would struggle with depression and alcoholism for much of his life. He became a frequent fixture on Japanese television, hosting a popular program called *The Saturday Show*. He hosted quiz shows, appeared on cooking shows and even introduced movies on prime time television. He suffered from a severe bout of depression in the late 1990s from being dropped from the cooking show *Gochisosama* and the illness and death of his mother. In June 2019, he passed away at his home in Tokyo of natural causes. Yu Fujiki often co-starred with Takashima in comedic roles. They frequently played a Laurel and Hardy-like pair including in *Atragon* and *King Kong vs. Godzilla*. Fujiki (1931-2005), a Tokyo native, was born Yuzo Suzuki. He was fencing champion in college at Doshisha University. Fujiki was accepted into Toho's New Face program in 1953. He was in the same class as Akira Takarada, Kenji Sahara and Momoko Kochi. His debut was in Honda's *Farewell Rabaul*. In the original Godzilla, he plays a tiny role as the *Eiko Maru*'s radioman. He played a large variety of comedic and dramatic supporting roles, including in Kurosawa's *The Lower Depths* and Naruse's *When a Woman Ascends the Stairs*. Appearing in more than 100 films, Fujiki became more successful as a television actor. His most popular role was on the beloved police procedural *G-Men '75* (1975-1982). He developed diabetes which caused him a myriad of health problems until his death in 2005.

Yoko Fujiyama (1941-) plays Jinguji's daughter Makoto. Fujiyama joined Toho straight out of high school. This was at the urging of composer Chuji Kinoshita, who was her teacher and his brother: director Keisuke Kinoshita. Fujiyama left show business in 1967 to marry. But she appeared in quite a few popular Toho films including some *Crazy Cats* and *Young Guy* comedies and Kurosawa's *Red Beard* (1965). Jun Tazaki plays Jinguji. For Honda he specialized in authority figures like military men, scientists and policemen. Rumor has it that the role of Jinguji may have been written with Toshiro Mifune in mind but this is unconfirmed. With a similar commanding voice and stern continence, Tazaki certainly invokes Mifune's war film roles like in *Storm Over the Pacific* (1960) and *Admiral Yamamoto* (1968). Tazaki (1913-1985) was born Minoru Tanaka in Aomori Prefecture, the son of a civil servant. He began acting straight out of high school, soon joining the stage troupe Pier Boys. His acting career was, as for many, interrupted by stints fighting in China. In 1942, he joined the comedic acting troupe Tampopo alongside Ichiro Arishima. He was drafted again in 1944 and fought in the army until the war's end. After the war, he began to transition from stage to screen. He acted in the stage version of *Gate of Flesh*. As a result, he was cast by director Masahiro Makino in his film adaptation. Taking on the stage name Jun Tazaki, he joined Shin Toho. It was at this point that he began to specialize in playing stern authority figures in period

pieces and war films. In 1957 he played General Heihachiro Togo in Shin Toho's controversial blockbuster *Emperor Meiji and the Great Russo-Japanese War*. Soon he contracted with Toho where he acted prolifically. In addition to sci-fi films, he appeared in works by Teinosuke Kinugasa, Akira Kurosawa, Masaki Kobayashi, Hiroshi Inagaki and Kihachi Okamoto. His final role was in Kurosawa's *Ran* right before his death by lung cancer in 1985.

Hideyo Amamoto plays the high priest of Mu. Amamoto (1926-2003) was one of Toho's finest character actors. For Honda, he often played flamboyant villainous roles, most notably the nefarious Dr. Who in *King Kong Escapes*. Amamoto was also a close friend and favorite actor of director Kihachi Okamoto. It was often joked that the two men looked like brothers. Amamoto was born in Fukuoka and after high school was drafted into the Imperial Army. He was rebellious against his superiors and was beaten brutally. After the war, Amamoto became a liberal anarchist, studying to be a diplomat at Tokyo University. He was disappointed by the post-war Japanese government and dropped out. Instead, Amamoto decided to pursue acting. He joined the Haiyuza Theater Company and in 1954, he began to appear in film roles as well. A notable early appearance was in Keisuke Kinoshita's *Twenty Four Eyes*. With a gangly appearance and distinctive voice, he became an in demand character actor; specializing in offbeat roles. By the 1970s, he was popular on television as arch villain Dr. Shinigami in Toei's *Kamen Rider*. One of his final roles was, fittingly, in

Shusuke Kaneko's *Godzilla, Mothra and King Ghidorah: Giant Monsters All-Out Attack* (2001). Amamoto had an adoration for Spain and its culture. After he died, his ashes were scattered on the banks of the Guadalquivir river there. The Mu Empress is played by Tetsuko Kobayashi (1941-1994) whose career was sporadic. Honda was unsure of who to cast in that role as most of the usual actresses didn't fit the mold. Keiji Tani, an assistant on the production, recommended Kobayashi, a friend, to Koji Kajita and Ishiro Honda. Honda was impressed by her audition and after several meetings gave her the part. It was decided to give the Empress red hair so the character would make a strong impression and to compliment her brash personality. Kobayashi was dedicated to the role and even applied her own makeup.

SFX

Eiji Tsuburaya's miniature work in *Atragon* is among his very finest, with impressive composites throughout. Due to the rushed schedule, Tsuburaya split special effects photography into three units. Tsuburaya handled shooting for "Unit A" while he recruited friend Keiji Kawakami to direct "Unit B". Kawakami (1912-1973) was a longtime associate of Tsuburaya's, dating back to *The War at Sea From Hawaii to Malay.* He had left Toho for Shochiku but still worked with Tsuburaya on occasion. He was the effects director on Shochiku's war film *Okinawa Kenji Corps* (1953), one of their first post-war films to use *tokusatsu*-style effects. For Tsuburaya Pro, Kawakami

directed the special effects for numerous *Ultra Q* episodes. Kawakami later went on to handle FX work on Shochiku's *The X From Outer Space* (1967), *The Living Skeleton* and *Genocide* (both 1968). Teruyoshi Nakano handled "Unit C" which shot location plates.

Designed by Shigeru Komatsuzaki, four models of the *Goten-go* were constructed. These were a one foot miniature, a three foot, a six foot one and a whopping 15 foot model built of metal and wood. The six foot model was used more frequently while the 15 foot miniature Goten-go had radio controlled mechanical parts. The "Zero Cannon" was an aerosolized smoke shot out from the miniature. The underwater shots of the *Goten-go* diving are especially beautiful. A short sequence showing it destroying a Muan warship was left on the cutting room floor.

One of the most jaw-dropping sequences in *Atragon* features Tokyo "imploding" from below during a Muan attack. This effect was accomplished by collapsing support beams placed underneath the miniatures. This caused them to fall apart and appear to implode. Explosives aided in this process and it was tricky to get right. It required precise mathematical calculation from Tsuburaya and his team. Manda, the giant sea serpent worshipped by the Muans, was added at the insistence of Tomoyuki Tanaka ala *Gorath*'s Maguma. Tanaka wanted a dragon-like monster in the film as it was to be released for the New Years' holiday season and the upcoming year, 1964, was the Year of the Dragon. Manda was executed as a wire controlled marionette; two were built.

Designed by Akira Watanabe, the puppets were modeled by Teizo Toshimitsu. Its sequences were shot on a dry set. As typical for Toho's special effects unit, light reflected through water tanks was used to create an undersea texture. The final explosion was done with the classic method of dumping paints in a water tank and flipping the image upside down. This technique was first used in *The Last War* and later used for an impressive underwater volcanic eruption in 1969's *Latitude Zero*.

MUSIC

Akira Ifukube's score is another example of his finest work. Memorable themes abound for the *Goten-go* itself and the Mu Empire. One track, *"The Volunteer Corps Swing Into Action"*, is among the most exhilarating military marches Ifukube composed. The Muans' choral chant was written by Ifukube himself. Similarly to Yuji Koseki's *"Song of Mothra"*, its lyrics were translated into a Pacific dialect.

REAL WORLD

The submarine Jinguji disappears in at the end of the war is the I-403. This is a nod to a genuine series of Imperial naval submarines. The I-400 class was laid down in 1943 as the tide began to turn against Japan in the Pacific. The Germans assisted in the construction of them, sending parts and components to the Japanese. Plans for most of the submarines were scuttled or abandoned, but the I-400, I-401 and I-402 made it to sea. They were some of the largest, most state of the art submarines ever built. The former two even contained built-in aircraft carriers to launch aerial attacks on U.S. forces. The I-403 was planned to be constructed but cancelled in October 1943.

THEMES AND MOTIFS

Director Ishiro Honda would bring humanistic subtext to *Atragon* inspired by his own feelings on Japanese nationalism. By the early 1960s, a romanticization of World War II-era *bushido* values was again on the rise. Fervently nationalistic writers like Yukio Mishima were becoming popular. Mishima (1925-1970) wound up attempting a coup d'etat at a Self Defense Force office before committing ritual suicide. A man with painful wartime experience, Honda was appalled by such neo-fascist ideologies. Honda and writer Sekizawa also drew influence from stories about the many Japanese "holdouts". These were soldiers who refused to surrender after the Pacific War's end. Many of these men hid on remote tropical islands or in jungles for years, believing themselves still carrying on the will of the Emperor. The last two known hold-outs, Hiroo Onoda and Teruo Nakamura, did not surrender until 1974. Captain Jinguji even utters a line associated with the *kamikaze*: *"I devote my life to my country"*. He is one of the most fascinating characters in Honda's films: torn between his patriotic duty and greater humanity.

Atragon was called *"an adult fairytale"* by assistant director Koji Kajita. It is among the most quintessential of director Ishiro

Honda's films in understanding his pacifistic mindset. Though based on a nationalistic novel, *Atragon*'s very message is an outright deconstruction of *The Undersea Warship*. There's an unusually deep subtext, darker than first glance, on Japan's wartime militarism. *Atragon* explores the spectre of its former aggression and fanatical collective mindset in a sincere and apologetic fashion. It is a film about Japan's collective struggle in letting go of its old war-like ways. The Mu Empire, a colonialist and Imperialist state which tries to conquer the world, resembles a dark satire of Imperial Japan. The final scene, where Jinguji allows the Mu Empress to die for her country, is poignant. Jinguji allows her to share her country's fate because he understands, but no longer shares, her nationalistic mindset.

RELEASE AND LEGACY

Honda and company finished the movie on time and budget. They celebrated, as usual, with a party at Honda's Tokyo home. *Atragon* did modestly successful business at the Japanese box office. It was the 13th highest grossing domestic film that year. *Atragon* would prove one of Toho's most popular and influential films. The Manda prop was later used in the episode *Grow! Turtle* in Tsuburaya Pro's *Ultra Q*. Manda itself would be back in 1968's *Destroy All Monsters*, actually double-billed with an edited version of *Atragon*. For *Destroy All Monsters,* the same prop was used, though a new head was constructed. *Atragon* would later strongly influence 1977's *The War in Space*. Its concept of a Japanese super

battleship saving humanity unquestionably influenced Yoshinobu Nishizaki and Leiji Matsumoto's *Space Battleship Yamato* franchise.

In 1995-96, a two volume OVA (direct-to-video *anime*) called *Super Atragon* was released. The episodes were directed by Kazuyoshi Katayama and Mitsuo Fukui, respectively. This is a modern updating more in line with Oshikawa's novel though it also borrows elements from Toho's film. Boasting some well animated scenes, it's an above average but unexceptional '90s anime. There's definitely strong influence from *Space Battleship Yamato* along with Hideaki Anno's *Nadia: The Secret of Blue Water*. The *Goten-go* would return outright in 2004's mind-numbing *Godzilla: Final Wars* and in *Sazer X the Movie: Fight! Star Warriors* the following year.

ALTERNATE VERSIONS

An export version of *Atragon* was produced, identical to the Japanese original. Called *Atoragon* in Toho's press materials, it was dubbed into English in Hong Kong by Ted Thomas' Axis International. Known dubbing cast includes Thomas as Jinguji, John Wallace as Kusumi and Linda Masson (suspected) as the Mu Empress.

American International Pictures acquired the film and changed its title to *Atragon*. It was released on a double bill with Ib Melchior's *The Time Travelers* on March 11, 1965. The U.S. cut runs 89 minutes and is fairly faithful to the Japanese version. A handful of expository dialogue scenes are edited out. These include a scene where Kusumi tells Makoto that her father was a patriot. A sequence where Makoto discusses her anxieties meeting Jinguji with Susumu while sailing to the island is also cut. Makoto and Jinguji's confrontation is shorter as well. The credits are mostly shifted to the end of the film rather than the opening. American International also did this with *The Lost World of Sinbad* (aka *Samurai Pirate*, 1963) and *Destroy All Monsters*. The English dubbing was done at Titra (soon to be Titan) and is a quality track. Dubbing cast includes Bernard Grant (Susumu), Lucy Martin (Makoto), Larry Robinson (Nishibe), Bret Morrison (Kusumi), Kenneth Harvey (Detective Ito), Jack Curtis (Mu Agent 23) and Peter Fernandez.

Toho reissued the film in 1968 as a co-feature for their new *Destroy All Monsters*. This re-edited version is shorter, running around 75:13. The most notable change is that the opening scene is excised, though a portion is reinserted as a flashback to the next sequence. The early scenes are mainly intact even including the "patriotism" exchange cut from the U.S. version. The most edits are done to the middle portion of the film and include a shortened journey to Jinguji's base on his island. The end of Jinguji's introductory scene is also cut. The Muan prayer scenes are cut and shortened and a military montage is edited out. The ending of the film feels more intact with most scenes shortened rather than excised outright.

AMERICAN HOME VIDEO HISTORY

Though occasionally aired on television, *Atragon* was an elusive film on U.S. home video for decades. It never got a stateside VHS release. It was finally released to DVD by Media Blasters in January 2006. This release included the uncut Japanese version. The Titra dub was noticeably absent, supplanted by the export track. *Atragon* has not been released to U.S. home video since.

Further Viewing:

(1969)
緯度0大作戦
Toho, *Director:* **Ishiro Honda**

Latitude Zero was one of the most ambitious films Toho and director Ishiro Honda attempted. It was to be a US/Japanese co-production based on a radio play by Ted Sherdeman filmed entirely in English. It stars an assortment of Hollywood players. These include the great Joseph Cotten as a Nemo-like submarine captain, the only man to work with Orson Welles, Ishiro Honda and Mario Bava. The antagonist is played by the mighty Cesar "Joker" Romero with Patricia Medina as his moll. *Latitude Zero* also stars Linda Haynes, later to appear in Jack Hill's cult classic *Coffy*. Richard Jaeckel also appears, fresh from his last trip to Japan where he battled *The Green Slime*. Sadly, the American producer Don Sharp's company went bankrupt as the stars arrived. This left Tomoyuki Tanaka with a handful of American stars but no budget. As a result, Toho took up the film's production costs themselves.

Many Japanese monster films such as the original *Godzilla* received recuts adding American stars to them and the Western talent available in Japan proved to be shaky at best. Toho thus began to import Hollywood actors to sell their films internationally. First it was Nick Adams in *Frankenstein Conquers the World* and *Invasion of Astro-Monster* (both 1965). Then came Russ Tamblyn in *The War of the Gargantuas* (1966) and Rhodes Reason in *King Kong Escapes* (1967). *Latitude Zero* was something of a last hurrah for these U.S./Japanese co-productions. Campy in the extreme, it's an uneven but fun film. As a result of the funding evaporating, there are a lot of corners cut. Some sets and costumes look like they came from a cheap episode of *Voyage to the Bottom of the Sea*. The monsters: consisting of a flying Gryphon, bat people and giant rats, are especially silly.

Another interesting yet frustrating aspect of *Latitude Zero* is that it was one of the only Japanese productions shot entirely in sync English. Toho did not employ the post-dubbed "everyone speaks their own language" technique of European or Hong Kong films. Even the Japanese thespians like Akira Takarada and Akihiko Hirata speak English. It's almost surreal to hear what these actors, usually dubbed or speaking Japanese, sound like talking in English in their actual voices. But the Japanese players clearly learned their lines phonetically. Their accents are so thick that many lines are difficult to understand. Takarada fares the best of the Japanese stars, but Akihiko Hirata, appearing in one scene as a doctor, is almost unintelligible. When *Latitude Zero* came to U.S. shores, the Japanese actors were not relooped. This is surprising considering many American distributors scrapped Toho's international English dubs as being too low quality.

Overall, *Latitude Zero* is a lot of fun though. The film's sense of aesthetic high camp is a trip. The monsters may fare poorly, but Eiji Tsuburaya's miniature work is fantastic; one of his last jobs before his death. The models are beautiful and the pyrotechnics plentiful. The optical work is polished and composite shots well executed. Early on, there's a gorgeous shot of an erupting underwater volcano created, as usual, with multicolored paint injected into a water tank and filmed upside down. The *Alpha* is beautifully designed by Yasuyuki Inoue. It would provide inspiration for the *Nautilus* in Hideaki Anno's anime series *Nadia: The Secret of Blue Water*. In addition, Akira Ifukube provides a thundering musical score, one of his very best. *Latitude Zero* is an uneven curiosity of a film, but perfect for lazing with on a Sunday afternoon.

THE WAR IN SPACE

(1977)

惑星大戦争

Toho, *Director:* **Jun Fukuda**

Among Western *tokusatsu* fan circles, *The War in Space* is fairly maligned. Overall, it's a lot more entertaining than its reputation suggests. In 1977, Tomoyuki Tanaka and special effects director Teruyoshi Nakano caught a preview screening of a new Hollywood film yet to open in Japan: *Star Wars*. Afterward, Tanaka turned to Nakano and said *"Make me a movie like THIS"*. Like *Atragon*, *The War in Space* was a hectic production. Plans for a new Godzilla film were scuttled and *The War in Space* was rushed into Toho's theaters instead by the New Years' holiday to beat out Japan's release of *Star Wars*.

If one puts its stigma as a "Japanese Star Wars rip-off" aside, *The War in Space* is a lot of stupid fun. It would be more respected if it had been made before *Star Wars*. A soft remake of *Battle in Outer Space* with elements of *Atragon*, *The War in Space* has few if any novel tropes. Early scenes are somewhat clumsily directed by Jun Fukuda. Yet Nakano's end of the film is surprisingly strong if one avoids comparing it to John Dykstra. The film's miniature work is gorgeous and there are some inventive shots. The *Atragon*-style *"Gohten"* is sleekly designed, again by Yasuyuki Inoue. Portrayed by ten and three foot models, it even features

a gunbarrel-style revolving missile launcher. That sort of fun is what Japanese science fiction is all about and *The War in Space* delivers this in spades. During shooting, so much colored concrete dust was blown around that the FX staff's skin began to change color.

The War in Space gets a lot more entertaining midway. Its Venus finale where Nakano's unit takes the stage is explosive fun. There's certainly homage paid to Hollywood's interstellar fare. The space suits are *2001*-influenced and there's a Chewbacca-inspired "space beast". Yet directors Fukuda and Nakano understand what *The War in Space* is: an old school Japanese special effects film. This is hardly a state of the art, trailblazing production like *Star Wars*. It's a classical *tokusatsu* flick with spaceships still hung from piano wires in front of lightbulbs meant to represent a starfield. The scenes inside the invading aliens' Roman-style ship have a Mario Bava-style weirdness with surreal architecture. *Godzilla vs. Mechagodzilla*'s Goro Mutsumi shows up in blue face paint and a Centurion costume. Add to this a rockin' score by Toshiaki Tsushima and you've got a silly but exhilarating picture. At its best, *The War in Space* is like a live action *Space Battleship Yamato* movie made in the classic Toho style. This is taken a step further in the *manga* adaptation that draws Yuko Asano's Jun just like *Yamato*'s Yuki Mori. *The War in Space* is far from one of Toho's best films but hardly on par with later disasters like *Bye Bye Jupiter*.

SHINICHI SEKIZAWA
The Fantasy Scribe

関沢新一
6/2/1920-11/19/1992

"If the story were very positive or even child-like, it would go to Sekizawa. Sekizawa had more of a humanistic touch. He has a very joyous and at times very humorous sensibility..."
-Ishiro Honda, from *Ishiro Honda: A Life in Film, From Godzilla to Kurosawa* (2017) by Steve Ryfle and Ed Godziszewski

Shinichi Sekizawa was Toho's other science fiction screenwriter. He was usually recruited for more hopeful stories with a fantastical flair. Sekizawa was a far younger man than Takeshi Kimura and known for an eccentric charm. He often wore kimonos in public rather than Western clothing and had an obsession with locomotive trains. Sekizawa was born in Kyoto. Like many of his contemporaries, he had a painful experience fighting at the brutal Pacific War front. Returning to Japan in 1946, he turned to almost eclectic pursuits. He was an assistant and writer to director Hiroshi Shimizu, including on *Children of the Beehive* (1948) and *Buddha's Children* (1952). He also studied *manga* under genre luminary Osamu Tezuka. In 1956 he wrote and directed an independent film called *The Fearful Invasion of Flying Saucers*. Distributed by Shin Toho after Daiei and Toho passed on it, it starred Tadao Takashima in an early role. *Flying Saucers* was believed to be a lost film until a 16mm print turned up at auction in 2010.

Sekizawa soon joined Toho as a screenwriter, one of his first films being *Varan* (1958). He wrote films in numerous genres including Kihachi Okamoto's 1960 *The Last Gunfight* and *Westward Desperado*. Yet after 1961's *Mothra* he began to specialize in fantastical science fiction scripts. He wrote more Godzilla entries than any other screenwriter. He was also a lyricist, ghost writing songs for films under the pseudonym Mamoru Yoshiike. These included some of the most popular tunes of Japan's original post-war idol, Hibari Misora. Sekizawa wrote a few *anime* films as well including Toei's *Jack and the Witch* and contributed to the pilot of Tsuburaya Pro's *Ultraman*. Tetsuo Kinjo, the Ultra series scribe, was something of Sekizawa's protege. Sekizawa also created and wrote the kaiju TV miniseries *Agon: The Atomic Dragon*. Filmed in 1964, *Agon* was not broadcast until 1968. This was due to legal red-tape from Toho who accused Sekizawa of breaching the "non-compete" clause in his contract. After the 1970s, Sekizawa largely retired. He devoted his remaining years to photographing trains and building models of them; a hobby he adored. In 1990, he received the government's Medal with Purple Ribbon for his achievements in screenwriting.

Selected Filmography (as screenwriter)

Children of the Beehive (1948) [assistant director]

Buddha's Children (1952) [assistant director]

The Fearful Invasion of Flying Saucers (1956) [director]

Varan (1958)

Battle in Outer Space (1959)

The Last Gunfight (1960)

Secret of the Teligian (1960)

Westward Desperado (1960)

Mothra (1961)

King Kong vs. Godzilla (1962)

Warring Clans (1963)

Atragon (1963)

Mothra vs. Godzilla (1964)

Dogora (1964)

Ghidorah, the Three-Headed Monster (1964)

Invasion of Astro-Monster (1965)

Ultraman *[episode 1]* (TV, 1966)

Zero Fighter (1966)

Ebirah, Horror of the Deep (1966)

The Killing Bottle (1967)

Jack and the Witch (1967)

Son of Godzilla (1967)

Agon: The Atomic Dragon *[episodes 1-4]* (TV, 1968)

Latitude Zero (1969)

All Monsters Attack (1969)

Godzilla vs. Gigan (1972)

Godzilla vs. Megalon (1973)

Godzilla vs. Mechagodzilla (1974) [original story]

MOTHRA vs. GODZILLA

Mosura tai Gojira "Mothra vs. Godzilla"
Toho, 4/29/1964 (*Showa 39*), 6 Reels (2,444 meters), 88:36, 35mm, TohoScope (2.35:1 anamorphic), Eastman color, monaural sound

Crew
Producers: Tomoyuki Tanaka, Sanezumi Fujimoto
Director: Ishiro Honda
Special Effects Director: Eiji Tsuburaya
Screenplay: Shinichi Sekizawa
Director of Photography: Hajime Koizumi
Music: Akira Ifukube
Assistant Director: Koji Kajita
Production Design: Takeo Kita
Editor: Ryohei Fujii
Sound Recordist: Fumio Yanoguchi
Sound Effects: Sadamasa Nishimoto
Sound Editor: Hisashi Shimonaga

Lighting: Shoshichi Kojima
Production Manager: Boku Morimoto
Assistant SFX Director: Teruyoshi Nakano
SFX Cinematography: Sadamasa Arikawa, Mototaka Tomioka
SFX Art Director: Akira Watanabe
SFX Lighting: Kuichiro Kishida
SFX Optical Photography: Yukio Manoda, Yoshiyuki Tokumasa
SFX Continuity: Hiroshi Mukoyama
SFX Production Manager: Tadashi Koike

Still Photographer: Jiro Tsuchiya

Cast
Akira Takarada *(Ichiro Sakai)*
Yuriko Hoshi *(Junko Nakanishi)*
Hiroshi Koizumi *(Professor Miura)*
Yu Fujiki *(Jiro Nakamura)*
Kenji Sahara *(Torahata)*
Emi Ito *(Twin Fairy)*
Yumi Ito *(Twin Fairy)*
Yoshifumi Tajima *(Kumayama)*
Jun Tazaki *(Editor)*
Kenzo Tabu *(Prefectural Assemblyman)*

Yoshio Kosugi *(Chief of Infant Island)*

Akira Tani *(Village Headman)*

Susumu Fujita *(JSDF General)*

Yutaka Sada *(School Principal)*

Ikio Sawamura *(Priest)*

Ren Yamamoto *(Sailor)*

Yasuhisa Tsutsumi *(Police Officer At Dock)*

Miki Yashiro *(Teacher)*

Shin Otomo *(Police Officer)*

Senkichi Omura *(Fisherman)*

Yutaka Nakayama *(Fisherman)*

Koji Iwamoto *(Fisherman)*

Koji Uno *(Fisherman)*

Takuzo Kumagai *(Fisherman)*

Jiro Tsuchiya *(Fisherman)*

Hiroshi Akitsu *(Fisherman)*

Kozo Nomura *(Soldier)*

Hideo Shibuya *(Reporter)*

Wataru Omae *((Happy Enterprises Employee))*

Toshihiko Furuta *(Soldier)*

Tadashi Okabe *(Soldier)*

Seishiro Kuno *(Aide)*

Mitsuo Tsuda *(JSDF)*

Terumi Oka *(Hotel Waitress)*

Koji Uruki *(Reporter)*

Kenzo Echigo *(Reporter)*

Yukihiko Gondo *(Happy Enterprises Employee)*

Koichi Sato *(Happy Enterprises Employee)*

Haruya Sakamoto *(Soldier)*

Hiroshi Takagi *(Happy Enterprises Employee)*

Keisuke Yamada *(Police Chief)*

Shinjiro Hirota *(Happy Enterprises Employee)*

Shigeru Sunagawa *(Fisherman)*

Ikuo Kawamura *(Transport Aircraft Pilot)*

Rinsaku Ogata *(Transport Aircraft Co-Pilot)*

Haruo Suzuki *(SDF Radioman)*

Haruo Nakajima *(Godzilla)*

Katsumi Tezuka *(Godzilla)*

Alternate Titles

Godzilla vs. the Thing (U.S.)

Godzilla vs. Mothra (U.S. video title)

Godzilla und die Urwelt-Raupen **[Godzilla and the Monster Larva]** (Germany)

Mothra contre Godzilla (France)

Godzilla contra los monstruos **[Godzilla vs. the Monsters]** (Spain)

Godzilla contra Mothra (Mexico)

Watang! Nel favoloso impero dei mostri **[In the Fabled Empire of Monsters]** (Italy)

Επιχείρησις Φούτζι Γιάμα **[Operation Mount Fuji]** (Greece)

Godzilla Contra a Ilha Sagrada **[Godzilla Against the Sacred Island]** (Brazil)

Mothra Contra Godzilla (Portugal)

Mothra möter Godzilla (Sweden)

Годзилла против Мотры (Russia)

Godzilla kontra Mothra (Poland)

"SEE the armies of the world destroyed! SEE the BIRTH of the world's most terrifying monster! SEE the war of the GIANTS!"
-U.S. poster (1964)

Mothra vs. Godzilla is among the very finest Godzilla sequels. It is a classic Japanese monster picture and signature Ishiro Honda and Eiji Tsuburaya production. Thematically expanding on both, *Mothra vs. Godzilla* manages to be a worthy follow-up to both the 1954 *Godzilla* and 1961 *Mothra*. Honda and Tsuburaya's teams are in top form; producing their most dynamic work.

PLOT

A typhoon batters coastal Japan's industrial areas. Reporter Ichiro Sakai (Akira Takarada) and his photographer Junko Nakanishi (Yuriko Hoshi) cover the clean-up. Junko finds a mysterious object appearing to be a huge scale in the debris. Soon afterwards, a giant egg drifts into a fishing village's waters. The villagers bring the egg to shore and sell it to entrepreneur

Kumayama (Yoshifumi Tajima). Biology Professor Miura (Hiroshi Koizumi) attempts to take samples for study. He is shut down by Kumayama, who also humiliates Junko.

Kumayama discusses plans to build an amusement park around the egg with his investor Torahata (Kenji Sahara). The Twin Fairies (Emi and Yumi Ito) of Infant Island visit the men, begging for the egg to be returned. The two men unmoved by their pleas, the Fairies barely escape. Sakai, Junko and Miura next encounter the Fairies in a nearby forest. The Twin Fairies explain that the egg belongs to Mothra. If it is not returned it will hatch into a larvae that will cause destruction. The trio meets with Kumayama and Torahata but they are again unswayed. The Twin Fairies return to Infant Island.

Sakai and Junko are next summoned to Miura's laboratory. He reveals that the strange object they discovered earlier was radioactive. They return to the beachfront where it was found. As Miura tests for radioactivity, Godzilla, who had been buried in the sand, resurfaces. The creature makes for Nagoya. It attacks the Yokkaichi industrial region and destroys Nagoya Castle. Sakai's fellow reporter Jiro Nakamura (Yu Fujiki) comes up with the idea that Mothra could defeat Godzilla. Sakai, Junko and Professor Miura travel to Infant Island to ask for Mothra's help. The chief (Yoshio Kosugi) and Twin Fairies refuse. After impassioned pleas from Junko and Sakai, Mothra chooses to help

them. However, the Fairies warn the trio that Mothra is nearing the end of her life.

BACKGROUND

After *King Kong vs. Godzilla* was a blockbuster hit, Toho was eager to continue the Godzilla series. A direct follow-up to *King Kong vs. Godzilla* was considered, as was a film pitting Frankenstein's Monster against Godzilla. The script for the latter would become *Frankenstein Conquers the World,* sans Godzilla, in 1965. Toho decided that pairing Mothra against Godzilla was their best bet. The early draft for *Mothra vs. Godzilla* by Shinichi Sekizawa, submitted on New Years Eve 1963, was significantly different. The characters of Junko and Torahata were absent and Dr. Miura had an apprentice. In place of Mothra's egg was a comatose Godzilla; wrongly believed to be dead and also exploited by Kumayama. The script was envisioned as a more direct sequel to *Mothra*. Godzilla revives and attacked that film's Rolisica. The Rolisican army fires powerful, new "Frontier Missiles" at Godzilla. Instead of Nagoya Castle, Godzilla destroys Himeji. The main characters also offer themselves as hostages to the Infant Islanders in exchange for Mothra's help. The finale was to be a confrontation between Godzilla and imago (winged) Mothra in Tokyo. Sekizawa revised this script with the input of Ishiro Honda. Godzilla's body was changed to Mothra's egg and a twist was added where the egg hatches into "twins".

PRINCIPAL PHOTOGRAPHY

Mothra vs. Godzilla is a monster picture where Honda and Tsuburaya's units are in top form and synergy. By this time, Honda and company were beginning to take a more serious note of Godzilla's appeal to children. Yet it was a sweet spot where the stories were still mature enough for adult audiences. For Honda, Akira Takarada, Yuriko Hoshi and Hiroshi Koizumi play a similar trio of protagonists to those in the original *Mothra*. Yoshifumi Tajima plays his most memorable role as the greedy but pitiful Kumayama. Kenji Sahara is once again cast against type as the slimy Torahata. To develop the character, Sahara spent time around real estate agents. To Honda and Sahara, Torahata was a symbol of human greed. When filming Torahata's pummeling, Honda and Sahara decided to give the character a bloody end. Though Honda warned him that being bloodied might *"wreck his cool guy image"*, Sahara didn't care. Honda was disappointed, however, in the Infant Island sequences. He wanted a bleaker, more desolate vision of the island than was seen in *Mothra*. Due to the lower budget he had to use scaled down interior sets with obvious artificial rocks.

SFX

In spite of the lower budget and fewer miniatures, Tsuburaya's team shines with some of their most creative work. Godzilla's new design is among the finest in the series. The suit was sculpted by Eizo Kaimai and the Yagi Brothers with its head made by Teizo Toshimitsu. The teeth and claws were made by Keizo Murase. The suit was made with input from Haruo Nakajima himself, built lighter than previous ones. Godzilla's appearance is softened with a feline quality. Yet it is still a terror to be reckoned with: a rampaging *yonaoshi* god heralding destruction and chaos. The suit, with slight modifications, went on to be reused in the next entry: *Ghidorah, the Three-Headed Monster* (also 1964). It also would be refurbished to play Gomess in the pilot episode of Tsuburaya Pro's *Ultra Q*. The suit's body was used to create Jirass in episode 10 of *Ultraman* as well.

Nakajima gives his signature Godzilla performance with a distinctive character that's almost mischievous. Nakajima improvised a now iconic moment where Godzilla, having emerged from seaside mudflats, shakes the sand from its skin. For Godzilla's Nagoya rampage, a detailed miniature of Nagoya Castle was built in the span of a week. Trouble was, it was constructed so well that Nakajima was unable to destroy it. The structure was partially repaired, weakened and another take was done. The scene was well salvaged in the edit, using footage from both takes. Tsuburaya's team shot background plates for the Nagoya sequence as well, somewhat in lieu of miniatures. Nakajima also had trouble destroying the miniature incubator around the Mothra's egg prop. The finished scene took a lot of coordination between Nakajima and the staff who manned the piano wires. Close-ups of the incubator being smashed were done with a separate prop tail. This was quite heavy; requiring two stagehands to operate.

One sequence that was filmed but cut from the Japanese version features a U.S.-led military force attacking Godzilla with "Frontier Missiles". These scenes were shot on location at the Nakatajima sand dunes in Hamamatsu. Ishiro Honda allegedly felt unsure of how Japanese audiences would react to a display of American military might on Japanese soil. It's said Honda's personal copy of the script had this scene later crossed out. It would be included in American International Pictures' U.S. version, *Godzilla vs. the Thing*.

The Mothra prop from the 1961 original was reused in some scenes, mainly the shots on Infant Island. Imago Mothra was scaled down considerably for this film to better match Godzilla's size. A new, larger and better made Mothra was built for most shots. This new marionette was almost twice as large as the original, with an eight foot body and 15 foot wingspan. The prop was given motorized, radio controlled parts to allow the legs and head to move. A motor, coupled with a Y-shaped wire brace, was also used to make the wings flap quicker and better than in the first *Mothra*. For the wide shot of Mothra's egg on the beach, a matte painting was used, but in most shots a miniature was used. For the shots of Mothra's egg "hatching", a second egg was constructed. This prop was created by molding glue and a calcium substance made from crushed oyster shells around a styrofoam orb. The styrofoam was then removed with a hot wire, creating a

hollow shell that was easy to crack. Two foot hand puppets were used to portray the larvae as they hatched. In the original, the larval Mothra was portrayed pantomime horse style, here Tsuburaya and his team built two sets of mechanical props. The first pair were built for the land scenes and were radio controlled, though augmented with wire. The second were for the water scenes, built with a motorized and rotating conveyor belt by engineer Sojiro Ijima. This created a self propelled up-and-down motion as the larvae swam. This mechanism would later be salvaged and re-used for the monster Namegon on *Ultra Q*. The beaks on all the Mothra props were wooden cores coated in rubber.

Tsuburaya's team shows even more ease in using the Oxberry printer this time around. The printer is used to almost seamlessly integrate the tiny Twin Fairies in with actor footage. The Fairies are better executed in scale than in *Mothra*, with oversized sets combined with the Oxberry composites. Sadamasa Arikawa's camera work throughout Tsuburaya's sequences is some of his most dynamic with inventive angles. Imago Mothra's battle with Godzilla is among Tsuburaya's masterworks as special effects director. It is a kinetically edited, Eisensteinian sequence with creative use of suits, marionettes, puppets and miniatures. The monsters are realistically manipulated. High speed photography is integrated to create a ferocious, chaotic effect. Puppets, though mismatched, are used for certain shots to make the battle more brutal. Arikawa objected to the use of the Godzilla puppet.

Tsuburaya was steadfast, saying it was necessary for the story. Arikawa and Tsuburaya got into one of the most heated arguments of their long working career, with Arikawa almost quitting. Years later, Arikawa got into a similar argument with his cameraman, Mototaka Tomioka, and realized his mentor was right. A lot more footage of the puppet in *Mothra vs. Godzilla* was shot; much of it left on the cutting room floor.

Another standout is the film's finale with the Mothra larva cocooning Godzilla. The cocoon silk was largely the same recipe as in *Mothra*. It was sticky and corrosive. Protection was required for the camera and it burned the skin of crew members. For offscreen shots, the mixture was poured into a cup with small holes on its top and placed into a large industrial fan. It would shoot out and solidify in the air as the fan spun. For close-ups of the material being fired from the Mothra larvae's mouths, a compressed air dispenser was built into the puppets' beaks akin to a silly string can. This substance could only be removed with gasoline which meant the Godzilla suit had to be soaked in it after shooting. For water shots, particularly the cocooned Godzilla plunging into the ocean at the end, the suit from *King Kong vs. Godzilla* was used.

MUSIC

Akira Ifukube's score is one of his very finest. It alternates from intense and heavy to poetic and ethereal. The *"Terror of Godzilla"* theme from *King Kong vs. Godzilla* is reused but expanded and reorchestrated to sound more menacing. Yuji Koseki's *"Song of Mothra"* is integrated by Ifukube as well. A standout is *"Sacred Springs"*, Ifukube's only song he ever composed for The Peanuts. Ifukube was less secure in his ability to compose songs for pop artists. This was a major reason why he had turned down Honda's offer to score the original *Mothra* three years prior. Regardless, *"Sacred Springs"* is a hauntingly beautiful piece. It would be impressively reworked for 1992's *Godzilla vs. Mothra*. During the scoring for *Mothra vs. Godzilla*, Honda and Ifukube had a rare professional disagreement. In a scene where, ala the 1954 original, Godzilla sticks its head over a hill, Ifukube thought the scene would play better with no music. Honda disagreed and wanted a variant of Godzilla's theme to play at that moment. When Ifukube would not renege, Honda inserted Godzilla's theme from an earlier scene without telling him. At a staff screening of the film, Ifukube shot Ishiro Honda a dirty look to which Honda returned his usual meek grin and shrug.

REAL WORLD

Mothra vs. Godzilla is among the most military heavy Godzilla films, featuring the army mounting an intricate defense. By this time, the American Sherman and Chaffee tanks had been phased out. The Japanese Self Defense Force developed their own novel tank, their first built post-war. The Type 61 started development in 1955 and began to be rolled out in 1961. Powered by a diesel engine and mounted with a 90mm cannon, it saw service in the SDF until the year 2000. It was supplanted by Type 74 and Type 90 tanks.

Mothra vs. Godzilla is the first kaiju film to feature Type 61 tanks. By this time, the involvement of the SDF was lessening and Honda had to use military exercise footage from *The Mysterians*. Tsuburaya used entirely miniature tanks for these scenes. These were not built from scratch but modified from commercial models bought at the local toy store.

THEMES AND MOTIFS

Mothra vs. Godzilla is a rare sequel to successfully expand upon not one predecessor but two. It's a *kaiju Empire Strikes Back* to the *Star Wars* of the 1954 *Godzilla* and 1961 *Mothra*. It effectively combines the anti-nuclear themes and "monster on the loose" tropes of *Godzilla* with the magical realism of *Mothra*. Sekizawa's script is darker than average for him with a biting satire on corporate greed. Whereas *Mothra* seemed to criticize Western capitalism, *Mothra vs. Godzilla* takes a universal focus. 1964 was when the Tokyo Olympics took place and Japan's economy was booming. The film's themes are a cautionary warning on the cost of the post-war economic miracle. While this is a bit ironic coming from a soon-to-be corporate giant like Toho, Honda and Sekizawa state it earnestly. The themes are similar to those in *King Kong vs. Godzilla*. Yet *King Kong vs. Godzilla* mocked such greed in a lighthearted fashion akin to Toho's popular *Company President* and *Salaryman* comedies. *Mothra vs. Godzilla* depicts corporate evil in a deadpan manner that would have made Erich Von Stroheim blush,

going full force as the villain is gruesomely beaten to a pulp.

RELEASE AND LEGACY

Mothra vs. Godzilla was not the hit *King Kong vs. Godzilla* was, making less than half of its gross. Among both Japanese and Western fans, however, it quickly became a favorite. It was re-released in Japan in both 1970 and 1980. The film was given a soft remake of sorts with *Godzilla vs. Mothra* in 1992. Both Godzilla and Mothra would return in *Ghidorah, the Three-Headed Monster*, released only eight months later.

ALTERNATE VERSIONS

Via producer Henry G. Saperstein, the rights of *Mothra vs. Godzilla* were sold to American International Pictures. Released widely on September 17th, 1964, the film was retitled *Godzilla vs. the Thing*. AIP did a creative ad blitz obscuring Mothra as Godzilla's foe. The art was painted by prolific horror poster and comic artist Reynold Brown. He painted Mothra as a tentacled beast behind a board marked "censored". The U.S. version runs around 88:11, with theatrical prints containing an overture in lieu of Toho's logo. It was double-billed with the Czech sci-fi film *Voyage to the End of the Universe*, also dubbed into English.

Godzilla vs. the Thing was the first U.S. version to contain minimal alterations. A scene showing Kumayama promoting his show to the public was cut. The *"Sacred Springs"* song is cut down and Kumayama being shot by Torahata is sanitized to remove blood. Ifukube's score, however, is not altered for this scene. It runs at a different sync, patching the moment of silence the Japanese version has before imago Mothra arrives. The final exchange between Sakai, Miura and Junko as the twin Mothras swim away is also cut. The most significant change is that the Frontier Missile sequence, excised from Honda's cut, is reinstated.

The English dub was recorded in New York by Titra Sound Studios. Dubbing cast includes Bernard Grant (Sakai), Kenneth Harvey (Miura), Larry Robinson (Nakamura), Paulette Rubinstein (Twin Fairy), Terry Van Tell (Twin Fairy), Jack Curtis (Torahata), Bret Morrison (Kumayama) and Peter Fernandez in several small roles. It is one of the very best classic dubs ever recorded for a Japanese monster picture. It features careful sync, realistic vocal performances and a lot of nostalgia for many.

For the winter 1970 Champion Matsuri Festival, *Mothra vs, Godzilla* was reissued in an edited version. Supervised by Ishiro Honda, the original negative was cut to save money. This presented preservation problems down the road. The Champion cut of *Mothra vs. Godzilla* runs 74:05. The lion's share of cuts are to dialogue scenes in Honda's end with Tsuburaya's portions of the movie left almost untouched. The opening of Sakai and Junko's introductory sequence early on is cut. The scene with the fishermen discussing what to do about Mothra's egg is cut in half. The openings and endings of many scenes are truncated. The

Twin Fairies' explanation of the egg being washed away in a hurricane is placed over the flashback as narration. A short segment showing the natives of Infant Island in this scene is also cut. Kumayama calling Torahata to borrow money from him is edited out. Junko mentioning to Sakai that Miura wants to see them to discuss the Godzilla scale is cut. The opening of the discussion the heroes have with Sakai's editor on how to stop Godzilla is also excised. The heroes arriving on Infant Island where they encounter a radiation poisoned sea turtle-like creature and are captured by the islanders is taken out. Later on, much of the first military briefing is cut along with the opening of the Kumayama-Torahata confrontation. The film's final reel is left mostly intact. The scene featuring the school principal begging for help to rescue the stranded class is cut down and rearranged slightly. Interestingly, bits cut from the U.S. version are left in. These include the complete *"Sacred Springs"* number and the heroes' final conversation as the Fairies and Mothras depart.

AMERICAN HOME VIDEO HISTORY

In 1989, *Mothra vs. Godzilla* was released to VHS and Betamax by Paramount Home Video. This television and video cut, retitled *Godzilla vs. Mothra*, was subtly different. There's some excised dialog and a new video generated title card. It was reissued by Paramount to VHS and laserdisc in 1994. Simitar acquired the rights soon after in 1998 and it was released to VHS and DVD. Some VHS versions and the DVD were early releases in widescreen format. Classic Media soon acquired the rights and released a barebones DVD of the old UPA TV master in 2002. A better DVD edition containing both the Japanese and U.S. versions followed in 2006. While the U.S. version was more complete than in the UPA master, it was sourced from an HDTV master cropped to 16:9. Classic Media reissued the disc in later years. In the late 2010s Janus Films acquired *Mothra vs. Godzilla*. First made available for streaming on FilmStruck and then The Criterion Channel, the film was included in 2019's *Godzilla: The Showa Era* Criterion set. Sadly, the U.S. version was not included.

Further Viewing:

(1964)

三大怪獣 地球最大の決戦

Toho, *Director*: **Ishiro Honda**

1964 was the Year of the Dragon in the Chinese Zodiac. It is fitting that it was not only the year where Toho released two Godzilla entries but heralded the introduction of tri-headed arch foe King Ghidorah. *Ghidorah, the Three-Headed Monster* is another classic monster mash from Honda and Tsuburaya. The film was rushed into production when Toho needed a film for the 1964 holiday season as Kurosawa's *Red Beard* was delayed. Like *Atragon*, production values are still top tier in spite of its hectic schedule. Bringing Godzilla, Rodan and Mothra together to battle a worse foe, it was a proto-crossover film before *The Avengers*

made it trendy. It was also the first major humanization of Godzilla, something even Honda had strong reservations about.

The human story is more engaging than average. It involves a princess (Akiko Wakabayashi) from a Tibet-like country targeted by assassins. She's possessed by an alien spirit from Venus and develops the ability to see the future. She soon predicts the arrival of world-destroying space monster King Ghidorah. Wakabayashi (1939-) was one of Toho's most lovely and talented actresses. With Audrey Hepburn-like beauty, she appeared in several foreign productions, most notably the 007 entry *You Only Live Twice*. Character player Hisaya Ito also makes an impression in his most notable role as the sociopathic assassin Malness. The role was written with Yoshio Tsuchiya in mind, but Ito more than makes it his own. In general, the human scenes are well integrated with Tsuburaya's FX work which takes the stage as the film proceeds.

While Tsuburaya's work is more uneven than in *Mothra vs. Godzilla*, there are two particular standout sequences. The first is a scene where King Ghidorah is explosively "birthed" from a fallen meteorite. This scene masterfully uses complex suitmation, ingenious pyrotechnics, miniature photography and even cel animation. Another well executed sequence shows King Ghidorah's gravity beams raining hellfire on Tokyo's buildings. The optical animation was once again done by Sadao Iizuka and is a colorful eyeful. These two scenes are among Tsuburaya's strongest and show off the beauty of the tokusatsu artform. The iconic King Ghidorah was designed by Akira Watanabe with the heads modeled by Teizo Toshimitsu. It was based on the eight-headed hydra-like *Yamata no Orochi* of Japanese folklore. Tsuburaya had brought the creature itself to life in 1959's *The Three Treasures*. His decision for Ghidorah to be golden was at the last minute, as the suit had already been painted green. Ghidorah was stuntman Koji Uruki in a suit which contained a metal bar for balance. Meanwhile, the heads, wings and tails were controlled by wire operators. For the impressive pantomime finale where the four monsters do battle, it took 25 staff members to operate the wires.

Ghidorah features a scene where, with the Twin Fairies as translator, baby Mothra tries to convince Godzilla and Rodan to battle beside her. This overt humanization of the monsters was the start of a new direction for the series. It was the final nail in the coffin, for now, of Godzilla as a nuclear parable. For the remainder of the *Showa* series, Godzilla was still a destructive *yonaoshi* god, but one humanity has struck a sort of truce with. Yet *Ghidorah, the Three-Headed Monster* is another classic entry from the series at its peak. The heavily edited U.S. version was often paired with the Elvis Presley vehicle *Harum Scarum*. The King of Monsters vs. the King of Rock must have been one surreal night at the drive-in. In re-runs, *Ghidorah* was also sometimes paired with *Doctor Who and the Daleks* and, a few years later, *Night of the Living Dead.*

AKIRA TAKARADA
The Gentleman

宝田明

4/9/1934-

Akira Takarada is one of Toho's most handsome and professional leading men with a Humphrey Bogart-like style. Known for his generosity to fans, anyone who has met Takarada can attest that he is a gentleman of the highest order. Akira Takarada was born on April 9th, 1934 in what is now North Korea. His father was an engineer and was soon transferred to Northern Manchuria. Takarada and his family lived in Harbin, Heilongjiang Province from the time he was two. As he was raised in North China, he speaks fluent Mandarin. When Japan surrendered, the Russians invaded. The Soviets showed little mercy to the retreating Japanese as the military had conducted medical experiments there. As his family fled in 1946, a 12 year old Takarada witnessed Russian soldiers raping a Japanese woman. Later, while searching for his brother, he was shot. It was an Imperial army doctor who removed the bullet from his body.

The Takaradas returned to Japan, settling in Murakami City in Niigata, the hometown of

Akira's father. After graduating from high school, Akira Takarada's good looks and natural talent got him accepted into Toho's New Face program. Takarada was in the Class of 1953. His classmates included Kenji Sahara, Momoko Kochi, Yu Fujiki and Masumi Okada.

His debut was in 1954's *And Then the Liberty Bell Rang*. Takarada's big break came soon after when director Ishiro Honda cast him in a leading role in the new monster film *Godzilla*. Takarada rocketed to fame and was soon an in-demand leading man at Toho. At his peak, he starred in seven pictures a year. He still found time to party, however and often went out drinking at Ginza. One of the most popular films he starred in was the 1961 romantic comedy *A Night in Hong Kong*. A co-production with Hong Kong studio Cathay, it paired Takarada with HK superstar Lucille Yu Ming. Takarada also appeared in a pair of follow-ups, *Star of Hong Kong* (1962) and *White Rose of Hong Kong* (1965). He also starred in Yasujiro Ozu's *The End of Summer* (1961) and made a return to the Godzilla series with 1964's *Mothra vs. Godzilla*. Takarada additionally played the role of spy Andrew Hoshino in 1965's *Iron Finger* (aka *100 Shot, 100 Killed*) and its 1968 sequel *Booted Babe, Busted Boss*.

In 1966, Takarada married beauty queen Akiko Kojima, the 1959 Miss Universe. They had a daughter, Michiru. After 1969's *Latitude Zero*, Takarada's contract at Toho expired. He mainly appeared on television dramas in the '70s. He was also active in plays, fittingly portraying Clark Gable's Rhett Butler in a Tokyo stage version of *Gone With the Wind*. He began to make a comeback to films in the '80s. In 1992 he appeared in Juzo Itami's *Minbo or the Gentle Art of Japanese Extortion*. He also returned to the Godzilla series that same year with Takao Okawara's *Godzilla vs. Mothra*. Takarada is also a frequent voice actor. He provided the Japanese voice for Jafar in Disney's *Aladdin*. Takarada reprised the role for Tokyo Disneyland attractions and in their *Kingdom Hearts* series of video games. His final appearance in the Godzilla series was 2004's *Godzilla: Final Wars*. He was cast in Gareth Edwards' 2014 *Godzilla* but his scene was cut from the film. Most recently, he appeared in *The Great Buddha Arrival* in 2019. In the meantime, Takarada is popular in the convention circuit where he is known for his kindness.

Selected Filmography (as actor)

And Then the Liberty Bell Rang (1954)
Godzilla (1954)
Half Human (1955)
On the Wings of Love (1957)
Samurai Saga (1959)
The Three Treasures (1959)
Storm Over the Pacific (1960)
A Night in Hong Kong (1961)
The Last War (1961)
The End of Summer (1961)
Star of Hong Kong (1962)
Chushingura (1962)
Mothra vs. Godzilla (1964)
Iron Finger (1965)
White Rose of Hong Kong (1965)
Invasion of Astro-Monster (1965)
Ebirah, Horror of the Deep (1966)
King Kong Escapes (1967)
Let's Go! Young Guy (1967)
Booted Babe, Busted Boss (1968)
Latitude Zero (1969)
The Legend of Plumeria (1983)
Tales of a Golden Geisha (1990)

Minbo or the Gentle Art of Japanese Extortion (1992)
Godzilla vs. Mothra (1992)
Aladdin (1992) [voice, Japanese version]

Kingdom Hearts (2002, video game) [voice, Japanese version]
Godzilla: Final Wars (2004)
Kingdom Hearts II (2005, video game) [voice, Japanese version]

Godzilla (2014) [scene deleted]
The Great Buddha Arrival (2019)

GAMERA THE GIANT MONSTER

大怪獣ガメラ

Daikaiju Gamera "Gamera, the Giant Monster"
Daei, 11/27/1965 (*Showa 40*), 7 Reels (2,164 meters), 78:33, 35mm, DaieiScope (2.35:1 anamorphic), black and white, monaural sound

Crew
Executive Producer: Masaichi Nagata
Producer: Hidemasa Nagata
Producer/Planning: Yonejiro Saito
Director: Noriaki Yuasa
Screenplay: Niisan Takahashi
Director of Photography: Nobuo Munekawa
Music: Tadashi Yamauchi
Art Director: Akira Inoue
Assistant Director: Shima Abe
Editor: Tatsuji Nakashizu
Sound Recording: Toshikazu Watanabe
Lighting: Yukio Ito
Production Manager: Hiroaki Ueshima
Special Effects: Yonesaburo Tsukiji
SFX Continuity: Kazufumi Fujii
Lighting: Mamoru Ishizaka
Miniatures: Haruo Sekiya
Assistant SFX Director: Kiyoshi Ishida
SFX Production Manager: Kiyoshi Kawamura

Still Photographer: Koichi Katsukake

Cast
Eiji Funakoshi *(Dr. Hidaka)*
Harumi Kiritachi *(Kyoko Yamamoto)*
Junichiro Yamashita *(Aoyagi)*
Yoshiro Uchida *(Toshio Sakurai)*
Michiko Sugata *(Nobuyo Sakurai)*
Yoshiro Kitahara *(Mr. Sakurai)*
Jun Hamamura *(Professor Murase)*
Kenji Oyama *(Minister of Defense)*
Munehiko Takada *(Soviet Representative)*
Yoshio Yoshida *(Inuit Chief)*
Jun Osanai *(Chidori Maru Captain)*
Daihachi Kita *(Chidori Maru Navigator)*
Kazuo Mori *(Chidori Maru Radioman)*
Koji Fujiyama *(Dock Foreman)*

Osamu Okawa *(Radar Technician)*
Ikuji Oka *(Fighter Pilot)*
Bokuzen Hidari *(Old Farmer)*
Fumiko Murata *(Farmer's Wife)*
Shigeru Kato *(Farmer's Grandson)*
Jutaro Hojo *(Self Defense Force Commander)*
Daigo Inoue *(Self Defense Force Adjutant)*
Takehiko Goto *(Self Defense Force Cessna Pilot)*
Chiduru Ko *(Stripper)*
Ryoko Oki *(Stripper)*
Kenichi Tani *(Policeman)*
Akira Shimizu *(Dancing Youth)*
Yasuo Araki *(Self Defense Force Soldier)*
Kenji Oba *(Self Defense Force Soldier)*
Ichigen Ohashi *(Mr. Ueda)*
Tatsushi Fujii *(Official at Haneda Airport)*
Yuji Moriya *(News Announcer)*
Kenichiro Yamane *(Geothermal Station Engineer)*

Tsutomu Nakata (*Toshio's Uncle*)
Wakayo Matsumura (*Customer*)
Misato Kawashima (*Teacher*)
Saburo Kurihara (*Ichiro*)
Tetsuro Takeuchi (*Japan Broadcasting Station Announcer*)
Shin Minatsu (*Sapporo Broadcasting Station Announcer*)
Rin Sugimori (*Police Station Chief*)
Shinichi Matsuyama (*Operator*)
Toichiro Kagawa (*Operator*)
Kyosuke Shiho (*Fish Seller*)
Shunji Sayama (*Fish Seller*)
Ken Nakahara (*Fish Seller*)

Shigeo Hagiwara (*Child at Lighthouse*)
Tetsu Furuya (*Child at Lighthouse*)
Osamu Maruyama (*Atomic Energy Research Institute Chief*)
Toshio Maki (*Atomic Energy Research Institute Staff*)
Kazuo Sumida (*Atomic Energy Research Institute Staff*)
Ichiro Ise (*Reporter*)
Shinji Sayama (*Reporter*)
Hajime Munechika (*Reporter*)
Tsukako Fujino (*Stewardess*)
M. Anabai
Richardson
Streihan
Ranson
Hank Brown (*U.S, Fighter Pilot*)

Hartman
Gunter Braun (*News Reporter*)
Teruo Aragaki (*Gamera*)
Kazuo Yagi (*Gamera*)
Shizuo Chujo (*Narrator*)

<u>Alternate Titles</u>
Gammera, the Invincible (U.S.)
Gamera (U.S. video title)
Gamera - Frankensteins Monster aus dem Eis **[Gamera - Frankenstein's monster from the ice]** (Germany)
El mundo bajo el terror **[The World Under Terror]** (Spain)
Gammera - O Monstro Invencível **[Gammera - The Invincible Monster]** (Brazil)
Гамера (Russia)

"GAMMERA! The super-monster that even the H-bomb cannot destroy!"
-Narrator (Jack Curtis), U.S. Trailer

Gamera, the Giant Monster is the first of Daiei's Gamera franchise; the longest running competitor to Godzilla. It's not a great film but is an important one. The production values are less polished than Toho's and director Noriaki Yuasa's style is pedestrian compared to Honda and Tsuburaya's. Yet *Gamera, the Giant Monster* boasts a starker tone than its sequels, aided by atmospheric black and white cinematography. The Gamera series would lose this and descend into child-oriented ridiculousness.

PLOT

In the Arctic, scientist Dr. Hidaka (Eiji Funakoshi), his assistant Kyoko (Harumi Kiritachi) and reporter Aoyagi (Junichiro Yamashita) arrive at an Inuit village. At the same time, planes from the communist bloc make threatening maneuvers near an American airbase. An U.S. Air Force pilot pursues the jets and shoots one down when fired upon. The downed jet was carrying a nuclear bomb, which then explodes. The explosion releases an ancient, turtle-like giant monster from the ice. The Inuit chief (Yoshio Yoshida) gives Hidaka a ceremonial stone with a painting of a monster turtle. The awakened Gamera attacks the expedition's icebreaker, the *Chidori Maru*, killing all aboard.

Back in Japan, UFO sightings have become commonplace. Toshio Sakurai (Yoshiro Uchida) is a young boy living in a lighthouse at Hokkaido. He is made by his father (Yoshiro Kitahara) and sister Nobuyo (Michiko Sugata) to release his pet turtle. Gamera soon appears at the lighthouse but saves Toshio from falling. Toshio becomes obsessed with Gamera as he believes his pet turtle transformed into the beast.

Gamera next makes for a thermonuclear power plant. It proves impervious to the Self Defense Forces' weaponry and consumes the plant's energy. Dr. Hidaka, advising the army, consults his colleague Professor Murase (Jun Hamamura). Murase recommends that cold temperatures could be used to slow the pace of the monster. The military uses freezing bombs on Gamera which slow its advance. The army then uses explosives to flip the creature on its back. As Hidaka and company rejoice at Gamera's apparent defeat, the creature pulls its legs in. Releasing flames, it then begins to spin. Gamera flies off before the dumbfounded scientists and military, revealing itself to be the UFO seen around Japan. The United Nations calls an international conference. At Oshima Island, Hidaka, Murase and company plan to lure Gamera to the island with petroleum. Gamera will then be guided to a rocket where it will be sealed up and shot into space. This is called the "Z Plan".

BACKGROUND

Like the original *Godzilla, Gamera, the Giant Monster* sprang from the cancellation of another project. Daiei's president, Masaichi Nagata (1906-1985), was inspired by the success of Toho's *King Kong vs. Godzilla* and Hitchcock's *The Birds.* Nagata wanted to produce a monster film of his own. Daiei, a studio with a "house style" as distinctive as Toho's, had produced a handful of prior special effects films. These included 1956's *Warning From Space*, 1960's *The Demon of Mount Oe* and 1962's *The Whale God.* Yet they had never produced a full scale *tokusatsu* monster film.

Production was announced on *Giant Rat Horde Nezura* in 1963. *Nezura* was to feature a swarm of giant rats, enlarged through a chemical foodstuff, attacking Tokyo. Due to the expense of using stop motion, FX director Yonesburo Tsukiji opted to use genuine sewer rats. This was just the logistical and hygiene nightmare one would imagine. Rats escaped, bred in the studio and engaged in cannibalism. Crew members beame deathly ill from tick bites. Finally locals living near the studio complained to the authorities. Production on *Nezura* was shut down by the Tokyo health department. Tsukiji's company was left in debt by the production as Masaichi Nagata was eager for a replacement project.

Ala Tomoyuki Tanaka, Nagata claims to have had a vision of a giant turtle soaring through the air as he flew home from the United States. Soji Ushio of P-Productions also claimed that Daiei plagiarized a concept he was pitching. Nagata formed a production committee and hired producer Yonejiro Saito. Saito in turn brought in screenwriter Niisan

Takahashi to flesh out the concept. Takahashi (1926-2015) wrote a pair of treatments before penning the full script. Takahashi would become the exclusive screenwriter for the next seven entries in the Gamera series. Originally Gamera was to be called "Kamera" (*kame* is Japanese for "turtle"). It was quickly realized that the pronunciation and *katakana* were identical to the Japanese word for "camera".

PRINCIPAL PHOTOGRAPHY

The relatively young Noriaki Yuasa was hired to helm *Gamera, the Giant Monster*. The rest of Daiei's stock of directors passed on the project. The then 32 year old Yuasa's directorial debut, *If You're Happy Clap Your Hands* (1964), was a critical disaster. Yuasa's once fledgling career was now on life support. Many believed he was assigned this project as a form of humiliation. Even outside Toho, Eiji Tsuburaya was revered in the Japanese film industry. To compete with him was seen as both foolish and disrespectful. Daiei even avoided giving their films a "special effects director" credit out of respect for Tsuburaya. Yuasa's direction in *Gamera* is rather pedestrian compared to Ishiro Honda's. Yet the moody black and white Cinemascope shooting by Nobuo Munekawa brings atmosphere. There is a stark, more serious tone to *Gamera, the Giant Monster* aided by the black and white aesthetic. This is in striking contrast to the silly, child-oriented entries to come.

Production on *Gamera, the Giant Monster* was trying on Yuasa. The film was made quickly. Shooting began in September 1965 and concluded on November 11th, only two weeks before its debut in Japanese theaters. Yuasa was often heckled by executives while screening rushes and fought with the special effects staff. At one point, someone yelled *"Do you really think you're going to be the next Tsuburaya?!"* to him. The budget was slashed. This is partially why the film wound up shot in black and white when most Japanese films were already in color. There were also frequent equipment breakdowns. At one point a Gamera prop exploded but no one was harmed. American military recruits from Yokota air base were used in the U.S. arctic base scenes. They are poor actors and their scenes slow the film. Unlike Toho who used synthetic snow, real ice and snow were used for the Arctic sequences on a refrigerated set. It melted, causing on-set flooding which delayed production further. The Daiei brass grew irritated as the film went over budget. They considered hiring personnel from Tsuburaya's unit to finish the FX. Yuasa persevered and delivered a finished picture in time, often sleeping at the studio to accomplish this.

As evident from the trailer and Takahashi's script, quite a bit of footage was left on the cutting room floor. One deleted scene shows Toshio refusing to play with his classmates and would have introduced him. A dream sequence where Toshio imagines a friendly Gamera was in the script. It's unknown if it was actually filmed. Gamera's Tokyo rampage was reduced. Pre-rampage scenes of panic and evacuation were excised. A short sequence in a strip club with two strippers complaining about having to evacuate before Gamera's foot comes through the ceiling was cut. It was probably for the sake of child audiences. Also cut was a scene in Tokyo's Sky Lounge hotel. In the Japanese trailer, a deleted subplot is shown where Gamera kidnaps Toshio, *King Kong*-style. It's unknown if this was filmed exclusively for use in the trailer or was to be included in the finished film.

ACTORS

Like Honda's monster films, the characters are a mix of scientists, military officials and journalists. The cast is headed by Eiji Funakoshi. Funakoshi (1923-2007) was born Eijiro Funakoshi. He wanted to be an artist but his father insisted that he study economics. He enrolled in Seishu University and graduated in 1944. Shortly after, he was drafted into the Imperial Navy. He survived the war and ran a photo shop in Tokyo. As a prank, his brother's friend, an actor at Toho, entered him into the Daiei New Face contest in 1947. Funakoshi was accepted and debuted in *The Second Embrace* that same year. At first he didn't take acting seriously, but by the '50s was one of Daiei's most popular players. He appeared in films by Mikio Naruse and particularly Kon Ichikawa. His most famous role was in Ichikawa's *Fires on the Plain* (1959). Another notable part he played was in Yasuzo Masumura's deranged *The Blind Beast* (1969). His son Eichiro Funakoshi (1960-) is also a famous actor.

Other notable actors include Bokuzen Hidari (1894-1971). Hidari was a freelance character actor who appeared in several Kurosawa films and Ishiro Honda's *The Human Vapor*.

Another veteran character actor, Jun Hamamura (1906-1995) plays Professor Murase in a campy wig. Hamamura was born in Fukuoka as Takeshi Takeuchi. He played numerous roles for Kurosawa, Ichikawa, Masaki Kobayashi, Shohei Imamura, Masahiro Shinoda and Nagisa Oshima. His other genre film appearances included *100 Monsters* (1968), *The Vampire Doll* (1970) and *Prophecies of Nostradamus* (1974). The actresses include Harumi Kiritachi (1942-2002) and Michiko Sugata (1945-). *Gamera* was one of Kiritachi's last films before she left the industry for a domestic life. Sugata was very prolific at Daiei, her sister was Nikkatsu starlet Kazuko Tachibana. Previously cast in *Nezura*, she also appeared in Kenji Misumi's *Sleepy Eyes of Death* (1965). She retired from acting in the early '70s, wedding Yomiuri Giants pitcher Makoto Kurata. Toshio is played by child actor Yoshiro Uchida (1953-). Later to become a popular singer, this was his film debut. He recently resurfaced and appeared in 2019's *The Great Buddha Arrival*.

SFX

The special effects work in *Gamera, the Giant Monster* is decent, if below Tsuburaya quality. The black and white cinematography helps hide the less polished quality better than in future entries. There is some quality miniature work largely on par with Tsuburaya's team. The 10 foot miniature used for the *Chidori Maru* in the picture's early moments looks especially good. Like the aborted *Nezura*, the special effects unit was supervised by Yonesaburo Tsukiji. Unlike at

Toho, however, Yuasa directed the unit, choosing camera angles. Tsukiji (1923-2012) became a camera operator at the beginning of World War II for the company Shinko Kinema. Shinko Kinema became Dai Nippon in 1942, producing propaganda for the Imperial government. That year, Tsukiji helped shoot a film about the Japanese victory at Hong Kong: *Hong Kong Strategy: Day of Britain's Defeat*, directed by Shigeo Tanaka. After the war, Dai Nippon became Daiei. When Eiji Tsuburaya was exiled from Toho thanks to the American Occupation, he took Tsukiji under his wing. Tsukiji assisted him on *The Invisible Man Appears* (1949). After Tsuburaya was called back to Toho, Tsukiji's first film supervising special effects was *Snow on Mount Fuji* (1952). He also assisted Toru Matoba for the FX shots in *Warning From Space* (1956) and worked on Shigeo Tanaka's 70mm historical epic *The Great Wall* (1962).

As with Godzilla, multiple Gamera suits and props were built. Most of these were molded by Equis Productions, run by the Yagi family who often worked for Tsuburaya's unit. Kanju Yagi's son Masao handled much of the construction for Gamera, along with Keizo Murase. Kanju died the same year *Gamera* was released. From his sickbed, he barked orders at Masao about ingredients and materials. They had to balance making Gamera turtle-like with building a viable monster costume. The suits were constructed from foam rubber and latex. The final, main and heaviest suit was six and a half feet tall. The suit was lighter than the Godzilla suits at the time, but still quite heavy. Gamera's fire,

unlike Godzilla's which was usually optically animated, was created with a propane torch. The suit had to be padded to protect the actors from the fire which added to its weight. A lighter suit was built for the non-fire breathing scenes. Also unlike Godzilla, Gamera was portrayed by many different actors. At first, Yuasa called in some college-age weightlifters. None of them lasted more than three days in the cumbersome suit. In the end, members of the FX crew drew lots to decide who had to get in the suit that day. During filming of a water scene near the end of the picture, a still powered light fell into the pool, almost electrocuting the person inside.

An early sequence set at a lighthouse invokes Eugene Lourie's *The Beast From 20,000 Fathoms*, incidentally distributed by Daiei in Japan. *Gamera, the Giant Monster* comes alive a bit more in later scenes. Gamera's flying scenes, some of the best in the film, presented a particular challenge. These scenes were expensive and difficult to film. Gunpowder was used to create the flames igniting from the creature's shell. Only a certain type of gunpowder worked and sometimes had to be special ordered. Four shell props were built, mainly by Keizo Murase, in case of damage from the heavy pyrotechnics. The gunpowder often didn't ignite properly and the prop frequently fell mid-take. The spinning effect was created by several piano wires affixed to the prop and attached to a motor. It had to be done carefully or the wires would snap, which they often did. The motor was unwieldy and difficult to turn on and off, so timing was tricky. Yuasa was not entirely satisfied with these scenes. He believed audiences would find the concept of a flying turtle daft. Gamera's nighttime attack on Tokyo is a good sequence. It mimics Godzilla's 1954 rampage, though it lacks the devastating sense of pathos. The film's miniatures were built mainly out of plaster and some left over from *Nezura* were used. Tiny reinforcement bars were built into many of them so they'd crumble realistically. The scene where Gamera knocks over Tokyo Tower was almost ruined as the miniature was pulled over too quickly. An insert was filmed and the bit was saved in the edit.

Pyrotechnics were used heavily in the production of *Gamera, the Giant Monster*. Rags were soaked in a mixture of kerosene and metal powder. Unlike at Toho, a considerable portion of the FX scenes were shot outdoors because of the heavy toxic smoke. The final "Plan Z" sequences are well executed. These were likely an influence on *The Return of Godzilla* two decades later. That film features Godzilla also lured into a trap by scientists on Oshima Island. After *Gamera*, Yonesaburo Tsukiji quit Daiei. He was frustrated with their lack of understanding of special effects. Noriaki Yuasa went on to handle the special effects entirely on subsequent entries.

MUSIC

Gamera, the Giant Monster's score was composed by Tadashi Yamauchi. Yamauchi (1927-1980) was a student of none other than Akira Ifukube. *Gamera*'s music is quite

effective and Yamauchi would be back to score 1967's *Gamera vs. Gyaos*. Incidentally, he was the brother of actor Akira Yamauchi (*Godzilla vs. Hedorah*) and writer Hisashi Yamauchi (*Pigs and Battleships*).

RELEASE AND LEGACY

In November of 1965, Yuasa screened the final cut of *Gamera, the Giant Monster* to Masaichi Nagata and other executives at Daiei. When the lights came up, Nagata said *"Amusing"*. *Gamera* proved a hit, billed with the Kyoto Daiei production *New Kerama Tengu: Battle At Gojizaka*. The lighthouse sequence where Toshio is saved from falling to his death screened well with children. As a result, the series was soon tailored to a child audience. The first sequel, *Gamera vs. Barugon* (1966), however, was a prestige A-picture aimed at adults.

ALTERNATE VERSIONS

Gamera, the Giant Monster was sold to Harris Associates, Inc. who partnered with World Enterprises Corporation to produce an Americanization. This version was titled *Gammera, the Invincible* and released on December 15th, 1966. It was often billed with either *The Road to Fort Alamo* or *Knives of the Avenger*, both directed by Mario Bava. Running around 85:41, it's another rare U.S. version longer than its Japanese counterpart.

Unlike *Godzilla, King of the Monsters!*, the Japanese footage is trimmed only slightly. Mainly cut is Aoyagi's affections toward

Kyoko, whom he calls his *"Goddess of Luck"*. The scenes with the amateur Americans are removed, supplanted with new Arctic base scenes. These new scenes are far better with professional actors such as Diane Findley, John Baragrey, Dick O'Neil and Mort Marshall. Genre veterans Brian Donlevy (*The Quatermass Xperiment*) and Albert Dekker *(Doctor Cyclops)* appear in later scenes. Donlevy (1901-1972) plays Chief of Staff General Arnold who helps the Japanese execute "Plan-Z". Dekker (1905-1968) portrays a supportive Secretary of Defense. These new scenes were directed by Sandy Howard (1927-2008) and shot by Julian Townsend. A handful of special effects shots unused in the Japanese version are put back into the film. A surf-rock *"Gammera theme song"* was added in the opening, club scene and ending. This song was performed by Wes Farrell and Artie Butler under "The Moons". Expository narration was added to the opening of the film as well.

The English dubbing for the Japanese scenes was done at Titan Productions in New York. Dubbing cast includes Bernard Grant (Dr. Hidaka), Larry Robinson (Aoyagi), Paulette Rubinstein (Kyoko) and Corine Orr (Toshio). Playing smaller roles are Kenneth Harvey (*Chidori Maru* Captain/Narrator), Peter Fernandez (Mr. Ueda), Jack Curtis and William Griffiths. In many ways, *Gammera, the Invincible* is a superior and more enjoyable version of the film. Footage was featured on a 2010 season 4 episode of AMC's popular show *Mad Men* (2007-2015). In it, Don Draper (Jon Hamm) and Lane Pryce (Jared Harris) see *Gammera,*

the Invincible on New Years' Eve. The scene is anachronistic, however, as the episode is set at the end of 1964.

In 1985, producer Sandy Frank (1929-) acquired the rights to *Gamera, the Giant Monster* along with four other entries. As the Japanese version had no export dub, he commissioned a new English dub and not a very good one at that. This dub was done at Anvil Studios in England and features the voices of Garrick Hagon and Liza Ross. This version, called *Gamera*, is almost identical to the Japanese version. The main difference is the addition of a new credit sequence over a watery backdrop. Frank was planning to release a colorized version of the film but wound up keeping it in black and white. It was shown twice on the comedic "riffing" show *Mystery Science Theater 3000*. *Gamera* was first used in the original season on local Minneapolis network KTMA. It was later featured on the third season of the show's run on Comedy Central, aired on June 8th, 1991.

AMERICAN HOME VIDEO HISTORY

Gamera, the Giant Monster has had numerous stateside home video releases in many formats. The Sandy Frank version was released to VHS and laserdisc by Celebrity in 1988. It was reissued in EP mode on their "Just For Kids" video label around 1991. These tapes featured a grating introduction from Noel Bloom Jr., the son of Celebrity's CEO. Meanwhile, *Gammera the Invincible* was offered by collector's video outlets for years like Sinister Cinema and Video Yesteryear. These were telecined from old

16mm prints. In 1999, Neptune Media released both *Gamera, the Giant Monster* and *Gammera, the Invincible* to tape. A DVD release was planned but scuttled. Regardless, this was a special occasion. It was one of the very first times a kaiju film was brought to stateside home video in Japanese with subtitles. Around 2003, Alpha Video released *Gammera, the Invincible* to DVD. This was an unauthorized release from a VHS source.

In 2007, *Gamera, the Giant Monster* was released by Shout! Factory to DVD, in Japanese with subtitles only. It was then released to Blu-ray in a set with *Gamera vs, Barugon, Gamera vs. Gyaos* and *Gamera vs. Viras* by Mill Creek in 2014, also subtitled only. Later that year, Mill Creek released a box set of the first 11 Gamera films. In August 2020, both *Gamera, the Giant Monster* and *Gammera, the Invincible* were included in Arrow Films' *Gamera: The Complete Collection*. Sandy Frank's dub is an audio option on the Japanese version.

Further Viewing:

GAMERA VS BARUGON

(1966)
大怪獣決闘 ガメラ対バルゴン
Daiei, *Director:* **Shigeo Tanaka**

Gamera vs. Barugon was released within a mere six months of the original. Thanks to the first's spirited performance, Masaichi Nagata gave it a lavish "A" picture budget. Yuasa, however, was not re-hired as director. Instead he ran the picture's special effects

unit. The esteemed Shigeo Tanaka stepped into the director's chair instead. Tanaka (1907-1992) was Daiei's most dependable veteran hitmaker, having made the lavish 70mm historical epic *The Great Wall* (1962). For *Gamera vs. Barugon*, a more adult tone was taken with darker plot threads and not a tyke in a baseball cap and short shorts to be seen. The cast is headed by Kojiro Hongo (1938-2013), Daiei's Kenji Sahara look-alike who appeared in three more Gamera films after this.

Gamera vs. Barugon is not a great film but is one of the better *Showa* Gamera movies. It features higher production values than usual. Of any of the vintage Gamera films, it has the most Toho-like vibe. Many of the classic Toho tropes are replicated. The monster is found on a South Pacific island ala *Mothra*. Maestro Chuji Kinoshita's score even sounds a little like Ifukube. *Barugon* features a similar cooperation between scientists and the military as Ishiro Honda's recent films. As in Honda's work, there are lengthy army operations to destroy the new monster. The miniature work is quite decent with the effects not hurt by the more revealing medium of Eastman color. There's a stunning sequence showing Barugon's gooey hatching that is easily Tsuburaya-quality. Gamera, of course, begins to show a benevolent side but hasn't yet turned into the "friend of all children". The monsters are treated more like *yonaoshi* gods brought about by greed with Gamera restoring Earth's balance.

The main flaw of *Gamera vs. Barugon* is that it's overlong and monotonous at a whopping

101 minutes. This is rectified somewhat by the shorter American television cut *War of the Monsters. Gamera vs. Barugon* was released on a double bill with Kimiyoshi Yasuda's Daiei Kyoto production *Majin*. It underperformed and as a result, the budgets were cut on subsequent films. Noriaki Yuasa was put back in charge of the series, which began catering increasingly to a child audience.

GAMERA VS GYAOS

(1967)
大怪獣空中戦 ガメラ対ギャオス
Daiei, *Director*: Noriaki Yuasa

Gamera vs. Gyaos is where Gamera officially became the "friend to all children" and is possibly the best of the *Showa* Gamera pictures. It strikes a nice balance between the darker tone of the first two films and the kiddie silliness to come. The bat-like "vampire *kaiju*" Gyaos is an inspired creation. It was designed by series art director Akira Inoue, sculpted by Masao Yagi and painted by Keizo Murase. While Yuasa's FX unit can't quite do it like Eiji Tsuburaya's, there are some gorgeous composites.

There's a precocious kid on hand, played by Naoyuki Abe, but his presence detracts little. Like *Barugon*, *Gyaos* features Toho-style scientists and army guys trying to stop the monsters. An aerial battle sequence in Nagoya is a highlight with some spirited FX work. *Gamera vs. Gyaos* also features a well staged final battle. One interesting aspect of Yuasa's Gamera films is that they were quite

gory. The monsters' blood was made outlandish colors so as to frighten children less. Tsuburaya, by contrast, hated on-screen bloodshed. He would angrily shoot down suggestions by his crew to make monsters bleed.

After seeing *Gamera vs. Gyaos*, Ishiro Honda himself sent a congratulatory New Years' card to director Yuasa and screenwriter Takahashi. Indeed, the Gamera series was more influential on Toho than they let on. By the late 1960s, Toho began catering its Godzilla series purely to child audiences as well. Tsuburaya's successor, Teruyoshi Nakano, also started to make his FX footage gorier. The Gamera series slid into fair ridiculousness with the next entry, *Gamera vs. Viras* (1968). Gyaos would be back in stock footage and in 1969's *Gamera vs. Guiron* before being reimagined in 1995's *Gamera: Guardian of the Universe.*

GAMERA VS GUIRON

(1969)
ガメラ対大悪獣ギロン
Daiei, *Director*: Noriaki Yuasa

The preceding *Gamera vs. Viras* took the series in a goofy, child-oriented direction. By *Gamera vs. Guiron*, the series and Yuasa's direction takes on an Ed Woodsian strangeness. *Guiron* is a fairly indisputably terrible picture. It is worth a mention, however, mainly for some oddly ghoulish moments. Some have called it *"Like a children's film written by Hannibal Lecter".* In what is one of the most deranged sequences ever created for a kid's movie, a "Space Gyaos" is gruesomely dismembered by knife-headed novel foe Guiron. Excised from American TV prints, the sequence invokes the later "Black Knight" gag in *Monty Python and the Holy Grail* (1975). There are also a pair of cannibalistic alien babes (Reiko Kasahara and Hiroko Kai) straight out of the darkest Brothers Grimm story. They try to literally eat the brains of the film's boy protagonists Akio (Nobuhiro Kajima) and Tom (Christopher Murphy). Tom's mother is played by Edith Hansen (1939-), an American expat heavily involved in nonprofit work in Japan. William Ross called her a *"truly horrible woman"* in Stuart Galbraith's *Monsters Are Attacking Tokyo.*

For *Gamera vs. Guiron,* the production values and budget have taken a dive and are far below even Toho's '70s films. Dull early scenes give way to subpar special effects sequences. The *tokusatsu* work by Yuasa is television grade as best and fairly shoddy, marred by especially poor composites. There's the occasional good shot but the special effects are mostly clunky. *Gamera vs. Guiron* is the kind of Japanese monster film that uninformed Americans often stereotype the genre as. *Guiron* is probably among the worst of the classic *Showa* Gamera films but fun ironically for its oddly twisted touches. The export English dub, recorded by a little known Japan-based firm called Pedro Productions, is so awful it almost has to be heard to be believed.

NORIAKI YUASA
The Kiddie Programmer

湯浅憲明

9.28.1933-6.14.2004

"During production, Mr. Yuasa would teach the child actors how to act not by memorizing their lines, but rather he would let them kind of act it out. He would tell them what was going on and then he would "be" the monster. The young actors responded very well to that."
- Kon Omura, *Monsters Are Attacking Tokyo* (1998) by Stuart Galbraith

Just as Ishiro Honda is the director associated with Toho's Godzilla films, Noriaki Yuasa is synonymous with Daiei's Gamera series. While far from the talent of Honda or Tsuburaya, Yuasa was a hard-working man who persevered. Yuasa would go on to direct seven Gamera entries, helming both the drama and *tokusatsu*

units. Yuasa was born in Tokyo and came from a show business family. His father was actor Hikaru Hoshi and his grandmother Meiji-era stage actress Hideko Azuma. Yuasa graduated from law school at Hosei University. He joined Daiei's Tokyo branch in 1957, working as AD under esteemed directors like Teinosuke Kinguasa, Umetsugu Inoue and Koji Shima.

Yuasa's directorial debut was the youth comedy *If You're Happy Clap Your Hands*. It was a critical disaster and Yuasa's career was now in jeopardy. When Daiei's new monster movie *Nezura* was shut down by the Tokyo Board of Health, Yuasa was hired as director for the replacement project. Called *Gamera, the Giant Monster*, the film was a sort of last chance for Yuasa and, many believed, a form of subtle humiliation. Indeed, Daiei almost hired Tsuburaya's unit to finish the film. Yuasa, however, proved up to the challenge. Working with special effects expert Yonesaburo Tsukiji, Yuasa delivered a hit monster picture. Daiei's president Masaichi Nagata now saw ample opportunity to create a franchise to rival Godzilla at Toho. For the sequel *Gamera vs. Barugon*, veteran hitmaker Shigeo Tanaka was hired. With Tsukiji and Toru Matoba's departures from Tokyo Daiei, Yuasa was put in charge of the special effects division and ran the FX unit for *Gamera vs. Barugon*.

Gamera vs. Barugon's box office returns were disappointing so Yuasa was put back in charge of the series. Under him, a more child-friendly tone was adopted, starting with *Gamera vs. Gyaos* (1967). With *Gamera vs. Viras* (1968), the series dove deep into child-oriented camp. That same year, Yuasa also directed *Snake Girl vs. the Silver Haired Witch*, a black and white kiddie horror flick double-billed with Kyoto Daiei's *Spook Warfare*. *Gamera vs. Guiron* (1969), *Gamera vs. Jiger* (1970) and *Gamera vs. Zigra* (1971) soon followed. Yuasa also kept busy doing special effects work for the war film *The Falcon Fighters* (1969), directed by Mitsuo Murayama and helming television episodes.

Yuasa soon began work on the next Gamera entry. However, Daiei went bankrupt late in 1971. An embittered Yuasa went to Daiei's FX warehouse and destroyed all the monster suits in storage. Yuasa continued his career directing for television. He directed episodes of such tokusatsu shows as *Iron King* (1972-73), *Electroid Zaborger* (1974-75) and *Ultraman 80* (1980). He returned to directing for the big screen with *Gamera: Supermonster* (1980). Unfortunately, this film suffered production issues and wound up mainly composed of stock footage from prior entries. He also made the theatrical special *Anime Chan* (1984) for Tsuburaya Pro. Later on in his career, Yuasa focused mainly on television and V-Cinema productions. His final film was 1996's *Cosplay Warrior Cutie Knight II*. He was not fond of Shusuke Kaneko's *Heisei Gamera* trilogy, which he saw as betraying the child-like spirit of his films. Yuasa passed away from a stroke in 2004.

Selected Filmography (as director)
If You're Happy Clap Your Hands (1964)
Gamera, the Giant Monster (1965)
Gamera vs. Barugon (1966) [special effects director]
Gamera vs. Gyaos (1967)
Gamera vs. Viras (1968)
Snake Girl vs. the Silver Haired Witch (1968)
Gamera vs. Guiron (1969)
The Falcon Fighters [special effects director]
Gamera vs. Jiger (1970)
I Am Five (1970)
Gamera vs. Zigra (1971)
Maturity (1971)
Iron King [episode 8] (1972-73, TV)
Electroid Zaborger [episodes 23, 24, 37, 38] (1974-75, TV)
Comet [episodes 1-3, 7-9, 11, 12, 15-17, 22-24, 27, 28, 31-34, 37, 38, 41-43, 46, 47, 50-53, 56,

57, 60-63, 66-68] (1978-79, TV)
Ultraman 80 *[episodes 1, 2, 5, 6, 9, 10, 13, 14, 17, 18, 21, 22,*

25, 26, 29, 30, 33, 34, 39, 40, 43, 44] (1980-81, TV)
Gamera: Supermonster (1980)

Anime-chan (1984)
Cosplay Warrior Cutie Knight II (1996)

INVASION OF ASTRO-MONSTER

怪獣大戦争

Kaiju Daisenso "The Great Monster War"
Toho/United Productions of America, 12/19/1965 (*Showa 40*), 7 Reels (2,580 meters), 94:19, 35mm, TohoScope (2.35:1 anamorphic), Eastman color, monaural sound

Crew
Producers: Henry G. Saperstein, Tomoyuki Tanaka
Director: Ishiro Honda
Special Effects Director: Eiji Tsuburaya
Screenplay: Shinichi Sekizawa
Director of Photography: Hajime Koizumi
Music: Akira Ifukube
Editor: Ryohei Fujii
Assistant Director: Koji Kajita
Production Design: Takeo Kita
Lighting: Shoshichi Kojima
Sound Effects: Sadamasa Nishimoto
Sound Recording: Wataru Konuma
Sound Editor: Hisashi Shimonaga
Production Manager: Masao Suzuki
Assistant SFX Director: Teruyoshi Nakano
SFX Cinematography: Sadamasa Arikawa, Mototaka Tomioka
SFX Art Director: Akira Watanabe
SFX Lighting: Kuichiro Kishida

SFX Opticals: Yukio Manoda, Sadao Iizuka
SFX Wire Work: Fumio Nakadai
SFX Production Manager: Tadashi Koike
Still Photographer: Kazukiyo Tanaka

Cast
Akira Takarada (*Kazuo Fuji*)
Nick Adams (*Glenn*)
Jun Tazaki (*Dr. Sakurai*)
Keiko Sawaii (*Haruno Fuji*)
Kumi Mizuno (*Miss Namikawa*)
Akira Kubo (*Tetsuo Torii*)
Yoshio Tsuchiya (*Xilien Commandant*)
Kenzo Tabu (*World Education Corporation President*)
Yoshifumi Taijima (*Military Commander*)
Yasuhisa Tatsumi (*Military Captain*)
Nadao Kirino (*Military Aide*)
Toru Ibuki (*World Education Corporation Employee*)
Koji Uno (*World Education Corporation Employee*)

Fuyuki Murakami (*Doctors' Representative*)
Toki Shiozawa (*Women's Representative*)
Gen Shimizu (*Minister of Defense*)
Somesho Matsumoto (*Priest*)
Takamaru Sasaki (*Chairman of Earth Committee*)
Minoru Ito (*Reporter*)
Saburo Iketani (*News Anchor*)
Noriko Sengoku (*Tetsuo's Aunt*)
Kazuo Suzuki (*Xilien*)
Mitsuo Tsuda (*Xilien*)
Takuzo Kumagai (*Xilien*)
Ryoji Shimizu (*Xilien*)
Hideki Furukawa (*Xilien*)
Yoshizo Tatake (*Xilien*)
Yutaka Oka (*Reporter*)
Masaaki Tachibana (*Scientist*)
Rinsaku Ogata (*Scientist*)
Goro Naya (*Glenn*, voice)
Haruo Nakajima (*Godzilla*)
Masaki Shinohara (*Rodan*)
Shoichi Hirose (*King Ghidorah*)

Alternate Titles
Monster Zero (U.S.)

Invasion of the Astros (U.S., Armed Forces)

Godzilla vs. Monster Zero (U.S., Video)

Invasion of the Astro Monsters (U.K.)

Befehl aus dem Dunkel [**Command From the Darkness**] (Germany)

Los monstruos invaden la Tierra [**Monsters Invade Earth**] (Spain)

La invasion de los astros monstruos (Mexico)

Invasion planete X [**Invasion From Planet X**] (France)

L'invasione degli astromostri (Italy)

A Guerra dos Monstros [**War of the Monsters**] (Brazil)

Avaruushirviöt hyökkäävät [**Space Monsters Attack**] (Finland)

Άστρο-Τέρατα Επιτίθενται [**Attack of the Astro Monsters**] (Greece)

Inwazja potworów [**Monster Invasion**] (Poland)

Годзилла против Монстра Зеро (Russia)

Canavarlar Geliyor [**Monsters Are Coming**] (Turkey)

Invazija iz Svemira [**Invasion From Space**] (Yugoslavia)

"In defense of Earth we're gonna fight 'till the last man, baby."
-Astronaut Glenn (Nick Adams)

Invasion of Astro-Monster is another fine Godzilla sequel representing the Honda and Tsuburaya team at top form. A pulp classic, it is a rare *kaiju* film where the humans take center stage and the monsters play second fiddle as lumbering plot devices. As with *Frankenstein Conquers the World*, the film is a U.S./Japanese co-production with American star Nick Adams imported as lead. With stunning space scenes and iconic alien antagonists, *Invasion of Astro-Monster* is a memorable 1960s Toho *tokusatsu* extravaganza.

PLOT

In 196X, unusual transmissions lead to the discovery of a mysterious new planet behind Jupiter named Planet X. Spaceship P-1 is dispatched to investigate the transmissions, piloted by Astronauts Fuji (Akira Takarada) and Glenn (Nick Adams). Scientist Dr. Sakurai (Jun Tazaki) is overseeing the mission from World Space Authority HQ. Fuji warns his sister

Haruno (Keiko Sawaii) not to jump into her relationship with inventor Tetsuo Torii (Akira Kubo) while he's away, irritating her. Torii has invented a rape-whistle style device called the Ladyguard Alarm that produces an obnoxious siren. A toy manufacturer called World Education Corporation expresses interest in buying it. Tetsuo and Haruno meet with its representative, Miss Namikawa (Kumi Mizuno) to sign the contract.

Fuji and Glenn approach Jupiter and land on Planet X, finding it deserted and desolate. Fuji soon loses contact with Glenn and finds their ship to have vanished. A mysterious voice commands Fuji to step into a cylindrical elevator. Taken deep underground, Fuji is reunited with Glenn and the two meet the denizens of the planet: the Xiliens. The Xilien Commandant (Yoshio Tsuchiya) introduces himself as the planet's surface is attacked by King Ghidorah. The Commandant reveals that Ghidorah has been ravaging their planet: turning it into a wasteland and driving them underground. He asks Fuji and Glenn to relay a message to Earth's leaders asking to borrow Godzilla and Rodan, who once drove King Ghidorah from Earth. In return, the Xiliens can give Earth's doctors a formula for a cancer cure. Fuji and Glenn return with the Commandant's message and Earth's leaders happily agree to his terms.

The military soon finds Godzilla in nearby Myojin Lake, exactly where the Xilien Commandant said it was. Xilien spacecraft soon emerge from the lake. The following morning, one of the spacecraft lands and the Xilien Commandant comes forth to meet with the leaders of humanity. As Dr. Sakurai criticizes them for operating on Earth without permission, the Commandant expresses his gratitude before proclaiming a national day of friendship. The remaining Xilien spacecraft capture Godzilla and Rodan. The monsters are sealed in bubble-like force-fields before they are carried away with electromagnetic waves. Fuji, Glenn and Sakurai accompany the Xilien Commandant back to Planet X. On Planet X, Godzilla and Rodan are released and do battle with King Ghidorah, driving it away. As the battle rages, Fuji and Glenn sneak off to investigate the Xiliens' base. They find that the planet is rich in gold reserves. The two see several Xilien women, all looking exactly like Miss Namikawa, before they are captured. The Xilien Commandant decides not to press charges on them and they are sent back to Earth with a tape supposedly containing the cure for cancer. Tetsuo meanwhile is being held by the Xiliens as the World Education Corporation is revealed to be a front.

The astronauts return to Earth and play the tape, which contains not a cancer cure but terms for Earth's conquest and surrender. As the world is gripped by civil unrest, Glenn confronts Namikawa who urges him to surrender and become a citizen of Planet X so they can marry. The World Education president and his men appear, killing Namikawa but not before she slips Glenn a note. Having received no reply from Earth, the Commandant threatens to unleash Godzilla, Rodan and King Ghidorah on Earth's cities. Glenn is taken to the Xiliens' island base and imprisoned with Tetsuo. As the military contemplates using nuclear weapons against the aliens, Dr. Sakurai and Fuji make an important discovery. They realize that a light ray can be used to interrupt the Xiliens' magnetic wave broadcasts controlling the monsters. Tetsuo finds the note Namikawa gave Glenn, revealing that the Xiliens have a weakness to loud noise.

BACKGROUND

Like *Frankenstein Conquers the World*, Invasion of is a co-production with American Henry G. Saperstein (1918-1998) and his company United Productions of America (UPA) featuring Nick Adams. UPA, purchased by Saperstein in 1959, was best known at the time for its animated works like *Mr. Magoo* and *The Gay Purr-ee* (1962). Saperstein's business associates wanted sci-fi films to show on television. Saperstein went to the Academy of Motion Picture Arts and Sciences library and asked *"Who makes the best science fiction films overseas?"*. His answer was *"Hammer in England or Toho in Japan"*. As Hammer had a reputation for being difficult to deal with, Saperstein chose to pursue Toho. Saperstein, going as far to learn Japanese business etiquette, struck a multi-picture deal with them in 1965. He was keen to take advantage of the yen's weak exchange rate in Japan at the time. Toho's decision to make Godzilla a more heroic character may well have been because of Saperstein's influence. Saperstein also purchased one of Toho's *International Secret Police* films, *Key of Keys* (1965). Woody Allen, in his feature length directorial debut, turned the film into the comedic proto-gag dub *What's Up Tiger Lily?* (1966). Additionally, Saperstein produced John Boorman's *Hell in the Pacific* (1968) with Lee Marvin and Toshiro Mifune.

PRINCIPAL PHOTOGRAPHY

Invasion of Astro-Monster is a direct sequel to the previous years' *Ghidorah, the Three-Headed Monster*. By this time, Godzilla was midway in its journey from foreboding villain to protector of Earth. A hesitant Honda had begun to humanize Godzilla in *Ghidorah* and *Invasion* features an even more anthropomorphic vision. At one point in *Astro-Monster*, the creature pauses to dance a jig (called the *"Gojira shie"*

in Japanese), a suggestion by Yoshio Tsuchiya opposed by Honda. The film's press materials would make particular use of this moment, even showing several of the actors doing the *shie*.

Invasion of Astro-Monster is special in that it brings to synthesis the George Pal-style sci-fi trappings of Honda's earlier *The Mysterians* and *Battle in Outer Space* and the monstrous theatrics of his *kaiju* pictures. The result is a pulpy invasion flick with monsters mixed in and a cinematic joy. Veteran Takeo Kita's (1907-1979) effective production design in *Invasion of Astro-Monster* is halfway psychedelic and retro-futuristic. Coupled with Hajime Koizumi's cinematography, nearly every shot looks like it could be an illustration in a pulp sci-fi magazine. The Xiliens are the series' most interesting aliens with creative costume design. Clad in leather, their wardrobe even includes elf-like boots. *Invasion of Astro-Monster* represents a zenith for '60s Japanese science fiction. As the old Paramount VHS cover would say it's a *"Japanese monster movie fan's ecstasy"*.

ACTORS

Invasion of Astro-Monster was Toho's second production to feature Hollywood star Nick Adams. Through Toho's partnership with Saperstein's UPA, he was brought to Japan for *Frankenstein Conquers the World* and *Invasion of Astro-Monster*. Adams (1931-1968) was by this time considered washed up. Born in Pennsylvania, he was a figure like Leonardo DiCaprio's Rick Dalton in Quentin Tarantino's *Once Upon in Time in Hollywood* (2019). Adams had been up for an Oscar for his role in *Twilight of Hono*r, even spending ten thousand dollars campaigning. The actor even arrived at the Academy Awards ceremony hours early and practiced his walk to the podium. He lost and took it hard, the TV cameras lingering on his expression of disappointment. He had fallen from his heights headlining the hit Western show *The Rebel*. Before his work in Japan, Adams had starred in *Young Dillinger*, directed, incidentally, by *Godzilla: King of the Monsters'* Terry Morse. This project was somewhat disastrous for Nick Adams as he began a torrid affair with his co-star Mary Ann Mobley which strained his friendships with buddies Robert Conrad and John Ashley. He had spoken out against appearing in foreign co-productions but was soon on his way to Japan when work in Hollywood dried up. After *Astro-Monster*, Adams would appear in one more film for Toho, the spy flick *The Killing Bottle* (1967), before his tragic death. Directed by Senkichi Taniguchi, it would be the last film in the *International Secret Police* series. In terms of other genre work, he appeared on the *Outer Limits* episode *Fun and Games* and in the 1965 British horror film *Die, Monster! Die!* with Boris Karloff. One of his last films was the low budget sci-fi film *Mission Mars* (1968). If Nick Adams' and actress Kumi Mizuno's chemistry seems authentic, it's because he was quite smitten with the actress. Nick Adams would often call Mizuno late at night and she would use a dictionary to understand him. Whether they had a genuine affair is unknown. During production of *Astro-Monster*, Adams proposed to Mizuno, who turned him down as she was already engaged.

On set, Adams worked from a different script than the Japanese actors. They spoke their lines in Japanese while Adams spoke English. In spite of this, the actors worked comfortably with Adams with few communication issues. Henry Okawa often acted as Adams' translator. Nick Adams had a good relationship with director Honda and the two highly respected one another. Adams would be dubbed into Japanese for Toho's original release. He was voiced by Goro Naya (1929-2013), best known as the voice of Inspector Zenigata in the *Lupin III* franchise.

Yoshio Tsuchiya is impressive as the Xiliens' calculating and sociopathic Commandant. For *Astro-Monster*, Tsuchiya helped create a language for the Xiliens, similarly to his turn in *The Mysterians*. This time, it was based on Germanic dialects and the language of the *Kappa*, a water monster prevalent in Japan's folklore. On the sets of *Frankenstein Conquers the World* and *Astro-Monster*, Tsuchiya was especially friendly with Nick Adams. Adams would bring an autographed photo of the actor back to his home in Los Angeles, placed on his wall as a memento. After this, Tsuchiya would play a few more roles for Honda and take a dark turn as a gay man who commits incest in Toshio Matsumoto's *Funeral Parade of Roses* (1969). Tsuchiya then became more active in television in the 1970s and '80s before returning to the Godzilla series in *Godzilla vs. King Ghidorah* (1991). Tsuchiya died of lung cancer in early 2017.

SFX

Eiji Tsuburaya's special effects footage, especially the film's space scenes, is stellar. It is reminiscent of prior sequences in films like *Battle in Outer Space* and *Gorath*. A new, less menacing Godzilla suit was built; the head sculpted by Teizo Toshimitsu. The suit would return in the following entry, *Ebirah, Horror of the Deep*. Its head was loaned mid-shoot to create the monster Jirass in episode 10 of *Ultraman*. The head was heavily repaired and the suit was used in the water scenes of several more Godzilla films. The Rodan and King Ghidorah suits from *Ghidorah, the Three-Headed Monster* were reused with minor repairs. The miniature work is stunning. The P-1 spaceship, designed by Akira Watanabe and Yasuyuki Inoue, is beautifully crafted and convincingly filmed. Inspired by NASA's then current Gemini program, the miniature was enormous: standing over ten feet tall. The Xiliens' saucers are notable miniature creations. Made from Fiber Reinforced Plastic (FRP), only two were actually built. They were filled with electrical wiring so they could light up. The cord powering them was cleverly hidden in the piano wire holding the models up.

The film's matting and composite work is lush with some of the finest such shots in the series. Tsuburaya's Oxberry printer once again shows its magic, with some seamless, painterly images juxtaposing fleeing crowds with the monsters. Fuchimu Shimakura's painted backdrops are particularly noticeable and impressive in this film. Shimakura would go freelance after 1970's *Space Amoeba*, but Koichi Kawakita called on him to paint the stunning space backdrops in 1984's *Bye Bye Jupiter*. Shimakura later worked as recently as on 2012's *God Warrior Appears in Tokyo*, *Ultraman X: The Movie* (2016) and *Howl From Beyond the Fog* (2019).

A flaw is a slight over-abundance of stock footage, particularly from *Rodan* (1956), during the monsters' climactic rampage. The film's budget was slashed to Honda's chagrin. Yet the newly shot destruction footage is high quality. A large-scale Godzilla foot was built that effectively flattens through bigger miniatures. *Invasion of Astro-Monster* was the final Toho *tokusatsu* film with the classic special effects team who worked on the original *Godzilla*. After this film, contracts would run out and the crew would be downsized. Art director Akira Watanabe left Tsuburaya's team to start his own company, Japan Special Effects Inc. Watanabe would go on to do special effects for Nikkatsu and Toei with *Gappa, the Triphibian Monster* (1967) and *The Green Slime* (1968). Eizo Kaimai and the Yagi family would also depart, founding Kaimai Productions and Equis Productions, respectively.

MUSIC

Akira Ifukube's score for *Invasion of Astro-Monster* is one of his most iconic and memorable. The main theme is a bombastic military march first introduced in the original *Godzilla*. Yet it actually stems from one of Ifukube's early compositions, composed for the Imperial government in 1943 as *"Kishi*

Mai" (*Hope's Dance*). Eerie and foreboding chords dominate the space scenes.

THEMES AND MOTIFS

Ishiro Honda and screenwriter Shinichi Sekizawa bring some interesting subtexts to the table. Honda always featured science in a positive light from the first *Godzilla* on. In this film, human ingenuity, coupled with scientific inquiry, saves the day. *Invasion of Astro-Monster* also features an implied interracial relationship between Nick Adams' Glenn and Kumi Mizuno's Namikawa. Though the latter is actually an alien, such a depiction was progressive for its time. After all, interracial marriage was frowned upon in Japan and would not be legalized in the United States for two more years. Similarly to *The Mysterians* and Mu Empire in *Atragon*, the Xiliens' fanaticism to authority, regimented existence and colonialist desire for conquest bring the darker side of Imperial Japan to mind. The Xiliens' destruction by sound is a likely nod to *Earth vs. the Flying Saucers* (1956), which featured visual effects by Ray Harryhausen. The same trope was later employed comedically in Tim Burton's *Mars Attacks!* (1996).

If *Invasion of Astro-Monster* has any flaws, it's some daftness in the screenplay. The Xiliens asking permission to transport Godzilla and Rodan doesn't make much narrative sense. If they were operating on Earth, couldn't they have captured the monsters and begun their invasion without the humans knowing? At the same time, this is '60s science fiction, so suspension of disbelief isn't hard.

RELEASE AND LEGACY

Invasion of Astro-Monster did spirited business, being the 10th highest grossing domestic film in Japan that year. Overall, it was a popular and influential entry. Rebooted versions of the Xiliens would return in 2004's atrocious *Godzilla: Final Wars* and in the recent Godzilla anime trilogy.

ALTERNATE VERSIONS

It's unclear if Toho commissioned an export version or not. There is a trailer with English supers on the film's Turkish DVD which hints at its existence. There are also anecdotal accounts of "a version where Nick Adams is dubbed by another actor". If this version existed it may be lost. The "international version", released on VHS in the United Kingdom and available as an audio track on Criterion's Godzilla Blu-ray set, is the Los Angeles recorded dub synced to the Japanese version.

On July 29th, 1970, after almost five years, the film came to American shores under the title *Monster Zero*. Saperstein had a falling out with American International Pictures' Sam Arkoff in 1966. This left him without a distributor for several of his movies. It was finally released by Maron Films on a double-bill with Honda and Tsuburaya's next co-production with Saperstein, *The War of the Gargantuas*. The film was left almost unaltered and now runs 93:01. The cuts amount to only a minute or so of material. These are mainly tidbits of the Xiliens speaking their own language, a brief exchange between Fuji and Glenn and a single FX shot of the saucers at Myojin Lake. The film was dubbed into English by Ryder at Glen Glenn Sound in Los Angeles. The dub was likely directed by Riley Jackson, credited as post-production supervisor. Marvin Miller dubs Fuji, having previously voiced Takarada in Brenco's version of *The Last War* (1961). Some slight sound design additions were made, including footfalls as Godzilla dances its *shie*. The biggest change between the U.S. and Japanese versions is the soundtrack. Ifukube's opening march over the credits is replaced with a more foreboding cue from later in the film. Despite being only a cosmetic change, this alters the movie's tone to a slightly darker one. It was rated "G" by the Motion Picture Association of America.

In spring 1971, Toho would release a re-edited version for their Champion Matsuri kiddie matinee program. The film was retitled *The Great Monster War: King Ghidorah vs. Godzilla* and cut by about 20 minutes, running 74:08. This cut replaces the early expository title card with narration, catering to its younger audience. The deleted scenes mainly amount to character development, cutting the subplot of Fuji's disapproval with Tetsuo. The bureaucratic scenes are almost completely removed from the film. The sequence where Glenn tells Fuji about having seen the Commandant on Earth is also removed. There's a slight rearranging of scenes, too, turning Tetsuo's first scene, where he annoys his aunt with the invention,

into a flashback. Many shots and lines of dialogue are cut from the remaining scenes to quicken pacing. More narration is also added in a few instances. As with *Mothra vs. Godzilla*'s Champion cut, a few moments cut from the U.S. version are still intact. These include the Xiliens speaking in their native tongue and Fuji and Glenn's exchange.

AMERICAN HOME VIDEO HISTORY

The U.S. version was released to American VHS and Betamax by Paramount Home Video in 1988. Retitled *Godzilla vs. Monster Zero*, this version had a new video generated title card. Simitar would release an unauthorized version around 1990. Paramount reissued the film again to VHS and laserdisc in 1994 with new cover art. Simitar would properly acquire the rights, releasing the film to VHS and DVD in 1998. It was one of the first Godzilla releases in widescreen format. Classic Media then licensed it, reissuing the film in 2007. This new DVD had both the Japanese and U.S. versions available in widescreen. They would repress this disc before their rights lapsed and Janus acquired them. Most recently, the film would be included in 2019's Criterion *Godzilla: The Showa Era* Blu-ray set.

Further Viewing:

(1968)
怪獣総進撃
Toho, *Director:* **Ishiro Honda**

Toho was ahead of the curve, producing a "cinematic universe" ensemble piece decades before it was cool. Long before the pixels of *Avengers: Infinity War* flickered on digital screens, *Destroy All Monsters* played in glorious 35mm around the world. It was intended to be the last Godzilla movie and a close to the *Showa* series. After two scaled down "island" entries by Jun Fukuda, it returned director Ishiro Honda to the series. Honda brings similar pulpy sci-fi elements to the table as in *Invasion of Astro-Monster*.

For *Destroy All Monsters*, the setting is now explicitly futuristic: the then far-off 1999. The scale is global as the monsters are set loose by a race of alien women on a multitude of international cities. The film is far from Honda at the top of his craft. With a barebones script by Takeshi Kimura, it feels a little cliched and painted by numbers. Honda had already better covered similar ground in films like *The Mysterians* and *Invasion of Astro-Monster*. *Destroy All Monsters*, however, reaches a level of spectacle the series had yet to depict. The working title was *Giant Monster Chushingura*, a nod to the epic Japanese folk story of the 47 Ronin. It features a whopping eleven giant monsters from the Godzilla series and beyond. Sadamasa Arikawa's special effects sequences are strong. Honda's retro-futuristic stylings are delightful and show a bit of *Star Trek* influence. The sequences set on the moon, featuring the sleek Mutsumi Toyoshima-designed space cruiser SY-3, invoke *Battle in Outer Space*. *Destroy All Monsters* was made the same year Kubrick's

2001: A Space Odyssey was released, also featuring the vivid depiction of a lunar base. While unable to measure up to *2001* in aesthetic perfection, *Destroy All Monsters'* moon sequences feature beautiful miniature work. Ifukube's score is one of his most memorable and aids the film's spectacle. There are two especially great scenes. The first is an ace destruction sequence, one of the series' finest. Here Godzilla and several other *kaiju* converge on a futuristic Tokyo. The film's finale pits the monstrous ensemble against arch enemy King Ghidorah and is particularly impressive. It's an operatic *Cirque du Soleil* of stuntmen in monster skins, piano wires and remote controlled mechanics.

If unoriginal in its tropes, *Destroy All Monsters* is an entertaining creature feature that never lets up in old school spectacle. The English dub by Titan Productions was released to American drive-ins by American International in 1969. It's one of the best English versions of a Japanese monster film. Sadly Toho has buried it due to legal concerns, preferring the awful Frontier export dub. If watching it in English, try to find the Titan track. *Destroy All Monsters'* box office was profitable enough that Toho decided to continue on with the series. This was albeit with reduced budgets and distributed in a kiddie matinee program called Champion Matsuri. *Destroy All Monsters* would also be the namesake for an experimental rock band. Founded in Detroit in 1973, their raw sound gave them a strong cult following.

KUMI MIZUNO
The Vamp

水野久美

1/1/1937-

"I didn't want to play women who were just beautiful and wholesome. I wanted to play real, strong women who had real problems."
- Kumi Mizuno, *Monsters Are Attacking Tokyo* (1998) by Stuart Galbraith

There is likely no more memorable actress in Japanese genre film than Kumi Mizuno. She had a certain *je ne sais quoi;* a mix of beauty, brains and acting chops. These set her apart, even from other beautiful stars like Yuriko Hoshi, Mie Hama and Akiko Wakabayashi. Mizuno was born Maya Igarashi in 1937 in Sanjo, Niigata Prefecture. Her parents owned a professional photo studio and laboratory. Mizuno was born prematurely after her mother fell down the stairs. She was at first interested in becoming her father's apprentice, but became interested in acting as a teenager. While attending high school, she was part of the drama club. She appeared in numerous school plays, including as Cordelia in *King Lear*. Her talent and beauty got her noticed and she was featured in *Junior Soriiyu* magazine.

In 1957 at the age of 20, she began her film acting career in Shochiku's *Crazy Society*. She soon moved to Toho the following year, appearing in Seiji Maruyama's *A Bridge For Us Alone*. She played supporting roles in popular films like Hiroshi Inagaki's *The Three Treasures* (1959) and Kihachi Okamoto's *Westward Desperado*. Numerous parts followed, both starring and

supporting, including Inagaki's blockbuster *Chushingura* (1962). With both beauty and acting skill, she was called the *"Françoise Arnoul of Japan"*. In the West, Mizuno became known for her roles in genre films. These included *Gorath* (1962), *Matango* (1963), *Frankenstein Conquers the World, Invasion of Astro-Monster* (both 1965), *The War of the Gargantuas* and *Ebirah, Horror of the Deep* (both 1966). Director Ishiro Honda was particularly fond of her. At one point, she was almost cast opposite Jack Palance in a cancelled historical epic set in ancient China.

On *Frankenstein Conquers the World*, she worked with Hollywood actor Nick Adams. Adams was smitten by this lovely Japanese actress. Adams would often call Mizuno late at night and she would use an English dictionary to try to understand him. They appeared together again in *Invasion of Astro-Monster* and *The Killing Bottle* (1967). At one point, Adams proposed to Mizuno, but she turned him down as she was already engaged. She married actor Manabu Yamamoto in 1966. The two divorced in 1969 and she remarried to Michio Igarashi in 1973.

Kumi Mizuno went freelance from Toho by the late '60s. She played supporting parts in a variety of films and television from herein. These included the musical comedy *Mysterious Robber Ruby* (1988) and Okamoto's *Rainbow Kids* (1991). In 2002, at the age of 65, she returned to the kaiju genre with *Godzilla Against Mechagodzilla*, directed by Masaaki Tezuka. She also appeared in Ryuhei Kitamura's *Godzilla: Final Wars* in 2004. Since then, she has remained active on the big screen and television.

Selected Filmography (as actress)
Crazy Society (1957)
A Bridge for Us Alone (1958)
A Holiday in Tokyo (1958)
The Spell of the Hidden Gold (1958)
Herringbone Clouds (1958)
The Three Treasures (1959)
One Day I... (1959)
Seniors, Juniors, Co-Workers (1959)
Lips Forbidden to Talk (1959)
Fox and Tanuki (1959)
Whistle in My Heart (1959)
Westward Desperado (1960)
The Gambling Samurai (1960)
Wanton Journey (1960)
Challenge to Live (1961)
The Merciless Trap (1961)
The Crimson Sea (1961)
Witness Killed (1961)
Counterstroke (1961)
Big Shots Die at Dawn (1961)
The Underworld Bullet Marks (1961)
Kill the Killer! (1961)
Gorath (1962)
Chushingura (1962)
The Crimson Sky (1962)
Operation X (1962)
Operation Enemy Fort (1962)
Weed of Crime (1962)
Matango (1963)
Samurai Pirate (1963)
Interpol Code 8 (1963)
Sink or Swim (1963)
Warring Clans (1963)
Whirlwind (1964)
Trap of Suicide Kilometer (1964)
Blood and Diamonds (1964)
Key of Keys (1965)
White Rose of Hong Kong (1965)
Frankenstein Conquers the World (1965)
Invasion of Astro-Monster (1965)
The War of the Gargantuas (1966)
Ebirah, Horror of the Deep (1966)
The Killing Bottle (1967)
Love is in the Green Wind (1974)
Mysterious Robber Ruby (1988)
Rainbow Kids (1991)
Graduation Journey: I Came from Japan (1993)
Godzilla Against Mechagodzilla (2002)
Godzilla: Final Wars (2004)
The Hundred Year Clock (2012)
Amanogawa (2019)

Tanin no Kao "Face of Another"
Teshigahara Productions/Tokyo Eiga/Toho, 7/15/1966 (*Showa 41*), 9 Reels (3,328 meters), 121:32, 35mm, Academy (1.37:1), black and white, monaural sound

Crew
Producers: Nobuyo Horiba, Kiichi Ishikawa, Tadashi Ono
Director: Hiroshi Teshigahara
Screenplay: Kobo Abe (also novel)
Director of Photography: Hiroshi Segawa
Music: Toru Takemitsu
Editor: Yoshi Sugihara
Art Directors: Masao Yamazaki, Arata Isozaki
Set Decoration: Kenichiro Yamamoto
Costume Design: Tamiko Moriya
Assistant Directors: Hideo Nagasawa, Yutaka Osawa

Makeup and Masks: Taichiro Akiyama
Lighting: Mitsuo Kume
Sound: Junosuke Okuyama
Sculptures: Tomio Miki
Continuity: Eiko Yoshida
Title Design: Kiyoshi Awazu
Still Photographer: Yasuhiro Yoshioka

Cast
Tatsuya Nakadai (Okuyama)
Machiko Kyo (Okuyama's Wife)
Mikijiro Hira (Dr. Hori)
Kyoko Kishida (Nurse)
Miki Irie (Girl with Scar)
Eiji Okada (Boss)

Minoru Chiaki (Apartment Superintendent)
Hideo Kanze (Mental Hospital Patient)
Kunie Tanaka (Mental Hospital Patient)
Etsuko Ichihara (Superintendent's Daughter)
Eiko Muramatsu (Secretary)
Yoshie Minami (Old Lady)
Hisashi Igawa (Man with Mole)
Kakuya Saeki (Brother of Girl with Scar)
Sen Yano (Psychiatric Patient)
Beverly Maeda (Singer at Bar)

"I see your face before me
Yet I no longer recognize you
Where are you?
Where are you?
The you I knew yesterday."
-Singer at Bar (Beverly Maeda)

Auteur Hiroshi Teshigahara and renowned novelist Kobo Abe followed the success of 1964's *Woman in the Dunes* with *The Face of Another*. Based on Abe's '64 novel of the same name, the book and film are loose but qualifiable science fiction. *The Face of Another* lacks the hallucinatory genius of *Woman in the Dunes,* but it is nonetheless a captivating picture. Like a *Twilight Zone* episode written by Kafka, it presents luminous black and white images and Nieztchian existentialism.

PLOT

The face of Okuyama (Tatsuya Nakadai) is burned in an industrial accident. His visage covered in bandages, Okuyama's wife (Machiko Kyo) rejects his advances. Pathologically frustrated, he turns to psychiatrist Dr. Hori (Mikijiro Hira). Hori offers to make Okuyama an experimental mask of space age material that is impossible to distinguish from a real face. Okuyama then rents an apartment as a hideout while he takes part in the mask experiment.

Okuyama sees a film about a young girl (Miki Irie) who bears a keloid scar on the right side of her otherwise beautiful face. A Nagasaki survivor disfigured in the blast, she works at a home for disabled veterans. She lives with her brother (Kakuya Saeki) and worries about the possibility of another war. Dr. Hori and Okuyama next scope out a man (Hisashi Igawa) with a distinctive mole on his face. They pay him 10,000 yen to use his skin as a model for the texture of the mask. The mask is next fitted to Okuyama. It is completely life-like, exceeding his wildest expectations. At a German-style beer hall, Hori and Okuyama toast to the mask's success. Hori warns Okuyama to be careful. He fears the mask could form a new persona in Okuyama's subconscious and plunge him into a dissociative state.

Okuyama does not tell his wife or boss (Eiji Okada) that he has the mask. He uses the alibi that he's *"away on business"* while living as a new man. In the mask, Okuyama rents another apartment in the same complex. He is dismayed when the superintendent's mentally handicapped daughter (Etsuko Ichihara) recognizes him. He fools the receptionist (Eiko Muramatsu) at his job, however. This gives him confidence. Against Hori's advice, Okuyama decides to use the mask to seduce his wife.

BACKGROUND

The Face of Another is the third collaboration between arthouse extraordinaire Hiroshi Teshigahara and novelist Kobo Abe. Teshigahara (1927-2001) was the son of Sofu Teshigahara (1900-1979), the founder of the Sogetsu school of *ikebana* (flower arranging). In spite of the traditionalism of ikebana, Sofu was a progressive man. He was a revolutionary figure in Japanese modern art, reimagining ikebana as floral sculpture. Sogetsu became the center of post-war Japan's modern art movement. Trained as a Picasso-style painter, Sofu's son Hiroshi attended the prestigious Tokyo University of the Arts. Hiroshi was expected to succeed his father as the head of Sogetsu but had a passion for filmmaking. He began making short form documentaries starting with 1953's *Hokusai*. In the basement of Sogetsu, Hiroshi would often have meetings with fellow artists. This was how he met novelist Kobo Abe. The two would form a group called the "Century Club". This group also included musician Toru Takemitsu who would become a collaborator as well. With many Japanese Communist Party members in their ranks including Abe, they were politically radical.

Abe and Teshigahara's first collaboration was 1962's *The Pitfall*, based on a short teleplay by the former. The pair soon got the world's attention with the masterwork *Woman in the Dunes* (1964), based on Abe's 1962 novel. A dark sociological parable stunningly executed, the film was an international sensation. *Woman in the Dunes* was a New Wave Japanese film of sorts. Teshigahara and Abe followed with *The Face of Another*, based on a 1964 Abe novel. Unlike the faithful *Woman in the Dunes*, *The Face of Another* makes significant departures from the text. The character of Dr. Hori was negligible in the book. In the film he becomes a major character and, according to Teshigahara, a mirror image of the protagonist. The sequences with Miki Irie's keloid-scarred *hibakusha* girl were but a short passage in the book. In the film, they become something of a "B-story". Irie had previously worked with Teshigahara on his short film *White Morning* (1965).

PRINCIPAL PHOTOGRAPHY

The Face of Another doesn't quite have the hypnotic power and aesthetic perfection of *Woman in the Dunes*. It is a less accessible picture but an unsettling parable that's nearly as powerful. In both, Kobo Abe's intellectual themes gel with Teshigahara's visual mastery to near perfection. Like *Woman in the Dunes*, the film boasts stunning monochrome cinematography. DP Hiroshi Segawa's black and white images are luminous and haunting. They focus on the *Invisible Man*-like visage of Okuyama's bandaged face in the early sections of the film. Teshigahara and Segawa's camera is voyeuristic. It lingers in apartment hallways, street alleyways and doorways. Some compositions look almost Kubrick-like. To illustrate the duplicity of Okuyama and his masked alter-ego, framing is often mirrored or repeated throughout. Soviet filmmaker Andrei Tarkovsky was particularly fond of Teshigahara's work. One gets the sense *The Face of Another* was influential on him, particularly for *Solaris* and *Stalker*.

The film's production design is striking, handled by Teshigahara's close friend, famed architect Arata Isozaki. Isozaki (1931-) became known for designing the Museum of Contemporary Art in Los Angeles and the Olympic Stadium in Barcelona. Dr. Hori's office is a remarkable set with an almost Escher-like aesthetic. Filled with severed ear sculptures by artist Tomio Miki, it features glass panels adorned with Langer's lines and da Vinci's Vitruvian Man. The scenes set in the German-style beer hall were filmed in an actual Tokyo gastropub that closed in the 2000s.

ACTORS

The cast includes some of Japan's finest players. Tatsuya Nakadai (1932-) needs no introduction to Japanese cinema fans. On par with Mifune as Japan's greatest thespian, he's starred in many films by great directors like Akira Kurosawa and Masaki Kobayashi. With a distinctive voice and gaze, he always gives a memorable performance. Machiko Kyo (1924-2019) needs no introduction either. Kyo was known for roles in Kurosawa's *Rashomon* (1950), Mizoguchi's *Ugetsu* (1953), Kinugasa's *Gate of Hell* (also '53) and the Hollywood *Teahouse of the August Moon* (1956). Here she, almost shockingly, plays a middle-aged modern woman. Her face beginning to show wrinkles, Kyo's role is a far cry from the prim, almost doll-like characters from the peak of her career. Dr. Hori is played by Mikijiro Hira. Hira (1933-2016), a native of Hiroshima, was one of Japan's premiere Shakespearian actors. Appearing in roles on stage, film and television, he received several honors from the Japanese government. The *Woman in the Dunes* herself, Kyoko Kishida (1930-2006), returns as Hori's nurse. Eiji Okada also has a small role as Okuyama's boss.

MUSIC

The Face of Another's soundtrack was composed by Toru Takemitsu. Takemitsu (1930-1996) also needs little introduction to Japanese film fans. He was a self taught, avant garde composer with a large body of work outside cinema. Takemitsu often handled his film scores like musical soundscapes. He became one of Japan's most in-demand composers. His scores include for Teshigahara, Masaki Kobayashi, Akira Kurosawa, Masahiro Shinoda, Mikio Naruse, Nagisa Oshima and Shohei Imamura. His music for *The Face of Another* is minimalistic, often relying on chords from a water organ to build suspense. It is punctuated by a catchy Austrian waltz; later sung in German by *Son of Godzilla*'s Beverly Maeda.

THEMES AND MOTIFS

The Face of Another is like a *Twilight Zone* episode directed by Ingmar Bergman and written by Franz Kafka. While loose science fiction, it nonetheless contains sci-fi themes owing their lineage to H.G. Wells and Robert Louis Stevenson. These are mixed with an existentialism akin to Kafka or Nietzsche. The film is rich in subtext, though some may find its frequent philosophical exchanges pretentious. Its themes are universal and take Kafkaesque concepts of identity to a logical extreme. A brief sequence where masked Okuyama makes faces before a mirror conveys this perfectly without words. There's subtle commentary on the rigid social roles in Japanese society. Jesuit missionary João Rodrigues Tçuzu is often quoted as saying that in Japanese society everyone has three faces. One face is for strangers, shown to the world. The second face is more intimate; for family and close friends. The third face is not shown to anyone and is the truest reflection of one's self. With face transplants and life-like masks now a reality for the disfigured, *The Face of Another* is relevant as ever. Japan's loss of identity (face) following World War II is also explored by Teshigahara and Abe. The sequences of the unnamed *hibakusha* girl: her face scarred by the Nagasaki bomb, are both disturbing and hauntingly beautiful.

The Face of Another bears similarities to George Franju's 1960 *Eyes Without a Face* and John Frankenheimer's *Seconds* (also 1966). All three films are alike in themes and black and white imagery. *Seconds*, itself based on a novel by David Ely, particularly parallels *The Face of Another*. *Seconds* features a depressed middle-aged man (John Randolph), unhappy with his marriage and job. He undertakes a state of the art plastic surgery operation: assuming a new identity (Rock Hudson). Like Nakadai's Okuyama, his subconscious is unable to accept this new persona. It leads to emptiness, a mental breakdown and ultimately, horrific tragedy. Hollywood's premiere DP James Wong Howe's monochrome visuals even resemble Hiroshi Segawa's at times.

RELEASE AND LEGACY

The Face of Another was viewed as a let down, particularly in the West, after the arresting *Woman in the Dunes*. Teshigahara and Abe would collaborate on one more film: 1968's *Man Without a Map*. Unlike prior films, made independently in black and white, it was produced at Daiei in color and 'scope: starring *Zatoichi*'s Shintaro Katsu. After 1972's *The Summer Soldier*, Teshigahara became more sporadic in his output. In 1980, he succeeded his father as head of Sogetsu and began to focus on bamboo installations over filmmaking. He still directed a handful of films, however. These include the documentary *Antonio Gaudi* (1984) and *Rikyu* (1989), based on the life of tea ceremony master Sen no Rikyu. *The Face of Another* has been re-appraised in recent years. It is now considered one of the best Teshigahara and Abe collaborations.

ALTERNATE VERSIONS

The Face of Another was released to U.S. arthouses and mostly harsh reviews on June 9th, 1967. This release was, presumably, intact and subtitled.

AMERICAN HOME VIDEO HISTORY

For years, *The Face of Another* was unavailable on any sort of home video format in the U.S. It was finally released to DVD by Criterion in July 2007 in a boxed set with *The Pitfall* and *Woman in the Dunes*. This set is out of print, but it is available to stream on the Criterion Channel.

Further Viewing:

(1959)
双頭の殺人鬼
Shaw-Breakston Enterprises/United Artists/Toei, *Directors*: George Breakston, Kenneth Crane

A more vulgar take on Louis Stevenson's *Jekyll and Hyde*, *The Manster* is classic Psychotronic cinema. The film was made in Japan in 1958 but not released stateside until '62. It paired American directors George Breakston and Kenneth Crane (*Monster From Green Hell*) with a mainly Japanese crew. *The Manster* has the artless tone of an American '50s B-picture but with a twisted stylization only found in Japanese horror.

Tetsu Nakamura plays his most memorable role as a 731-like mad scientist who conducts deranged mutation experiments. He's already turned his brother into a Morlock-like ape man. His wife is now a grotesque wrath who looks like a woodblock print of *Yotsuya Kaidan*'s Oiwa. Aided by seductive assistant Tara (the late, part-Chinese Terri Zimmern), his newest victim is American reporter Larry Stanford (Peter Dyneley). Larry gradually transforms from nice guy to adulterous alcoholic to murderous two-headed apeman. Hunted by Detective Aida (*Mothra*'s Jerry Ito), Larry's prehistoric alter-ego splits from him and the two do battle. Too bad Larry now faces a long and painful stint in the Japanese court system.

The Manster is an odd movie with Ed Woodsian strangeness but packed with unsettling moments. Kenneth Crane is no Orson Welles, but the special effects have a distinctively Japanese flair. Brits Peter Dyneley (later to do voice work on *Thunderbirds*) and Jane Hylton do surprisingly good American accents. *The Manster* is often remembered in terms of certain images and fever dream-like cinematic moments. These include Larry's hand sprouting werewolf-like hair, him finding an eye on his shoulder and the new head growing from him. The show-stopping "splitting" scene is straight out of a childhood nightmare. These grotesqueries tend to linger in one's subconscious. Sam Raimi later paid homage to *The Manster*'s finale in *Army of Darkness* (1992). In the U.S., the film was released on a double bill with Franju's *Eyes Without a Face*. *Eyes* was dubbed, had its gory operation scenes trimmed and was retitled *The Horror Chamber of Dr. Faustus*. While akin to serving lobster thermidor with Dinty Moore beef stew, it must have stricken Baby Boomers with gnarly nightmares. After *The Manster*, Crane (1907-1995), focused more on editing than directing. He would later cut 1967's *Venus Fly Trap* (aka *Revenge of Dr. X*), also filmed in Japan and written by Ed Wood.

KOBO ABE
The Existentialist

安部公房
3/7/1924-1/22/1993

"The certificates we use to make certain of one another: contracts, licenses, ID cards, permits, deeds, certifications, registrations, carry permits, union cards, testimonials, bills, IOUs, temporary permits, letters of consent, income statements, certificates of custody, even proof of pedigree. Is that all of them? Have I forgotten any? Men and women are slaves to their fear of being cheated. In turn they dream up new certificates to prove their innocence. No one can say where it will end. They seem endless."
-Entomologist Junpei Niki (Eiji Okada), *Woman in the Dunes* (1964)

One of Japan's post-war literary titans, Kobo Abe is best known for *Woman in the Dunes* (1962) and its film adaptation. Though primarily a modernist fiction writer, Abe left his mark on Japanese science fiction with novels like *Inter Ice Age 4* (1958) and *The Face of Another* (1964). He was born Kimifusa Abe in Tokyo in 1924, the son of Asayoshi Abe and Yorimi Imura.

Soon afterward, his father, a physician, returned to Japanese colonized Manchuria. Abe would go on to spend much of his childhood in Mukden (now Shenyang). As a child, he was a voracious reader and became obsessed with the works of Edgar Allen Poe. Other writers he grew to adore included Franz Kafka, Fyodor Dostoyevsky and Friedrich Nietzsche.

Abe returned to Japan to study at the prestigious Seijo High School. He suffered a pulmonary condition and went back to Mukden for a while. Abe graduated in 1943 and enrolled in Tokyo Imperial University to study medicine. This was partially at the urging of his father, but also to keep himself from being drafted into the military. Students in the arts were not spared from conscription. Medical students were, however, valuable to the war effort. Abe soon snuck back to Manchuria. His father died shortly after, killed by a typhus outbreak at his clinic. After Japan's defeat, Abe fled Manchuria, returning to Japan by boat with his father's ashes in 1946. He would never visit China again. He married Machi Yamada, an art student, in 1947. Married for life, she would go on to provide cover designs and illustrations for many of his books. In 1948, he finally got his medical degree, having failed the exam twice. He was only allowed to pass on the condition that he never practice medicine. This mattered little to Abe by now, who was determined to become a successful writer. By this time he had already professionally published poetry.

Abe soon joined the "Night Society", a group of post-war writers, artists and thinkers. These included novelist Yutaka Haniya and artist Taro Okamoto. Haniya was something of a mentor to Kobo Abe and helped him publish his early works. Abe was also a fervent Japanese Communist Party member. Kobo Abe's first novel, *The Guidepost at the End of the Road*, was published in 1948. Abe and his wife struggled financially around this time; he often sold his blood for extra money. His short stories *Dendrocacalia* (1949) and *The*

Crime of S. Karma (1951) began to garner notice. The latter won Abe the coveted Akutagawa Prize. Kobo Abe also began to dabble in playwriting around this time. In 1954, his daughter Neri was born. In 1956, Abe visited Czechoslovakia for the 20th Convention of the Soviet Communist Party. He began to grow disenchanted with communist ideology. The Polish Poznań protests and Soviets' invasion of Hungary only deepened this sentiment for him.

Starting in 1958, Abe released his science fiction novel *Inter Ice Age 4*, serialized in the journal *Sekai*. The book contained futuristic themes far ahead of its time such as on transhumanism, climate change and the dangers of artificial intelligence. In 1960, Abe took part in the protests against the new Anpo US-Japan Security Treaty. He was expelled from the Japanese Communist Party the following year for criticizing its support of the Soviet Union. Later in 1961, filmmaker and Sogetsu school heir Hiroshi Teshigahara began production on a film based on Abe's teleplay *Purgatory*. This movie, *The Pitfall*, was released by the Japan Art Theatre Guild in 1962.

Also in 1962, Abe wrote what would become his most famous novel: *Woman in the Dunes*. This story centered around an entomologist on vacation in a rural village. He is imprisoned in a pit with a young widow by the locals; forced to shovel sand to keep the town from being swallowed up. The novel won the Yomiuri Prize for Literature and was also adapted by Hiroshi Teshigahara. Both the book and film were a tremendous international success. The novel was released in the U.S. translated to English by E. Dale Saunders in 1964. Teshigahara's film garnered numerous accolades abroad. These included the Special Jury Prize at the Cannes Film Festival and nominations for Best Foreign Film and Best Director at the Academy Awards. Abe's following novels included the sci-fi existentialist allegory *The Face of Another* (1964) and the deconstructive detective story *The Ruined Map* (1967). Both were also adapted by Teshigahara in 1966 and '68 respectively. The latter, *Man Without a Map,* was Teshigahara and Abe's first studio picture. Produced at Daiei and starring famed actor Shintaro Katsu, it was a financial failure. Abe and Teshigahara soon parted ways after that.

After taking part in the planning committee for Expo '70, Abe founded the Abe Studio in 1971, a playhouse. He began to focus on writing, directing and putting on live theatre. He also wrote another of his most famous novels, 1973's *The Box Man.* This tells the story of an agoraphobic man who chooses to withdraw from the world by wearing a box. In 1977, Abe released *Secret Rendezvous,* later translated to English by Juliet Winters Carpenter. Abe also indulged in a love of photography and cameras along with music. He was said to particularly adore Pink Floyd. Abe was also made an honorary member of the American Academy of Arts and Sciences.

By the 1980s, Kobo Abe went into semi-retirement. Abe Studio ceased production due to his increasingly frail health though he continued novel writing. He published *The Ark Sakura* in 1984, his first book written on a computer. His final completed novel was 1991's *Kangaroo Notebook.* In late 1992 he suffered a cerebral hemorrhage during a writing session. He died of heart failure a month later in early 1993. His wife Machi died of cancer later that year. Abe's daughter Neri helped publish much of his unfinished work and biography. She tragically passed away in 2018.

Selected Filmography
The Pitfall (1962) [teleplay *"Purgatory"*]
Woman in the Dunes (1964) [screenplay/novel]
The Face of Another (1966) [screenplay/novel]

Man Without a Map (1968) [screenplay/novel *"The Ruined Map"*]
The Box Man (2002) [novel]

THE WAR OF THE GARGANTUAS

フランケンシュタインの怪獣
サンダ対ガイラ

Furankenshutain no Kaiju: Sanda tai Gaira "Frankenstein's Monsters: Sanda vs. Gaira"
Toho/United Productions of America, 7/31/1966 (*Showa 41*), 7 Reels (2,405 meters), 87:56, 35mm, TohoScope (2.35:1 anamorphic), Eastman color, monaural sound

Crew
Executive Producers (UPA):
Henry G. Saperstein, Reuben
Bercovich
Producers: Tomoyuki Tanaka,
Kenichiro Tsunoda
Director: Ishiro Honda
Special Effects Director: Eiji
Tsuburaya
Screenplay: Kaoru Mabuchi
(Takeshi Kimura), Ishiro
Honda
Director of Photography:
Hajime Koizumi
Music: Akira Ifukube
Editor: Ryohei Fujii
Assistant Director: Koji Kajita
Production Design: Takeo Kita
Lighting: Toshio Takashima
Sound: Sadamasa Nishimoto
Sound Recording: Norio Tone
Production Manager: Shoichi
Koga
Assistant SFX Director:
Teruyoshi Nakano
SFX Cinematography:
Sadamasa Arikawa, Mototaka
Tomioka
SFX Art Director: Yasuyuki
Inoue
SFX Lighting: Kuichiro Kishida
SFX Unit Production Manager:
Yasuaki Sakamoto
SFX Opticals: Hiroshi
Mukoyama
SFX Wire Work: Fumio
Nakadai
Monster Design: Toru Narita

SFX Modeler: Akinori Takagi
Still Photographers: Kazukiyo
Tanaka, Goichi Araki

Cast
Russ Tamblyn *(Dr. Paul
Stewart)*
Kumi Mizuno *(Dr. Akemi
Togawa)*
Kenji Sahara *(Dr. Yuzo
Mamiya)*
Jun Tazaki *(Major General
Hashimoto)*
Nobuo Nakamura *(Professor
Kida)*
Hisaya Ito *(Japan Coast Guard
Chief Izumida)*
Yoshifumi Tajima *(Coast
Guard Officer Hirai)*
Nadao Kirino *(Kazama,
General's Aide)*
Ren Yamamoto *(Sailor
Kameda)*
Kipp Hamilton *(Lounge
Singer)*
Tadashi Okabe *(Reporter)*
Yoshio Katsube *(Reporter)*
Minoru Ito *(Reporter)*
Yutaka Oka *(Reporter)*
Hideo Shibuya *(Reporter)*
Masaki Tachibana *(Reporter)*
Henry Okawa *(Doctor)*
Kyoko Mori *(Nurse)*
Ikio Sawamura *(Fisherman)*
Shoichi Hirose *(Mountain
Guide)*
Toku Ihara *(Diver)*
Yasuhisa Tsutumi *(Soldier)*

Mitsuo Tsuda *(Soldier)*
Kozo Nomura *(Soldier)*
Haruo Nakajima *(Gaira)*
Yu Sekita *(Sanda)*
Goro Mutsumi *(Dr. Stewart,
voice)*
Yasuhiro Komiya *(Baby
Sanda)*

Alternate Titles
*Frankenstein - Zweikampf der
Giganten* **[Frankenstein: Duel
of the Giants]** (Germany)
Kempeabernes sidste kamp
**[Last Battle of the Giant
Apes]** (Denmark)
Katango (Italy)
A Invasão dos Gargantuas
[Invasion of the Gargantuas]
(Brazil)
La guerre des monstres **[War
of the Monsters]** (France)
*Ο Πόλεμος των
Γκαργκακντούα* (Greece)
*La batalla de los simios
gigantes* **[Battle of the Giant
Apes]** (Spain)
La guerra de los gargantas
(Mexico)
Pojedynek potworów **[Duel of
the Monsters]** (Poland)
*Чудовища Франкенштейна:
Санда против Гайры* (Russia)
King Kongarnas krig **[King
Kong's War]** (Sweden)
Canavarlar Savaşı (Turkey)

"Frankenstein cannot be found in the ocean."
-Dr. Paul Stewart (Russ Tamblyn)

The War of the Gargantuas is a loose sequel to the previous year's *Frankenstein Conquers the World*. It is an extraordinary 1960s *kaiju* production with particularly inventive effects work and memorable twin creatures. *The War of the Gargantuas* manages to outdo its predecessor despite a barebones script and is influential on both sides of the Pacific.

Featuring unusually grotesque elements and thrilling monster sequences, it has become a signature Japanese monster picture.

PLOT

One stormy night, a steamer is attacked by a giant octopus off the coast of Miura Peninsula. A giant humanoid then appears and fends off the enormous cephalopod before attacking the ship. The sole survivor Kameda (Ren Yamamoto) tells incredulous authorities that the monster devoured his fellow crew and resembled the Frankenstein Monster thought killed at Mount Fuji. Divers soon find the men's clothing in shredded condition. Coast Guard chief Izumida (Hisaya Ito) contacts Frankenstein expert Dr. Stewart (Russ Tamblyn). Stewart and his assistant Akemi (Kumi Mizuno) had the original monster in captivity. They are adamant that Frankenstein couldn't live in the sea and that eating humans is against its gentle nature. More incidents occur at sea as the monster attacks a trawler and gets caught in a fishing net. Dr. Stewart's colleague Dr. Mamiya (Kenji Sahara) investigates, finding the monster's tissue on the wreck. Meanwhile, Stewart and Akemi head to the Japan Alps and find giant footprints there. Mamiya brings the tissue to biologist Dr. Kida (Nobuo Nakamura), who concludes that it matches Frankenstein.

The monster soon comes ashore at Haneda Airport on a cloudy day. It destroys a terminal and eats a woman before being driven away by the sun emerging. Mamiya concludes that the creature is sensitive to light as the military draws up plans to destroy it. The beast attacks a nightclub and tries to devour the singer before heading into the wilderness. The military electrifies the lake and attacks the monster with their new Maser Cannon death-ray weapons. The creature is almost killed, but another, mountain dwelling Frankenstein appears and saves it. The two monsters then disappear into the mountains. Akemi and Dr. Stewart conclude the mountain Frankenstein is the one they had in captivity. The military christens it Sanda and the aquatic Frankenstein Gaira.

Stewart, Akemi and Mamiya collect cell tissue from both monsters and conclude that they are essentially the same creature. Stewart theorizes that Gaira grew from Sanda's tissue that made its way out to sea as he escaped to Lake Biwa. Akemi and Stewart go hiking and Gaira attacks. Akemi then falls down a cliff. Sanda remembers and rescues her, breaking his leg while doing so. Gaira devours several hikers. Sanda, disgusted with his brother's human munching ways, attacks him with a tree trunk. The two monsters make their way to Tokyo with the military in hot pursuit.

BACKGROUND

Tomoyuki Tanaka would begin production on a sequel to *Frankenstein Conquers the World* in early 1966. Called *Frankenstein's Sons* and then *The Frankenstein Brothers*, it was the third collaboration with Henry

Saperstein's United Productions of America. Much of the previous film's creative team would return including Ishiro Honda and Eiji Tsuburaya. Nick Adams was unable to reprise his role and was to be replaced with Tab Hunter. Hunter unavailable, *West Side Story*'s Russ Tamblyn wound up cast instead.

PRINCIPAL PHOTOGRAPHY

Ishiro Honda and Takeshi Kimura's script is barebones. By this time, Kimura had started using the moniker "Kaoru Mabuchi" because he disliked writing monster pictures. There is little character development of any kind. The film relies entirely on its *tokusatsu* spectacle and unique monsters and oddly succeeds in that end. Its connections to *Frankenstein Conquers the World* are loose. It's clear Tamblyn, Kumi Mizuno and Kenji Sahara are playing characters Adams, Mizuno and Tadao Takashima portrayed in *Frankenstein*. Yet they have different names and their laboratory is stationed in Kyoto rather than Hiroshima. *Gargantuas* suffers from an underdeveloped script but is an iconic monster romp through sheer audacity.

Whereas Adams was respectful of the Japanese cast and crew, Russ Tamblyn was by accounts quite the ugly American. He disliked the film's script and took little of Ishiro Honda's direction. Rather than socialize with the Japanese cast, he holed up in his hotel suite with his wife. At one point, while shooting in the mountains, he walked off set and went rock climbing just because he felt like it. Because of his bitter experience

with Tamblyn, Honda was never especially fond of *The War of the Gargantuas*.

SFX

The War of the Gargantuas is unique because it contains some of Eiji Tsuburaya's very best special effects work. Though his attention was already split between Toho and Tsuburaya Pro, he really seemed to take this film to heart. If *Invasion of Astro-Monster* is Ishiro Honda at the top of his form, *Gargantuas* is Eiji Tsuburaya at his. The design work and art direction on Tsuburaya's end of the movie is particularly stellar. The film opens with a battle between Gaira and a giant octopus, a nod to the previous film's deleted ending. For *Frankenstein Conquers the World*, Saperstein had demanded an alternate ending where Frankenstein does battle with an inexplicable giant octopus that just shows up at Mount Fuji. He had loved Tsuburaya's octopus scene in *King Kong vs. Godzilla* and wanted something similar regardless of its value to the story. The sheer ludicrousness of the concept perhaps sinking in, Saperstein wound up rejecting the footage. It went unused in both Japanese and American prints. *The War of the Gargantuas'* opening is a far better executed octopus sequence. The same prop was used for both scenes along with an episode of *Ultra Q*. It was refurbished for its appearance in *Gargantuas* with lights added to its eyes.

The two Gargantuas were designed by Toru Narita (1929-2002). Narita was an artist and modeler known for his creature and mechanical designs in the *Ultraman* franchise. He started off as an uncredited builder on the original *Godzilla* and became a designer for Tsuburaya's team. Inspired by a Japanese myth about brother deities Umihiko and Yamahiko, the designs of the Gargantuas are nightmarish. Gaira is an especially unique creation. Reminiscent of Francesco Goya's famous painting *Saturn Devouring His Son*, he's like a freakish ogre you'd find under a fairy tale bridge hungering for unfortunate travelers crossing by. Haruo Nakajima gives a distinctive performance in the Gaira suit. The suit, built by the Yagi family, was more lightweight than the reptilian beasts he usually portrayed. This allowed him to be faster and more expressive. Nakajima's favorite *kaiju* role after Godzilla would always be Gaira until his dying day. Tsuburaya instructed assistant Eizo Kaimai to keep the Gaira suit "dirty" and seaweed was affixed to it to make it look lived in. Sanda is also unique: a redesigned, more feral version of the first film's Frankenstein Monster covered in fur. The two Gargantua masks, molded from the actors' faces by Teizo Toshimitsu, have the disturbing feature of using the actors' real eyes, giving them an unsettling humanity. Unlike dinosaurian kaiju who have slower paced, lumbering battles as a result of the heavy suits, the lighter nature of the Gargantua costumes allowed for faster, more violent fights. In the film's finale, the creatures have a full-on brawl like two angry drunk *yakuza* in a deathmatch. This was unsettling to Japanese audiences at the time.

The film's newest ray-gun weapons, the Type 66 Maser Cannons, would become an iconic staple of the kaiju franchise as well. They were not present in the original script and were added at Honda's suggestion. Designed by Mutsumi Toyoshima and Yasuyuki Inoue, they bring elements to synthesis of rays in previous films like *The Mysterians, Mothra* and *Invasion of Astro-Monster*. Iodine lamps were used to make them light up. Often via stock footage from *The War of the Gargantuas* itself, they would return in many films to come.

Gargantuas is notable as Yasuyuki Inoue's first film as main SFX art director; for years he had worked as Akira Watanabe's right hand man. Inoue (1922-2012) lost his foot in World War II, developing a love of furniture making in a rehabilitation program for wounded veterans. While visiting a set on Shin Toho's lot, the impoverished Inoue was given a free meal and returned the next day. When it was found out that he could build sets and miniatures, he was quickly hired. He would move to Toho; joining Tsuburaya's unit on the original *Godzilla* two years later. There he soon became a valued team member. Inoue was entrusted with choosing building materials and estimating costs. Mutsumi Toyoshima was a young designer recruited by Inoue in 1959. He would go on to create the Moonlight SY-3 in *Destroy All Monsters* (1968). Inoue's art direction of the miniatures in *Gargantuas* is particularly impressive. They are among the most realistic Tsuburaya's unit achieved. The artificial forests, valleys and cities are built with a particular attention to detail, being at a larger scale than usual. The forests were made of living miniature pines and nearly every single tree had unseen roots added. This was so they would look realistic if torn up by the suit actors.

The "Maser" attack sequence against Gaira is particularly thrilling. The scene is staged and edited excitingly, as is the film's final urban duel between the beasts. *The War of the Gargantuas* was to end more elaborately with the underwater volcano destroying Tokyo. The end sequence would have made it clear that the Gargantuas and their cells were destroyed. Honda was in favor of this. Tanaka, however, felt an extra destruction sequence would have been too expensive, though shots from *The Last War* were going to be used to supplement Tsuburaya's footage.

MUSIC

Akira Ifukube gives another one of his best scores, exhilarating and even powerful if a little repetitive in bits. His theme for the Gargantuas incorporates motifs of his previous title piece from *Frankenstein Conquers the World*. The *"Operation L March"* is one of Ifukube's most notable military marches, though perhaps overused on the soundtrack. Reorchestrated versions would go on to be re-used in *Godzilla vs. Mothra* (1992) and *Godzilla vs. Destoroyah* (1995).

RELEASE AND LEGACY

The War of the Gargantuas wound up one of Toho's most influential *kaiju* films after the original *Godzilla*. It has admirers on both

sides of the Pacific. *Batman* director Tim Burton has called it one of his favorites and Quentin Tarantino put nods to it in *Kill Bill Vol. 2.* Tarantino later screened the film at his New Beverly Cinema in Los Angeles. *Crank 2: High Voltage* (2009), directed by Mark Neveldine and Brian Taylor, features a loving comedic homage. In the film, Jason Statham and an opponent become giants and battle it out at a miniature power station *tokusatsu* style. *The Shape of Water* director Guillermo Del Toro has also sung the film's praises. It would be an inspiration on several sequences in his giant monster film homage *Pacific Rim* (2013). In Japan, the film's concept would inspire *manga* artist Hajime Isayama to create *Attack on Titan*. Later issues would feature a "Beast Titan" obviously inspired by Sanda. Special effects wizard and director Shinji Higuchi is another of the film's biggest fans. It was an influence on the human-eating Gyaos monsters in *Gamera: Guardian of the Universe* (1995) along with a tonal and aesthetic inspiration for his live action *Attack on Titan* duo-logy. American rock group Devo are also fans. They covered the lounge scene's show stopping number *"The Words Get Stuck in My Throat"* for their compilation album *Pioneers Who Got Scalped.*

Attempts to bring the Gargantuas back to the big screen have been made. Saperstein would try to get a *Godzilla vs. Gargantua* film off the ground in 1978 but plans fell through. Sanda and Gaira's dog-eared costumes would reappear on Toho's poverty row kiddie programs *Godman* (1972-73) and *Greenman* (1973-74). Gaira would reappear decades later in *Go! Godman*, a direct to video *Godman* spin-off made in 2008 in a new suit created by Fuyuki Shinada.

ALTERNATE VERSIONS

An export version, editorially identical to the Japanese cut, was made. The film was dubbed into English in Hong Kong, likely by Barry Haigh's firm Po Hwa Dubbing Company. Sources have attributed the dub to Tokyo's Frontier Enterprises, but it's clearly a Hong Kong job. It features the unmistakable voices of HK talent like Haigh, Lynn Wilson, Nick Kendall, Ian Wilson and Warren Rooke. The garbled voices and poor mixing is in line with the acoustics of these dubs, Frontier having better equipment. Most of the versions shown in Europe and elsewhere are edits of the export cut. Its dub script retains the Frankenstein references later deleted from the U.S. version. In Germany, the film was entitled *Frankenstein- Zweikampf der Giganten* (*Frankenstein: Duel of the Giants*). It did good enough business that German distributor Constantin Film began importing all its *kaiju* films retitled and dubbed so that Dr. Frankenstein was responsible for the monsters.

The War of the Gargantuas would not receive a U.S. release until 1970. It was paired with Toho and UPA's previous *Invasion of Astro-Monster* (retitled *Monster Zero*) and distributed by Maron Films. Unlike the former, the American version is considerably different. It is a rare US version significantly longer than the Japanese, running over four minutes more at 92:04. All references to

Frankenstein are obscured, the monsters now passed off as Yeti-like cryptozoological oddities. There are a significant handful of new and alternate sequences. The Japan Coast Guard calls Dr. Stewart's laboratory far earlier in the film. Stewart accompanies the police as they talk to the survivor of the first boat and investigate the wreckage. There's an alternate version of a dialog scene early on between Stewart, Akemi and Mamiya. An additional dialogue scene takes place later in the film where the monsters are compared to the Old Testament's Cain and Abel. A shot of the dead woman's bloody clothes falling to the ground is added to the Haneda airport scene. There are some added special effects shots and an additional line of dialog from Akemi toward the end of the film. The most profound changes are in the soundtrack. The film's score and sound design are overhauled in the U.S. version and not for the better. New foley is added in some instances and Ifukube's majestic score is tampered with. New music is added in portions (mainly from Ifukube's score for *Invasion of Astro-Monster*). The *"Operation L March"* is deleted, replaced with a cheap library track by Phillip Green called *"Terror Hunt"*. The cue was also used in the terrible indie *Zaat* (1972). Despite its people eating sequences, *The War of the Gargantuas* received a "G" rating from the MPAA.

AMERICAN HOME VIDEO HISTORY

The U.S. version of *The War of the Gargantuas* was first released on VHS and laserdisc in 1994 by Paramount/Gateway. It was released to DVD in 2008 by Classic

Media in a set with *Rodan*. This would contain both the Japanese version with subtitles, ported from Toho's DVD and a scan of the U.S. version. *Gargantuas* is currently not in print on American home video, though Janus Films now has the rights and a Criterion release is possible. It can be streamed on Starz, HBO Max and The Criterion Channel in the meantime.

Further Viewing:

FRANKENSTEIN CONQUERS THE WORLD

(1965)
フランケンシュタイン対地底怪獣
Toho, *Director*: **Ishiro Honda**

Frankenstein Conquers the World was another project seeded from the sale of Willis O'Brien's *King Kong vs. Prometheus* script to Toho. They had opted to substitute their own Godzilla for a Frankenstein-like monster in *King Kong vs, Godzilla*. Yet Toho entertained ideas of creating their own rendition of Mary Shelley's monster. Initially, they considered matching Frankenstein with *The Human Vapor*. This idea was scrapped and *Frankenstein vs. Godzilla* was then considered. In the end Toho decided on a solo project for Frankenstein. *Frankenstein vs. Godzilla*'s script would form the basis for the finished product, however as Godzilla was substituted for novel beastie Baragon.

Frankenstein Conquers the World presents Mary Shelley's creation through a distinct Japanese lens. The monster is reimagined, ala Godzilla, in the shadow of World War II. The film boasts a fantastic opening. The undying heart of Frankenstein's monster is smuggled out of Nazi Germany during the Fall of Berlin and sent by U-Boat to Imperial Japan. As army doctors in Hiroshima examine the deathless heart, Little Boy falls on the city. The heart is irradiated and, twenty years later, grows into a young waif. The boy has been terrorizing the local neighborhood and eating people's pets. The creature is taken in by a trio of doctors researching radiation: Drs. Bowen (Nick Adams), Kawaji (Tadao Takashima) and Togami (Kumi Mizuno). The boy (Koji Furuhata) grows gigantic and escapes their lab, fleeing into the mountains.

Frankenstein Conquers the World is a spirited and entertaining but uneven film. It feels like two movies in one. The first half is an effective and atmospheric horror film where Ishiro Honda's unit shines. The second is a sillier *kaiju* film dominated by Tsuburaya that doesn't quite measure up. The World War II-set opening scenes are Honda at the absolute top of his form. Early scenes featuring the Frankenstein Monster are also effective with a horror movie tone. Akira Ifukube's score is one of his most unique and eerie, his closest to a horror score. Eiji Tsuburaya's FX work in the middle act's scenes is subtle and well crafted. Tsuburaya and his crew especially enjoyed working on these scenes. They got to build the miniatures for these sequences at a much larger scale. Tsuburaya enjoyed the challenge of creating more sympathetic monster scenes where the creature interacted with Honda's actors directly. Takeshi Kimura's script features an empathetic depiction of the monster. It reimagines Shelley's literary titan as a *hibakusha* (A-bomb survivor). Yet Kimura and Honda's vision is oddly in line with Shelley's. Frankenstein's Monster, like Godzilla and the atomic bomb, is a perfect incarnation of science's misuse.

The film's second half introduces the dopey but endearing rabbit-eared *kaiju* Baragon as an adversary. From there, *Frankenstein Conquers the World* develops a charming ludicrousness. The final battle between the two monsters is overlong. Furuhata's Frankenstein, a recognizable actor in makeup, battling Nakajima's suitmation Baragon doesn't quite work. Tsuburaya had fun with these scenes, though Honda was uncertain about them. These sequences are pure spectacle and one is advised to shut off their brain and take in the kaiju carnage. There are some stellar composite shots that are among the best in Tsuburaya's career. The film's alternate ending, shot at the behest of Saperstein, is ridiculous but a trip. It features a giant octopus showing up at random to drag Frankenstein into a lake. The shooting for it was rushed and the octopus prop isn't well executed. It would be employed far more effectively in *The War of the Gargantuas.*

THE ENGLISH DUBBING DOSSIER

英語吹き替え

One of the most prevalent stereotypes of Japanese science fiction films is that they're "badly dubbed" into English. It's true that many of the English dubs of these films are no substitute for watching them in Japanese. Yet dubbing is hardly the boogeyman some make it out to be. Not only is dubbing necessary for multiple reasons, plenty of English dubs were and still are done with surprising aesthetic care. In the 1950s through the '80s, there were several hubs that produced English dubs of varying quality for Japanese films. These included New York City, Los Angeles, Tokyo, Hong Kong and even Rome. Today, dubbing for live action Japanese films is mainly undertaken by firms that specialize in voicing anime.

The original 1954 *Godzilla* was released to American screens as *Godzilla, King of the Monsters!* This version added American actor Raymond Burr into the mix and some scenes contained rudimentary dubbing. This was mainly done by Chinese-American actor James Hong. This early, partial dub was crude and was done without the use of loops. Later 1950s dubs fared a bit better. They were mainly done in Los Angeles. The dubs for the U.S. versions of *Godzilla Raids Again* and *Rodan* featured Hong, Keye Luke (*Gremlins*) and even early voice roles by *Star Trek*'s George Takei. Other 1950s dubs included *The H-Man*'s dub done in Los Angeles with voice giant Paul Frees. Another was *The Mysterians*, dubbed by Austrian businessman Peter Riethof in New York. New York would soon become a major hub for dubbing with the establishment of

Titra Sound Studios, renamed Titan in the mid 1960s.

Titra's offices took up three floors inside the National Screen Building at 1600 Broadway between 48th and 49th streets in Manhattan. They became one of the most in-demand dubbing studios in the U.S. Titra/Titan worked with a wide pool of clients from independent filmmakers to major Hollywood studios. Their talent was pooled from the local stage and soap opera acting scene. Actors who often dubbed for them included Peter Fernandez, Hal Linden, Lucy Martin, Jack Curtis, Bret Morrison, Kenneth Harvey and Bernard Grant. Titra's dubbing was known for its high quality. These English dubs were superior to the "export dubs" produced in Asia or even the work of ELDA in Rome. Titra's talent would spend days and sometimes weeks on a single dub. This was in stark contrast to Hong Kong groups that tended to dub a whole film in a night or two. Titra's English dubs of Japanese films are marred only by faux Asian accents some find problematic today. This may be part of why Toho is now suppressing these dubs, along with actor union royalty issues. Most famously, Titan did one of the first anime dubs for television: *Speed Racer*. They finally ceased operations in the 1980s.

By the early to mid 1960s, the Japanese studios began to produce "export dubs" recorded locally in Asia. These low quality dubs were often redone at Titra/Titan or in Los Angeles by the American distributors. Yet they allowed the films to be sold internationally at film markets with ease. Tokyo itself became a major dubbing hub. Many films were sent to William Ross' dubbing studio Frontier, established in 1964. Ross ran his studio using the freelance voices of Anglophone expats who lived in Tokyo. These included Burr Middleton, Cliff Harrington, Robert Dunham and Budd Widom. Many of these actors, including Ross, Harrington and Dunham, often played small on screen roles in Japanese films. Bill Ross dubbed more Japanese movies than anyone else and Frontier continued operations until the early 2000s. Another Japan-based dubbing studio was Pedro Productions, run by a man named Pedro Komiyama. These dubs were far below even Frontier's quality. They include the awful export dub for 1969's *Gamera vs. Guiron* and likely the one for *The X From Outer Space* (1967).

Another major dubbing hub in Asia was Hong Kong. The phrase "Hong Kong dub" is a joke of sorts and indeed, they are pretty poor. Yet unlike Tokyo where most of the Western expats were Americans, Hong Kong was an English colony. This gave the dubs a more unusual sound as they were written and performed in a standard "Mid Atlantic" English tone. Ted Thomas' Axis International was likely the first dubbing team in Hong Kong. Another was Po Hwa Dubbing Studio, run by Barry Haigh. By the 1970s, there were multiple dubbing groups competing for work. The Hong Kong dubbers were often employed as newscasters for local English language stations like Radio Television Hong Kong. For them, recording these dubs was a side gig to make extra money. RTHK correspondent Ron Oliphant would often write Axis' dubs. The performers would crowd around a microphone in a cigarette smoke filled apartment and voice projected film loops. This was usually after digging into a spread of Chinese food. Most of their work came from the nearby Hong Kong film studios such as Shaw Brothers, Cathay and Golden Harvest. Yet Japanese studios like Toho often enlisted their quick and cheap services when Ross' Frontier was occupied. Another HK dubbing studio was Voicetrax, run by a young entrepreneur named Matthew Oram. Toho began to use Oram's firm almost entirely for their export dubs by the mid 1970s and '80s. Other notable Hong Kong dub voices include Chris Hilton, Michael Kaye, Warren Rooke and Linda Masson. Vaughan Savidge also ran a group in the late '70s. He mainly dubbed low budget Taiwanese films however and never did any Japanese work.

By the 1980s, Ted Thomas largely retired from dubbing. Another Brit expat, Rik Thomas, was running a dubbing firm called Omni Productions. Yet another group was run by a woman named Annie Mathers. Frequent voices from this period included John Culkin, Warwick Paul Evans, Simon Broad and Suzanne Vale. Many expats left Hong Kong after the mainland Chinese handover in 1997, but dubbing continued on a smaller scale. Fittingly, the final *tokusatsu* film dubbed into English in Hong Kong was *Godzilla: Final Wars*. The dub is credited to Red Angel Media which still exists. In the mid 2000s, Rik Thomas sold Omni Productions and retired to Malaysia.

Another major dubbing hub in the 1960s through '80s was Rome, Italy. The largest dubbing studio in Rome was the English Language Dubbers Association or ELDA. Of course, they mainly dubbed the numerous B-pictures being produced in Italy at the time. These included *giallos*, Spaghetti Westerns, *peplums* and Eurospy pictures. Occasionally, however, they did work on

Asian films. American International sent several films to Rome for dubbing after rejecting their export tracks including *Gamera vs. Barugon* and *The X From Outer Space*. The biggest player in the Italian English dubbing scene was Ted Rusoff. The voice of Rusoff (1939-2013) can be heard in over a thousand films. Rusoff occasionally acted on screen as well. He appeared in Martin Scorsese's *The Last Temptation of Christ* and played the leader of the Pharisees in Mel Gibson's *Passion of the Christ*. English dubs were also on occasion recorded in England and France. The odd, unfamiliar dub for 1977's *The War in Space* is believed to have been recorded in Paris.

Back in the U.S., the music and movie industry capital of Los Angeles was a major English dubbing hub as well. LA recorded *tokusatsu* dubs, often done at Ryder Sound Services, featured the voices of esteemed talent like Paul Frees and Marvin Miller. Both Miller and Frees did frequent work for Disney. The final Los Angeles dub to date was for *Godzilla 2000*, voice directed by Michael Schlesinger. Though a mediocre Godzilla entry on its own, Schlesinger went the extra mile. He spent around a million dollars for one of the best modern English dubs. Schlesinger cast Asian-American talent to make the voices sound authentic and redid the sound design. Even the proud Toho has acknowledged his version as outright superior.

From the 1980s on, anime developed a following in the U.S. Dubbing it into English became an industry in itself. Occasionally, anime dubbing studios would do live action Japanese films. An early luminary was Carl Macek (1951-2010) and his company

Streamline. Streamline did a few live action films such as *Zeiram* (1991). Bang Zoom! Entertainment dubbed occasional live action films as well, often working with home video distributor Media Blasters. ADV Films was a major anime distributor founded in Houston, Texas in 1992. They did their own in-house anime dubs in addition to subtitled releases for works like *Neon Genesis Evangelion*. They created dubs for all three of the *Heisei Gamera* trilogy. Funimation, founded in the 1990s, has since become a giant in anime distribution. Funimation dubs the occasional live action film such as *Space Battleship Yamato, Attack on Titan* and *Shin Godzilla*. Today, fewer live action Asian films are dubbed into English and are almost never released into theaters dubbed. In today's industry, live action Japanese film dubbing overlaps almost completely with anime dubbing. Rather than cram multiple actors into a booth watching film or video loops, today these dubs are recorded with individual voice talent. They are then edited and mixed together digitally.

At a press release from Cannes last year, Toho made the confounding statement *"The Godzilla films produced by Toho have so far not been dubbed, with very few exceptions"*. This is a film series and genre where the "bad dubbing" is an aesthetic joke. The remark, coupled with the lack of English versions on the Criterion Blu-ray set, is perhaps an ominous giveaway. Toho likely plans to suppress and make most English versions of these films unavailable, supplanting them with crisp new dubs. This is unfortunate. These dubs are part of a moviegoing heritage and have an authenticity that newly recorded tracks don't. Though hated by purists and cinephiles, English dubbing has its place, especially for Japanese monster movies. A major audience for these films are children. Outside Japan, these films become far more accessible to their target audience dubbed. Would anyone reading this have become a Godzilla fan if they had to watch subtitled versions as a six year old? Dubbing allows younger audiences worldwide to experience and enjoy these films. Adults can now switch on the Japanese tracks with subtitles if they don't like dubbed movies.

Kaijuto no Kessen: Gojira no Musuko "Decisive Battle of Monster Island: Son of Godzilla" Toho, 12/16/1967 (*Showa 42*), 6 Reels (2,341 meters), 85:32, 35mm, TohoScope (2.35:1 anamorphic), Eastman color, monaural sound

Crew
Producer: Tomoyuki Tanaka
Director: Jun Fukuda
Special Effects Directors: Eiji Tsuburaya (supervising), Sadamasa Arikawa
Screenplay: Shinichi Sekizawa, Kazue Kiba
Director of Photography: Kazuo Yamada
Music: Masaru Sato
Editor: Ryohei Fujii
Assistant Director: Takashi Nagano
Production Design: Takeo Kita
Lighting: Eiji Yamaguchi, Shoshichi Kojima
Sound Editor: Minoru Kaneyama
Sound Recording: Toshio Ban, Shin Watari
Sound Effects: Hisashi Shimonaga
Production Manager: Yasuaki Sakamoto
Assistant SFX Director: Teruyoshi Nakano
SFX Cinematography: Yoichi Manoda, Mototaka Tomioka
SFX Art Director: Yasuyuki Inoue

SFX Lighting: Kuichiro Kishida
SFX Opticals: Hiroshi Mukoyama
SFX Wire Work: Fumio Nakadai
Still Photographer: Kazukiyo Tanaka
SFX Still Photographer: Kazukiyo Tanaka

Cast
Tadao Takashima *(Dr. Tsunezo Kusumi)*
Akira Kubo *(Goro Maki)*
Beverly Maeda *(Saeko Matsumiya)*
Akihiko Hirata *(Fujisaki)*
Yoshio Tsuchiya *(Furukawa)*
Kenji Sahara *(Morio)*
Kenichiro Maruyama *(Ozawa)*
Seishiro Kuno *(Tashiro)*
Yasuhiko Saijo *(Suzuki)*
Susumu Kurobe *(Meteorological Observatory Captain)*
Kazuo Suzuki *(Meteorological Observatory Pilot)*
Wataru Omae *(Radio Operator)*
Chotaro Togin *(Meteorological Surveyor)*

Osman Yusuf *(Submarine Officer)*
Seiji Onaka *(Godzilla)*
Haruo Nakajima *(Godzilla)*
Yu Sekita *(Godzilla)*
Masao Fukazawa *(Minilla)*

Alternate Titles
Frankensteins Monster jagen Godzillas Sohn
[Frankenstein's Monster Hunts Godzilla's Son] (Germany)
El hijo de Godzilla (Spain)
La Planète des monstres **[The Planet of Monsters]** (France)
Il figlio di Godzilla (Italy)
Στην Ζούγκλα των Χαμένων Τεράτων **[In the Jungle of the Lost Monsters]** (Greece)
Frankensteinin saari **[Frankenstein Island]** (Finland)
Syn Godzilli (Poland)
Godzillas son (Sweden)
Сын Годзиллы (Russia)

"Have you ever seen a monster hatched from a monster egg? No? You will! In Toho's production Son of Godzilla!*"*
-International poster

By the mid 1960s, the Godzilla series was transitioning to a child oriented focus while keeping its creative spirit intact. This is most apparent in *Son of Godzilla*, energetically directed by Jun Fukuda. It's an underrated and enchanting entry with a breezy Masaru Sato score and lush island locales. *Son of Godzilla* features well crafted effects work from Tsuburaya's cameraman Sadamasa Arikawa.

PLOT

On the remote Sollgel Island in the Pacific, United Nations affiliated scientists are conducting a large-scale experiment. Led by Dr. Kusumi (Tadao Takashima), they

are attempting to change the island's tropical climate through weather control. This would allow any land on Earth to be made fertile and save the world's population from Malthusian catastrophe. A reporter, Goro Maki (Akira Kubo), parachutes down to the island, hungry for a story. Kusumi and his assistant Fujisaki (Akihiko Hirata) begrudgingly allow Maki to stay on the condition that he cook and clean. That night, the camp encounters a giant praying mantis. The next day, while collecting greens for cooking, Maki encounters a native girl (Beverly Maeda). She vanishes under the water when he tries to photograph her.

The weather control experiment is ready to be conducted the following day. The test is at first going well, but then radio waves jam the equipment. This causes the experiment to go awry, creating intense heat and radioactive, boiling rains. After a few days, the heat and rain stops. As the men check the equipment for damage, the mantids attack, having grown even larger to giant size. The monster mantids, dubbed "Kamakiras" by Maki, unearth a gigantic monster egg. As the Kamakiras claw at the egg, it hatches into Minilla, a baby Godzilla and the source of the radio waves. The adult Godzilla soon appears from the sea and advances on Sollgel Island. It rescues Minilla from the Kamakiras, killing a pair of them and driving away another.

Maki next catches the native girl trying to steal his shirt. He pursues her into a cave and finds out that she's actually Japanese. Named Saeko Matsumiya, she's the daughter of a late Japanese doctor who stayed behind on the island after the war. With their camp destroyed by Godzilla, the scientists move their equipment into Saeko's cave. Soon afterwards, several of the scientists come down with a mysterious fever. Saeko and Maki go to collect mineral-rich red water that can cure the fever. They witness Godzila "tutoring" Minilla. The water cures the men, though the homesick Furukawa (Yoshio Tsuchiya) grabs a rifle in a delirious state and grazes Dr. Kusumi with a bullet. One day, Saeko is attacked by a Kamakiras while gathering edible plants in the jungle. Minilla comes to her rescue but accidentally awakens Kumonga, a gigantic monster spider. Kumonga tries to trap the scientists inside by spinning a web. Fujisaki soon makes contact with the U.N. who have already sent a rescue ship. Kusumi decides to conduct the experiment with the hope of freezing the monsters.

BACKGROUND

Godzilla's transformation from stand-in for the existential horror of the atomic bomb to a benevolent force was almost complete. For 1966's *Ebirah, Horror of the Deep*, Toho opted for a change of scenery, both literally and figuratively. Ishiro Honda stepped aside. The keys to the franchise were given to Jun Fukuda, an action programmer specialist. Eiji Tsuburaya was now splitting his time between Toho and his own television productions. He placed his DP, Sadamasa

Arikawa, in charge of the effects unit and took only a supervisory role. The locale was also changed from metropolitan Japan to the exotic South Pacific. While some find these entries inferior to Honda's classics, they have an underrated charm of their own. They successfully bring the Godzilla series in a new direction, even if it wasn't entirely better.

Tomoyuki Tanaka decided to create their next film around a baby monster. Along with children, Toho wanted to draw in a "date crowd" for the film. They figured a baby monster would bring in female viewers, perhaps tapping into the young Japanese woman's mothering instinct. Kazue Kiba, a woman, was brought in to assist Shinichi Sekizawa in writing the script. Kiba had previously submitted a proposal to Toho called *Two Godzillas: Japan S.O.S.* This is where the concept for a baby Godzilla sprang. Kiba was the first woman credited with a major creative, behind-the-camera role in a *tokusatsu* film. Minilla was named via a contest held by Toho where 8,211 applicants submitted name ideas for Godzilla's offspring.

PRINCIPAL PHOTOGRAPHY

Director Jun Fukuda opted for a far more human portrayal of the monsters than in prior entries. *Son of Godzilla* would be a final step in humanizing Godzilla. The nuclear horror who burned civilians to a crisp in 1954 was now rearing an adorably monstrous child. While it sounds embarrassing on paper, *Son of Godzilla* is so creatively executed that it's a standout entry.

Son of Godzilla takes the exotic locale of *Ebirah* a step further. Location sequences were filmed on the tropical U.S. territory of Guam. The actors all flew to Guam with the exception of Tadao Takashima. Takashima was afraid to fly and a local Filipino-Chinese man who resembled him was hired as a stand-in. The lush Guam locals add a lot in terms of realism and are well integrated with footage shot on Toho's lot. The main unit's cinematography by Kazuo Yamada is engagingly shot. Yamada would also lens *Samurai Rebellion* for Masaki Kobayashi that same year.

ACTORS

The cast features many classic Toho contract players such as Akira Kubo, Takashima and Akihiko Hirata. The name of Kubo's character, Goro Maki, would be reused in both 1984's *The Return of Godzilla* and 2016's *Shin Godzilla*. Yoshio Tsuchiya plays a dark turn as Furukawa, a scientist driven to madness by cabin fever and homesickness. Beverly "Bibari" Maeda (1948-) plays Saeko and was a relative newcomer. The daughter of an American G.I. and Japanese woman, she was raised in Kamakura. Maeda was a talented dancer and singer. She rose to prominence with an appearance in a Shishido cosmetics commercial at the age of 18. In 1968, she married folk singer Mike Maki and cancelled her contract with Toho, moving to the U.S. She divorced Maki in 1976 and returned to Japan where she's taken character roles ever since.

SFX

The special effects work by Sadamasa Arikawa is, overall, the finest solo job in his career. There are stunning composites throughout and the miniatures are excellent. For *Son of Godzilla*, a new, far larger suit was built by Teizo Toshimitsu and Yasuei Yagi. This was partially to emphasize Godzilla's size against Minilla's. This suit was so big that Haruo Nakajima had to be recast. In his stead, baseball player Seiji Onaka portrayed Godzilla. However, Onaka broke his fingers during a game. As a result, Yu Sekita, who played Sanda in *The War of the Gargantuas*, was brought in to finish the Godzilla scenes. Haruo Nakajima did portray Godzilla in water scenes, wearing the suit from the previous two films. The *Son of Godzilla* suit would later be reused for the water scenes in 1972's *Godzilla vs. Gigan*. An image of this suit was used for the cover of Blue Oyster Cult's hit single "*Godzilla*".

Minilla is an adorable and empathetic character, if fairly disliked. Newborn Minilla was portrayed by a two foot puppet in early scenes. Toddler Minilla is played by Masao Fukuzawa, better known as "Little Man Machan". Fukazawa (1921-2000) was a little person and professional wrestler. He had difficulty moving in the suit and walked in a wobbly manner. Arikawa, however, thought this only enhanced his performance and made it convincingly toddler-like. Arikawa had wanted Minilla's atomic breath to resemble a *shuriken* (ninja star). It was Eiji Tsuburaya who came up with the idea to have the baby monster puff atomic "smoke-Os". This

wound up one of the most iconic and memorable images in *Son of Godzilla*.

Son of Godzilla's other monsters are portrayed by intricate marionettes. The most brilliantly executed is the beastly spider Kumonga. Kamakiras and Kumonga were designed by Yasuyuki Inoue. Kumonga's puppet was modeled by Teizo Toshimitsu. The Kamakiras marionettes were built by Nobuyuki Yasumaru, who would be Toshimitsu's successor. The Kumonga prop was a whopping 18 feet long. Controlled by piano wire, it required 20 puppeteers for some shots. Each leg alone required two people. Kumonga's webbing was largely the same polystyrene recipe used to create Mothra's cocoon silk in earlier films. A similar dispenser was installed in the puppet's mouth. The wire-work and puppetry is highly dynamic and among the finest in the series.

The final sequence, where Godzilla and Minilla go into hibernation, has surprising pathos. For one of the first times in the Toho special effects oeuvre, one feels genuine empathy for the monsters. The fake snow used was a mix of styrofoam and paraffin. Arikawa chose paraffin as it slowly melted similarly to snow. The scene was originally longer with more narrative tension. Godzilla was to contemplate abandoning Minilla in the snow. The monster began to wade into the ocean before having a change of heart and turning around. A portion of this extended sequence can be seen in Toho's trailer.

MUSIC

The scores for both *Ebirah, Horror of the Deep* and *Son of Godzilla* are by Masaru Sato. His music was lighter, jazzier and less militaristic than Ifukube's. This is particularly notable in *Ebirah* and *Son of Godzilla*. Sato's breezy musical stylings well complement the films' dramatic changes in both locale and tone. It's hard to even imagine Ifukube scoring *Son of Godzilla*.

RELEASE AND LEGACY

Both of Toho's monster films for 1967, *King Kong Escapes* and *Son of Godzilla*, failed to set the box office ablaze. Toho thus began planning for the close to their '60s monster cycle: *Destroy All Monsters*. It did well enough that Tanaka decided to continue making Godzilla pictures for an exclusive child audience. The films, starting with *All Monsters Attack* in 1969, would now be distributed through Toho's Champion Matsuri program. Minilla would return in both *Destroy All Monsters* and *All Monsters Attack*. A similar Godzilla offspring appeared in the *Heisei*-era entries *Godzilla vs. Mechagodzilla II*, *Godzilla vs. Space Godzilla* and *Godzilla vs. Destoroyah*. Minilla itself would return in 2004's *Godzilla: Final Wars* alongside Kumonga and Kamakiras.

ALTERNATE VERSIONS

An export English version, identical to the Japanese save for English supers, was created. The English dubbing was done in Tokyo by William Ross' Frontier Enterprises. Dubbing cast includes Ross as Kusumi, Burr Middleton as Goro Maki and Suzuki, Carol Wyland as Saeko, Robert Dunham as Fujisaki, Cliff Harrington as Morio and Bud Widom as Ozawa. Middleton (1941-) was an American expat and actor born in Los Angeles. He was the grandson of Charles Middleton, best known as Ming the Merciless in the original *Flash Gordon* serials. He dubbed Akira Kubo again in the export *Destroy All Monsters*. Middleton left Japan in the early '70s and still plays bit roles on television to this day. His distinctive voice can be heard on a 2004 episode of *Star Trek: Enterprise*.

In 1969, *Son of Godzilla* was sold to American television by the Water Reade Organization. This version, running around 84 minutes, has minimal alterations. The main changes are the deletion of the film's opening scene. This scene features Susumu Kurobe (*Ultraman*) as a meteorological plane captain sighting Godzilla. The opening credits are textless, with no indication of who made the film. The rest of the film is left unaltered.

The English dub was recorded in New York by Titan Productions. Dubbing cast includes William Kiehl as Kusumi, Peter Fernandez as Goro Maki, Lucy Martin as Saeko, Kenneth Harvey as Furukawa and Larry Robinson as Ozawa. In both the Frontier and Titan dubs, Saeko is called "Reiko" and Kamakiras and Kumonga are called "Gimantis" and "Spiga". Peter Fernandez is one of the most notable voice actors who often worked for Titan. Fernandez (1927-2010) was best known as the voice of *Speed Racer* in its American dub, recorded at Titan. A World War II veteran, he started off as a prolific radio voice actor. Before long he became involved in voicing cartoons and dubbing foreign films. His voice can be heard in many animated shows up to his death, including *Batman: The Animated Series*, *Dexter's Laboratory*, *The Powerpuff Girls* and *Courage, the Cowardly Dog*. Fittingly, his career was capped by a small role in the Wachowskis' live action *Speed Racer* (2008).

For the August 1973 Champion Matsuri festival, *Son of Godzilla* was re-released in an edited version. This version is cut down to a brisk 65:50. Like the U.S. version, the opening sequence with Susumu Kurobe is cut. The early conversation between Morio (Kenji Sahara) and Furukawa is also edited out, as is the opening of Maki's parachute scene. A comedic scene where Maki soaks vegetables in a laundry crate is removed. The opening of a scene where Kusumi explains the experiment to Maki is also truncated. A musical montage showing experiment preparation is excised. A conversation between Kusumi and Fujisaki mentioning that Maki has dubbed the giant mantids "Kamakiras" is cut. Furukawa's first breakdown is removed with the film cutting straight to Godzilla surfacing in a choppy fashion. Later, a suspenseful scene where Maki and Saeko pass through Kumonga's valley is also cut. The ending of the sequence where Kusumi is shot by Furukawa is excised as is a bit showing preparations for the second experiment. As with the other Champion cuts, the special effects end of the film is almost entirely intact, as is the final reel.

AMERICAN HOME VIDEO HISTORY

Son of Godzilla was released to VHS stateside in 1987 by Video Treasures. Before that, there were unauthorized releases by Videoline and Hollywood Home Theatre. Later, *Son of Godzilla* was reissued in 1997 by Anchor Bay. In 2004, the film was released to DVD by Sony containing both Japanese audio and the export dub. In 2017, *Son of Godzilla* was acquired by Janus. It was eventually released to Blu-ray on Criterion as part of the *Godzilla: The Showa Era* set.

Further Viewing:

(1966)

ゴジラ・エビラ・モスラ　南海の大決闘

Toho, *Director*: **Jun Fukuda**

Ebirah, Horror of the Deep began life as *Operation Robinson Crusoe*, a project starring King Kong. The U.S. producers wanted Ishiro Honda to direct the film. Tomoyuki Tanaka, however, was adamant on Jun Fukuda as director. As Honda was occupied with his romantic comedy *Come Marry Me,* the project was retooled to star Godzilla instead of Kong. Like its successor, *Ebirah* is a very underrated entry and a lot of fun.

Fukuda's direction is more lively than Honda's clinical sensibility with stylistic flair.

A group of castaways led by on-the-lam bank robber Yoshimura (Akira Takarada) wash ashore on an island. Here, evil communist organization Red Bamboo is using the people of Infant Island as slaves to manufacture nuclear weapons. The monsters don't come into play until the middle of the second act. Godzilla battles giant mantis shrimp Ebirah who looks like something you'd eat in Japan. Mothra appears in the film as well, acting as a deus ex machina to save the protagonists as the island is spectacularly destroyed in a nuclear explosion. Emi and Yumi Ito were also unavailable for *Ebirah* and were replaced by second string twin duo Pair Bambi. The script by Shinichi Sekizawa is well written with one of the most engaging human plots in the Godzilla series. Newcomer Noriko Takahashi was to play the native girl Dayo and some scenes with her were even filmed. She ruptured her appendix and had to be hastily replaced by Kumi Mizuno. Akihiko Hirata shows up as a Red Bamboo lieutenant with an eye patch, an obvious nod to Serizawa.

Though credited as special effects director, Eiji Tsuburaya stepped back and left his DP Sadamasa Arikawa in charge of *Ebirah*. Arikawa's FX are spirited with particularly strong miniature work and pyrotechnics. There's even novel and highly dangerous underwater photography using the monster suits. One sequence, a nod to the pterodactyl scene in *King Kong*, features a giant condor. It's actually a redressed version of the Litra

puppet from *Ultra Q*'s pilot episode. Godzilla behaves in a very Kong-like fashion: being awakened by electricity and even taking interest in Dayo. It's as if writer Sekizawa crossed Kong's name out in the script and wrote "Godzila". Overall, however, *Ebirah, Horror of the Deep* is an underrated gem and entertaining entry. Ebirah would be back in *All Monsters Attack* via stock footage and 2004's *Godzilla: Final Wars*.

(1967)
大巨獣ガッパ
Nikkatsu, *Director:* **Haruyasu Noguchi**

Nikkatsu was a Japanese studio known for its crime-themed action potboilers. By 1967, the studio was beginning to struggle financially. At the same time, *kaiju* films were big money and nearly every Japanese studio was producing them. They played in theaters and sold merchandise in department stores. On television, multiple shows with guys in monster suits tackling each other competed for ratings. So with a generous government grant that wasn't really spent on the movie, Nikkatsu produced their sole *Showa*-era kaiju and *tokusatsu* production: *Gappa, the Triphibian Monster*. Also known as *Monster From a Prehistoric Planet*, *Gappa* is a well made but mediocre film with lightly satirical elements. At first glance, *Gappa* has strong parallels with the King Brothers' British production *Gorgo* (1961). Yet the screenwriters Ryuzo Nakanishi and Gan Yamazaki, in Stuart Galbraith's *Monsters Are Attacking Tokyo*, swore to have never seen *Gorgo*. True or not, the problem is that *Gappa* is a film that commits one of the worst cinematic sins: it's boring. It's not ridiculously awful like the same year's *The X From Outer Space*. Yet despite solid production values and some good scenes, *Gappa* lacks the magic of a Toho production.

The Gappa monsters, created by Eizo Kaimai, are fairly generic and the human characters are cookie cutter. *Gappa*, in addition, contains a ridiculously sexist coda. The female lead, moved by the parenthood of the Gappas, announces her decision to abandon the "working woman" lifestyle to "have babies". There is, however, a unique and particular "Japaneseness" to the film. As Patrick Macias would note in *Tokyoscope*, it features an especially apt snapshot of urban '60s Tokyo nightlife. Something about the film's aesthetic feels more "real" than Toho and Daiei's set-bound films.

The special effects footage by former Toho art director Akira Watanabe is well executed. Yet it lacks the creative *je-ne-sais-quoi* of the work being done by Tsuburaya and Arikawa at the same time. There's a good aerial attack sequence where a squadron of F-104 Starfighters engage the monsters. This is marred only by the top of the set being clumsily visible in one instance. The film's highlight is a lake attack with a beautifully executed and composed tidal wave sequence. The international version, which would languish on late night television in the U.S.,

contains five minutes of additional SFX shots. The Japanese version, however, feels better paced. *Gappa* is not a film recommended to *kaiju* novices but is definitely worth seeing once for aficionados.

(1969)
ゴジラ・ミニラ・ガバラ オール怪獣大進撃
Toho, *Director*: **Ishiro Honda**

One of the most reviled Godzilla movies, *All Monsters Attack* is indeed pretty bad. Yet amidst the unevenness there are deeper, more redeeming elements. Michael Weldon in his 1983 *Psychotronic Encyclopedia of Film* calls the film a *"Godzilla movie for six year olds"*. This is apt as both a criticism and fact. It revolves around a young boy, Ichiro, played by Tomonori Yazaki who had a very brief acting career. Ichiro is a monster loving kid with working class wage slave parents who are seldom home. He daydreams about hanging out with Minilla on Monster Island while watching stock footage of Godzilla battling other monsters. *All Monsters Attack* was Toho's most rushed genre film to date; it started shooting in October 1969 for a December release date.

Obviously, the direction was heavily influenced by Daiei's Gamera films. Ishiro Honda, however, brings a little more pathos to the table than Noriaki Yuasa would have. *All Monsters Attack* is actually at its strongest outside of its monster scenes. Shot in the industrial city of Kawasaki, the sequences showcasing Ichiro's alienation as a neglected latchkey kid in bleak urban desolation are the highlight. The monster scenes by contrast are embarrassing, a television-style "clipshow" of sorts. Eiji Tsuburaya was sickly and, unbeknownst to him, nearing the end of his life. He was also occupied with work on the *Birth of the Japanese Islands* exhibit at Expo '70, which he tragically wouldn't live to see. As such, he could not run the special effects unit. Ishiro Honda thus helmed the unit with assistance from Teruyoshi Nakano. Much of the screen time on Monster Island is stock footage from *Ebirah, Horror of the Deep* and *Son of Godzilla*. What new footage there is features goofy "bully" *kaiju* Gabara. These scenes are shot on limited sound stages and look quite cheap. Gabara resembles an *oni* of Japanese folklore, though Toho recently retconned him as "a mutated toad". Shinichi Sekizawa, amusingly, named him after Che Guevara. A reimagined version of the monster is set to return in 2021's new Godzilla *anime: Godzilla Singular Point.* The breezy soundtrack is by Kunio Miyauchi (1932-2006), best known for scoring the original *Ultraman* show.

Viewed as an adult, *All Monsters Attack* is more tolerable and even a bit fun if seen through a different lens. This is not a straight up monster movie. This is a film set in the real world, a place devoid of giant monsters, about a boy who uses them as a form of escapism. The climax, involving Ichiro kidnapped by and cleverly battling a pair of bumbling crooks, looks forward to 1990's *Home Alone.* In the U.S., it was released in 1971 as *Godzilla's Revenge.* While it replaces the abrasive vocal theme with a fun jazzy instrumental, it has one of the worst American dubs with voices that are particularly obnoxious and cartoony. Overall, *All Monsters Attack* is certainly not a high point in the *Showa* series and Honda's career. Yet who here reading this book can't relate to being a lonely, bullied kid who uses monster movies to escape our harsh, banal world?

TOHO'S COMPETITION

東宝の競争

by John LeMay

Everyone knows who Godzilla is. It's a name and brand synonymous with the Japanese variety of giant monsters. Fewer people know the name of Godzilla's home studio: Toho. It's a guarantee that the average *gaijin* (non-Japanese) wouldn't know the names of Japan's other prominent studios to release *kaiju* films. Gamera and the Power Rangers might ring a bell, but they sure won't know Gappa and Guilala.

Toho has become synonymous with *tokusatsu* thanks to Eiji Tsuburaya. Yet believe it or not, Tsuburaya's first sci-fi-based tokusatsu films were actually for rival studio Daiei. The first was relatively uninteresting and called *Rainbow Man* (1949). A noir film set around a spooky house, the main plot concerned the Maya family. Their mad scientist patriarch has created a drug that causes people to hallucinate a rainbow before they die. When this happens, the screen suddenly switches to color: shocking for post-war Japanese audiences.

More interesting was the same year's *The Invisible Man Appears*, where Tsuburaya got to recreate some scenes from Universal's 1933 film. It is not to be confused with Toho's 1954 film *The Invisible Avenger*, also with FX by Tsuburaya. It was a typical story of a scientist who invents an invisibility serum and goes mad due to his experiments. Daiei's later effort, 1957's *Invisible Man vs. The Human Fly*, was more notable. By this time, Tsuburaya was on contract at Toho and so did not work on the film. It featured multiple invisible men and women as the good guys, while several tiny fly men were the baddies. In addition, Daiei produced the surprisingly excellent sci-fi flick *Warning From Space* in 1956.

Another studio worth mentioning from this period was Shin Toho (or "New Toho"). The studio was founded by disgruntled Toho workers and had a busy horror film division. Most were period pieces based on Japanese folktales like Nobuo Nakagawa's *Ghost of Yotsuya* (1959). Yet there were a few contemporary ones including *Woman Vampire* (also 1959) and *Vampire Bride* (1960). *Woman Vampire* was also directed by Nakagawa. It was very much a response to the recent success of Hammer's *Horror of Dracula* in Japan. Shin Toho also

produced 1956's *Fearful Invasion of Flying Saucers*, directed by future Toho sci-fi scribe Shinichi Sekizawa. It had elements akin to *Atragon* (1963), which Sekizawa would one day pen. Shin Toho is most notable for debuting the first Japanese superhero on movie screens with *Super Giant* in 1957. Directed mainly by Teruo Ishii and starring Ken Utsui as the title character, they were released in serialized format. These films would be distributed stateside, edited into a quartet of feature length compilations. In these dubbed versions, "Super Giant" became "Starman". Shin Toho folded in the early 1960s. Ironically, their catalogue was recently bought by Toho.

Daiei, meanwhile, were making *tokusatsu* films with and without monsters well before Gamera or Majin. Daiei actually had two different production branches: the Tokyo branch and the Kyoto branch. The Tokyo branch produced their contemporary flicks and Kyoto their period films such as *Zatoichi*. The movies shot at the Kyoto branch tended to have better production values than the Tokyo chapter. A notable production from Kyoto was *The Demon of Mount Oe* from 1960, a horror-themed *jidai-geki* film. It features a notable sequence with a giant spider that's as well executed as Kumonga from *Son of Godzilla*. It also includes a gigantic ox creature that resembles the monsters from Italian *peplum* (sword and sandal) movies. There were other early Daiei effects films. *Invisible Tengu* (1960) transports the Invisible Man concept back to feudal times. *The Whale God* (1962) is best described as a Japanese take on Herman Melville's *Moby Dick*. *Wind Velocity 75 Meters* (1963) is a hurricane-themed disaster movie with elaborate FX work.

The success of Toho's *King Kong vs. Godzilla* in 1962 made Daiei take note of giant monster pictures. By 1963 they were developing their own *kaiju* film, also inspired by Hitchcock's *The Birds*. Daiei's film was titled *Giant Rat Horde Nezura*. The story concerned rats from Sasashima Island eating experimental food for astronauts. This mutates them into giants. Most were to be human sized, but there was going to be one that was *kaiju*-sized. A giant radio controlled rat monster was even built. At the film's end, the rats and their giant leader would swim to Tokyo and begin destroying the city. The threat is neutralized when the rats turn on each other and revert to cannibalism. Unfortunately for Daiei, this very thing happened when live rats were loosed on an expensive miniature Tokyo before cameras! The rats also infested the studio with fleas and ticks and began breeding. Before they knew it they had a major health concern on their hands and had to exterminate the vermin. Thus ended *Nezura*.

Daiei President Masaichi Nagata was left with miniatures but no film to feature them in. To use these miniatures, Gamera was born. The story bore some eerie parallels to how Godzilla was dreamed up in 1954. If you'll recall, Tomoyuki Tanaka was denied visas for the cast of his war movie *In Glory's Shadow* in Indonesia. On the plane back to Japan he looked out the window at the sea below and imagined a giant monster lurking in the depths. A decade later on a flight back to Tokyo, Nagata looked out his window and saw a cloud formation that reminded him of a turtle. So he created the flying fire-breathing turtle Gamera. Or so one version of the story goes. Another is that a flying turtle was created for the abandoned P-Productions TV series *STOP!* (as in stop-motion) and that Daiei stole the idea. Daiei's production of *Gamera, the Giant Monster*, released in 1965, turned out to be an immense hit for the studio. A typical monster on the loose story filmed in black and white, it featured a scene where a prominent child character is saved by the creature. The scene where the rampaging Gamera saves the boy wound up setting the tone for the entire series.

The first Gamera sequel, 1966's *Gamera vs. Barugon*, had a hard-boiled adult tone and featured no children. It also started out as a completely different movie. The initial pitch was for *Gamera vs. the Ice Men from Outer Space* wherein Gamera would battle icy aliens and a giant humanoid ice giant. Daiei didn't like the idea as a Gamera movie, but loved the concept of a humanoid giant. This led to the production of *Majin*, a period piece about a stone giant coming to life to punish evil doers.

Being a feudal epic, *Daimajin (Great Majin)* was filmed at the Daiei Kyoto branch to make use of the period sets and costumes. That year Daiei cranked out three Majin flicks in a row to round out a trilogy. There would have been more adventures for Majin except for two issues. First, the third film, *Majin Strikes Again*, had to be re-shot because of damage to the negatives. Second, *Majin Strikes Again* was not as big of a hit at the box office as the first two. Thus ended Majin's adventures on the big screen.

The same year that Majin wrecked feudal Japan, another rival studio, Toei, got in on the monster game. Their film was *Grand Duel in Magic*, better known as *The Magic Serpent*. Based on the beloved *Jiraiya* legend, it too was set in the feudal era. The movie opens with a dragon attacking a castle. It isn't seen again until the climax, when the human hero transforms into a giant toad monster to battle it. The film must not have set the box office afire, because Toei didn't make any similar films. The monster props were later reused on their TV series *Masked Ninja Akakage* (1967-1968). Though beaten to airwaves by *Ultraman* and *Ambassador Magma* the year before, it was still one of the pioneers in color *tokusatsu* shows on television. It was the first color ninja show on TV at least. As it was, Toei fared better with television monsters than they did on the big screen. Their TV series *Giant Robo* (1967-1968) got good ratings and was picked up in the U.S. as *Johnny Sokko and His Flying Robot*. The two aforementioned series were the first in a long line of tokusatsu TV hits for Toei. In 1966 Toei also produced *Water Cyborg*, released theatrically in Japan. In the U.S. it aired on TV as *Terror Beneath the Sea*.

On both TV and the big screen, 1967 was a big year for Japanese monsters. Thanks to a government loan program that encouraged studios to make tokusatsu films, nearly every studio made a kaiju film. Shochiku, one of the oldest and most respected studios in Japan, produced *The X From Outer Space*. Though that awful film was the best known of Shochiku's *tokusatsu* quartet, the films they produced in 1968 were superior. *Goke, Body Snatcher from Hell* had vampiric aliens hijacking an airliner. Director Hajime Sato took inspiration from Nostradamus' prediction about a king of terror falling from the sky. Lesser known is

Genocide which mixed up killer bees with an atom bomb on a Pacific island.

Nikkatsu's entry into the 1967 monster mash fared better than Shochiku. Whereas *The X From Outer Space* looked to the stars, Nikkatsu's *Gappa* went the prehistoric route. The monsters were uniquely designed saurians that were able to thrive on land, water or in the skies. Hence the international title: *Gappa, the Triphibian Monster*. The film took a page from the UK's *Gorgo*, focusing on the relationship between *kaiju* parents and their offspring. Incidentally, Toho's *Son of Godzilla* would do the same that year. Unfortunately, Nikkatsu would produce no sequels to *Gappa*. Instead they came upon hard times and began producing softcore pornography in the early 1970s.

Of course, Daiei put out another Gamera movie, *Gamera vs. Gyaos*. It went on to become the most successful entry in the series up until that time. Though they often get left out of the 1967 monster mash, Toei was in on it as well via *Yongary, Monster from the Deep*. Though made by Keukdong in South Korea, Toei was still involved in the production and distributed it in Japan.

1968 would see yet another rare Toei tokusatsu film on the big screen in the form of *The Green Slime*. Yet, the driving force behind the film were producers Walter Manley and Ivan Reiner. Toei and director Kinji Fukasaku were just along for the ride. 1968 would see Gamera still going strong in *Gamera vs. Viras*. It was double-billed with *100 Monsters*, a period *yokai* spook story. If one watches the Tokyo-made Gamera movie and the Kyoto produced *yokai* film back to back the difference in quality is noticeable.

100 Monsters' production values are far superior. *Gamera vs. Viras* features around 10-20 minutes worth of stock footage (depending on the version, one has an additional ten minutes). The double-bill was, however, a huge hit. Not only would Daiei produce more *yokai* movies, they would also ask Noriaki Yuasa if he could churn out two Gameras a year instead of one. He politely declined. Meanwhile, Toho was planning a big send off in the form of *Destroy All Monsters*. After that, Godzilla and company would transition to the small screen for an animated series from Filmation. Or so they thought.

The desperate competitors Toho and Daiei would go on to copy one another. Toho was disappointed in the box office returns for *Destroy All Monsters*. Yet they took note of the fact that Daiei made a profitable movie in the form of the stock footage laden *Gamera vs. Viras*. As the Godzilla TV series didn't pan out, Toho was desperate for a "New Year's Blockbuster". They produced their own stock-footage fest aimed at children: *All Monsters Attack*. There's little denying this child oriented Godzilla film was inspired by the success of Gamera. While Toho was let down by the box office of *Destroy All Monsters*, Daiei was watching. They modeled their next *Yokai Monsters* movie after *Monsters*, calling it *Spook Warfare*. In it, all the *yokai* from the previous film return along with some new ones. They battle Daimon, an evil Babylonian demon who tries to invade Japan. The film was double-billed with another Noriaki Yuasa film, *Snake Girl and the Silver Haired Witch*. Daiei would produce one last Yokai Monsters movie, the tired and uninspired *Along with Ghosts* (1969). It was double-billed with *Gamera*

vs. Guiron. In 1970, Daiei released what turned out to be their highest grossing Showa era Gamera movie: *Gamera vs. Jiger*. *Jiger* was billed with *The Invisible Swordsman*, an update of sorts on *Invisible Tengu*. The film even features a friendly *yokai* in it, though it's more of a spin-off than sequel to the Yokai Monsters films.

1971 saw the release of the last Gamera movie, *Gamera vs. Zigra*. Like Toho's *Godzilla vs. Hedorah*, released a week later, it had ecological subtexts. Daiei announced some big projects in late 1971. These included an unauthorized adaptation of Sakyo Komatsu's upcoming novel *Japan Sinks* and another Gamera sequel. Before they could be produced, Daiei went completely bankrupt. Angry unpaid staff then went on a rampage, destroying the old Gamera suit. Rumor has it that they even destroyed the suit for the unfilmed *Gamera vs. Two-Headed Monster W*.

Gamera was dead and Godzilla's box office numbers were on the decline. A new monster boom would take hold in Japan on the small screen. The 1971-72 TV season saw the triple whammy of *Return of Ultraman* (Tsuburaya Productions), *Spectreman* (P-Productions), and *Kamen Rider* (Toei). Of the three *Kamen Rider* secured the highest ratings and was the most popular among children. Like *Moonlight Mask* of the 1950s, Kamen Rider stayed human-sized unlike Ultraman and Spectreman. Perhaps children could relate to Kamen Rider and recreate his battles easier because he was smaller. This was the start of Toei's usurping of Tsuburaya Productions as king of the airwaves as far as monster fighting heroes went. The second wave of Ultra shows would peter out by 1975 when

Ultraman Leo ended its run. It was the same year that Godzilla also went into retirement. Yet Kamen Rider kept going strong throughout the 70s.

Despite their success with TV monsters, Toei faced a major blunder in theaters with 1977's *Legend of Dinosaurs and Monster Birds*. It was inspired by *Jaws* and likely the un-produced Toho movie *Nessie*. *Legend of Dinosaurs* featured a plesiosaur eating villagers around Mt. Fuji's Saiko Lake. A giant-sized rhamphorhynchus also joins the fray. The dinosaurs fight, Mt. Fuji erupts and presumably everyone dies. Tsuburaya Productions also had a dinosaur flop when they made the rare venture to theaters with *The Last Dinosaur*. A co-production with Rankin/Bass, who provided the American stars (Richard Boone and Joan Van Ark) while Tsuburaya provided the locale and effects. It was intended for theaters in the U.S. too, but when the investors saw it they decided to sell it to television. The ratings there were decent.

1980 saw three attempted revivals of old properties, none of which went as well as hoped. Tokuma Publishing had acquired Daiei and had Noriaki Yuasa make *Super Monster* (aka *Gamera*; *Supermonster*). The movie was more or less a stock-footage compilation movie. Yuasa grew disappointed as filming went on and changed the ending to have Gamera die. That same year, Yuasa also worked on Tsuburaya's Ultraman relaunch *Ultraman 80*. Though it was by no means a failure, it didn't reignite the Ultraman franchise just yet. That wouldn't happen until the 1990s. Last and least was Toei's attempt to revive the TV hero *Moonlight Mask*. *Moonlight Mask: The Movie* was an attempt to launch a new series by way of theatrical feature film. It was a huge flop and no TV series followed.

In 1993, Toei's tokusatsu would cross the Pacific in a big way. Israeli-American producer Haim Saban adapted *Zyuranger* (1992-1993) into *Mighty Morphin' Power Rangers*. By then, the Super Sentai series had been around for almost 20 years. Super Sentai sprang from the same genius who helped create *Kamen Rider*: Shotaro Ishinomori. The franchise debuted with *Goranger* in 1975, the very year that Godzilla and Ultraman went on hiatus. The first few iterations of the series didn't have giant mecha, just a costumed team of heroes fighting monsters. The giant robots would come later thanks to *Spider-Man*. In 1978, Marvel and Toei created a licensing agreement. This allowed each other the use of their characters in certain circumstances. In Toei's case, they had their own live-action *Spider-Man* series. Other than the Spider-Man suit used, the hero had little in common with Peter Parker. This Spider-Man was an alien who came complete with his own giant robot, called Leopardon, to fight monsters. The giant robot aspect proved popular and carried over into the next Super Sentai series, *Battle Fever J* (1979-1980). Both Japanese Super Sentai and the U.S. based Power Rangers are still running today.

By the early 1990s, Daiei had revived again. They were clamoring to restart Gamera since *Godzilla vs. King Ghidorah* (1991) had proven to be a hit. At first they toyed with an hour-long direct to video sequel to the Showa series that would bring back Yuasa and Takahashi. This led to a quasi-short film made up of test footage of Gamera fighting a giant cobra-*kaiju* named Garasharp. Daiei decided to go the *Batman* route. Like Warner Brothers with Tim Burton and Christopher Nolan, they had an up-and-coming director retrofit their IP into something edgier. Shusuke Kaneko made the universally loved *Gamera: Guardian of the Universe*. Released in 1995, its grosses didn't equal the Heisei Godzilla films, but the picture received a great deal more praise from Japanese critics. It was even labeled as the best made Japanese film of 1995.

A sequel, *Gamera 2: Attack of Legion*, was released the next year. *Gamera 3: Revenge of Iris* followed and underperformed at the box office. In 2002, Daiei was bought by Kadokawa Publishing which rebooted the series with the more kid friendly *Gamera the Brave* (2006). Their original hope was to coerce Toho into making a *Godzilla vs. Gamera* film with them. Toho declined. The enemy monster Zedus was designed as a take on Jirass, the Godzilla monster from the 1966 *Ultraman*, as a swipe at Toho's unwillingness to play ball. Though planned as part of an ongoing series, *Gamera the Brave*'s gross didn't warrant sequels. We're still waiting on a reboot to this day. In 2015, a proof of concept trailer was released, screening at conventions. This got fans' hopes up but the project was not green-lit. At the end of the day, Toho has long dominated Japanese genre films. Its competitors, however, have more than made their mark.

GOKE, Body Snatcher From Hell

Kyuketsuki Gokemidoro "Gokemidoro the Vampire"
Shochiku, 8/14/1968 (*Showa 43*), 6 Reels (2,292 meters), 83:48, 35mm, Shochiku Grandscope (2.35:1 anamorphic), Fujicolor, monaural sound

Crew
Producer: Takashi Inomata
Director: Hajime Sato
Screenplay: Susumu Takaku, Kyuzo Kobayashi, Soji Ushio (story)
Director of Photography: Shizuo Hirase
Editor: Akimitsu Terada
Music: Shunsuke Kikuchi
Production Design: Tadataka Yoshino

Assistant Director: Keiji Shiraki
Lighting: Tatsuo Aomoto
Sound Recording: Hiroshi Nakamura
Sound Effects: Masashi Matsumoto
Planning: Masayuki Fukuyama
Production Managers: Makoto Naito, Hisao Watanabe
Special Effects (P-Productions): Shinsuke

Kojima, Motoyuki Okada, Michio MIkami

Cast
Teruo Yoshida (*Ei Sugisaka*)
Tomomi Sato (*Kuzumi Asakura*)
Hideo Ko (*Hirofumi Teraoka*)
Masaya Takahashi (*Professor Toshiyuki Saga*)
Nobuo Kaneko (*Tokuyasu*)
Eizo Kitamura (*Gozo Mano*)

Yuko Kusonoki *(Noriko Tokuyasu)*
Kazuo Kato *(Dr. Momotake)*
Cathy Horan *(Mrs. Neal)*
Norihiko Yamamoto *(Matsumiya)*
Hiroyuki Nishimoto *(Airline Captain)*
Harold Conway *(British Ambassador)*

Keiichi Noda *(Gokemidoro, voice)*

<u>Alternate Titles</u>
Body Snatcher From Hell (U.S.)
Goke - Vampir aus dem Weltall
[Goke: Vampire From Space] (Germany)

Distruggete DC 59, da base spaziale a Hong Kong
[Destroy DC 59: The Space Base in Hong Kong] (Italy)
Goke - O Vampiro do Espaço (Brazil)
Гок, похититель тел из ада (Russia)

"What we're in for is going to blow our minds...Suicidal birds, the strange light, a flying saucer and now that wound on his face. We can't even imagine what's next!"
-Professor Saga (Masaya Takahashi)

Produced by Shochiku, known for its films by Yasujiro Ozu, *Goke, Body Snatcher From Hell* is the stand-out of its genre pictures. It is a bleak and misanthropic horror/sci-fi hybrid. At any moment, it can evoke the works of Nobuo Nakagawa, Don Siegel, Alfred Hitchcock, Ishiro Honda, Mario Bava and George Romero. Boasting unpolished but inventive FX work, *Goke* is one part grotesque alien invasion yarn, the other bitter Vietnam protest.

PLOT

During what was to be a routine flight from Haneda to Itami, co-pilot Sugisaka (Teruo Yoshida) of plane JA-306 notices that the sky is blood red. As flight attendant Kuzumi Asakura (Tomomi Sato) serves drinks, arms dealer Tokuyasu (Nobuo Kaneko) laments to politician Mano (Eizo Kitamura). The British ambassador has been assassinated and with him died any hope for peace in Asia. Mano asks if peace would harm Tokuyasu's best interests, to which the dealer's wife Noriko

(Yuko Kusonoki) agrees. A bird flings itself against the windows with a splatter, scaring American war widow Mrs. Neal (Cathy Horan).

The captain (Hiroyuki Nishimoto) receives a message from Haneda airport. The police have received a threat from a lunatic planning to commit suicide by blowing up the plane. Sugisaka and Asakura search everyone's bags. Psychiatrist Dr. Momotake (Kazuo Kato) immediately suspects a bomb threat and raises alarm. Sugisaka searches the bag of Matsumiya (Norihiko Yamamoto), finding only art prints. Another bird throws itself against the window with a torrent of blood. Matsumiya speculates that the birds are committing suicide. Astronomy professor Saga (Masaya Takahashi) theorizes that this is an omen foretelling of darker things. Asakura finds an unmarked bag. Sugisaka opens it, finding a vial of acid and a rifle.

His cover blown, an assassin on board named Teraoka (Hideo Ko) hijacks the plane. He orders the captain to head towards Okinawa as the radio reports a flying saucer has been seen over Japan. The glowing saucer appears and collides with the plane, disabling its controls as it crashes to the ground. Having crashed into a remote region, Sugisaka awakens. He finds the pilot dead and Teraoka seemingly so. Asakura has survived, along with most of the passengers. Matsumiya, who called in the bomb threat, attempts suicide but Sugisaka stops him. As the survivors decide what to do, order begins to break down as Asakura reveals that there's no food or water left. Teraoka awakens, taking Asakura hostage as Mano realizes that he assassinated the ambassador and is on the run.

As Teraoka flees into the wilderness with Asakura where they encounter the flying saucer. The spacecraft lures Teraoka towards it, slicing open his skull as Asakura faints from terror. Sugisaka finds Asakura unconscious and delirious. Dr. Momotake decides to hypnotize her to find out the truth of what happened to Teraoka. During hypnosis, she reveals that Teraoka, after having the vertical gash made on his head, was possessed by an amoeba-like alien. The creature entered his head through the wound. Matsumiya has a panic attack and causes Dr. Momotake to fall off a cliff by accident. The other survivors lock him up as Momotake comes face to face with Teraoka. The assassin,

transformed into a zombie-like vampire, kills Momotake and drinks his blood.

Teraoka next shows up at the crash site and Mrs. Neal insists he be given first aid. His wound reminds her of her dead husband, who died in Vietnam; his face torn open by napalm. Professor Saga is flummoxed by Teraoka's wound which despite its depth shows no sign of bleeding. Mano, fed whiskey by Tokuyasu, is suffering from extreme thirst. Tokuyasu tortures him by pouring out a canteen of water. He forces Mano to confess that he was bribed to pressure the government for a defense contract and that Noriko came along as a "treat". The two bicker before Tokuyasu forces everyone out of the plane at gunpoint. As he turns around, Teraoka is standing there. He tries to make the vampiric assassin leave too, but is overpowered as Teraoka feasts on his blood. Sugisaka breaks back into the wrecked plane, finding Tokuyasu dead. Saga notices his blood is drained as Noriko is taken away by Teraoka. Bringing her to the flying saucer, she is brainwashed.

The next morning, the survivors look for Noriko and find her standing atop a cliff. Possessed by the aliens, she speaks in a guttural voice. The invaders reveal themselves to be the "Gokemidoro" from a distant galaxy and state their intent to exterminate the human race.

BACKGROUND

Shochiku's first sci-fi romp was *The X From Outer Space* (1967), a shabby but entertaining *kaiju* flick about a giant chicken spawned from cosmic gunk. It did spirited business enough that Shochiku's president Shiro Kido wanted to make more such films. *Goke*'s initial concept came from a tokusatsu pilot shopped around by P-Productions, known for its work on the hit show *Ambassador Magma (The Space Giants)*, based on a *manga* by Osamu Tezuka. The concept would only vaguely resemble the finished product. It involved a benevolent alien who could transfer to humans. The villain was a monster, "Gokemidoro" spawned from bad airline food. At least some footage of the creature was filmed as proof of concept, its original design hairy with multiple arms. Like Godzilla, its name is a clever portmanteau. It came from Midoro pond, a locale known for its ghost stories, along with the English word "chemical". The "Go" came from Golgotha where Christ was said to be crucified. P-Productions' head Soji Ushio took the footage to Shochiku, who immediately green-lit the film. Screenwriter Kyuzo Kobayashi (1935-2006) started work on the script.

For director, producer Takashi Inomata turned to Hajime Sato at the suggestion of Kobayashi. Sato (1929-1995) was an economics student turned film director. He had helmed the atmospheric *Ghost of the Hunchback* (1965) and international sci-fi actioner *Terror Beneath the Sea* (1966), both for Toei. Sato brought in Susumu Takaku, a prolific television screenwriter. Takaku (1933-2009) was writing for spy show *Key Hunter* (1968-73) and would write anime like *Devilman* (1972-73). Sato and Takaku opted for a horror oriented story without a *kaiju*, taking scant elements from Ushio's concept. The writers considered setting the film in a mental hospital, but opted for a passenger plane. Sato drew inspiration from Nostradamus' famous prediction that *"The King of Terror will fall from the sky"*. Frederic Brown's sci-fi novella *The Mind Thing* (1961) was also a particular influence. P-Productions would stay on board to do the special effects.

PRINCIPAL PHOTOGRAPHY

Goke, Body Snatcher From Hell is a far cry from its roots as a child-oriented TV pitch. Sato's direction is stellar and the production design is excellent. Two Salvador Dali paintings are used in the opening: *Millet's Architectonic Angelus* (1933) and *The Resurrection of the Flesh* (1945). *Goke* was shot around Yori Daiei quarry in Saitama, known for its later use in Toei's superhero shows.

At any moment *Goke* can bring to mind the best work of better known directors. Hajime Sato was clearly well versed in the work of his contemporaries. Its tropes and bleak ending remind one of Don Siegel's classic *Invasion of the Body Snatchers* (1956). Sometimes it invokes the grotesque imagery and lighting schemes of Nobuo Nakagawa's 1960 *Jigoku (Hell)*. Its opening, involving suicidal birds splattering against airplane windows, brings to mind Alfred Hitchcock's *The Birds* (1963). Its story of marooned survivors turning on each other while facing a monstrous threat suggests Ishiro Honda's *Matango*. Its phantasmagorical images and space vampire concept invokes Mario Bava's *Planet of the Vampires* (1965). Finally, its apocalyptic atmosphere and Vietnam protest brings George A. Romero's *Night of the Living Dead* (also 1968) to mind.

ACTORS

Except for the amateur ex-pat Cathy Horan who is terrible, the acting is effective. Hideo Ko (1918-2009), better known as a French-trained chanson singer, plays the assassin/vampire. Ko would be called "Gokemidoro" by the neighborhood children for years to come, much to his annoyance. He was supposed to play the role throughout the film, but had to leave the shoot early due to a prior obligation. The script was rewritten to have the Gokemidoro pass on to Masaya Takahashi's Saga. Takahashi (1930-2014) would later appear in *Submersion of Japan* (1973) and as an elderly bicycle shop owner in *Godzilla, Mothra and King Ghidorah, Giant Monsters All-Out Attack* (2001).

Veteran actor Nobuo Kaneko (1923-1995) chews the scenery as despicable arms dealer Tokuyasu. He later played the narcissistic *yakuza* boss Yamamori in Kinji Fukasaku's *Battles Without Honor and Humanity* (1973-74). Kaneko was also a bureaucrat in *The Return of Godzilla* (1984). Teruo Yoshida (1936-) was a favorite of exploitation director Teruo Ishii. He and Ko would both

go on to appear in Ishii's *Yakuza's Law: Lynch* and *Horrors of Malformed Men* (both 1969). Actor Kazuo Kato (1928-?) plays the nihilistic psychiatrist Momotake who becomes Gokemidoro's first victim. After the war, Kato joined the Bungakuza Theater Troupe. One of his first appearances was in Akira Kurosawa's *I Live in Fear* (1955). He left Bungakuza in 1963 and became freelance, appearing on many television shows such as *The Guard Man* and *Key Hunter*. After appearing in Kurosawa's *Dodes'kaden* (1970), Kato often played supporting roles as government officials. This includes in *Submersion of Japan* (1973), *Prophecies of Nostradamus* (1974) and *Deathquake* (1980). Kato also appeared in Kurosawa's *Ran* (1985) and did a lot of voice dubbing for foreign films. It is unknown if he is still alive.

SFX

The special effects work from P-Productions is surprisingly inventive, supervised by Shinsuke Kojima.. They were more of a ragtag team than Tsuburaya or Noriaki Yuasa's units. Their work is a little unpolished as there are embarrassing shots involving unrealistic dummies. Yet there are many effective shots on par with Tsuburaya's best work. The glowing spaceship miniature is well executed. It was later refurbished to make the villainous Dr. Gori's ship on P-Productions' beloved *Spectreman* (1971-72). The shots where the Gokemidoro enter and exit the skulls of human hosts are rather incredible. A mixture of melted condoms were pumped out of well constructed replicas of actors Ko and

Takahashi's heads. It was played backwards for the effect of the creatures entering. A shot of the Saga vampire's dead body turning to dust and blowing away is also quite impressive. It exceeds the quality of the vampire disintegration scenes shot by UK studio Hammer. Designer Michio Mikami was later recruited by Hong Kong's Shaw Brothers to visualize *The Super Infra-Man* (1975).

MUSIC

The harsh but effective music is by Shunsuke Kikuchi (1931-), who would also score the next four Gamera films. He was born in Aomori Prefecture, the son of a fish shop owner. Kikuchi graduated from the Nihon University College of Art. His first score was for the 1961 Toei production *The Eight Enemy.* He became a popular composer, especially for television, composing the theme for *Key Hunter* (1968-1973). Kikuchi would go on to score Toei's *Kamen Rider* series as well as numerous *anime*, particularly the *Dragonball* franchise. Kikuchi also scored the beloved and decades long show *The Unfettered Shogun* (1978-2008). He has received numerous awards and honors, including a lifetime achievement award in 2015 at the Japan Record Awards.

THEMES AND MOTIFS

Goke, Body Snatcher From Hell is an ugly and misanthropic portrait of humanity. The film's ensemble cast shows us the monstrousness of people. Suffering from hunger, thirst and fatigue, they turn on each

in a way that would make Jean-Paul Sartre blush. Kazuo Kato's psychiatrist Momotake, early in the picture, proclaims that as a shrink he's fascinated to see a microcosmic breakdown of society. Like *Matango,* as more characters get picked off, the remaining get nastier. Politician Mano, not specified as liberal or conservative as its beside the point, starts the film as an upstanding man of the people. He becomes a vile monster. Mrs. Neal starts off as a sympathetic war widow before becoming a quintessential ugly American carrying a rifle around. Astronomer Saga begins as a rational, kindly man before going along with murder in the name of science.

Goke, Body Snatcher From Hell has a sense of rage over the Vietnam War. Direct references are made through Cathy Horan's war widow Mrs. Neal. Images of combat are flashed on screen. By 1968, the war was escalating with the Tet Offensive. Japanese on all ends of the political spectrum were unsettled by a horrific conflict in their relative backyards. Reference to the assassinations of figures like Martin Luther King, Malcolm X and the Kennedys is made with an ambassador's death, implied killed by Ko's assassin. No doubt, by 1968 it began to feel like the world was unraveling, especially in Japan. *Goke* trangressively suggests that maybe the Gokemidoro are giving humanity just what it deserves.

RELEASE AND LEGACY

Goke, Body Snatcher From Hell was released on a double bill with Kinji Fukasaku's *Black Lizard* in what must have been a wild night at the movies for any young Japanese Boomer.

Since then it has been a little influential. Its opening shot of a miniature jetliner against a blood red sky might look familiar. That's because Quentin Tarantino copied it almost verbatim for a scene in *Kill Bill Vol. 1* (2003) where Uma Thurman's Beatrix Kiddo flies to Tokyo. Another notable fan is Shinji Higuchi, who helped Tarantino coordinate *Kill Bill*'s Japanese leg of shooting. He was gleeful visiting the set the day the *Goke* shot was filmed. Higuchi paid homage to the film in his storyboards for *The End of Evangelion* (1997), a giant Rei Ayanami's head splitting open in a similar vertical gash. Goke was also referenced in an early 2021 episode of Mamoru Oshii's *VladLove;* in it the characters go to see a revival screening. Shochiku would make two more special effects driven films. First the *Carnival of Souls*-like *The Living Skeleton*, also featuring Nobuo Kaneko in a villainous role. They also released *Genocide*, written by Takaku. Both films were also distributed on a double bill.

ALTERNATE VERSIONS

Shochiku commissioned an export version, dubbed in Hong Kong by Ted Thomas' firm. For an HK job, it's unusually tolerable. The vocal cast includes Thomas as the pilot and Tokuyasu, Linda Masson as Asakura, Barry Haigh as Saga, Ian Wilson as Momotake and Michael Kaye as Mano and Matsumiya.

Linda Masson was a college student studying Chinese whom Ted Thomas recruited for dubbing. He wound up marrying her and she became a mainstay of his dubs. However, Masson had divorced Thomas by 1973.

Afterwards, she started a Hong Kong-based jewelry company and became quite wealthy. She continued dubbing with Barry Haigh and Matthew Oram, most recognizably voicing Katsura Mafune in *Terror of Mechagodzilla*. Haigh was a news anchor and radio personality from England. He also ran a dubbing group of his own. Michael Kaye was another British born newscaster who returned to England in the 1970s. Three of this dub's male voices would go on to provide English dubbing for martial arts sensation Bruce Lee. The unidentified voice actor who dubbed Sugisaka voiced Lee in the export version of *The Big Boss* (1971). Kaye and Haigh would dub him in *Fist of Fury* and *The Way of the Dragon* (both 1972), respectively.

Goke was not released stateside for nine years. In 1977, grindhouse distributor Pacemaker acquired it, putting it out on a double-bill with a re-issue of *The Bloody Pit of Horror* (1965). Retitled *Body Snatcher From Hell*, this version is almost identical to the export cut, using its dubbing. Only the credits are truncated, reducing the runtime by about a minute. There is no on screen information as to who made the film, the Shochiku logo replaced by a red title card crediting only Pacemaker. It was rated "PG" by the Motion Picture Association of America.

AMERICAN HOME VIDEO HISTORY

An early American VHS release was from VCR Video in 1984. Video Yesteryear and Sinister Cinema offered copies through the 1990s as well, made from an anamorphic scope print. Janus licensed the film in the mid

2000s. In 2012, Criterion, through its Eclipse label, released it in a DVD set called *When Horror Came to Shochiku*. This subtitled set also features *The X From Outer Space, The Living Skeleton* and *Genocide*.

Further Viewing:

TERROR BENEATH THE SEA

(1966)
海底大戦争
Toei/RAM Films, *Director:* **Hajime Sato**

Made with Italian money by Toei for American airwaves, *Terror Beneath the Sea* is known under a myriad of titles. These include *Water Cyborg* and *Agent X-2: Operation Underwater*. Amusingly called *"the usual"* by Leonard Maltin, *Terror Beneath the Sea* is quite uneven. Yet it boasts a pulpy tone and distinctive, Euro Cult-style direction from Hajime Sato. It features a mixed Japanese and Western cast headed by Shinichi (soon to be Sonny) Chiba. Chiba (1939-) needs little introduction. Born Sadao Maeda, he was a particular favorite of director Kinji Fukasaku. Chiba would soon start his own stunt organization: the Japan Action Club. He would become a martial arts sensation rivaling Bruce Lee in *The Street Fighter* (1974) and later appeared in Quentin Tarantino's *Kill Bill Vol. 1* (2003).

A pair of reporters (Chiba and Neal) are hunting for leads on mysterious humanoid sea monster sightings. In the process, they stumble upon an underwater base far beneath the surface of the ocean. Ruled by diabolical Dr. Rufus Moore (Erik Nielsen), its denizens are creating the underwater monsters. Called "Water Cyborgs", these creatures are surgically transformed humans to be Dr. Moore's soldiers for world conquest.

Terror Beneath the Sea is strongest when director Sato channels his beloved Italian genre directors. It boasts a psychedelia akin to Mario Bava's *Planet of the Vampires* or *Danger: Diabolik* (1968). Sato's aesthetic is unique: combining Toei's house "action" flavor with Antonio Margheriti-like stylings. If not for star Chiba and some unmistakably Japanese miniatures and suits, *Terror Beneath the Sea* could be mistaken for a European genre film. Aside from Chiba and a handful of others, its cast consists of mainly Caucasian players. Most were non-actors frequently cast as extras in Japanese films and television. They include Peggy Neal, Franz Gruber and Mike Daneen who all later fought *The X From Outer Space*. Andrew Hughes later appeared in Ishiro Honda's *Destroy All Monsters*. FX director Nobuo Yajima's spirited miniature work calls more attention to its Japaneseness as well. The film's *Creature From the Black Lagoon*-like beasties and submarines were designed by Toru Narita. Narita, however, had to use a pseudonym per his contract with Tsuburaya Pro. Toei later reused a *Water Cyborg* suit on an episode of *Akuma-Kun (Little Devil)*. The concept of humans engineered to survive underwater could be a nod to Kobo Abe's *Inter Ice Age 4*, due to be adapted by Toho that same year.

With a furiously paced finale, *Water Cyborg* also recalls old school Republic serials. Standing out are surprisingly grotesque "operation" scenes where the monsters are created. With clever effects, Sato lets his talent for directing atmospheric horror shine, foreshadowing his later *Goke*. One wonders if these sequences influenced the later *Island of the Fishmen* (1979) with Joseph Cotten. It should also be noted that *Water Cyborg* features an ahead of its time interracial romance between the Japanese Chiba and the blonde Peggy Neal, depicted casually. Neal (1947-) was an army brat and college student studying in Japan from Mississippi. Returning to the U.S., she lived in California for years where she sort of disappeared. In 2019 she resurfaced and appeared in *The Great Buddha Arrival*. *Terror Beneath the Sea* is messy but fun. Unsubstantiated rumor had it that the Japanese version is longer with "extra violence". This is not at all the case. In fact the US version contains a slightly extended ending. The next U.S./Japanese/Italian co-production from Toei was 1968's *The Green Slime*.

(1968)
昆虫大戦争
Shochiku, *Director:* **Kazui Nihonmatsu**

Genocide (aka *The War of the Insects*) was Shochiku's final genre film for decades. Directed by *The X From Outer Space*'s Kazui Nihonmatsu, it boasts a far better script, direction and effects work. Written by *Goke's*

Susumu Takaku, it has a similar grim tone and bleak view of humanity. Shit hits the fan when a B-52 bomber is downed by a ferocious swarm of bees. Crashing near Okinawa, the surviving airmen are stung to death by the bees, save for the PTSD-riddled Charlie (Chico Lourant). Islander Joji (Yusuke Kawazu) is framed for their murder as American colonel Gordon (Rolf Jesser) frantically pursues the missing nuke. Dr. Nagumo (Keisuke Sonoi) discovers that the insects have been bred by Anabelle (Cathy Horan), a misanthropic Holocaust survivor. She intends to unleash her vicious bees and wipe out humanity.

For a Japanese studio picture, *Genocide*'s political commentary is quite radical. Like *Goke*, *Genocide* explores hot-button political issues with nihilistic glee. Screenwriter Takaku drew particular inspiration from the then-recent Palomares incident. In 1966, a U.S. B-52 bomber collided with a craft refueling it and crashed off the coast of Spain. The four atomic weapons it was carrying took months to recover. Two of them partially detonated near the seaside village of Palomares, leaving nuclear contamination that persists to this day. *Genocide* also explores raw topics like Vietnam, drug addiction among G.I.s, the U.S. occupation of Okinawa and even the Holocaust. The film is a scathing indictment of 1960s U.S. foreign policy and by extension, human nature. Col. Gordon, ala *Mothra*'s Clark Nelson, is an almost grotesque "ugly American" caricature. All the more amusingly, he's played by the Germanic Rolf Jesser. Japanese studios casting Europeans in "American" roles was common as they knew the films would be dubbed into English abroad. The result lends a bizarro-world surrealness distinctive of Japanese pulp cinema.

Chico Lourant (1920-2015) plays the delirious and sympathetic Charlie; one of the first and few African-American characters in Japanese science fiction. Lourant was often called "Chico Roland" and confused with Willie Dorsey, another black expat actor. Born in Brazil, Lourant had fought in Korea, lived in Hong Kong and eventually found himself in Tokyo. Mistaken by a Japanese director for Sydney Poitier, he was cast in many films. His most notable role was likely in Koreyoshi Kurahara's *Black Sun* (1964). Joji is played by Yusuke Kawazu. Kawazu (1935-) was a popular freelance actor who appeared in films for Daiei, Toei and

Shochiku. He returned to the genre with appearances in *Godzilla vs. Mechagodzilla II* (1993), *Gamera 2: Attack of Legion* (1996) and *Gamera 3: Revenge of Iris* (1999).

The final reel of *Genocide* is a hallucinogenic trip with queasy macro-lens close-ups of bees stinging and biting their victims. Segments with giant, man-sized bugs were shown in the film's trailers, but excised. Shunsuke Kikuchi's score sounds almost identical to his work on *Goke* but well augments the sleazy tone. Keiji Kawakami's special effects work is imaginative. There are surprisingly good miniatures and Tsuburaya-quality composites. Capped in a doomsday finale ala *Goke*, most of the film's characters are so vile that their final annihilation feels almost cathartic. The message is similar: is humanity even worth saving?

KAIJU INVADE GREATER ASIA

怪獣攻撃東アジア

The *kaiju* and *tokusatsu* boom didn't just hit Japan. Its neighbors observed the success of such films in their native Japan and abroad. Many decided to try their hands at Japanese-style productions. Hong Kong, Taiwan, South Korea, Thailand, even the Hermit Kingdom of North Korea; all attempted monster movies of their own with varying levels of success. Often, they solicited the aid of Japanese technicians who were more than happy to lend their expertise. These productions tended to lack the polish of Japan's films. Yet they have a unique quality: combining Japanese

technical skill with the native aesthetics of many of these countries. Japan's cinematic influence on the rest of East Asia stretches back to the Imperial years and World War II. The Japanese brought cruelty and oppression to the Asian countries they conquered. They also brought better cinematic technology. In the interest of producing propaganda to deflate the local resistance, they modernized the industries of countries like China, Korea, Thailand, Malaysia, the Philippines and Indonesia.

By the mid 1960s, Japanese special effects and monster films were at peak popularity. In Japan, nearly every studio produced a monster film in 1967 and *kaiju* swarmed the airwaves. The first fellow East Asian country to cash on the Japanese monster boom would be South Korea. The Korean peninsula is one of Japan's closest neighbors and biggest international rivals. Greater Korea was brutally occupied by the Japanese from 1910 until 1945. After that, anti-Japanese sentiment was so bitter that Japanese media of any sort was banned in both Koreas. In South Korea, the ban was not relaxed until 1998. It is still illegal to air Japanese music and shows on the radio and television. Regardless, the South Korean film industry was impressed with Japan's monster boom. They made a pair of monster films in the same vein. The summer of '67 begat two Korean *kaiju*: *Space Monster Wang Mag Wi* and *Yongary, Monster From the Deep.*

Released first in June and produced by Seki Productions, *Wang Mag Wi* is a mysterious and sought after film. Shot in black and white, it concerns a giant alien monster sent by helmet-wearing space people to destroy Earth. The creature is first seen human-sized, kept in a cell by the aliens. It also features a young couple: an air force pilot (Nam Kung-won) and his bride-to-be (Kim Hye-kyeong), whose wedding is ruined by the beast. The creature, King Kong-style, spirits the bride away. Also involved is a vagrant boy who hides inside the monster's head. The monster is depicted *tokusatsu* style with a man in a suit and miniatures, though no Japanese technicians were involved. In general, the FX work is unpolished and well below the quality of any Japanese productions. *Space Monster*

Wang Mag Wi was directed by Kwon Hyeok-jin. It has been little seen except at film festival screenings courtesy of the Korean Film Archive. Due to rights issues, the KOFA is unable to release the film publicly.

The better known *Yongary, Monster From the Deep* came next in August, directed by veteran Kim Ki-duk (1934-2017). For this film, its studio, Keukdong, consulted Japanese technicians from Daiei and Toei. Yongary was a Godzilla-style monster woken by a nuclear test in the Middle East. The monster emerges in Korea from underground and wreaks havoc in Seoul. Ala Godzilla, Yongary is killed by a chemical compound from a young scientist (Oh Yeong-il). As in the Gamera films, there's an irksome young boy (Kwang Ho Lee) who takes a liking to the monster. The special effects were supervised by Kenichi Nakagawa and Toru Suzuki. Masao Yagi, who built the original Gamera suit, constructed Yongary. The Korean staff were given a crash course on how to do Japanese style special effects. The picture is a pretty awful one with some oddly disturbing moments, like showing Yongary bleeding from its rectum as it dies. Still, it made good box office in Korea. *Yongary, Monster From the Deep* was exported internationally, released in Japan by Toei. In the United States, it came to television in an English dubbed version courtesy of American International Pictures. The original Korean version is lost. All that remains of it is an incomplete print running only 48 minutes at the Korean Film Archive.

The greater Chinese island nation of Taiwan also made a fair share of *kaiju*-style pictures, though with a fantasy bent. Unlike

China and Korea, Taiwan has a favorable view of Japan. Though also occupied by the Japanese for decades, China's former leader Chiang Kai-shek turned the country into a haven for the last of the *Kuomintang* in 1949. Strategically, Chiang's regime turned negative public opinion away from Japan towards Mao's communist China. The Japanese became allies in the struggle against communism. Taiwanese cinema was in turn aimed at promoting the ideal of reclaiming the Mainland from the communists.

An early post-war Japanese/Taiwanese co-production was a film called *Feng Shen Bang* (1969), roughly translating to *List of the Gods*. It is a *wuxia* (Chinese swordplay flick) with strong fantasy elements. *Feng Shen Bang* was co-directed by none other than Tatsuya Yamanouchi (*Grand Duel in Magic* or *The Magic Serpent*). Like *Grand Duel*, it features a giant dragon. The special effects were handled by Equis Productions' Masao Yagi and Akira Suzuki. Other notable early Taiwanese wuxia/monster/fantasy films include *Young Flying Hero* (1970) and *Tsu Hong Wu* (1971).

Tsu Hong Wu, or *Founding of the Ming Dynasty*, was directed by Hsu Ta-Chun. It features a white ape, a red haired giant and a dragon, all executed *tokusatsu* style. The special effects technician for this film was none other than Koichi Takano of Tsuburaya Pro. Takano (1935-2008) was well known for his work on the Ultraman franchise. He would go on to work on more Taiwanese productions including *The Devil From the Bottom of the Sea* (1974). Special effects footage from *Tsu Hong Wu* and *The Devil* was re-used in a later Taiwanese

fantasy film, *The Fairy and the Devil* (1982).

In Thailand, a filmmaker named Sompote Saengduenchai began making his own tokusatsu-style films at his company, Chaiyo. Sompote (1941-) had actually met and been mentored by Tsuburaya himself while visiting Japan. He spent some time on the sets of *King Kong vs. Godzilla* and *Son of Godzilla*. Chaiyo's first film was *Tah Tien* (1973). *Tah Tien* was based on Thai folklore and featured a pair of giants named Yak Wat Jaeng and Yak Wat Pho. *Tah Tien* was a tremendous success at the Thai box office. This led to Chaiyo and Tsuburaya Pro collaborating on two Thai-Japanese co-productions.

The first was *Jumborg Ace and Giant* (1974). This teamed Yak Wat Jaeng from *Tah Tien* with Tsuburaya's Jumborg Ace. They battled their enemies Jum Killer and Yak Wat Pho. The film was co-directed by Sompote and Shohei Tojo. Tojo is credited exclusively in Japanese prints. Tojo (1939-) was a prolific director who specialized in television *tokusatsu* shows. He started at Tsuburaya and went on to direct a lot of Toei's programs. In particular, Tojo helmed numerous Metal Hero and Super Sentai episodes. *Jumborg Ace and Giant* would be exported in Taiwan with new actors as *Mars Men*. It did good enough business in Thailand and Japan to warrant another collaboration between Tsuburaya and Chaiyo.

That film, far better known, is *Hanuman vs. 7 Ultraman* (1974), or *The 6 Ultra Brothers vs. the Monster Army*. In this film, a gaggle of *kaiju* including Gomora from *Ultraman* and Dustpan from *Mirrorman* are awakened by a failed rocket test. They lay siege to Thailand. All that stands in their way is the Hindu monkey god Hanuman and all the current Ultramen. The Ultra Brothers and Hanuman (quite brutally) battle the monsters. As with *Jumborg Ace and Giant*, Shohei Tojo co-directed. Thai prints exclusively name Sompote as director whereas Japanese prints credit Tojo. The special effects were handled by Kazuo Sagawa. Sagawa later worked on *The Last Dinosaur* (1977), another international Tsuburaya co-production.

The Thai cut of *Hanuman vs. 7 Ultraman* is a lot longer at around 103 minutes whereas the Japanese version is only 79. The shortened Japanese version, not released until 1979, is far more palatable. Hanuman would be back in 1975's *Hanuman and the Five Riders* and 1984's *The Noble War*. The former used Kamen Rider footage without Toei's permission. *Hanuman vs. 7 Ultraman* was re-released in Thailand in 1984 as *Hanuman vs. 11 Ultraman*. This version used unauthorized footage from the compilation film *Ultraman Zoffy*. It was localized for the U.S. in 1985 as *Space Warriors 2000*. *Space Warriors 2000*, produced by Dick Randall, is possibly the worst Americanization of an Asian film in cinema history.

In the mid 1970s, Chinese film mogul Run Run Shaw also became interested in producing tokusatsu-style productions. Shaw (1907-2014), along with his older brother Runme (1901-1985), owned the monolithic Hong Kong studio Shaw Brothers. The sound of Shaw Brothers' logo fanfare was well known in Hong Kong. Like Toho, Shaw Brothers owned their own line of theaters and had a distinctive house style.

One could tell that a film of theirs was *"Another Shaw Production"* just by watching it. At their peak in the mid '70s, they were putting out dozens of films per year. They were known for their stagey yet polished martial arts films which were popular internationally. Yet they produced films in every genre from romantic comedy to horror. In total, over a thousand pictures were put out by Shaw Brothers over the decades.

The Shaw or Shao family was long in the movie business. Run Run's older brothers had started theater and film businesses in Shanghai in the silent era. Runme and Run Run started their own film production arms in Malaysia and Singapore. After the war, they rebuilt their business with gold and jewelry they had buried in their backyard. In 1957, Run Run and Runme started Shaw Brothers studios. They built a movie factory of sorts on 46 acres of land in Clearwater Bay. By 1961, they were the largest scale film production outlet in the world.

When looking to technologically modernize his company, Run Run Shaw turned not to Hollywood but to former adversary Japan. Veteran Japanese cinematographer Tadashi Nishimoto acted as technical consultant in the early 1960s. Nishimoto (1921-1997) had worked for Shin Toho including for horror director Nobuo Nakagawa. He convinced Run Run Shaw to adopt Cinemascope and Eastman color as standard like Japan's industry had done. Additionally, he spent years in Hong Kong, shooting many of Shaw Brothers' early classics under the Chinese name "Ho Lan-Shan". He trained the Chinese crew on sophisticated cinematography techniques. The films shot by Nishimoto included Yueh Feng's

Madame White Snake (1962), Li Han-Hsiang's *The Love Eterne* (1963) and King Hu's *Come Drink With Me* (1966). Yukio Miyake (1934-) or "Kung Mu To" was another Japanese cinematographer who shot many of kung fu director Chang Cheh's films. Run Run Shaw also employed Japanese directors for some of his productions. These included the prolific Umetsugu Inoue, along with Koji Shima and Akinori Matsuo. The Shaws even structured the way their studio was run off the "Big Five" in Japan, particularly Toho. The actors, directors, writers and technical craftspeople were exclusively contracted to Shaw Brothers.

By the mid '70s, Japanese superhero shows like *Ultraman* and *Kamen Rider* were popular on Hong Kong airwaves. The Shaws decided to make a similar Chinese superhero. The project became *The Super Infra-Man*, released in August of 1975. Shaw Brothers brought Japanese designer and sculptor Michio Mikami, from Equis Productions, on board. Mikami (1935-) started his career with Tsuburaya's unit on *Rodan* in 1956. Eventually, he ended up at Daiei where he helped design monsters from the Gamera films including Gyaos and Zigra. Going freelance, he also worked on *Goke, Body Snatcher From Hell* and *The Green Slime* (both 1968). By the '70s, Mikami was chief designer for Toei's *Kamen Rider* franchise. Afterwards, he would supervise the production design on *Message From Space* (1978). He was a pivotal force and supervising director on Go Nagai's *Supermarionation*-style show *X-Bomber* or *Starfleet* (1980-81). Mikami designed Infra-Man himself along with many of the film's monsters. He had creative differences with the Chinese crew whom he felt weren't doing a good job building the suits and sets.

While high camp, *The Super Infra-Man* is a ferociously entertaining film. It combines colorful Japanese-style monster theatrics with kinetic Chinese action and martial arts mayhem. Its director was then 33 year old Hua Shan (1942-), who later specialized in martial arts and crime thrillers. Danny Lee plays the lead, a young scientist named Lei Mai. Lee, or Lee Sau-yin (1952-), was a prolific actor at Shaw Brothers who started in Chang Cheh's *The Water Margin* (1972). He would later be known for his role in John Woo's *The Killer* (1989). In *Infra-Man*, Princess Elizibub (Terry Liu) attacks Earth with her gaggle of monsters. Lee's Lei Mai is transformed *Kamen Rider*-style into the titular character by Professor Liu (veteran kung fu baddie Wang Hsieh). Once transformed, *Infra-Man* leaps into action. He takes on creature after creature in one off-the-wall sequence after another. Like *Ultraman* and *Kamen Rider*, he has numerous superweapons at his disposal. They are handy in destroying the various *H.R. Pufnstuf*-like beasties he battles.

Infra-Man also stars young actress Yuan Man-Tzu (1957-) and Bruce Le (1950-). Le became famous for being something of a Bruce Lee impersonator. He starred in a string of "Bruceploitation" films after the iconic martial artist's death. *Infra-Man*'s DP was none other than Tadashi Nishimoto, who had shot *The Way of the Dragon* (1972) for Bruce Lee himself. *The Super Infra-Man* flopped badly in Hong Kong but was exported internationally. It was released by Joseph Brenner in 1976 as

Infra-Man with a English dub by Titan Productions.

In 1976, the Taiwanese studio Dominic Pictures produced an interesting tokusatsu-style film called *War God*. Unlike prior films of this sort, this had a contemporary setting and sci-fi elements. The Taiwanese government objected to Taipei being destroyed in a film. They feared it would make Taiwan look weak to the communists. So the setting of the film's urban destruction was changed to Hong Kong. *War God* concerns an invasion by Martian aliens who look like albino bugs. After laying waste to Hong Kong with their spaceship, they grow to gigantic size and stomp through the metropolis. A statue of Chinese folk hero Guan Yu comes to life, Majin-style, and battles the giant aliens. Directed by Chan Hung-Man, the special effects were once again handled by Koichi Takano. They're about on par with Japanese television, but *War God* has a distinctive weirdness that makes it pretty appealing. It has to be seen to be believed.

Also in 1976 came the U.S./South Korean co-production *A*P*E*. Produced by Taiwanese entrepreneur T.K. Yang, the film was a sleazy cash-in on Dino De Laurentiis' then in production *King Kong*. Badly shot in 3-D and atrociously directed by American Paul Leder, *A*P*E* is a premiere cinematic abomination. The film's budget was only $23,000 and looks it. *A*P*E* has rock bottom production values that make Ed Wood look like Stanley Kubrick. The special effects by Park Kwang Nam are among the worst in film history. The ape suit is awful; about on par with one you'd rent for a '70s costume party. *A*P*E* also tries to shamelessly cash in on *Jaws* as the ape battles a (live) shark early on. It features a mixed American and Korean cast headed by Joanna Kerns as the blonde Fay Wray ingenue. She later became known for her role on TV's *Growing Pains*. The truly terrible *A*P*E* managed to beat De Laurentiis' *Kong* in Korean and American theaters by several months. *The Blob*'s Jack H. Harris distributed it with the tagline/legal disclaimer *"Not to be confused with King Kong"*.

Shaw Brothers put out a *King Kong* cash-in of their own in mid 1977: *The Mighty Peking Man*. The Shaw Brothers wanted to make an outright Kong film but were unable to procure the rights to the monster. The film was directed by Ho Meng-Hua. Ho (1923-2009) was one of the most prolific and interesting directors employed at Shaw Brothers. His previous work includes *The Lady Hermit* (1971) with Cheng Pei-pei and the original *The Flying Guillotine* (1974). The depiction of the latter's title weapon, invented by Qing emperor Yongzheng to kill Han rebels, became iconic in Chinese popular culture. Ho was hired for *The Mighty Peking Man* as he had proved he could handle special effects laden films with the *Black Magic* series and *The Oily Maniac* (1976). Once again Shaw Brothers brought in talent from Japan to lend expertise. The special effects were handled by none other than Sadamasa Arikawa, Tsuburaya's cameraman and the former head of Toho's FX division. For *The Mighty Peking Man,* other Toho employees accompanied him to Hong Kong. Koichi Kawakita assisted and Mototaka Tomioka was special effects cinematographer. The Peking Man suit was constructed by Keizo Murase and bests Toho's Kong suits. Murase (1933-) built many monsters for Toho and Daiei particularly Baragon in *Frankenstein Conquers the World* and Titanosaurus in *Terror of Mechagodzilla.*

The film concerns an expedition into India headed by explorer Johnny (Danny Lee again). Johnny has a depressed death wish because his girlfriend left him for his brother. They discover the titular Peking Man, a giant Kong-like Yeti. Johnny also finds a girl named Samantha (Swiss actress Evelyn Kraft). Samantha is a Tarzanette of sorts who has been living in the jungle since her parents died in a plane crash. Johnny is love-struck by this blond beauty and brings Peking Man and Samantha back to Hong Kong. Ala King Kong, Peking Man gets loose and goes on the rampage. He climbs Hong Kong's Jardine House before being killed by the British army as Samantha dies in the crossfire. Prolific Chinese actor Ku Feng (1930-) also appears in the film as a sleazebag promoter responsible for Peking Man's rampage. He played both mentors and villains in numerous martial arts films. An amusing anecdote is that Ho's Chinese crew were miserable during the location shooting in India. They hated the food and barely ate until they could find a Chinese restaurant. At that point, director Ho remarked, he'd never seen his crew eat so much.

The Mighty Peking Man is one of the best East Asian pseudo-*tokusatsu* movies. It is marred only by *mondo*-style animal cruelty and a ridiculous love montage so corny it looks like a parody by Trey Parker and Matt Stone. Its Japanese-made special effects are quite decent. The budget was one of the biggest in Hong Kong film history at over a million U.S. dollars. Arikawa and company definitely took the film's King Kong-inspired

material to heart. The Shaws and director Ho had some conflict with the Japanese FX team. They were frustrated that Arikawa's crew were taking a long time to finish the special effects sequences. The Shaws wanted to get the film out before Di Laurentiis' *King Kong* was released in Hong Kong. Due to visa problems with the Japanese FX crew, the release of *Peking Man* was delayed until August of 1977. It was released in the U.S. in 1979 as *Goliathon* by World Northal. Northal distributed a good amount of the Shaws' kung fu fare to grindhouses.

On the subject of Arikawa, an interesting Taiwanese/Japanese co-production is *War of the Wizards* (1978). A fantasy *wuxia* film with sci-fi elements, it involves a scroll that grants wishes from space. It features several monsters including a giant phoenix. The film's lavish special effects work and some co-direction were done by Sadamasa Arikawa and shot by Mototaka Tomioka. The villainess, an evil goddess named Flower Fox, is played by Betty Pei-Tei. Pei-Tei had a chilling turn as a brothel keeper in Chu Yuan's *Intimate Confessions of a Chinese Courtesan* (1972), made for Shaw Brothers. American actor Richard Kiel (*The Spy Who Loved Me*) appears as her henchman. *War of the Wizards* was released in the U.S. in 1983 by 21st Century Film Corporation.

Sompote Saengduenchai's Chaiyo, meanwhile, continued to produce films. Thailand's own local *kaiju* film of sorts was *Crocodile* (1978). It was actually a Korean co-production with Han Jin Enterprises and co-directed by Lee Won-Se. Kazuo Sagawa of Tsuburaya Productions also acted as advisor for the special effects sequences. Paying homage to both *Godzilla* and *Jaws*,

Crocodile concerns a radiation spawned giant crocodile wreaking havoc in Asia. The wives and daughter of main characters Tony (Nard Poowanai) and John (Min Oo) are eaten by the monster. As in *Jaws*, they head out to sea to hunt it down and kill it, along with a Quint-like Japanese fisherman named Tanaka (Kirk Warren). *Crocodile* has some vicious on-screen animal abuse that will turn off many viewers. The American Humane Association has condemned the film. The Thai cut and U.S. version are almost different movies with the former having better editing. The 100 minute Thai version of *Crocodile* is overall a pretty decent monster on the loose film. The 90 minute American version, supervised by Dick Randall, is quite haphazardly assembled. It was released in the U.S. in 1981 by Herman Cohen's Cobra Media. Other Chaiyo monster films not mentioned include *Phra Rod Meree* (1981) and *Magic Lizard* (1985).

Years later, relations between Tsuburaya and Chaiyo disintegrated. Sompote proved himself to be quite the crook. In the mid '90s, he began to claim he owned the international rights to the Ultraman franchise. He cited that he had helped Eiji Tsuburaya invent Ultraman when looking at Thai statues as inspiration. Sompote also claimed Tsuburaya's late son Noboru had gifted him the rights. He went as far as to forge the Tsuburaya family's *hanko* seal on an obviously fake contract. Sompote became a controversial figure and litigation lasted for years. It was finally settled in 2018, when a Los Angeles court sided in favor of Tsuburaya Pro. Sompote was thus forced to relinquish rights to the Ultraman franchise.

Speaking of litigation, in 1980, the Hong Kong company First Films, best known for producing *The Master of the Flying Guillotine* (1975), announced a *kaiju* production of their own. The film was to be called *Star Godzilla*. First Films even took out an entire ad in Variety. *Star Godzilla* was to be directed by Hsu Futien and star Joey Fang and Charles Woo. The Variety ad poster not only featured a Godzilla-like creature, but also Anguirus and King Kong-like monsters and flying saucers. It would have no doubt been an off the wall Hong Kong monster bash akin to *Infra-Man*. Unfortunately, production was halted abruptly and nothing was heard of it hence. For years, Western fans believed that the film might have actually been produced. The truth is there is no evidence of its existence beyond the Variety ad. First Films flaunting their unauthorized use of a heavily trademarked character in the industry's biggest trade magazine was not the smartest move. A stern phone call from Toho's legal reps likely put an end to *Star Godzilla*.

An extremely obscure Taiwanese production is *Big Frog* or *Who Killed the Frog* from 1980. Little is known about it except that it involves a giant frog on the rampage. *King of Snake* (1984) is another Taiwanese monster movie. Directed by Hsu Yu-Lung, it concerns an obnoxious little girl named Ting-ting (Tracy Su). Ting-ting finds a snake that she makes her pet and names "Mosler". Mosler, having eaten a chemical called R19, gets bigger and bigger. It grows to giant size and rampages through the countryside before being killed by the army. *King of Snake* is a strange film. It seems unsure whether it wants to be a children's film about a little girl and her monster or a thriller with political intrigue and violent shoot-outs. It also features Danny Lee, this time as a scientist responsible for creating the monster. There's unauthorized stock footage from *Mothra*. The finale also shamelessly uses Morricone's ending theme from *Once Upon a Time in the West*. The special effects were handled by another Japanese technician: Gozo Matsui. Matsui (1934-2001) was a cinematographer and FX technician on many Taiwanese films. The effects work is about Japanese television quality with Mosler executed as a puppet. The execution is very mixed but the urban destruction at the end of the film is a little better. The best looking shots have Mosler wrapped around a tall building fending off jets. The puppet was sent to Japan and re-used in Kinji Fukasaku's *Legend of the Eight Samurai* (1983) by FX director Nobuo Yajima.

Several years later, in 1987, Joseph Lai's IFD bought the rights to *King of Snake*. He and director Godfrey Ho created *Thunder of Gigantic Serpent* from it. Lai and Ho (1948-) were known in the Hong Kong film scene for their low quality but profitable business model. They would buy up obscure East Asian films from Taiwan, the Philippines or South Korea. Ho then shot wrap-around scenes with Western actors like Richard Harrison. Lai and Ho as a result could make several films for the time and price of one. *Thunder of Gigantic Serpent* follows this formula exactly. Footage from *King of Snake* is intercut with material shot by Ho featuring actors Pierre Kirby and Edowan Bersma. Despite IFD's dubious pedigree, in some ways *Thunder of Gigantic Serpent* is more palatable than *King of Snake*. It has more tasteful music choices and improved pacing, though both versions are pretty awful.

Another odd production is *War of the God Monsters* or *The Flying Monster* (1984). Like Godfrey Ho's work, the film is a pastiche. This cheapo South Korean flick combined tokusatsu footage from Tsuburaya Pro's *Return of Ultraman* with scenes shot in Korea. *The Flying Monster* was an extremely obscure film before it was released to Blu-ray by SRS Cinema.

In North Korea, the despotic Kim Jong Il also wanted to get his film industry's feet wet with a *kaiju* production. Years prior, Kim had kidnapped South Korean director Shin Sang-ok and his ex-wife, actress Choi Eun-hee. Kim forced them to make propaganda films for his regime. Inspired by the success of Toho's *The Return of Godzilla*, Kim had much of that film's staff brought to North Korea. He tricked them into coming; making them think the shoot was in China. The film that resulted, made in 1985 and directed by Shin, was called *Pulgasari*. It was based on the Korean myth of the *Bulgasari*, a tapir-like monster that ravenously devours iron. The special effects were supervised by none other than Teruyoshi Nakano, with camerawork by Kenichi Eguchi. Pulgasari was designed by Ultraman monster creator Yoshio Suzuki and its suit was made by modeling veteran Nobuyuki Yasumaru.

The plot, similar to *Majin*, revolves around oppressed farmers in 14th century Korea. The farmer's tools are confisticated by a cruel governor (Pong-ilk Pak). An imprisoned elderly farmer, as he is starved to death, makes a doll of the Pulgasari out of rice. When his daughter (Chang Son Hui) cuts herself while sewing, it comes to life. Starting off doll-sized, it devours metal, getting bigger. It becomes child-sized (played by Minilla actor Masao Fukuzawa/Little Man Machan). It then grows human-sized and then gigantic (played by Godzilla actor Kenpachiro Satsuma). With Pulgasari's help, the farmers overthrow the governor, raising the ire of the King (Yong-hok Pak). Eventually, Pulgasari destroys the King's palace, winning a victory for the farmers. Yet Pulgasari's hunger for iron is insatiable and it devours the farmers' tools.

Politics aside, *Pulgasari* is actually a fairly good movie. It has solid production values for a film made in a nation known for prison camps and mass starvation. Nakano's FX work is quite good, on par with what he was doing in Japan at the time. The Japanese FX team's contribution elevates the movie with a good suit and quality miniatures. Its communist propaganda themes are definitely evident. The farmers' struggle is clearly meant to represent the proletariat vs. the elites. It's said Pulgasari itself represents unchecked capitalism, first helping the farmers and then turning on and consuming them. *Pulgasari* was Shin Sang-ok's final North Korean film. Shortly afterward, Shin and his wife escaped Kim's clutches. At a film festival in Austria they were able to take refuge in the American embassy. Amusingly enough, Shin would later remake *Pulgasari* in the U.S. as *Galgameth* (1996). *Galgameth* moves the setting to medieval Europe and gives the story a more child friendly tone. In Japan, *Pulgasari* was not released until 1998 to capitalize on Tristar's *Godzilla*.

One of the last films of this type was director and former comedian Shim Hyung Rae's *Yongary* remake. *Yonggary* was also intended as something of a cash-in to Tristar's *Godzilla*. It was the most expensive film made in South Korea up to that time and was hyped at the Cannes Film Festival. It even starred Hollywood actor Harrison Young (*Saving Private Ryan*). Originally, an elaborate suit was built but it was replaced with CGI for most shots. *Yonggary* opened in Korea in 1999 and Shim, not happy with the film, gave it extensive reshoots. He replaced even more of its practical FX with CG. It was re-released in 2001 and in the U.S. as *Reptilian*. Overall, it was well received in its native Korea but skewered abroad. Director Shim would later make another Korean *kaiju* film with a mostly Western cast: *D-War* (2007).

Since then, there have been a handful of monster and science fiction movies made outside Japan. The most prestigious is certainly Oscar golden boy Bong Joon-Ho's *The Host* (2006). The Japanese influence has lessened and most of these films are done with CGI. Yet it's clear that Japan's special effects and *kaiju* boom was more influential than many give credit. It inspired Japan's neighbors, all former wartime adversaries, to produce similar films. Politics and national grudges were put aside as Japanese technicians were consulted and brought to work on these productions.

GODZILLA VS. HEDORAH

ゴジラ対ヘドラ

Gojira tai Hedora "Godzilla vs. Hedorah"
Toho, 7/24/1971 (*Showa 46*), 6 Reels (2,335 meters), 85:17, 35mm, TohoScope (2.35:1 anamorphic), color, monaural sound

Crew
Producer: Tomoyuki Tanaka
Director: Yoshimitsu Banno
Screenplay: Yoshimitsu Banno, Kaoru Mabuchi (Takeshi Kimura)
Director of Photography: Yoichi Manoda
Music: Riichiro Manabe
Editor: Yoshitami Kuroiwa
Assistant Director: Heikichi Tsushima
Art Director: Yasuyuki Inoue
Sound Recording: Masao Fujiyoshi
Lighting: Fumiyoshi Hara
Continuity: Shoji Okawa
Optical Photography: Yoshiyuki Tokumasa
Optical Composites: Saburo Doi
Production Manager: Boku Morimoto
Still Photography: Kazukiyo Tanaka

Cast
Akira Yamauchi (*Dr. Toru Yano*)
Toshie Kimura (*Toshie Yano*)
Hiroyuki Kawase (*Ken Yano*)
Toshio Shiba (*Yukio Keuchi*)
Keiko Mari (*Miki Fujinomiya*)
Yoshio Yoshida (*Gohei*)
Haruo Suzuki (*JSDF Senior Officer*)
Yoshio Katsube (*JSDF Technical Officer*)
Tatsu Okabe (*Announcer*)
Kentaro Watanabe (*Announcer*)
Wataru Omae (*Police Officer*)
Tadashi Okabe (*Scholar*)
Shigeo Kato (*Construction Worker*)
Takuya Yuki (*Correspondent*)
Eisaburo Komatsu (*Non-Commissioned Officer*)
Yukihiko Gondo (*Helicopter Pilot*)
Haruo Nakazawa (*Youth*)
Kazuo Imai (*Mahjong Player*)
Saburo Kadowaki (*Mahjong Player*)
Masaki Shinohara (*Mahjong Player*)
Nobuo Katsura (*Mahjong Player*)
Haruo Nakajima (*Godzilla*)
Kenpachiro Satsuma (*Hedorah*)
Koji Uruki (*Hedorah*)

Alternate Titles
Godzilla vs. the Smog Monster (U.S.)
Godzilla vs. Hedora (Alternate English title)
Frankensteins Kampf gegen die Teufelsmonster **[Frankenstein's Fight Against the Devil's Monster]** (Germany)
Hedora, la burbuja tóxica **[Hedora, the Toxic Beast]** (Spain)
Godzilla contra monstruos del smog (Mexico)
Godzilla - Furia di mostri **[Godzilla: Fury of Monsters]** (Italy)
Godzilla kontra Hedora (Poland)
Οι Τελευταίες Στιγμές της Γης **[The Last Moments of Earth]** (Greece)
Годзилла против Хедоры (Russia)

"Pollution's hideous spawn dooms the earth to choking horror and pits GODZILLA VS. THE SMOG MONSTER.*"*
-U.S. poster (1972)

In early 1970, Eiji Tsuburaya passed away. In the wake of his death, Sadamasa Arikawa went freelance and Ishiro Honda focused on directing for television. The younger, newly promoted Yoshimitsu Banno stepped into the director role for 1971's *Godzilla vs. Hedorah*. The film represents a wild departure for the series in tone and style. Banno took a more auteurist tact with the special effects and live action units merged. Like a *kaiju The Wall*, *Godzilla vs. Hedorah* is a surreal "head film" as much as a monster picture. The first Godzilla entry to tackle a social issue since 1954, it switches stylistic gears whenever it pleases. With a dream-like aesthetic, *Godzilla vs. Hedorah* throttles from kiddie anime sequences to psychedelia to surprising grotesquery.

PLOT

Gohei (Yoshio Yoshida), a fisherman, gives marine biologist Dr. Toru Yano (Akira Yamauchi) a strange find. While trying to fish for shrimp he caught a tadpole-like creature. Later, a gigantic creature similar to the tadpole attacks an oil freighter at sea. Yano goes scuba diving near where the old man found the tadpole while his son Ken (Hiroyuki Kawase) waits for him. Ken suddenly encounters the monster, who burns his hand. Yano is then attacked by the creature underwater and his face is burned with corrosive acid.

Dubbing the monster Hedorah, Ken has a dream that Godzilla is coming to humanity's aid. Dr. Yano, meanwhile, discovers that the monsters are made of minerals and can merge. A larger Hedorah soon comes ashore, having evolved into an amphibious form. Meanwhile, Ken's uncle Yukio (Toshio Shiba) and his girlfriend Miki (Keiko Mari) party at a club. Yukio, on a drug trip, hallucinates his friends with fish heads. Hedorah feeds on smoke stacks at a nearby power station. Godzilla arrives on the scene as a piece of the monster oozes into the club, leaving a cat covered in toxic slime. Hedorah and Godzilla do battle, with Godzilla driving the pollution monster away.

Dr. Yano collects samples of the monster where it fought Godzilla. He identifies an element, Hedrium, that gives the creature its incredible power. Yano theorizes the monster came from a meteor. Hedorah next appears in broad daylight in a flying form. It spreads sulphuric acid mists through the air that asphyxiate and burn crowds of civilians. Ken's mother (Toshie Kimura) witnesses her physical education class fall to the ground, choking, as Hedorah flies overhead. Dr. Yano realizes Hedorah could be defeated by dehydrating it using electricity. The experiment is successful on a small Hedorah tadpole. The Self Defense Force thus begins construction of two giant electrodes. Yukio, meanwhile, plans a giant party on Mount Fuji to stand against pollution. As Yukio, Miki and Ken party atop Fuji, Hedorah appears in its largest and most fearsome form yet. Godzilla isn't far behind, however.

BACKGROUND

Eiji Tsuburaya's death changed a lot at Toho. Sadamasa Arikawa initially became head of Toho's special effects department. He resigned and went freelance after Toho refused to put an onscreen tribute to Tsuburaya in *Space Amoeba* (1970). Ishiro Honda also felt that making special effects films wasn't the same without Tsuburaya. He went into semi-retirement, only directing sundry television episodes. Additionally, much of Toho's talent let their contracts expire. This included the usual stock of actors. A huge creative void was left at Toho and a younger generation began to fill it. Arikawa's replacement as head of Toho's special effects department was Teruyoshi Nakano. Nakano was a fairly young man whose trademark would be his distinctive gasoline conflagrations.

For 1971's Godzilla entry, Honda's replacement as director was a protege: Yoshimitsu Banno. Born in Imabari, Ehime Prefecture, Banno (1931-2017) joined Toho in the mid '50s as an assistant director. He served under several esteemed filmmakers, including Akira Kurosawa on *Throne of Blood* (1957), *The Lower Depths* (1957), *The Hidden Fortress* (1958) and *The Bad Sleep Well* (1960). He directed the underwater photography unit in 1967's *Young Guy in the South Pacific,* part of the popular series starring Yuzo Kayama. In 1970 he created the Expo '70 attraction *Birth of the Japanese Islands.* The popularity of this motion

exhibit led to him being put in charge of the next Godzilla entry.

In developing *Godzilla vs. Hedorah,* now executive producer Tomoyuki Tanaka gave Banno relative free reign. Banno chose to focus on ecological horror for *Godzilla vs. Hedorah* as he felt it was a similar existential threat to nuclear weapons. Banno remembered a visit to a polluted beach near the industrial center of Yokkaichi where the very air smelled like rotten eggs. Banno was also obsessed with Rachel Carson's 1962 *The Silent Spring.* Carson's writings influenced the lyrics of *"Return Us the Sun"*, the movie's Bondian theme song by Keiko Mari. Banno was also inspired by a recent news story about high school girls in Tokyo collapsing due to smog from a nearby factory. He would pay direct homage to this incident in *Godzilla vs. Hedorah.* Hedorah was conceived as so powerful that Banno and screenwriter Takeshi Kimura couldn't think of a method to defeat it. It was sci-fi author Masami Fukushima who suggested using electrodes. Fukushima pointed to a news story about how rice paddies were being dried out with electricity in Hokkaido.

PRINCIPAL PHOTOGRAPHY

Godzilla vs. Hedorah's budget was significantly low. Director Banno was given only 35 days to shoot both the drama and special effects scenes. Complicating things further, the budget allowed for only one unit. In a rarity for the normally set-bound Toho films, only the *tokusatsu* miniatures, Dr. Yano's laboratory and the Go-go Club were sets. Nearly all the human footage was shot on location. This gives the movie a grittier feel.

Banno however, was determined to include imagery and aesthetic never seen in the Godzilla series before. The direction is certainly more auteurist than usual. In contrast to prior entries, *Godzilla vs. Hedorah* features unusual camera-angles, staccato editing and "far-out" cinematic technique. The tone is closer to surrealist works like Seijun Suzuki's *Branded to Kill*, Toshio Matsumoto's *Funeral Parade of Roses* and Shunya Ito's *Female Convict Scorpion: Jailhouse 41* than *King Kong vs. Godzilla*. *Godzilla vs. Hedorah* includes multiple screens, trippy animated sequences, musical numbers, manipulation of color saturation and fish-eye lenses. Only some of Nobuhiko Obayashi's hyper stylized films like 1977's *House* are more off-the-wall. In spite of some blatant low budget flaws like a poverty row Self Defense Force, *Godzilla vs. Hedorah* has an impressive level of atmosphere.

Godzilla vs. Hedorah features surreal images throughout like a fever dream. A mannequin, looking like a mangled corpse, lays in sludge-filled waters. A male protagonist, likely tripping on LSD, hallucinates his friends in the nightclub with fish heads. A kitten is left behind in Hedorah's wake, mewing as it sits covered in toxic slime. A quartet of men playing *mahjong* die screaming as a chunk of Hedorah flies through the window. As a crowd of youths party at Mount Fuji, a gaggle of elderly people watch them with stern expressions

from the bushes. *Godzilla vs. Hedorah* can shift gears at any second, with a weirdness akin to *Pink Floyd's The Wall* (1982).

Director Banno was inspired to feature a "Go-go Club" in the film by a similar venue called Mugen in Tokyo's Akasaka district. The club's psychedelic display was inspired by a projection at a gay bar in Chicago. It was created with colored lights shined through swirled salad oil in water. The tiny "tadpole" Hedorahs were portrayed by live fish. Banno also did the underwater photography himself. He was the diving stand-in for actor Akira Yamauchi as the two had similar physiques. Banno also courted *manga* artist Yoshiharu Tsuge to create the *anime* sequences. Tsuge had drawn a pollution-themed manga called *Salamander* that Banno was fond of. Tsuge, however, turned him down as he had social anxiety and did not want to animate in a group.

Godzilla vs. Hedorah exhausted its budget before shooting could be completed. A furious Tomoyuki Tanaka ordered the shoot halted. It was Ishiro Honda, in his typical diplomatic form, who intervened. He agreed to watch a rough cut of the film and give Banno feedback. Thanks to Honda's mediation, production resumed. Tanaka soon was hospitalized for a stretch.

SFX

The disgusting shots of a polluted bay that punctuate the film's credits and finale are not genuine. They were created by the special effects staff in Toho's "Big Pool". This was done by mixing dead fish and garbage into the pool and the stench was unbearable. For the special effects sequences, Yoshimitsu Banno and Teruyoshi Nakano worked as co-directors. The FX work is a mixed bag but the two men clearly learned a lot from each other. Banno and Nakano filmed frantically on the effects stage, averaging 30 shots a day.

Hedorah is an impressive creation and its forms were designed by art director Yasuyuki Inoue. Banno and Inoue based the shape of Hedorah's eyes off the human vagina. By this time, suit craftsman Teizo Toshimitsu had retired. Replacing him was his apprentice, Nobuyuki Yasumaru. Yasumaru built the various Hedorah suits and puppets and did excellent work. They have unsettlingly dead looking eyes and the enormous final form's suit looks convingly slimy. Built entirely from foam rubber, it was Toho's bulkiest monster suit to date. This hulking costume was worn by a young stuntman named Kengo Nakayama, better known as Kenpachiro Satsuma. Satsuma, would, of course, go on to portray Godzilla starting in 1984's *The Return of Godzilla*. The Godzilla suit from *Destroy All Monsters* is again recycled; inhabited once again by Haruo Nakajima. In spite of the heavy damage done to the suit on this film, it would return in even roughier shape in 1972's *Godzilla vs. Gigan*. Yasuyuki Inoue also built and designed the miniature electrodes which were based on a toaster in shape.

While Tanaka was staying at the hospital, unable to keep reign on production, Banno decided to add a scene that wasn't in the script. He and Nakano felt the picture's grim tone had to be offset. In this scene, Godzilla flies by propelling itself into the air with its ray, inspired by the swimming of seahorses. This preposterous sequence is a major flaw in the film and stops it cold. Banno and Nakano deliberately shot it so it could easily be cut from the movie. They got permission from most of Toho's brass save for Tanaka. By the time Tanaka was discharged, it was too close to release to cut the scene. Tanaka was incensed, frustrated that Banno went around him to get approval. Tanaka said *"Banno will never direct a special effects film again"*. This statement would be, sadly, prophetic.

MUSIC

The much maligned musical score for *Godzilla vs. Hedorah* was composed by Riichiro Manabe. Manabe (1924-2015), was a graduate of the Tokyo Institute of Technology and a student of Akira Ifukube and Sei Ikeno. This was not his first *tokusatsu* film score, he worked on a few installments of Shin Toho's *Super Giant*. He was a favorite composer of filmmaker Nagisa Oshima and scored his *Cruel Story of Youth* and *Night and Fog in Japan* (both 1960). In the '70s, he scored Michio Yamamoto's three "Bloodthirsty" films starting with *The Vampire Doll* (1970). He also composed music for the 1974 *pinku eiga Flower and Snake*. Though hated by fans, Manabe's offbeat score is oddly effective to *Godzilla vs. Hedorah*'s unusual aesthetic and vivid atmosphere. He'd be back to score *Godzilla vs. Megalon* in 1973.

RELEASE AND LEGACY

Despite Tanaka's frustrations, *Godzilla vs. Hedorah* did better than expected business. After going to Africa to shoot a documentary about famine, Yoshimitsu Banno would be back for *Prophecies of Nostradamus* in 1974. Though directed by Toshio Masuda, Banno's fingerprints can be seen in the film's heavy environmentalist bent. He also directed a second unit in New Guinea. Tanaka was impressed with his work on *Prophecies of Nostradamus* and gave Banno another opportunity to direct a Godzilla film in 1975. Tanaka was lukewarm, however, to Banno's pitch of a sequel to *Godzilla vs. Hedorah* set in Africa. As a result, Ishiro Honda stepped into the director's chair one last time for *Terror of Mechagodzilla*. *Godzilla vs. Hedorah* was later included in the 1978 book *The 50 Worst Films of All Time*. It also likely inspired a 1990 episode of the American cartoon *Captain Planet*.

Hedorah would be back in 2004's *Godzilla: Final Wars*. Around the same time, Banno tried to get a sequel filmed in IMAX, *Godzilla 3-D: To the Max*, off the ground. While Toho gave him their blessing, Banno had to look for investors himself. Pitched to Legendary Pictures, the project became Gareth Edwards' 2014 *Godzilla* and Banno received a producer credit.

ALTERNATE VERSIONS

An English export version was ordered by Toho and dubbed by Barry Haigh's group Po Hwa in Hong Kong. The voice cast includes Haigh as Yukio, Esma Wilson (suspected) as Toshie, Linda Masson as Ken, Lynn Wilson as Miki, Chris Hilton as the JSDF officer and Ian Wilson as the news anchor. With the exception of English supers, this version is identical to the Japanese version. Unlike in the U.S. version, the original Japanese *"Return Us the Sun"* song by Keiko Mari is intact. This version took American fans by surprise when it was unexpectedly broadcast in letterbox format on the Sci-Fi Channel in 1996.

In April 1972, American International Pictures released *Godzilla vs. Hedorah* stateside, retitled *Godzilla vs. the Smog Monster*. With lurid poster art, it was double-billed with AIP's *Frogs* in some areas. This must have been an eco-horror night at the drive-in to remember for any young Boomer or Gen-Xer. Amusingly, *Frogs* actually features a bit of "polluted bay" stock footage from *Godzilla vs. Hedorah*. Later, it was also billed with *The Thing With Two Heads* in other regions.

Godzilla vs. the Smog Monster, running around 85:01, has some subtle differences to the Japanese and export cuts. The first is that Keiko Mari's *"Return Us the Sun"* ditty over the opening credits is dubbed into an English song called *"Save the Earth"*. *"Save the Earth"* was performed by Adryan Russ and written by Hollywood lyricist Guy Hemric. The Toho logo fanfare is excised. The film cuts to a "THE END" card against black as Godzilla walks into the horizon. This obscures the Japanese and export cut's use of Hokusai's

"Great Wave Off Kanagawa" and implication that another Hedorah has arisen. Some Japanese text is replaced with English supers and there are slight music cue differences. Some 16mm television prints contain text from the Japanese version. A new English dub was performed at Titan Productions in New York. The dubbing cast includes Bernard Grant (Dr. Yano), Peter Fernandez (Yukio), Lucy Martin (Toshie) and Earl Hammond (JSDF Officer). This superior dub was directed by Lee Kresel, supervised by Salvatore Billitteri and edited by Eli Haviv. In general, it's also more accurate to the Japanese version's dialogue. *Godzilla vs. the Smog Monster* was rated "G" by the MPAA. The export cut was later re-rated "PG" on Sony's DVD in 2004.

AMERICAN HOME VIDEO HISTORY

Godzilla vs. Hedorah was released to stateside VHS and laserdisc as *Godzilla vs. the Smog Monster* in 1989 by Orion. An unauthorized VHS by Simitar was released a year later, made from the alternate 16mm television print. The film was not released again until 2004, this time to DVD by Sony. This version was the international cut with the choice of Japanese audio and the export English dub. Low quality, unauthorized versions of *Godzilla vs. the Smog Monster* also floated around on DVD from Cheezy Flix and Digital Disc. The latter was packaged with *Godzilla vs. Megalon*. In 2014, ADV's successor Kraken Releasing distributed *Godzilla vs. Hedorah* on Blu-ray and DVD. This release came from the same master as the Sony DVD and also contained Japanese and export English audio. In 2019, *Godzilla vs. Hedorah* was released as part of Criterion's *Godzilla: The Showa Era* box set. This release was made from Toho's own inferior HD master and contains the Japanese audio only.

Further Viewing:

GODZILLA vs. GIGAN

(1972)
地球攻撃命令 ゴジラ対ガイガン
Toho, *Director:* Jun Fukuda

Long before *The Rise of Skywalker*, *Godzilla vs. Gigan* was an early example of franchise "course correction". Jun Fukuda was put back in the director's chair and the story was changed back to the classic alien invasion narrative. *Godzilla vs. Gigan* features a *manga* artist (Hiroshi Ishikawa) who finds out that his new employers are man-sized space cockroaches from a distant nebula. They have built a base of operations in the guise of a kiddie amusement park. Naturally, they summon space monsters King Ghidorah and Gigan to do their bidding. Of course, Godzilla and Anguirus arrive to defend humanity.

Beginning life as a more ambitious treatment entitled *Godzilla vs. the Space Monsters*, *Godzilla vs. Gigan* suffers from unoriginal, tired tropes. The plot is preposterous: why would the aliens hire Gengo the *manga-ka* to begin with? The musical score lacks novelty too, being composed of Ifukube recordings from prior films. The work of Teruyoshi Nakano's FX unit is uneven; it would take a few more films for the special effects director to find his feet. Then there's the bevy of stock footage to pad the movie's runtime. The use of stock footage is typical in *Showa*-era Japanese studio filmmaking. However, *Godzilla vs. Gigan* and its successor *Godzilla vs. Megalon* go overboard with it. The heavy use of stock shots is distracting and can make one wish they were watching the older films instead. The *Destroy All Monsters* Godzilla suit is used once more, even after all the damage it endured at Yoshimitsu Banno's hands in *Godzilla vs. Hedorah*. The suit is in ratty shape with tears visible and bits of it flying off in shots. This would be Haruo Nakajima's final performance as Godzilla and as such is bittersweet. The old King Ghidorah suit is also re-used, though with renovations by Nobuyuki Yasumaru.

Yet there's also a lot to like in *Godzilla vs. Gigan*. The film is affectionately 1970s and a lot of silly fun. The avian cyborg Gigan is an intriguing creation. Illustrator Takayoshi Mizuki designed it, brought in by Nakano for some "new blood". Mizuki used such motifs as eagles, kimonos and even actor Yujiro Ishihara. Nobuyuki Yasumaru built the suit, installing an electric conveyor belt for its abdominal buzzsaw. The film's Godzilla Tower miniature is oddly iconic and well built by Yasumaru. While there are far better Godzilla entries, *Godzilla vs. Gigan* is entertaining, especially with a couple Sapporo tallboys. The Hong Kong export English dub comes ironically recommended for its nostalgia factor.

(1973)
ゴジラ対メガロ
Toho, *Director:* **Jun Fukuda**

Shot in only three weeks with the lowest budget yet, *Godzilla vs. Megalon* is a controversial entry. Fans are torn between whether it's the worst or second or third worst Godzilla movie. In reality, *Godzilla vs. Megalon* gets a worse rap than it deserves and is a step-up from *Godzilla vs. Gigan* in many ways. In the 1980s and '90s, *Godzilla vs. Megalon* was considered public domain by distributors. It was given hordes of low quality VHS releases and lampooned on TV's *Mystery Science Theater 3000*. These poor 16mm prints did the film few favors, hiding its impressive Cinemascope compositions. High definition transfers reveal a far more technically polished movie.

Godzilla vs. Megalon is more fun viewed in a mindset far removed from *MST3K*. It takes a certain refuge in its audacity. By now, the *Showa* Godzilla series was ridiculous to the point of anarchic. As such, *Godzilla vs. Megalon* is hard to hate. The movie suffers from an even more awkward use of stock footage than *Godzilla vs. Gigan*. There are entire minutes of *Megalon* devoted to stock scenes from better pictures. Yet the original material is lively. Director Jun Fukuda keeps the action at a good clip and has fun helming engaging car chases. Katsuhiko Sasaki and

Yutaka Hayashi play a pair of robot-building buddies with an intimacy that's almost homoerotic. Hiroyuki Kawase from *Hedorah* returns to play another Gamera movie-like tyke. The underwater Mu Empire-like Seatopia that sends Megalon to Japan as revenge for nuclear tests looks far more 1970s than ancient civilization. Commanded by an aging Robert Dunham in a toga, it features dancing high priestesses in granny panties. Teruyoshi Nakano's new FX footage is spirited. A scene of a draining lake early on is well executed and thrilling. It well integrates Nakano's miniature work with live action footage shot at Motusu Lake near Mt. Fuji. While filming this scene in frigid winter weather, director Fukuda kept warm by drinking whiskey. A sequence where cockroach monster Megalon smashes up a dam is also well done, with strong miniature work. There are inventive composite shots throughout. The urban destruction scenes are particularly weak, however and rely on sloppy use of stock shots. It seems like Nakano ran out of money and time before he shot them. The score by Riichiro Manabe is downright bizarro world but enhances the picture's '70s aesthetic. The film's *"Jet Jaguar! Punch!"* ending song, given a problematic faux translation on *MST3K*, was crooned by Masato Shimon. Shimon (1944-) was best known for singing numerous anime and tokusatsu theme songs.

Shinichi Sekizawa was given main credit as script writer. In reality he only wrote the story with Jun Fukuda actually penning the screenplay. A new Godzilla suit was made for what really counts as a guest appearance. The suits for new monster Megalon and robot Jet Jaguar were all constructed by Nobuyuki Yasumaru and his apprentice Tomoki Kobayashi. Jet Jaguar was originally called Red Alone and inexplicably grows to a giant size for the film's climax. Designed as a cross between Ultraman and Go Nagai's Mazinger Z, it was later paid homage to in an episode of *Neon Genesis Evangelion*. Jet Jaguar would return in 2021's *Godzilla: Singular Point*. Around this time, Toho also produced the TV show *Zone Fighter*. With an Ultraman-like family of heroes battling weekly monsters controlled by an alien overlord, *Zone Fighter* had frequent guest appearances by Godzilla. Many episodes were directed by Ishiro Honda and Jun Fukuda. *Godzilla vs. Megalon* is not a quality entry, but it is a lively and energetic one. The final reel is a shut-off-your-brain monster slugfest for everyone's inner eight year old. Godzilla's "drop kick" near the end of the picture was bitingly lampooned on *MST3K*. It is indeed an even more embarrassing moment than Godzilla flying in *Godzilla vs. Hedorah*. By this time though, things are so delightfully ludicrous that it works. *Godzilla vs. Megalon* first came to the U.S. in 1976 with a poster, inspired by De Laurentiis' *King Kong*, of Godzilla and Megalon atop the World Trade Center towers. Needless to say, it hasn't been used much since 9/11.

UNMADE
THE FILMS THAT GOT AWAY

未完成のSF映画

Willis O'Brien's *Creation, War Eagles* and *King Kong vs. Prometheus.* Alejandro Jodorwosky's *Dune.* David Lynch's *Return of the Jedi.* David Cronenberg's *Total Recall.* Ridley Scott's *I Am Legend.* Stanley Kubrick's *AI: Artificial Intelligence.* Neil Blomkamp's *Halo* and *Aliens* sequel. Guillermo Del Toro's *The Hobbit.* These "films" are legendary among genre fan circles. Yet they all have one thing in common: they were never actually produced. They exist only in the imagination of film goers. In Japanese science fiction cinema, many such unmade productions are also documented. Given the hectic production practices of the old school Japanese film industry, these projects are numerous. Here's a handful of unmade films that, if completed, would have made a memorable impact. These are films that you will never get to see. Yet it's fun to imagine them. Many have existing pre-production art to help in that aim. Some scientists believe that there are infinite alternate realities. Perhaps there's an alternative timeline or two where you can get Blu-ray copies of *Nezura, Nessie, A Space Godzilla* and *Invisible Man vs. the Human Torch.*

BRIDE OF GODZILLA (1955)
ゴジラの花嫁?
Toho

Bride of Godzilla was to be a follow-up to *Godzilla Raids Again.* It was also to be the first Godzilla entry and *kaiju* film produced in color. A treatment was submitted in June of 1955 by Hideo Unagami, who later penned the story for 1958's *The H-Man.* Unagami's treatment was fairly convoluted. The titular "Bride of Godzilla" was a giant humanoid robot built by a scientist to combat it. The plot revealed that Godzilla and Anguirus, who returns, were from a giant hollow cavern deep below the Earth. Also involved were mermaid people and a giant Archaeopteryx and chameleon.

This epic and labyrinthine story would have required a large budget and was likely scrapped for that reason. However, elements from the story were clearly used in the years to come. The giant Archaeopteryx likely inspired the following year's Rodan and the trope of Godzilla battling a giant robot formed the basis for 1974's *Godzilla vs. Mechagodzilla.* Coincidentally, the concept of giant monsters being from a "hollow Earth" under the ground was later used in Legendary's Monsterverse, introduced in *Kong: Skull Island.*

THE VOLCANO MONSTERS (1957)
AB-PT Pictures/Toho

Godzilla Raids Again was to have been given a similar treatment to *Godzilla, King of the Monsters!* and *Half Human.* That is, a full scale Americanization. Entitled *The Volcano Monsters*, it was to be a largely different film. Toho sold the rights for *Godzilla Raids Again* to AB-PT Pictures. They would also unsuccessfully collaborate with AB-PT around the same time with *Varan*. Producers Harry Rybnick, Edward Barison and Richard Kay opted to use the monster footage from *Raids Again* to create their own film.

Screenwriters Ib Melchior (*The Angry Red Planet*) and Ed Watson were hired to pen the script. *The Volcano Monsters* would have revolved around two giant dinosaurs on the rampage in San Francisco. To make liberal use of Tsuburaya's effects scenes, they would have spent a lot of time fighting in Chinatown. Toho even sent AB-PT newly made Godzilla and Anguirus suits so they could shoot more footage. However, AB-PT soon suffered financial woes. This spelled an end to *The Volcano Monsters* and left Toho with a half finished film in the form of *Varan*. The *Volcano Monsters* suits were, amusingly, never returned. Warner Brothers ended up with the rights for *Godzilla Raids Again* which became *Gigantis, the Fire Monster*. Rather than a full-on Americanization, it was dubbed, narrated and reedited.

GIANT RAT HORDE NEZURA (1964)
大群獣ネズラ
Daiei, *Director*: Mitsuo Murayama

Nezura has been mentioned in the *Gamera, the Giant Monster* review and in John's *"Toho's Competition"* article. Yet unlike all the other films on this list, a sizable portion of *Giant Rat Horde Nezura* was filmed. A trailer was even created, shown in Japanese

theaters. Portions of this trailer were broadcast on television in the 1980s.

Inspired by Hitchcock's *The Birds* and H.G. Wells' *The Food of the Gods, Nezura*'s failed production is truly infamous. It was directed by Mitsuo Murayama (*Invisible Man vs. the Human Fly*) from a script by Kimiyuki Hasegawa. What footage was filmed starred Ken Utsui, Keizo Kawasaki and Michiko Sugata who appeared in *Gamera* the following year. Yonesburo Tsukiji, who later supervised the effects for *Gamera, the Giant Monster*, was in charge of the FX unit. With stop motion considered too expensive, the film's FX crew opted to use live rats crawling over miniatures. At first, lab rats were purchased but they proved too docile. In the end, captured sewer rats were used. This was exactly the logistical and hygienic nightmare one would expect.

The rats were hard to wrangle, carried fleas, lice and ticks and bit crew members who had to be masked on set. The rats even engaged in frequent cannibalism. Many escaped and bred, causing vermin outbreaks at the studio. The miniatures had to be sprayed down with pesticides daily. Crew member Michio Mikami developed an allergic reaction from a rat-borne tick bite. He almost died in the hospital. Eventually, locals near the studio began to complain. Tokyo's health department thus shut production down. Perhaps owing to the animal cruelty involved, Kadokawa destroyed the surviving teaser trailer when they acquired Daiei's holdings in 2002. It's possible sections of the trailer still exist in video form somewhere in Japan as shots were broadcast on television. It has yet to turn up, however. Also in 2002, a direct to video film called *Nezulla: The Rat Monster* was produced. Directed by Kanta Tagawa, it was likely inspired by *Nezura*. Currently in production at Kadokawa is a film entitled *Nezura 1964*. This is a comedic docudrama inspired by the production of this film. Yukijiro Hotaru (*Gamera: Guardian of the Universe*) and Mach Fumiake (*Gamera: Supermonster)* are both appearing in it.

BATMAN VS. GODZILLA (1966)
バットマン対ゴジラ
Toho/20th Century Fox

Batman vs. Godzilla was proposed in late 1965 by Shinichi Sekizawa who wrote a treatment. It was an attempt to make another Hollywood/Toho crossover after the success of *King Kong vs. Godzilla*. The treatment featured The Dark Knight and Boy Wonder battling the King of the Monsters. Toho briefly considered this concept before shelving it; probably as too difficult to produce. Some negotiations with Fox, who owned the rights to Batman at the time, likely took place. Toho was also trying to partner with Fox for a planned adaptation of Sakyo Komatsu's *Virus* around that time. The Adam West *Batman* show would debut on airwaves shortly after.

A lot of questions remain about how the project would have been executed. Would it have starred Japanese actors as Batman and Robin or brought in Hollywood players? Would it have paired a Hollywood crew with Tsuburaya's FX unit? I admit, a timeline where Adam West and Burt Ward battled 60s *Showa* Godzilla is one I wish I lived in. Spurred to do more international productions, Toho would push forward with another King Kong film.

THE FLYING BATTLESHIP (1966)
空飛ぶ戦艦
Toho, *Director:* **Ishiro Honda**

Another unmade Sekizawa script, *The Flying Battleship* was to have been a spiritual follow-up to 1963's *Atragon*. Shigeru Komatsuzaki and Toru Narita did design work. Ishiro Honda and Eiji Tsuburaya were to have directed with Ifukube doing the score. The plot would have involved an evil organization called NOO headquartered in the Amazon. Attempting to conquer Earth, they are countered by U.N. space battleship Super Noah. The project was dropped for unknown reasons. Designs and plot elements, however, would be recycled for Tsuburaya Pro's *Mighty Jack* (1968).

INTER ICE AGE 4 (1966)
第四間氷期
Toho, *Director:* **Hiromichi Horikawa**

Woman in the Dunes (1964), based on a novel by Kobo Abe, was a huge international success. Its distributor Toho sought to adapt one of Abe's most ambitious early novels, the dark science fiction epic *Inter Ice Age 4*. Written in 1958, it covered many ahead of its time themes. These include transhumanism, the dangers of artificial intelligence and climate change. Kurosawa acolyte Hiromichi Horikawa, who later helmed 1970's *The Militarists*, was to direct from a script by Abe. The finale would have involved the world being submerged beneath the waves due to global warming; using Eiji Tsuburaya and his unit. It's unknown whether it would have been in black and white like Teshigahara's Abe adaptations or color.

Inter Ice Age 4 was dropped for unknown reasons after Abe turned in a first draft. It may have been due to the poor commercial and critical reception of *The Face of Another* that same year. The novel's climax of countries sinking into the sea may have influenced an author who was Abe's protegee of sorts: Sakyo Komatsu.

JAPAN'S APACHES (1969)
日本アパッチ族
Toho, *Director*: Kihachi Okamoto

Sakyo Komatsu's debut novel was *Japan's Apaches* in 1964. It told the story of outcast people in a post-apocalyptic, remilitarized Japan who scavenge scrap metal to survive. In what may have been influential on *Tetsuo: The Iron Man*, these scavengers start to live off metal as food. They become a new race and revolt against the fascistic government. Planned in the late '60s, Kihachi Okamoto was to direct from a script by author and *manga* artist Kazumasa Hirai (*Wolf Guy*). The popular comedy and jazz troupe the Crazy Cats were set to star. Okamoto was never happy with the script and Hirai became too busy to rewrite it. So the project was scrapped.

GAMERA VS. THE TWO-HEADED MONSTER W (1972)
ガメラ対双頭怪獣W
Daiei, *Director*: Noriaki Yuasa

As a child, one of my favorite books was Don Glut's 1980 *The Dinosaur Scrapbook*. In that book Glut mentioned a Gamera film after *Gamera vs. Zigra* that may or may not have been made. As a kid, I tried to find this film but soon realized it probably didn't exist. *Gamera vs. the Two-Headed Monster W* was indeed planned, announced and almost made. Noriaki Yuasa was once again in the director's chair. The new monster was designed and suits were constructed. Only one thing stopped it and that was Daiei's catastrophic December 1971 bankruptcy.

Rumor has it that angry employees or even Yuasa himself destroyed the suits in storage, including the new ones for this film. Little else is known about *Two-Headed Monster W* besides that it was to be filmed at the newly opened Miyazaki Zoo. Daiei's remnants were soon acquired by Tokuma Publishing in 1974. Years later, in 1991, Yuasa produced a similar proof of concept short film. Called *Gamera vs. Garasharp*, it was a special feature for a Gamera laserdisc set and is included in Arrow's Blu-ray box.

GODZILLA VS. REDMOON (1972)
ゴジラ・レッドムーン・エラブス・ハーフン 怪獣番外地
Toho/Tsuburaya, *Director*: Shohei Tojo

A co-production between Tsuburaya Pro and Toho, *Godzilla vs. Redmoon* was planned for release in the early 1970s. It would have featured a pair of monsters Red Moon and Erabus on the rampage in Okinawa. These two monsters were to mate and give birth to a baby monster named Hafun. Hafun is killed when a greedy entrepreneur tries to kidnap him. This sends his parents into a rage with Godzilla all that can stop them.

Toho were happy to lend their support to the production and show the film at Champion Matsuri. They were planning to loan the production the Godzilla suit from

Son of Godzilla. A script was written by native Okinawan Tetsuo Kinjo and Kazuho Mitsuta. The film was to have been directed by Shohei Tojo with Kazuo Sagawa in charge of the effects. Tojo would later co-direct the Chaiyo/Tsuburaya production *Hanuman vs. 7 Ultraman.* It's unknown why this project was cancelled but it wound up giving rise to Tsuburaya's *Daigoro vs. Goliath.* It's possible that *Godzilla vs. Mechagodzilla*'s Okinawan locale was also inspired by this attempted production. That Red Moon and Erabus were going to be played by the Daigoro's Mother and Goliath suits is a fandom myth. Those suits were designed and built specifically for *Daigoro vs. Goliath.*

INVISIBLE MAN VS. THE HUMAN TORCH (1975)
透明人間対火焔人間
Toho, *Director*: Jun Fukuda

Director Jun Fukuda and Toei screenwriter Masahiro Kakefuda spent years developing the script for *Invisible Man vs. the Human Torch. It* was planned for Fukuda to finally direct it on the heels of *ESPY*. The project didn't get very far, however, though concept art was made. It's a shame, as another science fiction actioner from Fukuda would have been a blast.

GODZILLA VS. HEDORAH II (1975)
ゴジラ対ヘドラ 2
Toho, *Director*: Yoshimitsu Banno

Tomoyuki Tanaka was impressed with Yoshimitsu Banno's contributions to *Prophecies of Nostradamus.* As a result, Tanaka decided to give Banno another chance at helming a Godzilla entry. Banno

first considered a concept called *Godzilla vs. Hitodah* with a pollution mutated starfish. However, he wound up pitching a direct sequel to *Godzilla vs. Hedorah.* This time another Hedorah was to show up in Africa, attracted by pollution from recent economic development. Banno was quite obsessed with Gualtiero Jacopetti and Franco Prosperi's *Africa Addio* (1966). He had recently worked on a 1973 documentary entitled *Cruel Famine Continent.*

Like *Godzilla vs. Hedorah* and *Prophecies of Nostradamus*, this would have been an interestingly offbeat film. Unfortunately for Banno, Tanaka didn't go for the idea. Perhaps the costly prospect of location shooting in Africa was the deal breaker. Banno wound up taken off the project. Ishiro Honda was thus coaxed out of semi-retirement to make a direct sequel to *Godzilla vs. Mechagodzilla.*

PROPHECIES OF NOSTRADAMUS II: FEAR OF THE KING OF TERROR (1975)
ノストラダムスの大予言 II 恐怖の大魔王
Toho, *Director*: Toshio Masuda

Prophecies of Nostradamus, in spite of its controversies, was one of Toho's biggest hits in 1974. As such, Tomoyuki Tanaka was keen on producing a sequel. *Prophecies of Nostradamus II: Fear of the King of Terror* was to bring back much of the original's core crew. This included director Toshio Masuda and special effects director Teruyoshi Nakano. The script was written by Masato Ide (*Ran*). It featured a reporter character named Tsutomu Goto, based on the author of the original's source material. He was to unsuccessfully try to make contact with Nostradamus' spirit. At the same time, an ominous UFO, the apparent King of Terror from Nostradamus' prophecies, appears over Japan. Owing to backlash from the first film, plans were scuttled.

CONTINUATION: SUBMERSION OF JAPAN (1976)
続日本沈没
Toho, *Director*: Shiro Moritani

Tanaka was also eager to make a sequel to his megahit *Submersion of Japan*. This follow-up would have brought back director Shiro Moritani and Teruyoshi Nakano. It was to have focused on the struggles of Japan's refugees overseas, climaxing with Onodera and Reiko Abe being reunited in Geneva. Toho announced the film on their production slate in 1974, '76 and '78. For unknown reasons the film never made it past pre-production.

REBIRTH OF GODZILLA (1977)
ゴジラの復活
Toho, *Director*: Jun Fukuda

In the late 1970s, Tomoyuki Tanaka established a "Godzilla revival committee". He would make several attempts to revive Godzilla before *The Return of Godzilla* was made. The one that came closest to production was *Rebirth of Godzilla*. Scripted by *Gappa* and *The War in Space*'s Ryuzo Nakanishi, details are conflicting on its plot. Some sources say it involved Godzilla battling terrorists hijacking a nuclear power plant. Others state it was to have been a straight-up remake of the 1954 original. Jun Fukuda was to direct and Teruyoshi Nakano would have helmed the special effects. It was nearly made, but then

Tanaka saw *Star Wars*. Like Toei's Shigeru Okada, he scrapped plans for a monster film and opted to swiftly develop *The War in Space* instead with the same team.

DEVIL MANTA (1977)
デビルマンタ
Toei, *Director*: Hajime Sato

After seeing Steven Spielberg's *Jaws*, Toei CEO Shigeru Okada was keen to produce a series of monster pictures. The first of these proposals became 1977's *Legend of the Dinosaur and Monster Bird*. The second was a space borne monster flick to be called *Devil Manta*. With designs by tokusatsu and manga god Shotaro Ishinomori, it would have been director Hajime Sato's first film since 1968's *Goke, Body Snatcher From Hell*. Nobuo Yajima was to helm the special effects unit. Production was abruptly halted when Okada saw *Star Wars*. Rather than make a space monster film, he changed the direction to space fantasy. Ishinomori and Yajima were kept on, but Hajime Sato was let go from the project. Kinji Fukasaku was hired and the film became *Message From Space*.

NESSIE (1978)
ネッシー
Toho/Hammer, *Director*: Bryan Forbes

A legendary unmade production, *Nessie* was to be an international co-op between Toho and England's own house of horror, Hammer. Production was announced in a lavish trade ad in Variety. The director was to be an Englishman, Bryan Forbes (1926-2013). Forbes, also a novelist and screenwriter, was best known for *The Stepford Wives* (1975). Teruyoshi Nakano was set to handle the special effects. It's unknown how the logistics of the production would have been handled or if *Nessie* was to be filmed in the UK or Japan. It's possible Forbes' unit would have shot in the UK while Nakano's team handled the special effects sequences back in Japan.

Production actually got pretty far with Yasuyuki Inoue even building some *Nessie* maquettes. The financially distraught Hammer pulled out of the project last minute. It's a shame. The two studios, both known for their stylized genre pictures, would have worked well together. It would probably have been more fruitful than Hammer and Shaw Brothers' *Legend of the 7 Golden Vampires*. Hammer soon went belly up after producing a 1979 remake of Hitchcock's *The Lady Vanishes*. Rumors that Nakano refurbished the Nessie prop for 1987's *Princess From the Moon* are false as pictures of Inoue's distinct maquettes have recently surfaced.

A SPACE GODZILLA (1979)
ア・スペース・ゴジラ
Toho, *Director:* **Nobuhiko Obayashi**

After the success of director Nobuhiko Obayashi's stylish horror thriller *House* (1977), a Godzilla project helmed by him was contemplated. In 1979, a two part story by Obayashi was published in the Japanese edition of Starlog magazine. Called *A Space Godzilla,* it was a detailed outline of his potential Godzilla project. Obayashi's vision of Godzilla would have been as trippy as *House* and made *Godzilla vs. Hedorah* look tame. As Tomoyuki Tanaka was particular about the Godzilla brand and thought even Banno's concepts were too strange, it's unlikely that *A Space Godzilla* was seriously considered.

The story in Starlog lists a potential crew for the project that includes most of *House*'s collaborators including DP Yoshitaka Sakamoto and the rock band Godeigo. The special effects were not to be helmed by Teruyoshi Nakano, but by Tatsuo Shimamura who later worked on 1989's *Tokyo: The Last War*. The plot for *A Space Godzilla* is possibly even more batshit insane than *House*. It involves Godzilla dying of diabetes and then traveling through space. Imagine the eclectic dream-like madness of *House* crossed with a *tokusatsu* version of the Stargate scene in *2001: A Space Odyssey*. The magazine articles do include a photograph of a model intended to be used in the film, so perhaps Obayashi was serious about getting it made. The Starlog articles were also published with Toho's approval. The article's illustrations were done by a little known at the time *manga* artist named Katsuhiro Otomo. Otomo would, of course, go on to become a giant of *anime* and manga with the seminal *Akira*. If you want to take in the full madness of what Obayashi's bizarre mind dreamed up, check out Kevin Derendorf's Maser Patrol blog. It contains a detailed translation by his Japanese-fluent fiancee Amanda.

GODZILLA: KING OF THE MONSTERS IN 3-D (1983)
Director: **Steve Miner**

Godzilla: King of the Monsters in 3-D was the first attempt to make an American Godzilla film. The talent behind it was 1980s Hollywood genre top tier. Steve Miner (*Friday the 13th Part II*) spearheaded the project and was to direct. Fred Dekker, later to write and co-direct *Night of the*

Creeps and *The Monster Squad,* penned the screenplay. Popular paleontological illustrator William Stout created the Godzilla design. Stout also storyboarded much of the film. Some of tinseltown's finest special effects experts were also attached. This included Rick Baker and stop motion maverick David Allen. Between the talent involved and the all practical effects '80s aesthetic, this may have been a more palatable Hollywood take on Godzilla than those to come.

Miner pitched the project to multiple studios but most balked at the budget. Miner was hardly an A-list director and the studios were hesitant as a result. As it goes, the project fizzled out. It certainly lit a fire under Tomoyuki Tanaka back in Japan. *The Return of Godzilla* was released only a year after *Godzilla: King of the Monsters in 3-D* was proposed. Interestingly, *The Return of Godzilla* has some plot parallels with Dekker's script. Both feature Godzilla destroying a Russian submarine and a nuclear missile fired by accident from a satellite.

MOTHRA VS. BAGAN (1990)
モスラVSバガン
Toho, *Director*: Kazuki Omori

After *Godzilla vs. Biollante,* Toho and writer/director Kazuki Omori set about development of a third *kaiju* film. At first they were planning to take a break from Godzilla and make a standalone Mothra picture pitting her against "Bagan". This was a sort of re-imagined version of Bakan from Tanaka's early *Return of Godzilla* treatment. *Mothra vs. Bagan* was, naturally, going to lead to a sequel pitting Bagan against Godzilla. Development got

quite far on *Mothra vs. Bagan*. Sachiko Suzuki and Shoko Aida of the J-pop duo WINK were even cast as new versions of the Twin Fairies. *Godzilla vs. Biollante* was a box office disappointment, however. Tomoyuki Tanaka and company thus grew wary of making a kaiju film without Godzilla. They opted to go in a different direction; bringing back classic Ghidorah for 1991's *Godzilla vs. King Ghidorah.*

The project would prove influential, however. Omori's script for *Mothra vs. Bagan* would provide the basis for 1992's *Godzilla vs. Mothra.* "Black Mothra" Battra replaced Bagan's role. Producer Shogo Tomiyama also considered using Bagan on more than one occasion. Among Godzilla aficionados, Bagan is oddly popular for an unproduced character. Mothra wound up getting her own standalone film, too. 1996's *Rebirth of Mothra* would beget two sequels.

MAI THE PSYCHIC GIRL (1991)
Carolco Pictures, *Director*: Tim Burton

Mai the Psychic Girl was to be based on the *manga* by Kazuya Kudo, one of the first ever fully published in the U.S. A live action, musical adaptation of *Mai the Psychic Girl* was spearheaded by the rock group Sparks starting in the late '80s. By 1991, they had a studio on board along with A-list director Tim Burton, fresh off *Batman.* Carolco Pictures, the studio involved, hoped for Burton to direct *Mai* after *Batman Returns.* Burton wanted to make *Ed Wood* first, however. As a result the rights expired. Multiple attempts to produce it have been made since, one with HK director Kirk Wong (*Crime Story*) attached. It's unknown if the film was planned to be a white-washed adaptation or not, but it's likely knowing '90s Hollywood.

In 2010, Tim Burton expressed renewed interest in directing *Mai the Psychic Girl*. It should also be noted that Takao Okawara's 1991 *Reiko, the Psyche Resurrected* likely drew quite a bit of inspiration from that manga.

GODZILLA (1995)
Tristar, *Director*: Jan De Bont

After what Tristar's stab at an American Godzilla movie became, this first iteration has taken mythical status in the fandom. Put into motion by producer Henry Saperstein, the deal with Toho was first made in 1992. A teaser trailer was attached to the end of 1993's *Godzilla vs. Mechagodzilla II*. It promised *"dynamic Hollywood filmmaking"* and *"ground-breaking visual effects"*. The project was scripted by Ted Elliot and Terry Rossio, one day to write *Shrek* and *Pirates of the Caribbean*. For directors, Tim Burton and Joe Dante were courted. *Godzilla* wound up in the hands of former cinematographer Jan De Bont. De Bont was in the midst of his directorial debut *Speed* (1994).

To revolve around Godzilla battling a giant "doomsday beast" Gryphon, De Bont's Godzilla got pretty far into development. Filming was set to commence in late 1994. A team headed by *Jurassic Park*'s Stan Winston produced a Godzilla design and maquette far more palatable than what Tristar ended up with. It was a look that still resembled its Japanese counterpart; retaining its "handsomeness". Extensive storyboards were also drawn. The film was

planned to contain 500 VFX shots, a cinematic record at the time. They were to be done by James Cameron's Digital Domain and Sony Imageworks after Industrial Light and Magic passed per their busy slate. Problems at Tristar's parent company Sony soon arose. These included the costly failure of *Last Action Hero* (1993). Then came the departure of long time project champion Peter Guber from Sony's leadership.

Having only made *Speed*, De Bont was still relatively green as a powerhouse director. He wanted Godzilla to be totally computer generated and the budget to be massive: just under $200 million. Sony's new brass balked at *Godzilla*'s monstrous budget, wanting it kept under $100 million. De Bont tried to pair down the film's budget but Sony began to rethink the project's direction. In the end, De Bont's *Godzilla* was canned just as the first sets were being built. We all remember how it ended. De Bont went on to direct *Twister* (1996). The project was revived under the (mis)direction of producer Dean Devlin and director Roland Emmerich. Both made their disdain for Japanese monster movies clear in interviews, so what resulted was unsurprising in hindsight. Terry Rossio would later contribute to *Godzilla vs. Kong* (2021).

GAPPA VS. GUILALA (1997)
ガッパ対ギララ
Shochiku

In a 1997 issue of G-FAN, it was said Shochiku had announced a film pitting Nikkatsu's Gappa against their Guilala from *The X From Outer Space*. Whether this was hearsay or if the project was seriously considered is anyone's guess. Guilala would finally be back in 2008's satirical *Monster X Strikes Back: Attack the G8 Summit* in 2008. Gappa, however, has not been seen since 1967's *Gappa, the Triphibian Monster*.

GODZILLA 2 (1999)
Tristar, *Director*: Roland Emmerich

Tristar wanted to produce a trilogy of American Godzilla films. Roland Emmerich and Dean Devlin approached screenwriter friend Tab Murphy (*Gorillas in the Mist, Last of the Dogmen*). Murphy was hired to pen a sequel treatment before the 1998 film was even picture locked. He was given relatively free reign on *Godzilla 2* and he submitted a treatment in October 1999.

Matthew Broderick's Nick Tatopolous was to have returned, along with Jean Reno's Philippe. Opening with a dissection of the previous film's creature, Nick finds the last surviving baby Godzilla has hatched. Taking pity on it as it imprints on him, he saves it from the military. Godzilla was to have reappeared fully-grown in the Australian outback and be raising another brood there. This second Godzilla was to take a benevolent role, protecting the world from a giant insect monster somewhat akin to Megaguiras. Also involved was a Dian Fossey-inspired lady scientist (*Godzillas in the Mist*, anyone?). Tab Murphy wanted to humanize Godzilla and give audiences more of an emotional connection with the monster. In the end, the treatment was never made into a script. Tristar thought the better of making a sequel due to the harsh critical backlash to *Godzilla '98*.

GODZILLA: REBORN (2001)
Sony/Toho, *Director*: Joe Dante

After the kibosh was put on a sequel to the 1998 film, *Godzilla 2000* (1999) was released to American theaters in the summer of 2000. It performed below Tristar's expectations. The subsequent Millennium entries were thus dumped directly to DVD. That didn't stop producer Michael Schlesinger from pitching an American sequel to *Godzilla 2000*. Schlesinger had creatively spearheaded the U.S. version of *Godzilla 2000*. The rights to one more Godzilla film still lay in Sony's hands. It would have been directed by *Gremlins'* Joe Dante for $20 million, paltry by Hollywood standards. The special effects were to be handled *tokusatsu*-style by a Toho special effects crew. Schlesinger penned a script which Toho approved, demanding only one change. In the original draft, Godzilla was killed mid-film and then resurrected through cloning. Toho had that changed to a simple coma. The film was to have a comedic tone akin to Dante's *Gremlins 2: The New Batch* or Tim Burton's *Mars Attacks!*. Shiro Sano's Dr. Miyasaka from *Godzilla 2000* was to return, along with an all-star slew of cult actors. Schlesinger and Dante wanted to cast Bruce Campbell, Jamie Lee Curis, Scott Bakula, Christopher Lee, Leonard Nimoy, Robert Picardo, Dick Miller and Ken Takakura.

Sony's Hollywood brass had yet another shakeup. The new heads were less than enthused with green-lighting a $20 million cult picture. As a result, Sony's rights to a Godzilla sequel soon expired. Legendary Pictures would next acquire the Godzilla rights via Yoshimitsu Banno's failed IMAX extravaganza *Godzilla 3-D: To the Max*.

NEON GENESIS EVANGELION (2004)
ADV Films/Weta

This ambitious but foolhardy project was announced to collective groans at Cannes in mid 2003. *Evangelion*'s U.S. distributor ADV Films aimed to make a live action adaptation of the iconic anime property. The film would have been shot in New Zealand with the participation of Peter Jackson's Weta Workshop, fresh off the Oscar-winning *Lord of the Rings* trilogy. ADV even commissioned quite a bit of art as proof of concept from the designers at Weta. This art was first unveiled in Newtype magazine and as a special feature on a DVD release of the *Evangelion* director's cuts. Much of the art, while quality, looked too Westernized, garnering a mixed response from fans. Weta co-founder Richard Taylor was interviewed in this segment. Taylor badly mangled the pronunciation of "Evangelion". Worse still, characters bore Anglicized names (Asuka Langley Soryu was "Kate Rose"). It was dreaded like climate catastrophe: a dumbed down, white-washed and CGI-drenched Hollywood take that vaguely resembled Hideaki Anno's opus. Anno was well aware of this project. At first he threw his support behind it but in more recent years has taken a skeptical attitude. In the interview, Taylor mentions that his team had an idea for the bullet casings from the Evangelions' guns to fall onto and crack pavement. A similar shot was featured in 2007's *Evangelion 1.0: You Are (Not) Alone*.

For years, ADV's Matt Greenfield shopped the project around to Hollywood studios. He continually promised that they were "close to a deal". A spec script was allegedly written by a popular sci-fi writer. It was said several "A-list directors" were interested. Who these people were has never been revealed. Some have alleged James Cameron was one of them. Anecdotally, ADV was hoping to get Peter Jackson. Robin Williams may also have been lobbying for the part of Gendo Ikari. It seems like ADV, a Texas-based company founded to distribute anime, were a little green on how the Hollywood system worked. In the end, ADV was tangled up in a lawsuit with Gainax. This killed any chance of the project getting off the ground. Rumors swirled a few years later that Michael Bay was interested in the property from a clickbait rag. Honestly, a sanitized Hollywood *Neon Genesis Evangelion* flick with a white-washed cast is not something any fan of the series would want to see. If one desires a Hollywood take on Japanese giant robots, *Pacific Rim* is your best bet. Netflix's recent acquisition of *Evangelion* does make one wonder if they might be considering a similar project ala Adam Wingard's *Death Note*. Weta was very passionate about working on *Evangelion*, but at least later got to do *Ghost in the Shell* and *Alita: Battle Angel*.

GODZILLA 3-D: TO THE MAX (2008)
Toho/Advanced Audiovisual Productions,
Directors: Yoshimitsu Banno, Keith Melton

Godzilla vs. Hedorah's Yoshimitsu Banno long had an interest in large format films. Banno himself helped develop a 70mm format called JAPAX. He even produced the very first JAPAX Film: *Breathe* (1985). In 2000, Banno founded Advanced Audiovisual Productions, a firm dedicated to large format movies. At the same time, he also itched to make another Godzilla movie. Banno thought Toho could be sold on the concept of a large format Godzilla film. Toho gave Banno their blessing and the rights to use the Godzilla brand, but left him to find investors elsewhere. Banno's first script, written in 2003, was a work of mad genius. Opening with children singing *Hedorah*'s ditty *"Return Us the Sun"*, it would have involved a new pollution monster, Deathla, appearing in the Amazon. Godzilla, who can fly again, battles Deathla across the globe and even in Disney World and at the 9/11 monument. It was to be a 40 minute short, filmed stereoscopically in 70mm IMAX 3-D. The project was to have been co-directed by Keith Melton, who had helmed the IMAX short *Cirque du Soleil: Journey of Man* (2000). *Captain EO*'s Peter Anderson was on board as DP and VFX director. *Blade Runner*'s Syd Mead was also tapped to design Deathla. Best of all, it was to have featured traditional, *tokusatsu* effects lensed in razor sharp 70mm IMAX. Eichi Asada (*Godzilla: Tokyo S.O.S*) was to supervise the special effects sequences. Seeing a soft remake of *Godzilla vs. Hedorah* with tokusatsu effects on a hundred foot curved screen in the splendor of IMAX sounds too amazing for our mundane world. It probably was.

In the mid to late 2000s, Banno and his team kept pushing the start of production back as they had difficulty finding investors. The film's website shut down in March of 2006, the month it was supposed to start shooting. The script went through numerous rewrites to make it more appealing to Hollywood executives. Eventually it was even decided to make Godzilla mainly computer generated. Around 2010, Banno went to Legendary Pictures looking for funding and they expressed interest. Legendary wanted, however, to make a feature length film for mainstream theaters. The project, as you can guess, became Legendary's 2014 *Godzilla*, directed by Gareth Edwards. Yoshimitsu Banno's name wound up on the movie as executive producer. However, Edwards' bland blockbuster bore little in common with the original concept. Undaunted, Banno tried to make a similar IMAX 3-D Gamera film but that project also fell by the wayside before his death in 2017.

SUBMERSION OF JAPAN

日本沈没

Nippon Chinbotsu "Japan Sinks"
Toho, 12/29/1973 (*Showa 48*), 12 Reels (3,935 meters), 143:36, 35mm, Panavision (2.35:1 anamorphic), Fujicolor, stereo

Crew	Special Effects Director:	Screenplay: Shinobu
Producers: Osamu Tanaka, Tomoyuki Tanaka	Teruyoshi Nakano	Hashimoto, Sakyo Komatsu (novel *Japan Sinks*)
Director: Shiro Moritani		

Directors of Photography: Hiroshi Murai, Daisaku Kimura
Music: Masaru Sato
Editor: Michiko Ikeda
Assistant Director: Koji Hashimoto
Production Design: Yoshiro Muraki
LIghting: Kojiro Sato
Sound Recording: Toshiya Ban
Production Manager: Takahide Morichi
Assistant Camera: Kenji Takama
SFX Cinematography: Mototaka Tomioka
SFX Art Director: Yasuyuki Inoue
SFX Lighting: Masakuni Morimoto
SFX Optical Photography: Takeshi Miyanishi
SFX Composites: Kazunobu Sanbe
SFX Engineering: Koji Matsumto
SFX Assistant Director: Yoshio Tabuchi
SFX Assistant Camera: Eichi Asada
Miniatures: Tadaaki Watanabe
SFX Production Manager: Keisuke Shinoda
Still Photographer: Yoshinori Ishizuki
SFX Still Photographer: Kazukiyo Tanaka

Cast
Keiji Kobayashi *(Dr. Yusuke Tadokoro)*
Hiroshi Fujioka *(Toshio Onodera)*
Ayumi Ishida *(Reiko Abe)*
Yusuke Takita *(Associate Professor Nobuhiko Yukinaga)*
Hideaki Niitani *(Katsushige Nakata)*

Tadao Nakamaru *(Kunieda)*
Kunio Murai *(Kataoka)*
Isao Natsuyagi *(Tatsuya Yuki)*
Tetsuro Tanba *(Prime Minister Yamamoto)*
Koichi Ito *(Minister of Foreign Affairs)*
Tatsuo Matsushita *(Minister of International Trade and Industry)*
Koji Kawamura *(Minister of Construction)*
Takeshi Yamamoto *(Minister of Transport)*
Kanta Mori *(Defense Secretary)*
Mizuho Suzuki *(Science and Technology Agency Director)*
Goro Tarumi *(Prime Minister's Aide)*
Toshio Hosokawa *(Chief Cabinet Secretary)*
Kazuo Kato *(Secretary Mimura)*
Nobuo Nakamura *(Envoy Nozaki)*
Shogo Shimada *(Watari)*
Yuriko Kado *(Hanae)*
Tetsuya Kaji *(Oceanologist)*
Shozo Inagaki *(Survey Team Member)*
Minoru Uchida *(Survey Team Member)*
Shiro Oki *(Survey Team Member)*
Kei Yoshinaga *(JMA Engineer)*
Makoto Miyajima *(Captain Tatsumaru)*
Yuji Osugi *(Navigator)*
Shigeru Kamiyama *(Operation Manager Yoshimura)*
Masaya Takahashi *(Professor Yamashiro)*
Jun Kondo *(Professor Oizumi)*
Hitoshi Takeuchi *(Professor Takeuchi)*
Hiroaki Ishii *(Science and Technology MInister)*

Kazuo Imai *(Prime Minister's Prefectural Chief)*
Yuzu Hayakawa *(Chairman of the Defense Agency)*
Shizuo Nakajo *(D1 Committee Member)*
Akira Nagoya *(D1 Public Safety Officer)*
Miwa Saito *(Prime Minister's Wife)*
Nitta Masagen *(Onodera's Brother)*
Masanobu Okubo *(Eldery Man)*
Andrew Hughes *(Prime Minister of Australia)*
Roger Wood *(Australian Official)*
Masateru Orui *(TV News Anchor)*
Tetsu Nakamura *(Japanese U.N. Representative)*
Taeko Hattori *(Ya-chan)*
Van Henry *(Chinese Envoy)*
Tetsuo Morishita *(Old Son)*
Takuzo Kumagai *(Disaster Prevention Center Director)*
Fumio Wada *(Countermeasure Headquarters Operator)*
Haruo Suzuki *(Helicopter Pilot)*
Jack Ongan *(U.N. Security Council)*
Franz Gruber *(U.N. Security Council)*
Charles Seams *(Dr. Eugene Cox)*
Junpei Natsuki *(Train Victim)*
Haruo Nakajima *(Prime Minister's Chauffeur)*

Alternate Titles
Tidal Wave (U.S.)
Panik über Tokio **[Panic Over Tokyo]** (Germany)
La submersion du Japon (France)

El hundimiento del Japón (Spain)
Morte no Sol Nascente **[Death of the Rising Sun]** (Portugal)
Pianeta Terra: anno zero **[Planet Earth: Year Zero]** (Italy)

S.O.S. Jorden sjunker **[SOS-Earth Sinks]** (Sweden)
SOS - maa vajoaa **[SOS - The Country Sinks]** (Finland)
A Submersão do Japão (Brazil)
Потъването на Япония (Bulgaria)

Zaglada Japonii (Poland)
Scufundarea Japoniei (Romania)
Dünyanin Sonu **[End of the World]** (Turkey)

"The Japanese are a young folk. Brought up comfortably on these four islands, they're still in an infancy. If they got into any trouble in the outside world, they could always retreat back to their homeland and sit like a baby in its mother's arms. From now on, the Japanese won't have any place to go back to, no one to depend on and will be dispersed among more hardened peoples."
-Dr. Tadokoro (Keiju Kobayashi)

Submersion of Japan is easily the finest Japanese special effects production of the 1970s. It boasts impressive FX by Teruyoshi Nakano and nearly Hollywood-quality production values. Director Shiro Moritani's subtext is somber. It addresses Japan's collective anxieties over its natural disasters and strained international relations. *Submersion of Japan* is based on a best-selling novel by apocalyptic sci-fi luminary Sakyo Komatsu. Its phenomenon is as iconic in Japanese pop culture as *Godzilla*. At the core of the film is a sense of existential horror at the loss of Japan's cultural identity.

PLOT

Near Japan, one of the Ogasawara islands has submerged beneath the sea. Geologist Dr. Yusuke Tadokoro (Keiju Kobayashi) investigates the area in the submersible *Wadatsumi*. Piloted by Toshio Onodera (Hiroshi Fujioka), the submarine finds unusual volcanic activity near the sunken island. Investigating further, they take *Wadatsumi* deep into the Japan Trench.

They notice further abnormalities along the seafloor and find that the base of Japan's land mass is eroding.

Returning home, Onodera's boss introduces him to a wealthy friend's daughter, Reiko Abe (Ayumi Ishida). The two hit it off. While they relax on the family's beach property, nearby Mt. Amagi erupts. With this eruption and Tadokoro's findings off the Japan Trench, Prime Minister Yamamoto (Tetsuro Tanba) grows concerned. He meets with Japan's geological community, including Tadokoro. The scientists explain that the Earth's mantle has begun to accelerate in movement. Tadokoro warns that because of this, a massive earthquake could be impending. Most of the other scientists and cabinet scoff at him, but Yamamoto takes note of the eccentric scientist's claims.

Tadokoro meets with Watari (Shogo Shimada) and his niece and caretaker Hanae (Yuriko Kado). Watari is a mysterious and wealthy elderly man with immeasurable political influence. Watari tells Tadokoro that each spring swallows build their nests around his house. Yet this spring the swallows have been absent. Tadokoro replies that a lot of animals, particularly birds, have been behaving strangely. Watari and Tadokoro both agree that this is likely an omen of disaster. Tadokoro next meets with officials Kunieda (Tadao Nakamaru) and Nakata (Hideaki Niitani). With the funding of Watari and blessing of Yamamoto, they begin execution of Tadokoro's D-Plan. D-1 is to complete the study into what's wrong with Japan's land mass. The officials agree to buy a French submarine for Tadokoro to complete this survey. The room suddenly shakes as the Kirishima undersea volcano erupts.

Onodera quits his job to pilot for Tadokoro. The French sub is used for another survey and the data that comes back is sobering. Tadokoro predicts that Japan is going to break apart and sink into the ocean completely. As Tadokoro comes to this conclusion, the worst earthquake in history strikes the Kanto area. Prime Minister Yamamoto tries to mobilize firefighting and rescue units as firestorms spread throughout Tokyo. Yet his efforts are ineffectual against this horrific disaster. The intense heat prevents authorities from getting close enough to put out the fires. Crowds of survivors make for the Imperial Palace, clashing with police. Yamamoto orders the Palace's gates opened. Tokyo is

completely destroyed and the death toll is an unimaginable 3.6 million.

Three months pass and a slight normalcy returns to Japan. Prime Minister Yamamoto, his wife having died in the quake, decides to factor Tadokoro's research into his official policies. Tadokoro and his team meet with Watari where he unveils the next phase of the D Plan: D-2. D-2 is a plan to save the Japanese people by evacuating them to other countries. Yamamoto begins to send envoys abroad. The Australian Prime Minister (Andrew Hughes) scoffs at the notion of accepting Japanese refugees. Watari explains to Yamamoto that some experts believe it might be best to do nothing, allowing Japan to commit collective suicide. Meanwhile, Nakata and the geology team inform Prime Minister Yamamoto of grim news. Their model shows that Japan is going to completely sink into the ocean in only 10 months.

BACKGROUND

Sakyo Komatsu began writing his iconic novel *Japan Sinks* in 1964. This was on the heels of his first two books *Japan's Apaches* and *Virus: The Day of Resurrection*. He was so enraptured in its story that he considered writing multiple volumes. The publisher kept him at two. *Japan Sinks* would take nine years for Komatsu to write and the first volume was not published until 1973. By this time, there was considerable ballyhoo. Sakyo Komatsu had mentioned he was writing it on a news show in 1972. Immediately afterward, struggling film company Daiei announced a film called *The Sinking of the Japanese Islands*, blatantly stealing Komatsu's concept. Executive Masaichi Nagata intended for this to revitalize Daiei's film production as the company had gone bankrupt. The project never came to light. It was likely due to Daiei's dire financial straits or legal action. At Toho, the cunning Tomoyuki Tanaka had scooped up the film and TV rights to this new novel before it was even published.

With one of the biggest budgets in Japanese film history, Tanaka brought in his company's finest talent; veterans of Akira Kurosawa and Eiji Tsuburaya's teams. This included esteemed screenwriter Shinobu Hashimoto and director Shiro Moritani. Hashimoto (1918-2018) could be the greatest screenwriter in Japan. Starting with Kurosawa's *Rashomon*, Hashimoto wrote many classic Japanese films. These included Kurosawa's *Seven Samurai, Throne of Blood* and *The Hidden Fortress*, Masaki Kobayashi's *Harakiri* and Kihachi Okamoto's *Japan's Longest Day*. He also directed a few films, including the war drama *I Wanna Be a Shellfish* (1959). Shiro Moritani (1931-1984) was another Kurosawa collaborator. Before earning his wings as director with 1966's *Zero Fighter*, he was assistant director on *Sanjuro, High and Low* and *Red Beard*. Teruyoshi Nakano, now in charge of Toho's special effects department, handled the mass destruction.

Hashimoto's screenplay is relatively faithful to the novel, though cutting down on the subplots and political intrigue. The most notable deletion is of one of the female characters, Maya, a bar hostess. Also deleted are subplots involving predatory Western capitalists stealing Japan's art and profiteering off its end. *Submersion of Japan*'s subsequent TV series would address more of these.

PRINCIPAL PHOTOGRAPHY

In stark contrast to *Godzilla vs. Megalon* that same year, the shoot for *Submersion of Japan* took four months. *Submersion of Japan* boasts almost Hollywood-grade production values. Director Moritani and writer Hashimoto bring Komatsu's themes exploring Japan's loss of cultural identity to vivid life. Technically, the film compares well with Hollywood's *Earthquake*, made the following year. Yet *Submersion of Japan* is a far better, more philosophical film than *Earthquake*. *Submersion of Japan*'s slow burn of building dread courtesy of director Moritani is unsettling. Many dialogue scenes are interrupted with earthquake tremors. This lends itself well to a feeling of impending doom.

ACTORS

Submersion of Japan has an all star cast. Keiju Kobayashi plays the eccentric Dr. Tadokoro. Born in Gunma Prefecture, Kobayashi (1923-2010) was one of Japan's finest character actors. He was a versatile and prolific player who appeared in 250 films. He played roles for a wide range of directors such as Kurosawa, Ozu, Naruse, Hiroshi Inagaki, Kihachi Okamoto and Kaneto Shindo.

Kobayashi played a bittersweet turn as a drunken salaryman turned writer in Okamoto's *The Elegant Life of Mr. Everyman* (1963). Later, he began to specialize in playing military figures and scientists. He portrayed Hideki Tojo in *The Militarists* (1970) as well as General Mitsuru Ushijima in *Battle of Okinawa* (1971). His Tadokoro is a brash man. Like Watari and Yamamoto, he is willing to go against Japanese social norms to save its people, even as his sanity unravels. His final scene with Tanba's Yamamoto is a poignant one. Kobayashi would later play Admiral Isoroku Yamamoto in *Imperial Navy* (1981) and Prime Minister Mitamura in *The Return of Godzilla* (1984).

Actor Hiroshi Fujioka (1946-) plays young submarine pilot Toshio Onodera. He was best known for playing *Kamen Rider* on television for Toei. For Toho, he later appeared in *ESPY* (1974), also based on a Komatsu novel and *Conflagration* (1975). He also played World War II aviator Saburo Sakai in *Zero Pilot* (1976). Ayumi Ishida (1948-), who plays love interest Reiko Abe, was a famous singer at the time. Ishida was starting to branch out into movies and television. Her single *"Blue Light Yokohama"* was #1 on Japan's charts in 1968. Veteran Toho actor Tadao Nakamaru appears as a government official who helps Tadokoro. Hideaki Niitani plays Tadokoro's trusted associate Nakata. Niitani (1930-2012) was best known for his role in Seijun Suzuki's *Tokyo Drifter* (1966). He was married to screen siren Yumi Shirakawa until his death. Actor Kunio Murai plays a supporting role as a researcher.

Murai (1944-) was born in Japanese-occupied Tianjin, China. He also appeared in *Godzilla vs. Gigan* the previous year. Known in Japan for dubbing Harrison Ford, he was back for *The Return of Godzilla* (1984) and *Godzilla, Mothra and King Ghidorah: Giant Monsters All-Out Attack* (2001).

SFX

The special effects sequences by Teruyoshi Nakano are nothing short of stunning. He truly earns his pedigree with this film. Though Nakano had been directing FX scenes since 1969, he was not yet credited as "special effects director". *Submersion of Japan* was his first film where, like mentors Tsuburaya and Arikawa, he was given that credit before director Moritani. The early underwater scenes with the *Wadatsumi* boast impressive miniature work. The Tokyo earthquake is an especially memorable scene, one of the best sequences of destruction Nakano orchestrated in his career. The tone is far more realistic than Nakano's Godzilla work and there's a disturbing human casualty element. Unlike most *kaiju* films, we see numerous civilians maimed and killed.

Later scenes, involving volcanic eruptions and typhoons, are well executed and inventively shot. Miniatures were built to vibrate and shake mechanically. Most impressive are satellite's eye view shots of the Japanese islands as they suffer volcanic eruptions and sink into the sea. To create these shots, Nakano's unit pumped beer onto miniature mockups. This created the effect of erupting volcanoes and submerging land. Shinji

Higuchi, Makoto Kamiya and their team lovingly paid homage to these shots in particular in their 2006 remake. Large quantities of beer were also mixed into Toho's "Big Pool" to make the tidal waves more realistic. Members of the FX crew would sip the water and get drunk. As the TV show was already planned, the television crew shot some B-roll footage on the special effects set of the movie to keep costs lower.

REAL WORLD

Japan is one of the most disaster prone countries on Earth. The fear of natural disasters is etched into Japan's collective subconscious. The great Kanto earthquake of 1923 left Japan devastated and Tokyo almost destroyed. The destruction was so appalling that the government considered moving Japan's capital elsewhere. It was the economic fall-out from Tokyo's destruction that helped fuel the rise of militarism in Imperial Japan. The great Kanto 'quake is as strongly etched into Japan's collective trauma as Hiroshima and Nagasaki. And unlike war, natural disasters cannot be prevented with peace treaties. In 1995, another earthquake hit Hanshin Prefecture, damaging the city of Kobe. Then, in March of 2011, Japan was rocked by a magnitude 9.1 undersea quake that caused near apocalyptic destruction. The Japanese still await another cataclysmic earthquake with an epicenter in the Tokyo region. This "big one" will cause billions in property damage and snuff out and upend many innocent lives. Additionally, Mount Fuji has not erupted since 1707. It is long overdue for a massive eruption. Ominously,

geologists have noted that the lava pressure inside Fuji has been rising over the last few decades. With the advent of climate change, Japan will also be hit particularly hard. As an island nation, it stands to lose a severe portion of its land if the Polar ice caps melt.

THEMES AND MOTIFS

Submersion of Japan's Polish poster is one of its best. Unlike others, which sell the film on its destruction sequences, the Polish one is minimalistic. It shows the image of a woman with a face like a *No* mask sinking underwater. This poster well sums up the underlying themes of both the book and film. *Godzilla* is about Japan's collective pain and guilt over its war experience. *The Last War* is about post-war Japan's collective feeling of helplessness over the dynamics of the Cold War. In contrast, *Submersion of Japan* is about Japan's trauma over its frequent natural disasters. Komatsu's *Virus: The Day of Resurrection,* also adapted to film, depicts the scenario of an unstoppable pathogen wiping out humanity. To the Japanese, *Submersion of Japan*'s concept of their cultural identity destroyed by disaster, is just as existentially terrifying.

Submersion of Japan and its novel were likely influential on 2016's *Shin Godzilla*. Both deal with how Japan is viewed internationally. The dilemma Japan faces, having to appeal to the rest of the world to take in Japanese citizens, is an interesting aspect. To beg and plead is something the reserved Japanese seldom do as neediness is particularly frowned upon in their culture.

Yet the once mighty Japan finds itself in a vulnerable position. At first, most countries turn a cold shoulder to Japan. The Australian Prime Minister, played by *Destroy All Monsters'* Andrew Hughes, makes a biting remark. *"If we have to accept things Japanese I would prefer them to be art treasures rather than people"*. The world's foreign powers relent but only after preventable loss of life. The trope of an eccentric scientist not believed until it's too late is a common one in Japanese science fiction. It stretches forward all the way to *Shin Godzilla*.

One of the film's more interesting characters is old Watari. He's played by veteran actor Shogo Shimada (1905-2004). In the U.S. version, he's misnamed as a member of the Imperial family. In both Komatsu's novel and Moritani's film, Watari is a shadowy figure. He's a powerful old man rumored to be nearly a hundred years old, having lived through the *Meiji, Taisho* and *Showa* eras. It's implied he belonged to a shadowy group like the Black Dragon Society. He now uses his wealth and intellect to manipulate politicians. It is his political machinations that allow the Japanese people to be saved. In the end, he decides to stay behind and die with Japan, representing the death of Japan's old, Imperial-era guard. Prime Minister Yamamoto, played by stalwart Tetsuro Tanba, is a member of the conservative Liberal Democratic Party. The LDP in Japan is quite analogous to America's Republican Party. They are even more culturally conservative yet also more liberal on science, infrastructure and healthcare. Like the characters in *Shin Godzilla*, the shrewd Yamamoto chooses to go against the political mainstream to save the people of Japan.

RELEASE AND LEGACY

Submersion of Japan was the biggest box office hit in Japan that year, grossing 1.64 billion yen and selling almost nine million tickets. Tomoyuki Tanaka was eager to make more disaster films. *Submersion of Japan* was followed-up with *Prophecies of Nostradamus* (1974). *Nostradamus* widened its scope to the entire world, concerning environmental catastrophe and nuclear war. Undaunted, Toho followed it up with *Conflagration* (aka *High Seas Hijack*, 1975). That film features an oil tanker hijacked by African revolutionaries who are planning to explode it in Tokyo Bay. Finally, in 1980, Toho put out *Deathquake*. In all three films, Teruyoshi Nakano let loose his unique brand of explosive destruction. More film adaptations of Komatu's novels would follow as well. These would include *ESPY* (1974), *Virus* (1980), *Bye Bye Jupiter* (1984) and *Tokyo Blackout* (1987).

Submersion of Japan's TV adaptation would air from October 6th, 1974 to March 30, 1975. In Japan, some fans prefer it to the film. With 26 hour long episodes, it presents a far less condensed version of Komatsu's novel. Keiju Kobayashi reprised his role as Dr. Tadokoro but most of the cast was different. So Yamamura played the Prime Minister, a role he played more than any other Japanese actor. Onodera was played by Takenori Murano. Reiko Abe was played by Kaoru Yumi, who starred in *Prophecies of*

Nostradamus and *ESPY* that same year. Incidentally, the show aired after *Army of the Apes*, another TV show based on material from Sakyo Komatsu.

Tanaka was also keen on making a sequel to *Submersion of Japan*. *Continuation: Submersion of Japan* was first announced in 1974. It was to bring back directors Moritani and Nakano, focusing on the plight of Japanese now scattered overseas. Onodera and Reiko were to reunite in Switzerland at the film's climax. The project was to be completed by 1976, but for reasons unknown languished in pre-production. It was finally shelved after 1978. In late 1998, Shochiku announced a new adaptation called *Japan Sinks 1999*. After the Hanshin earthquake of '95, interest in Komatsu's novel was revived. It was to be released in 2000 and Kazuki Omori (*Godzilla vs. Biollante*) was attached to direct. Shochiku abandoned the project due to its immense cost. The concept of a new adaptation stuck around however. In late 2005 Toho and TBS started production on *Sinking of Japan*. Its director was Gainax and Gamera FX wizard Shinji Higuchi, fresh off his alternate history epic *Lorelei*.

Sinking of Japan was poorly received, winning second place in the Japanese equivalent to the Razzies. It prompted a parody from tokusatsu-loving comedy director Minoru Kawasaki (*The Calamari Wrestler*). Called *The World Sinks Except Japan*, it came out in Japan only two months after *Sinking*. The film itself is an adaptation of a satirical novella written by Yasutaka Tsutsui (*The Girl Who Leapt Through Time,*

Paprika). It darkly parodies Japan's nationalism and xenophobia as it explores the opposite concept. As in what if the rest of the world sank into the ocean, leaving only Japan? Also in 2006, Sakyo Komatsu came out with a long awaited follow-up novel to *Japan Sinks*.

More recently, an *anime* version of *Japan Sinks, Japan Sinks 2020*, was released to Netflix. Directed by Masaaki Yuasa (*Devilman Crybaby*), it is an adaptation of Komatsu's novel mainly in-concept. It centers around a family affected by the cataclysm, going from a slice-of-life anime drama to apocalyptic chaos. Clearly, Komatsu's novel and its film adaptation *Submersion of Japan* have stood the test of time. Both remain hauntingly relevant.

ALTERNATE VERSIONS

An English dubbed export version of *Submersion of Japan* is unavailable. It's unknown if one exists. It's quite possible that Toho released a shorter export version internationally. The various European versions appear to be based on a cut running around two hours, making its existence possible. At the same time, there's little physical evidence like dubbed trailers or European video releases. *Submersion of Japan*'s international version remains an enigma.

In the U.S., *Submersion of Japan* was bought by Roger Corman's New World Pictures. At this time, Universal's *Earthquake*, directed by Mark Robson, was a top grossing film.

Submersion was re-edited into *Tidal Wave* to cash in on *Earthquake*'s success. Released in May 1975, *Tidal Wave* runs a paltry 81 minutes. Only around half of the Japanese footage remains. It opens with credits against a black screen with new music. A cut down version of the opening animation is used with narration. Large swaths of the plot are removed. This includes most of the character development, the entire D-Project subplot and the political intrigue. The early and later portions of the picture are more intact. The Tokyo earthquake scene is left relatively uncut and is the most intact portion of the film.

Like with Raymond Burr in *Godzilla, King of the Monsters!*, New World opted to add an American actor to the proceedings to help it sell. In this case: Lorne Greene, fresh from *Earthquake*. Greene plays a helpful U.S. Secretary of State who negotiates on behalf of the Japanese people. Like New World's later *Godzilla 1985*, the Americans' role in this version is glorified compared to the Japanese original. These short scenes were directed by Andrew Meyer. Meyer also seems to have written the English dub for the Japanese scenes. Eric Saarinen was DP for the American sequences. They also star Rhonda Leigh Hopkins as Greene's secretary. John Fujioka (a Japanese-American actor with no relation to Hiroshi) plays an emissary from Japan.

Tidal Wave's dub was done in Los Angeles. It is decently performed but its scripting badly loses the nuance of the Japanese dialog. Dubbing cast includes Marvin Miller, Susan Sennett, Ralph James and Joe Dante. Yes, the future director of *Gremlins* did some dubbing for this. Overall though, *Tidal Wave* is not recommended. It's an interesting curiosity, but only glimmers of the suspense and pathos of the Japanese version remain. It was rated "PG" by the Motion Picture Association of America.

AMERICAN HOME VIDEO HISTORY

Neither *Submersion of Japan* nor *Tidal Wave* have ever been released to U.S. home video. *Tidal Wave* did air quite a bit on television into the 1990s, however.

Further Viewing:

(1974)
エスパイ
Toho, *Director:* Jun Fukuda

Toho followed *Submersion of Japan* with another Komatsu adaptation, this time based on 1965's *ESPY*. The novel was likely inspired by Frank M. Robinson's 1956 *The Power,* adapted into a 1968 film by George Pal and director Byron Haskin. Toho had planned to make an adaptation of *ESPY* in 1967. To have been directed by Jun Fukuda, its cast would have included Tatsuya Mihashi, Makoto Sato, Mie Hama and Akiko Wakabayashi. The project was put on hold due to Wakabayashi's contract at Toho expiring. *Submersion*'s success and a visit by

Uri Geller to Japan influenced Tomoyuki Tanaka to revive it.

Short for "Esper Spy", *ESPY* concerns a clandestine organization of international spies with psychic powers. Headed by Hojo (*Young Guy*'s Yuzo Kayama) and Tamura (Hiroshi Fujioka), they use their powers in the service of world peace. Opposing them is Counter-ESPY, aiming to destabilize the world stage. They are led by the misanthropic Ulrov, played by *Lone Wolf and Cub*'s Tomisaburo Wakayama. *Terror of Mechagodzilla*'s Katsumasa Uchida plays his top assassin.

ESPY is a blast of a flick; thrilling with plenty of distilled 1970s weirdness. Filmed nearly back-to-back with *Terror of Mechagodzilla,* it features energetically directed action sequences by Jun Fukuda. The production values are far superior to his simultaneous Godzilla films. The cinematography is dynamic and polished. *ESPY*'s DP, Shoji Ueda, would become one of the best cinematographers in Japan, helping lens Kurosawa's films from *Kagemusha* on. *ESPY* also boasts impressive location shooting in Istanbul and Switzerland. These shots were done by a second unit run by Kenjiro Omori, who would go on to helm 1980's *Deathquake.* The score by Masaaki Hirao and Kensuke Kyo is catchy and European-style with Morricone-like arrangement. Teruyoshi Nakano's FX work is subtle in most scenes. It only takes center stage in an airplane sequence with heavy miniature work.

Prophecies of Nostradamus' Kaoru Yumi also stars; strutting in lingerie during an erotic dance sequence. Willie Dorsey, another African American expat, plays one of his most memorable roles. He would be back as an African terrorist in the following year's *Conflagration* (aka *High Seas Hijack*). His son is Michael Takahashi, the Japanese-American basketball player. *Woman in the Dunes*' Eiji Okada also appears as a Mideastern yogi. The handsome, Eurasian Masao Kusakari would return in another Sakyo Komatsu adaptation: *Virus* (1980). Toho courted Linda Blair, fresh from *The Exorcist,* to play a small role in the film as villainess Julie. Unfortunately, her agent advised her against it and singer Luna Takemura was cast instead.

The plot, with "good" psychics battling psychics that hate humanity and want to take over Earth, parallels the mutants in the X-Men comics. The first volume of *X-Men* came out in 1963 so it's unknown if it had any influence on Komatsu. At the end of the day, *ESPY* is a pulpy and entertaining spy flick, 1970s Japanese sci-fi style. Like other Toho '70s genre films, it has yet to get its due in Western fan circles. The version shown on U.S. television was slashed to ribbons; awkwardly shorn of its sex and violence by Saperstein's UPA. *ESPY* really makes one wish that Fukuda's planned *Invisible Man vs. the Human Torch* had materialized.

DEATHQUAKE

(1980)

地震列島

Toho, *Director:* **Kenjiro Omori**

Toho would revive its disaster film cycle with 1980's *Deathquake*. They had, earlier in the year, produced a TV movie called *Tokyo Earthquake Magnitude 8.1*. The cast led by Sonny Chiba, ratings were through the roof. So a lavish-budgeted theatrical film was quickly green-lit. *Deathquake*'s tagline goes *"I knew it would come someday, I just hoped it wouldn't be today"*. Like *Submersion of Japan*, it dwells on the existential horror eternally facing the people of Tokyo. That is, the possibility of another horrific earthquake on par with the great Kanto 'quake of 1923. Tokyo is overdue for a severe earthquake with an epicenter near the Kanto region. Such a 'quake would likely dwarf the devastation wrought by the 3/11 earthquake and tsunami in 2011. *Deathquake* proposes this, served with a mix of pathos and Irwin Allen-like spectacle.

Deathquake features an engaging script by Kaneto Shindo, director of *The Island*, *Onibaba* and *Kuroneko*. It concerns seismologist Dr. Kawazu (Hiroshi Katsuno), who realizes that the next Kanto earthquake is only a month away. Kawazu puts his career on the line as he desperately tries to convince his colleagues. Nobody listens of course, with the exception of his mistress (Yumi Takigawa, also in *Virus* that same summer). An intrepid young reporter (Toshiyuki Nagashima, later in *Gamera 2*) is also intrigued. The Prime Minister (Kentaro Kaji) is far more interested in improving his golf swing than listening to Kawazu's apocalyptic predictions. The trope of a rebellious outlier fighting to convince Japan's bureaucratic establishment the sky is falling foreshadows *Shin Godzilla*. Of course, Kawazu is right and a monstrous 7.9 magnitude quake turns Tokyo into a burning hellscape. In the end, Kawazu is trapped in a flooding underground subway with his soon to be ex-wife (*Lone Wolf and Cub*'s Kayo Matsuo). He has to make a sacrifice that might seem almost *kamikaze*-like to Western viewers.

Deathquake, until that point a family drama, springs to life once the tremors start. Teruyoshi "Bomber" Nakano's unit takes center stage and the film is possibly his fiery masterwork. The miniature shooting is top tier and the pyrotechnics so plentiful you can almost feel the heat. Nakano's work on *Deathquake* is like an intricate dance with burning gasoline and model buildings, barraging the viewer with one stunning *tokusatsu* conflagration after another. Director Kenjiro Omori's unit also produces footage that is suspensefully helmed. Tilting, rotating sets are used inventively to simulate tremors. The two units' footage is almost seamlessly integrated and the production values are stunning. As with much of Toho's output from this period, *Deathquake* is quite criminally underrated.

SINKING OF JAPAN

(2006)

日本沈没

Toho, *Director:* Shinji Higuchi

Shinji Higuchi's *Sinking of Japan* is, in general, a far less faithful and satisfying adaptation. *Sinking of Japan* is a pretty film, but a vapid one. Its Hollywood style production values and polished images can't make up for its screenplay. The script is predictable and plays on trite, Hollywood-style beats. *Sinking of Japan* lacks both the existential horror and haunting pathos of Moritani's original. The sense of dread is absent from all but a few sequences. Numerous characters are cut and new ones added. Reiko Abe is now a firefighter and played by *Battle Royale*'s Ko Shibasaki. In a Hollywood style ending, Onodera, played by former boy band member Tsuyoshi Kusanagi, saves Japan from sinking. This "happy ending" completely goes against the point of Komatsu's novel and the original film. There is but one scene of unsettling pathos involving the protagonist passing a line of bodies and a woman with a dead baby. This hauntingly looks forward to the coming earthquake and tsunami in March of 2011. If only *Sinking of Japan* contained more sequences like that one.

Sinking of Japan does have one major strength: its apocalyptic imagery is stunning. *Sinking*'s special effects shots by Makoto Kamiya are among the best ever produced in Japan. Kamiya (1965-) was mentored under both Koichi Kawakita and Higuchi and by this time earned his grit. The effects are on par with anything being produced in Hollywood; seamlessly blending practical FX with CGI. The film's dynamic computer-frosted visuals could almost be mistaken for news footage from the 3/11 tsunami and indeed have become more powerful since. Higuchi and company, including FX wizard Katsuro Onoue, would return with more life-like natural disaster imagery in *Shin Godzilla*.

Overall, however, *Sinking of Japan* is like a Japanese equivalent to Michael Bay's *Armageddon* or Roland Emmerich's *The Day After Tomorrow*. Those films embody everything that's wrong with Hollywood filmmaking. *Sinking of Japan* embodies everything that's wrong with the Japanese film industry. In both Hollywood and Tokyo, movies are produced too much by corporate committees.

SAKYO KOMATSU
The Doomsayer

小松左京
1/28/1931-7/26/2011

The Michael Crichton of Japan, Sakyo Komatsu was known for writing clever speculative fiction, often with apocalyptic overtones. Along with Shinichi Hoshi and Yasutaka Tsutsui, he was considered a post-war luminary of literary Japanese science fiction. He was born Minoru Komatsu in Osaka to an entrepreneur father. He was a sickly child unable to play sports, so he was a voracious reader. His older brother, later an engineer at Sanyo, inspired an interest in scientific study. His brother would allow young Komatsu to read his science manuals. World War II left an indelible impression on Komatsu, especially stories of youth his age used as cannon fodder and killed in Okinawa. After the war, he became interested in literature, especially classical Italian works like Dante's *Divine Comedy*.

Komatsu studied Italian literature at Kyoto University. He also became politically active, joining the Japanese Communist Party. Komatsu left the JCP after finding out that the Soviet Union was also testing nuclear weapons. Graduating college in 1954, his early career was difficult and full of hardship. He toiled writing amateur plays until the late 1950s. Afterward, Komatsu was inspired by author Kobo Abe and decided to try his hand at story writing. His first major short story was called *Peace on Earth*. It presents an alternate universe where World War II didn't end and the Allies mounted an invasion of the Japanese islands.

His next short story was *Memoirs of an Eccentric Time Traveler*. It won the top prize in a competition at Masami Fukushima's SF Magazine. Komatsu soon began writing his first novel: *Japan's Apaches*. Inspired by Korean "*sangokujin*" scavengers after the war, it tells the story of outcast youth in a post-apocalyptic Japan who survive by collecting scrap metal. *Japan's Apaches* was published in 1964 and became a bestseller. It has since become quite iconic in Japanese popular culture. *Virus: The Day of Resurrection* followed, also published in '64. Influenced by the novel and film *On the Beach*, this horrifying story features a space-borne pandemic wiping out humanity, leaving only researchers in Antarctica. Toho bought the rights for a film adaptation in 1965. They soon realized the project would be too expensive and need to be a co-production with Hollywood.

Other novels by Komatsu followed, including *ESPY*, about international spies with psychic powers. He soon became a beloved and acclaimed science fiction author. In 1970, Komatsu was a member of the committee of Osaka's Expo '70 exhibition. In 1973 he published his best known novel *Japan Sinks*. About the Japanese archipelago sinking into the sea due to tectonic plate activity, it became one of Japan's iconic science fiction stories. Toho scooped up the rights before it was even published and started work on film and television adaptations. *Submersion of Japan*, directed by Shiro Moritani, was released at the end of 1973. This successful film was followed by a television show that ran from 1974 to '75. In 1974, Komatsu's novel *ESPY* was also adapted into a film helmed by Jun Fukuda.

In 1980, ambitious producer Haruki Kadokawa mounted a massive adaptation of

Virus: The Day of Resurrection. Directed by Kinji Fukasaku, *Virus* was the biggest budgeted Japanese film in history. It was a commercial flop and released internationally in a heavily cut version. Earlier, in 1976, Toho had propositioned Komatsu for an original science fiction story to compete with Hollywood. He invited a group of his colleagues to brainstorm ideas. The result was *Bye Bye Jupiter*, published in 1982. This novel told the story of a spacefaring group of scientists trying to solarize Jupiter, opposed by a group of ecoterrorists. Toho produced a big budget adaptation in 1984 which Komatsu himself acted as co-director on. Though with stupendous FX work from Koichi Kawakita, the project, supposed to get international attention, was a creative disaster and flop. Komatsu's next novel was *Tokyo Blackout* (1985), adapted into a 1987 film directed by Toshio Masuda.

Komatsu became less prolific in his older age. In 2006, the same year another film adaptation of *Japan Sinks* was produced, he published a long awaited sequel, co-written with Koshu Tani. After the 3/11 earthquake and tsunami, he was interviewed. He said that he hoped Japan would evolve into a better country in its wake. Sakyo Komatsu passed away only three months later from pneumonia at the age of 80. His legacy is still relevant. In Japan, *Virus* has had a resurgence in popularity due to the COVID-19 pandemic. Additionally, a loose *anime* adaptation of *Japan Sinks* directed by Masaaki Yuasa was released in July 2020.

Selected Filmography
Submersion of Japan (1973) [novel *"Japan Sinks"*]
ESPY (1974) [novel]
Virus (1980) [novel; *"The Day of Resurrection"*]

Bye Bye Jupiter (1984) [director/screenplay/novel]
Tokyo Blackout (1987) [novel]
Sinking of Japan (2006) [novel *"Japan Sinks"*]
Japan Sinks 2020 (2020) [novel *"Japan Sinks"*]

GODZILLA vs MECHAGODZILLA

Gojira tai Mekagojira "Godzilla vs. Mechagodzilla"
Toho, 3/21/1974 (*Showa 49*), 6 Reels (2,309 meters), 84:17, 35mm, Cinemascope (2.35:1 anamorphic), Fujicolor, monaural sound

Crew
Producer: Tomoyuki Tanaka
Director: Jun Fukuda
Special Effects Director: Teruyoshi Nakano

Screenplay: Hiroyasu Yamamura, Jun Fukuda, Shinichi Sekizawa (*original story*), Masami Fukushima (*original story*)

Director of Photography: Yuzuru Aizawa
Music: Masaru Sato
Editor: Michiko Ikeda
Production Design: Kazuo Satsuya

Sound: Fumio Yanoguchi
Lighting: Masayuki Morimoto
Assistant Director:
Tsunesaburo Nishikawa
Production Manager: Keisuke
Shinoda
SFX Directors of Photography:
Mototaka Tomioka, Takeshi
Yamamoto
SFX Assistant Director; Koichi
Kawakita
SFX Art Directors: Toshiro
Aoki, Kan Komura
Monster Design: Akihiko
Iguchi
SFX Wire Work: Shoji Okawa
SFX Composites: Kazunobu
Sanpei
SFX Optical Photography:
Takeshi Miyanishi
Optical Animation: Masa
Kawana
Still Photographer: Kazukiyo
Tanaka

Cast
Masaaki Daimon *(Keisuke
Shimuzu)*
Kazuya Aoyama *(Masahiko
Shimizu)*
Reiko Tajima *(Saeko
Kanagusuku)*

Akihiko Hirata *(Professor
Hideto Miyajima)*
Hiroshi Koizumi *(Professor
Wagura)*
Beru-Bera Lin *(Nami
Kunigami)*
Masao Imafuku *(Tengen
Kunigami)*
Hiromi Matsushita *(Ikuko
Miyajima)*
Shin Kishida *(Agent Nanbara)*
Goro Mutsumi *(Black Hole
Alien Leader Kuronuma)*
Daigo Kusano *(Black Hole
Alien Agent Yanagawa)*
Takayasu Torii *(Agent
Tamura)*
Kenji Sahara *(Captain)*
Yasuzo Ogawa *(Foreman)*
Takamitsu Watanabe *(Black
Hole Alien)*
Takanobu Toya *(Black Hole
Alien)*
Koji Ozaki *(Black Hole Alien)*
Isao Zushi *(Godzilla)*
Kazunari Mori *(Mechagodzilla)*
Mamoru Kusumi
(Anguirus/King Caesar)

Alternate Titles
Godzilla vs. Bionic Monster
(U.S. original title)

Godzilla vs. Cosmic Monster
(U.S.)
King Kong gegen Godzilla
[King Kong vs. Godzilla]
(Germany)
Jättihirviöiden kaksintaistelu
[Duel of the Giant Monsters]
(Finland)
*Godzilla contre Mecanik
Monster* [**Godzilla vs. the
Mechanical Monster**]
(France)
Godzilla contro i robot
[**Godzilla vs. the Robot**] (Italy)
Ρομπότ εναντίον Γκοτζίλα
(Greece)
*Godzilla contra Cibergodzilla,
maquina de destruccion*
[**Godzilla vs. Cybergodzilla:
Machine of Destruction**]
(Spain)
Godzilla a Mechagodzilla ellen
(Hungary)
Godzilla kontra Mechagodzilla
(Poland)
*Годзилла против
Мехагодзиллы* (Russia)
Godzilla: Fezada Mücadele
(Turkey)

*"Mechagodzilla reminded people of the bad Godzilla of the 1960s. We couldn't have made Godzilla the bad
guy, because children wouldn't have liked it, so we created Mechagodzilla and acted out our feelings through
it."*
-Teruyoshi Nakano, *Monsters Are Attacking Tokyo* (1998) by Stuart Galbraith.

Godzilla vs. Mechagodzilla is one of the better entries of the waning 1970s era, mindless but unadulterated fun for one's inner ten year old. The film's thrills are a mile-a-minute as actor-driven action scenes keep an engaging human story going. All the while special effects director Teruyoshi Nakano brings the heat with explosive monster battles. *Godzilla vs. Mechagodzilla* is made primarily for children. Yet it has plenty of cinematic cool to please older children-at-heart with a taste for '70s camp.

PLOT

In Okinawa, while performing a traditional dance, Azumi royal descendant Nami (Beru-Bera Lin) has a prophecy of a giant monster attacking Japan. At the same time, Masahiko Shimizu (Kazuya Aoyama) finds a strange shard of metal while exploring Gyokusendo cave. His brother Keisuke (Masaaki Daimon), uncovers another cave at a construction site, actually an ancient ceremonial chamber. He meets archeologist Saeko (Reiko Tajima) whom he mistakes for a reporter. The two find the small statue of a monster inside along with a mural. This foretells Nami's prophecy but promises that *"When the red moon sets and the sun rises in the West, two monsters will arrive to save the people"*. Saeko concludes that the statue is likely King Caesar, a monster deity and guardian of the Azumi. As Keisuke and Saeko jet back to Tokyo, they meet a mysterious man claiming to be a freelance reporter (Shin Kishida). They then see a black cloud in the sky resembling a mountain, the first omen of the Okinawan prophecy.

Saeko and Keisuke take the statue and inscription to the latter's archeologist uncle Professor Wagura (Hiroshi Koizumi). Masahiko, meanwhile, brings the metal to scientist Professor Miyajima (Akihiko Hirata). Miyajima concludes that the metal must be a rare cosmic alloy called "space titanium". Wagura, meanwhile, translates the inscription on the statue. He discovers that the statue, placed on the Azumi's

sacred shrine, is key to awakening a monster named King Caesar.

A monster appearing to be Godzilla begins a rampage through Japan as Keisuke leaves to find his brother. Anguirus appears and attacks Godzilla, which baffles Keisuke as the monsters are supposed to be allies. Angurius is brutally beaten and has its jaw broken by Godzilla. It wounds the monster in the process, however, revealing a metal exoskeleton under Godzilla's skin. Keisuke finds a larger block of space metal in the rubble, which Miyajima concludes is also space titanium. As Godzilla attacks an oil refinery, another Godzilla surfaces from underground. The two beasts tussle and the second Godzilla reveals more metal exoskeleton under the skin of the first. Miyajima believes the first monster is a mechanical replica of the real Godzilla who has shown up to challenge it. Controlled by aliens from a Black Hole, their leader Kuronuma (Goro Mutsumi) burns off the rest of Mechagodzilla's disguise. Mechagodzilla badly injures the real Godzilla. Godzilla has inflicted enough damage however that the robot malfunctions and needs to be recalled.

Keisuke and Saeko return to Okinawa with the statue by boat. At the same time, Masahiko, Miyajima and his daughter Ikuko (Hiromi Matsushita) go to Gyokusendo cave in search of clues. They are captured by the Black Hole Aliens and brought to their underground base. Kuronuma coerces Miyajima into repairing Mechagodzilla by threatening to kill Masahiko and Ikuko. At sea, Keisuke is attacked by a Black Hole Alien called Yanagawa (Daigo Kusano), desperate to steal the statue. He shoots him in the face, revealing a grotesque, ape-like appearance. The alien agent is about to shoot Keisuke when he's shot dead by an unknown assailant, falling overboard with the statue. Keisuke and Saeko realize that the "reporter" is on the ship, whom they suspect shot the alien agent. Arriving in Okinawa, Keisuke reveals that he gave Saeko a decoy and had the real statue locked in the safe.

Keisuke and Saeko check on Miyajima and company at the hotel but find them missing and the hotel staff concerned. As Saeko guards the statue, Keisuke goes to Gyokusendo to rescue them. Miyajima, meanwhile, finishes repairs on Mechagodzilla. He is double-crossed by Kuronuma, who puts him, his daughter and Masahiko in an execution chamber designed to cook them alive. Keisuke is meanwhile attacked by another Black Hole Alien. He is saved by "the reporter" who reveals himself to be an Interpol agent named Nanbara. Taking the alien hostage, the two infiltrate their base where they rescue Miyajima and friends. They escape, but the Black Hole Aliens booby-trap their car with explosives. Nanbara realizes this and saves everyone's life. Ikuko notices that the moon is bright red as foretold in the prophecy. Miyajima, feeling intense guilt over having repaired Mechagodzilla, goes back in to disable it with Nanbara and Masahiko. At the Azumi shrine, the remaining company are cornered by Black Hole Aliens who have taken Nami and her grandfather Tengen (Masao Imafuku) hostage, demanding the statue. Keisuke is about to hand it over before they are shot by another Interpol agent, Nanbara's partner Tamura (Takayasu Torii). The statue is placed upon the sacred shrine as the sun appears to rise in the west (actually a mirage). King Caesar is freed from his mountain lair.

BACKGROUND

With the death of Eiji Tsuburaya, the departure of Ishiro Honda and the 1970s oil shocks, the Godzilla series was on life support. The films, their budgets slashed, were now made exclusively for Toho's kiddie matinee program, the Champion Matsuri Festival. Workaholic parents could drop their children off at the local Toho theater. Their kids could then be enraptured by *tokusatsu* TV episodes, *anime* shorts and usually a feature double bill. *Godzilla vs. Mechagodzilla*, while also shown at the Champion program, was released for Godzilla's 20th anniversary.

For *Godzilla vs. Mechagodzilla*, Tanaka allocated a higher budget than for the last two kiddie-oriented films *Godzilla vs. Gigan* (1972) and *Godzilla vs. Megalon* (1973). Their director, Jun Fukuda, would come back but a grittier tone was adopted. Fukuda and Teruyoshi Nakano wanted to bring Godzilla back to its roots, but Tanaka was adamant Godzilla stayed a protector of Earth. The character of Mechagodzilla was invented so

Godzilla could fight an evil version of itself. It was primarily inspired by the character of Mechani-Kong in *King Kong Escape*s (1967). The concept of Godzilla fighting a giant robot had also already been floated in Hideo Unagami's scrapped *Bride of Godzilla* treatment. Additionally, the staff were influenced by the recent popularity of Go Nagai's *manga* and anime *Mazinger Z*.

PRINCIPAL PHOTOGRAPHY

Godzilla vs. Mechagodzilla is unpretentious, distilled fun in cinematic form, a classic '70s B-picture executed to perfection. Jun Fukuda is a figure often derided as a *"poor man's Ishiro Honda"*, which couldn't be farther from the truth. Though Fukuda was something of a B-list director at Toho, he was a more stylish filmmaker than given credit. He employed more dynamic set-ups, handheld camerawork and staccato editing than Honda, who had a more conventional visual style. His two "South Seas" entries, *Ebirah, Horror of the Deep* (1966) and *Son of Godzilla* (1967) are underrated. Visually, *Godzilla vs. Mechagodzilla* is Jun Fukuda at his prime. His handheld shots, dynamic close-ups and brisk cutting bring Toei directors like Sadao Nakajima and Kinji Fukasaku to mind.

Michiko Ikeda's editing of the film is stellar. *Godzilla vs. Mechagodzilla* has a breakneck pace, balances its plot threads and keeps the audience on its toes between monster battles. The film's ape-like aliens are a possible nod to *Planet of the Apes* but could also be influenced by the villains of *Spectreman*.

ACTORS

The human scenes are well directed and more exciting than usual. Familiar faces Akihiko Hirata, Hiroshi Koizumi and Kenji Sahara make a welcome return. A standout is Shin Kishida as Agent Nanbara, cigarette in mouth as he oozes old school cool. Kishida (1939-1982), appeared as a regular cast member in Tsuburaya's *Operation: Mystery* (1968-69). He was known for his "Japanese Dracula" roles in *Lake of Dracula* (1971) and *The Evil of Dracula* (1974), both directed by Michio Yamamoto. Kishida, a native of Tokyo and member of the Bungakuza theatre troupe, played a variety of roles in contemporary and period pieces. He was a favorite of directors Kihachi Okamoto and Akio Jissoji. Tragically, esophageal cancer claimed his life at a young age. Goro Mutsumi also makes an impression as a hammy "big boss" villain. Mutsumi (1934-) was an actor from Kobe who had dubbed Russ Tamblyn into Japanese in *The War of the Gargantuas*. He'd be back to reprise the role, for all intents and purposes, in the next entry.

SFX

Teruyoshi Nakano's FX team was given a lot more money to work with on *Godzilla vs. Mechagodzilla* as Tanaka was quite proud of their work on *Submersion of Japan*. Mechagodzilla itself was designed by Akihiko Iguchi. Iguchi (1943-) was a brilliant visual artist responsible for many Ultraman monsters and would go on to create

Titanosaurus in the sequel. For the design of Mechagodzilla, Western knight armor was an aesthetic influence along with *kabuki* costumes. The suit was built by Nobuyuki Yasumaru, mainly of a polyethylene resin used in bathroom mats. Yasumaru and his assistant Tomoki Kobayashi tried to outdo their work on Jet Jaguar in *Godzilla vs. Megalon*. The suit was enhanced with car parts, including motorcycle tail lights for Mechagodzilla's eyes. The Godzilla suit from *Godzilla vs. Megalon,* also built by Yasumaru, was reused with some heavy renovations. The new monster King Caesar was inspired by ceremonial Okinawan statues of *shisa*, sacred creatures resembling a cross between lions and dogs. They are a cultural descendant of Chinese "guardian lions" per Okinawa's Chinese heritage.

Fresh off *Submersion of Japan*, Teruyoshi Nakano shows a confidence and competence with his special effects sequences that wasn't present in *Gigan* and *Megalon*. Liberally using his beloved pyrotechnics, he crafts dynamic monster scenes with a minimal use of stock footage. The script called for the disguised Mechagodzilla to do battle with U.S. Forces in Okinawa. Nakano opted to remove this sequence. Okinawa had been returned to Japan only two years prior and the presence of American forces there was still a hot button issue.

One sequence has Mechagodzilla raining a barrage of missiles and ray beams on Godzilla and King Caesar. This impressive scene feels like Nakano at top form. It's a masterful, Eisensteinian montage of well choreographed

suit work, pyrotechnics, miniatures and animated beams. The future head of Toho's FX division, Koichi Kawakita, was said to have had a major hand in this sequence. Perhaps taking a cue from rival Gamera director Noriaki Yuasa, Nakano was not afraid to hurt his monsters in contrast to his mentor Tsuburaya. The added bloodshed helps amp up the stakes.

MUSIC

Composer Masaru Sato returns to the series and creates an effective score: perfectly complimenting the film's breezy tone. Influenced by jazz and traditional Okinawan folk music, it makes use of themes he had composed for Kihachi Okamoto's war epic *Battle of Okinawa* (1971).

RELEASE AND LEGACY

Godzilla vs. Mechagodzilla would lead to a direct sequel, the even-better *Terror of Mechagodzilla* (1975). Ishiro Honda stepped back into the director's chair, crafting a more somber film than Fukuda. The two Mechagodzilla entries are a pair of fundamentally similar films made by very different directors, both bringing their stylistic flair to the table. Fukuda would soon return to the tokusatsu genre for the extrasensory spy thriller *ESPY* (1974) and the *Star Wars*-inspired *The War in Space* (1977).

Mechagodzilla would be back in 1993 for *Godzilla vs. Mechagodzilla II*, now a tool of humanity to defeat a hostile Godzilla. Another version, nicknamed *"Kiryu"* and again in the service of humans, appears in *Godzilla Against Mechagodzilla* (2002) and *Godzilla: Tokyo S.O.S.* (2003). King Caesar, along with cues from Sato's score, would return in *Godzilla: Final Wars* (2004), *Godzilla vs. Mechagodzilla* being a favorite of Ryuhei Kitamura. Recently, both the Black Hole Aliens and Mechagodzilla would be loosely recycled in the Godzilla anime trilogy (2017-18). A version of Mechagodzilla would also appear in Steven Spielberg's *Ready Player One* (2018) and another shows up in Legendary's *Godzilla vs. Kong* (2021).

ALTERNATE VERSIONS

An export version was commissioned, cut for cut the same as the Japanese. The dubbing was done in Hong Kong, though Toho started using a different firm at this point. They switched from Ted Thomas' group to Voicetrax, run by another HK-based entrepreneur named Matthew Oram (1946-). Dubbing cast includes Oram (Keisuke), Lynn Wilson (Saeko), Michael Kaye (Dr. Miyajima/Ship's Captain) and Michael Ross (Kuronuma). The English-born Oram was a horse racing enthusiast who would often invite his dubbing team to bet on races between takes. Like Thomas, he was an anchor for local English language news, as were many of the people who dubbed for him. He was a film critic for the South China Morning Post too, critically trashing many of the martial arts movies his firm dubbed badly into English. His son, Harry Oram, is an actor and martial artist in Hong Kong. Ross (1956-), despite dubbing villainous roles in kung fu films, was only a teenager at the time.

Most international versions were based on the export cut, the U.S. version included. *Godzilla vs. Mechagodzilla* had a colorful distribution history stateside. It was picked up by grindhouse outlet Cinema Shares in 1977. It would be first titled *Godzilla vs. Bionic Monster* (sic) and some prints were even shown with that title. Universal, creator of *The Six Million Dollar Man* and *The Bionic Woman*, came knocking on Cinema Shares' door with a cease and desist. The film was pulled and the title changed to *Godzilla vs. Cosmic Monster*. The American cut's differences are minor and the export dubbing is used. The main deletions include the opening credits and some human violence such as Yanagawa slashing Keisuke's hand with a knife during the boat segment. The film's very last scene showing Nami putting the statue in the shrine's catacombs while the heroes rejoice is removed as well. There's some rearranging to mask an awkward cut that actually improves the pacing, juxtaposing Keisuke and company racing to the shrine with Nanbara killing an alien. *Godzilla vs. Cosmic Monster* runs around 80:11, give or take a few seconds. It was rated "G" by the Motion Picture Association of America.

AMERICAN HOME VIDEO HISTORY

Godzilla vs. Mechagodzilla has had many American home video releases. In 1988, New World Pictures released the film, along with *Godzilla vs. Gigan*, to VHS and laserdisc. This was an uncut presentation of the export version, the Toho logo in all. This master was reissued on VHS by budget label Starmaker in 1992 in EP mode and then by Anchor Bay in 1997. The *Godzilla vs. Cosmic Monster* edit was put out in the '90s by UAV and Goodtimes Home Video, the latter edited down to just 60 minutes or so. Collectors' outlets Video Yesteryear and Sinister Cinema also put out versions telecined from 16mm prints. In 2004, *Godzilla vs. Mechagodzilla* was released to DVD by Sony, in widescreen with both Japanese and English audio for the first time. The disc went out of print but the film was acquired by Janus. It is now available on Blu-ray in Criterion's eight disc *Showa Godzilla* set, released in 2019.

Further Viewing:

TERROR OF MECHAGODZILLA

(1975)
メカゴジラの逆襲
Toho, *Director:* Ishiro Honda

In many ways an even better film than its predecessor, *Terror of Mechagodzilla* is a highlight of the '70s Godzilla entries. With Jun Fukuda occupied by *ESPY*, Tomoyuki Tanaka brought Yoshimitsu Banno on board as director for the 1975 Godzilla film. Tanaka was less than keen on his pitches. Director Ishiro Honda thus stepped back into the director's chair for the first time since 1970's *Space Amoeba*. A more conventional entry and direct sequel to *Godzilla vs. Mechagodzilla* was instead planned. Toho put out a story contest and the winner was Yukiko Takayama, a 29 year old screenwriting student. Takayama's early draft would feature

two giant dinosaur "Titans" who merge together for the climax. With feedback from Honda, the Titans were changed to a single monster: Titanosaurus.

Honda brings a more somber tone somewhat akin to the first *Godzilla*, aided by Ifukube's first original series score since *Destroy All Monsters*. The film is unusually grim with surprising violence and even nudity. This is all excised from the hacked-to-shreds U.S. kiddie matinee version. Akihiko Hirata returns as bitter mad scientist Dr. Mafune, though his performance is not helped by a bad Colonel Sanders wig. It's a role quite like his turn as archvillain Mr. K on Toho's series *Rainbowman* (1972-73). The lovely Tomoko Ai, fresh from *Ultraman Leo*, plays his cyborg daughter Katsura. She's a tragic character akin to Kumi Mizuno's Namikawa and her scenes are a high point. Like a sci-fi *Romeo and Juliet*, she has a doomed romance with protagonist Ichinose, played by Katsuhiko Sasaki, the son of *Seven Samurai*'s Minoru Chiaki. There are elements of transhumanist fetishism to Katsura's depiction. This looks ahead to robotic anime and manga characters like Masamune Shirow's Motoko Kusanagi or Yukito Kishiro's Alita. Goro Mutsumi all but reprises his role as the alien commander from the prior film. Veteran actor Toru Ibuki (1940-, *Ebirah, Horror of the Deep*) plays a sleazy role as his lieutenant. Unusually, the DP of Nakano's FX unit, Mototaka Tomioka, shot Honda's drama scenes as well.

Teruyoshi Nakano had now cut his teeth with stellar work on *Submersion of Japan* and *Prophecies of Nostradamus*. Here he crafts FX sequences that show a mastery not present in earlier '70s Godzilla films. Titanosaurus is one of Godzilla's most inspired foes, designed by Akihiko Iguchi and beautifully built by Keizo Murase. Titanosaurus' first Tokyo attack is a well executed and atmospheric scene. Surviving models from *Submersion of Japan* and *Prophecies of Nostradamus* were used to keep costs lower. Stock footage is employed, but more tastefully than in *Godzilla vs. Gigan* or *Godzilla vs. Megalon*. There's an impressive city smashing sequence where Mechagodzilla II renders miniatures to a pyrotechnic pulp. The film was simultaneously released in the U.S. to both TV and theaters. The theatrical cut, *The Terror of Godzilla*, was heavily censored for a "G" rating. This version cuts all human violence from the plot; resulting in a choppy

viewing experience. Thankfully it is no longer in circulation. UPA's TV version actually ran longer than the Japanese original and featured a lengthy prologue padded with footage from *Invasion of Astro-Monster*, along with *All Monsters Attack*. Sadly *Terror of Mechagodzilla* wound up the lowest attended Godzilla entry to date. When Godzilla wades off into the sea at the film's end, it would be going into hibernation for close to ten years. The *Showa* series would never really be outdone again. These films, *Terror of Mechagodzilla* included, are cinematic treasures. They hearken back to a time when you could forget the troubles of the world watching giant pantomime beasts fire rays at each other on a glowing screen. Today's audiences are too cynical.

JUN FUKUDA
The Action Director

福田純

2/17/1923-12/3/2000

"The original is the only one that's successful, that's really good. I give all of my Godzilla films a minus score."
-Jun Fukuda, *Monsters Are Attacking Tokyo* by Stuart Galbraith (1998)

A figure unfairly dubbed *"the poor man's Ishiro Honda"*, Fukuda was a talented program director in his own right. With a more dynamic visual style, he specialized in action-based movies. He was self deprecating about his work and thought his *tokusatsu* films were terrible. Jun Fukuda was born in 1923 in Jilin Province in Japanese-colonized Manchuria. His father worked for the South Manchuria Railway.

His family returned to Japan and he attended Nihon University. Fukuda would often skip the lectures to see movies. After World War II, he saw that Toho was recruiting assistant directors. He applied in 1946 and made the cut. For over 10 years, he labored under directors like Hiroshi Inagaki and Ishiro Honda.

Finally, in 1959, he was promoted to director with *It's Dangerous Playing with Fire*. His second film, *Secret of the Telegian* (1960), was science fiction based, pairing him with Eiji Tsuburaya. He began to specialize in moody crime thrillers, including *The Merciless Trap* (1961) and *The Weed of Crime* (1962). He also directed early entries in Toho's beloved *Young Guy* series with Yuzo Kayama. Fukuda began to show serious skill with his dark comedy actioner *Iron Finger* (1965). Also called *100 Shot, 100 Killed*, it starred Akira Takarada as a Bondian international spy.

After Honda passed on it, Toho was confident enough in Fukuda's abilities that he was given their newest monster picture in 1966. Called *Operation Robinson Crusoe*, it was planned to star King Kong. Rankin-Bass, who had the rights to Kong at the time, wanted Honda to direct and so pulled out of the project. Toho replaced Kong with Godzilla and the project became *Ebirah, Horror of the Deep* (aka *Godzilla vs. the Sea Monster*). Fukuda chose to work with Masaru Sato rather than Akira Ifukube to give the film a "lighter" tone. While Eiji Tsuburaya was credited as special effects director, his time was now divided with his television work at Tsuburaya Pro. As a result, the unit was mostly overseen by his right-hand man and DP Sadamasa Arikawa.

Fukuda returned for the following Godzilla entry. The even better *Son of Godzilla* (1967), partially filmed in Guam, retained its predecessor's island setting. Composer Sato and FX director Arikawa also returned.

Fukuda's next films included more entries in the *Young Guy* series. He also directed a follow-up to *Iron Finger* called *Booted Babe, Busted Boss* (1968). After Eiji Tsuburaya's death and Toho's refusal to put a tribute in *Space Amoeba*, Ishiro Honda switched to directing for television. Yoshimitsu Banno was placed in charge of the next Godzilla film, *Godzilla vs. Hedorah* (1971). As Tomoyuki Tanaka was displeased with the result, Jun Fukuda was tapped to helm the following entries. By this time, the series was being made for Toho's kiddie matinee program. *Godzilla vs. Gigan* (1972) and *Godzilla vs. Megalon* (1973) had far lower budgets than the '60s entries. The budget was increased slightly for *Godzilla vs. Mechagodzilla* (1974). Fukuda also directed the sci-fi spy thriller *ESPY* (1974), based on a novel by Sakyo Komatsu. Fukuda's last film at Toho was the *Star Wars*-inspired *The War in Space* (1977). Afterwards, he turned to directing for television. These included episodes of *Saiyuki "Monkey"* (1978-80) and documentaries. He died of lung cancer in 2000.

Selected Filmography *(as director)*
Samurai I: Musashi Miyamoto (1954) [assistant director]
Samurai II: Duel at Ichijoji Temple (1955) [assistant director]
Samurai III: Duel at Ganryu Island (1956) [assistant director]
Rodan (1956) [assistant director]
Yagyu Confidential (1957) [assistant director]
Ninjitsu (1958) [assistant director]
It's Dangerous Playing with Fire (1959)
Secret of the Telegian (1960)
The Merciless Trap (1961)
The Weed of Crime (1962)
Japan's No. 1 Young Guy (1962)
Young Guy in Hawaii (1963)
Tiger Fang (1964)
Iron Finger (1965)

Ebirah, Horror of the Deep
(1966)
Son of Godzilla (1967)
Booted Babe, Busted Boss
(1968)
Konto 55: Grand Outer Space Adventure (1969)
Konto 55: Grandchildren of the Ninja (1969)

Young Guy on Mt. Cook
(1969)
Freshman Young Guy (1969)
City of Beasts (1970)
Godzilla vs. Gigan (1972)
Godzilla vs. Megalon (1973)
Zone Fighter [episodes 1, 2, 6, 11, 17] (1973, TV)
Godzilla vs. Mechagodzilla
(1974)

Submersion of Japan
[episodes 1, 23, 26] (1974-75, TV)
ESPY (1974)
The War in Space (1977)
Monkey [episodes 1.2, 1.10, 1.19, 1.20, 1.23, 1.24, 2.1, 2.6, 2.25, 2.26] (1978-80, TV)

PROPHECIES OF NOSTRADAMUS

ノストラダムスの
大予言

Nostordamasu no Daiyogen "The Great Prophecies of Nostradamus"
Toho, 8/3/1974 (*Showa 49*), 9 Reels (3,081 meters), 113:51, 35mm, Panavision (2.35:1 anamorphic), color, monaural sound

Crew
Producers: Tomoyuki Tanaka, Osamu Tanaka
Director: Toshio Masuda
Special Effects Director: Teruyoshi Nakano
Screenplay: Yoshimitsu Banno, Toshio Yasumi (script *The Last War*), Ben Goto (book *The Great Prophecies of Nostradamus*)
Second Unit Director: Yoshimitsu Banno
Directors of Photography: Rokuro Nishigaki, Kaoru Washio
Music: Isao Tomita
Editor: Nobuo Ogawa
Assistant Director: Fumisake Okada
Production Design: Yoshiro Muraki

Lighting: Shinji Kojima
Sound Recording: Kanae Masuo
Production Manager: Hisayuki Murakami
Assistant SFX Director: Koichi Kawakita
SFX Cinematography: Mototaka Tomioka, Takeshi Yamamoto
SFX Art Director: Yasuyuki Inoue
SFX Lighting: Masakuni Morimoto
SFX Unit Production Manager: Keisuke Shinoda
SFX Optical Photography: Takeshi Miyanishi
SFX Opticals: Yoshio Ishii
Monster Design: Akihiko Iguchi
Stunts: Chihiro Mitsuishi

Dance Choreography: Kiyohiko Kawanishi
Still Photographer: Yoshinori Ishizuki
SFX Still Photographer: Kazukiyo Tanaka

Cast
Tetsuro Tanba (*Dr. Ryogen Nishiyama/Genta Nishiyama/Gengaku Nishiyama*)
Toshio Kurosawa (*Akira Nakagawa*)
Yoko Tsukasa (*Nobue Nishiyama*)
Kaoru Yumi (*Mariko Nishiyama*)
Kaori Taniguchi (*Orin*)
Yoshiro Aoki (*Kempeitai Officer*)
Katsu Ryuzaki (*Oone*)

Katsuhiko Sasaki (*Yoshihama*)
Shosei Muto (*Ihara*)
Jun Hamamura (*Kida*)
Kumeko Otowa (*Mrs. Kida*)
Tomoe Mari (*Kida's Daughter*)
Tappei Shimokawa (*Captain of Self Defense Force*)
Akihiko Hirata (*Botanist*)
Hiroshi Koizumi (*Zoologist*)
So Yamamura (*Prime Minister*)
Mizuho Suzuki (*Director of Environmental Agency*)
Taketoshi Naito (*Chief Cabinet Secretary*)
Sayoko Kato (*Tour Bus Girl*)
Mikizo Hirata (*Sanji Nakagawa*)
Tatsuo Nakamura (*Katsuko Nakagawa*)
Takashi Shimura (*Hospital Director*)
Masahiko Tanimura (*Tayama*)

Kazuko Inano (*Hamako*)
Kazuo Kato (*Scholar*)
George F. Flynn (*US Representative*)
Willie Dorsey (*African Representative*)
Franz Gruber (*Dr. Wilson*)
Tony Cetera (*American Research Scientist*)
Rolf Jesser (*German Research Scientist*)
Osman Yusuf (*Research Scientist*)
Isamu Sugii (*Soft-Bodied Human*)
Nobuyuki Nakano (*Soft-Bodied Human*)
Shunsuke Kariya (*Leader of Rioters*)
Goro Naya (*TV Newscaster*)
Kyoko Kishida (*Prophetess,* voice)
Shinji Nakai (*Narrator,* voice)

Alternate Titles

Catastrophe 1999: Prophecies of Nostradamus (alternate international title)
The Last Days of Planet Earth (U.S.)
La fin du monde d'après Nostradamus [**The End of the World According to Nostradamus**] (France)
Verdens sidste dag [**Last Days of the World**] (Denmark)
Catastrofe [Catastrophe] (Italy)
Katastrofen 1999 (Norway)
Apocalipsis 1999 [**Apocalypse 1999**] (Spain)
Weltkatastrophe 1999 [**World Catastrophe 1999**] (Germany)

"The splendor of many beautiful maidens... Never again will they be so brilliant."
-Century 10, Prophecy 98, *The Prophecies* (1555) by Michel De Nostredame

An elusive film due to a self imposed studio ban, *Prophecies of Nostradamus* is an offbeat eco-horror docudrama. While at times gleeful in its apocalyptic spectacle, the film is relevant. It accurately if melodramatically depicts a global civilization falling apart due to slow-building ecological catastrophe. Like screenwriter Yoshimitsu Banno's previous *Godzilla vs. Hedorah* (1971), it represents a plea for humanity to re-examine its relationship with the ecosystem.

PLOT

In 1853 Tokugawa Japan, teacher Genta Nishiyama (Tetsuro Tanba) is executed for using the prophecies of Nostradamus in his lessons, predicting the arrival of Commodore Matthew Perry's fleet. During World War II, his grandson Gengaku Nishiyama (also Tanba) is interrogated by a *kempeitai* officer for spreading predictions of Japan's defeat. In the modern day, his son Dr. Ryogen Nishiyama (also Tanba) is a pediatrician, environmental scientist and activist. Like his grandfather and father, Nishiyama is a student of Nostradamus, his family still owning a copy of *The Prophecies* passed down from Genta. As he notices children in his office in respiratory distress due to pollution from a nearby factory,

Nishiyama is visited by police. They warn him to stop flying his plane over the factory in protest.

As the news photographer boyfriend of Nishyama's daughter Mariko (Kaoru Yumi), Akira Nakayama (Toshio Kurosawa), returns from assignment in Africa, giant slugs appear. Nishiyama pleads with the army not to destroy them so they can be examined, but is ignored. Later, Nishiyama's wife Nobue (Yoko Tsukasa) tells him that local *yakuza* have been threatening them over his protest of the factory. Multitudes of dead fish next wash ashore on Japan's coasts, heralding the collapse of fishing stocks. Akira's fisherman father Sanji (Mikizo Hirata) tries to drown himself in despair. The strange occurrences continue, with a high percentage of deformed babies born in polluted areas. The daughter (Tomoe Mari) of Nishiyama's employee Kida (Jun Hamamura) is among the unlucky ones. She gives birth to a disfigured stillborn as her father laments.

After disturbing reports of atomic fallout on New Guinea, a United Nations expedition is dispatched to investigate. Two of Nishiyama's assistants, Oone (Katsu Ryuzaki) and Yoshihama (Katsuhiro Sasaki), go with the expedition. Nishiyama pleads with the Japanese government as the strange incidents intensify. People experience hallucinations and monster weeds appear in subways. Children develop superhuman abilities from a zinc mine's contamination. Egypt experiences a snowstorm and the Pacific freezes over due to haywire weather patterns from climate change. This strains the global food supply and causes international tensions. Undeveloped nations harbor resentment at rich countries for taking too much grain to feed livestock.

After the original New Guinea expedition disappears, Nishiyama leads a second UN expedition to try to rescue them. Trekking deep into the jungle, they find mutated, bird-eating plants and are attacked by ferocious bats. One of the men is then bitten by a radioactive leech. At nightfall, radiation disfigured natives attack their camp, engaging in cannibalism. Following them, Nishiyama and the others find the previous expedition. They are disfigured and radiation poisoned to delirium. The expedition mercy kills the men and buries them as Nishiyama despairs.

Soon, two SST jets soon explode in the stratosphere ripping apart the ozone layer. This results in a variety of ecological disasters as ultraviolet rays come streaming down. The rays cause injury to people, fires and then deluge and flooding takes place. After grain worldwide is affected, the Japanese government puts food rationing into effect, leading to mass riots. Tokyoites flood the freeways trying to escape the city, causing a traffic jam stretching miles. A reckless driver causes an explosive accident. This creates an endless chain-reaction of burning vehicles. Young people begin to commit suicide in alarming numbers.

Violent food riots take place in Tokyo but the Prime Minister (So Yamamura) holds off on calling the Self Defense Force in. Nobue, meanwhile, dies of a respiratory illness. As a city riots and Nishiyama mourns his wife's death, the smog becomes so intense that the sky's light refracts.

BACKGROUND

After the success of *Submersion of Japan*, producer Tomoyuki Tanaka was eager to make more disaster pictures. For their follow-up, rather than sink Japan under the waves of the Pacific, Toho put the entire world in their apocalyptic crosshairs. They used a recent bestseller on the French prophet Michel de Nostredame (Nostradamus) by journalist Tsutomu "Ben" Goto as the basis. The film was originally intended as a soft remake of *The Last War*, hence a screenwriter credit for Toshio Yasumi. It quickly became its own distinctive story. *Prophecies of Nostradamus* was directed by Toshio Masuda; once a specialist in gritty potboilers at Nikkatsu. After they switched mainly to making softcore pornography, Masuda went freelance. Making films for both Toei and Toho, he developed a reputation for being a hitmaker. He was fresh from directing *The Human Revolution* (1973), a top-grossing biographical drama on controversial *Soka Gakkai* founder Josei Toda, played by Tetsuro Tanba.

Another key player in *Prophecies of Nostradamus* is its screenwriter: Yoshimitsu Banno. Handed the reins to the Godzilla series, his entry, *Godzilla vs. Hedorah*, brought environmental destruction to the forefront as an existential horror like nuclear weapons. Tomoyuki Tanaka, who was hospitalized and couldn't keep tight rein on production, was displeased. Yet Banno was tapped to write *Prophecies of Nostradamus* and direct the film's second unit, mainly in the New Guinea sequence.

PRINCIPAL PHOTOGRAPHY

Early on, Yoshimitsu Banno and a crew of six flew to New Guinea to take location shots. Actor Tetsuro Tanba was somewhat known as a prima donna in that he didn't like to learn his lines. Director Masuda, who by now was used to working with him, had the cinematographers conserve the most film for Tanba's performance. Supporting actor Katsuhiko Sasaki (1944-) was frustrated that Masuda gave Tanba preferential treatment, ordering the actors to speed up their line readings to make time for Tanba.

The disturbing pair of deformed post-nuke mutant children seen near the film's end were designed by Akihiko Iguchi and modeled by Nobuyuki Yasumaru. Called "Soft-Bodied Humans" in official press, they were played by two actual children. The creatures are unsettling creations; bringing the end of the BBC docu-drama *Threads* to mind. Though Teruyoshi Nakano's FX team designed and built the suits, this sequence was helmed by Toshio Masuda's main unit.

Prophecies of Nostradamus is a film some would consider heavy-handed in its approach yet its science is relevant. Scientific advisers from the government were consulted for accuracy. Masuda's direction is melodramatic but the film is ahead of its time in dealing with issues like climate change and ecological catastrophe. While there was conjecture on such issues in environmentalist circles, they weren't political talking points yet. *Prophecies of Nostradamus*, like *The Last War*, also explores the concept of mutually assured destruction. Using stock footage from that film, it links environmentalist and anti-war sentiments. It theorizes that ecological disaster could cause disruptions in the food supply chain, straining international diplomacy and resulting in a third World War. Masuda would return to the theme of thermonuclear war for his anime opus *Future War 198X* (1982).

ACTORS

Tetsuro Tanba (1922-2006) plays the fiery Dr. Nishiyama. Tanba, who had played the Prime Minister in *Submersion of Japan*, was a noteworthy actor from Tokyo. He was a consummate professional who played a multitude of roles for Masaki Kobayashi, Shohei Imamura, Hideo Gosha, Masahiro Shinoda, Kihachi Okamoto, Kinji Fukasaku and others. He appears in the 1967 Bond entry *You Only Live Twice* as Tiger Tanaka. Tanba spoke better English than his colleagues, his years as a translator during the American occupation came in handy. Tanba was well known for his roles on TV's *Key Hunter* and *G-Men '75* and had an obsession with spiritualism. In later life he led an afterlife-themed religious movement called *Dai Reikai (Great Spirit World)*. He wrote

numerous books on the subject and produced two *Tetsuro Tanba's Great Spirit World* films. His very last role would fittingly be in Shinji Higuchi's *Submersion* remake *Sinking of Japan* (2006).

Renowned actress Yoko Tsukasa (1934-) also appears as Nishiyama's doomed wife. She was a veteran of films by Kurosawa, Ozu, Kobayashi and Hiroshi Inagaki. Kaoru Yumi (1950-) plays Nishiyama's daughter Mariko. She was a popular actress and singer, also appearing in Jun Fukuda's *ESPY* that same year. Unlike some of her contemporaries, she was not afraid to shed her clothes. Today, she is known for her exercise videos ala a Japanese Jane Fonda. She also held a government position as health advisor. Toshio Kurosawa (1944-) is another notable actor who frequently worked with both director Masuda and co-star Tanba. He appeared in Kihachi Okamoto's *Samurai Assassin* (1965) and *Japan's Longest Day* (1967). He also played a notable role opposite Meiko Kaji in *Lady Snowblood* (1973) and appeared in Michio Yamamoto's *The Evil of Dracula* (1974).

Actor So Yamamura more or less reprises his role from *The Last War* as the Prime Minister of Japan. Another noteworthy actor is Mizuho Suzuki (1927-) who plays the Environmental Secretary. Born in Manchuria, he often played authority figures and bureaucrats starting in *Submersion of Japan*. He would appear in more disaster and special effects films including Toei's *The Bullet Train* (1975) and Toho's *Conflagration* (also 1975), *Deathquake* (1980) and *The Return of*

Godzilla (1984). Suzuki did a lot of Japanese dubbing for television, voicing both Vito Corleone and Darth Vader. He also voiced Dr. Onishi in Katsuhiro Otomo's seminal anime masterpiece *Akira* (1988).

SFX

Teruyoshi Nakano returned to do the special effects and his unit started shooting in May 1974. Like *Submersion* he took this film to heart, doing some of his finest work as he nearly burned down Toho's backlot in the process. A shot of the countryside browning as the ozone layer is ripped open was created by spraying diluted sulfuric acid on miniature mountains planted with cedar buds. While Nakano's unit shot the ensuing forest fire, the blaze became out of control. Toho's entire Studio 7 burned to the ground and many props and suits in storage were ruined. Thankfully, no one was injured. Nakano's ever thrifty FX unit would use the rubble of Studio 7 for the later scene showing the aftermath of the destroyed Fukushima nuclear plant. Some of the charred debris was saved and used in later pictures.

One explosive scene, where miles of cars in a traffic jam explode in a firestorm, became a signature sequence for Nakano. He would reuse it in *The War in Space* (1977), *Deathquake* (1980) and *The Return of Godzilla* (1984). A later shot of a nuclear missile silo's door smashing open was done with a plaster miniature with weights placed inside it. Nakano's unit wrapped up their end of the shoot on June 30th, 1974.

MUSIC

Prophecies of Nostradamus also features a rocking score by synthesizer musician Isao Tomita (1932-2016), Japan's own Wendy Carlos. In addition to a plethora of film music and work on Osamu Tezuka's *Jungle Emperor* (1965-67), Tomita would go on to create beloved synthesizer re-orchestrations of classical works. This includes his Debussy album *Snowflakes Are Dancing* (1974) and take on Holst's *The Planets* (1976).

REAL WORLD

Yoshimitsu Banno's script asks the same question as in *Godzilla vs. Hedorah* but with more scope: could our present destruction of the ecosystem create problems for humanity in the future? Banno was particularly inspired by the infamous Minamata incident. A Japanese fishing village of the same name was poisoned for decades by mercury from a chemical plant's wastewater. The town's people and animals developed high rates of birth defects and cerebral palsy that became known as Minamata disease. It was an ongoing legal case in Japan until 2010. Banno includes pointed references to it in his script. Banno makes an outright mention of "Yusho disease". PCB, a chemical additive used as a preservative, sickened people in Southern Japan. He also references Yokkaichi City's asthma outbreak in the 1960s to '70s, caused by fumes from their petrochemical complexes.

One chilling scene shows an earthquake destroying the Fukushima Daiichi nuclear power plant, which floods the prefecture with radiation. On March 11, 2011, reality became stranger than fiction. A tsunami, caused by a massive earthquake off Japan's coast, would disable the emergency generators the plant needed to shut down. This resulted in the meltdown of three reactors and began one of the worst nuclear disasters since Chernobyl. Clean-up of the site will be on-going for decades. A prophetic nuclear power plant meltdown would also be featured in the "*Mount Fuji in Red*" segment in Akira Kurosawa's *Dreams* (1990).

THEMES AND MOTIFS

Prophecies of Nostradamus meditates on similar existential matters as Godfrey Reggio's non-narrative *Koyaanisqatsi* (1982). The difference is, *Koyaanisqatsi*'s images of whizzing freeways, factories, war machines and urban sprawl merely suggest what *Prophecies* outright asserts. Yet in spite of the film's almost gleeful pessimism, there is an element of humanism. *Prophecies of Nostradamus* holds some faith that humanity might solve these daunting challenges. It concludes fatalism is more part of the problem than solution.

RELEASE AND LEGACY

After the film's release, a group of Hiroshima survivors' activists complained to Eirin, Japan's equivalent to the MPAA, about two sequences. The first scene to draw their ire shows irradiated cannibalistic natives on the attack in New Guinea. The other features two deformed, elephant man-like mutant kids in a post-nuke world fighting over a snake they want to eat. The complaints soon prompted Toho to withdraw the film and re-release it with cuts.

As with *Submersion of Japan,* a television series adaptation of *Prophecies of Nostradamus* was planned. Some 16mm B-roll was even shot on Nakano's FX unit. Due to the film's controversy, plans for the show were scuttled. A sequel, scripted by Masato Ide (*Red Beard*), was also planned. It was to feature a fictionalized version of Ben Goto and involve a UFO appearing over Japan. *Prophecies of Nostradamus II* would also have brought back Masuda and Nakano. Again likely due to the controversy surrounding the first film, plans were scrapped.

Toho attempted to release *Prophecies of Nostradamus* to tape and laserdisc in 1986 but it was cancelled due to protest. Since then, *Prophecies of Nostradamus* has been under a self imposed in-studio ban by Toho itself, ala Disney's treatment of *Song of the South*. Toho has relegated the film to their vaults and interested fans must squint at an illegal copy made from a leaked video master. The closest Toho has come to releasing the film is a "drama CD" with only the film's audio. This is a shame, as *Prophecies of Nostradamus* is one of the most memorable Japanese special effects productions of the '70s. Its depiction of a civilization unravelling from the slow burn of ecological disaster has come to resemble our own world. Unsurprisingly, Hideaki Anno (*Neon Genesis Evangelion*) and Shinji Higuchi are major fans of this film. Toho's next disaster epic was *Conflagration* (1975), released as *High Seas Hijack* stateside. Masuda himself would return to the genre over a decade later for *Tokyo Blackout* (1987), based on a novel by Sakyo Komatsu.

ALTERNATE VERSIONS

Prophecies of Nostradamus is known for having a multitude of edits, there are at least seven distinct versions. The first alternate cut is the shortened Japanese reissue version which features an unknown number of edits. It is rumored to be about a minute and 45 seconds shorter. Confirmed edits are a segment where New Guinea natives feast on the body of one of the expedition members and the soft-bodied human sequence. A video copy is on file with the Library of Congress.

An export version was created despite its domestic controversies. Entitled *Catastrophe 1999: Prophecies of Nostradamus*, it features English dubbing by Barry Haigh's Po Hwa Dubbing Company in Hong Kong. Matthew Oram and Haigh dub Nishiyama and Akira and this version runs about 88:27. It also features the voices of Michael Ross and Linda Masson as Mariko. It has about 25 minutes of cuts to the drama scenes and subplots. The prologue showing Nishiyama's family history is excised, as is the Kida baby subplot and the Prime Minister's final speech. The latter creates a jarring jump in the soundtrack at the end. This shortened cut plays more like an exploitation film. The other international edits are based on this one. The German cut features some additional edits including the excision of the soft-bodied humans sequence. The French version shuffles scenes around, inexplicably moving the scene with Akira's father to near the end of the film.

In 1981, Henry G. Saperstein's UPA acquired the rights and would release a re-edit of the film to television called *The Last Days of Planet Earth*. This cut of the movie takes on the feel of a Sunn Classics production with a sloppy, Ed Woodsian editing style. It is mainly based on the international version, retaining its dub track but making cuts to nudity and gore. Fade-outs for television commercials are inserted. The most notable edit is the deletion of Mariko's dance sequence later in the film. The biggest change is an added narration track by TV actor Jack Ryland, who sounds like he's narrating a *Ripley's Believe It Or Not* special with a touch of Ed Wood's Criswell. These supplant a female voice's readings of the prophecies (by *Woman in the Dunes'* Kyoko Kishida) in the Japanese and international versions. The narration sometimes drowns out dubbed dialogue. There are some sound design changes with the soft-bodied humans given monstrous grunts and re-dubbed bits. Tidbits of the Japanese version are actually put back in, including a snippet of the Kida baby scene. A scene showing a sickly old man in a tree, temples and a tour bus is also reinstated. There is some new, exclusive footage of a transmission from New Guinea being received. This version, running 87:42, is recommended only as a curiosity.

AMERICAN HOME VIDEO HISTORY

Paramount/Gateway put *The Last Days of Planet Earth* on VHS and laserdisc in 1994. Toho was offering the film in its international sales catalogs in the 2000s, but no longer does. That makes a quality release nigh impossible for now.

Further Viewing:

(1987)
首都消失
Daiei, *Director:* **Toshio Masuda**

Tokyo Blackout (or *Capital Disappearance*), published in 1985, was one of Sakyo Komatsu's last major bestsellers. In 1977, Sakyo Komatsu had written a short story called *America's Wall*. Hauntingly relevant in today's time, it involves the United States cut off from the rest of the world via a magnetic cloud wall. Komatsu recycled the basic premise of this story for *Tokyo Blackout*. Instead of the U.S, a magnetic cloud surrounds Tokyo, sealing it off completely from the rest of Japan and the world. A revitalized Daiei, now under publishing mogul Yasuyoshi Tokuma, soon optioned the rights. Toshio Masuda stepped into the director's chair and Teruyoshi Nakano's unit from Toho was tapped to handle the special effects.

Tokyo Blackout is a daft but entertaining disaster flick. Yuko Natori heads the cast as an intrepid reporter and Masuda brings his typical melodrama to the table. It's certainly far from Masuda's best film and often veers into soap opera theatrics. Things become sticky when, naturally, the Americans and Soviets get involved. The English actors here are a nudge less awful than usual. Prolific superstar composer Maurice Jarre, best known for scoring David Lean's masterworks, was tapped for the soundtrack. In spite of his pedigree, Jarre's music is badly dated and feels inappropriate to the intended somber mood. Nakano's FX work is subtle but well executed. Its eye-catching optical effects are marred only by the occasional iffy composite. The magnetic cloud is convincing, 100 tons of dry ice were used throughout the shoot. There's impressive miniature work in an aerial sequence midway. *Tokyo Blackout* was, along with *Tokyo, the Last Megalopolis*, an early Japanese film to use high definition video for its VFX composites. The finale is pretty ludicrous. The novel's hints of the cloud being alien in origin are scuttled. *Tokyo Blackout* is a mediocre but enjoyably polished disaster picture. Director Masuda, however, brings a degree of atmospheric stylishness and production value that makes one wish Toho had put him in charge of a Godzilla entry.

DREAMS
(1990)
夢
Kurosawa Productions/Toho/Warner Brothers, *Director:* **Akira Kurosawa**

Included thanks to a few segments with loose sci-fi elements, Akira Kurosawa's *Dreams* (1990) is unforgettable. Though generally regarded as "lesser Kurosawa", it's one of the finest anthology films ever produced. Only an auteur director of Kurosawa's stature could make such a film. Indeed, in the hands of a lesser filmmaker, a movie like *Dreams* would be quite pretentious and self indulgent.

With *Dreams*, Kurosawa crafts lyrical, visual poetry, with each shot like a moving painting. Early segments like *"Sunshine Through the Rain"* and *"The Peach Orchard"* strongly invoke colleague Masaki Kobayashi's *Kwaidan* (1964). Capped with a jaw dropping ceremony sequence, *"The Peach Orchard"* illuminates Kurosawa's love of nature, foreshadowing the environmentalism of the following segments. *"The Blizzard"* is a highlight, feeling like a riveting survival drama crossed with *Kwaidan*'s *"Woman of the Snow"*. The characters' icy suffering is so vividly depicted that you can feel the cold.

"The Tunnel" is another standout. While many claim it was ghost-directed by Ishiro Honda, the truth is that Honda's role was likely more as an uncredited co-director. The segment certainly has some of his directorial stylings as well as being, most likely, based on one of his dreams. One of Honda's most eloquent quotes in Galbraith's *Monsters Are Attacking Tokyo* begins with *"My nightmares are almost always about war: wandering the streets, searching for something that's lost forever"*. *"The Tunnel"* can largely be summed up in that quote. A snarling feral dog that accosts actor Akira Terao's "I" seems

to almost represent a Jungian manifestation of Honda's war guilt. Regardless of who had the lions' share of creative input, *"The Tunnel"* represents Kurosawa's heartfelt tribute to a lifelong friend.

"Crows" is probably the film's weakest link but still fairly dazzling. It opens with a perfectly executed zoom shot. A flawless zooming shot is particularly difficult for a director, DP and their operators to pull off. Kurosawa nails it as if to boast *"Yes, I'm the greatest living director in the world"*. *"Crows"* is Kurosawa's tribute to the art of painting which he himself dabbled in heavily. Kurosawa, as a moody auteur director, clearly strongly related to the segment's subject: Vincent Van Gogh. Other aspects of *"Crows"* don't fare as well. Martin Scorsese's performance is a bit weak, his American accent is unconvincing. The VFX by Industrial Light and Magic, showing Terao's "I" exploring the scenery of Van Gogh's iconic paintings, is stunning. A few shots, however, have aged embarrassingly but they minorly detract from the whole.

"Mount Fuji in Red" is another segment that almost certainly had creative input from Ishiro Honda. It strongly invokes a *tokusatsu* disaster picture, particularly *Submersion of Japan*, directed by Kurosawa's protege Shiro Moritani. Yet there's an existential nightmarishness and emphasis on the human element not present in the Toho disaster film cycle. *"Mount Fuji in Red"* is particularly horrifying in the wake of the Fukushima nuclear disaster. *"The Weeping Demon"* piggybacks off the doomsday vibe of *"Mount*

Fuji in Red" with a hauntingly bleak feel all its own. It's reminiscent of the finale of *Prophecies of Nostradamus* crossed with Nobuo Nakagawa's *Jigoku*. It's capped in a particularly unsettling and beautifully executed long take. Finally, *"Village of the Watermills"* is a melancholy but contemplative segment. Depicting an anarcho-primitivist utopia where people view life as a gift more than a burden, it speaks of Kurosawa's deepest idealism. In contrast to previous segments illuminating his darkest fears, it makes for a lyrically beautiful close to the picture. Perhaps *Dreams* does seem like a disappointment next to *Seven Samurai* or on the heels of *Ran*, but it is a stunningly beautiful trip all its own.

TOSHIO MASUDA
The Hit Maker

舛田利雄

10/5/1927-

Toshio Masuda is one of the last surviving Japanese directors of his generation. Like Kinji Fukasaku, whom he collaborated with on the Japanese segments for *Tora! Tora! Tora!*, Masuda helmed a large assortment of blockbusters in every genre at Japan's biggest studios. Born in Kobe, the son of a sailor, he was expelled from school toward the end of World War II for being skeptical of militarism. After the war, he enrolled in Osaka University and studied Russian literature. He soon became interested in French cinema, so he joined the film program.

Upon graduation he joined Shin Toho as an assistant director. There he worked under such esteemed filmmakers as Umetsugu Inoue, Mikio Naruse and Nobuo Nakagawa. Inoue in particular was a mentor figure to Masuda. He would stay at Inoue's mansion and the two would collaborate on screenplays. Naruse was another mentor, teaching him cinematography. Moving to Nikkatsu, he worked as an assistant to Kon Ichikawa including on *The Burmese Harp* (1956). The following year, he was promoted to full-fledged director. His first film was *A Journey of Body and Soul* (1957). Masuda's earliest successful picture would be his third, *Rusty Knife* (1958), which starred Yujiro Ishihara and Akira Kobayashi. Masuda would develop a unique style of "Nikkatsu action" and secure a reputation as being able to produce quality hits on time and budget. During this time, he became known as *"The Emperor of Nikkatsu Action"*.

Masuda left Nikkatsu after producing a series of films with *Tokyo Drifter* star Tetsuya Watari. These included *Velvet Hustler* (1967) and *Gangster VIP* (1968). Nikkatsu would soon abandon its traditional fare, making softcore exploitation *"roman porno"* films to stay afloat. Masuda became freelance and in 1970, he directed a large portion of the Japanese segments for 20th

Century Fox's *Tora! Tora! Tora!* (1970). He initially turned the project down, but after Masaki Kobayashi and Kihachi Okamoto declined the job, he decided to take it. Masuda and Kinji Fukasaku replaced a disenchanted Akira Kurosawa. Productions like the bloody *chambara Shadow Hunters* (1972) and its sequel followed. He next helmed *The Human Revolution* (1973) for Toho, a biography of controversial *Soka Gakkai* sect leader Josei Toda. It was followed by a sequel in 1976. Masuda also directed the FX-filled doomsday flick *Prophecies of Nostradamus* in 1974.

At the same time, he became involved in *anime* productions, becoming one of the first directors to go back and forth between the live action and *anime* mediums. Masuda was brought onto *Space Battleship Yamato* by producer Yoshinobu Nishizaki. Nishizaki, a fan of Masuda's crime thrillers, wanted a live action influence. Masuda was too busy making *Nostradamus* to have much of a hand in the TV show, but he would direct several of the *Yamato* movies. He was an integral part of one of Japan's most iconic franchises.

In the '80s, a busy Masuda continued to make blockbusters for the major studios. He directed big budget war epics including *Port Arthur* (1980), *The Imperial Japanese Empire* (1982), *The Battle of the Sea of Japan* (1983) and *Zero* (1984). He also directed the romance dramas *High Teen Boogie* (1982) and *Loving* (1983). He would make more anime films such as *Future War 198X* (1982), *Odin* (1985) along with the disaster flick *Tokyo Blackout* (1987). His film *Company Funeral* (1989) was nominated for several Japanese Academy Awards and won him a Blue Ribbon Award for Best Director. Masuda's final feature film was *Heavenly Sin* (1992) which starred Omar Sharif. He has since been occasionally active directing for television.

Selected Filmography *(as director)*

The Burmese Harp (1956) [assistant director]
A Journey of Body and Soul (1957)
Rusty Knife (1958)
Red Quay (1958)
The Man Who Risked Heaven and Earth (1959)
The Brawler (1960)
Hana and Ryu (1962)
Red Handkerchief (1964)
Taking the Castle (1965)
Velvet Hustler (1967)
Gangster V.I.P. (1968)

Tora! Tora! Tora! (1970)
Shadow Hunters (1972)
Shadow Hunters: Echo of Destiny (1972)
The Human Revolution (1973)
Prophecies of Nostradamus (1974)
Blood (1974)
Continuing Human Revolution (1976)
Farewell to Space Battleship Yamato (1978)
Port Arthur (1980)
Be Forever: Yamato (1980)

The Imperial Japanese Empire (1982)
High Teen Boogie (1982)
Future War 198X (1982)
Battle of the Sea of Japan (1983)
Loving (1983)
Zero (1984)
Love: Take Off (1985)
Odin: Photon Sailer Starlight (1985)
Tokyo Blackout (1987)
Company Funeral (1989)
Doten (1991)
Edo Castle Rebellion (1991)
Heavenly Sin (1992)

THE LAST DINOSAUR

Kyokutei tankensen Pora-Bora "Underground Expedition Ship: Polar Boar"
Rankin-Bass/Tsuburaya Pro/Toho, 9/10/1977 (*Showa 52*), 106:07, 35mm, Spherical (1.85:1),
Fujicolor, monaural sound

Crew
Producers: Arthur Rankin Jr.,
Jules Bass, Noboru
Tsuburaya
Associate Producers: Masaki
Izuka, Kazuyoshi Kasai, Benni
Korzen, Kinshiro Okubo
Directors: Tsugunobu Kotani,
Alexander Grasshoff
Special Effects Director: Kazuo
Sagawa
Screenplay: William Overgard
Director of Photography:
Masaharu Ueda
Music: Maury Laws
Conductor: Kenjiro Hirose
Editors: Minoru Kozono,
Yoshitami Kuroiwa, Tatsuji
Nakashizu
Assistant Director: Shohei
Tojo
Art Director: Kazuhiko
Fujiwara
Lighting: Hisaki Yoneyama
Sound Mixer: Yuji Hiyoshi
Production Manager: Minoru
Kurita
Production Coordinator:
Kiyotaka Ugawa

SFX Cinematographer: Sadao
Sato
SFX Optical Composites:
Michihisa Miyashige
SFX Optical Photography:
Minoru Nakano
Assistant SFX Director:
Yoshiyuki Yoshimura
SFX Art Director: Tetsuzo
Ozawa
SFX Lighting: Yasuo Kitazawa
SFX Production Manager:
Kazuo Ohashi

Cast
Richard Boone (*Masten
Thrust Jr.*)
Joan Van Ark (*Francesca
'Frankie' Banks*)
Steven Keats (*Chuck Wade*)
Luther Rackley (*Bunta*)
Masumi Sekiya (*Hazel*)
William Ross (*Hal, Mother 1
Chief Technician*)
Carl Hansen (*Barney*)
Tetsu Nakamura (*Dr.
Kawamoto*)
Nancy Magsig (*Thrust's
Mistress on Plane*)

Don Maloney (*Mother 1
Captain*)
Vanessa Cristina (*Reporter*)
James Dale
Hyoe Enoki
Shunsuke Kariya (*Caveman
Chief*)
Gary Gundersen
Toru Kawai (*Tyrannosaurus*)
Katsumi Nimiamoto
(*Triceratops, front half*)

Alternate Titles
Der letzte Dinosaurier
(Germany)
Le Dernier Dinosaure (France)
*Viimeinen dinosaurus -
hirviöitten kuningas* [**The Last
Dinosaur: The King of
Monsters**] (Finland)
O Último Dinossauro (Brazil)
El último dinosaurio
(Columbia)
Ο Τελευταίος Δεινόσαυρος
(Greece)
Ostatni dinozaur (Poland)
Ultimul dinozaur (Romania)

"It's the last one!"
"So am I."
-Francesca Banks (Joan Van Ark) and Masten Thrust (Richard Boone)

A co-production between Tsuburaya Pro and Rankin-Bass, *The Last Dinosaur* is an underrated monster picture engagingly directed by Grasshoff and Kotani. It features a similar aesthetic to Kevin Connor's 1974 Edgar Rice Burroughs adaptation *The Land That Time Forgot*. *The Last Dinosaur* has deeper subtext than meets the eye and borrows literary elements from Burroughs, Sir Arthur Conan Doyle and even Herman Melville. It is accentuated by a strong lead performance from actor Richard Boone.

PLOT

Masten Thrust (Richard Boone) is the wealthy heir to an oil empire. His firm, Thrust Inc., drills for oil in the Arctic with the Polar Borer, a manned high tech drill. On one routine expedition, only geologist Chuck Wade (Steven Keats) comes back alive. He explains that his group was drilling through the icecaps and accidentally ended up in a volcanic basin. They were then attacked by a gigantic *Tyrannosaurus Rex,* with only Chuck escaping. Thrust has organized an expedition to this basin to investigate. Going with him are Chuck, his trusty Maasai tracker Bunta (Luther Rackley) and scientist Dr. Kawamoto (Tetsu Nakamura). Pulitzer Prize winning photojournalist Francesca "Frankie" Banks (Jon Van Ark) is selected to accompany them by the press pool. The sexist Masten refuses to take her along, but reneges after being seduced by her.

The Polar Borer is launched towards the basin. The company disembarks and sets up camp in this tropical prehistoric oasis as *pteranodons* fly overhead. Ashore, Frankie encounters a giant turtle before she and Masten are almost run down by a rampaging *Uintatherium.* The *Tyrannosaurus* attacks Masten, Chuck, Frankie and Bunta as they explore. Masten fires at the creature with a rifle he smuggled aboard the Borer. This enrages Chuck as Masten had promised the dinosaur would not be harmed. The group barely escape with their lives. The *Tyrannosaurus* next attacks and destroys the camp, killing Dr. Kawamoto who had stayed behind. The dinosaur grabs the Polar Borer in its jaws and tries to bury it in its boneyard. It awakens a *Triceratops* which it battles and overpowers, killing it with a bite to the neck. The group returns to find their camp destroyed and realize Kawamoto has been eaten. Masten vows to hunt and kill the *Tyrannosaurus* as the group realizes they're stranded as the Polar Borer's missing.

BACKGROUND

The Last Dinosaur is the first of several collaborations by Tsuburaya Pro and Rankin-Bass. Producers Arthur Rankin Jr. (1924-2014) and Jules Bass (1935-) had a long history of working with Japanese talent on their productions. Their company was first called Videocraft and early works were animated in Japan. Their iconic stop-motion opuses such as *Rudolph the Red-Nosed*

Reindeer (1964) and *Mad Monster Party* (1967) were also created in Japan. Calling the process "Animagic", they were animated by stop motion pioneer Tadahito Mochinaga. In addition, Rankin-Bass co-produced *King Kong Escapes* with Toho. Their later cel-animated works were also produced in Japan by Tezuka's Mushi Productions and Toru Hara's Topcraft. These include *Frosty the Snowman* (1969), *The Hobbit* (1977), *The Flight of Dragons* and *The Last Unicorn* (both 1982). Topcraft was where Hayao Miyazaki made *Nausicaa of the Valley of the Wind* shortly after. For *The Last Dinosaur*, Arthur Rankin supervised the script and co-ordinated the shoot. Jules Bass then handled the musical score and post-production.

PRINCIPAL PHOTOGRAPHY

The Last Dinosaur takes a while to get going. Early sequences focus on Thrust's grandiose persona. Yet it gets engaging once the characters end up in the film's Edgar Rice Burroughs-like lost world. The direction by Tsugunobu "Tom" Kotani and Alex Grasshoff is quite competent. Kotani mainly dealt with the film's aesthetics and directed the Japanese crew. Grasshoff, meanwhile, handled the American actors. Much of *The Last Dinosaur* was shot in the mountainous Kamikochi region, part of Chubu-Sangaku National Park in Nagano Prefecture. The weather was often miserable as it was shot during the area's rainy season. The film's tribe of cave people were played by Japanese actors, an interesting and effective choice. The location footage is cut together well with

the special effects unit's work. The climax is quite thrillingly edited.

ACTORS

The Last Dinosaur is surprisingly well acted. The film is driven by actor Richard Boone's impressive performance as Masten Thrust. Boone (1917-1981) was a Los Angeles native and World War II vet known for his Western roles. He was the star of the long-running show *Have Gun Will Travel* (1957-1963) and appeared in over 50 films. Some of his notable performances included as Pontius Pilate in 1953's *The Robe* and in John Wayne's *The Alamo* (1960). For Rankin-Bass, Boone would also voice Tolkien's iconic dragon Smaug in *The Hobbit* around the same time he appeared in *The Last Dinosaur*. By this time, Boone was struggling with alcoholism. Director Tsugunobu Kotani occasionally had to stop shooting because of Boone's hangovers. An aged Western star nearing the end of his life, Boone is perfectly cast as Thrust, a likable narcissist of sorts. Thrust's Friday-like tracker Bunta is played by basketball star Luther Rackley (1946-2017).

Joan Van Ark plays Francesca "Frankie" Banks. Frankie is a strong and feministic woman; the product of a progressive, modern world. As such, she plays well off Boone. Her character looks forward to Brie Larson's similar Mason Weaver in *Kong: Skull Island* (2017). Van Ark (1943-) also appeared in *Frogs* (1972). Character actor Steven Keats (1945-1994) plays Chuck, a more modern, intellectual man. Keats had appeared in the 1973 Boston crime thriller *The Friends of*

Eddie Coyle and in Michael Winner's *Death Wish* (1974) with Charles Bronson. Tragically he committed suicide. There's a love triangle of sorts between Masten, Frankie and Chuck that's well handled.

SFX

The special effects work is where *The Last Dinosaur* most shows off its Japaneseness. If the film were made in Hollywood by a different studio, stop motion effects would likely be employed. Tsuburaya Pro had actually considered using stop motion like their earlier show *Dinosaur Expedition Bornfree* (1976-77). They wound up settling for quicker, cheaper suitmation. Handled by Kazuo Sagawa (1939-), the effects are unconvincing but endearingly pantomime. It is comparable in aesthetic to the work done by Roger Dicken on Amicus' *The Land That Time Forgot*. The dinosaur suits were constructed from foam rubber. The *Tyrannosaurus Rex* is quite Godzillian. Its roar is even a re-mixed version of Godzilla's and the creature is played by Toru Kawai. Kawai had portrayed Godzilla only a few years prior in 1975's *Terror of Mechagodzilla*. He would go on to play Gamera in the little bit of original footage in *Gamera: Supermonster* (1980). A highlight is a gory *Triceratops* battle that made heavy use of piano wire. The *Tyrannosaurus* suit would be reused in Tsuburaya's later shows *Dinosaur War Izenborg* (1977-78) and *Dinosaur Corps Koseidon* (1978-79). *Izenborg* was later distributed stateside in a compilation feature called *Attack of the Super Monsters*.

The miniature work in *The Last Dinosaur* is well crafted. The staff went to particular lengths to make the miniature sets look lived in. Smoke machines were used to obscure wires and talcum powder was scattered in the boneyard set. A shot where a miniature helicopter lands was, amazingly, done by hand. In general, the FX work is more in line with television than a theatrical film. Some shots, however, are well on par with what Teruyoshi Nakano's unit at Toho was doing around the same time.

THEMES AND MOTIFS

Comic book author William Overgard's script is engagingly written. The plot follows the literary tradition of classic "lost world" stories. These include Jules Verne's *Journey to the Center of the Earth*, Sir Arthur Conan Doyle's *The Lost World* and Edgar Rice Burroughs' *Caspak* trilogy. Yet there's an oddly progressive subtext. Masten Thrust is a more complex character than first glance. His obsession with killing the *Tyrannosaurus* becomes akin to Captain Ahab's in Herman Melville's *Moby Dick*. As the catchy '70s theme song implies, he is the true *Last Dinosaur* of the title; a great white hunter far past his era and an aged cowboy whose salad days are behind him. In the end, he opts to stay behind to continue the Ahab-like pursuit of his ultimate trophy. His newfound companion is, fittingly, a primitive cavewoman. Beneath the surface of *The Last Dinosaur* is a morality play about a man too old fashioned for a changing world.

RELEASE AND LEGACY

Arthur Rankin and Jules Bass were keen on it being shown theatrically but *The Last Dinosaur* failed to entice a distributor stateside. It was released directly to television in the U.S, while Toho distributed the film some months later in Japan. This version played in English, subtitled in Japanese, though the film was later dubbed for TV. Several more Japanese co-productions with Rankin-Bass followed. All directed by Tsugunobu Kotani, these included *The Bermuda Depths* (1978), *The Ivory Ape* (1980) and *The Bushido Blade* (1981). The latter, influenced by *Shogun*, starred Richard Boone as Commodore Matthew Perry. The impressive supporting cast included Toshiro Mifune, Sonny Chiba, Mako, Tetsuro Tanba and James Earl Jones. Boone died shortly after production of *The Bushido Blade.* These films were all released as TV movies in the U.S., though some got theatrical distribution aboard.

ALTERNATE VERSIONS

The Last Dinosaur was released directly to television in the U.S. by ABC on February 11, 1977. This was over six months prior to its Japanese release in September. The U.S. version of *The Last Dinosaur* is cut down from its 106 minute international version to around 92 minutes. This was, presumably, to better fit it into a two hour slot. The scenes cut are mainly character development sequences. This includes an intimate scene between Masten and Frankie where she takes him into a bedroom and winds up showing him a slideshow of her photos. Also cut is a sizable portion of the film in the middle emphasizing the love triangle between Frankie, Masten and Chuck. Unlike Toho's 1.85:1 films which tended to be hard matted in camera, *The Last Dinosaur* was shot "open matte". This means the entire 35mm frame was exposed. The U.S. TV version has the matte opened and significantly more visual information on the tops and bottoms of the frame. Only the optical composite shots are cropped.

AMERICAN HOME VIDEO HISTORY

In the 1990s, *The Last Dinosaur* was released to VHS a handful of times by budget labels. These include Mintex Entertainment, Westlake Entertainment, Goodtimes Home Video, Alpha Video and Video Treasures. Some tapes featured the cut down 92 minute version and others the 106 minute international cut. In 2011, Warner Brothers released *The Last Dinosaur* uncut to DVD-R via their print-on-demand Archive line.

Further Viewing:

KING KONG ESCAPES
(1967)
キングコングの逆襲
Toho/Rankin-Bass/Universal,   *Director:* **Ishiro Honda**

King Kong Escapes was Rankin-Bass' first live action Japanese co-production. After the explosive success of *King Kong vs. Godzilla*, Toho were itching to make another Kong film as they still had the rights for five years. They attempted *Operation Robinson Crusoe*, but the American producers wanted Ishiro Honda for the project while Tomoyuki Tanaka had hired Jun Fukuda. As a result, Kong was replaced with Godzilla and the project became 1966's *Ebirah, Horror of the Deep*. Undaunted, Toho prepared another King Kong film with Honda and Eiji Tsuburaya at the helm. Elements from the concurrent *The King Kong Show* cartoon were used.

King Kong Escapes is hardly a top tier Honda monster movie but keeps you entertained with campy '60s hijinx. Hideyo Amamoto plays a particularly lip smacking baddie in Dr. Who. The U.S. version takes it one step further and has Paul Frees in full Burgermeister Meisterburger mode dub his voice. Amamoto would later play the similar role of Dr. Shinigami (Dr. Death) on TV's *Kamen Rider*. Madame Piranha is played by Toho siren Mie Hama. Hama (1943-) had previously encountered Kong in *King Kong vs. Godzilla* and was fresh off Bond girl stardom in *You Only Live Twice*. Rankin-Bass brought American B-lister Rhodes Reason to Japan to star, the brother of *This Island Earth*'s Rex Reason. Like Russ Tamblyn, Reason was mainly in it for a free trip to Japan and in interviews called Ishiro Honda a hack. The Fay Wray role is played by then-19 year old Linda Miller, a Pennsylvania-born expat model living in Japan at the time. Arthur Rankin chose Miller after seeing her in an ad spread in the magazine *Josei Seven*.

The original *King Kong* was one of Eiji Tsuburaya's favorite films to the point that he owned a print that he studied frame by frame. Here, he lovingly recreates *Kong* 33's iconic *Tyrannosaurus* battle in *tokusatsu* form. He even copies a shot or two verbatim. The Gorosaurus suit was the very first built by craftsman Nobuyuki Yasumaru, soon in charge of suitmaking in the 1970s. The Kong costume looks just as awful as the one in 1962, but is inhabited by Godzilla stuntman Haruo Nakajima. Nakajima does give a more ape-like performance. There's a lot of beautiful composite and miniature work, particularly in the Tokyo Tower finale. The FX work gets better and more imaginative as the film goes on. Mechani-Kong was built by Yasumaru's mentor Teizo Toshimitsu. The suit looks convincingly metallic and is far better executed. Indeed, Mechani-Kong proved an influence on Mechagodzilla. Toho showed an edited version of *King Kong Escapes* at their late 1973 Champion Matsuri Festival with a preview for *Godzilla vs. Mechagodzilla* attached. *Heisei* series FX director Koichi Kawakita particularly loved Mechani-Kong and years later wanted to bring it back in a Godzilla entry. Toho found out that the rights to anything Kong related came at a steep price and made *Godzilla vs. Mechagodzilla II* instead. Rankin-Bass, meanwhile, continued making Japanese co-productions for decades. *King Kong Escapes* wound up particularly influential on 2021's *Godzilla vs. Kong*.

LEGEND OF DINOSAURS AND MONSTER BIRDS

(1977)
恐竜・怪鳥の伝説

Toei, *Director:* **Junji Kurata**

The other Japanese dinosaur movie from 1977, *Legend of the Dinosaur and Monster Bird* is controversial. Stuart Galbraith, in *Monsters Are Attacking Tokyo*, calls it one of the worst Japanese monster films and *"without any redeeming values of any kind"*. *Legend of the Dinosaur* is a mess but far from that bad. It's better in Japanese and widescreen transfers reveal a film with surprisingly good production values. Toei had a unique "house style" quite different from Toho's, producing many crime and exploitation films in the 1970s. Toei was prolific on television with their *tokusatsu* output via the *Kamen Rider* and *Sentai* franchises. Yet they seldom produced theatrical *kaiju* films. *Legend of the Dinosaur and Monster Bird* is a monster flick produced in Toei's gritty aesthetic. The picture is laden with "dutch angles" and offbeat cinematography you'd seldom see in a Toho film. The atmospheric opening is superbly executed and stylishly directed by Kurata.

Tsunehiko Watase, often playing *yakuza* for Kinji Fukasaku, plays an intrepid geologist. He's trying to unravel the mystery of strange occurrences at Mount Fuji's Aokigahara Forest and Sai Lake. Aokigahara, nowadays, is best known as the "suicide forest" where Logan Paul comitted career suicide. Soon, a *Plesiosaur* shows up in Sai Lake and starts eating attendees of a country music festival being held at Fuji. *Legend of the Dinosaur* was primarily inspired by Steven Spielberg's *Jaws*. Toei CEO Shigeru Okada greenlit the film after seeing it. Toho was also at work on *Nessie*, an aborted co-production with England's Hammer. It's possible *Legend of the Dinosaur and Monster Bird* was also planned to compete with Toho's film. The similar American production *The Crater Lake Monster* was also made that same year. *Legend of the Dinosaur* would wind up being the most expensive Japanese film produced up to that time and the shoot took six months. The influence of *Jaws* is indeed apparent, with the "cardboard fin" gag even borrowed wholesale. As in *Jaws*, there's inventive use of underwater photography. Toei built their own giant pool just for the water attack sequences. In Toei fashion, there are some unsettling and surprisingly grisly moments. These, along with some nudity, are excised from Sandy Frank's U.S. version, amusingly released on Celebrity's "Just For Kids" video label.

Besides some horrible sexism, *Legend of the Dinosaur and Monster Bird* has a major flaw. Its effects work is surprisingly poor and unconvincing despite its budget. The monsters were made by Fuminori Ohashi right before he retired and are ineffective. They are stiff and poorly puppeteered. The final reel features the *Plesiosaur* doing battle with the monster bird of the title, a winged *Rhamphorhynchus*, as Fuji erupts. It is disappointingly disjointed. The film's potential, set up from the superb opening, crashes and burns in this inept finale. It's a shame, because *Legend of the Dinosaur and Monster Bird* would be a minor genre masterpiece with polished FX work. Oddly, the film was a huge hit in Soviet Russia. Okada would next greenlight a *Star Wars*-inspired film, *Message From Space*, that would fare better.

(1978)
バミューダの謎
Rankin-Bass/Tsuburaya Pro, *Director:* **Tsugunobu Kotani**

In *Monsters Are Attacking Tokyo*, Stuart Galbraith refers to *The Bermuda Depths* as *"more like a harlequin romance than a Gamera movie"*. Indeed, if it's a monster movie you're after, you'll be in for a disappointment as the film's monster turtle doesn't show up until well over an hour in. The second of Rankin-Bass' collaborations with Tsuburaya Pro, *The Bermuda Depths* was also released direct to television in the states but got a theatrical run in Japan. It swaps out the Doyle/Burroughs-style lost world tropes of *The Last Dinosaur* for Melvillian nautical stylings. *The Bermuda Depths* is overall a big step down from *The Last Dinosaur*: decent if unremarkable.

The Bermuda Depths boasts impressive underwater photography along with idyllic Bermuda locales. Save for the occasional insert of distinctively unreal Japanese FX work, it feels more like an American production. Leigh McCloskey, later to star in Dario Argento's *Inferno* plays Magnus, a dopey young man who has fallen head over heels for Jennie Haniver (*The Greatest American Hero*'s Connie Sellecca). Problem is, Jennie is actually a Calypso-like sea siren who drowned in the Bermuda Triangle in the 18th century. Carl (*Predator*) Weathers and the Santa Claus-like Burl Ives play notable supporting roles. *The Bermuda Depths* is slow to get going, though picks up some steam midway with a touch of lyrical beauty.

The final act strongly recalls *Jaws* with a maritime hunt for Jennie's monster sea turtle pet. Kazuo Sagawa's *tokusatsu* unit only takes command of the final 20 minutes of the picture. The FX footage shot in Japan isn't well integrated with the main unit's material filmed in Bermuda. *The Bermuda Depths* is capped with a downbeat end where several major characters die. That makes the film somewhat unique. Overall, *The Bermuda Depths* is a mixed but at times intriguing bag.

AKIO JISSOJI
The Tokusatsu Expressionist

実相寺昭雄

3/29/1937-11/29/2006

Something of an unsung hero in Western fan circles, Akio Jissoji was an eccentric talent in Japanese genre television and cinema. He is best known for directing some of the best *Ultra* series episodes. Jissoji also directed some very transgressive, psychosexual works far outside of the realm of children's entertainment. Along with Kihachi Okamoto, he was a major aesthetic influence on *Evangelion* director Hideaki Anno. Jissoji was born in Yotsuya ward in Tokyo. He spent his early childhood in Japanese occupied Qingdao, China before his family returned to Japan after the defeat. He spent the rest of his youth in what is now Kita ward in Tokyo. Jissoji attended Waseda University where he studied French literature. After graduation, he got a job with the TV studio Tokyo Broadcasting System (TBS) where he began to be an assistant director on live TV shows and Japanese soap operas.

Jissoji was promoted to director in 1961 at the age of only 24. His broadcasts became known for their artistic style early on. This caused friction between Jissoji and the station's brass. An usually styled broadcast with beloved idol Hibari Misora drew ire from her fanbase and nearly got him fired. In 1965, Jissoji began working with Tsuburaya Pro as TBS thought his odd sensibility would be more at home there. Eiji and Hajime Tsuburaya were indeed more receptive to his outside-the-box ideas. He wrote two scripts for *Ultra Q*, though neither were produced. He directed a television documentary on Eiji Tsuburaya at the same time. Jissoji also met and married actress Chisako Hara (1936-2020). The two would go on to have a daughter, Ako, born in 1967.

For Tsuburaya's subsequent show, *Ultraman*, Jissoji was put in charge of some of the *most memorable episodes. These include "The Underground Destruction Work", "My Home is Earth" and "The Monster Graveyard"*. Jissoji's episodes had something special to them. In stark contrast to many of the other directors who worked on the show, Jissoji used wide-angle lenses, expressionistic lighting and created visually stunning images on the lower budget of television. His melancholy *Ultraman* episodes began to get him some attention. Not all of the other directors liked his creative approach, especially Samaji Nonagase and Koichi Takano. The production staff were often frustrated by his unorthodox methods. It was thought his episodes were so Japanese that they made exporting the shows internationally difficult. Jissoji did several more interesting episodes for *Ultraseven* (1967-68), including the now suppressed *"From a Planet With Love"*. Jissoji also worked on Tsuburaya's horror-themed show *Operation: Mystery* (1968-69).

In 1969, Jissoji made his feature film directorial debut with *When Twilight Draws,* scripted by Nagisa Oshima. He followed this up with a series of surreal, almost experimental erotic dramas produced by the Art Theater Guild. These included his Buddhist trilogy *Mujo* (1970), *Mandala* (1971) and *Poem* (1972), along with 1974's *It Was a Faint Dream*. His next picture was *Utamaro's World* (1977), which told the story of famed printmaker Kitagawa Utamaro and his years making pornographic prints. Jissoji became less prolific in the '80s, but made a major comeback with 1988's *Tokyo: The Last Megalopolis* for Toho. A confusingly plotted, massively budgeted adaptation of a beloved novel by Hiroshi Aramata, it went on to become one of the top grossing films that year. The picture featured designs by *Alien*'s H.R. Giger along with an early use of high definition video technology for its compositing. The portrayal of character Yasunori Kato by actor Kyusaku Shimada has become quite iconic. Jissoji was next hired by Tsuburaya Pro to helm *Ultra Q the Movie: Legend of the Stars* (1990).

His following film *Walker on the Roof* (1992) was based on a novel by *Taisho*-era pulp author Edogawa Rampo. A huge influence on Jissoji and iconic figure, Rampo was something of the Agatha Christie of Japan. The film was extremely controversial for its full frontal nudity that was censored in Japanese prints. This was followed by another *Rampo*-based film, 1998's *Murder on D Street*. Jissoji also helmed episodes of *Ultraman Tiga* and *Ultraman Dyna*. Late in his career, he directed episodes of *Ultra Q: Dark Fantasy*, *Ultraman Max* and a segment of the anthology film *Rampo Noir* (2005). Even up to his death in 2006, Jissoji was extremely active on projects. He is buried at Somei Cemetery in Toshima, Tokyo.

Selected Filmography (*as director*)
Ultraman [*episodes 14, 15, 22, 23, 34, 35*] (1966-67, TV)
Ultraseven [*episodes 8, 12, 43, 45*] (1967-68, TV)
Operation: Mystery [*episodes 4, 5, 23, 25*] (1968-69, TV)
When Twilight Draws (1969)
Mujo (1970)
Mandala (1971)

Poem (1972)
It Was a Faint Dream (1974)
Utamaro's World (1977)
Ultraman (1979)
Tokyo: The Last Megalopolis (1988)
Ultra Q the Movie: Legend of the Stars (1990)
Walker on the Roof (1992)
Ultraman Tiga [*episodes 37 and 40*] (1996-97, TV)

Ultraman Dyna [*episode 38*] (1997-98)
Murder on D Street (1998)
Ultra Q: Dark Fantasy [*episodes 24, 25*] (2004)
Ultraman Max [*episodes 22, 24*] (2005)
Rampo Noir (2005) [segment *"Mirror Hell"*]

BLOOD TYPE : BLUE

ブルークリスマス

Blue Christmas
Toho, 11/23/1978 (*Showa 53*), 10 Reels (3,643 meters), 132:36, 35mm, Academy (1.37:1), color, monaural sound

Crew
Producers: Shinichi Shimada, Kenji Kakiuchi
Director: Kihachi Okamoto
Screenplay: So Kuramoto
Director of Photography: Daisaku Kimura

Music: Masaru Sato
Editor: Yoshitami Kuroiwa
Production Design: Kazuo Takenaka
Sound Recordist: Noboyuki Tanaka
Lighting: Shinji Kojima

Production Manager: Takehide Morichi
Still Photographer: Matsuo Yoshizaki

Cast
Hiroshi Katsuno (*Taisuke Oki*)

Keiko Takeshita (*Saeko Nishida*)

Tetsuya Nakadai (*Kazuya Minami*)

Eiji Okada (*Professor Mitsuhiko Hyodo*)

Kaoru Yachigusa (*Mrs. Hyodo*)

Harumi Arai (*Yuko Takamatsu*)

Yusuke Okada (*Kidokoro*)

Etsushi Takahashi (*Captain Sawaki*)

Masaya Oki (*Harada*)

Tetsuya Ushio (*Okamura*)

Eitaro Ozawa (*Godai*)

Shuji Otaki (*Takeiri*)

Shizuo Chujo (*Numata*)

Shinsuke Ashida (*Shuji Aiba*)

Ichiro Nakatani (*Chief of Staff Usami*)

Shogo Shimada (*Director Yoshiike*)

Kappei Matsumoto (*Director Suzuki*)

Tomo Nagai (*Production Director Shiro*)

Kunie Tanaka (*Kazuo Nishida*)

Hideyo Amamoto (*Representative*)

Shin Kishida (*Representative's Aide*)

Shigeru Koyama (*Agency Director*)

Shinji Ogawa (*Assistant Nakamoto*)

Yoshio Inaba (*Special Forces Commander*)

Toru Takeuchi (*Commander Tamura*)

Minako Okamoto (*Mrs. Minami*)

Yoji Matsuda (*Osamu Minami*)

Naoko Otani (*Girl in Coffee Shop*)

Daigo Kusano (*Underground Organization Leader*)

Toshitaka Ito (*Underground Organization Member*)

Ban Kojika (*Barber*)

Sachio Sakai (*Taxi Driver*)

Hugh Graham

Theodore Köber

John Mayer

Dieter Oeler

Curtis Bond

Gregg Bushta

Alain Daumalle

Chouard Pienick

Allen Lieb

Euginia D'Ambrosio

Bill Gold

Jean-Michel Dbernay

<u>Alternate Titles</u>
The Blue Stigma (alternate English title)

"When the time comes, global leaders will have to choose the safest way to minimize the problem. That is, to view the blue bloods as a menace and assure that all of humanity fears them. Politicians throughout history have chosen that path."
-Professor Hyodo (Eiji Okada)

Blood: Type Blue is a dark sci-fi parable by veteran director Kihachi Okamoto (*Samurai Assassin, Japan's Longest Day*). More a political thriller than a *tokusatsu* film, *Blood: Type Blue* unravels an engaging mystery. With a grim outlook on human nature, it tells the tragic story of human prejudice at its most base. The film has an epic scope, ensemble cast and is both well written and narratively compelling.

PLOT

Defense agency recruit Oki (Hiroshi Katsuno) gets his hair cut at a barber shop.

Meanwhile, Professor Hyodo (Eiji Okada) gives a talk at the Kyoto scientific conference. Hyodo claims proof of the existence of UFOs, drawing rage and consternation from other scientists there. Checking himself into his hotel, Hyodo is taken hostage by a group of American operatives. Unusual news rolls in as the Soviet Premiere "urgently" meets with the U.S. President at the White House. Minami (Tatsuya Nakadai), an investigative reporter for the Japan Broadcasting Company meets with correspondent Kidokoro (Yusuke Okada). Kidokoro noticed something odd about his girlfriend, up and coming starlet Yuko Takamatsu (Harumi Arai). She was at his apartment the other day, cooking. Yuko cut herself and her blood was bright blue.

Minami's boss Godai (Eitaro Ozawa) assigns him to look into Professor Hyodo's recent disappearance. Minami interviews Hyodo's wife (Kaoru Yachigusa) and laboratory assistant, both of whom have no idea of his whereabouts. The assistant points him in the direction of Professor Maehata who studies blood. Minami meets with Maehata's assistant Nakamoto (Shinji Ogawa). He says Maehata and Hyodo were doing research into squid blood, which is blue. While presenting his findings to Godai, Minami lets slip that Yuko Takamatsu's blood has apparently turned blue.

Professor Hyodo's house suddenly burns down. A young French student is next found to have developed blue blood. This is quickly covered up. UFOs are seen over Japan and the Self Defense Force is sent after them. Both the UFOs and pursuing jets vanish from radar. Godai confides in government official Takeiri (Shuji Otaki) that Hyodo is currently in the U.S. He's being held by a clandestine organization called "Blue Note". In Italy and Russia, babies are born with blue blood. Back in Japan, the international pop group The Humanoids arrive for the Tokyo leg of a concert tour to much fanfare. Aiba (Shinsuke Ashida), the Vice Minister of Defense, mentions to Chief of Staff Usami (Ichiro Nakatani) that the White House,

Kremlin and Japanese government have undertaken plans to exterminate those with blue blood.

Meanwhile, The Humanoids hold a press conference and Yuko attends their ensuing party. The party goers start smoking marijuana and are raided by the authorities. Yuko is arrested for possession. Later at a hospital in Tokyo, a baby is born with blue blood from a blue-blooded mother. A government representative (Hideyo Amamoto) and his aide (Shin Kishida) order the head doctor to murder the mother and child. Yuko's arrest gives JBC the perfect excuse to drop her from their show. A distraught Yuko then commits apparent suicide. The defense contractor Oki, meanwhile, finds out that friend Harada has disappeared in his jet with the UFOs. He begins to date a girl who works at the barbershop he frequents, Saeko Nishida (Keiko Takeshita).

Godai sends Minami to America to try to track down Professor Hyodo. Before his flight, Kidokoro confronts Minami, revealing that the marijuana was planted at The Humanoids' party as a conspiracy. One of the men handing out the marijuana was recognized by Yuko's manager as Oki. Kidokoro even suspects Yuko herself may have been assassinated. Another baby is born in Tokyo with blue blood, this time to a red-blooded mother and a blue-blooded father. Minami arrives in New York City and begins hunting for the whereabouts of Professor Hyodo. Kidokoro gives Minami a lead, telling him to contact an informant named Franco. Minami soon meets Professor Hyodo. He tells him the number of blue-blooded people are increasing around the world along with UFO sightings. Hyodo explains that the world's leaders are planning to exterminate the blue bloods. They are spreading propaganda to make the populace fear them. Hyodo reveals the truth about Blue Note to Minami. It's not a UFO investigation organization. It's a medical facility where blue bloods are lobotomized and experimented on. Realizing that they're being watched, Hyodo tells Minami to meet him at his apartment before he's spirited away. Minami is informed by the Japanese embassy that he will be arrested unless he returns to Japan.

BACKGROUND

In 1977, writer So Kuramoto published a story, *Blue Christmas,* in Kinema Junpo. It caught the eye of Toho's Tomoyuki Tanaka who decided to greenlight a film adaptation. Seasoned director Kihachi Okamoto was hired. Kuramoto turned his story into a screenplay with input from Okamoto. In Kuramoto's story, the blue blood in humans happened spontaneously. Okamoto had recurring dreams of encountering a UFO and so that element was added to make the film more clearly science fiction. It's possible Steven Spielberg's then-recent *Close Encounters of the Third Kind* was also influential on the concept.

PRINCIPAL PHOTOGRAPHY

The script's Christmas setting was problematic for production as the shooting schedule would not line up with the holiday season. Okamoto sent a cameraman out to film stock shots of holiday festivities in late 1977. Kuramoto's main condition was that the script not be altered. Okamoto found this exceedingly difficult with the script's intrigue and scope. Indeed, Toho contemplated releasing *Blood Type: Blue* as a TV mini-series rather than a theatrical movie. Okamoto was able to get Kuramoto to agree to cut several scenes. These include a sequence featuring the U.S. President lamenting at having to commit genocide. Early prints shown in certain Japanese cities may have contained the president scene.

Blood Type: Blue is a tense sci-fi thriller that is engagingly plotted. From samurai films like *Sword of Doom* and *Kill!* to his war films like *Desperado Outpost* and *The Human Bullet,* Kihachi Okamoto specialized in a dark wry satire. This is at the top form in *Blood Type: Blue.* Okamoto's direction and Kuramoto's script present a scathing commentary on human prejudice. The film evokes John Frankenheimer's best work like *The Manchurian Candidate* and *Seven Days in May.*

The cinematography by Daisuke Kimura, who shot the Sakyo Komatsu adaptations *Submersion of Japan* and *Virus,* is superb. Unlike many of Toho's '70s films which were shot anamorphic, *Blood Type: Blue* was filmed in Academy with more versatile spherical lenses. The use of shallow depth of field is impressive. The sense of scope is surprisingly epic with scenes shot on location in New York City and Paris. The New York scenes are unique. Though still an unusual view of America through a Japanese lens, the location shooting lends it more realism than prior depictions, often recreated on a soundstage with amateur expats. The film's depiction of military action is also quite realistic with authentic hardware. It should be noted that Toho's special effects unit is barely, if at all, employed for *Blood: Type Blue*. Whereas other directors would have Teruyoshi Nakano and company hang miniature UFOs from piano wire, Okamoto disliked working with special effects. As such, he sought to depict the film's phenomena in a minimalistic style.

ACTORS

The film features an ensemble cast with many of Okamoto's favorite players. These include Tatsuya Nakadai, Hideyo Amamoto, Kunie Tanaka, Shin Kishida and many others. Kunie Tanaka (1932-2021) was a very distinctive Japanese character actor. He was well liked by a handful of directors including Masaki Kobayashi, Okamoto and Kinji Fukasaku. Tanaka was best known for playing a comedic toadie to Yuzo Kayama in Toho's beloved *Young Guy* series. Lead Hiroshi Katsuno (1949-) was a young actor who got his start in television. He made an impression playing police detective "Texas" opposite Yujiro Ishihara on *Roar At the Sun* (1972-86). Later, he would appear in Toho's *Deathquake* (1980). Consummate Eiji Okada (1920-1995) appears in *Blood Type: Blue* as

well. He was best known for his roles in Alain Resnais' *Hiroshima Mon Amour* (1959) and Hiroshi Teshigahara's *Woman in the Dunes* (1964). He also appeared in wondrously awful *The X From Outer Space* (1967) along with Masahiro Shinoda's *Silence* (1971) and Toshiya Fujita's *Lady Snowblood* (1973). Veteran actress Kaoru Yachigusa also appears. For genre fans, Yachigusa (1931-2019) is best known for her role in *The Human Vapor* (1960). First a beloved Takarazuka Revue stage player, she appeared in numerous films including Hiroshi Inagaki's *Samurai* trilogy, Shiro Toyoda's *Snow Country* (1957) and Shinoda's *With Beauty and Sorrow* (1965). Prolific character actors Eitaro Ozawa, Ichiro Nakatani (1930-2004) and Hideji Otaki (1925-2012) are also on hand. The three starred in well over a hundred films each.

MUSIC

Masaru Sato, who often worked with Okamoto, does *Blood Type: Blue*'s soundtrack. Rare for Sato, it features haunting, electronic and synthesizer tones that enhance the film's unsettling tension well. Most memorable is a faux English pop song, *"Blue Christmas"*, by the Rolling Stones-like The Humanoids. The song, performed by popular singer and guitarist Char (born Hisato Takenaka), is quite an upbeat ditty. Juxtaposed with the dark and disturbing themes of *Blood Type: Blue*, it adds a sense of strong "mood whiplash" that is haunting. *Blood Type: Blue* features two iconic classical pieces: Bach's *"Jesus Bleibet Meine Freude"* and Handel's *"Messiah"*. Both later found their way onto *Neon Genesis Evangelion*'s soundtrack.

THEMES AND MOTIFS

Blood Type: Blue has a jet black view of human nature. Despite the lack of scientific evidence that the blue bloods represent any threat, the world's politicians are quick to persecute them. It's a classic example of a marginalized group seen as "the other" and targeted. This has been a theme throughout human history and still resonates in ongoing racial conflicts. In *Blood Type: Blue*, references to Nazi Germany are made outright. Director Okamoto and screenwriter Kuramoto hold no pretenses to the goodness of humanity. *Blood Type: Blue* is not a hopeful film. It's a simple story of human prejudice at its most cruel. It's as if the film's aliens turned people's blood blue to give humanity a test in empathy. A test humans miserably fail. Besides invoking the Holocaust, *Blood Type: Blue* foreshadows the HIV/AIDS epidemic. HIV would emerge only a few short years after the release of this film and bring similar stigma to the gay community worldwide.

RELEASE AND LEGACY

Blood Type: Blue was a dismal flop at the Japanese box office. It was also skewered critically. Domestic audiences were confused by the film's complex plot threads, multitude of characters and intricate motivations. Yet it did have its fans. Writer Minoru Tanaka called it the greatest Japanese film of the year. Another huge fan of the picture is director

Hideaki Anno. Anno put multiple references to the film in his *anime* masterwork *Neon Genesis Evangelion*. This includes the Angels' pattern being "blue" with the words *"Blood Type: Blue"* seen on NERV's computer monitors. A few shots from the movie were even copied wholesale.

ALTERNATE VERSIONS

Aside from limited release in a few Japanese American theaters in San Francisco, *Blood: Type Blue* was not released in the U.S. No known English dubbed version was made.

AMERICAN HOME VIDEO HISTORY

Blood: Type Blue was also never released to American home video in any format.

Further Viewing:

THE MAN WHO STOLE THE SUN

(1979)

太陽を盗んだ男

Kitty Films/Toho, *Director:* **Kazuhiko Hasegawa**

Another satirical political thriller with loose sci-fi elements, *The Man Who Stole the Sun* is a classic Japanese '70s film. The film is brilliantly written by Leonard Schrader (1943-2006), the brother of Paul Schrader (*Taxi Driver*) who spent years in Japan. He was later best known for his Oscar winning scripts for *Kiss of the Spider Woman* and *Mishima: A Life in Four Chapters*. *The Man Who Stole the Sun* is engagingly directed by independent filmmaker Kazuhiko Hasegawa.

The concept came about when Hasegawa (1946-) was visiting Los Angeles and met Schrader. He told Schrader that he was born in Hiroshima and in the womb was exposed to radiation from the bomb. The two were inspired to collaborate on a *Dr. Strangelove*-like political satire about nuclear weapons.

Famed pop singer Kenji "Julie" Sawada stars as gum-chewing science teacher Makoto Kido. Sawada (1948-) was a member of the Beatlemania rockabilly band The Tigers before becoming part of the supergroup Pyg. One of their most famous songs *"Flower, Sun, Moon"* was used in an episode of *Return of Ultraman*. Afterwards, Sawada went solo and became known as the *"David Bowie of Japan"*. David Bowie and Sawada would formally meet during one of Bowie's many Japanese outings. Like Bowie, he played the occasional film role in addition to his music career. Here, his character is an almost Alex DeLarge-level sociopath. Early on in the film Kido tests sleeping gas on his cat before using it to steal a gun from a police officer. Yet like Paul Schrader's Travis Bickle, he's an oddly likable anti-hero. He shows a few moments of humanity, such as later taking pity on his cat when it dies from ingesting plutonium. One day, while on a school field trip, his bus is hijacked by a crazy ex-Imperial Army veteran (Yunosuke Ito) who demands to see the Emperor. Grizzled police inspector Yamashita, played by screen *yakuza* don Bunta Sugawara, takes the hijacker out. After this, Kido snaps. He decides to, ala Walter White, use his science teacher knowledge for nefarious purposes. Rather than *Breaking Bad*, he opts to build his own atomic weapon. He robs plutonium from a nuclear power plant in a sequence that feels Tarkovsky-like. Much of the film's mid act is dedicated to surprisingly detailed bomb-making sequences. Kido builds a weapon of mass destruction with a disturbingly nonchalant glee.

Soon afterwards, Kido holds Tokyo at ransom, making incidental demands of the authorities. Yamashita is put on the case and determined to catch him. Kido calls himself "Number 9" to the police as he is the 9th body in the world to possess a nuclear weapon. Kimiko Ikegami (*House*) plays an opportunistic radio DJ who falls for Kido. She convinces him to demand that the Rolling Stones, banned from Japan due to drug charges, be allowed to play a concert in Tokyo. The driven ferocity of Kido and Yamashita is paralleled, leading to an equally ferocious confrontation between the two. The finale is bleak: Kido, now dying of radiation poisoning, detonates his DIY nuke.

The Man Who Stole the Sun had a large budget and difficult shoot. Assistant director Shinji Somai and his second unit were even arrested while shooting outside the Diet Building. The film's satire of nuclear destruction was considered in bad taste by many in Japan. There's a disturbing and especially controversial sequence where Kido poisons people at a public swimming pool with plutonium. Director Hasegawa was able to deflect these controversies with his *hibakusha* status. His direction builds tension throughout; a thrilling hostage sequence capping the first reel. Late in the picture, there's a masterfully executed car chase scene. Tautly edited, it's on par with anything by William Friedkin. The score by Takayuki Inoue is quite unsettling at times. It mixes foreboding chords with upbeat melodies, inducing mood whiplash. The cinematography by Tetsuo Suzuki is stunning and the production values are near Hollywood-quality. *Tokusatsu* fans will chuckle at an *Ultraman Leo* cameo.

Despite its controversies, *The Man Who Stole the Sun* would go on to win multiple awards at the Japanese Academy the following year. It is now a cult classic in Japan. Kenji Sawada's next big role would be as Christian samurai Amakusa Shiro Tokisada in Kinji Fukasaku's *Samurai Reincarnation* (1981). Years later, one of *The Man Who Stole the Sun*'s main musical cues would be reused in *Evangelion 2.0: You Can (Not) Advance* (2009). Shinji Higuchi storyboarded the film and *Man Who Stole* is one of his favorite movies.

KIHACHI OKAMOTO
The Satirist

岡本喜八
2/17/1924-2/19/2005

"Only half of my classmates survived the war and none of my childhood friends survived. I was the only one who came back. I developed this attitude that all this wasn't so much a tragedy as a comedy. You know, everything was so fucked up, everything was so sad it was funny."
-Kihachi Okamoto, *Monsters Are Attacking Tokyo* by Stuart Galbraith (1998)

Kihachi Okamoto was another versatile and prolific Japanese director. He was something of a Nippon Sam Peckinpah. Okamoto worked in many genres, though he specialized in samurai, war and gangster pictures, all peppered with his trademark wry humor and social satire. Okamoto was born in 1924 in Yokkaichi, Tottori Prefecture. He attended Meiji University, wanting to make films after seeing John Ford's *Stagecoach*. Upon graduation he was to join Toho as assistant director. The situation on the war front was worsening, however. The Japanese military was desperate for new recruits. Okamoto was thus drafted into the Army Corp of Engineers in 1943. He was part of the *"generation that never came back"*. By this time, young Japanese men in their teens and 20s were considered fodder for the Imperial war machine; often sent to die as *kamikaze*. Okamoto escaped this fate, but watching numerous friends die in air raids gave him a bitter insight into the ugliness of humanity. This theme would resonate in his work throughout his coming film career.

After the war ended, Okamoto was determined to be a film director and joined Toho as an AD. For over 10 years, he labored under directors such as Mikio Naruse, Ishiro Honda, Senkichi Taniguchi and Masahiro Makino. Toho liked some of his story ideas and in 1958 he was promoted to director. His first film was *All About Marriage*. He soon gained attention with *Desperado Outpost* (1959). It was a satirical war film and "Sukiyaki Western" of sorts set in Japanese occupied China. It was popular enough to lead to a sequel: *Westward Desperado* (1960).

In the 1960s, Okamoto made a name for himself with films like the noirish *The Last Gunfight* (1960) and the gangster musical *Ah Bomb* (1964). He also began to specialize in dark *jidai-gekis* like *Samurai Assassin* (1965) and *The Sword of Doom* (1966). His bizarre gangster flick *The Age of Assassins* (1967) got him some notoriety as Toho was hesitant to release it. In the late '60s, he directed the historical drama *Japan's Longest Day* (also 1967) and the samurai films *Kill!* (1968) and *Red Lion* (1969). Independently for the Art Theatre Guild, he directed the bitter World War II satire *The Human Bullet* (1968), his most personal film about the war. It was said Tomoyuki Tanaka courted him to direct a *tokusatsu* production. Okamoto refused as he disliked the genre and working with special effects. Okamoto was also to direct an adaptation of the novel *Japan's Apaches* by Sakyo Komatsu but the project fell through.

In the '70s, he directed films like the crossover *Zatoichi Meets Yojimbo* (1970) with Shintaro Katsu and Toshiro Mifune and the violent war drama *Battle of Okinawa* (1971). After 1977's *Sanshiro Sugata* and 1978's *Blood Type: Blue*, he left Toho and went freelance. He was credited as supervisor to the anime *Gatchaman* but was apparently uninvolved. Creator Hisayuki Toriumi was a huge fan and Okamoto allowed his name on the project to give it clout. Okamoto was also something of a mentor figure to younger director Nobuhiko Obayashi. His later films included the period musical *Dixieland Daimyo* (1986), *Rainbow Kids* (1991) and the international co-production *East Meets West* (1995). *Rainbow Kids* would net him the Japanese Academy Award for Best Director. His final film was *Vengeance For Sale* in 2002.

Okamoto died in 2005 of esophageal cancer. He is still an obscure director in the West but he does have admirers including John Milius (*Conan the Barbarian*, *Red Dawn*). Retrospectives on his work were held at the Berlin Film Festival in 2007 and São Paulo International Film Festival in 2008. Hideaki Anno is another huge fan. Anno has watched *Battle of Okinawa* over 100 times and interviewed Okamoto in 1996. He put pointed references to various Okamoto works in *Gunbuster*, *Neon Genesis Evangelion* and *Shin Godzilla*. In the latter, a photo of Kihachi Okamoto is used to represent the character Goro Maki.

Selected Filmography (*as director*)
Half Human (1955) [assistant director]
All About Marriage (1957)

Desperado Outpost (1959)
The Last Gunfight (1960)
Wayward Desperado (1960)
Blueprint of A Murder (1961)
Warring Clans (1963)

The Elegant Life of Mr. Everyman (1963)
Ah Bomb (1964)
Samurai Assassin (1965)
Fort Graveyard (1965)

The Sword of Doom (1966)
The Age of Assassins (1967)
Japan's Longest Day (1967)
Kill! (1968)
The Human Bullet (1968)
Red Lion (1969)

Zatoichi Meets Yojimbo (1970)
Battle of Okinawa (1971)
Aoba Shigereru (1974)
Sanshiro Sugata (1977)
Noisy Dynamite (1978)

Blood Type: Blue (1978)
Dixieland Daimyo (1986)
Rainbow Kids (1991)
East Meets West (1995)
Vengeance For Sale (2002)

VIRUS

復活の日

Fukkatsu no Hi "The Day of Resurrection"
Kadokawa/TBS Distribution/Toho, 6/28/1980 (*Showa 55*), 4,281 meters, 156:03, 35mm, Spherical (1.85:1), color, stereo

Crew
Producer: Haruki Kadokawa
Associate Producers: Yutaka Okada, Takashi Ohashi
Director: Kinji Fukasaku
Screenplay: Koji Takada, Gregory Knapp, Kinji Fukasaku, Sakyo Komatsu (novel *"Virus: The Day of Resurrection"*)
Director of Photography: Daisaku Kimura
Music: Teo Macero
Editor: Akira Suzuki
Art Director: Yoshinaga Yokoi
First Assistant Directors: Junnosuke Takasu, J. Anthony Robinow
Assistant Directors: Kenichiro Fujiyama, Kazuo Yoshida
Second Assistant Director: Jesse Nishihata
Gaffers: Hideki Mochizuki, Bob Gallant
Lighting Technicians: Isao Koyama, Shohei Iriguchi
Key Grip: Jim Craig
Camera Assistants: Masahiro Kishimoto, Toshifumi Nobusaka, Tsutomu Takada

Sound Mixer: Kenichi Benitani
Sound Recording: Minoru Nobuoka
Continuity: Mikoko Koyama
Assistant Art Directors: Fumio Ogawa, Masumi Suzuki, Lindsay Goddard, Masayoshi Omodaka
Casting: Shinichi Nakata, Howard Ryshpan, Masayoshi Omodaka
Propmasters: Don Miloyevich, Fernand Durand
Wardrobe: Arthur Rowselle
Makeup: Kathleen Mifsud
Production Managers: Isao Nagaoka, Susan A. Lewis, Katsumasa Amano
Special Effects Miniatures: Greg Jein, Michael Minor
Special Effects Assistant Director: Ichiro Higa
Transportation: Robert Bartman
Still Photographer: Takashi Ikeda

Cast
Masao Kusakari (*Dr. Shuzo Yoshizumi*)

Bo Svenson (*Major Carter*)
Olivia Hussey (*Marit*)
George Kennedy (*Admiral Conway*)
Chuck Connors (*Captain McCloud*)
Glenn Ford (*President Richardson*)
Henry Silva (*General Garland*)
Robert Vaughn (*Senator Barkley*)
Tsunehiko Watase (*Yasuo Tatsuno*)
Sonny Chiba (*Dr. Yamauchi*)
Isao Natsuyagi (*Dr. Nakanishi*)
Yumi Takigawa (*Noriko*)
Cec Linder (*Dr. Henri La Tour*)
Stuart Gillard (*Dr. Edward Meyer*)
George Touliatos (*Colonel Rankin*)
Stephanie Faulkner (*Sarah Baker*)
Kensaku Morita (*Ryuji Sanazawa*)
Toshiyuki Nagashima (*Akimasa Matsuo*)
Chris Wiggins (*Dr. Borodinov*)
Edward James Olmos (*Captain Lopez*)

Colin Fox (Agent Z)
Ken Pogue (Dr. Krause)
Ken Ogata (Dr. Tsuchiya)
Eve Crawford (Dr. Irma Ollich)
Nicholas Campbell (U.S. Radio Operator)
John Evans (Captain Nevsky)
John Granik (Dr. Turowicz)
John Bayliss (Major King)
Ava Hovanessian (Major Giron)
Ted Follows (Major Barnes)
Danielle Schneider (Secretary)
Diane Lasko (Secretary)
Laura Pennington (Secretary)
Julie Khaner (Secretary)
Larry Reynolds (Morisson)
David Gardner (Watt)
J. Roger Periard (Orderly)
Dan Kippy (Reed)
William Binney (Simmons)
Ron Hartman (Dr. Rogers)
Wally Bondarenko (East German Guard)
Jim Bearden (Stasi Officer)
Ken Camroux (Officer Jones)
Gordon Thompson (Nereid Radio Operator)
John Rutter (Nereid Sailor)

Alfred Humphreys (Nereid Sailor)
Peter Hepplestom (Periscope Operator)
Matt Hawthorne (Nereid Navigator)
David Griffiths (Nereid First Officer)
Michael Tough (Young Sailor)
Jan Muszynski (Ensign Smirnov)
Charles Northcote (T232 Sonar)
Mitsuko Oka (Yoshiko Tatsuno)
Etsutaka Kase (Asahi Tatsuno)
Ichiro Kijima (Dr. Tadokoro)
Takashi Noguchi (Hospital Intern)
Nenji Kobayashi (Hospital Intern)
Tayori Hinatsu (Nurse)
Keiko Ito (Nurse)
Tomoko Igarashi (Nurse)
Sachiko Sato (Nurse)
Sanae Nakahara (Mother)
Yukiko Watanabe (Daughter)
Richard Aryes (Little Man Spy)

Jefferson Mappin (Big Man Spy)
Dick Grant (Cessna Pilot)
Tyler Miller (Boy Cossack)
Charles Campbell (TV Narrator, voice)
Marcello Krakov (Toby Anderson, voice)
William Ross (Australian Weathering Team)
Joan Beldam (Gree)

Alternate Titles
Overkill - Durch die Hölle zur Ewigkeit [**Overkill: From Hell to Eternity**] (Germany)
Exterminio [**Extermination**] (Spain)
Ultimo rifugio: Antartide [**The Last Refuge: Antarctica**] (Italy)
Ameaça Planetária [**Planetary Threat**] (Portugal)
Livsfarlig virus [**Deadly Virus**] (Denmark)
Dødelig virus [**Lethal Virus**] (Norway)
Вирус (Russia)

"Well all he said was, it started out like a simple cold or flu mostly and then quickly turned into pneumonia. There were symptoms of other diseases as well. But he didn't think it was any of those things. He thought it was something else."
-Australian Weathering Team Member (William Ross)

The largest scale production in Japanese film history to that point, *Virus* brings another prophetic novel by Sakyo Komatsu to vivid life. This adaptation was helmed by Kinji Fukasaku, later known for the dystopian masterpiece *Battle Royale* (2000). Fukasaku, a prolific director who until then specialized in gangster films, crafts a sprawling apocalyptic epic. Difficult to watch in the wake of COVID-19, *Virus* combines the nightmares of biowarfare and nuclear annihilation. Fukasaku's best genre film, *Virus* boasts impressive first and final acts and a bleak tone coupled with top tier production values.

PLOT

In December 1983, the British submarine *Nereid* arrives in a deserted Tokyo Bay. All life in the city has perished. The

submarine's captain, McCloud (Chuck Connors), sends out a drone to see if the pathogen that killed Tokyo's inhabitants is active. He summons Japanese scientist Dr. Shuzo Yoshizumi (Masao Kusakari) to the bridge. Looking upon his decimated homeland, Yoshizumi sees the skeletal remains of an infant. He remembers his late girlfriend Noriko (Yumi Takigawa). She told him that she was pregnant before he left for Antarctica and the hellish pandemic that wiped out humanity took place. American military man Major Carter (Bo Svenson) boorishly mocks Yoshizumi. French doctor Henri La Tour (Cec Linder) informs McCloud that the virus is still active. He implores McCloud to let him take back a sample so he can study it and develop a vaccine. After some convincing, McCloud relents. The *Nereid* heads back to humanity's final stronghold, the continent of Antarctica. Yoshizumi remembers how this nightmare began.

In 1981, the creation of new viruses as biowarfare agents was banned internationally. Yet in Leipzig, East Germany in February of 1982, scientist Krause (Ken Pogue) meets with Z (Colin Fox) to hand over a sample of a terrifying new contagion. Krause believes that it will be studied by Dr. Leisener, an expert virologist. MM88, created by an American geneticist, is a virus lethal to all vertebrate life on Earth. It accelerates the growth of other viruses to deadly rates, killing its host in a matter of days. The Stasi, tipped off to Krause's theft of the virus by a guard, burst in, killing him. Z and his

men, actually American spies, escape by air with the viral sample. Their Cessna crashes in a mountainous region, releasing MM88 to the atmosphere.

A month passes. At the University of Maryland, Dr. Edward Meyer (Stuart Gillard), the creator of MM88, is visited by Col. Rankin (George Touliatos). Rankin informs Meyer that the spies he sent into East Germany never returned. When Rankin realizes that Meyer is planning to be a whistleblower, he has him committed to a mental hospital. Meanwhile, in Kazakhstan, livestock begin dying. In Italy, a mysterious plague breaks out. With a disturbingly high death rate, it becomes known as the "Italian flu".

By May of 1982, the Italian flu has spread worldwide. Members of the Japanese Antarctic weathering team at Showa Station make contact with the Australian team. They tell Drs. Nakanishi (Isao Natsuyagi) and Yamauchi (Sonny Chiba) of disturbing reports of the virus' spread in Uganda. One of the researchers, Yoshizumi, regrets his decision to leave his girlfriend Noriko who had revealed she was pregnant. Back in Tokyo, Noriko, a nurse, loses her child from the stress of dealing with the influx of patients. By June, in the United States, President Richardson (Glenn Ford) watches in horror. His country is devolving into mass civil unrest as this viral pandemic tears the country apart. Not only is there no effective vaccine but his health officials haven't even figured out which pathogen is responsible. Richardson's Chief of Staff General Garland (Henry Silva) believes that this outbreak is Soviet germ warfare. Garland wants to activate the ARS (Automatic Reaction System). This will trigger the launch of the country's nuclear arsenal upon impact of any Soviet missile.

By July, martial law has been declared in most countries. Japan's hospital system continues to be overwhelmed and the death toll is appalling. Noriko tells her senior physician, Tsuchiya (Ken Ogata) that the death rate has now reached 40%. The Japanese Self Defense Force is deployed to dispose of the dead with flamethrowers. In Antarctica, Yoshizumi's fellow researcher and friend Tatsuno (Tsunihiko Watase) receives a transmission from a five year old boy in New Mexico. Unable to help the child who commits suicide over the radio, Tatsuno becomes mentally unstable. Back in the U.S., President Richardson, with the help of Senator Barkley (Robert Vaughan) unearths a military conspiracy. The U.S. military was running a program called "Operation Phoenix" which involved the creation of pathogenic viruses. One lethal virus, MM88, was stolen and never recovered. Barkley reveals that Colonel Rankin had Dr. Meyer committed for threatening to blow the whistle. Meyer confirms that the Italian flu is MM88 and Richardson finds out his wife is dying from it. Meyer is tasked with the creation of a vaccine.

By September, most of the world's major cities have been decimated by the MM88 pandemic. Noriko, finding Tatsuno's wife dead, commits suicide with his son Asahi (Etsutaka Kase). Back in Antarctica, Tatsuno flees into the cold to die holding a picture of his wife and child. Dr. Meyer dies before being able to complete a vaccine. A dying Barkley and Richardson realize that because the virus can't thrive in cold, Palmer Station and the other Antarctic weathering teams must be unaffected. Richardson contacts the teams and informs them that most of humanity has succumbed to MM88. The Antarctic researchers are likely the last people alive. As Richardson dies, a delirious General Garland activates the ARS.

In November, U.S. Admiral Conway (George Kennedy) holds a meeting for all the wintering teams at Palmer Station. On the way, Nakanishi and Yoshizumi's snowmobile breaks down. They stop at the nearby Norwegian base, only to find all the members have shot themselves. Only one pregnant woman, Marit (Olivia Hussey), has survived. Yoshizumi stays behind with her as she's about to give birth. Nakanishi attends the conference, where Conway explains that 855 men and eight women are likely all that remains of humanity. Conway and company are informed that Marit has given birth to a baby girl. She names her daughter "Gree", which in Norwegian means the first light of the morning. The newly formed Federal Antarctic Council acts as Gree's collective godparent.

One of the women is sexually assaulted. The Council decides to assign the eight women to various sexual partners to help propagate humanity. A Soviet submarine, the *T-232*, makes contact with the Antarctic Council. Commanded by Ensign Smirnov (Jay Muszynski), they intend to land at the Soviet Station regardless of the fact that they are sick with the Italian flu. The submarine is intercepted and sunk by the *Nereid*, a British nuclear sub commanded by Captain McCloud. As the *Nereid* disembarked before the pandemic and none of its men are ill, Conway invites McCloud's company to join them.

A year later, the *Nereid* returns from its expedition to Tokyo in time for Christmas. Many of the women now cradle babies. Yoshizumi reunites with Marit, but their reunion is cut short as she has been assigned to spend the night with a young sailor. All this time, as a hobby, Yoshizumi has been working on predicting an earthquake. Major Carter notes that Yoshizumi's research predicts that Washington D.C. will be hit with strong tremors. Carter mentions that the American military activated the "ARS" system a year ago. Such an earthquake could trigger the missiles to launch. Soviet captain Nevsky (John Evans) reveals that the Soviet's similar system was also activated. One of the Soviet missiles is aimed at Palmer Station.

BACKGROUND

Author Sakyo Komatsu published his second full length novel, *Virus: The Day of Resurrection*, in 1964. This was on the heels of his debut *Japan's Apaches,* which tackled themes of racism in Japanese society and proto-transhumanism. The inspiration for *The Day of Resurrection* came from the recent sequencing of DNA by Francis Crick and James Watson. They had just been awarded the Nobel Prize in 1962. Komatsu thought that such a discovery had just as much potential for destruction as the splitting of the atom. Major influence on *The Day of Resurrection* also came from the novel and film *On the Beach. On the Beach* also depicts survivors living on a single continent after an apocalyptic event. Stanley Kubrick's then recent *Dr. Strangelove or How I Learned to Stop Worrying and Love the Bomb,* with its "doomsday machine" also inspired the concept of the "ARS" missile system.

In 1965, Toho sought to produce a big screen adaptation of *The Day of Resurrection.* Realizing the story was too large in scale to produce on their own, Toho aimed to co-produce the film with 20th Century Fox. They were also interested in co-producing a film pitting Godzilla against Batman. A deal with Fox could not be reached and both projects fell by the wayside. Physician turned sci-fi author Michael Crichton would write the similar *The Andromeda Strain* in 1969, made into a film by Robert Wise in 1971. The Hong Kong flu pandemic also took place in 1968 which brought the novel to mind for many Japanese.

By the mid 1970s, Haruki Kadokawa, heir to the Kadokawa Shoten publishing empire, had taken over his late father's company. Kadokawa (1942-) was determined to get into the movie business. His company's first film production was *The Inugamis* (1976), directed by Kon Ichikawa. Kadokawa's next films *Proof of the Man* (1977) and *Never Give Up* (1978) were two of the biggest hits in Japanese box office history. Kadokawa was beginning to develop the distinctive brand of making Hollywood-style Blockbusters in Japan. Ala a Japanese Jerry Bruckheimer, his movies were big budgeted and bombastic with high concepts and production values. Kadokawa Shoten had already published a reprint of *The Day of Resurrection*. Making a film adaptation was Haruki Kadokawa's dream. The successes of *Proof of the Man* and *Never Give Up* paved the way for Kadokawa to next produce *Virus*. Kadokawa was keen on making a large budget, lavish film with international cooperation. He courted Hollywood director John Frankenheimer to helm the film, but he wasn't interested. Kinji Fukasaku was thus chosen as director, though some felt he was not a good fit. At that point, the director was mainly known for his violent, gritty crime flicks at Toei. Shiro Moritani who had helmed *Submersion of Japan* (1973) lobbied for the role with Komatsu's blessing. Kadokawa was keen on Kinji Fukasaku however. He was a fan of his gangster pictures and felt Fukasaku had more experience working on international co-productions. Fukasaku had directed the

U.S/Japanese/Italian co-op *The Green Slime* in 1968. He later co-directed the Japanese sequences for Fox's *Tora! Tora! Tora!* (1970) after Akira Kurosawa dropped out. By this time, he was fresh off helming *Message From Space* (1978) with Vic Morrow. Daisaku Kimura, one of *Submersion*'s cinematographers, was hired as DP as a compromise to Komatsu.

Fukasaku and writers Koji Takada and Gregory Knapp significantly altered Komatsu's novel. In the book, MM88, ala Crichton's *Andromeda Strain*, is a space-borne pathogen discovered by astronauts and weaponized; the "MM" standing for *"Martian Murderer"*. In the film, it is entirely human engineered. Much of the exposition regarding the virus' development, theft and spread is altered, trimmed and simplified. In the book, the virus is stolen by the British and taken to the biowarfare lab in Porton Down rather than by the East Germans. The novel's size of the Antarctic community is close to 10,000 men and 16 women. This is in contrast to the film's 855 men and eight women.

PRINCIPAL PHOTOGRAPHY

In late 1978, after completing work on his *jidai-geki The Fall of Ako Castle*, Fukasaku and company began scouting locations. While visiting Antarctica, Fukasaku swam in the volcanic hot springs of Deception Island. It reminded him of the *onsens* back in Japan. With the largest budget in Japanese film history pushing $20 million, *Virus*' shoot was massive; taking place around the world throughout 1979. *Virus* was the first commercial film shot in Antarctica and the first time the continent was shot with 35mm cameras. Another Japanese crew would return a few years later to make the dog-themed drama *Antarctica* (1983). Many of *Virus'* interior sequences were filmed in Toronto, Canada. Other scenes were shot in Japan, Alaska and Chile. The crew also traveled to Machu Picchu in Peru. In total, Fukasaku's unit exposed a whopping close to 50 hours of footage for *Virus*.

Given its size and scope, the shoot for *Virus* was fraught with difficulties. Much of the Canadian crew working with Fukasaku's unit in Toronto had trouble with his direction. It did not help that Fukasaku spoke no English at all and was dependent on an interpreter, Toshiko Adilman. In stark contrast to the anarchic handheld camerawork of his yakuza films, Fukasaku shot *Virus* in a more static style. Working with Kimura as DP rather than his usual *yakuza* film cinematographers like Hanjiro Nakazawa likely influenced his decision for more "locked-down" camera work. The Canadians were frustrated by this as they had access to steadicams and dollies that Fukasaku often chose not to use. Chile's Navy supported the production, lending Fukasaku's unit one of their submarines, the *Simpson*, which portrayed the *Nereid*. The film's icebreaker was portrayed by the Chilean ship *Piloto Pardo*. Towards the end of the shoot in December of 1979, the Swedish passenger ship *Lindblood* was carrying much of *Virus'* cast and crew. They hit an underwater volcano, ran aground and the passengers had to be rescued by the Chilean Navy. This story made the front page of *The New York Times*.

ACTORS

Virus boasts an international ensemble cast including numerous American and Japanese players. There's George Kennedy (*Cool Hand Luke*) as Admiral Conway, fresh from the Airport series. Kennedy had previously appeared in *Proof of the Man* for Kadokawa. Noir and Western star Glenn Ford plays President Richardson. For the well directed White House scenes, Fukasaku had difficulty getting Ford to remember his lines. The crew had to hide cue cards all over the set. Robert Vaughn (*The Man From U.N.C.L.E.*) plays the cunning Senator Barkley who gets to the bottom of the "Operation Phoenix" conspiracy. Henry Silva plays the General Ripper-like Garland. Silva was a very prolific actor who played supporting roles in Hollywood films, including a memorable part in *Ocean's 11* (1960). He then switched to bigger roles in European films, mainly Euro Crime films from Italy.

One of *Virus'* flaws is that some of the Western roles are not convincingly cast. Former athlete and *Rifleman* star Chuck Conners is badly miscast as the British Captain McCloud. He attempts, at best, a kung fu dub-like mid-Atlantic accent. Interestingly, in Komatsu's novel, the *Nereid* is an American submarine. It sinks a British sub filled with infected crewmen instead of the Soviet *T-232*. Olivia Hussey (*Romeo and Juliet, Black Christmas*) plays the supposedly Norwegian Marit but speaks the Queen's.

Swedish American actor Bo Svenson appears as Major Carter. Svenson had taken over the role of sheriff Buford Pusser from Joe Don Baker for the *Walking Tall* sequels. He had also appeared in the 1977 Spaghetti war film *The Inglorious Bastards*. He and Kinji Fukasaku got along well and the two would keep in touch for years until Fukasaku's death. Svenson later appeared in *Kill Bill Vol. 2* (2004) and *Inglourious Basterds* (2009) for Quentin Tarantino. Edward James Olmos, best known for his role in Ridley Scott's *Blade Runner*, plays a small part as well. Canadian actor Cecil "Cec" Linder (*Goldfinger*) portrays Dr. La Tour. He also played Professor Roney in the 1957 BBC TV serial of Nigel Kneale's *Quatermass and the Pit*.

Virus' Japanese cast was just as high profile to Japanese audiences. Star Masao Kusakari (1952-) had already appeared in a previous Komatsu adaptation: *ESPY* (1974). The son of an American G.I. and a Japanese mother, his handsome Eurasian looks got him a gig as model for the cosmetics company Shishido. After *Virus*, he became a superstar for his role in Kadokawa's *Dirty Hero* (1982). Frequent Fukasaku collaborator Shinichi "Sonny" Chiba plays what amounts to an extended cameo. Consummate Ken Ogata plays a small role as a Japanese doctor dealing with the horrific pandemic. Ogata (1937-2008) is best known for his roles in Shohei Imamura's *Vengeance is Mine* (1979) and *The Ballad of Narayama* (1983). He played the lead of Yukio Mishima in Paul Schrader's *Mishima: A Life in Four Chapters* (1985). For Kinji Fukasaku, he later played swordsman

Musashi Miyamoto in *Samurai Reincarnation* (1981). He also appeared in Fukasaku's *House on Fire* (1986) and *Chaos of Flowers* (1988). Actress Yumi Takigawa (1951-) is best known for her role in Norifumi Suzuki's "pinky violence" classic *School of the Holy Beast* (1974). She had played the role of an abused *yakuza* moll in Fukasaku's previous *Graveyard of Honor* (1975). Takigawa later reunited with the director for 1992's *The Triple Cross*. Actor Tsunehiko Watase (1944-2017) plays the distraught Tatsuno. He was a favorite of director Fukasaku, often playing roles as young gangsters in his *yakuza* films.

SFX

The effective miniature work was done not by a Japanese *tokusatsu* crew but Hollywood's Greg Jein and Michael Minor. Both had just worked on *Star Trek: The Motion Picture* (1979). Jein (1945-) had won an Oscar for the alien spaceship in Spielberg's *Close Encounters of the Third Kind* (1977). He and Minor clashed with the Japanese crew, who wanted the mattes more brightly colored. Jein would continue to be one of Hollywood's premiere miniature-makers, with recent work on James Cameron's *Avatar* and Christopher Nolan's *Interstellar*.

REAL WORLD

During World War II, Japan was, interestingly, one of the first countries to understand the power of weaponizing biowarfare. Imperial military doctor Lt. General Shiro Ishii was obsessed with bioweapons research. This factored into the medical experimentation done at the Unit 731 facility in Northern Manchuria which he presided over. Ishii wanted to turn the tide of the Pacific War back in Japan's favor using a lethal strain of bubonic plague. Biowarfare attacks were actually carried out in China. Another germ warfare attack was nearly undertaken in Southern California. In exchange for his data, MacArthur's occupation forces did not charge Ishii or his associates with war crimes. It's unknown if Sakyo Komatsu drew any influence from any of this for *The Day of Resurrection*, but nonetheless it's interesting to note Japan's own history with bioweapons development.

The first act of *Virus* is disturbingly powerful at times, especially in wake of the COVID-19 pandemic. The virus is prophetically depicted as causing mass civil unrest. COVID-19, like MM88, is a virus with highly variable symptoms that starts as a cold or flu and then can progress to lethality. Hauntingly, a Reuters article dated April 14, 2020 reads *"'Isolated within isolation': keeping out coronavirus in the frozen Antarctic"*. Like COVID-19, in the novel MM88 starts spreading in China and then Italy. *Virus* also looks ahead to the HIV/AIDS epidemic, which began to make headlines shortly after the film's release. The science of *Virus* is overall, however, quite terrible. Any virologist worth their PhD will tell you a virus that is a death sentence for *"all vertebrate life on Earth"* would have trouble spreading far. Viruses need living hosts to propagate. This is why Ebola's high death rate actually makes it easier to contain and combat.

THEMES AND MOTIFS

Virus is without question Kinji Fukasaku's finest science fiction film. The film's prologue aboard the *Nereid* strongly invokes *On the Beach*. Scenes showing the viral pandemic emerging in Italy and overwhelmed medical staff in Japan are difficult to watch now. The early Japanese scenes show the most confidence from Fukasaku. One moment featuring topless girls dancing in a disco as they cough is especially unsettling. Excised from the export versions, it is the perfect image of a collapsing society that hasn't yet accepted its destruction. Fukasaku was inspired by the dread he felt during the height of the Cold War. In an interview for Stuart Galbraith's *Monsters Are Attacking Tokyo*, he said *"The Cuban Missile Crisis had threatened the whole world- it was a really dangerous period, not only for Japan. I wanted to reflect that feeling all over the world in* Virus".

Virus was a major milestone in director Fukasaku's career. It was his final step away from being a B-movie director towards a new status as a mainstream hitmaker. In spite of the production's large scale, Fukasaku brings his own style to *Virus*. There's a somber montage that rattles off the death tolls of each major city with title cards. Like contemporaries Kihachi Okamoto and Toshio Masuda, Fukasaku was fond of using heavy onscreen supers in his films. In *Battles Without Honor and Humanity* (1973), they introduce the labyrinthian cast of characters and appear on screen whenever a gangster is killed or arrested. In the later *Battle Royale*, title cards keep track of each student who dies in the film's brutal killing game. Like the memorials to the fallen *Battle Royale* students, *Virus'* title cards are an epitaph for humanity. In *Virus*, the world's leaders behave much like the yakuza families in *Battles Without Honor*. Rather than guns and knives, they hurl biowarfare agents and nuclear weapons at each other. Kinji Fukasaku had a clear disdain for U.S. foreign policy that is on vivid display here as well. His final script for 2003's *Battle Royale II* was quite ferociously anti-American in the wake of 9/11. It outright sympathizes with the Islamic terrorists the United States still fervently hunts.

Virus is quite an uneven film, however. Fukasaku's lack of an ear for English clearly affected his ability to direct the Western actors. The film loses a little steam midway for the Antarctic base sequences and there's a certain "strangeness" to some of the picture's lengthy English language scenes. The eight women having to act as prostitutes of sorts to hundreds of men is quite a problematic concept. Yet the wry Fukasaku makes how deranged he feels this is quite clear in an uncomfortable sequence. Olivia Hussey's Marit is shown about to bed a virginal young sailor "assigned" to her. Fukasaku's vision for *Virus* is arguably even bleaker than Komatsu's. In the novel, while Carter and Yoshizumi fail, another mission is able to stop the Soviet missiles from firing. Antarctica is thus spared and humanity begins to slowly rebuild by the end of the novel. In Fukasaku's

Virus, Dr. La Tour's vaccine is the film's only glimmer of hope. It's a slightly Ishiro Honda-like moment where science (almost) saves the day.

The final act of *Virus*, however, is quite incredible and Yoshizumi's multi-continent trek is hauntingly beautiful. The location shooting adds an impressive sense of scale. From both Fukasaku and Komatsu's ends, *Virus* has a strongly Buddhist subtext. This is hinted at in a bit where Yoshizumi picks up a copy of Buddhist scholar Alan Watts' *The Way of Zen* (1957) before leaving on the mission. It is also made clear in its Japanese title *The Day of Resurrection*. The story is ultimately about a mass cycle of death and rebirth. MM88, created in the aptly named "Operation Phoenix", brings about *yonaoshi* (world renewal) like a microscopic Godzilla. *Virus'* final, tranquil images are of Antarctic wildlife over the end credits. After the prior two-and-a-half hour marathon of death and destruction, these shots bring to mind this cycle. Life starts anew. Or as the film's theme song by Janis Ian states in an affectionately on-the-nose fashion: *"It's not too late to start again".*

RELEASE AND LEGACY

Virus was intended for release in December of 1979 but production ran over time and budget. The genre-bending sci-fi *jidai-geki* film *Time Slip* aka *G.I. Samurai* was thus distributed for the holiday season instead. *Virus* was shown at Cannes in May 1980 where it met a mixed reception. While author Komatsu had been skeptical of Fukasaku as choice for director, he was impressed by the finished product. *Virus* remained Komatsu's favorite film adaptation of his work until his dying day. When *Virus* was released in Japan the following summer, it did good business. Yet it was hardly the massive blockbuster Kadokawa had hoped for. Heavy competition came from Akira Kurosawa's *Kagemusha*. Additionally, Kadokawa and distributor Toho put out *Virus* the same day as the Japanese release of *Star Wars: The Empire Strikes Back*. Kadokawa had spent so much money on the picture that its Japanese gross wasn't nearly enough to break even. He pinned his hopes on international distribution. *Virus* wound up being released directly to video and television in a cut down version in the U.S. It had come a few years too late for the '70s disaster film boom. It was also a couple years too soon for the coming nuclear holocaust film renaissance starting with *The Day After*. Haruki Kadokawa would focus more on the Japanese market for future films. He went on to produce some of the most popular Nihon films of the '80s. Kinji Fukasaku's next major film and collaboration with Kadokawa was 1981's *Samurai Reincarnation,* based on a novel by Futaro Yamada. *Virus* has seen a strong resurgence of popularity in Japan due to the COVID-19 pandemic. It remains a hauntingly prophetic movie about humanity's self destructive potential.

ALTERNATE VERSIONS

Virus was exported internationally in a butchered version that runs 107:24. The editing in this version was credited to Pieter Hubbard. The film is reordered and no longer opens with the *Nereid*'s arrival in Tokyo Bay. This scene is shifted to the middle of the movie instead. Some international prints open with Yoshizumi's metaphysical "skeleton" conversation from the end of the film. Much of the near hour of deleted scenes are Japanese sequences, cut from the first act of the picture. These include a conversation between Krause and a guard at the East German facility, a discussion between the Japanese and Australian weathering teams about the pandemic and Noriko losing her child with Yoshizumi. Also cut are scenes of chaos in Japan and the scene where Tatsuno hears a five year old American boy commit suicide. Tatsuno's son taking sleeping pills on a motorboat with Noriko is cut. The Japanese version makes it clear that Yoshizumi is the main character. This is less obvious in the international version which credits the American stars before him. The *Nereid*'s arrival in Tokyo is shifted to the middle of the film with some new sound mixing. Tatsuno's suicide, oddly, is cut into this sequence. Many dialog and drama scenes in Antarctica are cut down. Appallingly, Yoshizumi's final "walk" is excised, though portions are shown, as mentioned, in the opening. The arresting shot of a skeletal Yoshizumi silhouetted against the sun is used for the title card. The international version ends with the nuclear missiles exploding, completely undermining *Virus'* narrative aim. This version is not recommended.

The cut released on American television and home video by Broadwood Entertainment would be the same as the international version. Yet there was one major change. Some of Yoshizumi's walk is reinstated into the finale. The film ends similarly to the Japanese version with him being reunited with Marit. While this version is more palatable, it's still a far cry from the Japanese original. It was rated "PG" by the MPAA.

AMERICAN HOME VIDEO HISTORY

Virus would be released to VHS several times in the states. Some of these releases include from Media Home Entertainment in 1984 and another from Starmaker years later. Eventually, the U.S. and export versions seemed to lapse into public domain as a bevy of unauthorized DVD releases began to pour out. Some of these included from Echo Bridge, Moonstone Pictures, Miracle Pictures, Diamond Entertainment, American Home Treasures and Reel Classic Films. In 2006, the Japanese version was finally released stateside by BCI. It was included in a set called the *Sonny Chiba Action Pack* paired with the Toei films *The Bullet Train* and *Golgo 13: Assignment Kowloon*. This is somewhat misleading as Chiba's role in *Virus* is largely an extended cameo. Nonetheless, this is, to date, the only release of the Japanese version.

Further Viewing:

(1968)

ガンマー第3号 宇宙大作戦

Toei/RAM Films/MGM, *Directors*: **Kinji Fukasaku, Katsuhiko Taguchi**

Kinji Fukasaku's first foray into science fiction was an international co-production shot at Toei Studios with Japanese staff and Western thespians. Made as an intended follow up to Antonio Marghereti's *Gamma One* series, *The Green Slime* is an indelibly campy 1960s Psychotronic flick. Like 1966's *Terror Beneath the Sea*, the film is a co-production with Italy's RAM Films.

It's the spacefaring retro future and an asteroid's headed for Earth. Military hardass Jack Rankin (Robert Horton) is sent on a mission to blow it up with estranged buddy Vince Elliot (Richard Jaeckel), commander of space station Gamma III. They're all the saltier because Elliot is engaged to Rankin's ex-flame (Luciana Paluzzi). As explosives are rigged, scientist in tow Dr. Halvorsen (Ted Gunther) finds a yucky green substance all over the space rock. Against far greater odds than Ben Affleck, they blast it and get away. On Gamma III, a speck of the space gunk stuck on a suit grows into a tentacled thingamajig that feeds on electricity and lethally jolts passerby. What's worse, shooting it spawns more monsters from its spilled blood. Soon the station is overrun and

Rankin and Elliot are at each other's throats over how to deal with this.

The Green Slime was the first genre production Fukasaku directed. He was brought in per his action background and reputation for budget efficiency. Fukasaku was interested in spinning the story as a subtle Vietnam parable but the backers wanted an artless programmer. With help from television helmer Katsuhiko Taguchi (later a force on *Kamen Rider*), Fukasaku delivered. Hints of Fukasaku's intended message remain. The protagonist Rankin is a "benevolent sociopath" who feels like a deconstruction of the classic John Wayne-style protagonist that actor Horton had played on *Wagon Train*. *The Green Slime* can seem like a proto-version of *Virus*, both mix unstoppable pathogens with Cold War commentary. Note that in *Virus* the character whose actions result in the titular MM88 being released is also named Rankin. The script for *The Green Slime* was actually co-written by Bill Finger, a co-creator of Batman.

The Green Slime is a rare *tokusatsu* picture with an entirely Western cast. Aside from the three leads, the supporting roles are a who's who of Japan's ex-pat community. There's Robert Dunham and William Ross, along with Budd Widom who often dubbed at Ross' Frontier. Frontier itself handled the looping for *The Green Slime*'s U.S. version. Cathy Horan (*Goke*), Linda Hardesty (*Ultraseven*) and Linda Miller (*King Kong Escapes*) also appear. Israeli Defense Force recruits stationed in Japan also took part,

fresh from the Six Day War. *The Green Slime* is hardly Kinji Fukasaku at top form. His direction is shockingly pedestrian considering his '70s *yakuza* films feature some of the most manic camerawork in cinema history.

The special effects work was handled by Akira Watanabe and Yukio Manoda, both of whom had a long history working for Eiji Tsuburaya's unit at Toho. The miniatures are decent if unremarkable. Inventive stop motion and visual trickery is here and there. The titular creatures look like Sid and Marty Kroft show rejects and were portrayed by school children. One gets the sense that perhaps Dan O'Banion was watching this on late night TV half in the bag while writing *Alien*. The Japanese version is considerably shorter at only 77 minutes. Co-featured with the anime *Pinocchio in Space* at the Toei Manga Festival, it has soundtrack differences with no rockin' *"Green Slime"* theme song. It also boasts a quickened pace axing the Horton-Paluzzi-Jaeckel love triangle subplot.

(1978)
宇宙からのメッセージ
Toei/United Artists, *Director*: Kinji Fukasaku

Kinji Fukasaku's next science fiction picture was made between his two *jidai-geki* films in 1978: *Shogun's Samurai* and *The Fall of Ako Castle*. In the mid 1970s, Toei's special effects division was mainly focused on their television properties like *Kamen Rider*,

Kikader and *Sentai*. President Shigeru Okada sought to revitalize their theatrical productions after seeing *Jaws*. One proposed project became *Legend of the Dinosaur and Monster Bird*, released in 1977. The other film Okada spearheaded was to be called *Devil Manta*. Hajime Sato (*Water Cyborg*, *Goke*) was set to direct the film with special effects by Toei's department head Nobuo Yajima. *Manga* and *tokusatsu* god Shotaro Ishinomori was brought in to design the monsters and *mecha*. Ishinomori (1938-1998) was best known for having created the influential anime and manga franchise *Cyborg 009*. This was along with many of Toei's flagship tokusatsu shows.

However, development on *Devil Manta* was halted. Okada witnessed the *Star Wars* boom in the U.S and subsequent popularity of *Space Battleship Yamato* in Japan. Frustrated that Toho beat him to the punch with their cash-in *The War in Space*, he changed the project's direction to a space opera. Hajime Sato was replaced with Kinji Fukasaku as Okada liked his angle to make the film a *"jidai-geki in space"*. Screenwriter Susumu Takaku was also replaced with Hiro Matsuda, who was working with Fukasaku on his current film *Shogun's Samurai*. Shotaro Ishinomori created around 500 designs. As inspiration, producer Yusuke Okada, screenwriter Matsuda and FX director Yajima went to Hawaii to see *Star Wars*. On the flight back, Matsuda came up with the idea to make the story an interstellar adaptation of Bakin Tozawa's classical novel *Satomi Hakkenden* to differentiate it. Director Fukasaku tried to avoid seeing *Star Wars*

before the shoot as he was worried he might copy it too much. His wife, however, dragged him to see it right before he began work on *Message From Space*.

Toei made their first production announcement in February of 1978 and a press conference soon followed. The tragically late Vic Morrow (*Dirty Mary, Crazy Larry*) and the up-and-coming Phillip Casnoff and Peggy Lee Brennan were recruited from Hollywood to head the cast. The budget was the highest in Japanese film history up to that time. Fukasaku's handling of such a budget no doubt influenced Haruki Kadokawa to hire him for *Virus*, which soon dethroned *Message* as the biggest budgeted Japanese movie. *Message From Space* is, overall, a very affectionately silly picture. As Patrick Macias says best in *Tokyoscope: The Japanese Cult Film Companion*, *"at any moment, it can change gears"*. *Message From Space* is a very aesthetically eclectic film. There's an oddly gritty feel in line with Fukasaku's *yakuza* movies that includes his trademark tilted camera angles and handheld shooting. A tavern sequence invokes the Mos Eisley cantina via the club in Fukasaku's earlier *Black Lizard* (1968). The film's art director who worked closely with Ishinomori was veteran Michio Mikami. The sequences with the villainous Gavanas showcase his work particularly. They resemble Mikami's sets for Princess Elizibub's base in Shaw Brothers' *The Super Infra-Man* (1975). Mikami would later incorporate similar motifs into *X-Bomber* (aka *Starfleet*) which he was a major creative force in. Mikio Narita, who plays archvillain Rockseia, often played yakuza dons for Fukasaku. Hideyo Amamoto appears, amusingly, in drag as Rockseia's mother. These scenes foreshadow Fukasaku's later fantasy *jidai-geki* like *Legend of the Eight Samurai* (1983), also based on *Satomi Hakkenden*.

Nobuo Yajima's FX work is a mixed bag. Yajima's unit lacks the innovative spirit of Nakano's at Toho, let alone John Dykstra or Dennis Murren's. Yet his team made use of some high tech equipment. This included a snorkel lens camera and a new video compositing system. This system, the ECG, was cheaper than printing composites on film and allowed for unlimited elements to be composited together. The drawback is that the film footage had to be transferred to video which resulted in fuzzier quality. This system was later used for the flying scenes in *Gamera: Supermonster* (1980), in Toei's metal hero shows like *Space Sheriff Gavin* (1982-83) and on Fukasaku's *Samurai Reincarnation* and *Legend of the Eight Samurai*. In spite of such advancements, the miniature work is shaky and generally below Toho quality. In the film's second half, the clunky but endearing FX work perks up. *Message From Space* feels a lot more rewarding in its *Star Wars*-inspired third act. The *"chicken run"* through the Gavanas' castle is almost cut-for-cut identical to the Death Star II run-through in *Star Wars: Return of the Jedi*. George Lucas, who was fond of Japanese genre films and kept an eye on his competition, almost certainly saw *Message From Space*.

The action-packed fight sequences in the Gavanas' castle were choreographed by star Sonny Chiba's Japan Action Club. These look forward to *Legend of the Eight Samurai*'s very similar finale. Chiba's protegees Hiroyuki "Henry" Sanada and Etsuko "Sue" Shihomi both play prominent roles. Sanada (1960-), after years of domestic period and martial arts films, would wind up one of the few Japanese actors to make a jump to Hollywood pictures. He would make appearances in 2003's *The Last Samurai*, 2013's *The Wolverine* and *Mortal Kombat* (2021). Shihomi (1956-) was best known for her role in *Sister Street Fighter* (1974). Chiba, Sanada and Shihomi often co-starred and would all return for *Eight Samurai*. *Message From Space* was a fair success and released to big screens in the States by United Artists later in '78. Dubbed into English in New York, it received savage reviews unfavorably comparing it to *Star Wars*. Toei would soon produce the spinoff TV series *Message From Space: Galactic Wars* which ran from summer 1978 to early '79. Episodes were compiled into the feature *Swords of Space Ark*, which, amusingly, aired on Pat Robertson's Christian Broadcasting Network.

TIME SLIP

(1979)
戦国自衛隊
Kadokawa/Toho, *Director:* **Kosei Saito**

Time Slip, aka *G.I. Samurai,* was in production at largely the same time as *Virus*. It's another big-scale mega production, this time based on a novel by Ryo Hanmura

(1933-2002), a popular SF writer. Inspired by *Star Wars*, Haruki Kadokawa wanted to make an SF-themed "youth movie" and mortgaged his house and took out a massive bank loan to help put up the budget. It's certainly a unique concept melding science fiction with Japan's popular *jidai-geki* genre, much akin to a sci-fi Western. *Time Slip*'s execution is quite flawed and clunky, though production values are top of the line.

During a routine exercise, a modern ensemble cast of Self Defense Force recruits led by the gruff Lt. Iba (Sonny Chiba) are thrust 400 years into the past into the middle of the *Sengoku* (Warring States) era and a classic *jidai-geki* scenario. At first the JSDF members bond with the local samurai, respecting them as fellow warriors. Iba develops a brotherly kinship with warlord Kagetora (*Virus*' Isao Natsuyagi) that comes off almost homoerotic in bits. He teaches him to fire a submachine gun as weirdly upbeat music plays. There are some fun action scenes as the SDF guys get tangled up in the *Game of Thrones*-like politics of the *Sengoku* era. Iba's sociopathic subordiante Yano (Tsunehiko Watase) and a group of followers run AWOL and commit some Nanjing-style raping and pillaging. This complicates things as Iba is forced to take them out. *Time Slip* turns into more of a straight up *jidai-geki* in its second half. Lt. Iba soon grows megalomaniacal and begins to lust over the simplicity of *Sengoku*'s old fashioned warface, complicating plans to return.

Overall, *Time Slip* is a fun, novel concept with very flawed execution. It is somewhat sluggishly paced and boring, feeling undeserving of its whopping nearly two-and-a-half hour runtime. Kosei Saito's direction is quite pedestrian and makes one wish that Kinji Fukasaku or even Junya Sato had helmed the picture instead. Parts of the film are uncomfortably rapey. Haruki Kadokawa was keen on getting support from the actual Japanese Self Defense Force for *Time Slip*. The SDF, amusingly, declined to participate as they were opposed to the script's depiction of recruits engaging in rape. As a result, the production had to make due with outdated equipment and build a Type 61 tank from scratch. *Kelly's Heroes* (1970), with Clint Eastwood and Telly Savalas, was another major influence on the production.

Better attributes include Iwao Isayama's striking cinematography. *Time Slip* is also well cast and includes a huge ensemble from Hiroshi "Monsieur" Kamayatsu, frequent samurai warlord and *yakuza* don Asao Koike, Shin "Dracula" Kishida, Hiroyuki "Henry" Sanada, Mizuho Suzuki, Miyuki Ono (*Evil Dead Trap*) and Mikio Narita. The film's highlight is easily a lengthy battle sequence like the finale of Kurosawa's *Kagemusha* crossed with the SDF porn of a *kaiju* film. This scene took 20 days to shoot and required the use of hundreds of horses, many imported from the United States. Sonny Chiba's Japan Action Club troupe trained the horses for an entire month before filming.

The soundtrack by anime composer Kentaro Haneda is occasionally ridiculous and features pop songs peppered in, giving *Time Slip* a feel akin to a Nihon *Top Gun*. *Time*

Slip's finale is surprisingly bleak. While the picture may have been a Hollywood style production, its ending is anything but as the heroic story anticipated by the viewer turns into a dour tragedy. Overall, *Time Slip* is a fair cinematic mess, though its action sequences by Chiba's Japan Action Club are impressive. *Time Slip* is at its best when its a dumb, no holds barred high concept actioner. Saito's next major jidai-geki for Kadokawa would be 1982's slightly better *Ninja Wars*. *Time Slip* was remade, more or less, as *Samurai Commando: Mission 1549* (2005), directed by the Millennium Godzilla series' Maasaki Tezuka and written by Harutoshi Fukui (*Lorelei*).

KINJI FUKASAKU
The Survivor

深作欣二

7/3/1930-1/12/2003

"I grew up surrounded by the ruins of war. Life was extremely difficult. It was like living in a constant state of violence. We had no food and such and without the help of the Americans, we couldn't get on with our lives. This was a great humiliation. As a boy aged 14 or 15, it had a tremendous impact on me."
-Kinji Fukasaku, *Tokyoscope: The Japanese Cult Film Companion* by Patrick Macias (2001)

Kinji Fukasaku was another maverick of Japanese cinema. Like a Japanese Howard Hawks, in his versatile career he walked a tightrope between fierce auteur and hit-making program director. Fukasaku was born in Mito, Japan. His 1975 film *Graveyard of Honor* told the story of a *yakuza* thug also from Mito. As a teenager during World War II, his class was put to work at a munitions factory. The factory was hit more than once by American bombers and his experiences there left a bitter scar. Fukasaku was 15 when the war ended and remembered the chaos of post-war Japan vividly. He consoled himself by going to see films, moved by Italian neorealist pictures by De Sica and Rosselini. Fukasaku soon entered the Nihon University College of Art where he studied screenwriting.

In 1954, he joined Toei as an assistant director, working under filmmakers like Masahiro Makino. Finally in 1961 he was promoted to director. Fukasaku's debut was a quartet of hour long actioners with future star Shinichi "Sonny" Chiba. Fukasaku and Chiba would form a long lasting friendship and work together again on numerous occasions in the coming decades. These were followed by the longer *High Noon For Gangsters* (aka *Greed in Broad Daylight*). More noirish films followed like *The Proud Challenge, Gangs vs. G-Men* (both 1962), *Jakoman and Tetsu* and *Wolves, Pig and Men* (both 1964). *Kamikaze Man: Duel at Noon* (1966) was Fukasaku's first color film. By this time, he developed a solid reputation at Toei for directing action films on time and budget. He married actress Sanae

Nakahara in 1965. The two were inseparable until Kinji's death.

Thanks to a clause in his contract, he was able to do freelance direction for other studios. In 1968 he made the gangster film *Blackmail is My Life* for Shochiku. It was followed by the garish crime thriller *Black Lizard*, starring drag queen performer and singer Akihiro Miwa. Fukasaku directed a follow-up, *Black Rose Mansion,* the following year. His ability to bring films in on schedule and under budget got him handed the reins to *The Green Slime* at Toei. A U.S./Japanese/Italian co-production, it was his first science fiction and *tokusatsu* film. Concerning titular green gunk spawning tentacled electric beasties on a space station, it featured an entirely Western cast. The stars included *Wagon Train*'s Robert Horton, *Thunderball*'s Luciana Paluzzi and *The Dirty Dozen*'s Richard Jaeckel. Fukasaku was not allowed to bring much directorial flair, but it was his first film to be exported internationally.

Fukasaku got another high profile international gig in 1970. Akira Kurosawa had dropped out of the U.S./Japanese co-production *Tora! Tora! Tora!* due to creative conflict with 20th Century Fox. Fukasaku and contemporary Toshio Masuda were brought on board to direct the Japanese sequences as both had good reputations for efficiency. Fukasaku focused on the action scenes as he disliked the script's gentlemanly portrayal of the Imperial brass. Far removed from Pearl Harbor's spectacle, in 1970 he also directed the tragic youth film *If You Were Young: Rage.* Inspired by Sam Peckinpah, he cultivated a darker style for his gangster pictures with *Sympathy For the Underdog*

(1971). He used his generous paycheck for *Tora! Tora! Tora!* to purchase the rights to a book by Shohei Tokisane. This became *Under the Flag of the Rising Sun* (1972). Alongside Masaki Kobayashi's *Human Condition* trilogy, it's one of the most scathing condemnations of Imperial Japan put to film.

Starting with *Street Mobster* in 1972, Fukasaku began to pioneer the *jitsuroku* (true crime story) subgenre of *yakuza* films. The film's actor, Bunta Sugawara, became another favorite player. Before Fukasaku, Japanese gangster pictures were *ninkyo* films. These were more stylized yarns depicting the protagonists akin to samurai, flawed but honorable. Ala Peckinpah's deconstruction of the old West, Fukasaku wanted something truer to his postwar experience. Quick and cheap to produce, these films were heavy on exploitation violence and mayhem. Yet they used avant-garde filmmaking methods that were almost arthouse. Fukasaku employed grotty locales, handheld shooting and titled angles to emphasize the world of chaos and brutality these gangsters thrived in. The plots were based on true crime stories that made headlines back in their day. Fukasaku's masterwork was his five film *Battles Without Honor and Humanity* (1973-74) saga. In Japan, it's considered the Nippon equivalent to Coppola's *The Godfather.*

While other Japanese studios struggled in the '70s, Toei developed a name with violent, low budget but innovative films from directors like Fukasaku. Trailers began to refer to him as *"genius director Kinji Fukasaku"*. More gritty gangster-themed films followed, such as three *New Battles*

Without Honor and Humanity films (1974-76), *Graveyard of Honor, Cops vs. Thugs* (both 1975), *Yakuza Graveyard* (1976), *Hokuriku Proxy War* and *Doberman Cop* (both 1977). In 1978, Fukasaku, wary of the traditionalism of the samurai genre, finally reneged. He directed a pair of *jidai-geki* films: *Shogun's Samurai* and *The Fall of Ako Castle*. He also directed the *Star Wars*-inspired space opera *Message From Space* that same year. The film was heavy on special effects and featured late American actor Vic Morrow. Fukasaku would occasionally direct for television as well. He did episodes of *Key Hunter, G-Men '75* and *Hattori Hanzo: Kage no Gundan*, among other shows.

Soon afterward, Fukasaku's career took a more commercial turn. He was hired by bigshot producer Haruki Kadokawa to direct *Virus*, an adaptation of a Sakyo Komatsu novel. Another co-production, *Virus* had the largest budget of any Japanese film. It was filmed all over the world and starred an international cast. By the 1980s, Kinji Fukasaku had rebranded himself as a mainstream hitmaker. He directed fantasy samurai films like *Samurai Reincarnation* (1981) and *Legend of the Eight Samurai* (1983), romances such as *Lovers Lost* and *Fall Guy* (both 1982) and even a musical entitled *Shanghai Rhapsody* (1984). Fukasaku became less prolific in the '90s, but returned to the crime genre with 1992's *The Triple Cross*. He also made *Crest of Betrayal* (1994), a horror/jidai-geki hybrid combining Japan's native *Yotsuya Kaidan* and *Chushingura* tales.

In 2000, he directed what would soon become his most notable film internationally: *Battle Royale*. Based on a dystopian novel by Koshun Takami, its premise attracted Fukasaku. It reminded him of watching his classmates die at the munitions factory during the war. In the wake of the Kobe child murders in Japan and the Columbine massacre in the U.S., *Battle Royale* was controversial. Politicians called for it to be banned and Japan's rating board, Eirin, insisted on giving it an "R-15" rating. The controversy only enticed audiences and *Battle Royale* was a massive hit. Fukasaku shot additional scenes for it and re-released it to theaters in 2001. He also branched into video games, directing the cutscenes in Capcom's *Clock Tower 3* (2002). Fukasaku had plans to direct a sequel to *Battle Royale*, but was soon diagnosed with prostate cancer. Undaunted, he intended to finish the film before he died. Tragically, his condition deteriorated after only one day of principal photography. Kinji Fukasaku passed away in January of 2003. He left his son Kenta at the helm to take over and finish the film, *Battle Royale II: Requiem*.

Selected Filmography (as director)

Wandering Detective: Tragedy in Red Valley (1961)
Wandering Detective: Black Wind in the Harbor (1961)
High Noon For Gangsters (1961)
The Proud Challenge (1962)
Gangs vs. G-Men (1962)
Gang Life (1963)
Jakoman and Tetsu (1964)
Wolves, Pigs and Men (1964)
Kamikaze Man: Duel at Noon (1966)
Rampaging Dragon of the North (1966)
Blackmail is My Life (1968)
Black Lizard (1968)
The Green Slime (1968)
Black Rose Mansion (1969)
Japan Organized Crime Boss (1969)
If You Were Young: Rage (1970)
Tora! Tora! Tora! (1970)

Sympathy for the Underdog (1971)
Under the Flag of the Rising Sun (1972)
Street Mobster (1972)
Outlaw Killers: Three Mad Dog Brothers (1972)
Battles Without Honor and Humanity (1973)
Battles Without Honor and Humanity: Deadly Fight in Hiroshima (1973)
Battles Without Honor and Humanity: Proxy War (1973)
Battles Without Honor and Humanity: Police Tactics (1974)
Battles Without Honor and Humanity: Final Episode (1974)

New Battles Without Honor and Humanity (1974)
Graveyard of Honor (1975)
Cops vs. Thugs (1975)
New Battles Without Honor and Humanity: The Boss's Head (1975)
Violent Panic: The Big Crash (1976)
New Battles Without Honor and Humanity: Last Days of the Boss (1976)
Yakuza Graveyard (1976)
Hokuriku Proxy War (1977)
Doberman Cop (1977)
Shogun's Samurai (1978)
Message From Space (1978)
The Fall of Ako Castle (1978)
Virus (1980)

Samurai Reincarnation (1981)
Lovers Lost (1982)
Fall Guy (1982)
Legend of the Eight Samurai (1983)
Shanghai Rhapsody (1984)
House on Fire (1986)
Chaos of Flowers (1988)
The Triple Cross (1992)
Crest of Betrayal (1994)
The Abe Clan (1995, TV Movie)
The Geisha House (1998)
Battle Royale (2000)
Clock Tower 3 (2002, video game) [cutscenes]
Battle Royale II: Requiem (2003) [honorary]

THE LITTLE GIRL WHO CONQUERED TIME

時をかける少女

Toki o Kakeru Shojo "The Girl Who Cut Through Time"
Kadokawa/Toei, 7/16/1983 (*Showa 58*), 104:12, 35mm, Spherical (1.85:1)/Academy (1.37:1, some scenes), black and white/color, stereo

Crew
Executive Producer: Haruki Kadokawa
Producer: Yorihiko Yamada, Kyoko Obayashi
Director/Editor: Nobuhiko Obayashi
Screenplay: Wataru Kenmochi, Nobuhiko Obayashi, Yasutaka Tsutsui (*novel*)
Director of Photography: Yoshitaka Sakamoto
Music: Masataka Matsutoya
Art Director: Kazuo Satsuya

First Assistant Director: Tadashi Naito
Assistant Director: Hideki Chiba, Akira Nakamura, Yojiro Nakamura, Shigeru Sakurada
Assistant Cinematographers: Shigeru Honda, Koichi Ishii, Hideo Ito
Assistant Art Directors: Chigumi Obayashi, Yu Yamada
Set Decorators: Nobuhiro Akitagaya, Yoshinao Tanaka
Props: Yoshio Fujii, Sadao Ota
Dolls: Mie Kuwahara

Assistant Editor: Ayako Imura
Sound Recording: Kazumi Imamura
Sound Designer: Shohei Hayashi
Recording Assistants: Yoshio Watanabe, Toshiaki Suzuki, Ken Okazawa
Gaffer: Akio Watanabe
Lighting Assistants: Kazuhito Eguchi, Keijiro Ishizaki, Itsuya Matsushima, Hiromasa Obata, Kenji Taniguchi
Continuity: Mihoko Kuroiwa

Hair and Makeup: Chieko Okano
Optical Composites: Akikata Okada, Takashi Yamada
Production Managers: Kazutaka Hattori, Michinori Sakamoto, Akio Sato
Still Photographer: Katsunori Endo

Cast

Tomoyo Harada (*Kazuko Yoshiyama*)
Ryoichi Takayanagi (*Kazuo Fukamachi*)
Toshinori Omi (*Goro Horikawa*)
Toshie Negishi (*Naoko Tachibana*)
Ittoku Kishibe (*Toshio Fukushima*)

Makoto Naito (*Tetsuo Yoshiyama*)
Wakaba Irie (*Noriko Yoshiyama*)
Akiko Kitamura (*Sadako Horikawa*)
Yukari Tsuda (*Mariko Kamiya*)
Yoko Yamashita (*Yoshiko Yoshiyama, age 7*)
Taizo Masumoto (*Takeo Haramichi*)
Hiroe Oka (*Yoshiko Yoshiyama, age 18*)
Mizu Arai (*Childhood Kazuko*)
Senjo Hirano (*Childhood Kazuo*)
Takeshi Kato (*Childhood Goro*)
Yoichi Takabayashi (*Clock Shop Man*)
Nao Asuka (*Woman in Mourning*)

Maiko Ogawa (*Student*)
Kiyomi Ishii (*Student*)
Ken Naito (*Student*)
Takashi Motoka (*Boy on Bicycle*)
Masuno Takahashi (*Old Woman in Field*)
Sumio Yamazaki (*Mr. Kyudo*)
Torao Horikawa (*Yajima*)
Yasuteru Takahashi (*Monk*)
Ken Uehara (*Masaharu Fukamachi*)
Takako Irie (*Tatsu Fukamachi*)

Alternate Titles

Girl of Time (alternate English title)

"When one finds a love that transcends reality, is that fortunate or not?"
-Opening Titles

Another Kadokawa production based on a popular novel by Yasutaka Tsutsui, *The Little Girl Who Conquered Time* is a beloved 1980s Japanese Blockbuster. It is directed by Nobuhiko Obayashi, best known for his quirky horror hit *House*. The film is an engaging high school drama that takes a sci-fi twist. *The Little Girl Who Conquered Time* doesn't reach the phantasmagorical heights of *House*. Yet it feels Spielbergian and boasts a heartfelt performance by newcomer Tomoyo Harada. The finale is a harshly bittersweet tearjerker.

PLOT

Kazuko Yoshiyama (Tomoyo Harada) is a 16 year old high school student. At a school ski trip, she meets a classmate named Kazuo Fukamachi (Ryoichi Takayanagi). When she returns to the class' meeting place, she notices Kazuo's ski set is missing. On the train ride back, Kazuo picks some wild grass. Months later, she's staying after class to clean the science room with Kazuo and another classmate, Goro Horikawa (Toshinori Omi). Alone, she hears a strange noise from the next room and feels the presence of a mysterious figure before tipping over a beaker of chemicals. Smelling a lavender-like scent, she faints. She is found unconscious by Goro and Kazuo. When she comes to, strange things begin to happen. On her way home from school, she stops at Kazuo's grandparents' house. In their greenhouse, she notes that Kazuo is cultivating lavender. The scent is exactly the same as what she smelled before passing out.

Kazuko goes to school two days later and leaves her club activities early. That night, an earthquake strikes. Kazuko notices that there seems to be a fire near Goro's house and speeds off to investigate. Thankfully, the soy sauce brewery belonging to Goro's family is unharmed. As Kazuko walks home, someone appears to assault her. She then wakes up in her bed. As she walks to school with Goro, the roof tiles of a temple fall on them. Kazuko reawakens in her bed again, thinking it's a dream. In school, she mentions what happened the prior night to Goro who doesn't remember it. In class, her teacher Mr. Fukushima (Ittoku Kishibe) assigns the same poem to interpret as the day before. Kazuko realizes she is repeating the previous day, as if in a time loop.

Kazuko once again leaves her club activities early. She tells Kazuo that she seems to be living the same day. The two remember an incident in their childhoods where they cut their hands on a broken mirror. As Kazuko predicts, the earthquake hits. Kazuko once more runs off to Goro's house and finds Kazuo there. Kazuo tells her that he believes she has developed the ability to "time leap" or teleport through time. When the two part, Kazuko notices Kazuo has no scar on his hand from the childhood accident.

BACKGROUND

Author Yasutaka Tsutsui first serialized *The Girl Who Leapt Through Time* in 1965. It was published as a novel by Kadokawa Shoten in 1967. The book was a sensation and was adapted into a television miniseries, *Time Traveler,* by NHK in 1972. The show's ratings were through the roof and later that year a sequel series, *Continuation: Time Traveler*, was aired. Tsutsui (1934-) is one of Japan's most esteemed post-war sci-fi novelists. Unlike the dour visions of friend Sakyo Komatsu, his work is strongly satirical. He was born in Osaka and was a child prodigy who loved *manga* and movies. Early influence came from the works of Jean Paul Sartre and Thomas Mann. Out of college, he started his own sci-fi *doujinshi* (fan magazine) called *NULL*. Some of his stories were printed in the popular *SF Magazine*. Besides *The Girl Who Leapt Through Time,* his most famous novel is 1993's *Paprika*, later adapted into an anime film by Satoshi Kon. He also created a parody of Komatsu's *Japan Sinks: The World Sinks Except Japan* (1973). This was adapted into a film in 2006 by Minoru Kawasaki. Tsutsui has also acted and recorded music. Personally, he is known for a dark and twisted sense of humor that often generates controversy. A Twitter post mocking a comfort woman statue with sexual innuendo drew condemnation from South Korean authorities and led to boycotts of his books. Tsutsui has claimed the comments were meant in an ironic nature and he was in fact making fun of Japanese nationalism.

In the 1980s, for his next film production, Blockbuster producer Haruki Kadokawa was keen on adapting Tsutsui's famous novel. He knew he had a surefire hit on his hands. For director, he chose Nobuhiko Obayashi, a stylish filmmaker whom he had a good relationship with. The two had first met in 1975, prior to Obayashi's directorial debut *House* (1977) at Toho. After *House*, Obayashi directed *The Adventures of Kosuke Kindaichi* (1979) and *The Aimed School* (1981) for Kadokawa. Obayashi was fresh off the beloved hit *Transfer Student* aka *I Are You, You Am Me*, a similarly themed film made at Shochiku. To lead *The Little Girl Who Conquered Time*, Kadokawa chose newcomer Tomoyo Harada (1967-), only 15 at the time and something of the Phoebe Cates of Japan. Harada had applied to a recruitment program that Kadokawa and Toei were having for *Ninja Wars* (1982). She was beat out by Noriko Watanabe for the role of the heroine, but Kadokawa was enchanted by this young actress. He gave her leading parts in the television series versions of *Sailor Suit and Machine Gun* and *The Aimed School*. Harada had loved Obayashi's previous *Transfer Student* and was excited to work with him.

PRINCIPAL PHOTOGRAPHY

As with *Transfer Student*, *The Little Girl Who Conquered Time* was mainly filmed at Nobuhiko Obayashi's hometown of Onomichi near Hiroshima. *Transfer Student, Little Girl* and Obayashi's 1985 film *Lonely Heart* became known as his *"Onomichi trilogy"*. *The Little Girl Who Conquered Time* was shot in only 28 days, a grueling pace for a big budget picture. The shoot was in three segments: the prologue at the ski resort, the studio in Tokyo and the exteriors at Onomichi. Shooting days often ran well into the night. The cast and crew frequently ate *tonjiru*, a type of Japanese pork soup, to keep their energy up. The cherry blossoms had yet to bloom for much of the shoot and were often added to shots with compositing. The sequence where Kazuko finds Kazuo on the cliff collecting plants was extremely dangerous to film; shot on a real cliff. Actor Ryoichi Takayanagi was nearly killed by an accident involving falling scaffolding.

The ski lodge opening of the film, filmed in black and white and academy ratio was shot at Joetsu Kokusai resort. It has an enchanting 1950s *Showa*-era feel. While the film doesn't reach the mad genius of *House*, Obayashi's direction is engaging. Tomoyo Harada's performance is quite strong and heartfelt. For a relative newcomer, it's an impressive turn. *The Little Girl Who Conquered Time* is stylish, though more subdued than the garish psychedelia of *House*. The cinematography by Obayashi's usual DP Yoshitaka Sakamoto is quite arresting. The images of temples and the rustic locales of Onomichi are lush. *The Little Girl Who Conquered Time* has a unique tone, somber yet lyrical in a way that invokes some of Steven Spielberg's smaller scale films. The film gets more stylized as it goes on and takes an unexpected hard sci-fi turn. Later scenes invoke the hyper-stylishness of *House* more.

The Little Girl Who Conquered Time concludes in a tear jerker finale. Its coda is beautiful but achingly bittersweet. This epilogue, also shot in Academy ratio, is not in Tsutsui's novel. It was added by Obayashi and screenwriter Wataru Kenmotsu. The film is capped with a masterfully executed Hitchcock-style dolly zoom. As intended, it makes the film's very sense of time and space feel distorted. The end credits feature a John Hughes-like gag where Kazuko "time leaps" through the movie as she sings the theme song.

THEMES AND MOTIFS

The themes in both the novel and film are enduring. They are evocative of later works like Harold Ramis' *Groundhog Day* (1993) and Christopher Nolan's *Interstellar* (2014). *The Little Girl Who Conquered Time*, starting off as a fairly straightforward school drama, takes a hard sci-fi turn. Its tropes include such quantum physics-based concepts of "time looping" and love transcending time. Director Obayashi's previous *Transfer Student*, which concerns two students swapping bodies ala Disney's *Freaky Friday*, had similar themes. The 1980 Hollywood production *Somewhere in Time*, based on a novel by Richard Matheson, was particularly influential on Obayashi.

RELEASE AND LEGACY

The Little Girl Who Conquered Time was the second highest grossing domestic film that year. Obayashi became known as the *"original idol film director"* and Tomoyo Harada one of the *"daughters of Kadokawa"*. The theme song, performed by Harada and

written by J-Pop luminary Yumi Matsutoya, was chart-topping. Matsutoya performed her own version and it was covered numerous times, even in Hong Kong by Cantopop singer Sandy Lam. Nobuhiko Obayashi would return to the science fiction genre with 1987's disastrous *The Drifting Classroom*. Cemented firmly in Japanese popular culture, Yasutaka Tsutsui's *The Girl Who Leapt Through Time* has been re-adapted on numerous occasions since. The next adaptation was a 1994 TV mini series starring Yuki Uchida. While on bail for his infamous high profile arrest over cocaine possession and smuggling, Haruki Kadokawa began development of another adaptation. Due to the arrest, he had been forced to resign from Kadokawa and so founded a new company. Kadokawa directed it himself and starred Nana Nakamoto as Kazuko. Released in 1997, this version was more faithful to the original novel and is set in 1965. Kadokawa was finally convicted in 2000 and sentenced to four years in prison.

The next major adaptation was 2006's *The Girl Who Leapt Through Time*. The film is an anime feature directed by Mamoru Hosoda, who later helmed the acclaimed *Summer Wars* (2009), *Wolf Children* (2012) and *Mirai* (2018). The character designs were by Yoshiyuki Sadamoto, best known for his work on *Neon Genesis Evangelion*. It's not a direct adaptation of the novel. More a spin-off set in the same universe, it does once again involve a high school girl learning to time leap. Another live action adaptation, *Time Traveller: The Girl Who Leapt Through Time*, was released in 2010. This film was actually a sequel to Tsutsui's novel. It stars Riisa Naka as Kazuko's daughter Akari. Naka also voiced the protagonist of the anime version. The most recent adaptation was a 2016 TV miniseries.

ALTERNATE VERSIONS

No known English dubbed version exists and *The Little Girl Who Conquered Time* was never given an official U.S. theatrical release.

AMERICAN HOME VIDEO HISTORY

The Little Girl Who Conquered Time is not available on American home video.

Further Viewing:
THE AIMED SCHOOL
(1981)
ねらわれた学園
Kadokawa/Toho, *Director:* **Nobuhiko Obayashi**

The Aimed School is another idol-based high school drama with light sci-fi elements from Kadokawa and director Nobuhiko Obayashi. Based on a young adult novel by Taku Mayumura, it stars Hiroko Yakushimaru (1964-), another *"daughter of Kadokawa".* *The Aimed School* is a major step down from the phantasmagorical genius of *House*, but boasts a similar, furiously eclectic aesthetic. Obayashi's direction is weaker though the film feels akin to a manga with flesh and blood actors. Fitting in with its live action manga vibe, it's a bit of a sports drama. As Yakushimaru was still attending high school

herself, Obayashi had to cram the shoot during her spring break. *The Aimed School* picks up when psychic schoolgirl protagonist Yuka Mitamura (Yakushimaru) is crossed by fellow psychic transfer student Michiru Takamizawa (Masumi Hasegawa). The film gets more fun with a flamboyant turn from character actor Toru Minegishi (later in *Godzilla vs. Biollante*). A VFX-filled dream sequence and finale brings *House*'s high octane cinematic insanity to mind. The picture only loosely follows the novel where male character Koji Seki (Ryoichi Takayanagi) is the main character. The character of Yuka was created to turn it into an idol vehicle for Hiroko Yakushimaru.

The Aimed School is overall not one of Obayashi's strongest films but is enjoyable. The plot of a psychic high school girl who squares off against an occult organization likely influenced Kazuya Kudo's iconic manga *Mai, the Psychic Girl*. *The Aimed School* would be Kadokawa's final film distributed by Toho. Haruki Kadokawa had a falling out with Toho as they paired *The Aimed School* with their own production *Blue Jeans Memory*. *Blue Jeans Memory* received heavier advertising from Toho, infuriating Kadokawa. Yakushimaru's next role would rocket her to superstardom in Japan: the gangster comedy *Sailor Suit and Machine Gun* (1981). She also later starred in Kinji Fukasaku's *Legend of the Eight Samurai* (1983). Years later, in 2012, an anime film adaptation of *The Aimed School* would be released entitled *Psychic School Wars*. This is more faithful to the novel with the character Koji Seki assuming protagonist status.

NOBUHIKO OBAYASHI
The Artsy Commercial Director

大林宣彦

1/9/1938-4/10/2020

As if 2020 wasn't awful enough, in April we lost Nobuhiko Obayashi, one of Japanese cinema's quirkiest luminaries. Obayashi's horror debut *House* (1977) has achieved a strong cult status in the West in recent years. Throughout his career, Obayashi managed to balance a distinct and oddball sensibility with strong commercial success. In addition to films, Obayashi cut his teeth on over three thousand television commercials. Nobuhiko Obayashi was born in early 1938 in Onomichi, Hiroshima Prefecture to a physician family. His childhood was idyllic but also bittersweet, overwrought by the chaos of wartime. This would be reflected in many of his films, often shot in Onomichi. His father was called to the war front when he was a year old as an army doctor so he was raised by his mother and grandparents. Obayashi loved filmmaking from a young age and made his first animation at the age of six with a still camera. He lost several childhood friends to the nearby Hiroshima bombing. By high school, he was enraptured by the early manga works of Osamu Tezuka. He also adopted a love of playing the piano, another frequent motif in his films.

Obayashi's father wanted him to be a physician and he nearly entered medical school at Keio University. In the end, he was accepted into Seijo University. Going to college in Tokyo, Obayashi lived in an apartment near Toho Studios. His next door neighbor was another future director, Yoichi Higashi. In college, Obayashi devoured films, often skipping classes to see them. He produced frequent student films on 8mm and met his wife Kyoko. Obayashi's early films garnered some awards and in 1960 he dropped out of college. In 1964, with Takahiko Iimura, Yoichi Takabayashi and Donald Richie, he started the experimental film collective Film Independent. Obayashi produced numerous experimental shorts in 16mm throughout the '60s. His most well known is the avant garde horror film *Emotion* (1966).

Obayashi was soon recruited by Dentsu, a television commercial firm and offered the job to direct advertisements. He accepted and would proceed to direct numerous commercials where he worked with Hollywood actors. His most famous was a spot for the perfume "Mandom" featuring Charles Bronson. He also did commercials with Sophia Loren, Catherine Deneuve, Ringo Starr, Kirk Douglas and Katharine Hepburn. Due to the multitudes of popular commercials Obayashi directed, Toho gave him an opportunity to develop a feature film. With the exception of ally Kihachi Okamoto, the veteran directors at Toho were irritated that a TV commercial director with no assistant experience was being given a feature film. Obayashi's feature length directorial debut was *House* (1977). *House* drew inspiration from sources as eclectic as Spielberg's *Jaws* and flights of fancy from Obayashi's young daughter. This film stunned audiences with its psychedelic visuals, stylized VFX work and lurid phantasmagoria. It netted Obayashi the Blue Ribbon Award for Best New Director and remains a cult classic both in Japan and abroad.

Obayashi followed *House* with several more films including *Visitor in the Eye* (1977) and *Adventures of Kosuke Kindaichi* (1979) for Kadokawa. His film *The Aimed School* (1981), which starred Hiroko Yakushimaru, began his penchant for being an *"idol film director"*. His next two films *Transfer Student* (1982) and *The Little Girl Who Conquered Time* were two of the biggest and most beloved Japanese Blockbusters of the 1980s. These two films, shot in Onomichi, cemented Obayashi's reputation as a stylish hitmaker. Subsequent 1980s Obayashi films included his sole anime *Kenya Boy* (1984) and *The Drifting Classroom* (1987), based on a popular horror manga by Kazuo Umezu. His 1988 *The Discarnates* was quite critically acclaimed and won several awards.

Chizuko's Younger Sister (1991), starring idol Hikari Ishida and also filmed near Onomichi, followed. Obayashi's film *Samurai Kids* (1993) won the Japanese Academy Award for best editing. *Sada* (1998), based on the infamous true story of Sada Abe, won the top award at the Berlin International Film Festival.

Obayashi continued to be active throughout the 2000s and into the 2010s. He directed a trilogy of anti-war films starting with *Blossoms to the Sky* (2014) and *Seven Weeks* (2014). He was diagnosed with terminal cancer in 2016 and given only a few months to live. He persevered, however and started production on his final film in the trilogy: *Hanagatami* (2017). This was something of Obayashi's magnum opus, a long standing pet project he had wanted to make since the 1970s. His final film was 2019's *Labyrinth of Cinema*, made as he was receiving cancer treatment. Sadly, the cancer finally claimed his life in April of 2020. Nobuhiko Obayashi leaves behind an exuberant filmography and an offbeat legacy as a commercial hitmaker with avant garde stylishness.

Selected Filmography (as director)
Onomichi (1963)
Eater (1963)
Complexe (1964)
Emotion (1966)
Confession (1968)
House (1977)
The Visitor in the Eye (1977)
The Adventures of Kosuke Kindaichi (1979)
The Aimed School (1981)
Transfer Student (1982)
The Little Girl Who Conquered Time (1983)
The Deserted City (1984)
Kenya Boy (1984)
Lonely Heart (1985)
Four Sisters (1985)
His Motorbike, Her Island (1986)
Bound for the Fields, the Mountains, and the Seacoast (1986)
The Drifting Classroom (1987)
The Discarnates (1988)
Beijing Watermelon (1989)
Chizuko's Younger Sister (1991)
Samurai Kids (1993)
Turning Point (1994)
Goodbye For Tomorrow (1995)
Sada (1998)
I Want to Hear the Wind's Song (1998)
The Last Snow (2002)
The Reason (2004)
Casting Blossoms to the Sky (2012)
Seven Weeks (2014)
Hanagatami (2017)
Labyrinth of Cinema (2019)

THE RETURN OF GODZILLA

Gojira "Godzilla"
Toho, 12/15/1984 (*Showa 59*), 7 Reels (2,833 meters), 103:19, 35mm, Spherical Panavison (1.85:1, hard matted), color, Dolby Stereo

Crew
Executive Producer: Tomoyuki Tanaka
Co-Producer: Fumio Tanaka
Producer: Tadahiko Maeda
Director: Koji Hashimoto
Special Effects Director: Teruyoshi Nakano
Screenplay: Shuichi Nagahara, Tomoyuki Tanaka (*treatment*)
Director of Photography: Kazutami Hara
Music: Reijiro Koroku
Editor: Yoshitami Kuroiwa
Production Design: Akira Sakuragi
Lighting: Shinji Kojima
Casting Director: Tadao Tanaka
Chief Assistant Director: Takao Okawara
Assistant Director: Kensho Yamashita
Production Manager: Takahide Morichi
Assistant Cinematographers: Takashi Wakiya, Takehisa Takarada
Costume Design: Kenji Kawasaki
Assistant Art Director: Ken Sakai
Set Decoration: Akio Tashiro

Construction: Yoshiki Kasahara
Lighting Assistant: Akira Oba
Electrician: Hideo Inagaki
Makeup: Fumiko Umezawa
Sound Recording: Nobuyuki Tanaka
Assistant Editors: Junko Shirato, Sae Toshima
Negative Cutter: Fusako Takahashi
Computer Graphics: Hiroshi Tsuchiya
Video Assist: Toshifumi Sakata
Maintenance: Kazuo Suzuki
Sound Assistant: Noboru Ikeda
Dolby Consultant: Mikio Mori
Key Grip: Shunji Yokota
SFX Cinematography: Takeshi Yamamoto, Toshimitsu Oneda
SFX Art Director: Yasuyuki Inoue
Assistant SFX Director: Eichi Asada
SFX Lighting: Kohei Mikami
SFX Animation: Takeaki Tsukuda, Yoshio Ishii
Suit Modeler and Builder: Nobuyuki Yasumaru

Animatronics: Shunichi Mizuno
SFX Wire Work: Koji Matsumoto, Mitsuo Miyagawa
SFX Pyrotechnics: Tadaaki Watanabe, Mamoru Kume
SFX Composites: Yoshikazu Manoda
SFX Production Manager: Masayuki Ikeda
SFX Lighting Assistant: Kasuji Watanabe
SFX Production Assistant: Shinji Higuchi
Still Photographer: Yoshinori Ishizuki
SFX Still Photographer: Takashi Nakao

Cast
Keiju Kobayashi (*Prime Minister Seiji Mitamura*)
Ken Tanaka (*Goro Maki*)
Yasuko Sawaguchi (*Naoko Okamura*)
Shin Takuma (*Hiroshi Okumura*)
Yosuke Natsuki (*Professor Makoto Hayashida*)
Taketoshi Naito (*Chief Cabinet Secretary Hirotaka Takegami*)
Tetsuya Takeda (*Vagrant*)

Eitaro Ozawa (*Finance Minister Kanzaki*)
Mizuho Suzuki (*Foreign Minister Emori*)
Junkichi Orimoto (*Defense Minister Mori*)
Shinsuke Mikimoto (*Kakurai, Chief of Staff*)
Mita Mori (*Land Agency Minister Okochi*)
Nobuo Kaneko (*Home Affairs Minister Isomura*)
Kiyoshi Yamamoto (*Science Agency Minister Kajita*)
Takeshi Kato (*International Trade Minister Kasaoka*)
Yoshifumi Tajima (*Environmental Minister Hidaka*)
Kunio Murai (*Secretary Henmi*)
Kenichi Urata (*Secretary Ishimaru*)
Hiroshi Koizumi (*Professor Minami*)

Kei Sato (*Chief Editor Godo*)
Takenori Emoto (*Desk Editor Kitagawa*)
Takero Morimoto (*Newscaster*)
Takashi Ebata (*Yahata Maru Captain*)
Chiyuku Ishihara (*Fisherman*)
Shigeo Kato (*Radioman*)
Shinpei Hayashiya (*Photographer Kamijo*)
Sho Hashimoto (*Akiyama, Captain of Super-X*)
Kenji Fukuda (*Super-X Lieutenant*)
Yumiko Tanaka (*Akemi*)
Shin Kazanaka (*Uno*)
Koji Ishizaka (*Nuclear Power Station Guard*)
Hiroshi Kamayatsu (*Priest on Train*)
Walter Nichols (*Rosenberg, American Ambassador*)
Alexandr Cairis (*Chevsky, Russian Ambassador*)

Luke Johnston (*Col. Kasirin*)
Dennis Falt (*Soviet Submarine Captain*)
Kenpachiro Satsuma (*Godzilla*)

Alternate Titles
Godzilla 1985 (U.S.)
Godzilla - Die Rückkehr des Monsters **[Godzilla: Return of the Monsters]** (Germany)
El retorno de Godzilla (Spain)
Le retour de Godzilla (France)
O Regresso de Gozilla (Portugal)
El retorno de Godzilla 1986 (Mexico)
Godzilla vender tilbake **[Godzilla Returns]** (Norway)
Godzilla'nin Dönüşü (Turkey)
Годзилла (Russia)

"Godzilla is a warning, a warning to every one of us. When mankind falls into conflict with nature, monsters are born."
-Professor Hayashida (Yosuke Natsuki)

After a nearly ten year hiatus, executive Tomoyuki Tanaka was eager for Godzilla's return to the silver screen. Attempts had been made as early as in 1977, but all failed to materialize. Production would finally begin on *The Return of Godzilla* in 1984. Erasing all continuity after the '54 original, it brings the monster back to its antagonistic roots. The picture also boasts better production values and a darker tone reflecting escalating Cold War anxieties. *The Return of Godzilla* is like a prototype of the modern "gritty reboot", popular since Christopher Nolan's *Batman Begins* (2005) and JJ Abrams' *Star Trek* (2009). It's a particularly well made entry successfully taking Toho's franchise in a mature direction.

PLOT

A few months after a volcanic eruption on Daikoku Island, the fishing vessel *Yahata Maru No. 5* is caught in a ferocious storm. The crew sees a blinding flash of light before the ship disappears. Shortly after, reporter Goro Maki (Ken Tanaka) discovers the derelict ship while out sailing. Climbing aboard, he finds the crew murdered and drained of their blood but a young fisherman, Hiroshi Okumura (Shin Takuma), unconscious and alive. He is attacked by a giant sea louse responsible for killing the crew. Okumura, regaining consciousness, kills it with a hatchet. Maki questions Okumura on deck. He tells Maki that before they were attacked by the monster louse, the crew encountered a giant creature at sea.

Hayashida (Yosuke Natsuki) interviews a hospitalized Okumura. Hayashida becomes convinced that Okumura's monster is a new or revived Godzilla. Prime Minister Mitamura (Keiju Kobayashi) is informed of Godzilla's return by his aide Takegami (Taketoshi Naito). Worried about mass panic, he imposes a media blackout. Maki is furious as his chief editor Godo (Kei Sato) refuses to publish his story. Godo suggests that he talk to Hayashida for additional information. While conducting his interview with Hayashida, Maki meets Okumura's sister Naoko (Yasuko Sawaguchi). Naoko still believes her brother to be lost at sea. Maki tells Naoko that her brother has been rescued. She fights her way into the hospital where they are reunited. Maki and his photographer Kamijo (Shinpei Hayashiya) gleefully take photographs to use in their scoop.

At the same time, a Soviet submarine in the Pacific is attacked and destroyed by Godzilla. The Russians blame the U.S. and tensions between NATO and the Warsaw Pact mount. A satellite image of Godzilla, taken near the site of the sub's destruction,

proves its responsibility. Mitamura makes Godzilla's existence public to save the world from nuclear war. Maki's article goes to print and Naoko is disgusted by his exploitation of her and her brother. The Self Defense Force, meanwhile, plans to use an armored battleship called the Super-X against Godzilla. Hayashida fully expects Godzilla to attack a nuclear power plant soon.

As predicted, Godzilla comes ashore near Shizuka Prefecture's Ihama plant. Destroying the plant as Hayshida, Maki and Okumura watch, Godzilla consumes the reactor's radioactive core. The creature departs as a flock of birds fly overhead. Hayashida hypothesizes that a reptile such as Godzilla may have a migratory homing instinct like birds do. Okumura notes that Godzilla departed when birds appeared. Hayashida concludes that they could use the frequency of birds as a lure for Godzilla. He sends Okumura to Mount Mihara on Oshima Island to do a geological survey of the volcano with friend Minami (Hiroshi Koizumi). Minami concludes that a volcanic eruption could be triggered without damage to local communities. Hayashida presents a plan to the Prime Minister's skeptical cabinet to lure Godzilla to Mihara with bird calls and then seal it in the volcano. Mitamura agrees to put Hayashida's plan in place as "Plan B" if the Super-X is unable to bring the creature down. Hayashida tells Maki and Okumura that he is doubtful the monster can ever be killed. He plans to bury it in the volcano to keep it bay for humanity's sake.

The American and Russian ambassadors arrive in Tokyo and meet with Mitamura. Both urge him to allow the use of nuclear weapons against Godzilla on Japanese soil. Mitamura refuses, much to their consternation. As his cabinet discusses the nuclear option with some in favor, Mitamura asks the American president and Russian premiere if they could drop nuclear bombs on Washington D.C. or Moscow. Swayed, they back off. Russian colonel Kasirin (Luke Johnston), deactivates the launch control aboard freighter *Balashevo*, covertly anchored in Tokyo Bay. The military soon sights Godzilla on its way to Tokyo.

BACKGROUND

When Godzilla waded off into the sunset at the end of *Terror of Mechagodzilla*, it was heading into a nine year cinematic hiatus. The film's low box office, along with the '70s oil shocks driving up the cost of film production, made Tomoyuki Tanaka decide to pull the plug on the series. Yet after only a few years, Tanaka was eager to bring Godzilla back to the screen. A multitude of comeback projects for the monster were planned but wound up shelved. These included *Rebirth of Godzilla*, pitched in 1977. Written by Ryuzo Nakanishi, it was rumored to be a straight-up remake of the 1954 original or to involve Godzilla battling terrorists at a nuclear power plant. The film, to be directed by Jun Fukuda, was dropped in favor of *The*

War in Space to beat out *Star Wars* in Japanese theaters. Another was *Godzilla vs. Gargantua* in 1978, a co-production with Saperstein's UPA that was to be a crossover with *The War of the Gargantuas*. *Godzilla vs. the Devil*, an entry to cash in on the popularity of occult horror hits like *The Exorcist* and *The Omen*, was also rumored. Most likely, it was never seriously considered. Director Nobuhiko Obayashi, fresh off the phantasmagorical horror hit *House*, also proposed his own Godzilla film: *A Space Godzilla*. Next came a proposal from Akira Murao and Tanaka himself in 1980: *The Resurrection of Godzilla*. The story was elaborate, involving Godzilla fighting Bakan, a mythical Chinese monster. The project was dropped by Toho for being too expensive.

Tanaka would try once more in 1984 but scrapped the treatment this time. He commissioned writer Shuichi Nagahara to script a solo project for Godzilla, dispensing with the continuity from 1955 on. Nagahara's script is a decent if formulaic story that is both a direct sequel and soft remake of the 1954 original. It shares some similar tropes: both open with a ship attacked at sea. Both also have a reporter and a brooding scientist who defeats Godzilla.

Tomoyuki Tanaka was keen on Ishiro Honda returning as director but Honda turned the offer down. He was already occupied assisting Akira Kurosawa on *Ran* and had no interest in making more *kaiju* films. Koji Hashimoto (1936-2005) wound up in the director's chair, fresh off *Bye Bye Jupiter* (also 1984). Hashimoto had labored as an assistant director for years, including on *Submersion of Japan* under Shiro Moritani. He rose to the position of director by Moritani's untimely death before *Jupiter* could be filmed. *The Return of Godzilla* would be his last film as director, though Toho considered bringing him back for 1991's *Godzilla vs. King Ghidorah*. Hashimoto wound up relegated to producer until his death.

ACTORS

Akihiko Hirata was set to play Professor Hayashida but died of cancer shortly before principal photography. His replacement was Yosuke Natsuki (1936-2018), veteran of *Dogora* and *Ghidorah, the Three-Headed Monster* (both 1964). Naoko is played by Yasuko Sawaguchi, winner of Toho's 1984 Cinderella contest. She would return for the following entry, *Godzilla vs. Biollante* (1989). Versatile Keiju Kobayashi plays Prime Minister Mitamura, another player from *Submersion of Japan*. Kei Sato appears in a small role as Maki's editor Godo. Sato (1928-2010) was another consummate professional with a distinctive voice. He appeared in numerous films throughout the decades for some of Japan's greatest directors including Masaki Kobayashi, Kaneto Shindo and Nagisa Oshima.

SFX

In the 1950s and '60s, Tsuburaya's FX unit only faced serious Western competition from the likes of George Pal and Ray Harryhausen. That was until the release of Stanley Kubrick's *2001: A Space Odyssey* (1968). By the 1980s, times were different now and technical standards higher. Iconic effects driven films were now coming out of Hollywood one after another from the *Star Wars* trilogy to *Blade Runner* to *Ghostbusters*. For *The Return of Godzilla*, Teruyoshi Nakano returned as special effects director, given the largest budget of his career. His unit would shoot more footage than had ever been lensed before for a *tokusatsu* film. For decades, Japanese films did not have a high shooting ratio. This was due to frugality left over from the war where Japanese DPs tended to be conservative about exposing film. In the '80s this began to change. State of the art video and optical printing technology allows for better, almost seamless compositing.

Taking a cue from Dino De Laurentiis' *King Kong*, a much publicized animatronic "cybot" Godzilla was built, standing at 16 feet tall. Composed of a robotic armature with polyurethane skin, it contained a whopping three thousand computer controlled moving parts. The Godzilla "cybot" cost nearly half a million dollars to build. Using it in lieu of a suit was considered, but that proved technically difficult. The cybot would be used for expressive close-ups of Godzilla's head. Tanaka, Hashimoto and Nakano decided to bring back old school suitmation techniques. With more money and technology, the Godzilla suit was built with space age materials. It was designed, modeled and constructed by Nobuyuki Yasumaru, each part made with precision from urethane molds. It also featured animatronic add-ons to make the monster more expressive. This new Godzilla borrowed design elements from the 1955 and 1964 suits. Like the very first suit in 1954, it took two months to create. A giant Godzilla foot was also built to interact with fleeing extras, but some of its shots aren't well executed.

The hulking 240 pound suit was built for stuntman Hiroshi Yamawaki but he was unable to commit. Kenpachiro Satsuma (1947-) was hired as his replacement. Satsuma was a factory laborer who became a stuntman at Nikkatsu. After the studio went *roman porno*, he moved to Toho. There he played Hedorah and Gigan in the 1970s. Paralleling his predecessor Nakajima, he suffered brutally during *The Return of Godzilla*'s shoot. Satsuma lost 12 pounds during filming, was cut by the suit's electric cables and electrocuted by its animatronic parts. The water scenes in Toho's "Big Pool" were terrifying to film for Satsuma and he nearly drowned on several occasions. Satsuma based his performance on the mannerisms of various animals. These included Komodo dragons, elephants, lions and crocodiles. His movement was also inspired by Japanese *No* opera. Nonetheless, like Nakajima, he was a trooper and would be back to play the monster on many more occasions.

On *The Return of Godzilla*, Hashimoto and Nakano bring a nearly Hollywood-level attention to detail. There is the occasional embarrassing shot, but Nakano's work here feels like a magnum opus. SFX art director extraordinaire Yasuyuki Inoue was also back one last time to design the miniatures. His work is stunning, Inoue's facsimile Shinjuku

is like an anime city. Inoue obsessively studied photos of the metropolis as he recreated it in miniature form. To make the monster intimidating amongst Tokyo's modern skyscrapers, Godzilla's size was increased from 50 to 80 meters. As a result, the miniatures were built at a smaller, less detailed scale. Yet Nakano, Inoue and company succeed at making them look impressive, in part through atmospheric lighting. The *Yahata Maru* in the film's opening is a gorgeous miniature. Inoue also designed the Super-X. A computer controlled model, its shape was an homage to Inoue's flying Hedorah design.

This was one of Nakano's last jobs before his swan song *Princess From the Moon* (1987). As a new team would take over, it's satisfying to see one last film from the *tokusatsu* old guard, finally given a big budget to play with. It is fitting that *The Return of Godzilla* is both the first film in what is now called the *Heisei* series but the final entry released in the *Showa* era. Nakano is, however, unable to resist his stock footage habit. There are shots from *Submersion*, *Prophecies of Nostradamus* and *Deathquake*, but they are used in an unobtrusive manner. Despite increased technology and Hollywood-style polish, the SFX footage still feels Japanese.

MUSIC

Akira Ifukube was unavailable so Reijiro Koroku was tapped to create a new score for the film. His music, like monster themes composed by Ghibli's Joe Hisashi, feels timeless yet brings a modern flair to Godzilla.

It's a shame Koroku did not return for more entries. Perhaps taking a cue from production partner turned rival Haruki Kadokawa, Toho began putting pop songs over the end credits of their films in the 1980s. The credits in *The Return of Godzilla* roll over a sappy but fun '80s pop ballad called *"Goodbye Godzilla"*, sung by the Dutch pop trio The Star Sisters.

THEMES AND MOTIFS

There is a darker subtext akin to 1961's *The Last War* relating to Japan's feeling of helplessness during the Cold War. The 1980s were its tumultuous finale with Ronald Reagan's hawkish attitude exacerbating tensions with Russia. In September 1983, a Soviet missile base's computer identified incoming American missiles by mistake. Had its staffer Lt. Col. Petrov not kept a cool head, much would be different today. Nuclear holocaust themed movies became in vogue again. These included *The Day After* (1983), *Testament* (1983), *Threads* (1984) and *When the Wind Blows* (1986), the latter two from England. In *The Return of Godzilla*, the world is almost destroyed when Godzilla takes down a Russian sub. The American characters have a blithe attitude toward Japan, seeing it as a tributary state worth sacrificing to stop Godzilla. Later, as a result of Russia's covert meddling, a nuke is fired from orbit at Godzilla and almost wipes Tokyo off the map. Similar to *The Last War* and 1980's *Virus*, there's a frustrated sentiment toward these superpowers as they play three-dimensional chess with nuclear weapons, the fate of the world hanging in the

balance. The Three Mile Island nuclear disaster was also recent news. It no doubt had an influence on another sequence where Godzilla attacks a nuclear power plant.

Ken Tanaka's Goro Maki, named after Akira Kubo's similar character in *Son of Godzilla*, has a Hollywood-style character arc. He starts off as a hotshot reporter who will do anything to get the perfect scoop. He exploits Hiroshi and Naoko's reunion for a good story. As the story goes on, he falls for Naoko and develops as a character. He's given a juicier story in Kazuhisa Iwata's tie-in *manga* adaptation of the film. A character named Goro Maki would later appear in *Shin Godzilla* (2016). Ala *Shin Godzilla*, there is a bureaucratic element to *The Return of Godzilla* foreshadowing that film. Like *Shin Godzilla*, the picture prominently features government meetings with the Prime Minister and each of his cabinet introduced with onscreen supers. Similarly, the U.S. and Russia pressure Japan to let them nuke Godzilla, the government and military are ineffectual and a scientific plan saves the day.

RELEASE AND LEGACY

One production assistant took an early job on Nakano's special effects unit at the age of 18. He was tasked with helping control the tail of Satsuma's costume. That young man's name was Shinji Higuchi, the future co-director of *Shin Godzilla*. This was also far from the last *kaiju* related gig for Shinpei Hayashiya, who plays a small role as Maki's photographer. Hayashiya (1955-) would go on to become an esteemed "fan filmmaker", directing *tokusatsu* films on a shoestring budget. He made an unofficial sequel to Kaneko's Gamera trilogy, *Gamera 4: Truth* (2003). His other films, released direct to video, include *Deep-Sea Monster Reigo vs. the Battleship Yamato* (2005), *Raiga* (2009) and *God Raiga vs. King Ohga* (2019).

The Return of Godzilla did decent though not remarkable business. Tanaka began swift development of a sequel but put it on ice after the massive box office failure of *King Kong Lives*. It would be five years until the next entry. With *Godzilla vs. Biollante* (1989), the series would get even better before descending into the formulaic.

ALTERNATE VERSIONS

Little known to many, the first alternate version was its Japanese home video version. The Japanese theatrical cut had a different audio mix. They are subtle, but the home video mix has some substantial changes in foley and music editing. The biggest is its deletion of Godzilla letting out an anguished scream as it plunges into Mount Mihara. The theatrical sound mix is only available on a rare and long out of print "drama LP" on vinyl.

An export version, identical in runtime to the Japanese but with English supers, was made. The dubbing is by Matthew Oram's Voicetrax in Hong Kong. Dubbing cast includes Oram as Hayashida, Barry Haigh as Mitamura and the vagrant, John Culkin as Maki and Warwick Paul Evans as Okumura. Elizabeth Oram, Matthew's Filipino-Chinese

wife who was now helping him run his firm, provides the voice of Naoko. Culkin (1961-) is a British HK-based radio and TV personality still active today. He dubbed Jackie Chan several times in export versions, including *Police Story* (1985). Culkin also worked with every single Hong Kong-based dubbing group including for Vaughan Savidge, Rik Thomas and Annie Mathers. He can be seen on screen in the actioner *The Man From Holland* (1986). Evans (1954-) is another English expat who was a news anchor as his day job. He appeared in Bruce Lee's *Game of Death* (released in 1978) when he first visited Hong Kong in 1973. He also played Dracula in a low budget HK horror flick called *The Gate of Hell* (1981).

Toho offered the film to American distributors in early 1985, asking for several million dollars. Though a deal was almost made with MGM, the big studios passed. Toho wound up selling the film for half a million to New World, an independent distributor founded by Roger Corman, now under new management. Under Corman, they had released Toho's *Submersion of Japan* as *Tidal Wave* in 1975. Again, New World opted for a full scale Americanization. They put producer Tony Randel (*Hellbound: Hellraiser II*) in charge. Randel (1956-) did not think the special effects were up to snuff for American audiences. He decided on a comedic approach playing up its camp value. Raymond Burr was brought on board to reprise his role as Steve Martin from *Godzilla: King of the Monsters!* He appears in new scenes directed by R.J. Kizer (*Hell Comes To Frogtown*) but refused to do comedic lines.

The comic relief was deadened as a result, but some humorous lines still remained, mostly given to actor Travis Swords. What resulted was called *Godzilla 1985*, named after *Frankenstein 1970*. While having a strong cult following, it is one of the most drastically altered versions of a tokusatsu film.

Running around 87:31, *Godzilla 1985* dubs the Japanese scenes into English, makes heavy cuts and rearranges many sequences. The 91 minute runtime often cited is because *Bambi Meets Godzilla* (1969) was shown before the theatrical and early video versions. The dubbing is well performed and synced, a huge improvement over the export track. Written by Lisa Tomei, it features the voices of Tony Plana (Maki), Paul Wilson (Hayashida), Lara Cody (Naoko), Andy Goldberg (Okumura) and Greg Snegoff. The sound mix and design is significantly overhauled. Koroku's score is left fairly untampered but music by Christopher Young from *Def Con 4* supplants it. Scenes completely cut include: a scene where Maki speaks to his editor on the phone along with the scene of Okumura being questioned by Hayashida. Naoko berating Maki for exploiting her and Okumura is taken out. The scenes with Prime Minister Mitamura's cabinet discussing the use of nuclear weapons and him explaining how he talked to the Americans and Russians are also cut. Also removed is a later sequence romantically developing Maki and Naoko after they are left alone in Hayashida's laboratory. Many other scenes are shortened, some significantly. These include Maki's tussle with the sea louse. This is actually a major improvement as uneven shots are removed. The scenes where Maki talks to his editor and interviews Hayashida are shorn of their openings. The sequence with Maki telling Naoko her brother is alive and Naoko's reunion with him both have their endings removed. The scene with the ambassadors is moved to much earlier in the picture and severely truncated. Godzilla's attack on the bullet train is shortened. A cameo of TV personality and singer Hiroshi "Monsieur" Kamayatsu is removed that would have gone over Americans' heads. A scene showing a Russian envoy calling the Foreign Minister is cut, supplanted by a new scene with the American characters.

Editorially, scenes are rearranged, particularly leading up to and during Godzilla's early rampage. *Def Con 4* cues are added to the military preparation sequences which originally had no music. The scene where Hayashida voices his insights on Godzilla is placed far later in the film, right before Godzilla resurfaces in Tokyo Bay. The altered *Balashevo* sequence is placed after the military's attack rather than before and both halves of the scene are merged. Mismatched footage of Godzilla attacking the crowds in Shinjuku is added before it advances into Yurakucho. Shots from later in the film are added to make Godzilla appear more aggressive in certain scenes. Godzilla also fires its heat ray at the Super-X when it first encounters it rather than to retaliate. Godzilla falls over sooner with no intercutting between the Russian missile firing. The reshuffling of scenes causes a major continuity error. Godzilla is shown standing upright on the Prime Minister's bunker screen after it had collapsed. There are also new lines of dubbed dialogue not in the export version. These include the jet pilots making comments as they fight Godzilla (*"Sayonara Sucker!"*). The helicopter Godzilla destroys is dubbed to be a newscaster named "Koji Takahashi". Michael Spence took on the job of re-editing the Japanese version and cutting together the new scenes.

There are about 10 minutes of Kizer's new scenes. Steve Dubin was director of photography. Like *King of the Monsters!*, Raymond Burr shot his footage quickly, though the entire shoot took three. There are a few scenes at Steve Martin's home, including one with his grandson Kyle (Justin Gocke) playing with a monster toy. Most of the new sequences are set in the Pentagon featuring actors Warren Kemmerling, James Hess and Travis Swords as army brass. These scenes feature heavy product placement for Dr. Pepper, who did tie-in commercials with Godzilla. Swords' character Major McDonough got the remaining comedic lines and is especially obnoxious. His worst jokes (*"That's quite an urban renewal program..."*) come off like a teenager doing a bad *Mystery Science Theater 3000* impression. The American military men are tied into the main plot when they agree to launch the counter missile for the Japanese. A 4K scan of a 35mm print done by devoted fans reveals these scenes were filmed open matte making use of the full frame. The Japanese scenes by contrast were hard-matted in camera.

The most frustrating change is to the scene where the missile is launched from the *Balashevo*. Through editing and a newly shot close-up, Kasirin's actions are completely changed. Rather than sacrificing his life attempting to stop the missile, he actually launches it. This, combined with the added American military scenes, gives the film a conservative and hawkish tone. Allegedly Randall was pushed for these changes by New World's brass. Poignant narration from Burr is put at the end of the film before the end credits. The "scream" is used; Toho provided New World with their original theatrical mix. Both songs in the film are deleted from the soundtrack: *"Goodbye Love"* by actress Sawaguchi and *"Goodbye Godzilla"* by The Star Sisters. Finally, the opening and ending credits are completely different. The opening credits to *1985*, a sort of fiery slashing spelling out the word "Godzilla", are impressively done and an improvement. The end credits are set to a medley of Koroku and Young pieces against black. By contrast, the Japanese and export credits linger on shots of Mount Mihara as *"Goodbye Godzilla"* blares.

Godzilla 1985 was released to American theaters on August 23rd, 1985, rated "PG" by the MPAA. It was a critical and commercial failure, opening to savage reviews. It was even nominated for two Golden Raspberry awards. Godzilla films would not get stateside theatrical releases for quite some time. *Godzilla 2000* (1999) would be the next Japanese entry to play in American theaters.

Godzilla 1985 was released to VHS, betamax and laserdisc soon after by New World Video. It was re-distributed to VHS by Starmaker around 1992 and Anchor Bay in 1997. New World's original release contained *Bambi Meets Godzilla*. Starmaker and Anchor Bay's did not. Anchor Bay planned to release *Godzilla 1985* to DVD in the early 2000s but plans fell through due to rights issues with the *Def Con 4* cues. *The Return of Godzilla* was finally released to DVD and Blu-ray in 2016 from Kraken Releasing, an offshoot of anime distributor ADV Films. A 5.1 remix of the international dub was included, but *1985* was not.

Further Viewing:

THE EIGHT-HEADED SERPENT STRIKES BACK

(1985)
八岐之大蛇の逆襲
Daicon Film, *Director*: **Takami Akai**

After taking early jobs on *Bye Bye Jupiter* and *The Return of Godzilla*, Shinji Higuchi took the *tokusatsu* industry by storm. His first professional special effects director job was on this feature length fan film produced by Daicon Film, soon to be Gainax. Directed by classmate Takami Akai, *The Eight-Headed Serpent Strikes Back* has a low budget rawness like a proto-Shinpei Hayashiya flick. The actors are obvious amateurs, the film is post-synced poorly and the costumes look cheap. Ala the later *Gehara*, *The*

Eight-Headed Serpent Strikes Back straddles between satire and loving tribute. Yet the picture comes to life when Higuchi's FX takes the stage. Elevating the film, they're astoundingly good effects sequences with impressive production value. Using old school methods, Higuchi's footage is on par with, if not better than, Toei's television shows of the time.

Shot in public parks without a permit, lots of low cost, low tech ingenuity was used. Higuchi shows his talent for striking visuals right out of the starting gate. The famed *Yamata no Orochi* is reimagined as a sort of cyberpunk biomech, predating Gainax's later *Evangelion*. Built from styrofoam with a wire mesh skeleton, Orochi is executed through a mix of hand puppets and a suit. Like the old school Ghidorah suit, the costume's heads were puppeteered on wires. Higuchi's intricate miniature work is fairly jaw-dropping. Higuchi and Akai's ragtag crew made detailed models from household materials while listening to Godzilla soundtracks. *The Eight-Headed Serpent Strikes Back* also began Higuchi's ingenuitive technique of building miniatures tailored for the shot rather than full miniature sets. Higuchi would go on to employ this in the *Heisei Gamera* trilogy. There's one scene, where a tank battalion cuts through a shopping arcade, that's a particular miniature marvel. *The Eight-Headed Serpent Strikes Back* is one of the best amateur tokusatsu films to come out of Japan. Being shot on 16mm definitely aids the film. One gets the sense it wouldn't be nearly as effective in a modern prosumer digital format.

TERUYOSHI NAKANO
The Pyrotechnician

中野昭慶

10/9/1935-

"At first, I hated what I was doing, but later on I realized that special effects are the core of movie making."
-Teruyoshi Nakano, *Monsters Are Attacking Tokyo* (1998)

Nicknamed "Shokei", Teruyoshi Nakano is another underappreciated talent. He was promoted to head of Toho's special effects unit during a difficult time. Like Jun Fukuda he earned an undue rap. His special effects work is known for two things: explosions and stock footage. Yet he learned from his mistakes, composing better scenes as his career went on.

Nakano was born in Japanese occupied Andong, Manchuria before the outbreak of the Second Sino-Japanese War. His father worked for the South Manchuria Railway. After World War II, Nakano's father was taken as a prisoner of war. His mother and he were repatriated to Japan. As an adolescent, he lived in Niihama and Kyoto. His mother had a job at the local theater so he was able to get discounted movie tickets. As a schoolboy, he would go to the theater several times a week. He enrolled at Nihon University's art department where he studied screenwriting. Upon graduation, he joined Toho as an assistant director.

Early films he worked on were Shue Matsubayashi's *Submarine I-57: Will Not Surrender* and Hiroshi Inagaki's *The Three Treasures* (both 1959). Both films had effects work by Eiji Tsuburaya. Seeing Tsuburaya's unit in action, he was inspired by their creativity. After three years as an assistant director on the main units, he was allowed to join Tsuburaya's team with *Gorath*. *Attack Squadron* and *Matango* were his first films as assistant director to Tsuburaya where he was credited.

Finally, in 1969 he was given his first special effects director assignment. The project was, fittingly, titled *Crazy Big Explosion*. It starred Toho's comedy troupe the Crazy Cats. He also co-directed the monster scenes in *All Monsters Attack* with Ishiro Honda, as Tsuburaya was unable to take part. Tsuburaya passed away shortly after in January 1970. Initially, Sadamasa Arikawa took over as chief of Toho's special effects department. Toho refused to put a title card in *Space Amoeba* dedicating the film to Eiji Tsuburaya. An enraged Arikawa quit, leaving Nakano as his successor.

At first, Nakano was not credited as special effects director despite running the units. In 1971, he worked on *Battle of Okinawa* with Kihachi Okamoto and *Godzilla vs. Hedorah* with Yoshimitsu Banno. Banno took the auteurist tact of supervising Nakano's scenes on set and choosing the camera angles. He next did the FX on *Godzilla vs.*

Gigan (1972) and *Godzilla vs. Megalon* (1973) along with television work. On the latter two, he had to rely on stock footage as the budgets had been slashed. While he is often derided for this, keep in mind that the use of stock footage was a Toho trademark and common in Japanese studio filmmaking. Nakano loved his explosions to the point that he was known as "Bomber Nakano" on set. He had a specific recipe his team used for their distinctive orange-green conflagrations. They mixed high octane leaded gasoline with copper sulfite.

On *Submersion of Japan* (also 1973), he earned his pedigree. Not only did he do impressive work on par with Tsuburaya's, he was finally credited as full fledged "special effects director", his name placed before director Shiro Moritani. He continued his career with *Godzilla vs. Mechagodzilla*, *Prophecies of Nostradamus, ESPY* (all 1974), *Terror of Mechagodzilla, Conflagration* (both 1975), *The War in Space* (1977) and *Phoenix* (1978). At one point in *Nostradamus'* production, his cinematic pyromania got him in some trouble. His unit caused a large fire on Toho's lot. This blaze destroyed quite a few vintage props, including the Mogera costume from *The Mysterians.*

He continued his career in earnest in the '80s on films like *Deathquake* (1980) and *Imperial Navy* (1981). The latter contained an impressive finale where the legendary battleship *Yamato* is destroyed in a torrent of flames. Nakano regarded this as his magnum opus of sorts. He also did shots in *Port Arthur* (1980), *The Imperial Japanese Empire* (1982) and *The Battle for the Sea of Japan* (1983) for Toshio Masuda. In 1984, he returned to the Godzilla franchise with *The Return of Godzilla.* Nakano, along with veteran art director Yasuyuki Inoue, would make their most impressive entry yet. Using high tech methods like a giant "cybot" Godzilla, Nakano redefined *kaiju* destruction.

In 1985, Nakano was asked by North Korean despot Kim Jong Il to supervise the FX on the monster flick *Pulgasari.* He agreed, thinking they were shooting in China. Kenpachiro Satsuma came with him to play the titular monster. Its director, South Korean Shin Sang-ok, had been kidnapped by Kim and forced to make propaganda since 1978. Nakano and Satsuma describe the experience in North Korea as tense but claim they were treated well. Nakano realized the Japanese team was under surveillance when he offhandedly mentioned that he missed Japanese beer. The next day, the exact brand of beer he spoke of was in the set's cooler. Kim let Nakano return to Japan and he was FX director for two more films: *Tokyo Blackout* and *Princess From the Moon* (both 1987). After *Princess*, Toho forced him out, allowing Koichi Kawakita to take over. Nakano designed amusement park rides, including at Tokyo Disneyland until he fully retired in 2001.

Selected Filmography
Submarine I-57 Will Not Surrender (1959) [assistant director]

The Three Treasures (1959) [assistant director]

Storm Over the Pacific (1960) [assistant director]

The Human Vapor (1960) [assistant director]

Mothra (1961) [assistant director]

The Man in Red (1961) [assistant director]
Sanjuro (1962) [assistant director]
Gorath (1962) [assistant special effects]
King Kong vs. Godzilla (1962) [assistant special effects]
Attack Squadron (1963) [assistant special effects director]
Matango (1963) [assistant special effects director]
Atragon (1963) [assistant special effects director]
Mothra vs. Godzilla (1964) [assistant special effects director]
Dogora (1964) [assistant special effects director]
Ghidorah, the Three-Headed Monster (1964) [assistant special effects director]
Retreat From Kiska (1965) [assistant special effects director]
Frankenstein Conquers the World (1965) [assistant special effects director]
Crazy Adventure (1965) [assistant special effects director]
Invasion of Astro-Monster (1965) [assistant special effects director]
Zero Fighter (1966) [assistant special effects director]
The War of the Gargantuas (1966) [assistant special effects director]
Ebirah, Horror of the Deep (1966) [assistant special effects director]

King Kong Escapes (1967) [assistant special effects director]
Son of Godzilla (1967) [assistant special effects director]
Destroy All Monsters (1968) [assistant special effects director]
Admiral Yamamoto (1968) [assistant special effects director]
Crazy Big Explosion (1969) [special effects]
Latitude Zero (1969) [assistant special effects director]
Battle of the Japan Sea (1969) [assistant special effects director]
All Monsters Attack (1969) [assistant special effects director]
The Vampire Doll (1970) [special effects]
Space Amoeba (1970) [assistant special effects director]
Battle of Okinawa (1971) [special effects]
Godzilla vs. Hedorah (1971) [special effects]
Godzilla vs. Gigan (1972) [special effects]
Godzilla vs. Megalon (1973) [special effects]
The Human Revolution (1973) [special effects]
Submersion of Japan (1973) [special effects director]
Godzilla vs. Mechagodzilla (1974) [special effects director]

Prophecies of Nostradamus (1974) [special effects director]
ESPY (1974) [special effects director]
Terror of Mechagodzilla (1975) [special effects director]
Conflagration (1975) [special effects director]
Continuing Human Revolution (1976) [special effects director]
The War in Space (1977) [special effects director]
Firebird (1978) [special effects director]
Port Arthur (1980) [special effects]
Deathquake (1980) [special effects director]
Imperial Navy (1981) [special effects director]
The Imperial Japanese Empire (1982) [special effects]
Lake of Illusions (1982) [special effects]
Battle of the Sea of Japan (1983) [special effects]
The Return of Godzilla (1984) [special effects director]
Pulgasari (1985) [special effects consultant]
Tokyo Blackout (1987) [special effects director]
Princess From the Moon (1987) [special effects director]

HEISEI

平成

January 8th, 1989 to April 30th, 2019

On January 7th, 1989, Emperor Hirohito finally died. His son, Akihito, succeeded him and ushered in the *Heisei* era. In stark contrast to *Showa*, *Heisei* began fortuitously for Japan. Only in later years did it become stormier. Japan entered the Heisei era as a premiere economic superpower. The bubble economy began to burst, however, by the mid 1990s. Japan's veneer was further shattered by incidents such as the 1995 Hanshin earthquake, the sarin gas subway attacks by the Aum Shinrikyo cult and the 1997 Kobe child murders. With the September 11th, 2001 terrorist attacks in the U.S., the world was plunged into uncertainty. Japan kept a low profile as a country throughout the 2000s, though its relations with neighboring countries declined. Controversy over the government's diminishment of its wartime misdeeds made occasional news. In 2006, the right wing Shinzo Abe was elected Prime Minister. Though he lost the next election, he was elected again in 2012. Japan under Abe became more assertive and hawkish as its relationship with its neighbors further disintegrated. On March 11, 2011, the archipelago was hit by the strongest recorded earthquake in its history. This caused devastating destruction and a massive tsunami. It also led to the Fukushima Daiichi Nuclear Plant disaster, the worst nuclear accident since Chernobyl. Populism was on the rise in both Japan and elsewhere: Abe would go on to become the longest serving Prime Minister in Japanese history. Additionally, the surprise black swan events of Brexit in the United Kingdom and Donald Trump's election as U.S. President shook the world.

In Japanese science fiction, popular tokusatsu and anime franchises kept going strong. A new generation of filmmakers born in the post-war recovery inherited the mantle. As old *Showa* directors like Ishiro Honda passed, filmmakers like Kazuki Omori, Shusuke Kaneko and Hideaki Anno stepped into their roles. Teruyoshi Nakano retired and a new generation of special effects wizards emerged under the guidance of Koichi Kawakita and prodigy Shinji Higuchi. As technology increased, the *tokusatsu* artform became integrated with computer generated images. The *Heisei* era finally ended with the abdication of Emperor Akihito, ushering in the *Reiwa* era under his son Naruhito.

TETSUO THE IRON MAN

鉄男

Tetsuo "The Iron Man"
Kaijyu Theatre, 7/1/1989 (*Heisei 1*), 4 Reels, 67:19, 16mm, Academy (1.37:1), black and white, monaural sound

Crew
Producer/Director/Writer/ Editor/Lighting/Production Design/Special Effects: Shinya Tsukamoto
Directors of Photography: Shinya Tsukamoto, Kei Fujiwara
Music: Chu Ishikawa

Assistant Director/Costumes: Kei Fujiwara
Sound: Mitsuo Tsukuda, Masaharu Goto, Koji Sato
Production Assistants: Nobu Kanaoka, Hiroyuki Kojima, Tomoko Ishigami, Tomoko Kodaka, Shozin Fukui, Hideyo Nagao, Tsunekazu Shibuya, Junko Sato, Midori Nukata

Cast
Tomorowo Taguchi *(Man)*
Kei Fujiwara *(Girlfriend)*
Shinya Tsukamoto *(The Guy)*
Nobu Kanaoka *(Woman)*
Naomasa Musuka *(Doctor)*
Renji Ishibashi *(Vagrant)*

"Your future is metal!"
-The Guy (Shinya Tsukamoto)

Tetsuo: The Iron Man is one of Japan's most ferociously original independent films. Highly experimental, it goes straight for the throat and never lets go. Mixing body horror with cyberpunk, it defies genre but features enough sci-fi elements to include. With an offbeat grotesquery often compared to David Lynch's *Eraserhead*, it's like a deranged version of the *Ultra Q* episode *Kanegon's Cocoon*.

PLOT

The Guy, a strange man who fetishizes metal (director Shinya Tsukamoto) enters his hideout in an industrial area. He cuts open his leg and inserts a rusted pipe. Later, his wound becomes infected and fills with maggots. Running down the street, a car hits him. Soon afterward, the driver (Tomorowo Taguchi) is shaving. He discovers a metallic pimple on his face that squirts blood when touched. Talking to his traumatized girlfriend (Kei Fujiwara) on the phone, she mentions that she's felt strange ever since the accident. On his way to work, he gets off the subway and sits next to a bespectacled woman (Nobu Kanaoka). The woman finds a strange hunk of metal and flesh on the ground. Touching it, it latches onto her hand like a parasite. Possessed by the Guy, she attacks and chases the protagonist through the subway. He is able to escape by stabbing her with a pen, but she pursues him to a garage. Taking on the face of the Guy, she accosts him. The protagonist, displaying unusual strength, pummels her to death.

The protagonist then becomes physically ill. His body starts to transform into metal as he has a disturbing dream. In it, a succubus-like figure resembling his girlfriend sodomizes him with a penile hose protruding from her groin. Returning home, he finds the metal pimple on his face has grown into a patch of wires. He makes love to his girlfriend, though she is hurt by the metal growths on him. The man grows delirious as she erotically eats, hearing only the sounds of metal. His penis then transforms into a power drill as his metamorphosis accelerates. He hides in the bathroom as his entire body transforms. His girlfriend forces her way in and screams in horror as she sees his disfigured face. He attacks her and tries to rape her with his drill penis. She burns his face with a hot frying pan before stabbing him in the groin. Sticking a fork in an electric socket, the electricity heals him. He comes after her once more and she stabs him in the neck. She then commits suicide in a torrent of a blood by allowing his penis to penetrate her.

The Guy, in his hideout, flashes back to a doctor (Naomasa Musuka) trying to treat his wounds. It is revealed that he implanted a piece of metal in his brain. Meanwhile, the protagonist's transformation continues. He receives a phone call from the Guy who threatens him. He then flashes back to the hit and run accident. It is revealed that his girlfriend and him left the Guy for dead in the woods before having sex. The protagonist tries to electrocute himself by sticking a fork in a power outlet but it only energizes him. The Guy soon arrives at the protagonist's apartment as the whole room begins to rust. The Guy takes possession of the girlfriend's body and attacks him. Emerging from her corpse, he shows the protagonist a vision of an apocalyptic world where humans are devoured by machines.

BACKGROUND

The 1980s were something of a heydey for independent genre films. Daring young filmmakers ran around remote areas and shot horror epics on shoestring budgets. Some of these would-be directors like Sam Raimi and Lloyd Kaufman wound up embraced by Hollywood. On the other side of the Pacific, *Tetsuo: The Iron Man* follows this same tradition. As with many independent features, *Tetsuo* was a project years in the making. The film's concept of man mutating into machine began life as a stage play called *The Phantom of Regular Size*. It was inspired by the urbanization of the Kanto area, which director Tsukamoto found unsettling. A self-taught filmmaker, he had been making films on Super 8mm since adolescence. By the early '80s, Tsukamoto temporarily abandoned filmmaking to work at an ad agency. During this time, he got into putting on plays. Tsukamoto started an offbeat drama troupe called Kaijyu *(Sea Beast)* Theatre, ala a Japanese equivalent to John Waters' Dreamlanders.

In 1986 he got back into filmmaking and produced an adaptation of *Phantom* in color Super 8. Most of his troupe came on board and Kaijyu Theater became a film company, which it remains to this day. More amateurish than *Tetsuo*, the 18 and a half minute *The Phantom of Regular Size* would form a blue-print for it. It features the same plot along with an identical cast. Like in *Tetsuo*, Taguchi's unnamed, bespectacled male protagonist is attacked by a woman (Kanaoka) with a metallic hand on the subway. His penis becomes a power drill in *Phantom*, too, which kills his girlfriend (Fujiwara) and he is accosted by Tsukamoto's Guy. As in *Tetsuo*, the two do battle and merge into one uber-being before going forth to destroy the world.

Tsukamoto's next film, made on Super 8 in 1987, was *Adventure of Denchu Kozo* (or *Adventure of Electric Pole Boy*). It wound up winning the top prize at the PIA Film Festival where Nagisa Oshima was a judge. Bits of *Denchu Kozo* were used on the television set in *Tetsuo*. Tsukamoto was encouraged and decided to take on a more ambitious project. He hoped to make something that could be sold in a video store. He returned to the concept of *The Phantom of Regular Size* and retitled it *Tetsuo*, the *kanji* for which translates to "*Iron Man*". Tsukamoto began to re-film it, switching from color Super 8 to black and white 16mm. By this time, he had quit his job at the ad agency to focus on filmmaking. This enraged his father who kicked him out of the house.

PRINCIPAL PHOTOGRAPHY

The black and white cinematography in *Tetsuo: The Iron Man* not only invokes Tsukamoto's favorite show *Ultra Q* but helps hide the film's paltry budget. Tsukamoto would shoot *Tetsuo* for 18 months from September 1987 to early 1989. Much of the film was shot in friend Kei Fujiwara's apartment. The factory locale for *Tetsuo*'s finale was shot next door to Fujiwara's residence in a derelict building slated for demolition. Fujiwara (1957-) is an under-appreciated talent: a filmmaker, stage actress and performance artist. To Tsukamoto, she was an essential figure in the production of *Tetsuo*. Without her Tsukamoto would have likely never completed the film. Not only did she provide her apartment and act in *Tetsuo*, but she assisted in camera operation, cinematography and lighting; manning the camera whenever Tsukamoto was on-screen. Fujiwara would not follow Tsukamoto to his bigger productions after the success of *Tetsuo*. Instead, she began her own directing career, making the disturbing *Organ* (1996).

During the lengthy shoot, Tsukamoto took the role of a genuine auteur, supervising every aspect of production. He's credited as producer, writer, director, partial DP, editor, production designer, special effects technician and gaffer. He brought a team of volunteer production assistants on board to assist. Most of them lived at Fujiwara's during the shoot. One of these PAs, Shozin Fukui (1961-), had made a short called *Gerrorist* (aka *Vomit Terrorist*). He would go on to direct two features also melding grotesquery and cyberpunk: *964 Pinocchio* (1991) and *Rubber's Lover* (1996). As the shoot for *Tetsuo* droned on, the production assistants abandoned it one by one, put off by the harsh working conditions. Actor Taguchi (1957-) chose to live off-set to stay out of the shoot's politics and keep a better relationship with Tsukamoto, instead biking from his parents' house where he lived. Tomorowo Taguchi was a punk singer of sorts turned actor. He was part of a band called Bachikaburi and met Tsukamoto for the stage version of *Denchu Kozo*.

SFX

Despite its shoestring budget and technical crudeness, *Tetsuo*'s special effects are well executed. They are best described as "hardware store *tokusatsu*". *Tetsuo*'s repulsively effective makeup and prosthetics were made by mixing scavenged computer parts with latex. These bits were often affixed to Taguchi with tape. For full body shots of the "Iron Man", a crude monster suit was fashioned akin to the *tokusatsu* films Tsukamoto adored. This was a jumpsuit with layered metallic parts glued to it. The "power drill" and gore effects are convincing. The art direction is stellar for a low budget film with the Guy's disturbing lair well put together, filled with various hunks of metal, pipes and cables. The film's stop motion effects are impressive and fluently animated. *Tetsuo*'s finale in particular is an indie tour-de-force, a seamless mix of prosthetics, pyrotechnics and stop motion. Many of these stop motion effects were done by Tsukamoto solo after much of his crew bailed from production. The merged final form was placed on a truck and driven around Tokyo. *Tetsuo* is also filled with complex time lapse photography and a technique called "pixelation". Played back, it gives the effect of rapid movement across a landscape.

MUSIC

Chu Ishikawa's score is cacophonous but effective. The late Ishikawa (1966-2017) was something of a Japanese Trent Reznor, already part of an industrial band called Zeitlich Vergelter. His music is like peak Nine Inch Nails via post-punk anarchist collective Godspeed You! Black Emperor. Tsukamoto was looking for someone to score the film and was given tapes of Ishikawa's work which he liked. Initially Ishikawa tried making music with metal tools but the results left something to be desired. Tsukamoto would go on to collaborate with Trent Reznor himself twice. First on a TV spot for MTV Japan and then on 2009's *Tetsuo: The Bullet Man*.

THEMES AND MOTIFS

Tetsuo: The Iron Man is not for the squeamish, but for those who relish cult cinema, it's savage fun. Its stark monochrome images are grotesque and the "power drill penis" sequence is vile. It mixes the DIY indie-horror spirit of Sam Raimi's *The Evil Dead* and Peter Jackson's *Bad Taste* with a dark psycho-sexuality ala Cronenberg. Cronenberg's *Videodrome* and *The Fly* were particularly influential on Tsukamoto. Often cited as an example of cyberpunk, Tsukamoto has acknowledged Ridley Scott's *Blade Runner* as an early influence on *Tetsuo*'s concept of urban dehumanization. Artists such as Hans Bellmer, H.R. Giger and Marshall Arisman were influential on the film's aesthetic. Its hyperkinetic tone puts it in a similar category to contemporary Japanese indies like Sogo Ishii's *Crazy Thunder Road* and *Burst City* and Shigeru Izumiya's *Death Powder*. Sequences in Katsuhiro Otomo's landmark anime masterpiece *Akira* likely influenced the film as it was made, both feature a "Tetsuo" character undergoing grotesque metamorphosis. At its heart it feels most in line with Tsuburaya's *Ultra Q*, beloved by Tsukamoto as a youth. An iconic episode, *Kanegon's Cocoon*, features a thrifty boy obsessed with money. He is transformed into a monster named Kanegon who must eat coins to survive. *Tetsuo* feels like a twisted *Ultra Q* episode for adults. Like *Kanegon*, it centers around a protagonist's Kafka-esque transformation, juxtaposing mundane reality and outlandish fantasy.

Some have picked up on homoerotic overtones to the film. By the film's end, the dynamic between Taguchi's protagonist and Tsukamoto's villain, who literally "unite", could easily be interpreted as sexually charged. In Japanese, the word for unite also means to engage in sexual intercourse. This is drilled in even more with a dream sequence showing the protagonist sodomized by a succubus with a penis-like attachment. There is another dream sequence towards the film's end showing the two men naked, their arms conjoined with a tube-like growth.

RELEASE AND LEGACY

The production took a mental toll on Tsukamoto, who was so enraged by the end of the shoot that he contemplated burning the negatives. Yet he persevered and submitted it to the Tokyo International Fantastic Film Festival, where it proved a hit. The festival's director, Yoichi Komatsuzawa, got the film accepted into Rome's Fanta Festival. It won the Grand Prix there before being sold internationally. It was also released on video in Japan by JHV (Japan Home Video). Tsukamoto had completely run out of money in post-production and needed to hire a sound designer. It was JHV who provided completion funds in exchange for the home video rights.

Tetsuo would prove influential. Darren Aronofsky cited it as a major influence on his debut *Pi* (1998). Tsukamoto was now an in-demand director. His next stop would be the professionally made horror yarn *Hiruko the Goblin* (1991) for Shochiku. He returned to the *Tetsuo* concept with two "sequels". The first was *Tetsuo II: Body Hammer* (1992), this time in 35mm and color. More a soft remake, the film features Taguchi again. Despite a higher budget and more polished production values, it's a step down. Even more underwhelming would be the 2009 *Tetsuo: The Bullet Man*. Digitally shot in English and poorly acted, it is a far cry from the original.

ALTERNATE VERSIONS

Tetsuo's only alternate version is called "The First Cut" and was available on a Japanese DVD release. An early workprint and assembly version of the movie, it runs 77:24. In general, most of the added runtime is simply because the editing pace is slower. Many scenes feature additional coverage removed from the final edit. The scene where the protagonist is pursued by the possessed woman is far longer with additional bits. These include a shot where the woman dances a jig outside the garage. A short scene where the protagonist tears up drywall underground afterward is added. The sex scene between the man and his girlfriend is longer and more graphic. The most significant addition is a segment of the doctor flashback. The doctor tries to amputate the Guy's infected leg and is killed. During their confrontation, there is an added exchange between the protagonist and the Guy. The Guy talks about his metal implants rusting and homo-erotically licks the protagonist. The sound mix is significantly different: less of Ishikawa's score is added and many sound effects are missing or alternative. Some of the music cues appear to be demo versions. Lines of dialogue were re-recorded in post, mainly Tsukamoto's lines in the final *"Our love can destroy this fucking world"* conversation. Overall, this cut is far less polished and effective but an interesting curiosity.

Tetsuo: The Iron Man was given a theatrical arthouse release stateside with English subtitles by Original Cinema in 1992.

AMERICAN HOME VIDEO HISTORY

Tetsuo: The Iron Man was released to VHS by Fox Lorber that same year, as well as laserdisc by Lorbor and Image Entertainment. On this release, it was paired with Greg Nickson's short film *Drum Struck* (1992). It was released to region 1 DVD by Image in 1998 and then by Tartan Video in 2005. Most recently, it was included in a Blu-ray box from Arrow Video called *Solid Metal Nightmares*. It also includes many of Tsukamoto's other films including *Denchu Kozo, Tetsuo II, Tokyo Fist, Bullet Ballet, A Snake of June, Vital* and *Haze*.

Further Viewing:

ADVENTURE OF DENCHU KOZO (1987)
電柱小僧の冒険
Kaijyu Theatre, *Director*: Shinya Tsukamoto

A 47 minute mini-feature made before Tsukamoto took on *Tetsuo, Adventure of Denchu Kozo* is far less polished. Yet it's a major step up from *The Phantom of Regular Size*. It features much of both films' casts including Taguchi, Tsukamoto, Kanoka and Fujiwara. *Denchu Kozo* was based on a stage play that Kaijyu Theatre had put on and reused many of the play's props. It concerns a bullied young man (Nariaki Senba) with a utility pole growing from his back. Having built a DIY-time machine, he's whisked into a bleak future to battle *yakuza*-like vampires. Shot on color Super 8 rather than black and white 16mm, its execution can be clunky. Yet the film has moments scattered throughout of mad genius prefiguring *Tetsuo*. *Denchu Kozo* truly comes to life in its impressive climax. The final ten minutes make vivid use of stop motion, pixelation, handcrafted sets and visual effects done on a shoe-string budget. *Denchu Kozo* is a spirited early film from an up-and-coming renegade filmmaker.

TETSUO II
BODY HAMMER

(1992)

鉄男II

Kaijyu Theatre, *Director*: Shinya Tsukamoto

Tetsuo II: Body Hammer is less of a sequel to *Tetsuo* than a bigger budgeted, more ambitious color remake. Like the first film, it features a man, played by Tomorowo Taguchi, who turns into a machine. Tsukamoto's "The Guy" also returns, this time leading a gaggle of nasty skinheads. The men provoke Taguchi's protagonist into killing his young son, leading to his transformation into a living weapon. Like *Tetsuo*, the protagonist and Guy do battle. Both also conclude with the transformed and merged characters rolling through the streets of urban Japan. *Tetsuo II* boasts a stronger narrative and character development than the original. The cyberpunk sci-fi elements are harder and there's more world building. This is actually counterproductive. The original *Tetsuo* works because of its batshit insane "WTF factor" and surreal lack of a traditional narrative. *Tetsuo II*, by contrast, feels a little overthought and less cohesive and powerful.

There is, however, a lot to like in *Tetsuo II* and many hauntingly nightmarish moments. The highlight is a disturbing black and white flashback sequence showcasing the protagonist's childhood trauma. Under the tutelage of a sociopathic father (played by the Korean-Japanese Sujin Kim), he is transformed into a killing machine. Finally, he gruesomely turns on his creator. The finale boasts striking images as well, like the protagonist extending pipe-like tentacles into the heads of screaming skinheads as his horrified wife (Nobu Kanaoka) looks on. The ending draws strong aesthetic influence from *Blade Runner*, invoking its climactic confrontation between Harrison Ford's Deckard and Rutger Hauer's Batty. *Tetsuo II* swaps out the gritty monochrome of the original for a slicker, proto-teal and orange look. This is less novel and effective, but the film is still a lot better than 2009's awful *Tetsuo: The Bullet Man*.

SHINYA TSUKAMOTO
The Indie Maverick

塚本晋也

1/1/1960-

"It's strange. Part of me loves a city like Tokyo, but part of me would happily destroy it..."
-Shinya Tsukamoto (1992)

A disciple of David Cronenberg, Shinya Tsukamoto is one of Japan's most distinctive independent filmmakers. Tsukamoto is best known for the cult classic *Tetsuo: The Iron Man* (1989) and for his unmistakingly hyperkinetic style and eccentric personality. He was born on New Years' Day in 1960 and grew up in Tokyo. As a boy, he was captivated by Tsuburaya's *Ultra Q*. A loner, he identified with the story of *The Ugly Duckling*. His father, who worked in advertising, got him a Super 8mm camera when he was 14. His first film was a crude adaptation of a Shigeru Mizuki *manga*. He also put on plays as a student. His independent, 8mm filmed opuses grew in ambition until his college years. One of these amateur efforts was even two hours long. After college, he became disenchanted with filmmaking. He put his focus towards working at an ad agency shooting commercials. Tsukamoto even worked on an advertisement featuring La Toya Jackson.

Around this time, he started an underground theater troupe called Kaijyu Theater. This consisted of him and others including Kei Fujiwara and Nobu Kanaoka. They would put on offbeat plays inside homemade tents they constructed. One play, *Adventure of Denchu Kozo*, was especially well received. For this play, he met Tomorowo Taguchi, a young actor and punk singer who became a favorite thespian of his. Tsukamoto had learned a lot making commercials and itched to make a film adaptation of *Denchu Kozo*. Thus Kaijyu Theater became a filmmaking troup. Their first project was the experimental *The Phantom of Regular Size* (1986), based on another play they performed.

The short, made in color Super 8, was well received enough that Tsukamoto continued on. He quit his job at the ad agency to focus on filmmaking. This move enraged his father who kicked him out of the house. Tsukamoto's next project in 1987 was a 47-minute mini-feature adapting *Adventure of Denchu Kozo* for the screen. With creative FX work, an entertaining pace and an impressive finale, it won admirers. The film would go on to win the top prize at the PIA Film Festival. The panel included Nagisa Oshima (*In the Realm of the Senses*) and future *kaiju* directors Kazuki Omori and Shusuke Kaneko. Tsukamoto longed to make a more horror-driven film and was eager to have his work sold in video stores. In late 1987, he started shooting a longer version of *The Phantom of Regular Size* in black and white instead of color. This project would become his most famous: *Tetsuo: The Iron Man*.

Tetsuo was a difficult production. It took a tremendous emotional toll on Tsukamoto and strained his relationships. By post-production, he was out of money and most of his friends weren't speaking to him. Japan Home Video, however, was impressed with what he had done so far and gave him completion funds. *Tetsuo: The Iron Man* won the top award at Rome's Fanta Festival and secured international distribution as a result.

Tsukamoto thus became an in-demand talent. His next project, made for Shochiku, was *Hiruko the Goblin* (1991) based on a *manga* by Danjiro Moroboshi. He followed that up with a color and 35mm semi-sequel to *Tetsuo: Tetsuo II: Body Hammer*. Quentin Tarantino courted him to make a Hollywood adaptation of *Tetsuo*, but the project never made it past planning. His next film was *Tokyo Fist* (1995). Critically acclaimed, it was a hyper violent boxing story starring Tsukamoto and his brother Koji. It won the top prize at Tokyo Sundance. He followed that up with *Bullet Ballet* (1998), a brutal neo-noir shot in black and white. Next came the higher budget *Gemini* (1999), based on an Edogawa Rampo novel and distributed by Toho. *A Snake of June* followed, premiering at the Venice Film Festival in 2002. *Vital* starring Tadanobu Asano came next in 2004 to more critical acclaim.

Tsukamoto has made a myriad of pictures since, switching to digital over film. These include the short *Haze* (2005), *Nightmare Detective* (2006) and *Nightmare Detective 2* (2008). He directed a third Tetsuo film, *Tetsuo: The Bullet Man* in 2010, but it was poorly received compared to the first two. He also helmed *Kotoko* in 2011 and a new adaptation of the World War II novel *Fires on the Plain* by Shohei Oka in 2014. His most recent film is *Killing*, his first *jidai-geki*, made in 2018. Additionally, Tsukamoto is an actor. Besides playing frequent onscreen roles in his own films, he has appeared in *Dead or Alive 2* and *Ichi the Killer* for Takashi Miike, *Marebito* for Takashi Shimizu, *Shin Godzilla* for Hideaki Anno and *Silence* for Martin Scorsese among others.

Selected Filmography

Genshi-San (1974)
Flying Lotus (1979)
The Phantom of Regular Size (1986)
Adventure of Denchu Kozo (1987)
Tetsuo: The Iron Man (1989)
Hiruko the Goblin (1991)
Tetsuo II: Body Hammer (1992)
Tokyo Fist (1995)

Bullet Ballet (1998)
Gemini (1999)
Sakuya: Slayer of Demons (2000) [actor]
Dead or Alive 2: Birds (2000) [actor]
Ichi the KIller (2001) [actor]
Blind Beast vs. Killer Dwarf (2002) [actor]
A Snake of June (2002)
Vital (2004)
Marebito (2004) [actor]

Haze (2005)
Nightmare Detective (2006)
Nightmare Detective 2 (2008)
Tetsuo: The Bullet Man (2010)
Kotoko (2011)
Fires on the Plain (2014)
Shin Godzilla (2016) [actor]
Silence (2016) [actor]
Killing (2018)

Gojira tai Biorante "Godzilla vs. Biollante"
Toho, 12/16/1989 (*Heisei 1*), 7 Reels (2,948 meters), 104:31, 35mm, Spherical (1.85:1, hard matted), color, Dolby Stereo

Crew
Executive Producer: Tomoyuki Tanaka
Producer: Shogo Tomiyama
Director: Kazuki Omori
Special Effects Director: Koichi Kawakita
Screenplay: Kazuki Omori, Shinichiro Kobayashi (original story)
Director of Photography: Yudai Kato
Music: Koichi Sugiyama, Akira Ifukube *(themes)*
Conductor: David Howell
Editor: Michiko Ikeda
Production Designer: Shigekazu Ikuno
Art Director: Akio Tashiro
Sound Recording Mixer: Kazuo Miyauchi
Sound Effects Editor: Shinichi Ito
Lighting: Takeshi Awakibara
Electrician: Hideo Inagaki
Assistant Directors: Hideyuki Inoue, Hiroshi Kubo, Kazuhiko Fukami
Costume Design: Kenji Kawasaki

Additional Cinematography: Takashi Wakiya
Assistant Editor: Miho Siga
Lighting Assistant: Kohei Mikami
Sound Recording Assistant: Sadakazu Saito
Script Supervisor: Yukiko Eguchi
Hair Stylist: Harumi Ueno
Construction: Yoshiki Kasahara
Props: Eiji Suzuki
Production Manager: Takahide Morichi
SFX Director of Photography: Kenichi Eguchi
SFX Art Directors: Tetsuzo Ozawa, Takashi Naganoma
Assistant SFX Directors: Kiyotaka Matsumoto, Toshiki Chiba, Makoto Kamiya
Lighting: Kaoru Saito
Suit Makers: Nobuyuki Yasumaru, Fuyuki Shinada
Wire Work: Koji Matsumoto
Pyrotechnics: Tadaaki Watanabe, Mamoru Kumi
Assistant SFX Photography: Hiroshi Kidokoro

SFX Continuity: Yoshiko Hori
Creature Designs: Atsuhiko Sugita, Noritaka Suzuki, Shinji Nishikawa
Mechanical Design: Hiroshi Yokoyama
Motion Control: Ryoji Kinoshita, Kenichi Abe
Optical Photography: Yoshiyuki Kishimoto, Noriaki Hojo
Video Effects: Kenji Hagiwara
VFX Animators: Mitsuaki Hashimoto, Hajime Matsumoto
Computer Graphics: Tetsuo Oya, Tanihisa Kame
Mattes: Kazunobu Mihei, Fumi Yamamoto
VFX Coordinators: Toshihiro Ogawa, Katsuji Mizawa
Still Photographer: Yoshinori Ishizuki
SFX Still Photographer: Takashi Nakao
Production Assistants: Takaya Fukuzawa, Satoshi Fukushima

SFX Production Assistants:
Taro Kojima, Masaya
Kobakura
VFX Production Assistants:
Takashi Yamabe, Mitsuharu
Umano

Cast
Kunihiko Mitamura *(Kazuhito Kirishima)*
Yoshiko Tanaka *(Asuka Okochi)*
Masanobu Takahashi *(Major Sho Kuroki)*
Megumi Odaka *(Miki Saegusa)*
Toru Minegishi *(Col. Goro Gondo)*
Ryunosuke Kaneda *(Seizo Okochi)*
Koji Takahashi *(Dr. Genichiro Shiragami)*
Yasuko Sawaguchi *(Erika Shiragami)*
Toshiyuki Nagashima *(Engineering Director Yamamoto)*
Yoshiko Kuga *(Chief Cabinet Secretary Keiko Owada)*
Manjot Beoi *(Saradian Agent SSS9)*
Koichi Ueda *(Joint-Chief of Staff Yamaji)*

Kosuke Toyohara *(Super X Operator)*
Kyoka Suzuki *(Super X Operator)*
Takashi Hunt *(John Lee)*
Derrick Holmes *(Michael Low)*
Hirohisa Nakata *(Defense Minister Minoru Koyama)*
Katsuhiko Sasaki *(Science and Technology Director Takeda)*
Kenzo Hagiwara *(Chief of Ground Staff)*
Kazuyuki Senba *(Chief of Naval Staff)*
Koji Yamanaka *(Chief of Air Force)*
Aydin Yamanlar *(Abdul Saulman)*
Hiroshi Inoue *(Self Defense Force)*
Kazuma Matsubara *(Self Defense Force)*
Ryota Yoshimitsu *(Self Defense Force)*
Satoru Kawaii *(Self Defense Force)*
Yasunori Yumiya *(Self Defense Force)*
Shin Tasuma *(Akiyama, Director of Giant Plant Monitoring)*
Shu Minagawa *(Military Official)*

Hajime Matsuoka *(Military Official)*
Soichiro Sakata *(Military Official)*
Soleiman Mehdizade *(Sirhan)*
Abdullah Helal *(Saradian Researcher)*
Kurt Cramer *(Commando)*
Brien Uhl *(Commando)*
Robert Corner *(Commando)*
Beth Blatt *(American Newscaster)*
Makiyo Kuroiwa *(Nurse)*
Haruko Sagara *(TV Reporter)*
Hiromi Matsukawa *(Newscaster)*
Demon Kogure *(TV Host)*
Isao Takeo *(Super X Maintenance)*
Kenpachiro Satsuma *(Godzilla)*
Shigeru Shibasaki *(Godzilla)*
Yoshitaka Kimura *(Godzilla)*
Masashi Takegumi *(Biollante)*

Alternate Titles
Godzilla - Der Urgigant
[Godzilla: The Giant]
(Germany)
Godzilla Contra-Ataca
[Godzilla Returns] (Portugal)
고질라 1990 **[Godzilla 1990]**
(South Korea)

"Godzilla and Biollante aren't the real monsters. The people who create them are..."
-Dr. Shiragami (Koji Takahashi)

Toho hit a real home run for their follow-up to *The Return of Godzilla*. *Godzilla vs. Biollante* pits Godzilla against a genetically engineered horticultural horror also made by misuse of science. *Godzilla vs. Biollante* was the first entry produced in the *Heisei* Imperial era. Fittingly, it would bring together a new team headed by Kazuki Omori and FX director Koichi Kawakita. Like *The Empire Strikes Back, Aliens* and *Terminator 2: Judgement Day, Godzilla vs. Biollante* both compliments and expands upon its predecessor.

PLOT

In the aftermath of Godzilla's 1985 attack, a military team gathers its cellular tissue for scientific use. A group of covert American operatives gather Godzilla cells as well. Discovered by the Japanese team, they shoot their way out. They are then killed by SSS9 (Manjot Beoi), an agent from the Arab Republic of Saradia, who takes the cells back to his country. Dr. Shiragami (Koji Takahashi) is a Japanese scientist working there with his daughter Erika (Yasuko Sawaguchi). He tells his superior Zalman (Aydin Yamanlar) that he plans to use the Godzilla cells to genetically engineer wheat that can be grown in the desert. This will make the Arab world able to produce grain. On the day he's set to begin work on this project, the American genetics firm Bio Major bombs his research lab in retaliation. Erika is killed in the explosion.

Five years later, Shiragami returns to Japan a bitter and broken man. He's become obsessed with a rose bush, believing that it harbors the spirit of his daughter. The daughter of his colleague Okochi, Asuka (Yoshiko Tanaka), brings over a young psychic named Miki Saegusa (Megumi Odaka). She tries to speak to the rose bush with her ESP but is unable to communicate. Asuka's father Seizo Okochi (Ryunosuke Kaneda) is trying to start a Nobel Prize winner sperm bank and wants to research the Godzilla cells. Asuka's boyfriend, a scientist named Kazuhito

Kirishima (Kunihiko Mitamura) is opposed to these projects.

Mount Mihara, where Godzilla was sealed five years prior, begins to show signs of activity. Miki's class at a center for children with psychic abilities have vivid dreams of Godzilla's return. The Japanese government prepares countermeasures in case the monster returns. Colonel Goro Gondo (Toru Minegishi) and young Col. Sho Kuroki (Masanobu Takashima) are put in charge. They fly Miki over Mt. Mihara and with her ESP, she detects that Godzilla has awoken. The government begins development of "anti-nuclear energy bacteria" to have ready when Godzilla appears. The bacteria was developed to clean up nuclear accidents. It has the potential to sedate or kill Godzilla but can only be made from Godzilla cells. Koroki asks Dr. Shiragami to create the bacteria but he refuses the offer. The Japanese-gathered cells, stored at the Okochi Foundation, are shown to Kirishima. Kirishima warns Okochi that anti-nuclear bacteria could shift the balance of power by neutralizing nuclear stockpiles. Mt. Mihara erupts which causes a small earthquake on the mainland. Shiragami's beloved rose bush is ruined in the tremors. Shiragami agrees to make the anti-nuclear bacteria on the condition that he keep the Godzilla cells in his lab. To save his rose bush, Shiragami implants the cells into it.

As Godzilla begins moving in Mt. Mihara, the military unveils the new Super-X2. It has improved armor and a synthetic diamond "fire mirror" that reflects Godzilla's heat-ray. Bio Major agents Lee (Takashi Hunt) and Low (Derrick Holmes) break into Shiragami's laboratory to steal the data on the anti-nuclear bacteria. A shoot-out ensues as SSS9 shows up, also after the data. Suddenly, monster plant vines attack the agents. Low is killed and Lee escapes with SSS9 also getting away. Kirishima and Shiragami find the severed vine, along with a large hole in the wall. Bio Major next sends the Japanese government a terroristic threat. They demand that the anti-nuclear bacteria be turned over. If not, they will blow up Mt. Mihara and release Godzilla. Gondo dismisses it as a bluff but after Bio Major sets off a warning explosion on Mihara, the government decides to give in. Meanwhile, Shiragami's plant monster, a giant rose creature, appears at Lake Ashinoko. Shiragami christens it "Biollante" after Norse mythology. Kirishima and Gondo next deliver the bacteria to Agent Lee. Both parties are intercepted by SSS9, who shoots Lee dead and steals the bacteria. Gondo and Kirishima try to disarm the remote detonator in Lee's truck but are unable to. Godzilla is released from Mt. Mihara to raid Japan once more.

Godzilla heads down the Uraga Channel towards Tokyo, destroying a naval battalion. The Super-X2 is sent after the monster. It proves effective in combat at first, diverting Godzilla's path. It is soundly defeated when the fire mirror melts from the intense heat of Godzilla's ray. Godzilla comes ashore at Odawara and heads toward Biollante at Lake Ashinoko. The two monsters do battle but Biollante proves vulnerable to Godzilla's ray. The creature erupts into flames and its heart explodes. Yet Biollante's spirit seems to survive the duel, leading Shiragami to conclude that the monster is immortal. Godzilla next heads toward the city of Osaka.

BACKGROUND

In 1985, Tomoyuki Tanaka was unsure of what direction he wanted to take the Godzilla franchise in. Toho thus put out a story competition. Fans from all over the world submitted ideas and two stories were decided on as finalists. The first was by an American, James Bannon. It involved Godzilla battling a devious supercomputer in a cyberpunk future. The second was by Shinichiro Kobayashi. Kobayashi (1955-) was a dentist by trade but occasionally penned scripts for television. He wrote an episode of Tsuburaya's *The Return of Ultraman* when he was only in high school. His submission involved Godzilla battling two genetically engineered abominations made from its cells. These were a giant rat named Deutalios and a monster plant called Biollante. Toho went with Kobayashi's treatment. Bannon's treatment would be developed sans Godzilla into *Gunhed*, also released in 1989.

Kobayashi was influenced by John Wyndham's 1951 novel *The Day of the Triffids* in particular. His concept was heavily rewritten for the final product by writer/director Omori. Kazuki Omori (1952-) was a former med student turned film director. His breakout was a dark comedy based on his medical school experience: *Disciples of Hippocrates* (1980). Toho decided this up-and-coming director was perfect to revitalize the franchise and he was awarded the job in 1986. The film was then delayed for several years after the dismal box office of *King Kong Lives* spooked Tanaka. Omori focused on several projects with idol Yuki Saito in the meantime. These included *Totto Channel*, a biopic of beloved TV personality Tetsuko Kuroyanagi. The delays were also because pre-production was exhaustive. The rat monster Deutalios was axed, replaced with an earlier "rose form" for Biollante. Biollante was redesigned a hundred times. The final design was created by Shinji Nishikawa and modeled by Fuyuki Shinada. Special effects director Koichi Kawakita also had input into the script: the monster battles were his baby. High tech *mecha,* including redesigned Maser Cannons, were added at his suggestion.

PRINCIPAL PHOTOGRAPHY

Finally, cameras began rolling on *Godzilla vs. Biollante* in August of 1989. The last shots of Godzilla submerging itself into the sea were shot in freezing November weather at Toho's "Big Pool". *Godzilla vs. Biollante* is a symbolic film, in many ways the first "modern Godzilla movie". By 1989, Emperor Hirohito had passed away, bringing the *Showa* era to an end. His son, Akihito, ascended the Chrysanthemum Throne and ushered in the *Heisei* era. Reflecting this, for *Biollante*, Toho's old guard handed the reins

to a younger generation. Tomoyuki Tanaka's involvement in these films lessened before his death. Production was now overseen mainly by younger producer Shogo Tomiyama (1952-). Teruyoshi Nakano passed the baton of Toho's FX department head to Kawakita after *Princess From the Moon* (1987). Directors like Ishiro Honda and Jun Fukuda had long since retired, leaving younger upstarts like Omori in charge. *Godzilla vs. Biollante* is the first entry with fresh, second generation talent and it shows.

Godzilla vs. Biollante has a creative energy and vibrancy that the series would soon lose. It's even more polished than *The Return of Godzilla* with production values closer still to the Hollywood tier. Omori had only minor affection for the Godzilla series. As a teenager, he stopped seeing Godzilla films and started watching 007 entries instead. Indeed, his screenplay mixes Bondian intrigue in at every turn. Yet Omori's direction has a nice balance. He has some reverence for the best entries but is just enough of an "outsider" to create something unique. There's a quirky, almost Ridley Scott-like attention to detail. The film's aesthetic is a perfect late '80s sweet spot where computer graphics were introduced but practical effects reign supreme. *Godzilla vs. Biollante* also has an unusual sense of realism. This is reflected in touches like a "Godzilla memorial" cocktail lounge, a cameo by metal singer Demon Kogure and a Yuki Saito concert interrupted by Godzilla's advance. The tone is more sardonic than *The Return of Godzilla* which was played dead serious. Whereas *Return* treated the Prime Minister with reverence, in

Omori's more cynical script his successor is *"Too busy with the opposition for Godzilla"*. This foreshadows touches that directors like Shusuke Kaneko and Hideaki Anno would bring to the genre in later years. With atmospheric cinematography by Yudai Kato, *Godzilla vs. Biollante* is one of the last entries to feel cinematic. After this, the series would adopt a bland, TV movie-like aesthetic, with each film barely distinguishable from the last.

ACTORS

The cast includes Kunihiko Mitamura and Yoshiko Tanaka, alongside newcomer Megumi Odaka. Mitamura (1953-) would return to the kaiju genre playing Ayana's ill-fated father in *Gamera 3: Revenge of Iris* (1999). Yoshiko Tanaka (1956-2011) was best known for her poignant role as a Hiroshima survivor in Shohei Imamura's *Black Rain* (1989). She would return to the Godzilla series for a different role in *Godzilla vs. Mothra* (1992). Tragically, she succumbed to breast cancer in 2011, leaving behind a heartbreaking message to her fans on YouTube. Actress and idol Megumi Odaka (1972-) won Toho's Cinderella contest in 1987. Her first appearance was in *Princess From the Moon*. Odaka, at first afraid to touch the Godzilla suit, would reprise the role of Miki Saegusa in the next five sequels. Miki is one of the franchise's more notable characters. She is given a juicier backstory in the *manga* adaptation by Tatsuyoshi Kobayashi. In that, her parents were killed in Godzilla's 1985 Tokyo attack. Odaka would become extremely popular with fans on both sides of the Pacific. In 2015 she was out

walking near her home in Kamata ward. The streets were blocked off by *Shin Godzilla's* shoot. She was stopped by a police officer who said *"You can't go through here, they're filming a Godzilla movie"*. Other notables include Masanobu Takashima as Sho Kuroki and Toru Minegishi as Gondo. Takashima (1966-) was the son of *Showa* legend Tadao Takashima. The character of Sho Kuroki returned in *Godzilla vs. Destoroyah* (1995) but played by Takashima's brother Masahiro. Minegishi (1943-2008) was a character actor who appeared in countless dramas and *jidai-geki* films. Active up until his death, he was married to Tomoko Ai, who played Katsura Mafune in *Terror of Mechagodzilla*. This was also the first Godzilla role for actor Koichi Ueda. Ueda (1941-) would appear in every subsequent Godzilla entry until *Godzilla: Final Wars*.

SFX

The execution of Koichi Kawakita's special effects end represents him at the top of his form. Once again, more special effects footage was shot for *Godzilla vs. Biollante* than any other entry up to that time. Kawakita's unit also made the heaviest use of robotics and radio controlled miniature helicopters yet. The Godzilla suit was redesigned in line with Kawakita's vision. Built once more by Nobuyuki Yasumaru, this Godzilla was sleeker than the last with some mammalian features. The Godzilla design motif for the subsequent *Heisei* entries would stay in line with this one. Kawakita sought to improve on the cybot used in *The Return of Godzilla*. While impressive, it was a little mismatched with footage of the suit. Kawakita instead built an animatronic upper body in the same scale as the suit. This was used for similar expressive close-ups and is far better matched.

For the first time in Japanese cinema history, the Hollywood technique of shooting VFX composites on 70mm was used for some shots. Before digital technology, composite shots had to be done optically by reprinting. Composites made on 35mm would suffer generational loss and often appear grainy and soft in projection. Using 70mm allowed for sharper composites that looked better on the big screen. These shots in *Godzilla vs. Biollante* are among the most stunning in the entire series.

Biollante's first battle with Godzilla is impressive. Kawakita wanted a fierce fight and it was well shot by FX cameraman Kenichi Eguchi. Biollante's tentacle-like vines were manipulated the old fashioned way: through large amounts of piano wire. Kawakita's team experimented with stop motion animation to make the battle more dynamic. It didn't match the rest of the sequence well so the idea was discarded. Given the amount of footage shot, there are several deleted FX scenes. The most notable is a poetic sequence showing hills of flowers blooming around Godzilla after Biollante's defeat. Due to scale and pacing issues, it was cut late in production. Another impressive scene is Godzilla's nautical battle with the navy and Super-X2. It was once again shot in Toho's "Big Pool" used primarily for its war films. A makeshift ceiling was built and light reflected from it to make the water's texture

more realistic. The amount of pyrotechnics and water-based filming made these scenes dangerous to film. Kenpachiro Satsuma had to wear goggles to protect his eyes. Eguchi built a raft and positioned the camera high above it to get the bird's eye shots of Godzilla he wanted. He fell right into the pool holding expensive camera equipment on several occasions.

Like *Godzilla Raids Again, Godzilla vs. Biollante* moves its urban destruction from Tokyo to Osaka. Godzilla's explosive Osaka rampage is among the most impressive in the entire series. A good portion of it was used as a gag in Tim Burton's *Mars Attacks!* Like the Nagoya castle miniature in *Mothra vs. Godzilla*, the miniature Twin Tower demolished by Godzilla was too well built. Satsuma couldn't crumble it in one take so its demolition had to be filmed three times. All three takes were edited together to give the illusion of the building being quickly destroyed. Stock footage used in the film is minimal, but some *Deathquake* (1980) footage is peppered into this sequence.

Yet the film's greatest FX scene is Godzilla's final, gruesome tussle with Biollante. *Little Shop of Horrors* (1986) was clearly an influence on this final form. Biollante also vomits up green sap like a kaiju Regan MacNeil. It was an incredible feat of engineering that put even the climax of *Destroy All Monsters* to shame. Ingeniously constructed by Fuyuki Shinada, evolved Biollante was an intricate suit crossed with a marionette that took 20 people to operate. In certain shots, the entire FX crew along with visitors from Omori's unit had to pull the strings. Kawakita, however, was uncertain of how to end the battle. His idea was to have Biollante devour Godzilla and purge the creature of humanity's sin. Much of this effect was done with *anime*-style hand drawn animation. Kawakita thought the cel animation stuck out like a sore thumb alongside the live action footage. So Biollante was made to simply return to the sky. The last shots of Godzilla in the water were filmed while the movie was editing. The scene in *Godzilla 2000* (1999) where Orga tries to devour Godzilla was an homage to this discarded ending.

MUSIC

The film features a contemporary score by Koichi Sugiyama. Sugiyama (1931-), is known both for his *anime* and video game music and his vocal denial of Japan's war crimes. The music is controversial among fans, but works in the context of a "modern" Godzilla movie. Biollante's theme is atmospheric and effective with eerie, sharp chords. The Super-X2 motif is similarly arranged to John Williams' *Superman* theme. The music well compliments Omori's more "Hollywood-style" direction. Some Ifukube pieces are sampled for nostalgia sake. Like Koroku before him, Sugiyama was also not brought back for subsequent entries as Ifukube would return. Ifukube's work on the next few entries was dependable but stale: consisting of re-orchestrated themes from the *Showa* era.

THEMES AND MOTIFS

The themes in *Godzilla vs. Biollante* are intriguing and deeper than at first glance. It is one of the most science-based entries, invoking the classic "misuse of science" trope. Kobayashi felt the concept of Godzilla battling another monster was tired. Like Yoshimitsu Banno with *Godzilla vs. Hedorah*, he felt that an effective adversary would have to be something just as existentially terrifying. As a result, he focused the story on genetic engineering as it has the same potential for weaponization as nuclear technology. It's a clever science fiction concept. Indeed, genetic engineering is still a controversial science. The film's American megafirm Bio Major even bears some similarity to Monsanto, known for its genetically modified crops and control over the food supply. The trope of nefarious Westerners would also play into Omori's subsequent *Godzilla vs. King Ghidorah*.

There's also subtext to *Biollante* involving the divide between the young and old, between progress and conservatism. In Japan, people in classrooms and workplaces develop a *senpai-kohai* relationship. The older colleague, the *senpai*, acts as a mentor to the younger *kohai*. This can be seen in the idealistic Kirishima's relationship with the more jaded Shiragami. It can also be seen in Col. Kuroki's interaction with Koichi Ueda's Yamaji, a high ranking chief of staff. He is contemptuous of Kuroki because of his brashness despite his *kohai* status. Yamaji then warms up to Kuroki after his tactics win the battle.

RELEASE AND LEGACY

Godzilla vs. Biollante was a moderate flop at the Japanese box office. It faced tough Christmas competition from Tim Burton's *Batman*. Despite stunning poster art by Noriyoshi Ohrai, audiences favored the Caped Crusader. Toho thus decided to course correct. Omori was kept on but they were determined to pair Godzilla with a more familiar foe for his next outing. As a result, stalwart villain Ghidorah was brought back for *Godzilla vs. King Ghidorah* (1991). That film was far more successful at the box office. Afterward, the series would massively decline in creativity and quality. Toho opted for a "safer" approach and Kawakita slipped into burn-out.

ALTERNATE VERSIONS

Toho commissioned an English dubbed export version from Omni Productions, another Hong Kong based firm. It was run by Richard "Rik" Thomas and his Chinese wife. Rik Thomas was a former British special forces member who served tours in the Congo and Vietnam. After a deployment, he stopped off in Hong Kong and was drinking at a pub. He was approached and asked to do film dubbing and before long, he had his own company. Known for his raspy voice and snarky personality, he appears on screen in the HK rom-com *My Darling, My Goddess* (1983).

The English dub for *Godzilla vs. Biollante* has its nostalgic fans. Recorded at a facility in Kowloon that now appears abandoned, it's badly mixed. It also includes a serious scripting gaffe where Okochi says *"The bodies belonged to two of Bio Major's agents"* when only one was killed. The scenes with amateurish English speaking actors play better in the dub. In the Japanese version the poor line readings give the scenes a rawness. In this English dub these characters sound more like Americans. The dub, however, plays the film too straight, partially losing the sardonic tone of the Japanese version. Rik Thomas dubs Gondo and is surprisingly convincing. Other dubbing cast includes Chris Hilton as Kirishima, Suzanne Vale as Asuka, Warren Rooke as Shiragami, Ellen Dyer (suspected) as Miki and Simon Broad as Okochi along with several others.

The Devon, England-born Hilton, who died in 2013, was notable. Despite having an almost boyish voice, he was a heavy set bearded man compared to Santa Claus. He worked as a news commentator for Radio Television Hong Kong. On English HK airwaves in the 1970s and '80s, he gave opinions on controversial political matters and moderated a talk show called *Here and Now*. He can be seen on screen in the 1985 film *Dog Tags*, though amusingly, his voice is dubbed. Hilton often provided the voices of Ti Lung and Gordon Liu in Shaw Brothers movies. He also dubbed Jackie Chan in *Snake in the Eagle's Shadow*. This was hardly his first Godzila or Toho role. He voiced Zan Fujita's Fumio Sudo in *Godzilla vs. Gigan*, Katsuhiko Sasaki's Goro Ibuki in *Godzilla vs. Megalon* and Hiroshi Katsuno's Kawazu in *Deathquake*. Warren Rooke is another familiar voice to both kung fu and *kaiju* fans. An Australian, he was also a correspondent for RTHK. He is heard in numerous martial arts films, playing everything from villains to comic relief. Rooke also dubbed Yutaka Hayashi's Jinkawa in *Megalon*. He left Hong Kong for Malaysia after the Mainland Handover.

Suzanne Vale (1954-) was another British-born expat who, for her day job, was a weather woman and news anchor. She moonlighted with stage acting and film dubbing. She has a small on-screen role in the made for TV *Spider Man: The Dragon's Challenge* (1979), filmed in Hong Kong. Her best known dubbing role was likely voicing Sally Yeh in the English version of John Woo's *The Killer* (1989). She left Hong Kong to pursue an acting career in Los Angeles in 1990, making *Biollante*'s dub one of her last. Simon Broad (1963-) is an active voice artist to this day and still resides in Hong Kong. Born in New Zealand, he came to Hong Kong as a teenager and got into dubbing for extra money. He worked with Vaughan Savidge, Matthew Oram, Annie Mathers and Rik Thomas. His voice is most associated with actor Chow Yun Fat. He dubbed Chow in numerous films including *The Killer* and *Hard-Boiled* (1992).

The export version is almost cut for cut the same as the Japanese version with the simple addition of English supers. The only other minute change is that the English end credits cut to black midway. The Japanese credits, by contrast, stay on the shot of Biollante in Earth's orbit.

There is a unique bootleg version of *Godzilla vs. Biollante* from the 1990s. It could be considered one of the first real fan edits. It is mostly in Japanese with subtitles but cuts to the dub for the scenes with English speaking actors. It also removes the entire subplot of Bio Major releasing Godzilla. In this version, Godzilla emerges from Mihara spontaneously.

AMERICAN HOME VIDEO HISTORY

Godzilla vs. Biollante was sold to Miramax but the stateside release was tied up in a lawsuit with Toho. The suit was settled and the film released directly to American pay television, VHS and laserdisc in 1993. It was given a "PG" rating by the MPAA for, amusingly, *"Traditional Godzilla Violence"*. The VHS and laserdisc from HBO Video were, unusually, the uncut export version in widescreen format. The film would not be released on U.S. home video again until 2012. Echo Bridge, sublicensing it from Miramax, released it on DVD and Blu-ray with both the Japanese track and English dub. The discs have since gone out of print.

Further Viewing:

(1989)
ガンヘッド
Toho/Sunrise, *Director*: Masato Harada

The other finalist for the Godzilla story contest was by American James Bannon.

Bannon's story was a cyberpunk take of sorts on Godzilla, no doubt influenced by recent Ridley Scott and James Cameron films. Godzilla was to do battle with a powerful supercomputer in a dystopian, high tech future. Toho went with Shinichiro Kobayashi's idea for their Godzilla entry, but reworked Bannon's concept sans Godzilla. The result was *Gunhed*, released the summer before *Godzilla vs. Biollante*. To produce *Gunhed*, Toho would partner with Sunrise, the company behind *Mobile Suit Gundam*. Kazuhiko Hasegawa (*The Man Who Stole the Sun*) was considered as the director. In the end actor/writer/director Masato Harada was chosen.

While more popular in Japan, *Gunhed* is treated with pariah status in American fans circles. Some even consider it *"the worst film ever produced by Toho"*. The truth is that it's hardly that bad and a lot of fun thanks to the contributions of Koichi Kawakita. *Gunhed*'s script is pretty awful with cliched tropes and bad dialog. Yet the film is well executed, especially from Kawakita's end. *Gunhed* boasts surprisingly good production values, impressive sets and a good sense of atmosphere. Something between a live action Super Robot *anime* and cinematic video game, *Gunhed* is one of the few cyberpunk *tokusatsu* films. This gives it a unique novelty. Each sequence feels like a different "game level" to be beaten. While that's not exactly high art, it's pretty exhilarating fun. Naturally, there was a tie-in video game and *manga* produced, the latter by Kia Asamiya (*Silent Möbius*). Both were arguably more popular than the film.

Gunhed's cast is led by Tadao Takashima's son Masahiro, who later appeared in two Godzilla entries and developed an S&M fetish. Hollywood actress Brenda Bakke (*Tales From the Crypt: Demon Knight, L.A. Confidential*) appears; speaking her lines in English. She's not great, but light years ahead of the average *gaijin* in a Japanese film. Character actor and singer Mickey Curtis (1938-, *Fires on the Plain*) has what amounts to an extended cameo early on. The aesthetic influence of films like *Alien, Blade Runner, The Terminator* and *Aliens* can be felt in every scene. There's even a pair of Newt-like orphaned scavenger kids. While a little slow paced, *Gunhed* is the most "aesthetic" of any *tokusatsu* film.

Gunhed comes to life when the titular *mecha* is launched by Takashima's Brooklyn in its second half. It's daft but thrillingly executed by Koichi Kawakita's unit at top form. Gunhed itself was designed by Shoji Kawamori, known for his work on the *Macross* franchise. Kawakita's FX for the second half is dazzling and the robotics and motion control work employed is impressive. Masaharu Ogawa of Ogawa Modeling built the mechas at varying scales. Kawakita, a serious gear-head and robot lover, clearly took *Gunhed* to heart. Before his death, he produced *Gunhed 2025*, a proof of concept short included on DVD with the film's surprisingly popular model kits. Sadly *Gunhed* tanked at the Japanese box office. The film's export version, amusingly, credits the film to "Allen Smithee", a dubious pedigree indeed. Yet *Gunhed* itself is underrated.

(1991)
ゴジラVSキングギドラ
Toho, *Director*: Kazuki Omori

Godzilla vs. King Ghidorah would be the last entry directed by Kazuki Omori, given a lot less creative freedom this time around. While a major step down from *Godzilla vs. Biollante*, there are interesting themes present. *Godzilla vs. King Ghidorah* is a meditation on both Godzilla's legacy and Japan's economic power. A group of time traveling leftists from the future arrive in modern day Japan. They go back in time to 1944, erasing Godzilla from existence. The Futurians then create a new version of King Ghidorah to ravage Japan. Japan has become the richest nation by the 23rd Century and weakening it will redistribute the world's income. Yet a recreated Godzilla resurfaces once more to battle Ghidorah.

Though better than much of what was to come, *Godzilla vs. King Ghidorah* lacks novelty. Omori, even more so than in *Godzilla vs. Biollante*, wears his Hollywood fetish on his sleeve. *Godzilla vs. King Ghidorah* pays homage to recent blockbusters by James Cameron, Robert Zemeckis, Steven Spielberg and John McTiernan. Akira Ifukube's score is moving yet unoriginal,

consisting of previously composed cues from the *Showa* era. Even pieces from his soundtrack for Daiei's *Majin* are pilfered. The film is not helped by hazy, bland cinematography by Yoshinori Sekiguchi. It feels less cinematic than Yudai Kato's work in *Biollante*. The time travel logic is so mind bending that few in the Godzilla fandom can agree on it. Did the Futurians create the Godzilla that already existed or was Godzilla erased from history and then recreated?

Koichi Kawakita's effects work is among his most eclectic. It's a mixed bag, however and where his work began to appear uninspired. The World War II Godzillasaurus sequence is a highlight aside from the occasional sloppy shot. Filmed at a bigger scale, it feels like a melding of Kawakita's kaiju work and his effects on war films like 1976's *Zero Pilot*. Kawakita's Ghidorah sequences are less effective. Ghidorah's attack on Fukuoka is inferior to Eiji Tsuburaya's similar sequence in *Ghidorah, the Three-Headed Monster*. Though made 27 years prior, Tsuburaya's footage feels far more visually dynamic. The King Ghidorah suit, though built by veteran Keizo Murase, looks stiff, boasting a bland, Western-style design. There are also some anime-like visuals and a sense of "aesthetic" that brings Kawakita's work on *Bye Bye Jupiter* and *Gunhed* to mind. The finale features benevolent Japanese Futurian Emmy (Anna Nakagawa) battling Godzilla "Super Robot"-style in a resurrected, cyborg "Mecha King Ghidorah". One of robot-loving Kawakita's most thrilling FX sequences, it's the movie's highlight. The miniature work, however, suffers due to Godzilla's increased height. Kawakita's footage on *Godzilla vs. King Ghidorah* oddly looks more convincing in the low resolution of VHS tape.

Godzilla vs. King Ghidorah has been accused of nationalism. CNN even broadcast a news story on the controversy. At first glance, the film is almost comically right wing, even more so than *Shin Godzilla*. With evil white men from the future trying to put Japan in its place, the film peddles a problematic "poor Japan" narrative. Japan is depicted as becoming such an economic powerhouse that it annexes entire continents, arguably feeding into its old colonialist fantasies. The Japanese Emmy turns on her Western comrades, helping her people when she feels her "Yamato spirit" stirring within. Ishiro Honda even criticized Omori, feeling the political message was out of line with the Godzilla series' values. Yet Omori has denied his intent to make a hawkish film. The film's sentiment is perhaps taken too much at face value. Once again, the Hong Kong recorded English dub obscures Omori's wry satire. *Godzilla vs. King Ghidorah* is just as much a warning to modern Japan as it is conservative propaganda. It tells Japan not to get too comfortable in its newfound economic prosperity. It warns the Japanese to be mindful of how powerful they become, lest they raise the ire of the rest of the world once more. Godzilla takes the role, once again, of a rampaging *yonaoshi* god. It returns to set Japan straight when the country becomes so proud it disrupts the world's balance. Indeed, Japan's bubble economy soon burst and the country was plunged into a mild recession by the mid '90s. Despite *King Ghidorah*'s

immense box office success, Omori left his role as Godzilla director behind, focusing on other projects. He stayed on as screenwriter, however, for *Godzilla vs. Mothra* (1992) and *Godzilla vs. Destoroyah* (1995), only doing the latter because his home was destroyed in the Kobe earthquake. Subsequent entries would mainly be directed by journeyman Takao Okawara, who brought little in the way of stylistic flair or engaging storytelling.

GODZILLA VS MECHA GODZILLA

(1993)
ゴジラVSメカゴジラ
Toho, *Director*: **Takao Okawara**

Released the same year as Steven Spielberg's *Jurassic Park* and promoted as the 40th anniversary Godzilla film, *Godzilla vs. Mechagodzilla II* is an otherwise pedestrian entry. It is elevated, however, by the contributions of special effects director Koichi Kawakita. Director Takao Okawara and DP Yoshinori Sekiguchi's footage is bland and TV movie-like. Some of the actors do, however, make an impression, including then-pop idol Ryoko Sano, character actor Daijiro Harada and Akira Nakao as the gruff General Aso. Nakao (1942-) had previously appeared in Michio Yamamoto's *The Vampire Doll* (1970). He would return in the subsequent two entries. *Showa* stalwarts like Kenji Sahara, Tadao Takashima and Yusuke Kawazu are also on hand. Canadian expat and actress Shelley Sweeney plays a memorable role, though, like her expat contemporaries, she can't act a lick. The film's Baby Godzilla, created by Masakazu Amaki and portrayed by Hurricane Ryu, is well executed and empathetic. *Godzilla vs. Mechagodzilla II* was cut down heavily before theatrical release and the Toho laserdisc contained many of the deleted scenes. Most of them dramatically improve Okawara's half of the film and should not have been cut.

Godzilla vs. Mechagodzilla II comes to life, however, whenever Koichi Kawakita's unit takes the stage. The robot-loving Kawakita clearly took this film to heart. The early battle between Godzilla and Rodan is a mixed bag with some beautiful shots but just as many clunky ones. Rodan is given an appealing redesign by Shinji Nishikawa and modeler

Shinichi Wakasa, though the creature lacks the majesty of its *Showa* series counterpart. Typical of the gear-headed Kawakita, the animatronic work is superb and a major strength. Each of the monsters had expressive animatronic heads built for close-ups. Mechagodzilla's launch is a stunning sequence and once again, strongly invokes Kawakita's prior work on *Gunhed*. The picture truly leaps to life during Mechagodzilla's explosive battle against Godzilla. Amusingly, Kawakita's unit used more gunpowder on *Godzilla vs. Mechagodzilla II* than on any prior Godzilla entry. Overall, the film is dumb fun and easily the most tolerable of Okawara's entries thanks to Kawakita's contributions. It has little of interest, however, outside of its impressive monster battle sequences.

KOICHI KAWAKITA
The Gear-head

川北紘一
12/5/1942-12/5/2014

"James Cameron said to me films are living things. They change as they go through the various stages of production."
-Koichi Kawakita (1994)

Koichi Kawakita was an especially interesting figure in Toho's special effects history. Kawakita started off as a talented young effects director. As time went on, he produced increasingly bland special effects work as Toho began to favor formula over creativity. He was born in 1942 in Chuo, Tokyo. As a teenager, he saw *The Mysterians* and was captivated. He longed

to work for Toho and follow in his idol Eiji Tsuburaya's footsteps. In college, he interned at Toho. When they offered him a job at the special effects department, he jumped at the chance and dropped out of school. The first film he worked on was *Gorath* (1962). He started shooting matte composites and helping to draw animated rays in the films to come. He helped Sadao

Iizuka create the A-cycle rays in *Invasion of Astro-Monster* (1965) and the Maser beams in *The War of the Gargantuas* (1966). He also did work for Tsuburaya Pro on *Ultra Q* (1966). After Eiji Tsuburaya passed away, he worked on opticals for *Godzilla vs. Hedorah*.

His first special effects director jobs were on episodes of *Ultraman Ace* (1972), *Ultraman Taro* and *Zone Fighter* (both 1973). He also assisted Teruyoshi Nakano on *Godzilla vs. Mechagodzilla, Prophecies of Nostradamus* (both 1974) and *Conflagration* (1975). With *Mechagodzilla*, he did some uncredited second unit FX direction. The sequence where the monster robot fires a torrent of beams at Godzilla and King Caesar was largely his. In 1976 he saw his dream come true when he was put in charge of the World War II drama *Zero Pilot* as special effects director. *Zero Pilot*, to his passing, was Kawakita's favorite film he worked on. He was allowed to experiment and given a lot of creative freedom by Toho. Using radio-controlled model Zero planes, Kawakita did superb work. He assisted Nakano again on *The War in Space* and Sadamasa Arikawa on the Hong Kong production *The Mighty Peking Man* (both 1977).

In the 1980s, he was assigned to more projects as special effects director. These included the WWII themed Australian/Japanese co-production *The Highest Honor* (1982) and *Zero* (1984) by Toshio Masuda. His superb FX work on the disastrous *Bye Bye Jupiter* was the film's saving grace. He also worked on Kensho Yamashita's *Nineteen* (1987). By the late '80s, he had taken over Toho's special effects division. He directed the unit on two

films in 1989 that would define his career: *Gunhed* and *Godzilla vs. Biollante*. His work on *Biollante* impressed fans. Sadly both films were box office flops and Kawakita took this hard.

He won a Japanese Academy Award for his work on *Godzilla vs. King Ghidorah*. Afterwards he was put in charge of the special effects for the rest of the *"VS"* Godzilla series. Though his work on *Godzilla vs. Mechagodzilla II* (1993) was a major step up, his scenes became sloppier and uninspired. It was an open secret that Kawakita struggled with alcoholism and drinking affected his work. He also was less enthusiastic about Takao Okawara's directing style. By *Yamato Takeru* and *Godzilla vs. Space Godzilla* (both 1994), his work contained some embarrassing composites and FX gaffes. Bandai figures were even used in wide shots in *Godzilla vs. Destoroyah*. After the abysmal *Rebirth of Mothra II*, Toho put Kenji Suzuki in charge of their FX unit. Kawakita then went into semi-retirement.

Afterwards, Koichi Kawaita continued his career designing amusement park rides. He also taught film at the Osaka University of the Arts. Kawakita did some special effects work for television such as for the Gransizers franchise. He would work on its feature film *Sazer X the Movie: Fight! Star Warriors* (2005), directed by old collaborator Kazuki Omori. Kawakita also involved himself in independent projects through his newly founded company Dream Planet Japan. These included *Kawaii Jenny* (2007) and *God of Clay* (2011). He was quite busy and still trying to get projects off the ground up until his death. Right before he died, Kawakita was a guest at the annual

G-FEST convention in Chicago. One memorable anecdote is that he took time out in the hotel lobby to play "monster fight" with some children and their Bandai figurines. For a man who spent a long career staging monster battles, this felt like a bittersweet bookend to his life.

Selected Filmography
"Ultraman Ace" (1972-73, TV) [special effects director, *episodes 21, 22. 25. 26. 27, 30, 31, 36, 37, 40, 41*]
"Zone Fighter" (1973, TV) [special effects director, *episodes 3, 4, 8, 10, 14, 15, 16, 25*]
"Ultraman Taro" (1973, TV) [special effects director, *episodes 6, 7*]
Godzilla vs. Mechagodzilla (1974) [assistant special effects director]
Prophecies of Nostradamus (1974) [assistant special effects director]
Conflagration (1975) [assistant special effects director]
Zero Pilot (1976) [special effects director]
The Mighty Peking Man (1977) [assistant special effects director]

The War in Space (1977) [assistant special effects director]
"Megaloman" (1979, TV) [special effects director, *episode 7*]
"Monkey" (1979, TV) [special effects director, *episodes 2.9, 2.12, 2.14, 2.15*)
The Highest Honor (1982) [special effects director]
Bye Bye Jupiter (1984) [special effects director]
Zero (1984) [special effects director]
Toho Special Effects Outtake Collection (1986) [director]
Nineteen (1987) [special effects]
Gunhed (1989) [special effects director]
Godzilla vs. Biollante (1989) [special effects director]
Godzilla vs. King Ghidorah (1991) [special effects director]

Godzilla vs. Mothra (1992) [special effects director]
Godzilla vs. Mechagodzilla II (1993) [special effects director]
Monster Planet of Godzilla (1994) [director]
Yamato Takeru (1994) [special effects director]
Godzilla vs. Space Godzilla (1994) [special effects director]
Godzilla vs. Destoroyah (1995) [special effects director]
Rebirth of Mothra (1996) [special effects director]
Rebirth of Mothra II (1997) [special effects director]
Sazer X the Movie: Fight! Star Warriors (2005) [special effects director]
"Kawaii Jenny" (2007, TV) [director]
God of Clay (2011) [director]
Gunhed 2025 (2013) [director]

KERBEROS PANZER COPS

Keruberosu: Jigoku no Banken "Kerberos: Watchdogs of Hell"
Bandai Visual/Fuji TV/Shochiku, 3/24/1991 (*Heisei 3*), 95:31, 35mm, Spherical (1.85:1), color, Dolby Stereo

Crew
Executive Producers: Shigeru Watanabe, Noboru Yamada
Producers: Sumiaki Ueno, Daisuke Hayashi
Assistant Producers: Hisashi Hashimoto, Koichi Uchida
Planning: Chuko Hayakawa, Tadashi Oka
Director/Screenplay: Mamoru Oshii
Director of Photography: Yosuke Mamiya
Music: Kenji Kawai
Music Producer: Takeshi Minematsu
Art Director: Tsunemitsu Tezuka
Designer: Kamui Fujiwara
Mechanical Designs: Yutaka Izubuchi

Sound Design: Shizuo Kurahashi
Sound Mixing: Shujo Inoue
Sound Recording: Shinji Minoru
Lighting: Yoshimi Hosaka
Lighting Assistants: Takashi Mizuno, Shigeru Izumiya
Editor: Seiji Morita
Assistant Editors: Hideaki Takahashi, Hisao Ariga, Ryuichi Shibamoto
Negative Cutters: Masaki Sakamoto, Sachiko Miki
Continuity: Yoshihiro Akase
Costume and Armor Modeling (Kerberos): Fuyuki Shinada
Special Effects Supervisor: Takahisa Notomi
Hair and Makeup: Mayumi Shoji, Yuko Takamori

Still Photographer: Haruhiko Higami

Cast
Yoshikazu Fujiki (*Inui*)
Eaching Sue (*Tang Mie*)
Takashi Matsuyama (*Hayashi*)
Shigeru Chiba (*Koichi Todome*)
Keinosuke Suzuki
Takayuki Kitamura
Sho Sadakata
Masaru Ikeda
Ryoichi Tanaka
Kazumi Tanaka
Yutaro Mitsuoka
Joji Nakata
Masashi Sugawara
Masamichi Sato
Koji Tsujitani

"Even if a wolf takes the guise of a man and lives among them, he can never be truly human."
-Hajime Handa (Yukihiro Yoshida), *Jin-Roh: The Wolf Brigade* (1999)

Stray Dog: Kerberos Panzer Cops is the second installment in a trilogy of films spearheaded by Mamoru Oshii. Best known for iconic anime works like *Patlabor* (1989) and *Ghost in the Shell* (1995), Oshii's contributions to the live action realm are surprising. Set in a dystopian alternate Japan, the films delve into complex and relevant themes including police militarization, trauma and societal decay. *Stray Dog* is a prequel to Oshii's 1987 *The Red Spectacles*. It is richer, boasting an impressive opening and lyrical midsection that unravels with tragic inevitability. The stunning finale combines John Woo-style bullet ballet with kinetic action of Oshii's best anime; executed live rather than with painted cels.

PLOT

In an alternate universe, Japan was occupied by Nazi Germany rather than the United States. In the post-war years, a militarized police force called the Kerberos unit was established to maintain public order. By 1995, with the opposition crushed and eroding public opinion, the Kerberos unit was ordered to disband and stand down. The unit resists this order, however and makes a last stand at their headquarters. Inui (Yoshikatsu Fujiki) wanders through the chaos. He sees superior officer Koichi Todome (Shigeru Chiba) board a helicopter to escape. Inui feels betrayed at Koichi's flight. The military then seizes the headquarters and the rebellion is extinguished. The members of the Kerberos unit, Inui included, are given jail sentences.

After three years, Inui is released with good behavior and leaves Japan for Taiwan. Hayashi (Takashi Matsuyama), Inui's contact with the shadowy Fugitive Support Group, tells him that Koichi Todome has also fled to Taiwan. Hayashi is actually an agent of the Public Security Division looking for Koichi. They are concerned that he intends to start a new Kerberos cell and return to Japan. Inui tracks down Tang Mie (Sue Eaching), a Taiwanese girl who was involved with Koichi. Inui moves in with her and the two start searching for Koichi.

In the idyllic Taiwan countryside, Inui and Tang find Koichi working as a prawn fisherman. Inui and Koichi fight but soon make peace. With money from Tang having sold her condo, the three rent a house and decide to move in together. Inui and Koichi work as laborers and for a time, things are good. The dynamic starts to break down, however. Soon Inui is approached by Hayashi who is well aware that he has found Koichi. He offers Hayashi a deal: surrender Koichi to be extradited to Japan and he can stay in Taiwan with Tang Mie. Refuse and both he and Koichi will be hunted down and apprehended.

BACKGROUND

By the mid 1980s, anime luminary Mamoru Oshii was starting to make waves in his career after directing the first two *Urusei Yatsura* films. His original video animation *The Angel's Egg* unsettled, perplexed but captivated its audience. After a failed project with fellow anime titans Hayao Miyazaki and Isao Takahata, Oshii joined the collective Headgear. Headgear's fellows included writer Kazunori Ito, manga artist Masami Yuki, mechanical designer Yutaka Izubuchi and character designer Akemi Takada. Together they got to work developing a new anime franchise: *Patlabor*. While *Patlabor* was in development, Oshii would get to work on a different, similarly themed project: the *Kerberos* saga. It began with a radio drama and continued with Oshii's very first live action movie: *The Red Spectacles* (1987).

The Red Spectacles tells the story of Koichi Todome, played in live action by Shigeru Chiba, a prolific anime voice actor. *The Red Spectacles* is actually set last in the series' timeline and details Koichi's return to a collapsing Japan. It was, interestingly, released the same year as Paul Verhoeven's similarly themed *Robocop*. Oshii followed *The Red Spectacles* with some *manga* volumes before making a follow-up prequel: *Stray Dog*. During pre-production, Oshii and his crew narrowly avoided tragedy as they went to Taiwan to scout locations. Oshii missed his flight which wound up crashing.

PRINCIPAL PHOTOGRAPHY

Unusually for a Japanese film, a good part of *Stray Dog* was shot in Taiwan and around half the film's dialogue is in Mandarin Chinese. The budget for *Stray Dog* was far bigger than the low budget *The Red Spectacles*. For *The Red Spectacles*, only three armored Kerberos uniforms were produced. With *Stray Dog*, modeler Fuyuki Shinada manufactured fifty of them. Shinada had built and would go on to build many kaiju for Koichi Kawakita, Shinji Higuchi and Makoto Kamiya's *tokusatsu* units. These included Biollante, Legion, Iris and Godzilla.

Compared to *The Red Spectacles, Stray Dog* is a better executed picture. Oshii shows more command of the live action medium with long steadicam-based takes including a *Paths of Glory*-like shot in the opening. The impressive pre-credit sequence expands upon *The Red Spectacles'* opening. Montages of urban Taipei invoke a similar sequence in Oshii's later *Ghost in the Shell*. The Taiwan locales are stunningly photographed. The country seems like an idyllic paradise compared to the hellish dystopian Japan seen in *The Red Spectacles* or the later *Jin-Roh*. The midsection of the film is lyrical and even dream-like. It has elements of *mono-no-aware* like much of Oshii's work. *Stray Dog's* dreamy peace is harshly broken with a disturbing sequence. Covered in an unbroken wide shot, Inui and Koichi brutally assault each other over the possession of the latter's gear.

Stray Dogs' finale is jaw dropping. It blends Hong Kong-style bullet ballet with the kinetic action of Oshii's *Patlabor* or *Ghost in the Shell* made live. The sequence was actually filmed in Hong Kong as Oshii wanted to film with genuine machine guns which is illegal in Japan. Oshii desired to use an old German MG34. He had to settle for a smaller MG42 per Hong Kong's own firearms restrictions. Oshii's time in Hong Kong shooting this sequence would no doubt influence *Ghost in the Shell*. The sequence is a haunting bloodbath; its gun toting, white-faced agents are a surreal visual much in line with Oshii's anime work. The scene also looks forward to the blood-drenched ending of Oshii's later live action *Nowhere Girl* (2015).

MUSIC

The sense of *mono-no-aware* is aided by Oshii's longtime musical composer Kenji Kawai. Kawai (1957-) dropped out of a nuclear engineering course in college to study music. He soon became one of anime's top composers, beginning with haunting work on the four part original video animation *Vampire Princess Miyu* (1988). Soon he began to branch into live action composing with his score for Hideo Nakata's *Ring* (1997). He even moved into scoring Hong Kong cinema with his work on Tsui Hark's *Seven Swords* (2005) and the *Ip Man* series.

THEMES AND MOTIFS

For the *Kerberos* saga, Oshii creates a universe that is as fascinating as it is disturbing. Made clearer in 1999's *Jin-Roh*, Japan had sided with the Allies rather than the Axis, the latter winning WWII. The Japanese were then occupied by Nazi Germany instead of the U.S. The stormtrooper-like helmets and Germanic motifs of the Kerberos unit is a dead giveaway. Oshii clearly has strong feelings on the militarization of police. Throughout history, the implementation of militarized police units is common in dysfunctional societies. Imperial Japan had the *Kempeitai*, Nazi Germany the Gestapo, East Germany the *Stasi*, Soviet Russia the KGB and Maoist China the Red Guard. Similar themes can be seen in Oshii's *Patlabor* along with his earlier *Dallos* (1983). *Dallos* depicts overworked lunar laborers oppressed by a brutal Earth-governed police force. In the United States, where stories about police brutality make frequent headlines, Oshii's themes cut deeper than most will admit.

Mamoru Oshii, however, also sympathizes with those conditioned into this brutality. The director is a dog lover who has owned many Basset hounds and highly empathizes with canines. He sees the Kerberos cops as akin to abused feral dogs without a master. This is made clear with their very name: *Kerberos*. Kerberos (Cerebus) was the three-headed hound in Greek mythology who guarded the gates of Hades. In Japan, the pre-war story of Hachiko is myth-like in status. Hachiko (1923-1935) was an *Akita* dog who waited for his master at Shibuya station every day. When his master, a college professor, died prematurely, he continued to wait, in vain, for the man for nine years. Hachiko's loyalty was revered amongst the

Japanese and used in Imperial propaganda. A statue of the dog was built at Shibuya station in the spot where he waited. It is amusingly destroyed in 1999's *Gamera 3: Revenge of Iris*. Oshii seems to have mixed feelings about this mindset; finding such conditioning appalling while admiring its victims for their fierce loyalty. *Stray Dog* takes the hound motif even further. The opening credits are juxtaposed over footage of dogs. The main character's very name is "Inui" which could be translated as "Doggie". Tang Mie takes Inui and Koichi in like a young girl taking in a pair of strays. Both *The Red Spectacles* and *Stray Dog* also revolve around the theme of trauma. Ultimately, Inui and Koichi are unable to let go of their traumatic conditioning. This leads both to a tragic finale tinged with inevitability.

RELEASE AND LEGACY

Oshii's next live action film was the dark meta-comedy *Talking Head* (1992). Afterwards he focused more on anime works with *Patlabor 2* (1993) and *Ghost in the Shell*. He returned to the Kerberos saga with 1999's *Jin-Roh: The Wolf Brigade*. An anime feature, it was originally to also be live action. Oshii did not direct it but wrote the screenplay. His protege Hiroyuki Okiura stepped into the role. *Jin-Roh*, made with much of *Ghost in the Shell*'s core team, takes us further back into the history of the Kerberos unit. It shows a post-World War II Japan in a state of urban civil war. Oshii would follow it up with more manga volumes and *Jin-Roh* received a Korean remake in 2018: *Illang: The Wolf Brigade*. Today, the themes of these films remain hauntingly relevant in a news cycle dominated by civil unrest and police brutality.

ALTERNATE VERSIONS

Stray Dog: Kerberos Panzer Cops was not dubbed into English.

AMERICAN HOME VIDEO HISTORY

Stray Dog: Kerberos Panzer Cops was released stateside directly to DVD in 2004 by Bandai. The film was made available in both a standalone edition and in a boxed set with Oshii's other films *The Red Spectacles* and *Talking Head*. This disc has long since gone out of print.

Further Viewing:

The Red Spectacles

(1987)

紅い眼鏡

Omnibus Promotion, *Director*: **Mamoru Oshii**

Mamoru Oshii's first stab at a live action feature is less polished than his anime work. Yet it boasts impressive production values for its budget. *The Red Spectacles* was to be a low budget film shot on 16mm but wound up filmed in 35mm, dramatically increasing the cost. Much of the cast and crew had worked with Oshii on *Urusei Yatsura*. This included producer Shigeharu Shiba and up-and-coming writer Kazunori Ito. Most of

the cast, including leads Shigeru Chiba, Machiko Washio and Hideyuki Tanaka were anime voice actors who seldom performed on screen. Producer Shiba wound up mortgaging his home to come up with the budget.

Mostly in black and white with an impressive color opening and ending, *The Red Spectacles* is chock full of unsettling moments. It boasts an impressively bleak atmosphere. Its dystopian Japan is a disturbing, collapsing society akin to '80s era communist countries, intentional on Oshii's part given his love of Soviet bloc cinema. Oshii would reach higher heights with *Stray Dog*, yet he translates his aesthetic sensibility well to the live action medium. *The Red Spectacles* doesn't reach the quality of his anime work but there are stunning compositions. Oshii composes his shots similarly to his anime, but with actors and sets rather than painted cels. There's an impressively tense confrontation between Chiba's Koichi and Washio's Midori uncomfortably framed in static wide shots. The film suffers from an occasional sense of monotony and is punctuated by odd slapstick humor that is almost kabuki vaudeville. It's disjointedly dream-like in a manner almost akin to the work of David Lynch. This winds up a clever trick by writer Ito and director Oshii.

The Red Spectacles comes alive in its hauntingly beautiful finale which ties in with *Jin-Roh*. In its moving final moments, once again trauma is a main theme. Toho actor Hideyo Amamoto plays a small but noticeable role in the film. *The Red Spectacles* was composer Kenji Kawaii's first of many collaborations with Oshii. His score, particularly for the finale, is eerily beautiful. Amusingly, the production had run out of money by the time they needed to shoot the reveal of the titular red glasses falling from Koichi's suitcase. They could not afford to buy the necessary amount of eyeglass frames. Oshii's crew put out a call for fans to donate glasses frames to the shoot in exchange for a promotional sticker.

Avalon

(2001)
アヴァロン
Deiz/Bandai Visual/Nippon Herald Films, *Director*: Mamoru Oshii

Mamoru Oshii's first film since *Ghost in the Shell* is a sumptuous, if confusing visual feast. *Avalon* is a tribute to his love of Polish cinema, Oshii being quite fond of directors like Jerzy Kawalerowicz and Andrzej Wajda. *Avalon* was filmed in Poland with an all Polish cast and a mixed-Polish/Japanese crew. This included a Polish DP. Perhaps emboldened by the Wachowskis' recreation of his imagery in *The Matrix*, Oshii crafts his most polished live action film to date. The influence of *The Matrix* along with David Cronenberg's *eXistenZ* is quite apparent. Ala the *Kerberos* films, it's set in a collapsing society with decaying infrastructure. Dystopia is a near fetish for Mamoru Oshii. Here, young people obsessively play an illegal virtual reality game: Avalon. Ash (Małgorzata

Foremniak), who looks like a far more convincing live action Motoko Kusanagi than Scarjo, is a star Avalon player. She pursues the mysterious Bishop (Dariusz Biskupski) through the higher levels of the game, aiming to unlock its secrets and gain wealth and notoriety.

Oshii would spend half a year in Poland making *Avalon* and the Polish military even lent him support. Principal photography took 44 days, mainly in Warsaw, Krakow and Vatsaf. *Avalon* can be a bit of a slog but is filled with stunning visuals. Its action sequences translate Oshii's anime style to live action with the most confidence yet. The film feels more Polish in many ways, but its mechanical designs and anime-like imagery betray its Japaneseness. The VFX is quite impressive in some scenes, shaky in others. Oshii's team used a newly developed video processing software called "Domino" by Quantel. This technology was also being implemented on contemporary Hollywood productions such as *The Lord of the Rings* trilogy, *Star Wars* prequels and *Sin City*. The dynamic surround sound mix was done at Skywalker Sound. *Avalon* is capped in a surreal finale with a gleefully bleak, ambiguous ending. Overall, *Avalon* is an underappreciated gem and an interesting, unusual film. Oshii would switch back to the anime medium for his subsequent *Ghost in the Shell 2: Innocence* and *The Sky Crawlers*. He then made a live action follow-up set in the same universe: the poorly received *Assault Girls* (2009).

MAMORU OSHII
The Visionary

押井守

8/8/1951-

"I think overall, making a movie is like putting a stamp on the world. Every time I make a movie, I feed in elements to make sure it's my movie. I'm marking poles like a dog does."

-Mamoru Oshii

One of Japanese animation's greatest luminaries, Mamoru Oshii is best known for anime classics like *Patlabor* and *Ghost in the Shell.* Yet he has left a significant mark on live action Japanese science fiction as well. His live action work is no less striking or personal. Oshii was born in Tokyo, the youngest of four siblings. His father was a police detective. Oshii was a rebellious student and often skipped school to see movies and engage in student activism. He also liked to make 8mm films. Unlike many of his contemporaries, who grew up on a diet of old school *tokusatsu* and anime, Oshii devoured European art films as a youth. One of his favorite films is *La Jetee* (1962) by Chris Marker and seeing it was a seminal experience. Oshii has a particular love of Ingmar Bergman and Polish cinema, though he also adores Ridley Scott's *Blade Runner* and Peter Jackson's *Lord of the Rings* trilogy. In high school, a truant officer paid a visit to Oshii's home. His furious father confined him to a mountain lodge as punishment.

In 1970, Oshii was accepted into Tokyo Gakugei University. He rarely attended classes and devoured films, having to repeat a year due to his poor grades. In 1976, he finally graduated. He first took a job at a radio company but they would not pay him so he quit after close to a year. Oshii became an animator and storyboard artist at Tatsunoko soon after. He worked on *Yatterman* (1977-79), the comedic *Time Bokan* series and *Zenderman* (1979-80). Oshii directed episodes of all under Hisayuki Toriumi. Following his mentor Toriumi, Oshii moved to Studio Pierrot. One of his first major directing jobs was on *The Wonderful Adventures of Nils,* based on Swedish author Selma Lagerlöf's famous children's book.

In 1981, Oshii was put in charge of *Urusei Yatsura,* a popular new anime show based on a manga by Rumiko Takahashi. His work on *Urusei Yatsura* rocketed him to notoriety. He would act as showrunner for three years and helmed the first two feature films: *Urusei Yatsura: Only You* (1983) and *Urusei Yatsura 2: Beautiful Dreamer* (1984). Also with Studio Pierrot, Oshii would create the first direct-to-video anime or OVA (original video animation): *Dallos* (1983). A sci-fi story of oppressed laborers rising up at a lunar colony, it bore themes of class warfare and police militarization.

These would come to define later Oshii works.

At mentor and fellow luminary Hayao Miyazaki's recommendation, he was considered to direct the next *Lupin the Third* movie. In the end the project was cancelled as the studio brass found his ideas "nonsensical". His next film, made at Studio Deen, was *The Angel's Egg* (1985). It would be a surreal, disturbing OVA rife with Biblical symbolism designed by genius illustrator Yoshitaka Amano. *The Angel's Egg* gained Oshii fame though its reception was critically mixed. Sequences were used in the post-apocalyptic Australian film *In the Aftermath* (1987). Following *The Angel's Egg,* Oshii worked with Miyazaki and Isao Takahata on developing a film called *Anchor*. His dour sensibilities, however, were at odds with the whimsical stylings of Miyazaki and the project was canned.

Soon afterward, Oshii's friend, screenwriter Kazunori Ito, invited him to join the collective Headgear. Their first work was the *Patlabor: Early Days* OVA. This gave rise to a feature film, *Patlabor: The Movie* (1989) and a TV series later that year. These were his first anime works made at Production I.G., where he would produce the bulk of his work from herein. Around this time, Oshii also dabbled in live action with *The Red Spectacles* (1987). This was the first installment in his dystopian *Kerberos Panzer Cops* series. Like colleague Hideaki Anno, Oshii would dabble in live action film repeatedly over the years; going back and forth between animated works. He would follow up *The Red Spectacles* with a prequel: *Stray Dog: Kerberos Panzer Cops* (1991). This was followed by a live action

dark meta comedy called *Talking Head* (1992).

An acclaimed sequel to *Patlabor* soon followed in 1993. In 1995, Oshii would direct what became known as his signature work, *Ghost in the Shell*. Based on a manga by Masamune Shirow, *Ghost in the Shell* won wide international acclaim. It gained notable admirers such as James Cameron and *The Matrix*'s Lana and Lilly Wachowski. Oshii took a hiatus from directing after *Ghost*, though he wrote the script for *Jin-Roh: The Wolf Brigade* (1999). He returned with the live action Polish-Japanese co-production *Avalon* (2001).

Oshii next made a long awaited return to anime with *Ghost in the Shell 2: Innocence* (2004). The Wachowskis tried to recruit Oshii to direct a segment of their anthology *The Animatrix*. He was too busy with the production of *Innocence* to accept. *Innocence* had a mixed reception with many fans finding it a let down compared to the original. Yet, it went on to be one of the few anime films shown at Cannes; competing for the prestigious Palme D'or. Shortly after, Oshii was due to collaborate with Kenta Fukasaku on a live action film called *Elle is Burning*. The project was sadly dropped as being too expensive. Oshii's next anime feature was the dystopian war drama *The Sky Crawlers* (2008), which was nominated for the Golden Lion at the Venice Film Festival. He also re-released *Ghost in the Shell* in 2008 with redone animation, CGI and sound design.

In the last decade, Oshii has focused his attention mainly on live action films. First came *Assault Girls* (2009) with Rinko

Kikuchi. Set in the same universe as *Avalon*, it got a fairly negative reception. His next major live action films were *Garm Wars: The Last Druid*, his first film shot in English, along with the drama *Nowhere Girl* (2015). His 2017 miniseries *A Sand Whale and Me* was aired on Cartoon Network's Toonami. Also in 2017, *Ghost in the Shell* was given a live action Hollywood remake starring Scarlett Johansson and directed by Rupert Sanders. Oshii returned to anime with the recent TV series *VladLove*. Its release was delayed by the effects of the COVID-19 pandemic, but the first episode was given an advanced streaming debut on December 18, 2020. He also has a feature film anime adaptation of Baku Yumemakura's novel series *Chimera* in the pipeline. Oshii is a noted dog lover who particularly adores Bassett hounds. His daughter, Tomoe Oshii, is married to writer and filmmaker Otsuichi.

Selected Filmography

"Ippatsu Kanta-kun" (1977-78, TV) [animator, director]

"Yatterman" (1977-79, TV) [animator, director]

"Gatchaman II" (1978-79, TV) [animator, director]

"Zenderman" (1979-80, TV) [animator, director]

"The Wonderful Adventure of Nils" (1980-81, TV) [animator, director]

"Urusei Yatsura" (1981-84, TV) [chief director]

Urusei Yatsura: Only You (1983) [director]

Dallos (1983) [director/screenplay]

Urusei Yatsura: Beautiful Dreamer (1984) [director/screenplay]

The Angel's Egg (1985) [director/screenplay]

The Red Spectacles (1987) [director]

Twilight Q (1987) [segment *"File538"*, director/screenplay]

Mobile Police Patlabor (1988) [director]

Patlabor: The Movie (1989) [director]

MAROKO (1990) [director/screenplay]

Stray Dog: Kerberos Panzer Cops (1991) [director/screenplay]

Talking Head (1992) [director/screenplay]

Patlabor 2: The Movie (1993) [director]

Ghost in the Shell (1995) [director]

Jin Roh: The Wolf Brigade (1999) [screenplay]

Avalon (2001) [director]

Ghost in the Shell 2: Innocence (2004) [director/screenplay]

The Sky Crawlers (2008) [director]

Assault Girls (2009) [director/screenplay]

The Next Generation -Patlabor- (2014) [director/screenplay]

Garm Wars: The Last Druid (2014) [director]

Nowhere Girl (2015) [director]

"Sand Whale and Me" (2017, TV) [director]

"VladLove" (2020-21, TV) [director]

ゼイラム

Zeiramu "Zeiram"
GAGA Communications/Crowd Inc./Toho, 12/21/1991 (*Heisei 3*), 96:40, 35mm, Spherical (1.85:1), color, Dolby Stereo

Crew
Executive Producers: Hiroshi Ichida, Shigeki Takeuchi
Producers: Yoshinori Chiba, Koichi Sugisawa
Director: Keita Amemiya
Screenplay: Keita Amemiya, Hajime Matsumoto
Director of Photography: Hiroshi Kidokoro
Music: Koichi Ota, Nakaji Kinoshita
Editor: Koichi Sugisawa
Art Directors: Akihiko Iguchi, Toshio Miike
Assistant Directors: Junichi Furusho, Wataru Kashibuchi, Aya Wakabayashi, Nobuyuki Oka
Lighting: Yoshimi Hosaka
Character Design: Keita Amemiya
Costume Design: Katsuya Terada
Action Coordinator: Mitsuo Abe
Stunts (Iria): Mei Daihashi
Stunts: Akira Ohashi, Makoto Yokoyama, Yuji Kobayashi, Kazuhiro Yokoyama, Toshimoto Takazaki, Eiji Kobayashi, Keiichi Ishiyama, Masahiko Mitsukoshi, Hisato Ifuku, Kenichiro Tamayori, Hiroshi Yoshida
Car Stunts: Yorimitsu Tada
Sound Engineers: Musei Ozawa, Hiroya Kozuki, Osamu Takemura
Sound Recording: Ikuko Shimaki
Sound Mixer: Yoshinori Matsumoto
Visual Effects Coordinator: Hajime Matsumoto
VFX Supervisor: Hiroshi Onodera
Cinematography Assistants: Masashi Sasaki, Takahide Mashio, Shinji Nakata, Satoshi Murakawa, Seijiro Fujita, Katsumi Arita
Lighting Assistants: Hokoku Hayashi, Takashi Mizuno, Shigeru Izumiya, Ikuo Hosoya, Yuji Tanabe
Zeiram Creator: Takayuki Taketani
Zeiram Suit Creator: Koichi Nagata
Iria Armor: Kenzo Okamoto
Final Zeiram Puppet: Yusuke Takayanagi
Special Make-up: Kazuhiro Sawa
Property Master: Norimichi Suzuki
Hair and Make-up: Hajime Iwasaki, Nanami Okada
Gun Effects: Yukitomo Tochino
Miniatures: Kame Ogasawara, Izumi Negishi, Kenichi Ueda, Yoshinori Muraishi, Kenji Kawaguchi
Puppetry: Kazuji Kosugi
Production Manager: Sadao Kan
Still Photography: Yu Mamizu, Sotaru Kimura, Yoshihiro Uehara

Cast
Yuko Moriyama (*Iria*)
Kunihiro Ida (*Teppei*)
Yukijiro Hotaru (*Kamiya*)
Masakazu Handa (*Bob, voice*)
Mizuho Yoshida (*Zeiram*)
Yukitomo Tochino (*Murata*)
Riko Kurenai (*Mama*)
Naomi Enami (*Electronic Store Manager*)
Mayumi Aguni (*Liliput*)
Masakazu Katsura (*Passerby*)

Alternate Titles
Zeram (U.S. Title)

> *"The people of Earth are about to be visited by some guests. While they're here, try and make them feel welcome."*
> -U.S. video spot

One of the finest *tokusatsu* works of the 1990s, *Zeiram* is an inspired and underappreciated gem. Creatively directed by Keita Amemiya, it boasts solid production values on a limited budget. With impressive practical effects and atmosphere throughout, Amemiya brings a unique design sense. Melding tokusatsu with cyberpunk, Amemiya's aesthetic blurs the line between the live action and anime realms. The action is breathless and *Zeiram* is high octane entertainment from beginning to end.

PLOT

Bioengineered alien killing machine Zeiram (Mizuho Yoshida) escapes confinement. Bounty huntress Iria (Yuko Moriyama) and her computer sidekick Bob accept the assignment to track her down to a planet called Earth and capture or destroy her. In Tokyo, Kamiya (Yukijiro Hotaru) and Teppei (Kunihiro Ida) are bumbling employees of an electric company. Kamiya encounters Iria on the street after she drops an apple. With computer parts bought in Akihabara, Iria sets up base in an abandoned warehouse. She creates an alternate dimension called a "Zone" to entrap Zeiram.

After being tipped off that someone is stealing electricity, Kamiya and Teppei discover Iria's base as the culprit. Kamiya accidentally transports Teppei into the

Zone just as Zeiram arrives on Earth. Kamiya confronts Iria and is also accidentally transported into the Zone. Iria then traps Kamiya in a containment unit. As she destroys the capsule Zeiram arrived in, a flummoxed Teppei encounters the creature. Zeiram fires her enormous gun at Teppei. As Teppei flees, Zeiram creates a clone soldier called Lilliput (Mayumi Aguni) and sends it in pursuit.

Iria encounters Zeiram and lures her to a warehouse. Zeiram is able to easily escape Iria's first trap. Iria finds that Zeiram is impervious to weapons as she's using a shield. Iria next dons her battle suit, despite Bob's advice not to fight Zeiram in close combat. Zeiram proves a brutal foe but Iria outwits and traps her. As Iria is about to seal her in a force field, Zeiram clones another Lilliput to distract her. Though Iria takes the Lilliput down, Zeiram escapes and clobbers her. In the nick of time, Iria grabs her containment unit generator and seals Zeiram.

Teppei finds Iria. She frees Kamiya and shows him and Teppei that they're inside an alternate dimension. As Bob is about to transport Zeiram so Iria can claim her bounty, a Lilliput attacks. Iria and the Lilliput are accidentally transported out of the Zone. The creature damages Iria's transporter before being killed, leaving

Teppei and Kamiya stranded in the Zone with Zeiram.

BACKGROUND

Director, designer and illustrator Keita Amemiya is a unique talent. His distinctive aesthetic combines *tokusatsu*, cyberpunk and traditional *jidai-geki* stylings. With *Zeiram*, he shows off his talent as a new force to be reckoned with. Amemiya had cut his teeth with his debut, the direct-to-video *Cyber Ninja* (1988). He was eager to make another film and felt more confident in his abilities. At first, he wanted to make a sequel to *Cyber Ninja* but plans fell through.

The working title for *Zeiram* was *HP9999*. Amemiya wanted to make a film in line with his sensibilities but that also pleased audiences. Amemiya conceived of the monster when imagining someone in an Edo-era sedge hat walking in a modern city at night. He found this mental image both unsettling and intriguing. Originally, Amemiya wanted actor Kunihiro Ida, who had worked with him on *Cyber Ninja*, in the lead role. The producers, however, wanted a prominent female part to give the film more sex appeal. So the bounty huntress character Iria was created. Ida wound up playing a supporting role as Teppei. Amemiya started shooting *Zeiram* immediately after directing the first two episodes of the *Sentai* show *Jetman* (1991-92).

PRINCIPAL PHOTOGRAPHY

Made on a limited budget, *Zeiram* was a grueling and difficult shoot. The film was mainly shot at night which was hard on the cast and crew. One shooting day ran for 37 hours straight. *Zeiram* was additionally filmed almost entirely on location. The first scenes filmed were of Iria at the Akihabara neighborhood in Tokyo, a tech nerd and *otaku* culture hub. The reliance on location shooting made weather a huge problem. Many of the film's images are shrouded in atmospheric mist. Heavy amounts of mineral oil-based smoke were used to create it. The local residents who had hung their clothes out to dry often got them drenched in oil.

Zeiram boasts breathless action sequences and exciting fight choreography. Stunt doubles were used fairly extensively, especially for actress Yuko Moriyama. A stunt involving explosions near a motorbike was dangerous for all involved. A "shock rope" was attached to the stuntman that snapped prematurely. The motorbike almost hit *Zeiram* performer Mizuho Yoshida.

ACTORS

The gorgeous Yuko Moriyama (1968-) plays Iria. She disliked her armored costume as it gave her bruises, but she got used to it in time. Moriyama was also quite startled when firing her prop gun for the first time as the blanks used were quite loud. Moriyama's Iria is a likable heroine; an anime warrior girl crossed with a little Ellen Ripley or Sarah Connor. Yukijiro Hotaru plays Kamiya, the older of the two bumbling electricians. Hotaru (1951-) was born Kiyoshi Watanabe and first appeared in softcore *pinku eiga* films. After *Zeiram*, Hotaru became close friends with director Amemiya. He appeared in many of his subsequent works including *Zeiram 2, Mechanical Violator Hakaider, Moon Over Tao* and the *Garo* franchise. Hotaru also played Inspector Osako in Shusuke Kaneko's *Heisei Gamera* films. He went on to play small roles in Kaneko's *Pyrokinesis* (2000) and *Godzilla, Mothra and King Ghidorah: Giant Monsters All-Out Attack* (2001). Hotaru also appeared in Kiyoshi Kurosawa's *Cure* (1997). Actress Moriyama learned a lot from working opposite the more seasoned Hotaru.

SFX/VFX

Zeiram is an underappreciated film directed very creatively by Amemiya, who brings a unique sense of design to the picture. The costumes are inventive. The computer graphics and futuristic monitor displays boast an appealing sense of cyberpunk "aesthetic". Zeiram herself is an impressive creation. She was designed by Amemiya with input from the art director, Toho veteran Akihiko Iguchi. The creature combines motifs reminiscent of illustrators H.R. Giger and Yoshitaka Amano. The alien monster's "main unit" is an unsettling, *No* mask-like alabaster face that should be more iconic than it is. The face was often manipulated through impressive puppetry. Though lost on viewers, according to director Amemiya, Zeiram was intended to be female. The feminine quality of her "face" is supposed to be a dead give

away. Unusually hulking for a *tokusatsu* monster, Zeiram is played by Mizuho Yoshida. Yoshida (1965-) went on to portray quite a few kaiju in the coming years. These included Legion in *Gamera 2: Attack of Legion* (1996), Dagahra in *Rebirth of Mothra II* (1997) and Godzilla in *Godzilla, Mothra and King Ghidorah: Giant Monsters All-Out Attack*.

Zeiram boasts dazzling practical effects throughout. Much of the puppeteering for the Zeiram "main unit" was done with old school wire work. Later scenes feature Jim Danforth-style stop motion animation and grotesque Rob Bottin-like puppetry. invoking John Carpenter's *The Thing* (1982). Unsurprisingly, numerous members of Amemiya's crew for *Zeiram* went on to join Shinji Higuchi's effects unit for the *Heisei Gamera* films. This included DP Hiroshi Kidokoro, art director Toshio Miike, VFX supervisor Hajime Matsumoto and engineer and technician Izumi Negishi.

RELEASE AND LEGACY

Zeiram is an inspired picture. It is a strong highlight of both director Amemiya's career and '90s tokusatsu cinema. Keita Amemiya wanted to create several sequels to Zeiram. He would largely fulfill that goal. A six episode original video animation was released in 1994 as *Iria: Zeiram the Animation*. This anime prequel was directed by Tetsuro Amino (*Macross 7*). It details Iria starting out as a bounty hunter and her first encounter with Zeiram. This somewhat contradicts the original film, which claims to be Iria's introductory battle with the monster. A proper sequel directed by Amemiya, *Zeiram 2*, followed shortly after in late 1994. *Zeiram 2* brought actors Moriyama, Hotaru and Ide all back. Additionally, Amemiya's film *Moon Over Tao* (1997) was originally conceived as a *Zeiram* sequel set in feudal Japan.

ALTERNATE VERSIONS

Zeiram was dubbed into English by Carl Macek's Streamline Pictures, a pioneer in dubbing anime. The dub was recorded at Screenmusic Studios (now Studiopolis) in Los Angeles. It was directed by Macek and written by Steven Kramer. It's a quality dub though it changes the nuance of the Japanese dialog significantly. Voice cast includes Edie Mirman as Iria, Robert Axelrod as Kamiya, Steve Bulen as Teppei, Jeff Winkless as Bob and Steve Kramer as Murata.

Robert Axelrod (1949-2019) is worth mentioning. He was a prolific voice actor from the 1980s to his death and did a lot of English dubbing for anime. He also played many onscreen bit parts such as in the popular sitcom *Family Matters* (1989-1998) and Chuck Russell's 1988 remake of *The Blob*. Axelrod was best known for providing the voice of Lord Zedd on *Mighty Morphin' Power Rangers* (1993-95). Keita Amemiya helmed several sentai episodes that were Americanized for that program.

AMERICAN HOME VIDEO HISTORY

Zeiram was released dubbed to VHS and laserdisc by Fox Lorbor in May 1994. It was later released to DVD by Image Entertainment in 1998. In 2006, it was released to DVD by Media Blasters with both Japanese and English audio tracks, bundled with its sequel *Zeiram 2*.

Further Viewing:

ZËIRAM 2
(1994)
ゼイラム2
Bandai Visual/Embodiment Films, *Director*: Keita Amemiya

Zeiram 2 is a worthy but flawed sequel. It is more ambitious than its predecessor but doesn't come together as well in execution. Having just helmed a pair of *Kamen Rider* films, Keita Amemiya got more creative freedom this time around. His aesthetic in *Zeiram 2* drifts more towards *jidai-geki* than sci-fi cyberpunk. After an intriguing off-world opening, the film brings back the main players including the bumbling Kamiya and Teppei along with a more mature Iria. Zeiram, of course, is back too in a new form resembling a *kitsune* (fox) spirit and can now fly. It's never made that clear if this Zeiram is a new unit or a resurrected version of the original. An obnoxious sidekick character called Fujikoro (Sabu), introduced in the anime, makes trouble for Iria. It somewhat contradicts the anime's portrayal of him where he is older and less antagonistic. A *"Daikannon"* statue is featured prominently in *Zeiram 2*. In the likeness of a Chinese princess canonized by Buddhist scholars, there are many such statues in Japan, some taller than the Statue of Liberty. The statue's interiors make a video game-like environment for the film's climactic action sequences.

A highlight of *Zeiram 2* is an impressive scene where Iria is surrounded by a mob of alien bounty hunters. The extras for this scene were recruited from an ad in B-CLUB magazine and allowed to bring their own costumes. As with the first *Zeiram*, the picture features superbly executed puppetry and animatronics. The ending makes heavier use of CGI. It gets arguably even more surreal than the first film as emotions run in a high stakes climax. Overall though, *Zeiram 2* is clunkier than the original and fails to reach the first *Zeiram*'s heights. A finale where Teppei gets married, built up throughout the film, is never actually shown. Narratively this feels like a letdown. Amemiya's next stop was the *Kikaider* spin-off *Mechanical Violator Hakaider* (1995).

(1995)
人造人間ハカイダー
Toei, *Director:* **Keita Amemiya**

Mechanical Violator Hakaider is an edgy and stylistic reboot of Shotaro Ishinomori's *Kikaider* franchise as only Keita Amemiya could make. The film takes Kikaider's arch nemesis Hakaider and turns him into an Eastwood's "Man With No Name"-style anti-hero. Opening with an amusing riff on

Toei's logo, Hakaider (Yuji Kishimoto) soon arrives in the disturbingly dystopian Jesustown, run by the androgynous, Hitleresque Gurjev (Yasuaki Honda). It's not Amemiya's best film, but with special effects supervision by Nobuo Yajima's protege Shuichi Kokumai, there are intriguing images throughout. Hakaider's transformation from human to robot invokes *Tetsuo: The Iron Man*. There's also a stunning dream sequence involving guerilla girl Kaoru (Mai Hosho) that looks like a Yoshitaka Amano illustration brought to life. A motorcycle chase resembles the early moments of Katsuhiro Otomo's *Akira* via a Toei Metal Hero show.

Hikaider comes alive, however, with its impressive finale. The picture's final 15 minutes are a visually stunning tour-de-force that utterly redeems what, up until that point, had been a mixed bag. The brutal duel between Hakaider and Gurjev's android Michael is a memorable highlight. As with the *Zeiram* films, there is a very creative and effective use of stop motion animation. You can certainly see, however, why the film offended Toei's brass. The theatrical release of *Mechanical Violator Hakaider* was heavily edited. Amemiya's director's cut runs a whopping 26 minutes longer but is far more palatable. *Mechanical Violator Hakaider* would be the final production the legendary Shotaro Ishinomori directly worked on.

(1997)

タオの月

Bandai Visual/Shochiku, *Director:* **Keita Amemiya**

Conceived as a *Zeiram* sequel, *Moon Over Tao* is another underrated gem from Keita Amemiya. It was produced for Shochiku's *"Cinema Japanesque"* project. This short-lived series was intended to showcase creatively directed and unconventional Japanese films. Along with 1979's *Time Slip*, *Moon Over Tao* is one of the few films to successfully combine the science fiction and *jidai-geki* genres. Kon Ichikawa had attempted it with his *Tale of Bamboo Cutter* adaptation *Princess From the Moon* (1987) but failed miserably. Amemiya, by contrast, produces a wild picture with a stunning sense of atmosphere.

Samurai retainer Hayate (*Godzilla 2000's* Hiroshi Abe) and military general turned monk Suikyo (*Gamera 2's* Toshiyuki Nagashima) are sent on a mission. They must collect information on a mysterious metal that produces swords sharp enough to slice rock. Teenage ninja girl Renge (Sayaka Yoshino), meanwhile, encounters a trio of battling aliens. The mortally wounded Kuzto (Yuko Moriyama) warns Renge that something called the "Makaraga" must not be awakened. She then gives Renge a device called the "Tao" that can seal it away. Renge, Hayate and Suikyo track the metal to Kakugyo (Takaaki Enoki), a sociopathic

wizard monk and former colleague of Suikyo. With an army of bandits and swords made from the meteoric metal, Kakugyo plans to conquer Japan. He also has the embryonic Makaraga in his possession as it was found with the metal. Kakugyo awakens it with human blood and it grows into a man-eating monstrosity. The creature gets larger and larger the more "people food" it devours and only the Tao can stop it.

Moon Over Tao is, like *Zeiram*, a very aesthetically rich film. It's origins as a *Zeiram* sequel show. Both involve a female alien played by Yuko Moriyama trying to retrieve a living alien bioweapon. *Moon Over Tao* merely transplants these tropes to the novel setting of *Sengoku* Japan. With an eclectic feel, *Moon Over Tao* can switch gears at any moment. Oftentimes it feels like a live action version of Yoshiaki Kawajiri's seminal anime actioner *Ninja Scroll* (1993). It helps that Hiroshi Abe's Jubei-like swordsman looks like a samurai anime protagonist made flesh. Early fight scenes involving Moriyama resemble modern *wuxia* like Tsui Hark's *Zu Warriors* (1983), Ronny Yu's *The Bride with White Hair* (1993) or Wong Kar-wai's *Ashes of Time* (1994). Other moments feel akin to Kinji Fukasaku's fantasy samurai films such as *Samurai Reincarnation* (1981) and *Legend of the Eight Samurai* (1983). *Moon Over Tao* comes to life in its bloodsoaked finale. The picture takes on the feel of a *Sentai* episode crossed with Daiei's *Majin* via pre-Tolkien Peter Jackson's *Braindead* (1992). The alien creature Makaraga is executed well and much akin to the *Heisei Gamera* monsters. This is unsurprising as many of the FX staff were now also part of Shinji Higuchi's team. A full sized model was built for some shots, an expressive puppet created for close-ups and the full body shots were done with CGI. The CGI is dated but not bad for a Japanese film made in 1997. Sadly, *Moon Over Tao* flopped at the Japanese box office and wound up one of Amemiya's last major theatrical films. From here, he would focus mainly on television properties like *Tekkouki Mikazuki* (2000) and *Garo* (2005-06).

KEITA AMEMIYA
The Aesthetician

雨宮慶太
8/24/1959-

By the late 1980s, a "New Wave" of *tokusatsu* filmmakers born in the post-war prosperity began to take the reins from the old guard. These included Kazuki Omori, Shusuke Kaneko, Shinji Higuchi and Keita Amemiya. Amemiya, a self proclaimed "adult boy", is one of the most creative modern tokusatsu figures. A talented illustrator as well as a filmmaker, his aesthetic and sense of design is distinctive. Amemiya's style bridges old and new. It effectively combines anime-style cyberpunk, traditional tokusatsu and even *jidai-geki* flourishes. Unsurprisingly, he has been involved in anime productions as well as tokusatsu works.

Born in Urayasu City, Chiba Prefecture, Amemiya adored tokusatsu television as a boy. At 11, he became obsessed with Toei's new show *Kamen Rider*. He also credits seeing *Star Wars* as a pivotal inspiration. Shortly after, in 1978, Amemiya entered the Asagaya College of Art. He dropped out in 1981 to make a short film. Called *Sweet Home* and not to be confused with Kiyoshi Kurosawa's movie, it made some waves. He established a company called Cloud Co., Ltd

in 1983. Through some connections, he got his first design job on the Toei Metal Hero show *Space Wolf Juspion* (1985-86). He did more designs on the following shows: *Time Warrior Spielban* (1986-87), *Superhuman Machine Metalder* (1987-88), *Mobile Cop Jiban* (1989-90) and *Space Police Winspector* (1990-91). He also contributed designs to *Kamen Rider Black* (1987-88) and *Kamen Rider Black RX* (1988-89). Additionally, Amemiya did designs for the animated U.S/Japanese co-production *Ultraman: The Adventure Begins* (1987) for Tsuburaya Pro. In 1986, he married Yumiko Amaya. Amaya herself would go on to direct 1994's *Nostradamus: The Prophecy*. The two had a daughter, Naomi Amemiya, an occasional actress.

Keita Amemiya's directorial debut was the direct-to-video *Cyber Ninja* (1988). Namco was working on a video game of the same name and wanted to make a tie-in film. Amemiya had some connections with Namco and convinced them to let him direct. *Cyber Ninja* made a splash at the Tokyo International Film Festival. Amemiya began to develop a reputation as a rising talent. Additionally, he assisted in optical animation for Toho's *Gunhed* (1989). Toei's brass was quite impressed with Amemiya's work on *Cyber Ninja*. He was made head director of their new *Sentai* show *Jetman* (1991-92), helming over a dozen episodes. Amemiya would also direct a pair of episodes for the following sentai show *Zyuranger* (1992-93). *Zyuranger* would be purchased by Saban and Americanized into *Mighty Morphin' Power Rangers*. Amemiya's two episodes, *"The Devil's Park"* and *"Beware of Shaved Ice"* became *"Itsy Bitsy Spider"* and *"Power Ranger Punks"*. At the same time, Amemiya commenced production on his first theatrical feature *Zeiram*. He began shooting it only days after finishing work on the pilot episodes of *Jetman*. With inventive special effects and highly creative direction, *Zeiram* caught international attention. Amemiya was now a force to be reckoned with in the tokusatsu industry.

The next several years were extremely busy for Keita Amemiya. He directed a pair of *Kamen Rider* films for Toei. This was followed swiftly by a *Zeiram* sequel in 1994 and *Mechanical Violator Haikaider* (1995). *Haikaider* was a spin-off of Shotaro Ishinomori's popular show *Kikaider*. The film makes Kikaider's nemesis Hakaider into the protagonist. Amemiya was given almost unlimited creative freedom for *Hakaider*. Toei came to regret this decision and Amemiya would not direct another one of their properties again. Amemiya focused on the novel medium of video games in the meantime. He worked on such games as Super Nintendo's *Treasure of the Rudras* (1996) and Playstation's *PAL: Shinken Densetsu* (1997). Amemiya returned to directing with 1997's *Moon Over Tao*. This genre-bending minor masterpiece was a box office failure.

Amemiya would largely switch to TV work from herein. His next project was directing the six episode *Tekkouki Mikazuki* (2000). He also helped conceive the anime show *Tweeny Witches* (2004-05). Keita Amemiya was pivotal to the creation of the horror-themed tokusatsu show *Garo*; the first series ran from 2005 to 2006. He has stayed active in the *Garo* franchise to this day, helming many of the spin-off films. Additionally, Amemiya has continued to be quite active in video game designs. He's worked on such games as the *Onimusha* series, *Final Fantasy XIV* and *Shin Megami Tensei IV* (both 2013).

Selected Filmography
"Space Wolf Juspion" (1985-86, TV) [character design]
"Time Warrior Spielban" (1986-87, TV) [character design]
"Ultraman: The Adventure Begins" (1987, TV) [character design]
"Superhuman Machine Metalder" (1987-88, TV) [character design]
"Kamen Rider Black" (1987-88, TV) [character design]
Cyber Ninja (1988) [director]
"Kamen Rider Black RX" (1988-89, TV) [character design]
Gunhed (1989) [animation]
"Mobile Cop Jiban" (1989-90, TV) [character design]
Lady Battle Cop (1990) [character design]
"Space Police Winspector" (1990-91, TV) [character design]
"Jetman" (1991-92, TV) [director/character design, *episodes 1, 2, 19, 20, 23, 24, 32, 33, 36, 37, 44, 45, 50, 51*]

Zeiram (1991) [director/screenplay/character design]
"Zyuranger" (1992-93, TV) [director, *episodes 25-26*]
Kamen Rider ZO (1993) [director/character design]
"Mighty Morphin' Power Rangers" (1993) [original director, *episodes 12, 23*]
Steel Hagane (1994, video game) [character design]
Kamen Rider J (1994) [director/character design]
Zeiram 2 (1994) [director/screenplay/character design]
Mechanical Violator Hakaider (1995) [director/character design]

Treasure of the Rudras (1996, video game) [character design]
PAL: Shinken Densetsu (1997, video game) [director/character design]
Dual Heroes (1997, video game) [director/character design]
Moon Over Tao (1997) [director/screenplay/character design]
"Tekkouki Mikazuki" (2000, TV) [director]
Onimusha 2: Samurai's Destiny (2002, video game) [character design]
Onimusha 3: Demon Siege (2004, video game) [character design]
"Tweeny Witches" (2004-05, TV) [concept/planning]

"Garo" (2005-06, TV) [director/screenplay]
Meatball Machine (2006) [creature design]
G-9 (2006) [director/screenplay]
"Kamen Rider Decade" (2009, TV) [character design, *episodes 26-27*]
Garo: Red Requiem (2010) [director/screenplay]
Shin Megami Tensei IV (2013, video game) [character design]
Final Fantasy XIV (2013, video game) [character design]
Garo: Kami no Kiba (2018) [director/screenplay]
Garo: Gekkou no Tabibito (2019) [director/screenplay]

Gamera: Daikaiju Kuchu Kessen "Gamera: Giant Monster Air Battle"
Daei/Nippon TV/Hakuhodo, 3/11/1995 (*Heisei 7*), 2,616 meters, 95:32, 35mm, Spherical (1.85:1), color, Dolby Stereo

Crew
Executive Producer: Yasuyoshi Tokuma
Production Representatives: Hiroyuki Kato, Seiji Urushido, Shigeru Ono
Producers: Tetsuya Ikeda, Toshio Hagiwara, Hatsuhiko Sawada
Planning: Naoki Sato, Hidehiko Takei, Hiroshi Morie, Nobuko Suzuki
Producer: Tsutomu Tsuchikawa
Line Producer: Miyuki Nanri
Associate Producers: Daisuke Kadoya, Jiro Kijima, Chihiro Takahashi
Director: Shusuke Kaneko
Special Effects Director: Shinji Higuchi
Screenplay: Kazunori Ito
Director of Photography: Junichi Tozawa
Music: Ko Otani
Music Producer: Mitsunori Miura
Art Director: Hajime Oikawa
Editor: Shizuo Arakawa

Assistant Director: Shozo Katashima
Sound Recording: Yasuo Hashimoto
Lighting: Sosuke Yoshikado
Casting: Yoshinori Suzuki
In Charge of Production: Ryo Ueno, Yoshiyuki Oikawa
Assistants to the Director: Masaki Hamamoto, Hideaki Murakami, Futoshi Sato
Talent Supervisor: Takashi Inoue
Camera Assistants: Yoshihito Takahashi, Shinji Kugimiya, Shinji Suzuki, Tsutomu Tada
Lighting Assistants: Masahiro Kudou, Seichirou Mieno, Hiroshi Tanabe, Tomo Minamisono, Takaharu Yamauchi
Recording Assistants: Satoshi Ozaki, Hisashi Kamike
Art Assistants: Gen Ishii, Noriko Akiyama
Set Decoration: Keiichi Hasegawa, Eiji Kaneko
Property Masters: Takayuki Suzuki, Toshiaki Takahashi, Yukie Oikawa
Equipment: Keiji Yoshinuma, Takahashi Kubono
Construction: Akihiro Hayakawa
Special Equipment: Masato Yoshiga, Takashi Mikami, Kouji Sakamaki, Kenji Nakashizu
Costumes: Noriko Baba, Yoshinobu Nagata
Makeup: Masami Kinjo
CRT CG: Manabu Niwa
Stunts" Wataru Tagaya
Editing Assistant: Mototaka Kusakabe
Sound Effects: Yukio Hokari, Akihiko Okase
Music Mixer: Teruhiko Oono

Re-recording: Koshirou Jinbo
Recording Studio Staff: Masumi Ishii, Chiaki Tachikawa, Tomeyuki Shimono
Print Timing: Toshikazu Ogura
Advertising Producer: Masaru Yabe, Tomofumi Arashi
Production Advertising: Takeshi Kobayashi
Publicists: Shuuzou Matsumoto, Mikio Ono
NTV Public Relations: Noriko Tachimatsu
Production Direction Youichi Arishige
Transportation: Yukinori Kaneko, Akio Hakamada, Kiyotaka Urushibata, Hideo Kobayashi, Noboru Matsuzaki, Hiroaki Kawabata
Gotenba Location Supervisor: Magosaku Osada
Production Supervisors: Mitsunori Sakai, Takafumi Hamaoka
Production Management: Ken Ikehara, Masanori Takeuchi
Second Unit Director of Photography: Akira Maeda
Second Unit Camera Assistants: Nobuyasu Kita, Tomohiro Nishimura
Second Unit Lighting: Masayuki Okao
Second Unit Lighting Assistants: Kazuya Ando, Hiroshi Aoki
Assistant Editor: Isao Tomita
SFX Cinematography: Hiroshi Kidokoro
SFX Art Director: Toshio Miike
SFX Lighting: Hokoku Hayashi
Monster Suit Construction: Tomoo Haraguchi
Practical Effects: Izumi Negishi

Visual Effects Supervisors: Hajime Matsumoto, Mitsuhara Haibara
SFX Editing: Shinichi Fujima
SFX Continuity: Junko Kawashima
Assistant SFX Director: Makoto Kamiya
In Charge of SFX Production: Masaya Kajikawa
Assistant SFX Directors: Kazuki Makazaki, Kenichi Takei, Keisuke Ota
Photographic Assistants: Akira Murakawa, Takahide Mashio, Yukio Komiya, Masujirou Kuratomi
SFX Lighting Assistants: Takashi Mizuno, Toshihiko Ootsuka, Shigetaka Yonezawa
SFX Art Assistants: Masato Inatsuki, Hiroshi Samukawae, Hideyoshi Amano, Kaoru Iwamitsu, Masahiko Tani, Keigo Okada, Nahoko Seki, Hitoshi Takanohara
SFX Stage Setting: Tomoyuki Takagi
Special Equipment: Daisaku Shimura, Kiyotaka Tanaka
Suit Construction Assistants: Hisashi Oda, Miki Takahama, Hidenori Yamaoka, Susumu Sano, Rikiya Sou
SFX Carpentry: Yumiko Noda
Animatronics: Tatsuya Abe, Masayuki Kurahashi, Shigeaki Ueda, Tetsuaki Maru, Yutaka Kiyosawa
Poly-molding: Haruto Miyazaki
Asst. Gymnastics Instructors: Kenichi Ueda, Yoshinori Muraishi, Kenji Kawaguchi, Atsushi Tsuji
Editing Assistant: Hirofumi Okuda
SFX Production Management: Yoshiaki Taro, Takayuki

Niihara, Hiroshi Adachi, Mitsuru Hagiawa, Hiroshi Iwatani

VFX Lighting: Yoshimi Hosaka

VFX Lighting Assistant: Shigeru Izumiya

Gymnast: Osamu Hatakeyama

Assistant Gymnasts: Toshiyuki Yajima, Fumiharu Sakata, Kenji Sugata

Motion Control Photography: Sadanori Inaba, Haruhiko Aizawa

Effects Animation: Mitsuaki Hashimoto, Akihiro Nishiyama

CG Images: Atsunori Sato

Matte Artist: Keisuke Kamitono

Rotoscope: Tomoko Shindo, Mizuho Yoshida

Photographic Effects: Osamu Izumiya, Teruo Tsuda, Takafumi Uchida

Optical Effects: Tetsuo Kaneko, Takanori Sato, Yutaka Ishikawa, Yoshio Shibata

Digital Effects: Takashi Kawabata, Tadao Fumishita

Video Effects: Nobuya Ishida

Computer Graphics: Misako Saka, Yoshishige Matsuno, Shinji Yamamoto, Hiroshi Arima, Hidenori Hayashi

Frame: Junji Kojima

Monster Design: Mahiro Maeda

Storyboards: Hyoue Ishida

Still Photography: Makoto Hisaida

Assistant Still Photographer: Kenji Takama

SFX Still Photographer: Miho Ishizuki

Still Photography Assistant: Seijiro Fujita

Cast

Tsuyoshi Ihara *(Yoshinari Yonemori)*

Shinobu Nakayama *(Mayumi Nagamine)*

Akira Onodera *(Naoya Kusanagi)*

Ayako Fujitani *(Asagi Kusanagi)*

Yukijiro Hotaru *(Inspector Osako)*

Hirotaro Honda *(Mr. Saito)*

Hatsunori Hasegawa *(Colonel Satake)*

Kojiro Hongo *(Captain of the Nojima)*

Akira Kubo *(Captain of the Kairyumaru)*

Takashi Matsuo *(Taxi Driver)*

Yoshihiko Hakamada *(Michiya)*

Tomiko Ishii *(Grocery Store Owner)*

Jun Fubuki *(Shopping Woman)*

Yasuo Kanechika *(Policeman on Himegami Island)*

Masahiko Sakata *(Officer at Dome)*

Masato Yasuo *(Nagasaki Helicopter Captain)*

Kiyokazu Inoue *(Chishima Maru Crewman)*

Masashi Ueda *(Officer behind Dome)*

Miyuki Fuji *(Correspondent)*

Haruyasu Oi *(Old Man at Bridge)*

Satoshi Masae *(Firefighter at Bridge)*

Miyako Wada *(Mother at Bridge)*

Takito Horiuchi *(Kid at Bridge)*

Hiroshi Atsumi *(Correspondent in Office)*

Mika Suzuki *(Correspondent)*

Nanako Shindo *(Zoo Employee)*

Sarina Kaori *(Reporter on Himegami Island)*

Koutaro Takeshita *(Young Man on Train)*

Mitsuko Aoki *(Girl on Train)*

Yuka Sakano *(Yukino)*

Takeshi Yano *(Investigator on the Kenzaki)*

Takumi Matsui *(Kairyumaru Crewman)*

Yoko Ooshima *(Woman in Otoko Island Shop)*

Yuichi Mayama *(Newscaster)*

Yuko Kimura *(Newscaster)*

Kenji Wakabayashi *(Newscaster)*

Minako Nagai *(Newscaster)*

Izumi Ogami *(Reporter)*

Akemi Nakamura *(Correspondent at Dome)*

Hisanori Koba *(Reporter at Dome)*

Minoru Tamura *(Newscaster at Train Station)*

Yutaka Natsuki *(Reporter)*

Tetsu Watanabe *(Captain at Mt. Fuji)*

Hiroyuki Watanabe *(Co. Commander at Tenohman)*

Naoki Manabe *(Gamera)*

Jun Suzuki *(Gamera)*

Yumi Kaneyama *(Gyaos)*

Alternate Titles

G1 (informal)

"What if giant monsters appeared in the real world? We started from that assumption."
-Shinji Higuchi, *The Making of Gamera: Guardian of the Universe* (1995)

Daiei, now owned by publishing mogul Yasuyoshi Tokuma, brought Gamera back to the big screen with 1995's *Gamera: Guardian of the Universe*. It is easily the best Japanese monster film since the peak of the Honda/Tsuburaya years. Director Shusuke Kaneko and young special effects genius Shinji Higuchi bring forth a "Kaiju New Wave". They add modern flourish while keeping reverence to the spirit of Honda and Tsuburaya. With the most realistic tone in a kaiju film yet, *Gamera: Guardian of the Universe* is fairly incredible filmmaking. It is close to Steven Spielberg's *Jurassic Park* in production value.

PLOT

The *Kairyumaru*, a transport ship carrying plutonium, collides with a mysterious atoll off the coast of the Philippines. This atoll appears to be drifting and heading towards Japan. A mission is dispatched to investigate the atoll, led by Naoya Kusanagi (Akira Onodera). Young navalman Yoshinari Yonemori (Tsuyoshi Ihara) was on the Kairyumaru's support ship the *Nojima*. He insists on accompanying the expedition. Meanwhile, ornithologist Mayumi Nagamine (Shinobu Nakayama) goes to Himegamijima, an island in Goto archipelago. Reports keep coming in of attacks by giant birds and her senior has disappeared. She and police inspector Osako (Yukijiro Hotaru) investigate a village allegedly destroyed by the birds. Nagamine finds a giant bird pellet containing the glasses of her missing senior professor.

At the same time, the scientists explore the atoll. They find mysterious amulets on the ground which appear to be made of the mythical metal orihalcum and a large stone slab covered in ancient runes. The slab fractures into pieces as the atoll suddenly shakes and breaks apart. The expedition is thrown into the water by the force. Yonemori sees a gigantic, turtle-like monster awaken underwater as he realizes the atoll was alive. Nagamine, meanwhile, encounters the giant bird monster. In a helicopter, she uses a camera flash to drive it away. Osako and Nagamine realize that there are three monster birds.

The government, led by EPA secretary Saito (Hirotaro Honda) attempts to capture the giant birds with Nagamine's assistance. She has the creatures lured to Fukuoka's Payday Dome with cow carcasses, intending to tranquilize and entrap them. Two of the monsters are successfully captured. Yonemori arrives at the capture site and tells the military that the larger monster turtle is on its way to Fukuoka. The other monster bird escapes to the harbor. The giant turtle surfaces and kills it with a fireball from its fanged mouth. As the turtle approaches the stadium, the captured bird creatures emit a mysterious laser beam that cuts their cages open. They escape, but the monster turtle takes off by igniting flames from its legs in hot pursuit.

Kusanagi and Yonemori translate the runes from the stone slab. They decide to call the giant turtle Gamera and the monster birds Gyaos. Yonemori gives Kusanagi's daughter Asagi (Ayako Fujitani) one of the orihalcum amulets. It glows as she touches it and Asagi inadvertently forms a psychic bond with Gamera. The government agrees to use the monster names but disagree that the Gyaos are more dangerous. The Gyaos next attack the Kiso Mountains at Gifu Prefecture. Yonemori and Nagamine, trying to save a stranded boy, are nearly killed. Gamera arrives on the scene and destroys another Gyaos, learning only one alive.

The Self Defense Force next mounts multiple attacks on Gamera and Asagi runs away from school. Watching the military fire on Gamera at Mount Fuji, she suffers the same wounds. The final Gyaos is drawn to the scene and lacerates Gamera with its laser beam. Gamera retreats into the sea and Asagi collapses. Kusanagi visits a hospitalized Asagi, who explains that *"She and Gamera must rest"* before falling into a coma. Yonemori and Nagamine consult with biologist Michiya (Yoshihiko Hakamada), Nagamine's college junior. He explains that the Gyaos have perfect duo chromosomes. This ominous data suggests they were genetically engineered and can reproduce aesexually. Nagamine believes that the Gyaos were created by an ancient Atlantean civilization. After they became too difficult to control, Gamera was then created to destroy them. The Gyaos have been reawakened due to pollution and climate change.

The last Gyaos is able to triple in size and attacks Tokyo, killing and eating a train full of people. The military tries to kill Gyaos with missiles, but destroys Tokyo Tower instead. Gyaos builds a nest in Tokyo Tower's ruins as night falls on the city. Kusanagi and Asagi arrive in Tokyo to inform the group that Gamera has reawakened and is on its way to challenge Gyaos.

BACKGROUND

After the bankruptcy of Daiei in the early '70s, the company was acquired by publishing mogul Yasuyoshi Tokuma in 1974. Tokuma (1925-2000) was later a pivotal figure in the foundation of Studio Ghibli. He was eager to bring back Daiei's stalwart monster Gamera. Tokuma Daiei's first attempt at a new Gamera film was *Gamera: Supermonster* (1980). Noriaki Yuasa was brought back for a fairly atrocious film composed of stock footage and vapid nods to the newest Hollywood blockbusters. Tokuma wanted to make another Gamera film after Toho's *The Return of Godzilla* (1984) but the project was slow in development. Finally, the success of Toho's *Godzilla vs. King Ghidorah* (1991) made Tokuma decide to move forward with a new Gamera picture.

Shusuke Kaneko was chosen as director. Kaneko had started out directing softcore pornography at Nikkatsu. He broke out with the youth drama *Summer Vacation 1999*

(1988) and dark vampire comedy *My Soul is Slashed* (1991). He was a long time *kaiju* fan, loving Godzilla films on the big screen and *Ultra Q* on TV as a boy. Kaneko had campaigned for the job to direct 1992's *Godzilla vs. Mothra*, but Toho had already hired Takao Okawara. *Anime* writer Kazunori Ito, another kaiju fan since youth, was brought on to pen the screenplay. Ito (1954-) was fresh off his work on the first two *Patlabor* films by Mamoru Oshii. In 1995, the same year *Gamera* was released, he also wrote Oshii's iconic *Ghost in the Shell*. Ito later would become an integral part of the *.hack* franchise. Shinji Higuchi, only in his mid 20s, was hired to direct the special effects sequences. At the age of only 19, Higuchi had worked on the low budget indie kaiju flick *The Eight-Headed Serpent Strikes Back*. It was so well made it was sold to Bandai. Kaneko was impressed with Higuchi's sequences in this film and gave him the job for *Gamera* as a result. Higuchi had also done quite a bit of anime storyboard work for his friends at Gainax like Hideaki Anno.

With a talented team in place, production finally began around late 1993. The first press conference was held on April 25, 1994. Kaneko was dismayed by the film's relatively low budget, less than half of Toho's concurrent Godzilla films. He contemplated directing the picture with a comedic angle. Yet after reading Ito's script, Kaneko was so impressed he decided to take up the challenge of making the best monster movie he could. Kaneko and Higuchi decided to envision the film from the starting point of *"What if giant monsters existed in the real world?"*.

Kaneko wanted to turn a formerly child-oriented franchise into one with a more adult tone. The characters of Gamera and Gyaos are brought back in reimagined form, but the tone couldn't be more different from Noriaki Yuasa's films. Daiei's brass was initially against this. They wanted Gamera to remain a child friendly monster. Kaneko asked them *"How does Gamera tell the difference between children and adults?".* When they couldn't answer, Kaneko was allowed to make Gamera the guardian of humanity rather than just children. Yuasa himself, though he visited Higuchi's special effects unit, did not like the film or its sequels. He felt they were too far off from the child-like spirit he had intended for the franchise. Daiei was also against the idea of Gamera being created by an ancient civilization. Ito had even put an implication in the script that Gamera was biomechanical. Daiei reneged after Kaneko threatened to quit the film. The hint at Gamera being mechanical was removed as a compromise. Originally, the script was also to feature five Gyaos. Lions Mansions, a luxury apartment complex in Tokyo, was to have been destroyed and made into Gyaos' nest instead of Tokyo Tower. There were also several more battles between the Self Defense Force and Gamera that were cut for budgetary reasons.

PRINCIPAL PHOTOGRAPHY

Director Kaneko brings a fresh style to *Gamera: Guardian of the Universe*. It is reverent of the classics but trends in a new, progressive direction. In a 1996 interview with Steve Ryfle, Kaneko claims that he often thought about how Ishiro Honda would have directed each scene and emulated it. References to classic kaiju films are numerous in *Gamera: Guardian of the Universe*. The first actor seen on screen is Kojiro Hongo, the star of several *Showa* Gamera films. This is followed swiftly by a cameo from Toho stalwart Akira Kubo. Early scenes on Himegamijima invoke both *Godzilla* (1954) and *The War of the Gargantuas* (1966). At one moment during the shoot, Kaneko and his crew looked through their black and white video assist monitor at a shot of the destroyed island village. They joked that it looked just like Odo Island in *Godzilla*. Later scenes with Gyaos nesting in a destroyed Tokyo Tower draw heavy influence from *Mothra* (1961). It should be noted that Kaneko wrote an 1981 episode, *"Mrs. Swallow and Mrs. Penguin"*, of the TV anime *Urusei Yatsura*. In it, a giant swallow builds a nest on Tokyo Tower similarly to Gyaos.

The Self Defense Force lent their full support to *Gamera: Guardian of the Universe*. The Air Defense Force, however, only agreed to give support provided a scene with an F-15 jet crash was removed. The staff was careful not to show too much damage to air units in the next two Gamera entries.

ACTORS

The cast is headlined by Shinobu Nakayama's adorable young scientist Dr. Nagamine. Nakayama (1973-) was a music idol turned actress. She had previously played a small role in Takao Okawara's *Godzilla vs.* *Mechagodzilla II* (1993). Nakayama had also played a major supporting part in *Fist of Legend* (1994) with Jet Li. Steven Seagal's half-Japanese daughter, Ayako Fujitani, plays Asagi Kusanagi. The character of Asagi was inspired by the subsequent Godzilla films' Miki Saegusa. Kaneko and Ito, however, thought they could better execute the trope of a girl with a psychic link to the monster. Kaneko has a fondness for attractive female protagonists, treading an awkward line between fetishism and feminism. Nonetheless, Nagamine and Asagi are the most empowered female characters in a *kaiju* flick yet.

SFX/VFX

The most astounding aspect of *Gamera: Guardian of the Universe* is Shinji Higuchi's special effects work. Only 28 years old during filming, Higuchi shows near mastery of his craft. Produced as mentor Koichi Kawakita's unit made the embarrassing *Godzilla vs. Space Godzilla*, Higuchi's footage was made for half the budget but looks infinitely better. Like Kaneko with Honda, Higuchi shows reverence to Eiji Tsuburaya's legacy but adds his own novel flair. Higuchi and his unit strived for aesthetic realism at all cost and the miniature work is dazzling. Higuchi and art director Toshio Miike devised a clever method to create impressive miniatures on the film's tight budget and the Daiei lot's limited space. In the old days, Tsuburaya's unit built their miniature cities ahead of time, before blocking shots. Koichi Kawakita's crew at Toho still did things that way. The ingenious Higuchi storyboarded and blocked his shots first. He then had Miike build partial, scale miniatures around the shot plans. This helped save money but still get an impressive result. Miike built his miniatures to a stunning level of detail. His team put many everyday touches on their tiny sets often ignored by other builders. These included hanging laundry, detailed signs and offices inside the most prominent models. A lot of thought and care was put into making the miniatures look lived-in. Approximately forty miniature buildings were constructed in total. Higuchi's unit shows an innovative spirit akin to John Dyskstra's team on *Star Wars*.

The creatures were designed by Mahiro Maeda. Maeda (1963-) had already contributed designs to *Ultraman: The Ultimate Hero* or *Ultraman Powered* (1993), along with Higuchi and Miike. His sleek re-designs of classic *Ultraman* monsters are a highlight of the otherwise creatively disastrous show. Maeda brings the same aesthetic to Gamera and Gyaos. He and Higuchi wanted to create a more sea turtle-like Gamera but Daiei insisted on a traditional depiction. Maeda would be allowed to incorporate the sea turtle motif in his Gamera designs for the next two entries. Mahiro Maeda was also an occasional anime director, his debut being 1998's *Blue Submarine No. 6*. He is best known for his anthology segment *The Second Renaissance*, a short animated prequel to *The Matrix*. Maeda also later contributed design work to George Miller's *Mad Max: Fury Road* (2015).

The suits were built by Tomoo Haraguchi. Haraguchi (1960-) also occasionally dabbles in directing horror-based works. These include *Mikadroid* (1991), *Sakuya, Slayer of Demons* (2000) and *Death Kappa* (2010). The suits are among the finest constructed yet. They are expressive, life-like and made from superior materials. Similarly to Kawakita's unit, an animatronic Gamera puppet was built for close-ups. Rudimentary Gyaos props were also made to interact with the live actors on Kaneko's unit. Higuchi's team sought to give Gamera more of a personality in their footage. They struggled with portraying Gyaos, Higuchi wanting a more agile creature than its 1967 counterpart. Gyaos was played by actress Yumi Kameyama, one of the first women to act inside of a monster suit. Higuchi wanted his monster battles to be ferocious wrestling matches. He and his DP Hiroshi Kidokoro made a point to lens their shots mainly from street level. To emphasize the monsters' size, Kidokoro often framed the creatures against mundane objects as a reference point. Despite technological advances, Tsuburaya's old school piano wire techniques were still occasionally used. Drawing influence from the anime of Hayao Miyazaki, Higuchi sought to create the most impressive aerial sequences in the genre to date. *Gamera: Guardian of the Universe* also made heavier use of blue and green screens than Kawakita's work did.

Gamera: Guardian of the Universe's finale is nothing short of jaw dropping. The monster scenes were mainly shot on an outdoor stage with natural light. For some shots, an Innovision "snorkel lens" was used to make the miniatures seem larger as it had an impressively wide focal length. With a deep focused aperture, it required a lot of light and fires would occasionally start on set. For the scene where Tokyo Tower is blown up, two miniatures were built at different scales. It took three takes to get the miniature to collapse correctly. One wide shot at the end of this sequence shows Gyaos nesting in the fallen tower against a vivid sunset. It feels like quintessential Shinji Higuchi. Like another mentor, Teruyoshi Nakano, Higuchi shows a taste for explosions. Higuchi's engineer Izumi Negishi used a variety of gunpowder and gasoline recipes. Negishi strived to make his explosions distinctive, varied and realistic. He perfected the classic Tsuburaya-era technique of loading bead-like containers with gunpowder and detonating them electrically. Higuchi opted to increase the size of the explosions as the film's dramatic tension built. The final stunt of a billowing petrochemical explosion before Gamera was extremely dangerous for suit actor Jun Suzuki. For Gyaos' explosive death, a smaller "Kapok" doll was built and then blown up by Higuchi's crew. In total, principal photography for the FX sequences lasted 101 days. The sole flaw of Higuchi's FX work is some dated CGI, rendered with a Silicon Graphics Indigo, a Macintosh and an IBM. Koichi Kawakita saw *Gamera: Guardian of the Universe* and was extremely impressed, congratulating Higuchi. The young man who had worked as a production assistant for Kawakita on *Bye Bye Jupiter* had now outshone his mentor.

MUSIC

Ko Otani (1957-) provided the score for *Gamera: Guardian of the Universe*. In addition to often working with Kaneko, Otani scored such anime as *City Hunter, Gundam Wing* and *Outlaw Star*. He also scored video games like *Shadow of the Colossus*. His music is perfectly suited to the film's tone, alternating between suspenseful and heroic themes.

THEMES AND MOTIFS

The script contains a multitude of references to classical Japanese mythology. Asagi's pendant was based on the *magatama*. They are curved beads found in prehistoric Japan and strongly associated with the Shinto religion. The *magatama* is used similarly in *Blue Seed*, a 1994-95 anime TV series based on a *manga* by Yuzo Takada (*3x3 Eyes*). The surname Kusanagi, as well, is associated with Shinto legends. The *Kusanagi no Tsurugi* is a sword said to have been used by *Susano-o* to kill the mythical hydra *Yamata no Orochi*. The *Kusanagi no Tsurugi* and a *magatama* called the *Yasakani no Magatama* are two of the three Imperial Regalia or Three Treasures of Japan. These are sacred heirlooms passed down through the Imperial family. It was screenwriter Kazunori Ito who chose to incorporate these fantastical and religious elements. There is also slight political satire showing backlogged bureaucracy, the invocation of Article 9 of Japan's Constitution and crashing stock markets. This foreshadows 2016's *Shin Godzilla*, co-directed by Shinji Higuchi.

RELEASE AND LEGACY

Gamera: Guardian of the Universe premiered at the Yubari International Fantastic Film Festival in February 1995. In general release, distributed by Toho, it did good enough business that Daiei quickly commissioned a sequel. Critically, it was well received; one of the few kaiju movies to make trade mag Kinema Junpo's list of the best Japanese films that year. *Gamera 2: Attack of Legion* would follow in 1996 and would bring back Kaneko, Higuchi and actress Fujitani.

ALTERNATE VERSIONS

Gamera: Guardian of the Universe was sold to ADV Films, an anime distributor based in Houston, Texas. ADV gave the film a small theatrical run in April 1997. The English dub was recorded in Texas by ADV. It was produced by John Ledford and written and directed by Matt Greenfield. Voice cast includes Aaron Krohn as Yonemori, Tiffany Grant as Nagamine, Amanda Winn Lee as Asagi, Tristan MacAvery as Kusanagi, Paul Sidello as Osako, Rick Peeples as Saito and Rob Mungle as Colonel Satake. Supporting voices include Spike Spencer, Kimberly Yates, John Swasey, Phil Ross, Marcy Rae, Kim Sevier, Guil Lunde, Brett Weaver, Laura Chapman, Sue Ulu and Allison Keith. It's a fairly well produced dub, marred only by an irritating original song, *"Gamera Always Wins"*. The same staff also produced the original English dub for *Neon Genesis Evangelion* which Shinji Higuchi, incidentally, also had a hand in.

There is an alternate, British version of the film with a different dub recorded in England by Arrival Films with thick accents. Released around 1997, it bizarrely replaces sections of Otani's score with obnoxious techno rave music. Dubbing cast includes Lara Clancy as Nagamine, Chris Harvey John, Roy Ward and Charlotte Bellamore. This version is recommended only as a curiosity.

AMERICAN HOME VIDEO HISTORY

Gamera: Guardian of the Universe was released to VHS and laserdisc by ADV in 1998. It was then distributed to DVD in 2003 with both Japanese and English tracks. In 2010, it was released to Blu-ray by Mill Creek, paired with *Gamera 2: Attack of Legion*. Mill Creek would later redistribute the film in two sets in 2011 and 2014. In 2020, Arrow included Kadokawa's 4K remaster on their *Gamera: The Complete Collection* Blu-ray boxed set chock full of impressive special features.

Further Viewing:

(1995)
ゴジラVSデストロイア
Toho, *Director:* **Takao Okawara**

As Shusuke Kaneko and Shinji Higuchi worked on *Gamera 2*, Takao Okawara and Koichi Kawakita gave us a final film in the *Heisei* (VS) series. *Godzilla vs. Destoroyah* is a clunky picture with an awe-inspiring final ten minutes. Originally called *Godzilla vs. Ghost Godzilla*, it boasts a far stronger half from Koichi Kawakita than director Okawara. The human scenes are uninteresting and flatly directed. Actor Toshiyuki Hosokawa was originally to play a major role but dropped out midway through shooting and was replaced by Saburo Shinoda. Shout-outs to the original 1954 *Godzilla*, including the presence of Momoko Kochi, feel hollow and only remind one just how much better that film is. Kazuki Omori penned the script and his directorial talents are missed. Omori, however, still leaves behind his signature Hollywood influence in the form of nods to *Alien* and *Jurassic Park*. The human scenes are not coordinated very well with Kawakita's end of *Destoroyah*.

Koichi Kawakita's FX work is overall a mixed bag but a far more satisfying one than Okawara's bland human scenes. There are some genuinely embarrassing shots. Some composites show leisurely crowds and traffic fleeing the monsters, but that is likely more the fault of Okawara who shot those elements. A JSDF attack sequence features Bandai toys of the crab Destoroyah monsters used in wide shots and some flying scenes are poor. However, there are also plenty of stunning shots and sequences. Kenpachiro Satsuma plays a sickly, dying Godzilla in agonizing pain with surprising pathos. The Godzilla costume was outfitted with hundreds of tiny light bulbs to create a burning effect and carbon dioxide gas was used to produce steam. Satsuma nearly died from suffocation and needed to use an oxygen tank for much of the shoot. A sequence with yet another Super-X unit battling Godzilla with freezing weapons is a highlight and once more invokes *Gunhed*. Additionally, an impressive mechanism was built for crab form Destoroyah's Xenomorph-style double-jaw. Godzilla Junior is a massive design improvement over Little Godzilla and the suit is well built by Tomoki Kobayashi. A battle between Junior and Destoroyah is a standout with better, larger scaled miniatures.

Destoroyah is an uninspired if mildly interesting creation with multiple forms similar to Hedorah. Its final form is frustratingly reminiscent of Space Godzilla, though with demonic motifs that stress the film's apocalyptic overtones. There were several deleted effects scenes, most notably a scene where Godzilla finished off Destoroyah in battle. It was discarded because Kawakita thought it would take away from Godzilla's ensuing death by meltdown. *Godzilla vs. Destoroyah* comes alive in its final moments which almost redeem it. Scored with one of Ifukube's few original pieces for the *Heisei* series, Godzilla's death is a beautiful, Eisensteinian sequence that might make you shed a tear or two. This incredible scene is driven mainly by Kawakita's unit. Okawara's, by contrast, just films and edits in static close-ups of the actors. *Godzilla vs. Destoroyah* is, overall, an uneven mess capped in some surprisingly heartrending moments.

GAMERA
THE BRAVE

(2006)
小さき勇者たち〜ガメラ
Kadokawa/Shochiku, *Director*: Ryuta Tasaki

After the superb *Gamera 3: Revenge of Iris,* plans for a *Gamera 4* were scuttled. Underwhelming box office and renewed financial issues for Daiei were to blame. In 2002, Kadokawa acquired Daiei and its holdings. They were keen to make a *Godzilla vs. Gamera* movie with Toho's collaboration, but Toho declined their offer. They wound up going back to the drawing board with a more child friendly return to Gamera's roots. *Gamera the Brave* is an interesting film in that it feels like a medium between Shusuke Kaneko and Noriaki Yuasa's styles. The spirit and tone is much in line with Yuasa's work. Yet it boasts a polished aesthetic and borrows visuals from Shinji Higuchi's FX work for the *Heisei* trilogy.

In 1973, Gamera self destructed itself to save humanity from a horde of Gyaos as young Kosuke watched. 33 years later, Kosuke (Kanji Tsuda) is a bitter widower whose son, Toru (Ryo Tomioka) still mourns his dead mother. Kosuke neglects Toru as he's busy running a newly reopened restaurant. One day, Toru finds a mysterious egg atop a large gem. The egg hatches into a baby turtle which Toru names "Toto" after a nickname his late mother gave him. Toto begins to grow impressively. At the same time, a giant monster, the man-eating Zedus, appears at sea and attacks Toru's village. Toto grows to an enormous size and attacks Zedus. It drives Zedus away, but soon the military captures Toto. As Toru's childhood friend Mai (Kaho) undergoes heart surgery, Toru and friends sneak away to Nagoya to save Toto.

Gamera the Brave is directed by Ryuta Tasaki, who did a lot of work for the recent *Kamen Rider* franchise. The film is tolerable, but far from the quality of Shusuke Kaneko's more mature entries. It's a little sappy and the child-focus is strong. Yet the kid protagonists are a lot more likeable and less abrasive than in Yuasa's films. The cinematography is lush and polished. *Gamera the Brave*'s tone is similar to Toho's *Rebirth of Mothra* trilogy but the execution is far better. Ryo Tomioka's Toru is a well developed protagonist and the early character-driven scenes are more effective than the sound and fury of the monster sequences. Toto's early turtle form is irresistibly adorable and impressively executed. These scenes used actual baby African spurred tortoises frosted with CGI. Animal rights activists in Japan were concerned about the treatment of these tortoises on set. They also worried that the film would inspire children to adopt them, resulting in mass abandonment. As a result, the end credits of *Gamera the Brave* put a disclaimer urging children to think twice before getting one as a pet. The scenes with Toru and the growing Toto are a highlight of the film and quite reminiscent of the classic *Ultra Q* episode *Grow! Turtle*.

The special effects scenes by Isao Kaneko (no relation to Shusuke) are well done. Tomoo

Haraguchi returned to model the puppets, props and suits. They are extremely well crafted. Gamera/Toto's foe, Zedus, is a nod to *Ultraman*'s Jiras, frilled neck in all. According to rumor, the use of a Godzillian monster was something of a bird to Toho for refusing a crossover film. Zedus is even played by Mizuho Yoshida, who played Godzilla in 2001's *Godzilla, Mothra and King Ghidorah: Giant Monsters All-Out Attack*. Keeping in step with Yuasa's penchant for kaiju gore, *Gamera the Brave* boasts some surprisingly grisly moments for a kids' movie. Zedus devours passerby in what are some of the most nightmarish human-munching scenes

since Gaira satisfied his "people food" craving in *The War of the Gargantuas*. The final scenes copy Shinji Higuchi's work significantly in style. They are somewhat tiresome and cliche contrasted with the well directed, character-driven early sequences. *Gamera the Brave* is somewhere between the Kaneko trilogy and Masaaki Tezuka-directed Godzilla films in quality. It boasts impressive moments but there are better modern kaiju flicks. Sadly, *Gamera the Brave* tanked hard at the Japanese box office. This regrettably put the kibosh on a *Majin* reboot to be directed by *Audition*'s Takashi Miike.

NORIYOSHI OHRAI
The Illustrator

生頼範義
11/17/1935-10/27/2015

A film's poster is an under-appreciated aspect of the cinematic experience. Where would the *Star Wars* or *Indiana Jones* franchises be without Richard Amsel or Drew Struzan to sell them? As a boy, I remember finding the tape for *Godzilla vs. Biollante,* which used Ohrai's poster art, in a suburban mall's video store. I was amazed by and even a little frightened of this dynamic art on the cover. Later, I found an imported Japanese book with the posters for the '90s Godzilla films, clearly by the same artist. These detailed, graphic illustrations wound up being more exciting than the movies themselves. Some years later, I realized that the genius responsible had a far more versatile career. Noriyoshi Ohrai's credentials branch their tendrils

from Godzilla to *Star Wars* to *anime* to Sakyo Komatsu to *Metal Gear Solid*.

Best called the Japanese Drew Struzan, his art is arguably even more masterful. Born in Akashi City in Hyogo in 1935, Ohrai's family evacuated to Kagoshima during the war. After high school, Ohrai would study fine art at the Tokyo University of the Arts. He wound up dropping out, but soon began working as a successful illustrator in 1962. One of his first movie poster jobs was for the Toei *yakuza* film *Tosei-Nin Retsuden,* directed by Shigehiro Ozawa. In the 1970s, he did his first work for Toho. Ohrai painted posters for *Submersion of Japan* (1973) and *Prophecies of Nostradamus* (1974). He also illustrated the jackets for Kazumasa Hirai's *Wolf Guy* and *Genma Taisen* novels.

Around 1980, Ohrai's career blossomed and he became the most in-demand illustrative painter in Japan. George Lucas saw a piece Ohrai had done of *Star Wars* in a magazine and was impressed. Lucasfilm thus commissioned Ohrai to paint the international poster for *The Empire Strikes Back*. He won the Seiun Award for Best Art the same year. During this period, Ohrai also contributed poster art for *Virus* (1980) and *Future War 198X* (1982). The former was also used for repressings of Sakyo Komatsu's novel. In 1983, he illustrated the cover of a Toho special effects film reference book. This got him the job to paint one of the posters for 1984's *The Return of Godzilla*. Ohrai would go on to create the art

for eight more films in the Godzilla series. He also contributed art to the *Macross* and *Gundam* franchises and did the Japanese posters for *The Road Warrior* and *King Kong Lives*. His poster for *The Goonies* was used by Warner Brothers for its U.S. release. Ohrai even did album art for the rock band Lazy and metal singer Misako Honjo.

In later life, Ohrai contributed art for several entries in Konami and Hideo Kojima's beloved *Metal Gear Solid* video game series. Some of his last film posters were for *Godzilla: Final Wars* (2004) and *Sinking of Japan* (2006). He died of pneumonia in late 2015 at the age of 79. His masterfully painted, striking images are missed on both sides of the Pacific even as, in film promotion, lush illustrations are supplanted by photographic collages.

Selected Filmography

Tosei-Nin Restuden (1969) [poster art]

Submersion of Japan (1973) [poster art]

Prophecies of Nostradamus (1974) [poster art]

Tentacles (1977) [Japanese poster art]

Star Wars: The Empire Strikes Back (1980) [international poster art]

Virus (1980) [poster art]

The Road Warrior (1981) [Japanese poster art]

Hot Sleep of the Beasts (1981) [poster art]

Future War 198X (1982) [poster art]

The Beastmaster (1982) [poster art]

The Return of Godzilla (1984) [poster art]

The Goonies (1985) [poster art]

Runaway Train (1985) [Japanese poster art]

King Kong Lives (1986) [Japanese poster art]

Tokyo Blackout (1987) [poster art]

Mobile Suit Gundam: Char's Counterattack (1988) [poster art]

Godzilla vs. Biollante (1989) [poster art]

Ronin-Gai (1990) [poster art]

Doomed Megalopolis (1991) [cover art]

Godzilla vs. King Ghidorah (1991) [poster art]

Godzilla vs. Mothra (1992) [poster art]

"Ultraman: The Ultimate Hero" (1993, TV) [video release art]

Godzilla vs. Mechagodzilla II (1993) [poster art]

Godzilla vs. Space Godzilla (1994) [poster art]

East Meets West (1995) [poster art]

Godzilla vs. Destoroyah (1995) [poster art]

Godzilla vs. Megaguirus (2000) [poster art]

Metal Gear Solid 2: Sons of Liberty (2001, video game) [Japanese cover art]

Metal Gear Solid 3: Snake Eater (2004, video game) [Japanese cover art]

Godzilla: Final Wars (2004) [poster art]

Sinking of Japan (2006) [poster art]

Gamera 2: Region Shurai "Gamera 2: Legion Invasion"
Daiei/Nippon TV/Hakuhodo, 7/13/1996 (*Heisei 8*), 99:33, 35mm, Spherical (1.85:1), color, Dolby
Digital 5.1 channel sound

Crew
Executive Producer: Yasuyoshi Tokuma
Producers: Tsutomu Tsuchikawa, Naoki Sato
Production Representatives: Hiroyuki Kato, Seiji Urushido , Shigeru Oho, Kazuto Kojima, Kazuhiro Igarashi
Producers: Tetsuya Ikeda, Takeshi Hosaka, Hatsuko Sawada, Naomasa Tsuruta
Planning: Kai Shimada, Hidehiko Takei, Yoshiro Yasunaga, Joji Tsutsui, Koji Ishida
Associate Producers: Seiji Okuda, Daisuke Kadoya, Naoya Fujimaki, Chihiro Takahashi, Tatsuhiko Sakamoto
Line Producer: Miyuki Nanri
Director: Shusuke Kaneko
Special Effects Director: Shinji Higuchi
Screenplay: Kazunori Ito
Director of Photography: Junichi Tozawa
Music: Ko Otani
Art Director: Hajime Oikawa
Editor: Shizuo Arakawa

Assistant Director: Shozo Katashima, Hideaki Murakami, Futoshi Sato, Hisashi Kimura
Sound Recording: Yasuo Hashimoto
Lighting: Sosuke Yoshikado
Casting: Yoshinori Suzuki
Set Decoration: Keiichi Hasegawa, Eiji Kaneko
Sound Effects: Shinichi Ito, Aya Kojima
Gun Stunts: Yukitomo Tochino
Production Manager: Kensei Mori
SFX Cinematography: Hiroshi Kidokoro
SFX Art Director: Toshio Miike
SFX Lighting: Hokoku Hayashi
Monster Suit Construction: Tomoo Haraguchi
Monster Suit Construction (Queen Legion): Fuyuki Shinada, Takuya Yamabe, Kenichi Sekine
Monster Suit Construction (Soldier Legion): Shinichi Wakasa
Practical Effects/Stunts: Izumi Negishi

Visual Effects Supervisors: Hajime Matsumoto, Mitsuhara Haibara
SFX Editing: Shinichi Fujima
SFX Continuity: Junko Kawashima
Assistant SFX Director: Makoto Kamiya
In Charge of SFX Production: Masaya Kajikawa
Assistant SFX Directors: Kazuki Makazaki, Keisuke Ota
Monster Designs: Mahiro Maeda, Shinji Higuchi
Still Photography: Daisaburo Harada

Cast
Toshiyuki Nagashima (*Colonel Yusuke Watarase*)
Miki Mizuno (*Midori Honami*)
Tamotsu Ishibashi (*First Lieutenant Hanatani*)
Mitsuru Fukikoshi (*Obitsu*)
Ayako Fujitani (*Asagi Kusanagi*)
Yukijiro Hotaru (*Osako*)
Zen Kajihara (*Mano*)
Tomorowo Taguchi (*Ishida, subway driver*)
Yuka Sakano (*Yukino*)

Takeshi Yoro (*Professor of Veterinary Medicine*)

Hatsunori Hasegawa (*Colonel Satake*)

LaSalle Ishii (*NTT Nazaki*)

Bengal (*Midori's Father*)

Kazue Tsunogae (*Midori's Mother*)

Yusuke Kawazu (*Akio Nojiri*)

Hiroyuki Okita (*Sasai*)

Akiji Kobayashi (*Senior Sergeant*)

Hiroyuki Watanabe (*Colonel Ono*)

Kazunaga Tsuji (*General Bando*)

Hiroshi Okochi (*Sapporo Odori Command Center Regiment Leader*)

Shunsuke Takasugi (*Howitzer Operator*)

Yasuyoshi Tokuma (*Chief Cabinet Secretary*)

Yoshiaki Umegaki (*Sapporo Riot Police Platoon Leader*)

Hiromasa Taguchi (*Public Bath Patron*)

Kazunori Nobutori (*Monitoring Base Leader*)

Masato Nagamori (*Sapporo Subway Department Chief*)

Yukitomo Tochino (*Man Clinging to Telephone Pole*)

Touta Tawaragi (*Captain of the Umigiri*)

Tasuku Unou (*Transport Helicopter Pilot*)

Yukio Shirabe (*Correspondent at Defense Base*)

Kohei Kowada (*Correspondent at Defense Base*)

Miyuki Komatsu (*Reporter in Sapporo*)

Negishi Daisuke (*Sapporo News Helicopter Cameraman*)

Yuko Miwa (*Tatebayashi News Helicopter Reporter*)

Hana Kawadzu (*Mother in Sendai*)

Aki Maeda (*Little Girl in Sendai*)

Ayako Sekiya (*Special Newscaster*)

Masako Yabumoto (*Newscaster*)

Akira Ohashi (*Gamera*)

Mizuho Yoshida (*Queen Legion, front*)

Toshinori Sasaki (*Queen Legion, back*)

Tomohiko Akayama (*Soldier Legion*)

Yuji Kobayashi (*Soldier Legion*)

Yoshiyuki Watanabe (*Soldier Legion*)

Akihiro Nakata (*Soldier Legion*)

Brien Uhl

Alternate Titles

G2 (informal)

Gamera 2: The Real Guardian of the Universe (working English title)

Gamera vs. Legion (alternate English title)

Gamera 2: Advent of Legion (alternate English title)

Gamera 2: Assault of Legion (alternate English title)

> *"And he asked him, What is thy name? And he answered, saying, My name is Legion: for we are many."*
> -Mark 5:9, *The Holy Bible, King James Version* (1611)

An arguably even better film than its predecessor, *Gamera 2: Attack of Legion* once again boasts almost Spielbergian production values. Director Shusuke Kaneko shines in suspenseful early scenes that bring his horror work to mind. Yet it is Shinji Higuchi and his talented team that truly impress as *Gamera 2: Attack of Legion* gets going. Higuchi's FX work is even more inventive than in the first film; boasting one stunning shot after another.

PLOT

A year after the Gyaos' attack, NASA scientists detect a massive volley of meteorites hurtling towards Earth. A particularly large meteorite crash lands near Shikotsu Lake in Hokkaido. In its aftermath a strange aurora appears over the area. The Japanese Self Defense Force mobilizes to investigate the impact site. Also investigating are Sapporo Science Center curator Midori Honami (Miki

Mizuno) and director Akio Nojiri (Yusuke Kawazu). Honami and Nojiri discuss the impact with Colonel Yusuke Watarase (Toshiyuki Nagashima) and Lieutenant Hanatani (Tamostu Ishibashi). They reveal that in their investigation they found no sign of a meteorite, only a crater. Honami proposes that the meteor somehow moved. Watarase and Hanatani realize it may be possible when the impact crater shows skid marks.

Outside Sapporo, unusual phenomena occur over the next several days. Security guards at a brewery encounter an insectoid monster. Obitsu (Mitsuru Fukikoshi), a technician at NTT Hokkaido's network, discovers that their fiber-optic cables have disappeared. Honami investigates the brewery with Watarase and Hanatani. They discover that all of the bottles have been disintegrated but the beer was left behind. Honami views a police interview tape with one of the witnesses, Osako (Yukijiro Hotaru). Osako claims to have seen a creature disintegrating the bottles. Hanatani shows Honami silicon powder recovered from the scene. They conclude that the bottles were all broken down into silicon.

Five days later, a subway train in Sapporo is attacked by the same type of insectoid monster seen in the brewery. In addition, a gigantic flower erupts from buildings in the center of the city. The Sapporo police rescue survivors of the attack and close the subway off. Watarase's platoon soon arrives to investigate the subway tunnels. They witness several creatures crawling through them. Honami proposes that the monsters are an insect-like "colony," in a symbiotic relationship with the flower or "pod". She concludes that both arrived from space in the meteor shower. Honami theorizes the creatures' colony breaks down silicon and feeds it to the pod. In turn this gives off high amounts of oxygen.

The Defense Force prepares to blow up the now flowering pod by planting explosives in the subway tunnels. The blast will be amplified by the heightened oxygen levels and the pod will be destroyed. Honami believes that the colony must spread to other worlds by making the pod launch a seed into space. Suddenly, Gamera surfaces from the Sanriku coast. Gamera lands in Sapporo and inhales the increased oxygen around the pod before blasting it with a plasma fireball. Gamera approaches the pod and uproots it, then destroys it with another fireball. As Gamera appears victorious, hordes of the alien creatures pour out from the tunnels and climb onto him. Gamera collapses to the ground. Some of the creatures are distracted by a nearby electrical transformer and climb off Gamera as he escapes and flies back to the ocean. Shortly after, a gigantic insectoid monster bursts from the ground and flies into the sky.

Watarase and Obitsu meet with Honami at her apartment to discuss the behavior of the creatures, now dubbed the "Legion" after a passage in the Bible. They determine that the Legion communicate through electromagnetic waves. Watarase notes that the subway passengers killed by the Legion were carrying electronic devices. They come to the conclusion that the Legion must see any electrical signals which interfere with their communication as a threat. The three theorize that the Legion are drawn to urban areas due to the high concentration of electromagnetic waves.

After a *pachinko* parlor is attacked by Soldier Legion, a second pod appears in Sendai. Due to Sendai's warmer climate, the pod flowers faster and is ready to seed before the Defense Force can destroy it. Evacuation begins, with civilians boarding helicopters at an airfield outside the city. Honami is escorted to one of the choppers. Before she can board, Gamera is seen flying overhead. As he approaches Sendai, two spear-like claws burst from the ground and knock him from the sky. Panicked civilians rush into the helicopters, knocking down Yukino (Yuka Sakano), a young woman on crutches. Honami and the girl's friend help her into the helicopter. They watch as a gigantic Queen Legion emerges from the ground and attacks Gamera. Honami sees Yukino's friend watching the battle clutching a distinctive comma-shaped bead. She realizes that the girl is Asagi Kusanagi (Ayako Fujitani).

Gamera holds the Queen Legion back, allowing the helicopters to safely take off. In the process, Gamera is stabbed in the shell by one of Legion's horns. The horn on Queen Legion's head splits open and

fires a beam which obliterates surrounding buildings and blasts off part of Gamera's shell. Gamera, wounded by Legion's assault, collapses. Queen Legion burrows underground and vanishes. Gamera gets back on his feet and limps into downtown Sendai to stop the pod. He knocks the pod over and throws himself on it as it seeds. This triggers an explosion that completely destroys Sendai. Amid the rubble, Gamera sits lifeless, appearing to have perished in the blast. Honami predicts that the Legion will likely head to Tokyo next. With Gamera no longer able to stop them, the JSDF sets up a defense line outside of Tokyo. Honami brings Asagi to the airport to fly home, but Asagi insists that Gamera is not dead and won't let the Legion win.

BACKGROUND

In 1995, a sequel to *Gamera: Guardian of the Universe* was swiftly green lit by Daiei. *Gamera 2: Attack of Legion* started development shortly after the first film's release. Director Shusuke Kaneko and screenwriter Kazunori Ito contemplated using old school adversary Viras as Gamera's foe, but opted for a novel threat. The Legion were named after a passage from the book of Mark. In the New Testament, they are a demonic horde that Jesus Christ exorcises. Author William Peter Blatty would also pay homage to this passage in his *Exorcist* sequel *Legion*, adapted into *The Exorcist III* (1990). Ito wanted to include another aerial sequence in the script but Shinji Higuchi talked him out of it. Higuchi felt he could not improve on the flying sequences in the first film and so another would be redundant.

PRINCIPAL PHOTOGRAPHY

The cameras started rolling on *Gamera 2: Attack of Legion* in late 1995. The first sequences shot were footage of the Self Defense Force mobilization for later in the picture. Kaneko had wanted friend Mamoru Oshii to direct these shots but he was unavailable. Live tank rounds were fired for the shots of the artillery attack on Legion. Kaneko and Ito wanted to give the Self Defense Force a more flattering role in *Gamera 2*. They were inspired by the heroism shown by SDF recruits during the Hanshin earthquake earlier that year. Invoking the classic films of Ishiro Honda, scientists and the military work closely in *Gamera 2*.

Gamera 2: Attack of Legion was shot in the dead of winter. Its bleak, colder aesthetic is a nice contrast to the summery feel of the first film. In contrast to Toho's fairly set bound films, Shusuke Kaneko's unit liked to shoot on location. This helps give his Gamera films, especially *Gamera 2,* an unusually realistic feel. Junichi Tozawa's cinematography is far more cinematic than the mediocre work of Toho's DPs at the time. The first actor sequence shot by Kaneko's unit was the airfield scene, filmed at Kisarazu air base.

Lurid early sequences involve the "Soldier Legion" on the attack. These invoke Kaneko's prior horror work such as *My Soul is Slashed* (1991) or his *Necronomicon* (1993) segment. The "J-Horror" vibe is especially noticeable in a scene where a Soldier Legion is dissected by scientists. These sequences, as the monsters are human-sized and interact with the actors, were shot mainly by Kaneko's unit. The Soldier Legion suits were built by Shinichi Wakasa of Monsters Inc. Wakasa (1960-) first worked as a modeling technician on Tsuburaya Pro's *Ultraman 80* (1980). He provided the grisly makeup FX for Toshiharu Ikeda's brutal *Evil Dead Trap* (1988) and Kaneko's *My Soul is Slashed*. He became an in-demand suit maker when he was hired by Koichi Kawakita's unit on *Godzilla vs. Mechagodzilla II* (1993). He built Rodan and assisted in construction of the Mechagodzilla suit. He also built the Space Godzilla and Destoroyah suits for the next two Godzilla films and worked on all three *Rebirth of Mothra* movies. He would go on to produce most of the Godzilla suits for the Millennium series, starting with *Godzilla 2000* (1999). The Soldier Legion suit actors had to crawl on all fours. The claw-like "arms" were affixed to them separately. Hand puppets were also used for some close-up shots.

For the Legion attack sequence in the brewery, the bottles were lifted up by fishing line and beer was pumped onto the floor. The first take didn't go as planned as the beer came out onto the floor too quickly. The staff swiftly cleaned up the mess and practiced it a bit more; nailing it in the second take. As Kaneko's unit filmed, children would approach his crew and ask if they could meet Gamera. Kaneko amusingly brings kids back into the fold for a scene in the ruins of Sendai. One of the little girls given a close-up is Aki Maeda. Maeda would go on to appear as young Ayana in *Gamera 3: Revenge of Iris* and star in Kinji Fukasaku's *Battle Royale* (2000).

ACTORS

The film's cast is headed by actor Toshiyuki Nagashima. Nagashima (1956-) has had a surprising amount of tokusatsu film appearances. He debuted in the *manga*-based 1977 basketball drama *Dokaben*. He then played supporting roles in such films as Fukasaku's *Virus*, Kenjiro Omori's *Deathquake* (both 1980) and Shue Matsubayashi's *Imperial Navy* (1981). Nagashima also appeared in Paul Schrader's *Mishima: A Life in Four Chapters* (1985) and *Godzilla vs. Biollante* (1989). He would go on to play small roles in *Godzilla vs. Megaguirus* (2000) and *Godzilla Against Mechagodzilla* (2002). Ayako Fujitani returns and Miki Mizuno plays another cute and intelligent lady scientist. She's no relation to Kumi Mizuno whose real name was Maya Igarashi. Nonetheless her role is one that would have been played by Kumi if this were a '60s Honda film. Mizuno (1974-) would go on to appear in the *Bayside Shakedown* series of films starting in 1998. Veteran actor Yusuke Kawazu appears as well. For genre fans he starred in Shochiku's *Genocide* (1968) and appeared in *Godzilla vs. Mechagodzilla II*. *Tetsuo: The Iron Man*'s Tomorowo Taguchi also cameos as an ill-fated subway conductor. Yukijiro Hotaru's Osako returns in something of an extended cameo.

SFX/VFX

Gamera 2: Attack of Legion truly comes alive when Shinji Higuchi's special effects unit takes the stage. His crew's work on *Gamera 2* is even more inventive than in the first film. Higuchi made a point to make his FX sequences novel, not merely repeating what came before. Art director Toshio Miike outdoes his already stunning miniature work on *Gamera: Guardian of the Universe*. Miniature buildings were once again built to astonishing detail. Early scenes involve the Legion spawning through a monster flower growing out of a building. These are a loving homage to one of Kaneko and Higuchi's favorite *Ultra Q* episodes, *The Mammoth Flower*. Many miniature composites are almost flawlessly executed. One scene the effects crew wanted to do better was Gamera's landing which Higuchi thought should be "awe-inspiring". A flying Gamera prop was built with sea turtle-like "flipper wings". Propelled by a crane, it could eject steam from its hind shell. To create the contrails of flying Gamera, a powerful dry ice machine was used. It was called the "baked sweet potato cart" by the crew as it resembled such a vendor stall in Japan.

Queen Legion is an inspired creation, looking like a cross between the Arachnids in Paul Verhoeven's *Starship Troopers* and a seafood delicacy you'd eat in Japan. The creature was designed by Mahiro Maeda and Higuchi. Higuchi opted to make Legion bigger and more powerful than Gyaos to ramp up the narrative stakes. Queen Legion's suit was built mainly by Fuyuki Shinada. This meticulously constructed costume was an engineering marvel and one of the finest ever built. Shinada (1959-) got his start on Shizuo Nakajima's fan film *Wolfman vs. Godzilla* (1983). This got him hired by Kawakita's unit at Toho where he helped build the elaborate Biollante suits in *Godzilla vs. Biollante* under Nobuyuki Yasumaru. He built the "Kerberos" armor on Mamoru Oshii's films *The Red Spectacles* (1987) and *Stray Dog* (1991). Shinada also made the Godzillasaurus in *Godzilla vs. King Ghidorah*. He would go on to be a pivotal designer and suit-maker for the Ultraman franchise. Additionally, he built a memorable Godzilla suit for Kaneko's *Godzilla, Mothra and King Ghidorah: Giant Monsters All-Out Attack* (2001).

Legion's suit ingeniously perfected the "pantomime horse" style used before in tokusatsu. It employed two suit actors: Mizuho (*Zeiram*) Yoshida in front and Toshinori Sasaki facing backwards. Unlike previous pantomime horse style suits, it utilizes the two actors almost seamlessly. Animatronic parts were also added to the suit to make its claws and mandibles move. As Higuchi's unit tested the Queen Legion suit in a Tokyo park, onlookers were flummoxed. A new, redesigned Gamera suit was built by Tomoo Haraguchi as well. This suit was given more mechanical parts than the first one. The neck was attached with a brace to actor Akira Ohashi so Gamera could now turn his head more easily. Miniature puppet versions of Gamera and Legion were also used. These were mainly for wide shots where using the full-sized suits would have been impractical.

For a scene where Gamera is covered by swarms of soldier Legion, a different suit was used and covered with tiny Legion models. The crew called it *"Fuzzy Gamera"*. The first battle between Gamera and Queen Legion is an astounding sequence where Higuchi takes center stage. Especially with a shot of industrial oil tanks exploding around Gamera, engineer and pyrotechnician Izumi Negishi again outdoes himself. The scene where Sendai is wiped off the map in an apocalyptic conflagration is a stunning pyrotechnic sequence. It feels like a spiritual successor to Eiji Tsuburaya's nuclear annihilation of Tokyo in *The Last War* (1961). For the close-up of Gamera screaming as the city explodes, a battle-damaged animatronic top half was built. Large amounts of smoke were pumped towards it. Higuchi was especially proud of a moving shot from the perspective of a jeep during this sequence.

Gamera 2: Attack of Legion boasts an exhilarating climax even stronger than *Gamera: Guardian of the Universe*'s. This pulse pounding finale is Kaneko and Higuchi at top form. Like Honda and Tsuburaya before them they coordinated their units' work effectively. Higuchi was excited about depicting Gamera fighting alongside the Self Defense Force and his enthusiasm shows. It recalls the creative spirit of his early work on *The Eight-Headed Serpent Strikes Back* (1985) while also looking forward to the military spectacle of *Shin Godzilla*. For an impressive sequence where Queen Legion obliterates a tank regiment, a shock rig had to be built around DP Hiroshi Kidokoro and the camera. The scene where Gamera's abdomen opens and fires a plasma blast was created with an animatronic under-shell controlled by remote control. For the shots of Legion's destruction, another "Kapok" doll was built and blown up by Higuchi's unit. This had to be done outdoors per safety. It was integrated with a bluescreen shot of the suit which was made to "disintegrate" with CGI. This shot was one of the last filmed by the FX unit. The VFX in *Gamera 2* is a major step up from the shots in the first film.

REAL WORLD

The Japanese Self Defense Force were even more heavily involved in the production of *Gamera 2*, lending Kaneko a lot of equipment and soldier extras. The tanks used in *Gamera 2* are Type 74 and Type 90s. The Type 74 was created to supplant the Type 61 tanks seen in many classic *Showa* monster pictures. Though designed in the 1960s and manufactured in the '70s, Type 74 tanks were not brought into use until 1980. They are featured prominently in *The Return of Godzilla* (1984). These tanks are still in minor use in the Japanese Self Defense Force. They have been largely supplanted by superior Type 90 and Type 10 units. The Type 90 tank was the state of the art successor to the Type 74 and is still in heavy deployment in the Self Defense Force today. The tanks are seen prominently in subsequent kaiju eiga, including *Gamera 3: Revenge of Iris* (1999) and 2016's *Shin Godzilla*.

LEGACY

Though the effects work was once again praised, *Gamera 2: Attack of Legion* was only a modest success at the box office. Shusuke Kaneko would take a break from directing kaiju eiga with *The Haunted School 3* (1997) and *F* (1998). However, one more sequel would be greenlit soon after: *Gamera 3: Revenge of Iris*. This would bring Kaneko, Higuchi and much of their creative team back for a superb finale to the trilogy.

ALTERNATE VERSIONS

Gamera 2: Attack of Legion was initially acquired by Disney through Tokuma. However, Disney apparently had little interest in distributing the film and the rights lapsed. The film would not be released until 2003, put out directly to DVD by ADV Films. ADV commissioned their own in-house English dub recorded in Texas. It was written and directed by Kyle Jones. Vocal cast includes Jay Hickman as Colonel Watarase, Shelley Calene-Black as Honami, Christopher Patton as Obitsu, Illich Guardiola as Hanatani and Luci Christian as Asagi. Supporting voices include Don Armstrong, John Kaiser, Lisa Singerman, Charles Kennedy, Jason Douglas, Hilary Haag, Heather Le Master, Tejas Englesmith, Don Armstrong, Lisa Singerman, Jason Douglas, Ryan Walsh, Rob Mungle, Marty Fleck, John Swasey, Adam Conlon and Paul Sidello. The voice cast did a redneck "gag dub" called *"Lake Texarkana Gamera"*. Included as a special feature on ADV's DVD and the later Arrow Blu-ray set, it isn't terribly funny.

AMERICAN HOME VIDEO HISTORY

ADV released *Gamera 2: Attack of Legion* on DVD in 2003. This was its first stateside home video release with Japanese and English dub tracks. In 2010, it was picked up by Mill Creek and released to Blu-ray in a double feature with *Gamera: Guardian of the Universe*. It was later included in two boxed sets by Mill Creek; one for only the *Heisei* trilogy in 2011 and the other for the entire Gamera series in 2014. In 2020, the 4K remaster done by Kadokawa was included on Arrow's impressive and quick to sell out *Gamera: The Complete Collection* Blu-ray set.

Further Viewing:
MIKADROID

(1991)
ミカドロイド
Toho, *Director:* **Tomoo Haraguchi**

Released through Toho's direct-to-video "Cineback" series, *Mikadroid* is the directorial debut of Gamera suit maker Tomoo Haraguchi. The concept began life in 1989 as *Mikado Zombie*. *Mikado Zombie* was to involve a Japanese Imperial Army soldier rising from the dead as a ghoul. Haraguchi and company had even begun modeling the props and makeup prosthetics. Then pedophilic serial killer Tsutomu Miyazaki was arrested. The case was so horrific that it caused a moral panic in Japan ala America's concurrent *"Satanic Panic"*. As Miyazaki had numerous horror films in his video collection, public opinion turned against the genre for a time. The PR-conscious Toho thus pulled the plug on *Mikado Zombie* only a day before shooting was set to begin. Toei offered make the film on their rival "V-Cinema" line, but Haraguchi, a huge fan of Toho tokusatsu films, was determined to make a film at Toho. He retooled the concept into more of a science fiction story and was greenlit.

Mikadroid isn't a great film, but it's stylish and fairly effective. It features a well directed World War II opening invoking Japan's medical experimentation. There's a visual shoutout to the original *Godzilla* and this black and white sequence has a bit of a Shinya Tsukamoto vibe. Up-and-coming director Kiyoshi Kurosawa cameos in this scene as a *kempeitai*. The film cuts to the present with an Imperial Japan-made cyborg super-soldier reawakening after decades. It soon starts killing clubgoers in the parking garage of a *Juliana's*-like discotek. In spite of Toho's reluctance to produce a horror film, strong "J-Horror" elements remain. This is most apparent in a twisted sequence where the Mikadroid flays a woman with a *katana* as she spins like a bloody ballerina. The legendary Akio Jissoji was one of *Mikadroid*'s producers and his fingerprints are quite visible. *Ultraman*'s Sandayu Dokumamushi even has an extended cameo. *Mikadroid* boasts interesting subtext on Japan's dark wartime history haunting its frivolous "bubble economy" present.

Yoriko Doguchi stars as a whiny club girl who finds her inner Sigourney Weaver by the end. The middle act drags a bit, but the *Mikadroid* itself is an inspired creation; a sort of steampunk cyborg. The creature was played by Hurricane Ryu who later portrayed several monsters in the *Heisei* Godzilla series for Kawakita. The suit's mechanics were engineered by Izumi Negishi, by far an unsung hero of the '90s tokusatsu scene. The ending kicks back into high gear as Shinji Higuchi, only 25 at the time, lets loose his visual genius. His unit's shots are easily theatrical film quality. *Mikadroid*, shot on 16mm, is still only available sourced from ¾" video tape masters. This is a shame as the film would be better appreciated in a new scan. Tomoo Haraguchi's next film wouldn't be for nine more years: *Sakuya, Slayer of Demons* (2000), also with Higuchi's collaboration.

(2000)
クロスファイア
Toho, *Director*: Shusuke Kaneko

Based on a pair of popular novels by Miyuki Miyabe, *Pyrokinesis* (aka *Crossfire*) is an effective J-Horror flick with a light sci-fi flourish. The picture was directed by Shusuke Kaneko in the wake of *Gamera 3* and it's interesting to see a genre film by him devoid of a special effects unit. As usual for Kaneko,

Pyrokinesis is well directed. There's an intriguingly experimental video-shot prologue delving into protagonist Junko (Akiko Yada)'s childhood. Ala Drew Barrymore in *Firestarter*, Junko can create hellish conflagrations with ESP. After her friend Kazuki (Hideaki Ito) has his little sister (Maya Hamaoka) murdered by a gaggle of juvenile delinquents, Junko seeks revenge using her powers. There's also a heavy police procedural element as intrepid detective Chikako Ishizu (Kaori Momoi) and her partner Makihara (Ryuji Harada) are hot on the tails of both the murderers and Junko. Toshiyuki Nagashima also appears in a rare villainous turn as a corrupt police chief who meets with an agonizing end.

Pyrokinesis is a little slow to start but comes alive once Junko seeks her vengeance. The finale is particularly impressive and the burning sequences boast an imaginative melding of visual effects and practical makeup by Shinichi Wakasa. Wakasa creates some Hollywood quality grisly burned corpse props. Kaneko's love of and fetishism for strong but pretty female leads is definitely in play here with Wada's Junko. She's depicted with a pathos invoking Yoshio Tsuchiya's Mizuno in *The Human Vapor*. *Pyrokinesis* is, overall, far from a masterpiece but it was having made this film for Toho that got Kaneko the job for their next Godzilla entry.

SHUSUKE KANEKO
The New Wave

金子修介
6/8/1955-

"I said 'What would Mr. Honda do if he were here?'."
-Shusuke Kaneko, 1996

The only director to have helmed entries in both the Gamera and Godzilla franchises, Shusuke Kaneko was at the forefront in a "New Wave" of *kaiju* cinema. Yet like his spiritual predecessor Ishiro Honda, he is a more versatile filmmaker than given credit. Born in 1955, his parents Tokuyoshi and Shizue Kaneko were fervent Japanese Communist Party members. His father continued to protest the Vietnam War until Kaneko was in high school. As a boy, Kaneko loved monsters, seeing *Mothra* (1961) at a young age was pivotal for him. He enjoyed Godzilla films on the big screen and Tsuburaya Pro's *Ultra Q* on television. Young Kaneko even made his own monster encyclopedia. He produced his first 8mm film at the age of 16 in 1971. Kaneko studied education at Tokyo Gakugei University. There, future *anime* director Mamoru Oshii was his *senpai* (upperclassman). In 1978, he graduated and got a spot at Nikkatsu as an assistant director. Nikkatsu had long abandoned mainstream fare and was producing softcore *"roman porno"*. Due to Japan's strict censorship laws regarding nudity, the actors had to wear flesh-colored patches to hide their pubic hair. Kaneko's first job as AD was the uncomfortable task of covering the male actors' crotches with these patches. Around this time, Kaneko

would also write for Oshii, mainly on the anime show *Urusei Yatsura* (1981-86).

In 1984, Kaneko was promoted to director with the roman porno *Wet and Shooting*. He also made connections acting as assistant director on the popular mainstream films *The Family Game* (1983) and *Main Theme* (1984). More pictures at Nikkatsu followed and even in the erotica arena, Kaneko's talent shined. Several early erotic films of his won awards at film festivals, though Kaneko eventually went freelance. His major breakout came in 1988 with the youth drama *Summer Vacation 1999*. This film was his first to be exported internationally. He would also direct the vampiric horror/comedy *My Soul is Slashed* in 1991 for Toho. In 1993, Kaneko directed a segment of Brian Yunza's H.P. Lovecraft-themed anthology *Necronomicon*. *The Cold*, shot in English, was based on Lovecraft's short story *Cool Air*.

Kaneko's next major break came when he won the job to reboot Daiei's Gamera franchise shortly after. Working with young FX maverick Shinji Higuchi, he directed *Gamera: Guardian of the Universe* (1995) to critical acclaim. The two returned for a sequel, *Gamera 2: Attack of Legion*, which was also well received. After directing *The*

Haunted School 3 (1997) and *F* (1998), he helmed a final film in the trilogy. *Gamera 3: Revenge of Iris* (1999) is considered one of the finest Japanese monster films since the original *Godzilla*.

After he directed *Pyrokinesis* (2000) at Toho, producer Shogo Tomiyama offered him the job to helm the next Godzilla film. Kaneko couldn't pass this up, though he was hampered a bit by studio interference. Nonetheless, Kaneko's *Godzilla, Mothra and King Ghidorah: Giant Monsters All-Out Attack* was regarded as one of the best Godzilla entries in decades. Subsequent films included *A Song of Love* (2002) and a sequel to Ryuhei Kitamura's *Azumi: Azumi 2: Death or Love* (2005). He also directed for television often and did episodes of *Ultra Q: Dark Fantasy* (2004) and *Ultraman Max* (2005). Kaneko's next major project was a double decker live action adaptation of Tsugumi Ohba's popular *manga Death Note*. Released concurrently with an anime adaptation in 2006, it was a box office hit. Kaneko followed this up with another manga adaptation, *Pride*, in 2009. Through the 2010s, Kaneko has continued directing, mainly focusing on drama films. His children, Suzuyuki and Yurina Kaneko, both followed their father into the film industry.

Selected Filmography *(as director)*

"Urusei Yatsura" (1981-82, TV) [screenplay]

The Family Game (1983) [assistant director]

Main Theme (1984) [assistant director]

Wet and Shooting (1984)

Minna Agechau (1985)

Mischievous Lolita: Attacking the Virgin From Behind (1986)

Last Cabaret (1988)

Summer Vacation 1999 (1988)

Who Do I Choose? (1989)

Hong Kong Paradise (1990)

My Soul is Slashed (1991)

Necronomicon (1993) [segment *The Cold*]

It's Summer Vacation Everyday (1994)

Gamera: Guardian of the Universe (1995)

Gamera 2: Attack of Legion (1996)

The Haunted School 3 (1997)

F (1998)

Gamera 3: Revenge of Iris (1999)

Pyrokinesis (2000)

Godzilla, Mothra and King Ghidorah: Giant Monsters All-Out Attack (2001)

A Song of Love (2002)

"Ultra Q: Dark Fantasy" (2004, TV) [*episodes 3, 7*]

"Ultraman Max" (2005, TV) [*episodes 1, 2, 35, 36*]

Azumi 2: Death or Love (2005)

God's Left Hand, Devil's Right Hand (2006)

Death Note (2006)

Death Note 2: The Last Name (2006)

Pride (2009)

Messiah (2011)

The Centenarian Clock (2012)

The Sacrifice Dilemma (2013)

Jellyfish (2013)

Danger Dolls (2014)

Scanner (2016)

Linking Love (2017)

Matchmaking Cruise (2017)

Gamera 3: Iris Kakusei "Gamera 3: Evil God Iris Awakens"
Daiei/Nippon TV/Hakuhodo, 3/6/1999 (*Heisei 11*), 107:39, 35mm, Spherical (1.85:1), color, Dolby Digital 5.1 channel sound

Crew

Executive Producer: Yasuyoshi Tokuma
Producers: Tsutomu Tsuchikawa, Naoki Sato, Miyuki Nanri
Production Representatives: Hiroyuki Kato, Kazuhiko Ishikawa, Shigeru Ono, Naomasa Isoda
Associate Producers: Seiji Okuda, Naoya Fujimaki
Director: Shusuke Kaneko
Special Effects Director: Shinji Higuchi
Screenplay: Kazunori Ito, Shusuke Kaneko
Director of Photography: Junichi Tozawa
Music: Ko Otani
Music Producer: Haruyuki Yamamoto
Music Production: Kentaro Matsumoto, Yoshio J. Maki, Shuta Tonosaki
Music Mixer: Toshiyuki Yoshida
Production Designer: Hajime Oikawa
Editor: Isao Tomita
Gaffer: Yoshikaku Sosuke
Assistant Directors: Hideaki Murakami, Koji Yamaguchi, Masahiko Yamakawa, Shintaro Horikawa, Yusuke Kubota
Assistant Cinematographers: Shinji Kugimiya, Yasuhiro Shimizu, Yoshihiro Kinoshita, Yoshiyuki Watanabe
Art Director: Hayato Oba
Set Decoration: Toshiaki Takahashi, Kazuyoshi Sawashita, Takayuki Suzuki
Props Master: Yukie Oikawa
Sound Recording: Yasuo Hashimoto
Recording Assistant: Satoshi Ozaki, Hisashi Ueie, Yoshimitsu Suzuki
Sound Effects: Shinichi Ito, Aya Kojima
Sound Editor: Naoko Asari
Coordinating Engineer: Masashi Tara
Lighting Assistants: Seiichiro Mieno, Hiroshi Tanabe, Tomoo Nanzono, Toshiyuki Fukugawa, Kota Sato
Lighting Preparation: Takaomi Sugiura, Shinichi Kurata
Editing Assistant: Koji Hara
Negative Cutting: Ayumu Ishikawa
Script Supervisor: Shobara Haru
Practical Effects: Katsuro Onoue
Animatronics Operation: Toyonaka Yokoi, Toru Nakayama
Hair Stylist: Misa Muramatsu
Costumes: Junko Ishikawa
Makeup: Yoko Nakamura
Makeup Assistant: Kazumi Takahashi
Continuity: Chikako Nakabayashi, Masahiro Mototo, Ryuichi Matsumura
Stunt Coordinator: Mitsuo Abe
Production Manager: Kensei Mori
Line Producer (A.S.P. Unit): Kazutoshi Wadakura
Line Producer (Philippines Unit): Hiroshi Onishi
Assistant Line Producer (Philippines): Toshinori Otake
Assistant Director (Philippines): Arturo Soquearta
Production Manager (Philippines): Larry Ocampo
Location Manager (Philippines): Tsuyoshi Tsuda
SFX Cinematographer: Satoshi Murakawa
SFX Art Director: Toshio Miike
SFX Lighting: Hokoku Hayashi
Assistant SFX Director: Makoto Kamiya

Monster Suit Construction: Tomoo Haraguchi
Practical Effects: Izumi Negishi
Visual Effects: Hajime Matsumoto
SFX Editor: Hiroshi Okuda
SFX Script Supervisor: Junko Kawashima
SFX Production Manager: Masaya Kajikawa
Second SFX Assistant Directors: Yuichi Kikuchi, Shigetsugu Saito, Tadashi Yokokura
SFX Assistant Cinematographers: Seiei Iioka, Yukio Komiya, Takashi Nakano, Yuji Okabe, Masayuki Nakazawa
SFX Lighting Assistants: Shigeru Izumiya, Yoshinobu Ikegaya, Shigeru Yonezawa, Shizuko Motoyanagi, Mitsuru Ogawa
SFX Art Assistants: Masato Inamura, Yoshiyuki Kasuga Hiroshi Sagae, Keigo Okada Akihiro Tsujikawa
SFX Props Master: Tomoyuki Takagi
Monster Design: Mahiro Maeda, Shinji Higuchi
Animatronics: Tatsuya Abe
Monster Suit Construction and Molding (Iris): Fuyuki Shinada
SFX Continuity: Yuki Hoshino
VFX Coordinators: Ken Yoshioka, Ken Uemura
Technical Director (Visual Science Institute): Akihisa Watanabe
Gyaos Modeler/3D Animator: Kazuya Sakagami
Gamera Modeler/3D Animator: Masayuki Watanabe
3D Animator: Shoichi Shimizu

VFX Production Manager (Visual Science Institute): Sadamu Sudo
VFX Continuity: Hiroshi Matsui
Technical Director (Digital Frontier): Kenichi Kobayashi
Iris Modeler/3D Animator: Yoichi Mori
Still Photographer: Miki Nakaoka
SFX Still Photographer: Junji Saito

Cast
Shinobu Nakayama (*Mayumi Nagamine*)
Ai Maeda (*Ayana Hirasaka*)
Aki Maeda (*Young Ayana*)
Ayako Fujitani (*Asagi Kusanagi*)
Yu Koyama (*Tatsunari Moribe*)
Nozomi Ando (*Miyuki Moribe*)
Takahiro Ito (*Satoru Hirasaka*)
Senri Yamazaki (*Mito Asakura*)
Toru Tezuka (*Shinya Kurata*)
Yukijiro Hotaru (*Tsutomu Osako*)
Hirotaro Honda (*Masaki Saito*)
Kei Horie (*Shigeki Hinohara*)
Norito Yashima (*Sakurai*)
Yusuke Kawazu (*Akio Nojiri*)
Kunihiko Mitamura (*Ayana's Father*)
Kazuko Kato (*Ayana's Mother*)
Nijiko Kiyokawa (*Moribe's Grandmother*)
Yukie Nakama (*Female Camper*)
Daisuke Honda (*Male Camper*)
Katsuhisa Namase (*Yawata Marine Insurance Representative*)
Aimi Takemura (*Tomomi*)
Yui Kobayashi (*Sanae*)
Nikki Soraneko (*Natsuko*)

Hiroyuki Watanabe (*Colonel Ono, 37th General Division Regiment Commander*)
Yu Tokui (*Resident of Nara*)
Hikaru Ijuin (*Police Officer in Kyoto*)
Masahiro Noguchi (*Constable in Nara*)
Tomoko Kawashima (*Shibuya Office Lady*)
Asumi Miwa (*Shibuya High School Girl*)
Satoru Saito (*Shigeki's Father*)
Toshie Negishi (*Shigeki's Mother*)
Tomorowo Taguchi (*Doctor*)
Masasuke Hirose (*Kairei Chief*)
Tamotsu Ishibashi (*Kairei Crew*)
Shoji Kokami (*Kairei Crew*)
Rita Kosegawa (*Kairei Crew*)
Takaya Kamikawa (*Air Force Controller*)
Tsuyoshi Shimada (*Air Force Controller*)
Kenjiro Ishimaru (*Air Force Senior Controller*)
Masahiko Tsugawa (*Air Force Commander*)
Makoto Kakeda (*Homeless Man*)
Yukitomo Tochino (*Homeless Man*)
Ao Santo (*Homeless Man*)
Osamu Shigematsu (*Street Interviewee*)
Katsuko Nishina (*Street interviewee*)
Takashi Nishina (*Self-Defense Force*)
Tarou Oumiya (*TV Director*)
Ikkei Watanabe (*TV Director*)
Hitoshi Kusano (*TV Performer*)
Ryoko Ozawa (*TV Performer*)
Mika Takanishi (*Newscaster*)

Takao Masuda *(Special News Announcer)*
Yoshifumi Funatsu *(Special News Announcer)*
Kumiko Tsunoda *(Special News Announcer)*
Fumio Matsunaga *(Special News Announcer)*

Shinobu Matsumoto *(Weathercaster)*
Miyuki Komatsu *(Reporter in Shibuya)*
Nanako Kaneko *(Interviewer)*
Hirofumi Fukuzawa *(Gamera)*
Akira Ohashi *(Iris/Trauma Gamera)*

Alternate Titles
G3 (informal)
Gamera III: Incomplete Struggle (Alternate English title)
Gamera 1999: The Absolute Guardian of the Universe (Alternate English title)

"For Gamera 3, *I didn't want to repeat anything from the first two films. I tried thinking as creatively as I could and pushed my team to do the same.""*
-Shinji Higuchi (2002)

For their third and final *Heisei* Gamera film, Shusuke Kaneko and Shinji Higuchi upped the ante. *Gamera 3: Revenge of Iris* is an almost flawless Japanese monster picture, possibly the finest ever produced. Like a *tokusatsu* film directed by Ridley Scott in his prime, the production values are astounding. Higuchi's unit dominates much of the movie with astonishing images and one jaw dropping sequence after another. *Gamera 3: Revenge of Iris* pulls off for giant monsters what Christopher Nolan's *The Dark Knight Rises* tried and failed for masked superheroes. Going to even higher heights than its predecessors, it satisfyingly ties up the trilogy and brings its motifs full circle.

PLOT

Three years after the Legion's attack, the Gyaos have returned. Dr. Mayumi Nagamine (Shinobu Nakayama) visits a Gyaos-besieged village in the Philippines. Off the sea of Japan, a mass graveyard of Gamera skeletons is found. Government spiritualist Mito Asakura (Senri Yamazaki) and computer designer Shinya Kuraya (Toru Tezuka) have an agenda of their own. Asukura believes Gamera to be an evil spirit that must be stopped *"To prevent Heaven and Earth's destruction."*

A teenage girl named Ayana Hirasaka (Ai Maeda) is haunted by memories of her parents' death during Gamera's battle against Gyaos four years prior. She hates Gamera and blames him for the loss of her parents. One night at Shibuya ward in Tokyo, a pair of Gyaos appear and are attacked by Gamera. In this heavily populated area, Gamera's crusade causes massive casualties and property damage. An estimated twenty thousand lives are lost. The Japanese government thus orders Gamera's destruction. Ayana, meanwhile, discovers a giant stone egg in a cave where a demon called the *Ryuseicho* is said to dwell. The egg hatches into a small, tentacled creature. Ayana names it Iris after her family's dead cat and seeks to raise the creature to take revenge on Gamera.

Iris grows aggressive and begins to pray on small animals, sucking their life force with its tentacles. It soon absorbs Ayana into a giant cocoon. A classmate, Tatsunari Moribe (Yu Koyama) frees her. Iris soon goes on the rampage, killing much of their village. Having absorbed the energy of the villagers, Iris grows into a larger form and does battle with the Self Defense Forces. They are unable to stop its advance and soon the creature takes flight. The monster flies towards Kyoto, pursued by the Air Defense Force. Iris is attacked in midair by Gamera and the two monsters do battle in the sky. The Self Defense Force, however, views Gamera as the greater threat. They knock the creature out of the air with a missile strike.

Iris then descends upon Kyoto where Asakura has taken Ayana. Nagamine and Asagi Kusanagi (Ayako Fujitani) take custody of Ayana and try to get her out of Kyoto. They are unable to leave the city, however, when an incoming typhoon shuts down travel. Gamera arrives in Kyoto and attacks Iris. The creature is able to deflect Gamera's fireballs, however and Kyoto burns. Iris soon gains the upper hand over Gamera, impaling him with its spear-like arms. The two monsters crash into Kyoto Station and Asakura and Kurata are killed. With Gamera badly wounded, Iris absorbs Ayana once more as Moribe tries to rescue her.

BACKGROUND

Despite *Gamera 2: Attack of Legion*'s slightly disappointing box office, Yasuyoshi Tokuma greenlit another entry in the series. Development began in 1998 with production meetings starting in March. Making Gamera's foe an aquatic monster was considered as Higuchi wanted to do an underwater battle. However, Higuchi felt beaten to the punch by mentor Koichi Kawakita in *Rebirth of Mothra II* (1997), so such plans were scrapped. The budget for *Gamera 3* was larger than the first two films, though still a nudge below Toho's productions. As a viewer, it's impossible to tell. *Gamera 3* looks as though it has a budget of $90 million rather than $9 million.

The final film in a trilogy tends to be considered a let down. After two films of build up, there's often a feeling of *"This is all?"* at the conclusion. *Star Wars: Return of the Jedi* is a classic example. While a decent film on its own merit, it feels like a notable step down from *The Empire Strikes Back*. With the *Heisei Gamera* series, director Shusuke Kaneko and special effects director Shinji Higuchi break this trend. *Gamera 3: Revenge of Iris* does what a third film in a trilogy is supposed to do: it brings the films' themes full circle while heightening the stakes and spectacle. *Gamera 3* is one of the most perfectly executed monster pictures alongside Ridley Scott's *Alien* (1979). Produced in the immediate wake of the Roland Emmerich *Godzilla*, it feels like Kaneko and Higuchi saying *"This is how giant monsters are really done"*.

PRINCIPAL PHOTOGRAPHY

Location scouting for *Gamera 3: Revenge of Iris* took place in late March 1998. The shoot commenced in May. The film's opening would be shot on location in the Philippines. Kaneko's direction yields an impressive attention to detail and the picture is gorgeously shot. Junichi Tozawa's images of rural Japanese locales are lush and *Gamera 3* feels the most polished of all three films.

For the Shibuya sequence, Kaneko and Higuchi's units closely collaborated in a manner strongly invoking Honda and Tsuburaya in the classic Toho years. Many shots were complex composites of footage filmed by both crews. Both Higuchi and Kaneko's units made use of green screens, which generally have superior compositing abilities to blue screens. These shots were storyboarded in particular detail. Extras were yanked through the air on pulleys in front of green screens in foreground elements for one of the most impressive composites. The shot of the unwitting worker in the shattering telephone booth was done with a shaking platform with shock matts for the falling actor.

The Kyoto Station sequence was shot in the real train station and began shooting in late June 1998. To create the effect of the typhoon's torrential downpour, a rain machine was used and water was hosed onto the actors and extras. CGI was used to enhance the rain in some shots. Light was reflected at the actors with a cross-shaped mirror to give the effect of flash from explosions during the monsters' battle. Norman England, a *Fangoria* correspondent, ex-pat and friend of Kaneko, was an extra in this sequence. England (1958-) later directed his own tokusatsu short film called *The iDol* (2006) and the documentary *Bringing Godzilla Down to Size* (2008).

The scenes with Ai Maeda's Ayana interacting with the infant Iris feature an intricate animatronic puppet. These scenes were directed by Kaneko's unit with Higuchi's supervision. Kaneko's J-Horror roots once again show with sequences of Iris gruesomely draining its victims' life-force. A stylish scene where the creature attacks a young female camper was filmed with the actress and camera on a moving platform. The Self Defense Force once more lent strong support to the production of *Gamera 3*. JSDF soldier extras participated in the scene where the army battles Iris.

The scene in the rubble of Kyoto Station where Ayana is absorbed into Iris was shot in early July. The scene made heavy use of green screen compositing and both practical and digital effects. The dynamic shot of Moribe's family sword flying through the air after being thrown at Iris was done with the prop on a moving, rotating rig. The sword was intended by Kaneko and Ito as a stand-in for the legendary *Kusanagi no Tsurugi*, used to defeat the hydra *Yamata no Orochi*. For Ayana's absorption by Iris, Ai Maeda was hung with wires over a green screen. The shot of her inside Iris was done with the camera affixed to a rotating rig. Kaneko's unit wrapped shooting on August 20th, 1998. Higuchi's team, meanwhile, still had another three weeks of shooting to do.

ACTORS

Actress Miki Mizuno from *Gamera 2* was to return and reprise her role; teaming up with Nakayama's Nagamine and Fujitani's Asagi. She was written out of the film due to scheduling conflicts. Yasuyoshi Tokuma was adamant on up and coming idol Nozomi Ando to play the role of Ayana. Shusuke Kaneko was keen on Ai Maeda, the older sister of Aki Maeda. Aki, incidentally, also appears as a younger version of Ayana. In the end, a compromise was reached with Ando given a supporting role as Moribe's sister Miyuki. Her fate is left uncertain in the finished film, but a deleted scene shows that she and Moribe's grandmother survived Iris' attack. The teenage Maeda's Ayana is like a female anime protagonist come to life She later appeared in Kenta Fukasaku's *Battle Royale II: Requiem* (2003).

SFX/VFX

Particularly in the final act, it is Shinji Higuchi's special effects team that utterly dominates the film. *Gamera 3: Revenge of Iris* is just as much of Higuchi's film as Kaneko's and many would argue more-so. It's an open secret that this caused friction between the two men but how much so is unknown. After the first two films, Higuchi strived for novelty in *Gamera 3*. As many scenarios had been exhausted with *Gamera: Guardian of the Universe* and *Gamera 2*, Higuchi pushed his

team to think extra creatively. Once again, Mahiro Maeda designed the monsters. His company Gonzo would also provide some CGI for the film. A new main Gamera suit was built by Tomoo Haraguchi with even more animatronic enhancement; it could open and close its mouth mechanically. Fuyuki Shinada modeled Iris and directed the building of its various suits and puppets. The main Iris suit had an electric light installed in its head. Electric dial controlled lights were also placed inside Iris' abdomen. Toshio Miike also refined his miniature building process even more. The models were often built in pieces that could be assembled as needed for the shot. Higuchi's unit started filming on June 1st, 1998 when work began on the Shibuya sequence. Higuchi would proceed to work so hard that he often slept in the studio.

The Shibuya destruction sequence is stunning in its realism and feels like Higuchi's masterwork as a special effects director. He depicts a burning Gyaos fall from the sky, ala Nostradamus' King of Terror, on what seems to be a normal evening in downtown Tokyo. It takes the concept of *"What if a monster appeared in the real world"* to its zenith. Higuchi was the most enthusiastic about this sequence and it shows. He sought to create a more realistic vision of Gyaos in *Gamera 3* and was much happier with the new designs. The flaming Gyaos prop was filmed outdoors and suspended from a wire hung from scaffolding. For the wide shot of Gamera landing: location plates, actor footage, CGI and miniatures were all blended seamlessly. The shot of Gamera descending to the ground was done by suspending the empty suit with ropes with some smoke blown into the shot for good measure. It had to be done almost ten times before Higuchi was happy with it. A separate Gamera foot was built for the shot of it crashing onto the street. It didn't fall correctly on the first take. The miniature was repaired and it was done again. Actor footage shot by Kaneko and cracking debris elements were composed into the shot. Dry ice was pumped into the mouth of the Gamera suit to give the effect of its breath. This tended to make suit actor Hirofumi Fukuzawa lightheaded.

The injured, mutilated Gyaos was mainly portrayed by a hand puppet while the explosion engulfing the Hachiko statue was done on a sideways set outdoors. The Hachiko model was built at half scale by the late sculptor Hiroshi Sagae. The shot of Gamera amongst the burning buildings was extremely dangerous to film and Fukuzawa had to be covered in a flame retardant gel. The most impressive composite shot shows people flying through the air as the city explodes. This was done with numerous elements including miniatures, genuine pyrotechnics, CGI frosting and the green screen shots of actors on pulleys for the foreground. For the distant elements, Barbie dolls were thrown against a green screen. For the effect of charred bodies flying through the air, tinfoil dolls were built and spray-painted black before being blown up. All in all, this incredible sequence took both units months to film. Higuchi's unit devoted the entire first month of principal photography to this scene.

The next major sequence to be filmed by Higuchi's unit was the air battle, which began shooting in late June. For *Gamera 3*, improved CGI gave Shinji Higuchi more creative freedom and was used the most in this scene. The digital workflow was dramatically improved for this film. Iris' aerial movement was inspired by squid, a nod to how Higuchi had wanted it to be an underwater monster. Yet Higuchi made a point to not use CGI as a shortcut. The CGI is the film's weakest link, but it is the most innovative done in Japan up to that time. Puppets of flying Gamera and Iris were used for close-ups and the clouds were created with smoke machines and dry ice. Footage of live missiles being fired were shot with the JSDF's cooperation. The shots of Iris rampaging through the forest and battling the Self Defense Force were done outdoors in natural light. Like Ghidorah, Iris required heavy wire work for its tentacles which were also enhanced with CGI.

Gamera 3's fiery Kyoto finale is another technical marvel driven by Higuchi's unit. It was filmed mainly in August of 1998. Numerous shots blend explosions, CGI, real cityscapes, miniatures and monster suits. Gamera's impressive landing was done with a camera placed on a dolly track and miniatures on a conveyor belt. Sand was sprayed at the monster suits to give the effect of rain bouncing off them. The stormy sky behind the monsters was not digital; Higuchi's unit used a magic lantern-like projector painted with black waves. CGI sparks were added to the fires to give the effect of wood burning, as Kyoto has more wooden buildings than other cities in Japan. Hand puppets were used for close-ups of the monsters grappling and the Kyoto Station miniature was built to a particularly large and detailed scale. Higuchi wanted the monsters to fight in a confined area to increase the feeling of narrative tension.

Models of Gamera's shell were built for shots of it being pierced by Iris. The shots of Gamera and Iris breaking through Kyoto Station were accomplished almost entirely with practical effects. Genuine locales, the actresses, the suits, puppet replicas, miniatures, pyrotechnics and live debris were all masterfully blended into an eye popping composition. For close-ups of Gamera's hand being pierced by Iris, a separate glove was built. Another large hand was created for shots of Gamera lowering Ayana to the ground. The concept of Gamera taking out Iris with a "flame fist" was a martial arts film nod, specifically to the Jimmy Wang Yu film *The One Armed Boxer* (1971). The Kyoto Station explosion was a masterwork of pyrotechnic engineering from Izumi Negishi. An even larger Kyoto Station miniature was built and blown up outdoors. Higuchi's only regret is that he had to use a static camera position. He felt it was smart to do so given the variables of working with explosions. Higuchi finally would get to do a moving explosion shot in 2000's *Sakuya: Slayer of Demons*. The final shot is an impressive mix of a Gamera model, real locale, genuine pyrotechnics and CGI frosting.

Later scenes shot by Higuchi's unit include the "Trauma Gamera" shots from Ayana's flashback early in the picture. These made use of a modified *Gamera 2* suit with heavy amounts of smoke blown at it. *Tokusatsu* modeling veteran Toru Suzuki (1930-2012) visited *Gamera 3*'s set and directed the model building for this scene. Suzuki, another unsung hero of the medium, had done *tokusatsu* work for nearly every studio. He joined Shintoho in 1948 where he became friends with Yasuyuki Inoue and Yoshie Irie. Over the course of the 1950s, '60s and '70s, he worked for Eiji Tsuburaya, Noriaki Yuasa and Nobuo Yajima's effects units. Suzuki was one of the founding members of Equis Productions and also worked on Toei's *Sentai* and *Metal Hero* franchises. This was along with South Korean and Taiwanese films such as 1977's *Heroes of the Eastern Skies*. Katsuro Onoue, Izumi Negishi and Toshio Miike had all been mentored by Suzuki.

The final footage shot by Higuchi's crew was in mid September of 1998; namely the pyrotechnic elements for the film's final shots. These giant flames were made by setting large rubber tires on fire. This had to be filmed in the remote region of Tochigi and regardless, the locals complained about the smell. With *Gamera 3: Revenge of Iris*, Shinji Higuchi shows himself to be a visual genius. Higuchi reveals a mastery of old school filmmaking techniques with a foot in the future and innovative streak. His images are like Eiji Tsuburaya's finest work with a Douglas Trumbull-like attention to detail. In the 1960s, it was Toho who produced the far more innovative special effects pictures. Noriaki Yuasa's Gamera films did not hold much of a candle to Honda and Tsuburaya's best opuses. With the 1990s *Gamera* trilogy, Kaneko and Higuchi flipped the dynamic and Toho and Daiei's places. If Ishiro Honda and Eiji Tsuburaya had lived to see *Gamera 3*, they would have been proud to see the evolution of their legacy.

THEMES AND MOTIFS

For *Gamera 3*, Kaneko and screenwriter Kazunori Ito opted for a more supernatural tone than the harder sci-fi of the previous film. The *yonaoshi* god motif used throughout the *kaiju* genre's history is all but explicitly referenced. The monsters are truly destructive gods battling to decide human society's fate. Kaneko would take this theme even further in his following *Godzilla, Mothra and King Ghidorah: Giant Monsters All-Out Attack* (2001). Ito's script is the most engaging of the three films and has the highest narrative stakes. Kaneko, Ito and Higuchi wanted to give *Gamera 3* a more apocalyptic tone for its release in 1999. This was, after all, the year Nostradamus prophesied that *"The King of Terror would fall from the sky"*.

Gamera 3: Revenge of Iris presents a Japan that, by this time, is quite weary of monster attacks. At one point, a returning Mr. Saito (Hirotaro Honda) says to Nakayama's Nagamine: *"Why do giant monsters have to keep attacking Japan?"*. In the *kaiju* genre, such a line of dialogue feels almost meta. Yet it works in line with the trilogy's realism and

Kaneko and Ito's intent is clear. *Kaiju* have become another regular disaster the populace lives with and tolerates now; like Japan's frequent volcanic eruptions and earthquakes.

RELEASE AND LEGACY

Daiei had the intention of making a fourth Gamera film, but box office results fell short. That didn't stop fan filmmaker Shinpei Hayashiya from making his own DIY conclusion, *Gamera 4: Truth*. Toho certainly took note of these films as both Kaneko and Higuchi would helm Godzilla entries in the coming years. After the death of Yasuyoshi Tokuma, Daiei financially crumbled again and was sold to printing and film monolith Kadokawa in 2002. Kadokawa rebooted the series in 2006 with *Gamera the Brave*. That film brought the series back to its kiddie matinee roots and was a dismal flop. Since then, Gamera has been dormant. In 2015, Kadokawa teased Gamera's return with a proof of concept short shown at conventions. The project has so far failed to materialize. Yet, given Toho's plans to continue making Godzilla movies for the foreseeable future, it's pretty inevitable that Gamera will make a comeback.

ALTERNATE VERSIONS

Gamera 3: Revenge of Iris was released directly to DVD by ADV Films in 2003. ADV commissioned their own English dub recorded in Texas and written and directed by Kyle Jones. Voice cast includes Tiffany Grant (Dr. Nagamine), Kelli Cousins (Ayana), Cameron Bautsch (Moribe), Luci Christian

(Asagi Kusanagi), Paul Sidello (Osako), Jason Douglas (Kurata) and Christine Auten (Asakura). Supporting vocal cast includes Paul Locklear, Alex Harter, Andy McAvin, Bob Biggerstaff, Victor Carsrud, Tony Oller, Cynthia Feaster, Rick Peeples, Jessica Boone, Vic Mignogna, Hal Raleigh, John Tyson, Mike Yantosca, Vickie Barosh and David Parker.

AMERICAN HOME VIDEO HISTORY

ADV's DVD of *Gamera 3: Revenge of Iris* was its first stateside home video release. The disc contained Japanese and English dub tracks, along with an obnoxious gag commentary by "Gamera". In 2011, it was picked up by Mill Creek and released to Blu-ray in a standalone edition. It was also included in two boxed sets by Mill Creek; one for only the *Heisei* trilogy in 2011 and the other for the entire Gamera series in 2014. In 2020, the stunning 4K remaster done by Kadokawa was included on Arrow's *Gamera: The Complete Collection* Blu-ray set.

Further Viewing:

GODZILLA
MOTHRA AND KING GHIDORAH
GIANT MONSTERS ALL-OUT ATTACK

(2001)
ゴジラ・モスラ・キングギドラ 大怪獣総攻撃
Toho, *Director:* **Shusuke Kaneko**

After Shusuke Kaneko directed *Pyrokinesis* (2000) for Toho, Shogo Tomiyama gave him the chance to helm his own Godzilla film. The previous Godzilla entry, *Godzilla vs. Megaguiras* (also 2000) was a massive flop, so Toho wanted to take the franchise in a different direction. *Godzilla, Mothra and King Ghidorah: Giant Monsters All-Out Attack* is light years ahead of the other Millennium entries. These range from decent (*Godzilla Against Mechagodzilla*) to unmitigated cinematic disasters (*Godzilla: Final Wars*). The film's flaws are mainly due to studio interference as Kaneko was given less creative freedom. As is known, Kaneko originally wanted the film to feature Anguirus, Varan and Baragon as Godzilla's foes. He was made to swap out Anguirus and Varan for more stalwart characters King Ghidorah and Mothra. This hardly wrecks the film, but it's pretty clear that *GMK* would have worked better with those monsters. Additionally, Gamera trilogy cinematographer Junichi Tozawa did not join Kaneko. Instead the director had to make due with the lazy eye of *Heisei* Godzilla DP Masahiro Kishimoto. Kaneko was also given a more rushed production schedule than for *Gamera 3*, which definitely hurt the film. *GMK* lacks the flawless execution of the latter two Gamera films. Shinji Higuchi's assistant on the Gamera trilogy, Makoto Kamiya, takes up his mantle. Kamiya has learned his close friend and mentor's craft well and composes special effects scenes in Higuchi's mold. Much of Higuchi's team returned to work under Kamiya including

Toshio Miike and Izumi Negishi, but his presence is missed.

Godzilla, Mothra and King Ghidorah: Giant Monsters All-Out Attack features a stronger element of social satire than the three Gamera films and the strongest fantasy elements of any Godzilla picture. It takes the *yonaoshi* god motif common in *kaiju* films to a logical conclusion of sorts with Godzilla as a literal Jungian manifestation of Japan's trauma and guilt. *GMK* is the only Godzilla film to outright acknowledge Japan's wartime misdeeds and is riddled with darkly comedic moments. Chiharu Niiyama plays a cute female protagonist in the vein of a Millennial Yuriko Hoshi. The legendary Hideyo Amamoto plays one final kaiju film role, he had worked with Kaneko before on his vampire comedy *My Soul is Slashed* (1991). During the shooting of *GMK*, the left wing Amamoto raged as the U.S. invasion of Afghanistan took place. There's an amusing cameo with Ai and Aki Maeda paying homage to Mothra's Twin Fairies.

Fuyuki Shinada creates a particularly memorable and interesting take on Godzilla, a hulking hellbeast inhabited by *Zeiram*'s Mizuho Yoshida. Kaneko deliberately made his Godzilla almost invincible as a protest against Devlin and Emmerich. *GMK* comes alive for Baragon's battle against Godzilla, a highlight of the picture. Baragon is portrayed by stuntwoman Rie Ota who gives a spirited performance. Ko Otani supplies a synth-laden score allegedly inspired by Italian horror rock maestros Goblin. While Higuchi is missed, a stunning sequence storyboarded by him pitting Godzilla against the Self Defense Force is another standout. Makoto Kamiya and Toshio Miike, who served under both Kawakita and Higuchi, built the miniatures with a mix of both men's methods. Model cityscapes made for *GMK* would wind up used for *Kill Bill Vol. 1* (2003) for Uma Thurman's Bride's *tokusatsu*-inspired plane landing. Assistants Yuichi Kikuchi and Kiyotaka Taguchi would soon become *tokusatsu* figures themselves. Kikuchi helmed the effects for the following entry: *Godzilla Against Mechagodzilla* (2002). *GMK*'s finale is clunky in parts, superbly executed in others as Kamiya finds his feet as FX director. *Godzilla, Mothra and King Ghidorah: Giant Monsters All-Out Attack* is overall a step down from *Gamera 3* but still one of the best Godzilla movies in years.

SHORT SUBJECTS: 25 TOKUSATSU FILMS
(under half an hour)

短編映画

by Kevin Derendorf

The movies Jules covers in this book are indeed essential. However, they have something else in common: they're all feature-length. In today's busy world, there are times when you want a snack-sized dose of Japanese special effects. A *tokusatsu* single serving to squeeze into a lunch break or last few moments of an evening, when a whole movie is too much. For that, we have the medium of the short film. In addition to their brevity, they have the advantage of experimental creative freedom less constrained by financing. *Tokusatsu* shorts are the preferred venue for up-and-comers that reflect their future filmmaking opuses.

Despite this, short features are under-discussed, footnotes among their high-profile cinematic siblings. To mirror the theme of this book, I selected twenty-five special effects shorts, running the gamut of silly to serious, spanning decades, purpose, and subject matter. Since monsters are my preoccupation, they take a disproportionate focus.

The criteria I'm using:

• To be consistent with the live-action focus of this book, these shorts must be live-action. This rules out *Negadon: The Monster from Mars, Cencoroll,* the Daicon opening animations, segments for the Japan Animator Expo and more.

• Shorts must be under half an hour. Sadly this rules out *Howl from Beyond the Fog, The Red Crow and the Phantom Ship* and *Gemu.*

• Western-made fan films such as *Showdown of the Godz, Marlin Man* and *Sword of the Dead* have been excluded for focus and concision.

• Lost, presumably destroyed film shorts have been excluded. The idea should be that the reader can hypotheticaly seek the films out, even if it's a significant hunt.

Ramayana (ラーマーヤナ, *1942 (probably), dir. unknown, 18 minutes)*

Any fan can point to a certain Toho production from November 1954 as the genesis of kaiju eiga as a pop-culture phenomenon. Yet many also recognize that there were Japanese giant monster movie dry-runs leading up to *Godzilla*'s debut. These include *Giant Buddha Travels the Country* and more. One such footnote is the 1942 Toho short *Ramayana,* based on the Indian epic. Adapted by *Gekko Kamen* creator Kohan Kawauchi and with special miniature effects, though uncredited, by the future god of *tokusatsu,* Eiji Tsuburaya. He was Kawauchi's boss in the Toho puppetry and special effects department at the time. Unlike Tsuburaya's later work, where human actors were composited into miniature sets, everything here is achieved in camera. With no human actors, marionettes are used throughout for a *Thunderbirds* meets *Sinbad* flavor. The picture has dancing skeletons, flying monkeys, bodily dismemberment and a fire-breathing giant whose rampage evokes what *Attack on Titan* would be doing seven decades later.

Daicon Films' Return of Ultraman (帰ってきたウルトラマン, *1983, dir. Hideaki Anno, 26 minutes)*

Anime fandom would have you believe that the spiritual origins of studio Gainax were with the 1981 opening animation for the Daicon III convention. As landmark as that short was (the Daicon IV short even more so), it's only a piece of the puzzle. The project would never have happened had Hideaki Anno, Takami Akai, and Hiroyuki Yamaga not become friends at Osaka University of Arts. They began producing buzzworthy fan films, which is how they landed the Daicon gig in the first place. Of that batch, few are as infamous as the series of Ultraman shorts that Anno starred in. Anno, a diehard Ultra-manic, played the title character in plain clothes. He battled classmates standing in for aliens, with only the crudest special effects. Yet the shorts incorporated sound effects, music and camera angles in line with Tsuburaya's franchise to great comedic effect.

After the group blew up from Daicon and began getting industry work, they didn't entirely abandon their independent passion projects. Daicon Film produced a number of fan projects, of which *Return of Ultraman* is the best known. The short was made as a promotion for Daicon IV. As with the college shorts, it features Anno himself as Ultraman, wearing jeans and a jacket. However, this time there are elaborate miniatures and a decent kaiju for him to battle. The design work is intricate. The staff made detailed technical schematics for the various ships and the defense base used. At first the movie was marketed as *"Return of Unoretramaso"*. In katakana that looks very close to *Ultraman* ala how The Asylum will make a *Transmorphers* movie when a *Transformers* entry comes out. Anno's later successes allowed the film to get licensed DVD releases from Tsuburaya in 2001,

giving it quasi-canonical status. The Anno *Ultraman* has even had action figures made.

There were several other shorts produced during this time. These culminated in the original feature *The Eight-Headed Dragon Strikes Back* and the foundation of Gainax:

• Takami Akai's *Patriotic Sentai Dai-Nippon (Aikoku Sentai Dai-Nippon)* was the first tokusatsu spoof in 1982. This 19-minute short Super Sentai parody features team members themed around stereotypically Japanese motifs like *harakiri, geisha* and *sukiyaki*. There were plans to follow it up with a short titled *Communist Sentai Dai-Russian*, but they never materialized.

• *Kaiketsu Noutenki* is the most revisited of their live action works, a parody of 1977's *Kaiketsu Zubat*. It had short installments in 1982, 1984 and 1988, with the hero even going to San Francisco and Seoul. Actor Yasuhiro Takeda made convention appearances in his *Noutenki* ("scatterbrain") costume at least until 2001. It's no coincidence that the book chronicling the history of the Daicon/Gainax studio is called *The Noutenki Memoirs*.

• There was also a Gerry Anderson-style puppet movie titled *The Big Hill of Gonzaless (Hayauchi Ken no Boken)*. It is almost never spoken about. It is not covered in the *World of Daicon Films* book, doesn't appear to have ever gotten a home video release and it doesn't have the future Gainax regulars on the staff. Still, a 40-minute puppet movie made contemporary to Daicon's *Return of Ultraman* is something worth tracking down.

S.F.3.D. Original Video: Nutrocker (1985, *dir. Shinichi Ohoka, 27 minutes*)

S.F.3.D (now called *Maschinen Kreiger ZbV 3000*) is a classic example of a success story from the bubble economy years. It began as a series of science fiction stories concocted by Ko Yokoyama for the model kit magazine Hobby Japan between 1982 and 1986. The post-apocalyptic mecha pastiche caught on with readers. They began clamoring for kits of the various war machines invented for the series. Despite a lack of new material, merchandise has continued circulation over the decades, both domestically and internationally. Its popularity is to the point that a Hollywood movie adaptation was announced in 2017 from *It* producer Roy Lee. If the film is produced, it will not be the first time that the universe of giant robot blitzkrieg would see film. It was done back in 1985 with *Nutrocker*.

Nutrocker was an interesting experiment in Tsuburaya Productions' long hiatus between Ultraman shows (1981-1996). During this time, they were branching out into other science fiction, fantasy and horror works. It's a brief adventure within the larger *S.F.3.D.* universe. It focuses on one pilot (American actor Tristan Hickey) stranded in hostile territory, struggling to make it out against nasty hover tanks. The piece is all in English and features some excellent miniature work. It has just enough sci-fi worldbuilding that it would appeal to the fans of *Robot Jox* and its numerous semi-spinoffs. The only thing likely keeping it off American VHS shelves in the 1980s was the short runtime. If the Hollywood movie happens, a resurgence in interest is possible.

The Phantom of Regular Size (普通サイズの怪人, *Futsu Size no Kaijin, 1986, dir. Shinya Tsukamoto, 19 minutes*)

This is covered earlier in this book, but *The Phantom of Regular Size* is very much a beta version of *Tetsuo: The Iron Man*. The same way that *Down to Hell* was to *Versus* or *Anatomia Extinction* is to *Tokyo Gore Police*. The piece was a major part of Shinya Tsukamoto's transition from stage theater back into moviemaking. It was done, much like Tetsuo, with his accomplices from the Kaijyu Theatre troupe. The piece has the same cast, the same locations, the same frenetic avant garde energy, the same pulsing style of soundtrack, and the same premise. Yet it is on a shorter timescale and in color 8mm. As experimental as *Tetsuo* is, *Phantom*, by nature of being a dry-run, is even more so. Tsukamoto himself says that he wasn't trying to express any idea with the film, making it in some ways an even more raw, inexplicable experience.

The Phantom of Regular Size led directly to the same crew producing *Adventure of Denchu Kozo*. Based on one of Kaijyu Theatre's plays, it won an award at PIA. The panel included future Godzilla directors Shusuke Kaneko and Kazuki Omori. That win was the push to turn Kaijyu Theatre into a full movie production house. The troupe immediately turned around to create *Tetsuo*, which remains a cult classic to this day.

Godzilla vs Mito Komon (ゴジラ対水戸黄門, *1991, dir. Shinya Takeshita, 12 minutes*)

There's no doubt that the Ultraman fan films that Hideaki Anno created at Osaka University of Arts were minimalist masterpieces. His underclassman Shinya Takeshita brought things to another level in this fan film a decade later. Takeshita does everything in the piece. He plays multiple characters from the *Mito Komon* TV series, as well as Godzilla, Daimajin, Ghidorah and Ultraman. Only editing, body language and a scant few pieces of cardboard distinguish one from the other. He even plays electrical towers and provides the entire soundtrack via a cappella chanting. Considering the recent comedic YouTubers debating themselves with multiple characters, he was ahead of the curve. Even them you seldom see get into wrestling matches between doppelgangers.

Ultraman vs. Kamen Rider (ウルトラマンVS仮面ライダー, *1993, dir. Keita Amemiya, 9 minutes*)

Made for the 25th anniversary of *Ultraman* and the 20th of *Kamen Rider*, a crossover TV special between Japan's most iconic heroes seems improbable today. Yet it was a reasonable event during a relatively dormant period for both characters. The special was mostly a documentary. The final 9 minutes feature a mini-movie by Keita Amemiya, whose *Kamen Rider ZO* theatrical film had premiered a week beforehand. The short has two fantastic original monster designs who battle the original Ultraman and Kamen Rider respectively. The two creatures merge and require Rider to grow gigantic for a team-up. Seeing the two heroes share a screen was no doubt a dream come true for a generation of children. The execution was strong, if ephemeral.

Monster Planet of Godzilla (怪獣プラネットゴジラ, *Kaiju Planet Godzilla, 1994, dir. Koichi Kawakita, 18 minutes*)

One of the best Japanese 4D theme park rides along with *Godzilla vs. Evangelion, Monster Planet of Godzilla* was an attraction at Sanrio Puroland from March 18, 1994 to July 1, 1998. The original version was 3D, with vibrating seats and smokey odors to enhance the stereoscopic effects. Unfortunately, neither this nor Megumi Odaka's sequences with companion Hello Kitty were preserved for home video. A 2D version was included in the Godzilla Final Box, while a 3D one was an extra on deluxe Japanese releases of the 2014 *Godzilla*. It's a shame that it's not available more widely. Even at its brief runtime, it is a more entertaining experience than the same year's 40th anniversary picture: *Godzilla vs. Space Godzilla*.

The video's first 10 minutes are a trivia quiz that kept theme park attendees engaged while waiting for the ride. Miki Saegusa (Odaka, reprising her role from the films) introduces us to the premise. We'll be riding a spaceship called Earth to an alien planet to investigate the disappearance of a different ship. Said disappearance was caused by the planet being inhabited by Godzilla, Mothra and Rodan. They are then accidentally transported back to Tokyo through shenanigans. The monsters duke it out and destroy numerous landmarks. These include the Wako department store seen in the original *Godzilla* and Tokyo Station, which was spared Godzilla-related damage until *Shin Godzilla*.

Being a Kawakita picture, the mechanics of the ship designed by Shinji Nishikawa and dock are filmed lovingly. The monsters also engage in numerous beam battles and there are a lot of sparks when they grapple, all to Ifukube music. The Godzilla suit and Mothra/Rodan puppets are recycled from the previous movies. Unlike most of the Heisei-era material, they are scaled with Godzilla a traditional 50 meters in height. This allows for better detail on the miniature buildings and military hardware. Being a Sanrio project may have had something to do with the kid-friendly premise that the monsters only become violent through human intervention. That's not exactly off the brand's thematics at the time either.

Archangel Thunderbird (超天使雷鳥, *Cho Tenshi Raicho, 1998, dir. Kevin Davies & Tony Luke, 21 minutes*)

I'm bending my rules a little to include *Archangel Thunderbird*. It was created as a pilot for Sci-Fi Channel UK, with an English-speaking cast and director. It's worth bringing up both because it's an underrated and interesting short but also was the joint brainchild of creature designer extraordinaire Yasushi Nirasawa and graphic artist Tony Luke. Nirasawa was responsible for *Garo, Gokaiger, The Great Yokai War* and *Godzilla: Final Wars'* Gigan design. Luke had broken new ground in 1993 by getting the comic *Dominator* printed in Kodansha's Afternoon. It was the first British work printed in a Japanese manga anthology. With wild-but-crude visuals and relentless pacing, *Archangel Thunderbird* feels more akin to a hyperactive music video than a narrative drama. It has a palpable anime influence that, combined with religious controversy, probably doomed its network prospects.

Set in 2012, London has been overrun with all manner of enormous demonic creatures, led by the somewhat-hidden Baal (voiced by author Neil Gaiman). The professor to predict their arrival and mount a resistance is Dr. John Churchill (Doug Bradley, better known as *Hellraiser*'s Pinhead). He learned about the invasion by reading the Necronomicon, as well as Baal's weakness. Churchill and his sidekick Rob (Adrian Bunting, in his only screen role) trek across London, avoiding various beasts, to meet up with Miki Manson (scream queen Eileen Daly), a *"lunatic with six personalities"*. Her unique mental state allows her to merge with (i.e. pilot) the ancient, multi-formed defense creature Archangel Thunderbird in exchange for having her way with Rob. The monster Dygon (who initially looks like a Tyrannosaurus with a Zeiram face in her chest, later powering up to look like Necrosan from Primal Rage) attacks our heroes. Just in the nick of time Archangel Thunderbird awakens. The show ends by giving us a demo of the Archangel's six forms as it dispatches Dygon while London burns around them.

Nirasawa pulled out all the stops for *Archangel Thunderbird*. The title creature gets six forms, including very Guyver-esque stat sheets in the Necronomicon that flash on-screen when transformations occur. Not to mention two forms for Dygon and several different creatures are shown rampaging early on. Personal favorites include the saucer-headed, scissor-handed skeletal cyborg and the winged horse-man with eye lasers. The stop-motion animation was done with atypical puppets. They're made of resin to capture the aesthetic of Nirasawa's figures and garage kits, with articulation added where it's needed. This is in contrast to the usual approach of soft material over a wire or armature frame. The result, while not state-of-the-art, is better than one would expect, especially considering the project's low-budget nature. These models are much more articulated than any reasonable action figure would be. It's hard to watch the battle and not feel compelled to go looking for its non-existent toy line afterwards.

Geharha: The Dark and Long Hair Monster
(長髪大怪獣ゲハラ, *Chohatsu Daikaiju Gehara, 2009, dir. Kiyotaka Taguchi, 21 minutes*)

Geharha has an interesting genesis as a rare movie conceptualized via live television. In April 2008, all-round artist Jun Miura hosted an NHK talk show where a group of panelists reviewed various *kaiju* design submissions. The selected entrant, from 22 year-old Shinya Nemoto, was a creature covered with long, black hair as popularized by the *nu-kaidan* movement with movies like *The Ring*. It sported the name "*Geharha*" (a pun on "*hage*", which is Japanese for "bald"). With that as a base, Miura and producer Shinji Higuchi got to work fleshing it out into a full movie. Future tokusatsu wunderkind Kiyotaka Taguchi, Higuchi's protégé for nearly a decade, stepped into the director's seat.

Geharha is an undeniable tribute to classic Toho. It generally riffs on stock plots, from the monster rising from the ocean in the first minutes. Ken Osawa (*Video Girl Ai, Reiko: The Psyche Resurrected*) plays a reporter who goes to investigate the Geharha shrine (written with the kanji for wool) where the creature was awakened. We

get a cameo from Tomorowo Taguchi (*Tetsuo*) as a priest. Shiro Sano (*Godzilla 2000*) plays a scientist trying to stop the monster. He does this while spouting profound clichés ("*Humans are the scariest monsters, after all*" or "*If we don't stop environmental destruction, another Geharha will appear*"). These usually elicit an awkward pause or annoyed look from his coworkers. Kanji Tsuda (*Gamera the Brave)* and Hiroyuki Watanabe (*Ultraman Gaia, Gamera: Guardian of the Universe*) also show up as a fisherman and a military commander.

The twist on the standard parody (mostly channeling *Varan the Unbelievable*) is that this is a hair monster. The picture has a lot of fun with that. Geharha's victims immediately turn bald. We have a recovery scene (like the one in *Rodan*) where one, unresponsive in a bed, is triggered by the sight of hair. Hair wrapping around everything is the monster's signature weapon, as is poison gas released by burning it. A very Marker-light-like super-weapon is rolled out to combat it, predictably looking like a giant hair dryer.

It's a fun ride, with A-grade miniature work and clever use of Akira Ifukube's concert pieces to give it the Godzilla-but-not-Godzilla vibe. It would be an excellent pastiche of 50s *kaiju* flicks, but, as a final twist, the "End" *kanji* is interrupted by an alien invasion. This kicks things into the 1960s and over-the-top. The last thing we're treated to is a fake trailer for a sequel, *Geharha: Monster Martial Law* (was Shingo Maehata's *Zella: Monster Martial Law* inspired by it?). It features a barrage of quick cuts, everything from an *Invasion of Astro Monster*-style saucer with force bubble to an Ultraman transformation pose to a *Submersion of Japan*-ish sea of hair. This is all set to Immediate Music's "Redrum", a certain nod to the trailer for *Godzilla: Final Wars* which used the same song. There's even a line at the climax where a character remarks that they're human, as in the *Final Wars* trailer.

God of Clay (ねんどの神さま, *Nendo no Kamisama, 2011, dir. Koichi Kawakita & Nobuaki Sugimoto, 11 minutes*)

God of Clay was a sort of last hurrah for an era. It was filmed in the Toho Built special effects studio, founded by Eiji Tsuburaya, right before it shut down. It's also a bit of a transition for Koichi Kawakita. Kawakita was moving into a teaching capacity, aiding his Osaka University of Arts students on projects like *Apollo Knight, Warrior Goddess Kanan* and the TV miniseries *Gunbot*. The effects work here is solid and the short's anti-war message is on-point. Unfortunately, since it is based on a book by Masamoto Nasu, licensing issues prevent it from being widely distributed. A similar situation to Daisuke Sato's much-touted adaptation of Ray Bradbury's *The Fog Horn*.

The movie deals with two children who, after losing their parents to WWII, create a clay idol of a god that hates warfare. One of the kids grows up to become a weapons manufacturer himself. The other prays until the god comes to life and confronts its long-lost creator. The lumpy, somewhat straightforward design of the titular god makes sense as something that a child would sculpt. In execution as a giant that absorbs artillery into its amorphous hide; it's effectively intimidating. It's a shame that

the picture has been locked away due to Dream Planet and the book's licensor not being able to come to terms. The cam rip taken at one of the two public screenings has done it no justice.

Go! Go! Godman & Greenman (行け！行け！ゴッドマン & グリーンマン, *Ike! Ike! Godman & Greenman, dir. Masaaki Tezuka, 2008, 21 minutes*)

From three-time Godzilla director Masaaki Tezuka, this is basically a spoof of the short 1970s superhero shows *Godman* and *Greenman*. Those programs were notoriously cheap, however. So *Go! Go! Godman & Greenman* actually features a better plot and better effects than the source material had. Recycling of classic Toho monsters on the programs (e.g. King Kong, Gorosaurus, Minilla, Sanda, bat people) was frequent. As a nod, the green gargantua Gaira is used as one of the villains' lackeys, to great comedic effect.

Giant God Warrior Appears in Tokyo (巨神兵東京に現わる, *Kyoshinhei Tokyo ni arawaru, 2012, dir. Shinji Higuchi, 10 minutes*)

To say that the God Warrior sequence in Miyazaki's *Nausicaa of the Valley of the Wind* was formative for Hideaki Anno is an understatement. It was an early opportunity for the young animator to handle an entire scene in a professional motion picture by himself. He also kept aspects of the hulking humanoid body horror that carried over into future hits such as *Nadia: The Secret of Blue Water* and *Neon Genesis Evangelion*, as well as a trademark purple beam. Yet as depicted in the movie, it's a weaker, dying, blobby form. It's nothing like the elaborate full-glory God Warriors depicted in

Miyazaki's manga. Those had never been realized on film. When Anno and lifelong friend Shinji Higuchi partnered in 2012 to put on a special effects museum exhibit, the God Warrior was an easy pick for a short subject. The short's objective is to demonstrate just what practical special effects can accomplish.

The effects work is up there with Higuchi's best efforts in the Gamera trilogy. It features elaborate sets of downtown Tokyo, complete with tiny details and even moving animals. All of this gets wiped out by the colossal God Warriors. They spew lasers from their mouths to melt the cityscape, hover on their wings of light, and advance in front of huge explosions. The latter spectacularly recreates one of the anime and manga's most iconic shots. One could point to this short as a dry-run for *Shin Godzilla*, particularly the iconic nighttime attack sequence.

The short was included on Japanese releases of *Evangelion 3.33*. Woefully, due to licensing restrictions with Studio Ghibli, it is not available in North America. The short was successful enough, even as an obscure bonus feature, that it's had several pieces of merchandise made. These include an articulated Figma of the God Warrior itself.

Earth Defense Force 3 PORTABLE THE COMMERCIAL (地球防衛軍3, *Chikyu Boeigun 3, 2012, dir. Minoru Kawasaki, 4 minutes*)

Japanese video games are big business. The marketing departments get hot talent to direct their commercials like Keita Amemiya for *Genpei Toumaden* and George Romero

for *Resident Evil 2*. To represent this niche of short filmmaking, I give you the ad for *Earth Defense Force 3*, a game in the *Earth Defense Force* series. It wears its inspiration on its sleeve by sharing a name with the Japanese title of *The Mysterians*. The franchise also sprang out of the unsuccessful ashes of the video game adaptation of *Tekkoki Mikazuki*, but that's another story. The games' penchant for setting humans against oversized arthropods has always been a bit tongue-in cheek. So who better to advertise it than director Minoru Kawasaki (*The Calamari Wrestler, Outerman, Monster X Strikes Back*), whose zany brand of comedy combines *tokusatsu* and slapstick?

This commercial features scenes right out of the games. Mobile infantry in high-tech armor go up against giant ants dropped from even larger flying saucers. This is complete with acid sprays, explosions and even a romance subplot. In true Kawasaki fashion, the cast includes some tokusatsu veterans. These include Koji Moritsugu (*Ultraseven*), Shunichi Okita (*Ultraman Ace*), Masami Horiuchi (*Ultraman Nexus*) and idol Risa Yoshiki. It also features unbearably awful performances by *gaijin* performers. This is a trait so consistent across his works that it must be an intentional comedic flourish.

Gingham Check (ギンガムチェック, *2012, dir. Joseph Kahn, 7 minutes*)

In an overview of short films, it'd be negligent to not mention at least one music video. Those can be some of the best-produced shorts out there. It's little surprise that Tsuburaya Productions has lent their staff and characters to a number of music videos over the years. These include from Science of Sound Special Players, OxT, Kaiju Girls and the Taiwanese band Mayday. They even produced a short spot to George Michael's *"Last Christmas"*. Yet this pales in comparison to working with AKB48. Japan's hottest musical act, AKB48 has become an empire. They have their own video games, TV shows, *anime*, movies (including Shusuke Kaneko's *Linking Love*), restaurants and countless spinoff groups. Several members appeared in 2012's movie *Ultraman Saga*. It's little wonder that the tables later flipped when the *kaiju* Golza appeared in one of their videos.

The video is from veteran MV director Joseph Kahn. Kahn has directed for Eminem, Britney Spears, Backstreet Boys, Jennifer Lopez, Lady Gaga and many more. It's a fun mash-up that features the band cutting back and forth between different genres. These include cop drama, spooky *yurei* movie, drag-racing delinquent flick and *kaiju* eiga. Several genre faces make appearances in the piece. These include *Kamen Rider Kiva*'s Kouhei Takeda and future *Ultraman Orb* star Hideo Ishiguro as love interests. Heisei Godzilla regular Akira Nakao plays a police captain.

Day of the Kaiju (怪獣の日, *Kaijū no Hi*, 2014, dir. Kazuhiro Nakagawa, 30 minutes)

Kazuhiro Nakagawa was an assistant director on *Shin Godzilla*. In places, *Day of the Kaiju* feels very much like a dry run for that project.

It deals with the political and bureaucratic fallout when a giant monster, defeated by the military, washes up in a seaside community. In some ways, the postmodern premise of the film is not really new. The dissection of a beached Godzilla takes up a large chunk of Nobuhiko Obayashi's unproduced *A Space Godzilla* film proposal from 1979. Hiroshi Yamamoto's *MM9* stories, starting in 2005, follow a group of *kaiju* meteorologists who rarely see the front lines of any monster battles. Nakagawa's mentor Shinji Higuchi actually adapted *MM9* for television in 2010. This sort of concept will always work on some level. It logically follows if you're setting out for a realistic portrayal of a fantastic world. For this, Nakagawa was inspired by the true complications involved in disposing of whale carcasses. He decided to scale it up for the *kaiju* genre.

Of course, the similarities of cleaning up whale guts and decontaminating a beach of nuclear waste was not lost on the director. One of the goals of the picture was to have this monster serve as an allegory for Fukushima in the way that Godzilla was one for the hydrogen bomb. Politicians argue about how the international community is observing them and make sloppy assumptions in hopes of looking better. Press conferences assure the public that *"Giant Life Form Number One"* is dead and everything is safe. An engineering team works on containment for the monster's body. Average civilians weigh in via protests and social media, it all has real-life counterparts in the 3/11 aftermath. Thus, many of the same elements also worked their way into *Shin Godzilla*. On top of that, there are shots identical to those in the Toho picture. These include the whole cast looking into the camera while the display of a computer monitor is superimposed on top of them and two characters conversing while leaning on a railing, looking at the incapacitated monster. Both pictures have the youthful, outspoken, pessimistic-but-correct protagonist. There's even a gag about how smelly one team member has become from working late hours. Higuchi proudly introduced the film that his assistant director was shopping around. He must've been taking notes as well.

ULTRAMAN n/a *(2015, dir. unknown, 3 minutes)*

A piece of footage apparently promoting a 50th anniversary project of Ultraman was posted on Tsuburaya Productions' YouTube channel on July 16, 2015. It ended in a stinger implying that something was coming on July 6, 2016. The piece showed a photorealistic CGI Ultraman and Zaragas duking it out in Shibuya. It certainly seemed like a trailer for an upcoming film, but so far the most that has come out of it is a figurine. Further confusing things, our colleague Alex Rushdy visited the home office of FIELDS (Tsuburaya's parent company). He was told that there was never any plan for a feature film. The short was just TsuPro testing out CGI for an AR project. Tsuburaya's office looks out over Shibuya and would make a cool venue to superimpose monsters over. It seems like a lot of effort for a gimmick only accessible via a private office building. Perhaps they were saving face by covering up another project that went south.

Nevertheless, it's a cool Ultraman redesign, even with the controversial toes. Hopefully some of the approaches present here carry over into *Shin Ultraman* and similar future endeavors.

Gamera *(2015, dir. Katsuhito Ishii, 4 minutes)*

Similar to *ULTRAMAN n/a*, *Gamera* is a 2015 short celebrating a major kaiju's 50th anniversary. It got reported everywhere as a trailer for a new feature film, and then there has been silence ever since. It's a shame that nothing more has come from this project. On top of looking great, it has a top-notch director (Katsuhito Ishii of *Taste of Tea and Funky Forest*) and composer (Kenji Kawai: *Patlabor, Ip Man*). The glimmer of hope is that Ishii's anime movie *Redline* (which he wrote but didn't direct) was in production for seven years. Even that window is growing eclipsed. however.

The short plays like a trailer and goes for a darker tone akin to the Heisei-era Gamera pictures. It features a swarm of Gyaos, as has become standardized by the Trilogy and Gamera the Brave, attacking Tokyo "ten years ago". You see a young child running for his life as his father urges him to run faster with promises of video games and snacks. Many have pointed to this as a comedic take, but to me it just reads as a parent desperately trying anything to give his kid a little edge, especially when he gets devoured onscreen. Gamera saves the child by graphically torching the birds. We cut to ten years later as the same kid, now grown, witnesses Gamera preparing to vanquish a new monster, a quadruped with some inventive energy weapon.

The teaser was intended to exploit the success of the 2014 *Godzilla*. That likewise had a proof-of-concept short featuring a kaiju not actually in the film. Kadokawa showed the piece off at New York Comic Con on October 8. This came with a baffling statement about how they were trying to raise money for the film. As if they are not a billion-dollar multimedia conglomerate who could finance whatever they please, even with polished creature CG by Japanese standards. They handed out T-shirts and fliers to promote the short. Evidently even the strong reception it received wasn't enough to move things forward.

Gundam Behind the Front *(2016, dir. Senzo Ueno, 8 minutes)*

Mobile Suit Gundam has a spotty track record in live action adaptation. Fandom is quick to lash out at attempts like *G-Saviour* and the *Gundam 0079: The War for Earth* video game, saying nothing of the Legendary film if it happens. Yet even amongst the difficult to please Gundam community, one live action piece has a general consensus of "getting it". This is *Gundam Behind the Front*.

The piece is a mockumentary set some time after the one-year war that defines the franchise. It interviews survivors about 50 years afterward with a Federation veteran speaking English and a Zeon one speaking Russian. Make of that what you will, but it's interesting that generally live action Gundam attempts have been English-heavy. There's not really much in the way of action, just testimonial to the horror of war and pleading to not forget the wonders of Earth. All thematically on-point for the series. The piece ends with some clips from the *anime* and the life-size RX-78 Gundam that used to be on display in Odaiba. It's surprisingly mellow for what's essentially a commercial for a museum and model kit line.

If you want more action-packed live action Gundam, there's always the model kit

commercials that Koichi Kawakita directed in the 1980s.

Sand Whale and Me *(2017, dir. Mamoru Oshii, 25 minutes)*

Sand Whale and Me is technically a series of five shorts, all produced for Adult Swim. Watching them together they make a single 25-minute experience, shorter if you skip the credits. The miniseries is part of a minor cinematic universe constructed by Mamoru Oshii. It started with the *Assault Girl* segment in the anthology *Eat and Run: 6 Beautiful Grifters* (2007). This was a sequel to 2006's *Female Fast Food Grifter*, which was a spinoff from *The Secret Lives of Fast Food Grifters*, which itself can be traced back to 1987's *The Red Spectacles*, and before that, surprisingly, to an episode of *Urusei Yatsura*. That was followed up with *Assault Girl 2*, a segment in the 2008 anthology *Kill*. It was then followed by the 2009 theatrical feature *Assault Girls*, which features a pre-*Pacific Rim* Rinko Kikuchi. Further muddying things, elements of this world appear to be taken from Oshii's 2001 film *Avalon* and 2014 *Garm Wars*. It appears that somewhere there's a larger picture that only Oshii himself is privy to.

The series features KFC (Hinako Saeki) wandering an alien planet seeking monstrous sand whales to hunt as in Assault Girls. Yet the limited plot is almost inconsequential. The piece is almost entirely an aesthetic exercise. The whole thing replicates the feel of a video game in live-action, with stilted motions, menus popping up at character actions and displays of character level and health. It's all accompanied by Kenji Kawai's haunting majestic score which feels out of a game and gorgeous costume design by Dango Takeda. The end result shows off both Oshii's eye for "cool" and his quirky sense of humor, too often under-appreciated by western critics. Also, there's no dialog, which is a massive improvement over the phonetic English in *Assault Girls*.

Paleonaut *(2017, dir. Eric McEver, 16 minutes)*

Slightly off-track from the other titles mentioned here, *Paleonaut* is a title I'd not be aware of had I not met director Eric McEver at a tokusatsu-themed bar. We wound up chatting about independent film projects, such as his work helping out on Daisuke Sato's *Howl from Beyond the Fog*. Eric gave me a copy of his own short, and I absolutely loved it, so I'm paying that forward now.

The picture is essentially about a colonist training in a time-travel program to go settle in the distant past. While we do get a miniscule glimpse of some dinosaurs towards the end, it's more about the angst of traveling back in time and the isolation of leaving the world you know including a potential budding romance. It ends with the mind-bending notion of realizing your own death has already taken place epochs before. It's high-concept, even if the notion of time-traveling colonists is problematic. It may prove a more character-focused diversion from your usual routine.

Female Weapon 701 (女兵器701, *Onna Heiki 701, 2017, dir. Kiyotaka Taguchi, 5 minutes)*

Fans of short films should definitely follow the *Tetsudon* anthology series. The annual, self-described "foolish" series began in 2014

with *Fool Japan: ABCs of Tetsudon*. It ever since has stressed collecting low-budget, independent films around a single theme. Naturally, *kaiju* and giant heroes are a recurring motif but 2017's anthology, *Tetsudon: Kaiju Dream Match*, was dedicated to the theme exclusively. It also attracted the most attention, with 28 shorts across nearly two hours. The likes of Yoshihiro Nishimura (*Tokyo Gore Police*), Hideki Oka (*Ultraman Saga*), Kengo Okuno (*Tokyo Abandonment Order Garateia*), and Bueno (*Gun Caliber*) participated with Sion Sono also showing up as an actor. Naturally Kiyotaka Taguchi, as a leader of practical *kaiju* effects in the modern era, was immediately involved. His short uses the *kaiju* that was designed as a mascot for the anthology.

The piece has a robot pilot in the midst of a battle against a *kaiju*. She accidentally knocks down the side of a love hotel, catching her boyfriend and friend in bed together. The battle is completely put on hold while she confronts the two-timer. The rampaging monster looks on perplexed. It's humorous, especially when considering that it features a couple of Ultraman actors (Haruka Momokawa and Takaya Aoyagi) who wouldn't be allowed to address such content on a children's show. The robot design is just a giant version of actress Misaki Izumi with some fancy gauntlets and goggles but iconic. It is a memorable piece of the anthology as a whole that it's always featured on the posters. Quite a few who've seen the short comment that they wish it were a whole series.

Kaiju Dream Match has never been released on home video. Taguchi, however, has released a Blu-ray collection of *Female*

Weapon 701 along with *Zone*. That contains his segment from *ABCs of Tetsudon* and *Delta* (his segment from 2015's *Tetsudon: Fool Japan*). Taguchi would go on to spearhead the Amateur Kaiju Movie Contest, so the process may have been inspirational.

ZVP *(2017, dir. Junya Okabe, 8 minutes)*

The very premise of this delightful short might be considered a spoiler. If you wish to proceed with reading this, do so at your own risk. *ZVP* was a fan-film short that Junya Okabe and his studio Blast did around the time of their *Silver Kamen/Super Robot Red Baron* crossover flick *Bravestorm*. It is also a crossover, celebrating anniversaries of two iconic film franchises. Namely the 55th anniversary of Zatoichi and the 30th of Predator. It's much more than a Predator-appears-in-samurai-times spin, though. Most of the short features Shun Sugata as the titular blind swordsman slashing his way through a far more colorful assortment of adversaries than any proper Zatoichi movie has. It feels like it could easily be part of the same world as *Basilisk* or *Ninja Scroll*. Assassins have anachronistic cyborg enhancements from chaingun chests to hot-iron katanas. The alien adversary doesn't appear until the end, but is still awesomely realized. It makes you wonder how even a professional studio could be blowing so much money on a fan production. The answer, most likely, is that this is a demo reel to get people talking. Official or not, this is still one of the greatest things to happen to the Predator franchise since the original picture, even counting a short-lived cross promotion with *Baki the Grappler*. It's a go-to for any Zatoichi marathon as well.

Godzilla Appears in Sukagawa (ゴジラ須賀川に現る, *Godzilla Sukagawa ni Genru, 2018, dir. Kenji Suzuki, 14 minutes*)

Much hullabaloo has been made about a Godzilla short produced for Godzilla's 64th anniversary, only available for viewing at the Eiji Tsuburaya Museum in Sukagawa. It features a reconstructed version of the original 1954 Godzilla costume and is directed by Kenji Suzuki (special effects director for *Godzilla 2000* and *Godzilla vs. Megaguirus*). I've heard fans say things like *"This is how Toho should do their next theatrical release"*. I have to disagree, because I think it's worth explaining and tempering people's expectations. While this is a fun little short, it's not, and I imagine was never intended to be of theatrical quality. Some museums do have theatrical-quality shorts, like the Ghibli museum, but that's practically an amusement park. The Tsuburaya museum is basically a library that takes up half a floor of a community center. There's no proper theater to watch the short like Ghibli or the Tezuka museum have, just a TV in the corner that plays it on loop. It's pretty cool for what it is and admission is free. Because it's hard to get there and the short is elusive elsewhere, it often gets misconstrued as what people want it to be, rather than what it actually is.

The short starts with Godzilla approaching the museum in the daytime. That was mostly done by superimposing Godzilla over static shots of the neighborhood, while you see local residents running away in panic. Some of them are looking at the camera or laughing, but I'm sure it was a fun project for the community ala the Dojo Studios movies produced at G-FEST. Sukagawa residents can go see themselves, their neighbors and their kids running from Godzilla and have a good chuckle at it.

Then it turns to night and we get the model work that was in a more widely-seen Boss Coffee commercial the same year. Some maser tanks roll out and Godzilla melts them with his breath. This part fares way better than the earlier "Godzilla photoshopped into the street outside" scenes. Yet the miniatures are sparse. It still feels like something filmed on a set for a TV production, not a proper movie. Again, that's cool for what the short was made for, a promo for the museum. If they had been selling the short, I would certainly have bought a copy. It probably won't be available as something other than a special feature on a larger release.

Kaiju Ward Gallas (シリーズ怪獣区 ギャラ ス, *Series Kaiju-ku Gyarasu, 2019, dir. Ryotaro Kogushi, 17 minutes*)

Gallas (as it is commonly Romanized) is another mysterious *tokusatsu* dead-end. This was first announced as a new series for Toei's *Tokusatsu Fan Club* streaming service. It even has the word *"Series"* in the title implying that more pieces are on the way. Yet, over a year later, there has been no follow-up on exactly what the project was intended to be. What we have gotten seems like it could be the first episode of an *Ultra Q*-like anthology, so it's interesting to watch and speculate on what could have been.

The short starts with a shadowy traveling saleswoman (*Hurricaneger*'s Nao Nagasawa) welcoming us to the *"Kaiju Ward"*. Likely to have been the brand, before *"Gallas"* appears as the name of the segment. The name, while shared with soccer star William Gallas, likely comes from the shrieking *"gya"* (like in Gyaos) and *"karasu"*, meaning "crow". It's no surprise that the piece features a giant crow monster. We cut to the inside of a bar, where a man (*Kyuranger*'s Keisuke Minami) dumps his girlfriend (Makoto Okunaka) and hits on the saleswoman. In a very J-horror "woman scorned" twist, the ex-girlfriend merges with a crow spirit. The giant monster stalks the poor guy across the city, to some of the best miniature effects work Toei has ever produced. Perhaps the project was too ambitious for the meager budget of a niche streaming service. That said, we can still appreciate the short that did get produced.

Godziban (ゴジばん, *2019, dir. Jun Shimazaki, 10 minutes*)

Toho is one of the most iron-handed entities when it comes to the depiction of their IP in the West. Yet they actually have a long tradition of fan engagement campaigns that get folded into canon. These include the Children Monster University contest that led to the creation of Jet Jaguar in *Godzilla vs. Megalon* and the script contest where *Godzilla vs. Biollante* was devised. The latest example of this sort of creative crowdsourcing is the *GEMSTONE Creators Audition*. This was a joint venture between Toho and Alphaboat to find new talent via YouTube and social media. Their inaugural competition in February of 2019 was to make a fan film focusing on Toho's most recognizable icon: Godzilla. The prize for the selected submission was 3 million yen. More importantly, this is one of the cases where artists reap the rewards of exposure: Shinji Higuchi was a judge and the winners were offered opportunities to develop projects with Toho.

Naturally, over 1000 hopeful amateurs applied to the Godzilla *GEMSTONE* competition. One of six winners was the puppet troupe Atelier Koganemushi. They had previously done the 2004 puppet play *Gekigodzi* and a Godzilla-Gamera-Ultraman- Kamen Rider crossover for the 1996 Hero Festival. They also did the Ultraman tie-ins *Ultra P*, *Ultramanland* and *Ultraman M730*, the AKB48 collaboration *Unfortunate Sentai Tanaminshii* and puppet effects for the adaptation of Junji Ito's *Marronnier*. From their reward for their submission, *Monster Puppet Theater Godziban*, the troupe was able to spin out a weekly series. This ran on YouTube for 12 episodes. They also did a live performance at the 2019 Godzilla Festival. The cute, quirky show consists of various shorts. These include hijinks with the three Godzilla brothers (Godzilla, Little and Minilla), a small second-form Shin Godzilla (*Kamata-kun*) getting into improbable situations with various human actresses, Jet Jaguar cartoons and Hedorah as an old man.

While on the subject, the other *GEMSTONE* submissions are worth checking out as well. Many have also pointed out similarities between the Godzilla design in the also award-winning *G vs. G GEMSTONE* short from Takuya Uenishi and Hikaru Yamane and the cameo Godzilla makes in the *Shinkansen Henkei Robo Shinkalion* movie. Uenishi and Yamane had both contributed to *Shin Godzilla*'s animation and the former actually got to work on *Shinkalion* based on the success of *G vs. G*. The contest doesn't only benefit its champions. All finalists get their work posted on YouTube, bringing attention to artists who otherwise may not get it. For example, by submitting a short of Godzilla fighting his original character Lequio, Hironobu Nakashima was able to bring attention to his work. That started a crowdfunding campaign for a *Lequio* DVD release. Director Hiroto Yokokawa also got noticed for his somber, contemplative submission *Hedorah: Silent Spring*. This was anticipating his wider kaiju debut *The Great Buddha Arrival*. While the second *GEMSTONE* audition was focused on promoting Japanese tourism, the third one will be focused on Ultraman. It's exciting to see what may materialize from that round of submissions.

Honorable Mentions

•Giant Beast Planet (1974)

A pitch reel for an unproduced Tsuburaya show. This was their first foray into the combined miniature/anime "stereoscopic animation" technique that their later shows *Bornfree* and *Izenborg* deployed.

•The Time Tunnel (1974)

The Time Tunnel is also kind of a prototype for *Bornfree*. This 14 minute short combines live actors with stop motion monsters in what's probably the closest to a Harryhausen effect as Japan's ever gotten. The director, Minoru Kujirai, worked for Toei animation doing *anime* before transferring to Tsuburaya in the 70s. He wound up working on both *Giant Beast Planet* and *Bornfree*, not to mention *Ultraman Leo*, *Aztekaiser* and *Tokyo: The Last Megalopolis*.

·The Baby Monster Which Mako Picked Up Resembles a Crab but Seems Very Exuberant (1983)
This was Minoru Kawasaki's piece inspired by *E.T.* The short's winning combination of "monster + cute young girl" led to the creation of *Terrestrial Defense Girl Iko* and thus his professional fame.

·Buddhism Force Buddhaman (1983)
A Super Sentai spoof playing on religious themes. Buddhist heroes fight against Abrahamic alien invaders. This was followed up with the feature-length *Buddha Powers* (2003), in which an Ultraman-sized Buddha battles aliens.

·"Modzilla Raids Again" on What a Fantastic Night (1983)
A comedy sketch that is both Akihiko Hirata's final *kaiju* appearance and Yoshiko Tanaka's first.

·All of Mighty Lady (1984)
The first entry of the long-running *Mighty Lady* franchise, distributed by Daiei during their stint between Gamera films.

·Appleseed Prelude (1988)

A live action, three-minute tie-in to the OVA version of Masamune Shirow's *manga*.

·Gamera vs Garasharp concept movie (1991)
A bonus feature on the Gamera laserdisc collection summarizing a movie that Noriaki Yuasa would have liked to make.

·Kamen Rider World (1994)
A theme-park attraction bringing together the two heroes from Keita Amemiya's Kamen Rider movies. This was also his first outing filmed in 3D. There is also a Super Sentai World and Toei Hero Daishugo that crosses Super Sentai and Metal Heroes.

·Wanigon vs. Gamaron (2000)
A crossover of two characters produced for Nitto plastic model kits in the 1960s.

·Rolling Bomber Special (2001)
Part of the *SMAP* Short Films series, this Super Sentai spoof sees a team of heroes challenging a regular civilian who has no idea what they're talking about.

·The Messenger (2002)
Ryuhei Kitamura's contribution to the *Jam Films* anthology. This has elements

that he would later use in Longinus, as well as star Kazuki Kitamura who would go on to feature in his *Godzilla: Final Wars*. *Jam Films* has many memorable segments, but this was selected because it's the first in the collection.

·Skullman: Prologue of Darkness (2007)
The live-action prologue of the *Skull Man* anime series based on Shotaro Ishinomori's proto-Kamen Rider dark hero. It was not included on the North American DVD release of the show, which is a shame.

·Gunhed 2025 (2013)
A new short movie by original *Gunhed* effects director Koichi Kawakita. It is available exclusively as a DVD packaged with Gunhed model kits. Kawakita had directed a number of commercials for Gundam kits throughout the 1980s, so this was in some ways a return to his roots.

·Space Monster Numaguirus (2015)
A kaiju short that was Takayuki Hosonuma's graduation project. He has since gone on to a commercial career, including filming ads for the giant girl *manga* *OniDeka*.

•Z: The last summer on earth (2015)
A zombie short from *Undertaker*'s Naoyoshi Kawamatsu.

•Jet Jaguar- Project M11 (2016)
A fan-film pitting an edgy version of *Godzilla vs. Megalon*'s Jet Jaguar against a more Terminator-like M11 from *Godzilla vs. King Ghidorah*. Robert Scott Field reprises his role. Made by Overload Films of *Zella* and *Gemu*.

•Tokyo Abandonment Order Garateia (2016)
A *kaiju* movie made by Osaka University of Arts in response to the success of alumni Hideaki Anno with *Shin Godzilla* and the passing of its professor Koichi Kawakita. Since then, the Gunkan Web group have created the Gasaking mascot for Mitsuwa marketplace, participated in the *Tetsudon* anthology, and done some interesting work on the hero *Saberlcon*.

•

The Return of Izenborg (2017)
A special documentary on Tsuburaya's cult hero made for Arabic TV. This features a new effects sequence directed by Kiyotaka Taguchi.

C∧SSHERN

Kyashan "Casshern"
Shochiku, 4/24/2004 (*Heisei 16*), 141:56, Digital, HD (1080p), 2K Digital Intermediate (2.39:1), color, 6.1 channel sound

Crew
Producers: Hideki Miyajima, Toshiharu Ozawa, Toshiaki Watanabe
Associate Producers: Chiaki Noji, Makoto Tanaka
Line Producer: Hirohisa Muroki
Director/Director of Photography/Editor: Kazuaki Kiriya
Screenplay: Kazuaki Kiriya, Dai Sato, Shotaro Suga, Tatsuo Yoshida (anime *Casshan*)
Assistant Director of Photography: Shozo Morishita
Music: Shiro Sagisu
Production Design: Yuji Hayashida
Art Directors: Yoshihito Akatsuka, Yutaka Motegi
Lighting: Yoshimi Watabe

Assistant Director: Shorei Noma
Costumes: Michiko Kitamura
Makeup and Hair: Ryoji Inagaki
Concept Design: D.K.
Storyboards: Shinji Higuchi
Character Design: Tomo Hyakutake
Sound Recording: Masahito Yano
Sound Effects: Akihiko Okase
Sound Editor: Mizuki Ito
Visual Effects Supervisors: Toshiyuki Kimura, Koji Nozaki
CGI Supervisor: Haruhiko Shono
Lead Lighting Artist: Kaori Doi
Action Director: Yuta Morokaji

Cast
Yusuke Iseya (*Tetsuya Azuma/Casshern*)
Kumiko Aso (*Luna Kozuki*)
Akira Terao (*Dr. Kotaro Azuma*)
Kanako Higuchi (*Midori Azuma*)
Fumiyo Kohinata (*Dr. Kozuki*)
Toshiaki Karasawa (*Burai*)
Hiroyuki Miyasako (*Akubon*)
Mayumi Sada (*Sagure*)
Jun Kaname (*Barashin*)
Hidetoshi Nishijima (*Lieutenant Colonel Mikio Kamijo*)
Mitsuhiro Oikawa (*Kaoru Naito*)
Susumu Terajima (*Sakamoto*)
Hideji Otaki (*General Kamijo*)
Ryo (*San Ikegami*)
Maya Tsuruta (*Burai's Wife*)
Tetsuji Tamayama (*Sekiguchi*)
Yoko Moriguchi (*Mrs. Kozuki*)
Tatsuya Mihashi (*Dr. Furoi*)
Goro Naya (*Narrator*)

"There are always two sides to the story. I really wanted to say that we all have the seeds to do evil deeds, yet (are) capable of so much love."
-Kazuaki Kiriya (2008), Vantage Point Interviews

Casshern was one of the first quality live action *anime* adaptations. It is similar to Kerry Conran's *Sky Captain and the World of Tomorrow* (also 2004) but far better. *Casshern* is based on Tatsunoko's iconic *Robot Hunter Casshan* but represents a strong departure from its subject material. Director Kazuki Kiriya turns it into a grim parable about racial prejudice invoking Japan's wartime past. *Casshern* was also the first Japanese film to use a "digital backlot" workflow. With this, Kiriya creates an unreal but beautiful aesthetic, each frame like a *manga* panel brought to life.

PLOT

In a fascistic future, a five decade war between the East Asian Federation and Europa has ended with the Federation victorious. As a pocket of resistance arises in Eurasian Zone 7, the Federation mobilizes its army to snuff it out. The half century of war has caused heavy pollution and the populace of the Federation is not faring well. Sickness, mutation and deformity is widespread among the population. Dr. Azuma (Akira Terao) gives a presentation to the government, a military junta run by General Kamijo (Hideji Otaki). He claims to have discovered Neo-Cells in a primitive race of people. These are powerful mutant stem cells that can be used to grow tissue,

organs and cure any disease. Azuma is rebuffed, but bureaucrat Kaoru Naito (Mitsuhiro Oikawa) approaches him on behalf of the military, offering him unlimited funding. Azuma agrees when Naito suggests he could use this research to heal his ailing wife, Midori (Kanako Higuchi).

Azuma's son Tetsuya (Yusuke Iseya) gets engaged to his colleague Dr. Kozuki's daughter Luna (Kumiko Aso). The Azumas, Kozuki (Fumiyo Kohinata) and Luna pose for a family portrait, but an argument erupts. Dr. Azuma is enraged at Tetsuya for choosing to abandon his medical career and enlist in the military. Tetsuya is soon deployed to Eurasian Zone 7 where he is forced to murder civilians. Eventually, he is killed by a grenade booby trapped in a civilian's corpse.

Having not heard from Tetsuya for months, Azuma invites Dr. Kozuki to his lab for a demonstration. His Neo-Cell research is close to finished, but the grown organs are still not usable. Midori, by now, is almost blind. She has a vision of Tetsuya's spirit before an army messenger informs her of his death. The system in Azuma's laboratory malfunctions as a bolt of lightning strikes the facility. This causes the Neo-Cells to fuse together into human-like beings. The first Neo-Sapien (Toshiaki Karasawa) stands before Azuma. A terrified Naito orders the military to exterminate them but the leader and others escape the massacre. Luna encounters one of them (Hiroyuki Miyasako) and seeing that he's mute, she takes pity and hides him. The surviving Neo-Sapiens hijack a car and take Midori as a hostage. Azuma submerges Tetsuya's body into his Neo-Cell pool, resurrecting him. Kozuki and Luna flee with Tetsuya.

The Neo-Sapiens, meanwhile, flee to Zone 7, trekking through a contaminated forest and mountain range. At Kozuki's home, Tetsuya is in fragile condition with musculature overdeveloped enough to burst his skin. Kozuki puts him in a battle armor prototype he designed as life support. In Zone 7, the four surviving Neo-Sapiens take up residence in an abandoned castle where they find a horde of deactivated robots. The leader Burai vows to exterminate humanity. Reactivating the robots, they begin attacks on the Asian Federation.

Neo-Sapien Sagure arrives to kidnap Kozuki to work in their robot factories. The newly armored Tetsuya battles Sagure and defeats her. Dr. Kozuki dies, mortally wounded by Sagure. Luna and Tetsuya escape but come face to face with Burai's robot army. Tetsuya destroys many of his robots before taking on Burai himself.

Kamijo's son Mikio (Hidetoshi Nishijima) stages a bloody coup against his father. He takes command of the Federation, mobilizing it for war against the Neo-Sapiens. Sagure dies from her wounds battling Tetsuya as the Neo-Sapiens lament, vowing revenge. Tetsuya begs Luna to leave so she'll be safer. She then faints, sickened by the polluted forest. They are found by the kindly Dr. Furoi (Tatsuya Mihashi) who takes them to a village in Zone 7. This village happens to be the same one that Tetsuya and his battalion massacred. Regardless, Furoi treats Luna and saves her life. The people of Zone 7 are not terrorists and are merely treated brutally by the fascist Federation over racism and land disputes. As men from the town want to kill Tetsuya, Furoi tells him about "Casshern", a deity the locals used to believe in. The military soon arrives and begins massacring the villagers once again. Tetsuya defends the Zone 7 villagers from the army. This draws the attention of the Neo-Sapiens. Barashin (Jun Kaname), desperate to avenge Sagure, battles Tetsuya. Barashin brutally stabs him as Luna is mistaken for a villager and taken away by the army. Healing from his wound, Tetsuya takes on the name Casshern.

BACKGROUND

Casshern was based on *Robot Hunter Casshan*, an *anime* created by Tatsunoko founder Tatsuo Yoshida. It aired on Fuji TV from 1973 to '74. Yoshida (1932-1977) was one of the great luminaries of the *anime* medium. He created such iconic franchises as *Speed Racer* and *Gatchaman (Battle of the*

Planets). He tragically passed at the age of only 45 from liver cancer. Yet his company Tatsunoko, co-founded with his brothers, lives on; still one of Japan's premier anime producers.

Casshern is directed by Kazuaki "Kazz" Kiriya. Kiriya (1968-) was educated in the U.S. at Parsons School of Design. He got his start in graphic design, making album covers. Kiriya then branched out to directing music videos. One video he made for J-Pop sensation Hikaru Utada in 2002 was called *Sakura Drops*. Something of a dry run for *Casshern*, the video blended footage of Utada shot against a green screen with surreal computer generated imagery. Kiriya and Utada would marry soon afterward. Utada, later to sing end credit songs for the *Evangelion* Rebuilds, would provide *Casshern*'s theme song. Kiriya approached Tatsunoko Productions about doing a live action *Casshan* film. His reel and work on *Sakura Drops* swayed its brass.

PRINCIPAL PHOTOGRAPHY

Director Kiriya was a fan of *Robot Hunter Casshan* as a boy. The live action *Casshern*, however, is quite different from its source material. The film changes the main villians from evil androids to biologically created Neo-Sapiens. In the anime, the Burai character is a malfunctioned android that turns on humanity. In this film, he is a bitter medical abomination created by Azuma's experiments. Likely, by the time *Casshern* was in planning, the trope of man vs. machine was a little tired. *The Matrix* sequels and

Terminator 3 were dominating the box office and director Kiriya wanted to create something that stood out. The character of Dr. Azuma is also far darker as he was heroic in the child-oriented show. In the anime, Casshan even has a helpful robot dog named Friender. While the original video animation remake *Casshan: Robot Hunter* (1993) darkens the tone, it stays somewhat faithful. *Casshern*'s feel is darker and its themes more philosophical. Nonetheless there are shout-outs to the anime. The show's classic helmet is seen in Dr. Kozuki's armory and Dr. Furoi's dog is named Friender. *Casshern* was originally going to be a much lower budgeted film. The budget was increased significantly when Shochiku got involved to produce the picture.

Casshern was in production almost simultaneously with *Sky Captain and the World of Tomorrow* but released a few months earlier. Like that film and Robert Rodriguez' *Sin City*, *Casshern* was filmed mainly with actors in front of green screens. This technique, called a "digital backlot", was gaining popularity at the time. It now represents standard practice for many VFX sequences in Hollywood.

Principal photography on *Casshern* lasted only two months. During shooting, actor Hiroyuki Miyasako suffered conjunctivitis from having to rise from a pool with his eyes open. Star Yusuke Iseya broke his arm near the end of shooting as well, temporarily putting the brakes on production. *Casshern* would also be an early Japanese film to be digitally recorded. This is the movie's weakest link. The high definition equipment used was designed more for television production than films. As a result, parts of *Casshern* can look a little bit raw and "direct to video". The action choreography by Yuta Morokaji is impressive, akin to Yuen Woo-Ping's work.

ACTORS

The film features esteemed actor and Kurosawa veteran Akira Terao (1947-) as Dr. Azuma. *Zatoichi* and *Tora San* veteran Kanako Higuchi (1958-) plays Midori. It would also mark the last appearance of Tatsuya Mihashi (1923-2004), who died shortly after release. He was best known for playing Commander Genda in *Tora! Tora! Tora!* (1970). His esteemed career also includes Honda's *The Human Vapor*, Kurosawa's *The Bad Sleep Well* and *High and Low* and numerous Toho crime and spy flicks.

VFX AND POST PRODUCTION

When the film gets going, *Casshern*'s computer processed images are stunning and creative; looking like manga panels brought to life with living, breathing actors. *Casshern* contains over two thousand VFX shots. Post-production was a brutal six month race to the finish line for the 34 year old Kiriya, who also shot the movie. The all-digital nature of the film might be a turn off for some, but like *tokusatsu*, it has a fantastical unreality. Similar to *Sky Captain*, the film's aesthetic is unique. It's a "*Showa* steampunk" look combining the feel of Imperial Japan with retro futurism. One of the film's action

sequences was storyboarded by Shinji Higuchi. His work on the picture is unmistakable, bringing an additional dynamism to its images. Director Kiriya was impressed with Higuchi's storyboards but the VFX crew looked at how complex they were with dread.

MUSIC

The music by Shiro Sagisu is quite moody and effective. Sagisu (1957-) is a triple threat: a record producer and composer, particularly for anime. The son of Tomio Sagisu (Soji Ushio), the founder of *tokusatsu* studio P-Productions, Sagisu began composing and producing songs in the early 1980s. An early score was for Noburo Ishiguro's four part OVA *Megazone 23*. Most famous are his collaborations with Hideaki Anno. Sagisu first composed the music for Anno's Jules Verne-inspired *Nadia: The Secret of Blue Water* (1990-91). Best known is his score for Anno's beloved/infamous *Neon Genesis Evangelion* (1995-96). Sagisu would also provide the soundtrack to *His and Her Circumstances* (1998-99). He went on to score much of Anno's subsequent work along with Shinji Higuchi's *Attack on Titan* duology (2015).

THEMES AND MOTIFS

When re-writing the story of *Casshern*, Kiriya was inspired by *Hamlet* and Dostoevsky. While not a fan pleasing adaptation of its original material, it stands on its own. Released after the U.S. invasion of Iraq, the film presents a powerful anti-war narrative.

Kiriya turns a run of the mill robot anime from the 1970s into a poignant story about racial prejudice. There's some apparent self examination of Japan's darker past along with commentary on Japan-China relations. The film's aesthetics suggest a *Man in the High Castle*-like future where Japan won World War II. The brutal "Zone 7" war flashbacks bring to mind Japan's atrocities in China. Like the Chinese, the denizens of Zone 7 are the ancestors of the Japanese living in the Federation. They are treated as subhuman by the Federation's people. The subplot involving Zone 7ers used for medical experimentation invokes Unit 731. The film's final plea is egalitarian: a naive yet charming *"We're all human, let's stop the fighting"* coda.

RELEASE AND LEGACY

Casshern was not entirely well received in Japan. It was voted "second worst" at the Bunharu Kichigo Awards, Japan's equivalent to the Razzies. Fans of the anime franchise, in general, were not pleased. This is a shame as *Casshern* is a breathtaking, creative and oddly moving film. It is one of Japan's better live action anime adaptations precisely because of its interpretative approach to the source material. *Casshern* was better received in the West and caught Hollywood's attention, however. Kiriya would eventually direct *Last Knights*, a 2015 Hollywood adaptation of *Chushingura* set in Medieval Europe. It starred A-listers Clive Owen and Morgan Freeman but was critically skewered. *Last Knights* lost any chance at commercial success due to the failure of Carl Rinsch's competing

47 Ronin adaptation with Keanu Reeves. The *Casshan* franchise would also get a reboot in anime form with the TV show *Casshern Sins* (2008-09).

ALTERNATE VERSIONS

The only known alternate version of *Casshern* was released directly to U.S. region 1 DVD by Dreamworks in October 2007. It's in Japanese with subtitles but is cut by a whopping 24 minutes; now running only 117 minutes. This version also has subpar subtitles and is not recommended.

AMERICAN HOME VIDEO HISTORY

The Dreamworks DVD was *Casshern*'s only U.S. home video release to date.

Further Viewing:

(2005)
ローレライ
Fuji TV/Toho, *Director*: Shinji Higuchi

Lorelei (aka *The Witch of the Pacific Ocean*) is based on a 2004 novel, *Shusen no Lorelei*, by Harutoshi Fukui. It blends alternate history Pacific War theatrics with science fiction. Fukui (1968-), called a Japanese Tom Clancy, was inspired to become a novelist by the works of Sakyo Komatsu. He worked as a security guard while penning his early novels. Fukui reached fame with his acclaimed 1999 novel *Aegis*. By 2005, three adaptations of

Fukui's novels were in production, with *Lorelei* the first. Often credited as Shinji Higuchi's directorial debut, this is actually inaccurate. Higuchi's first film as director was the straight-to-video *Mini Moni the Movie: A Sweet Adventure* (2002). *Lorelei* is one of Higuchi's most palatable films as solo director. It's a well made sci-fi/war epic with high production values.

Lorelei centers around Commander Masami (Koji Yakusho), a navalman disgraced for opposing kamikaze attacks. After the bombing of Hiroshima, Masami is put in command of submarine I-507 by the Imperial Navy. The submarine, a last minute gift from Nazi Germany, has a mysterious high tech sonar called the "Lorelei System". This is actually powered by a human being, Paula Atsuko Ebner (Yu Kashii). A Jewish-Japanese girl, she was experimented on in a concentration camp. Masami is given the objective to stop a third atomic bomb from being dropped on Tokyo. Yet Colonel Asakura (Shinichi Tsutumi) has his own ideas, planning to force Japan to surrender and turn over the Lorelei System.

Lorelei has some disturbingly neo-fascist elements but is well produced and entertaining. The film's plotting is tense and its pacing engaging. The special effects and VFX work is very anime-style with the climax even featuring storyboarding by Hideaki Anno. It boasts a nice mix of miniatures and CGI that, while not Hollywood quality, is endearing. Veteran modeler Toru Suzuki assisted in construction of the miniature I-507, one of his last jobs before his death in 2012. The composites haven't aged perfectly. Yet many are not far off from those in Peter Jackson's *King Kong*, released the same year. The influence of Wolfgang Petersen's *Das Boot* is apparent with claustrophobic submarine interiors. Higuchi and company also pay homage to old school war film directors like Shue Matsubayashi and Kihachi Okamoto. Matsubayashi's *Submarine I-57 Will Not Surrender* (1959) was a particular influence on both author Fukui and director Higuchi. *Lorelei*'s submarine, the "I-507", is only one digit away from that film's "I-57".

Lorelei certainly has its flaws. The biggest is that, ala Higuchi's later *Shin Godzilla*, the film presents a hawkish "Japan as victim" take. There's a subtle air of revisionist history and problematic depiction of Imperial Japan. *Lorelei* is both the modern equivalent and the antithesis to Ishiro Honda's *Atragon*. In *Atragon*, a proud and jingoistic Imperial navalman puts his nationalism aside. Jun Tazaki's Captain Jinguji chooses to fight for the sake of the world, not just Japan. Koji Yakusho's Masami, by contrast, is a humanist disgusted by Imperial Japan's use of suicide missions. In the end, to save his beloved Tokyo, he finds himself deploying those very tactics. Yet *Lorelei* is not outright jingoistic propaganda. It's a little more complicated and humanistic and Harutoshi Fukui has denied his intent to write a conservative story. *Lorelei* is ultimately about Japan's survival instinct. The film's American soldiers are sympathetic and the English-speaking actors are better than average for a Japanese film. This is because Higuchi had those scenes shot in Hollywood by American Cellin Gluck.

Lorelei also acknowledges Japan's complicity to Nazi Germany with disgust. Historically, however, Imperial Japan's medical experimentation was more scientifically advanced than the Nazis', not less.

The film's musical score is also a little overbearing and Hollywood style. Yet *Lorelei* especially comes to life for its thrilling finale. The film was a box office success in Japan and the 9th highest grossing film of 2005. As director, Higuchi showed promise with *Lorelei*. His subsequent work, however, tends to leave something to be desired with sundry highlights like *Giant God Warrior Appears in Tokyo*. Fukui, meanwhile, became an influential figure in the *Gundam* franchise. If you don't blink, you can see *Gundam* creator Yoshiyuki Tomino cameo in *Lorelei* as a naval officer.

SHINJI HIGUCHI
The Prodigy

樋口真嗣

9/22/1965-

"I originally envisioned much finer images than those we ended up creating, but budgetary constraints forced me to make a large number of changes."
-Shinji Higuchi, 1995

In his book *Tokyoscope* Patrick Macias called Shinji Higuchi the *"Gen-X answer to Eiji Tsuburaya"*. Indeed, like Tsuburaya, Higuchi has a tremendous talent for creating dynamic, compelling images. In addition to his special effects and directing careers, he is often called upon to draw *anime* storyboards. Born in 1965 in Tokyo, he grew up loving Toho's special effects films. His father took him to see *Submersion of Japan* and *Prophecies of Nostradamus* and a young Higuchi was blown away. He began to entertain dreams of getting into *tokusatsu* filmmaking. *The Human Vapor* and *Matango* were also particular favorites. Entering college, he joined Daicon Film, soon to become iconic anime studio Gainax. He would draw storyboards for some of their early works.

This would include their breakout *Daicon IV Animation* for the Nihon SF convention. He then worked as a production assistant for Koichi Kawakita and Teruyoshi Nakano's FX units on *Bye Bye Jupiter* and *The Return of Godzilla* (both 1984).

His big break would come shortly after, doing special effects for the feature length *The Eight-Headed Serpent Strikes Back*. Directed by Takami Akai, this independent film combined sci-fi tropes with the Japanese myth of *Yamata no Orochi*. It was considered impressive enough that Bandai bought its rights. Only in his early 20s, Higuchi was on the map as a rising talent. His storyboarding skills became in demand and he worked on anime and live action films. These include *The Wings of*

Honneamise (1987), *Tokyo, The Last Megalopolis* (1988), *Gunbuster* (1988-89), *Tetsuro Tanba's The Great Spirit World* (1989) and *Ultra Q The Movie: Legend of the Stars* (1990). In 1991, he helped out friend Tomoo Haraguchi with the special effects on *Mikadroid*. A modest budgeted film released directly to video, his work on it bolstered his career even further.

Higuchi also worked on Tsuburaya's attempt at an American Ultraman show, *Ultraman: The Ultimate Hero* (1993). He and friends Mahiro Maeda and Toshio Miike provided creature and mechanical designs. Recreating classic monsters from their childhood, they worked under Hollywood creature guru Kevin Hudson. The show was not purchased for airing in the U.S. and was something of a creative disaster. Yet their designs and the work of Hudson's team stand out. In 1993, at the age of only 28, Higuchi won the job to direct the special effects unit for Shusuke Kaneko's reimagining of Gamera. *Gamera: Guardian of the Universe* took him from rising talent to best special effects director in Japan. The effects sequences won universal acclaim and were produced on less than half the budget Kawakita was working with on the simultaneous Godzilla entries. Traditionally, the miniatures for *tokusatsu* sequences are built before camera angles are chosen. Higuchi planned his shots ahead of time. Model maker Toshio Miike then built the miniatures specifically for the shots. This kept the budget down while still allowing for impressive scale. Higuchi was brought back as special effects director on *Gamera 2: Attack of Legion* (1996) and *Gamera 3: Revenge of Iris* (1999). His work for each entry was more impressive than the last. All the while, he helped friend Hideaki Anno

with his masterwork *Evangelion*. Higuchi storyboarded certain episodes and helped script others. He also shot parts of the live action sequence in *The End of Evangelion*. Other work included the TV movie *Space Cargo Remnant 6* (1996), supervised by *Ghost in the Shell*'s Mamoru Oshii.

Higuchi continued his work as special effects director into the 2000s. He worked on *Sakuya, Slayer of Demons* (2000), *The Princess Blade* and Seijun Suzuki's *Pistol Opera* (both 2001). His feature length directorial debut was the little known *Mini-Moni the Movie: A Sweet Adventure* (2002). He also did storyboards for *Dragonhead* (2003), *Casshern* and Anno's *Cutie Honey* (both 2004). Additionally, he acted as production coordinator for the Tokyo leg of Quentin Tarantino's *Kill Bill Vol. 1*. Tarantino would use Toshio Miike's miniatures from *Godzilla, Mothra and King Ghidorah: Giant Monsters All-Out Attack* for shots of The Bride arriving in Tokyo.

In 2004, he started work on his next major film as director, *Lorelei*. Like a *tokusatsu Das Boot*, it was an alternate history World War II yarn based on a novel by Harutoshi Fukui. Higuchi's following project was *Sinking of Japan* (2006), an effects filled remake of *Submersion of Japan*. Its reception was very mixed, winning the Japanese equivalent of a Golden Raspberry. Higuchi followed it up with a remake of Kurosawa's *The Hidden Fortress: The Last Princess* (2008). He also storyboarded the "Operation Yashima" finale for Anno's *Evangelion 1.0: You Are (Not) Alone* (2007). He would provide storyboards for the next two *Evangelion* Rebuilds as well. Higuchi directed the stunning short film *God Warrior Appears in Tokyo* (2012) for

Anno's tokusatsu exhibition at the Tokyo Museum of Modern Art. This 10 minutes of destruction is Higuchi at top form, using practical techniques almost exclusively. He also co-directed *The Floating Castle* (also 2012), an adaptation of Ryo Wada's *jidai-geki* novel.

In 2014, he took up the task of adapting Hajime Isayama's *Attack on Titan* manga and anime to live action. This was ironic; Higuchi's scenes involving the Gyaos in *Gamera: Guardian of the Universe* were one of Isayama's main influences on *Titan*.

Higuchi's double-decker adaptation enraged some fans for its lack of faithfulness to the source material. Its visuals however, using a combination of old school *tokusatsu* effects and modern CGI, are stunning. With the two *Attack on Titan* films still in production, Toho hired Higuchi to direct their upcoming Godzilla film. Higuchi convinced Hideaki Anno to write it and co-direct. The two began filming *Shin Godzilla* with *Attack on Titan: The End of the World* not even picture-locked. Higuchi's next project is *Shin Ultraman*, also written by Anno.

Selected Filmography

Bye Bye Jupiter (1984) [production assistant]

The Return of Godzilla (1984) [production assistant]

The Eight-Headed Serpent Strikes Back (1985) [special effects]

Royal Space Force: The Wings of Honneamise (1987) [storyboards]

Tokyo, The Last Megalopolis (1988) [storyboards, continuity]

Gunbuster (1988-89) [storyboards]

Tetsuro Tanba's Great Spirit World (1989) [storyboards]

Ultra Q The Movie: Legend of the Stars (1990) [storyboards]

Nadia: Secret of Blue Water (1990-91, TV) [storyboards/co-director]

Mikadroid (1991) [special effects]

Otaku no Video (1991) [storyboards/live action segments]

"Ultraman: The Ultimate Hero" (1993, TV) [creature and mechanical design]

Gamera: Guardian of the Universe (1995) [special effects director]

Neon Genesis Evangelion (1995-96, TV) [storyboards/screenplay]

Gamera 2: Attack of Legion (1996) [special effects director]

Space Cargo Remnant 6 (1996) [special effects]

Neon Genesis Evangelion: The End of Evangelion (1997) [storyboards/live action sequences]

Gamera 3: Revenge of Iris (1999) [special effects director]

Sakuya, Slayer of Demons (2000) [special effects director]

The Princess Blade (2001) [special effects]

Pistol Opera (2001) [special effects]

Mini-Moni the Movie: A Sweet Adventure (2002) [director]

Dragonhead (2003) [storyboards, VFX design]

Casshern (2004) [storyboards]

Cutie Honey (2004) [storyboards]

Lorelei (2005) [director]

Sinking of Japan (2006) [director]

Evangelion 1.0: You Are (Not) Alone (2007) [storyboards]

The Last Princess (2008) [director]

Evangelion 2.0: You Can (Not) Advance (2009) [storyboards]

The Floating Castle (2012) [co-director]

God Warrior Appears in Tokyo (2012) [director]

Evangelion 3.0: You Can (Not) Redo (2012) [storyboards]

Attack on Titan (2015) [director]

Attack on Titan: The End of the World (2015) [director]

Shin Godzilla (2016) [co-director/VFX director]

Shin Ultraman (2021) [director]

SPACE BATTLESHIP YAMATO

Uchu Senkan Yamato "Space Battleship Yamato"
Toho/TBS/MBS/Robot Communications/Shogakukan, 12/10/2010 (*Heisei 22*), 138:34, 35mm,
Super 35, 2K Digital Intermediate (2.39:1), color, 6.1 channel sound

Crew

Executive Producers: Kazuya Hamana, Toshiaki Nakazawa
Co-Executive Producers: Hiroyuki Ishii, Takaaki Kabuto, Osamu Kamei, Akio Kobayashi, Hideki Matsuda, Masaji Nakao, Ryuichi Tatsumi, Kaori Watanabe, Yoshishige Shimatani
Producer: Nobuhiro Azuma
Line Producer: Shoichi Takeuchi
Director/VFX: Takashi Yamazaki
Screenplay: Shimako Sato, Yoshinobu Nishizaki (story), Leiji Matsumoto (story)
Director of Photography: Kozo Shibasaki
Editor: Ryoki Miyajima
Music: Naoki Sato
Music Producer: Kozo Araki
Music Coordinator: Daigo Mizoguchi
Music Engineer: Mikio Obata
Production Design: Anri Jojo
Art Directors: Masahide Nakazawa, Tetsuji Tatsuta
Assistant Cinematographer: Eiji Mukoyama

Gaffer: Sosuke Yoshikado
Sound Editing: Hitoshi Tsurumaki
Sound Effects: Kenji Shibasaki
Foley Artist: Akihiko Okase
Wardrobe: Rin Ishikawa
Hair/Makeup: Michiyo Miyauchi
Additional Hair Stylist: Kent Richard
Production Manager: Ichiro Nobukuni
Post-Production Manager: Kenny Kusaka
VFX Supervisor: Kiyoko Shibuya

Cast

Takuya Kimura (*Susumu Kodai*)
Meisa Kuroki (*Yuki Mori*)
Tsutomu Yamazaki (*Captain Juzo Okita*)
Toshiro Yanagiba (*Shiro Sanada*)
Naoto Ogata (*Daisuke Shima*)
Hiroyuki Ikeuchi (*Hajime Saito*)
Shin'ichi Tsutsumi (*Mamoru Kodai*)
Maiko (*Aihara*)

Reiko Takashima (*Doctor Sado*)
Toshiyuki Nishida (*Hikozaemon Tokugawa*)
Toshihiro Yashiba (*Yasuo Nanbu*)
Kazuki Namioka (*Saburo Kato*)
Takumi Saito (*Akira Yamamoto*)
Takahiro Miura (*Furuya*)
Kensuke Owada (*Kenjiro Ota*)
Kana Harada (*Sasaki*)
Junpei Ito (*Isaoka*)
Saya Ishikawa (*Shima's Wife*)
Seiji Hino (*Akagi*)
Ippei Sasaki
Miyu Sawaii (*Higashida*)
Bunki Suguira (*Shimada*)
Natsuhi Ueno (*Tobita*)
Yuichiro Hirose (*Segawa*)
Megumi Shoji (*Hoshino*)
Ryohei Aoki (*Jiro Shima*)
Yosuke Asari (*Ando*)
Yumiko Fujito (*Saito's Mother*)
Isao Hashizume (*Heikuro Todo*)
Kisuke Iida (*Nanba*)
Marika Matsumoto (*Nishina*)
Keisuke Minami (*Kazuhiko Sugiyama*)

Jun Mizukami (*Sukeharu Yabu*)
Kenji Motomiya (*Space Cavalier*)
Kazuki Muramatsu (*Nishio*)
Satoshi Nikaido (*Okita's Son*)
Shunsuke Oe (*Young Susumu Kodai*)
Takeru Taniyama (*Young Mamoru Kodai*)
Mae Otsuka (*Operator*)

Koichiro Takami (*Akira Nemoto*)
Maki Yamabayashi (*Inoue*)
Toshie Yanagi (*Honjo*)
Masato Yamaguchi (*Crew*)
Masato Ibu (*Dessla*, voice)
Isao Sasaki (*Narrator*)
Kenichi Ogata (*Analyzer*, voice)
Miyuki Ueda (*Iscander*, voice)
Ebizo Ichikawa

Teruyuki Kagawa
Keisuke Kamimura
Kazuki Kitamura
Hironori Koyama
Misaki Saijo
Kenta Suga
Tetta Sugimoto
Moe Tanaka
Yoji Tanaka
Madoka Terukina

"In April of 1945, the battleship Yamato set sail to bring a ray of hope into a time of utter despair. We do the same. The coordinates we were sent may be a trap. We may only be playing into the enemy's hands. But as long as there is one faint ray of light in the dark, as long as we have even a chance, we must go forward. That is the destiny of any ship named Yamato."

-Susumu Kodai (Takuya Kimura)

Space Battleship Yamato is one of Japan's biggest pop sci-fi phenomena alongside *Godzilla*. It is as iconic in Japan as *Star Wars* in the West. *Returner*'s Takashi Yamazaki brings Leiji Matsumoto and Yoshinobu Nishizaki's *anime* cels to vivid life. His *Space Battleship Yamato* bears a heavy Hollywood influence and plays into certain frustrating modern Japanese film trends. Nonetheless, it is an entertaining adaptation that does its monolithic source material justice. In spite of its Hollywood stylings, it still captures the property's unique "Japaneseness".

PLOT

In the year 2194, Earth is attacked by a mysterious alien force called the Gamilas. Five years later, humanity mounts a counter attack near Mars. The Gamilas are impervious to the Earth Defense Force fleet's weapons and most of the ships are destroyed. Corporal Mamoru Kodai (Shinichi Tsutsumi) sacrifices his life aboard his ship the *Yukikaze* so Captain Juzo Okita (Tsutomu Yamazaki) and his crew can escape.

The Earth has been lethally irradiated and a despairing humanity has retreated underground. Mamoru's brother Susumu (Takuya Kimura) scavenges the poisoned surface for scrap metal he sells to the military. One day he's hunting near the ruins of the World War II battleship *Yamato* when a projectile from space falls near him. Knocked unconscious, he awakens and finds the radiation around him gone along with an alien device. Susumu is rescued by Okita's returning crew. They find the device seems to contain schematics and coordinates. An enraged Susumu, learning of his brother's death, confronts Okita. He tries to deck Okita, but is hit by pilot Yuki Mori (Meisa Kuroki). Dr. Sado (Reiko Takashima) notes that Susumu has taken a lethal dose of radiation and yet survived.

As Okita returns, he finds out that the radiation is moving underground and humanity could be dead in a year. The coordinates in the capsule point to a far away planet called Iscander. Noting that Susumu survived a lethal dosage, Okita believes that on Iscander lies the secret to eliminating the radiation plaguing Earth. The battleship *Yamato* is rebuilt and retrofitted into a space battleship with a warp drive devised from the alien schematics. A call for volunteers with military and spacefaring experience is put out. Susumu Kodai, who once flew in a fighter squadron, re-enlists once more. The Gamilias launch a missile at Earth, targeting the *Yamato* before it can launch. Captain Okita orders the alien Wave Motion Cannon to be fired at the missile. Susumu aims it and destroys the projectile. The *Yamato* emerges from the explosion unscathed, winning its first victory against the Gamilias.

As the *Yamato* sets off on its journey of hope, Susumu is reunited with his former squadron members: the Black Tigers. He also meets Yuki who is still bitter towards him. The *Yamato* successfully manages to warp through space but Gamilas warships follow them in pursuit. As the Wave Motion Cannon is powered by the ship's warp engine core, the *Yamato*'s crew are unable to fire it. Okita decides to warp once the engine is recharged. The squadron is ordered to engage the Gamilas. Yuki

launches her fighter first, insistent on destroying the fleet herself. The Black Tigers soon join her and with the help of the *Yamato* the Gamilias fleet is destroyed. Yuki's ship is damaged by debris and her engine fails. Susumu goes after her, disobeying Okita's order to return to his post. Susumu successfully rescues Yuki and the Yamato warps just in time to evade an enemy barrage. For disobeying Okita, Susumu is put in the brig.

As the *Yamato* prepares to warp out of the Milky Way, Okita allows the crew members to contact their families on Earth. Shima (Naoto Ogata) tells Yuki why Susumu left the squadron. He caused an accident that led to the deaths of his parents and nearly killed Shima's pregnant wife. The *Yamato* warps and finds an abandoned Gamilas fighter craft adrift. As this happens, Okita has a heart attack. Dr. Sado tells Okita that his heart disease has progressed and he may not survive the voyage. The crew inspects the Gamilas ship and is attacked by its still-living pilot. The creature is seemingly killed, but its essence possesses one of the men: Saito (Hiroyuki Ikeuchi). Calling itself Dessla, the creature reveals that the Gamilas are part of a hive mind. They are not destroying the Earth, but terraforming it so they can live on it.

Susumu visits Okita, who thrusts him into the role of acting captain. The captured Gamilas fighter becomes a homing beacon, giving away the *Yamato*'s position. The Gamilas soon attack and crew members are trapped below deck. Susumu fires the

Wave Motion Cannon and destroys the main Gamilas ship. But a surviving Gamilas stealth fighter attaches itself to the lower hull and is primed to explode. Thinking quickly, Susumu orders Yuki to take out the lower deck, killing the trapped crew but saving the *Yamato*. Wracked with guilt, Susumu speaks with Captain Okita who tells him to persevere. Susumu then confronts Yuki and apologizes for giving the order. The two share a passionate embrace.

The *Yamato* soon arrives at Iscander but is attacked by a volley of Gamilas missiles. One of these projectiles obstructs the muzzle of the Wave Motion Cannon, disabling it. Unable to defend the ship, Susumu makes the hasty choice to randomly warp. The *Yamato* survives the warp and winds up on the other side of Iscander. Susumu and crew are surprised to see that this side of the planet is lifeless like the irradiated Earth. They realize that Iscander and Gamilas are the same planet. The crew suspects a trap, but Susumu decides to mount an attack with the Black Tigers.

BACKGROUND

To call *Space Battleship Yamato* the *Star Trek* of Japan is no exaggeration. Existing in television *anime, manga*, original video animation, anime movie and live action film forms, it's an iconic property. It was initially conceived by producer Yoshinobu Nishizaki. Nishizaki (1934-2010) was eager to produce a hit space anime TV show. He originally

envisioned a darker concept, a sort of interstellar version of *Lord of the Flies*. He hired manga artist and animator Leiji Matsumoto to help him develop the project. Matsumoto (1938-), conceived a different story. An optimistic tale where Japan's most famous battleship is retrofitted with alien technology and sent on a journey of hope.

Nishizaki liked Matsumoto's take. *Space Battleship Yamato* was made into a 26 episode series animated by Academy Productions and Group TAC. It ran from October 6th, 1974 to March 30th, 1975. On the first run, it was not a ratings sensation. Yet in 1977, a compilation film running just over two hours long was released. It was the same summer *Star Wars* was top movie in the 'states, so space operas were on everyone's mind. The *Space Battleship Yamato* movie wound up grossing more in Japan than *Star Wars* itself. While the U.S. was gripped with breathless anticipation for *The Empire Strikes Back*, Japan experienced its own "*Yamato* fever". The franchise created numerous fans. It was influential on many future anime works including Yoshiyuki Tomino's *Gundam*, Shoji Kawamori's *Macross* and Hideaki Anno's *Nadia: Secret of Blue Water* and *Neon Genesis Evangelion*.

Droves of media followed. First came a theatrical film conclusion to the series, *Farewell to Space Battleship Yamato*, released in 1978. The finale, where Susumu Kodai sacrifices himself and the *Yamato* is destroyed to save Earth, angered fans. The film was thus retconned and removed from official canon. A new series, *Space Battleship Yamato II*, was made continuing the adventures of the *Yamato*. This aired from October 1978 to April 1979. *Yamato: The New Voyage*, came out next, a TV movie spin-off in 1979. Another theatrical film directed by Toshio Masuda, *Be Forever Yamato*, was released in 1980. A third and less well received series, *Space Battleship Yamato III*, aired from October 1980 to April '81. It suffered from budget cuts and a truncated story arc. The original franchise was wrapped with one final movie: *Final Yamato* (1983). With a whopping over two and a half hour run time, it satisfyingly wrapped all the story's loose ends and grossed 1.72 billion yen.

In the U.S., the first two *Space Battleship Yamato* shows came to stateside television in an edited and dubbed version called *Star Blazers*. The characters' names were Anglicized and the rebuilt *Yamato* became the "Argo". The cuts mostly consisted of sanitizing the show for child viewing. Cuts for violence and sexuality were actually minimal. Amusingly, Dr. Sado's alcoholism is removed, his sake becoming "spring water". References to World War II are also taken out, though the ruins of the *Yamato* are still referred to by name. *Star Blazers* first aired in California and was particularly popular there.

Since *Final Yamato*, many attempts to reboot the franchise have been made. Such attempts were hampered by a legal dispute over ownership between Nishizaki and Matsumoto. A sequel OVA, *Yamato 2520*, was produced by Nishizaki in the mid '90s with design work from *Blade Runner*'s Syd Mead. It had to be prematurely ended when

Matsumoto sued. A television anime called *New Space Battleship Yamato* also failed to make it past pre-production. An OVA called *Great Yamato No. Zero* instead was produced in 2004 as Nishizaki settled with Matsumoto. Nishizaki produced and directed a feature film continuation of the Yamato saga, *Yamato: Resurrection*, in 2009. It was planned to be the first of several films but the franchise wound up going in a different direction.

All this time, plans for a live action movie adaptation were also afoot. In the 1990s, Disney had interest in producing a live action *Star Blazers* movie. The film would have only vaguely resembled the show. As is typical of live action anime films in Hollywood, it languished in pre-production hell for years. The live action rights reverted to Nishizaki after Michael Eisner left Disney as CEO. Nishizaki began developing a live action film version in 2005 with TBS. Production was formally announced at U.S. anime convention Otakon.

Shinji Higuchi was courted as director. Higuchi was unavailable so popular hitmaker Takashi Yamazaki was a natural choice. Yamazaki (1964-) made the breakout sci-fi hits *Juvenile* (2000) and *Returner* (2002). *Returner* beat out *Star Wars Episode II: Attack of the Clones* at the Japanese box office and was released stateside. This was followed by the beloved *Always: Sunset on Third Street* based on Ryohei Saigan's manga. It was a massive hit and begat a sequel which featured a Godzilla-themed dream sequence. The script for *Space Battleship Yamato* was written by Shimako Sato. Now the wife of Yamazaki, Sato (1964-) is a talented filmmaker in her own right. A graduate of the London International Film School, she directed the first two *Eko Eko Azarak* horror films.

Space Battleship Yamato was an early Japanese film to employ digital pre-visualization in lieu of drawn storyboards. While some productions still prefer hand drawn boards, more VFX-heavy films, especially in Hollywood, use computer-based pre-viz. Crude digital mock-ups of scenes and special effects shots are created in pre-production. These can sometimes be useful to the animators as a basic structural skeleton for the finished film's CG modeling.

PRINCIPAL PHOTOGRAPHY

There are marked differences between the *anime* and live action versions of *Space Battleship Yamato*. In the anime, Yuki Mori is the only female crew member. In the live action version there are numerous female officers on board. Dr. Sado was changed to a woman, though the character's comical alcoholism and pet cat is kept. Deck officer Aihara is also now female, played by the Japanese American Maiko. Susumu Kodai, played by SMAP's Takuya Kimura (1972-), is more rebellious. He's surlier and less respectful to Okita than his anime counterpart. Kuroki's live action Yuki Mori is also feistier than the demure anime girl.

Director Yamazaki was given a 22 million dollar budget, one of the largest in Japanese film history. Principal photography for *Space Battleship Yamato* began on October 12, 2009. Plot-wise, Sato's script does not attempt the foolhardy task of condensing three seasons and several movies of material into one film. Instead, Takashi Yamazaki and Shimako Sato give us a condensed version of the story with *Star Wars*-like beats. This was a smarter approach. The ending, however, invokes the controversial finale of *Farewell to Space Battleship Yamato*. In both, Susumu Kodai sacrifices himself and the *Yamato* to save humanity. Takashi Yamazaki's style also brings a strong Hollywood influence to the project. He directs with Ridley Scott-like polish and augments his shots with lens flair ala JJ Abrams. Abrams' *Star Trek* (2009) had just been released when *Space Battleship Yamato* began production. It was likely a significant influence. Both films repackage iconic properties in sleek, audience-pleasing fashion. Kimura's cockier reimagining of Susumu Kodai is akin to *Star Trek*'s new Captain Kirk played by Chris Pine. There's a sleek superficiality to *Space Battleship Yamato* that is a little irritating. It has some of the annoying "made by committee" hallmarks of modern Japanese cinema and Hollywood high concept filmmaking. It ends with a corny song by Steven Tyler: a saccharine, Micheal Bay-like touch it could have done without. Yet *Space Battleship Yamato* is saved by its relentless "fun" factor and relative faithfulness to the source material.

ACTORS

The grizzled Captain Okita is played by stalwart character actor Tsutomu Yamazaki (1936-). Yamazaki's breakout role was as the kidnapper in Kurosawa's *High and Low* (1963). He also appeared in *Red Beard* (1965) and *Kagemusha* (1980) for Kurosawa. For Juzo Itami, he appeared in *The Funeral* (1984), *Tampopo* (1986) and *A Taxing Woman* (1987). Yamazaki was also in Hiroshi Teshigahara's *Rikyu* (1989). The voices of Kenichi Ogata, Masato Ibu, Miyuki Ueda and Isao Sasaki can be heard. All four did voice work for the original anime series.

VFX AND POST PRODUCTION

Principal photography for *Space Battleship Yamato* lasted only a few months. The extensive VFX by Yamazaki's own Shirogumi, however, took far longer. Takuya Kimura saw James Cameron's *Avatar* as post production began. This inspired him to lobby to improve the quality and lavishness of the CGI. The influence of *Avatar* can be seen in the Gamilas/Iscander scene. Kimura even agreed to sacrifice part of his salary to keep the film from going over budget. The *Yamato* herself was not a miniature but completely computer generated. In a rarity for a Japanese film, there are dozens of shots that are entirely VFX. The live action footage shot by Yamazaki on-set makes heavy use of green screens. The film's compositing is nearly Hollywood quality. The CGI modeling and texture is extraordinary. The numerous explosions were particularly complicated. They required the animation of countless

elements and particles. CGI is more of an artisan craft than given credit, requiring strong aesthetic talent and spatial knowledge in its animators. It's quite apparent Yamazaki's team took *Space Battleship Yamato* to heart.

REAL WORLD

The *Yamato* herself was a masterwork of modern warship building. In Japan, the battleship occupies a sentimental cultural significance akin to the *Titanic* in the U.S. Laid down in 1937, she was built at Kure Naval Base. She was the pride of both the Imperial Navy and the Japanese people themselves. The *Yamato* was launched in summer of 1940 and commissioned after Pearl Harbor. Armed with 45 Calibre Type 94 naval guns, the largest ever affixed to a warship, she was a floating fortress. She became the flagship of the Japanese Combined Fleet and it was from her bridge that Admiral Isoroku Yamamoto commanded the Battle of Midway. After the defeat at Midway, the tide turned badly against Japan and its navy. In April 1945, during Japan's disastrous defense of Okinawa, the *Yamato* was sent on a suicide mission to protect the island. The crew was to beach the *Yamato* on Okinawa's shores and fire its cannons at the U.S. fleet until destroyed. The ship did not make it. The Americans intercepted radio transmissions and learned of *Yamato*'s whereabouts. She was spotted, attacked and eventually sunk off the coast of Kyushu. Most of her crew fought to the death and did not survive. Like the *Titanic*, undersea expeditions to examine the wreckage with the newest technology are often undertaken.

THEMES AND MOTIFS

Space Battleship Yamato is a thematically rich Japanese pop culture property. It combines a fairy tale militarism like *Star Wars* with the science and egalitarianism of *Star Trek*. Its soft nationalism rubs some audiences outside of Japan the wrong way. The very concept of a battleship from Imperial Japan salvaged and turned into humanity's last salvation could be considered problematic. Yet *Space Battleship Yamato*'s nationalism is harmless and humanistic at its heart. It's a story of Japan's *"Yamato spirit"* saving the world rather than conquering it; used for good instead of fascistic evil.

For Yamazaki's live action film, the nationalism is sharpened up a bit. The themes are a little more aggressive in line with the attitude of modern Japan. Yet the humanism underlying *Space Battleship Yamato*'s themes is overall preserved. While Yamazaki's film adopts a Hollywood flavor, the unique "Japaneseness" is not lost. The sense of soft nationalism is a little bit more aggressive compared to the anime. The *Yamato*'s role in World War II is mentioned affectionately. Susumu Kodai and other characters' sacrifices are also *kamikaze*-like to Western eyes. Yamazaki's following *The Eternal Zero* would be accused of outright jingoism and glorifying the kamikaze. Yet context is important. Unlike a kamikaze pilot, Kodai sacrifices his life not for the nationalistic honor of his country but to save the human race. The Japanese spirit, at its best, is about laying down one's life for a cause greater than the self. *Space Battleship Yamato* is humanistic and not jingoistic at heart. Yamazaki's film, overall, preserves this mindset.

RELEASE AND LEGACY

At the box office, the film was a massive success in Japan. It far outgrossed the prior year's *Yamato: Resurrection*. In Japan it even beat out *Harry Potter and the Deathly Hallows Part I*. Only a month prior to the live action film's release, Yoshinobu Nishizaki passed away. The franchise was thus given a complete reboot with *Space Battleship Yamato 2199*. This was a condensed remake of the anime's first season with state of the art animation. It was released as both a series of compilation films and on television from 2012-13. This was followed by a remake of the second season, *Space Battleship Yamato 2202*, in 2017. Takashi Yamazaki, meanwhile, followed the success of *Yamato* with a third *Always* film in 2012 and the aforementioned World War II drama *The Eternal Zero* (2013).

ALTERNATE VERSIONS

Space Battleship Yamato was distributed in the U.S. by Funimation through its "Giant Ape" subsidiary. It got a small theatrical run starting in October 2013. The English dubbed version is competent. It uses Funimation's stock of anime dubbers including Trina Nishimura as Yuki Mori.

Space Battleship Yamato was released to American DVD and Blu-ray in 2014.

Further Viewing:

Returner
(2002)
リターナー
Fuji TV/Robot Communications/Toho, *Director*: Takashi Yamazaki

Takashi Yamazaki's debut *Returner* beat out both Lucasfilm's *Attack of the Clones* and Ghibli's *The Cat Returns* at Japan's box office. It's a stylish, slick and polished little movie. With Hollywood style writing, *Returner* is predictable but brilliantly directed by Yamazaki. Teenaged soldier Milly (Anne Suzuki) is sent back from an apocalyptic future to prevent war with a race of aliens. She teams up with Triad hitman Miyamoto, played by Taiwanese-Japanese superstar Takeshi Kaneshiro. They soon find out that humans were the cause of the war, with a shipwrecked baby alien found that's more in line with *E.T.* than *Independence Day*. The creature is kidnapped by sociopathic mob boss Mizoguchi (Goro Kishitani), whom Miyamoto has a long, dark history with.

Returner is far from perfect, but is a quality piece of high concept cinema that shows off Yamazaki's promise as director. Feeling like a sci-fi thriller helmed by John Woo, *Returner* boasts a stylish flourish akin to Hong Kong action films. This is melded with Hollywood-style tropes and nods to *The Matrix*, Steven Spielberg and *12 Monkeys*. There are poignant moments, such as Milly breaking down in tears from her first hot meal in who knows. The English actors in the future flashbacks are amateurs, but give better than average performances for *gaijin* in a Japanese genre film. Kishitani's vile Mizoguchi feels akin to a character in a John Woo film. Indeed, the ensuing bullet ballet and fight choreography expertly copies the HK style. *Goke*'s Masaya Takahashi appears as an elderly, Mandarin-speaking Triad don. The CGI aliens are surprisingly impressive for a 2000s Japanese film. Katsuro Onoue, soon Shinji Higuchi's right hand man, had a major hand in the practical end of the visual effects. *Returner*'s plot gets more engaging as it goes along. The ending is very Hollywood style but with a tinge of Japanese bittersweetness. Overall, *Returner* cemented Yamazaki's reputation as an up-and-coming directorial force ala a Japanese JJ Abrams.

ALITA
BATTLE ANGEL
(2019)
20th Century Fox, *Director*: Robert Rodriguez

Alita: Battle Angel languished in pre-production hell for so long that a timeline where it exists as a released movie seems wrong. Nonetheless, it was worth the decades-long wait. *Alita* is based on Yukito Kishiro's acclaimed *manga Gunnm*. Kishiro

(1967-) was inspired by Osamu Tezuka's *Astro Boy* and Ridley Scott's *Blade Runner*. He imbued *Gunnm* with ahead of its time transhumanist themes. The live action film began production in the hands of James Cameron. Cameron was shown the anime OVA adaptation in the mid 1990s, courtesy of Guillermo Del Toro, and became obsessed with it. He spent 15 years developing the project, with the script alone taking five years to write. By the 2000s, CGI technology had advanced, spearheaded by motion capture technology Weta Digital developed for Peter Jackson's *The Lord of the Rings* trilogy. Cameron finally felt comfortable bringing *Alita* to the screen. Ultimately, he chose to make *Avatar* instead. He almost gave up on *Alita* after he decided to spend the remainder of his career on the *Avatar* sequels. Cameron then had a conversation with friend Robert Rodriguez. He was impressed with Rodriguez' enthusiasm for the project and hired him to direct.

Rodriguez adapts Kishiro's graphic panels with the same reverence he did Frank Miller's in *Sin City*. He mimics James Cameron's aesthetic style while adding his own flourish. It's most noticeable in a bar brawl sequence invoking *Desperado* and *From Dusk 'Till Dawn*. As is typical of anything with Cameron's name on it, the production values are Hollywood top tier. The VFX by Weta, happy to be making a live action anime film after the aborted *Evangelion*, is mind blowing. The "uncanny valley" quality of Alita herself was criticized by some. But as a cyborg and live action anime girl, her unreal, giant eyes work. Actress Rosa Salazar does the motion capture with the same enthusiasm of Andy Serkis with Gollum and *Planet of the Apes*' Caesar. She even studied Kishiro's manga panels for her performance. In many ways, *Alita: Battle Angel* is a superior and more faithful adaptation of the manga than its 1993 anime counterpart.

If there are any flaws, *Alita* follows some irritating modern Hollywood trends. The dialog is clunky. The film is also awash in a stereotypically cyberpunk teal and orange color grade. *Alita* could also have used a Japanese thespian or two. The music is predictably Hollywood and feels ingenuine compared to the haunting score by Kaoru Wada in the OVA. Yet the images by best-in-the-biz DP Bill Pope are finely textured. The film, for a Hollywood production, is passionately reverent to its subject material. At the end of the day, *Alita: Battle Angel* is the best live action anime adaptation made outside Japan. It is everything Rupert Sanders' *Ghost in the Shell* (2017) is not.

CINEMATIC DISASTERS
OR SAYONARA X OF THE DRIFTING FINAL WARRIORS ON TITAN II: THE WORST OF THE WORST

SF映画の災害

"We gratefully acknowledge the kamikaze pilots for clearing the runways during production."
-*Space Warriors 2000* (1985)

This book is primarily about the best that the Japanese science fiction film genre has to offer. For this segment, we're taking a quick break from enthusiasm to focus on the *worst*. Not all Japanese sci-fi films are created equal. Some are pretty bad. Then there's a final tier of unique, premiere cinematic disasters. As a filmmaker, I know there are many ways a film can go rotten. Writing or directing isn't easy and few filmmakers set out to make a bad movie. You don't always hit one out of the park in spite of your best intentions. Filmmaking can even seem like a streak of dumb luck to the unitiated. A competent director paired with a bad script or who is a poor fit for the material can produce a dumpster fire. Some of these films are wrongheaded in every aspect of their execution. Others are competent on a technical level, but crash and burn with story which makes them even more embarrassing. There are even films that seem to have perfect ingredients on paper and yet in execution produced hot messes.

THE X FROM OUTER SPACE (1967)
宇宙大怪獣ギララ
Shochiku, *Director:* **Kazui Nihomatsu**

There's guilt in putting this one here. Unlike other films on this list, in "so bad it's good" entertainment value, *The X From Outer Space* is a blast. But so are films like *Robot Monster, Plan 9 From Outer Space* and *The Horror of Party Beach*. *The X From Outer Space* is a turkey in every respect. This is ironic as the monster Guilala resembles a giant repilitian turkey. It also features a hilariously bad musical score by Taku Izumi and a script so terrible it's hard to believe it took three people to write it. The actors are a mix of competent native thespians like Eiji Okada and amateur *gaijin* like Franz Gruber and Peggy Neal. They do their best to keep a straight face through this utter silliness. Guilala was named and designed by a schoolchildren's contest, with the winner being a submission from a 12 year old girl. Her prize was a trip to Europe. The production values aren't great. The miniature work is poor. The monster sequences are television quality save for the occasional creative Cinemascope composition.

The film is at its most entertaining, ala a campy *Lost in Space* episode, when it focuses on '60s-style retro futurism. This is a gleaming vision of the future with trendy cocktail lounges on the moon. It's hard to believe that while this hokey mess was being produced in Japan, Stanley Kubrick was working on *2001: A Space Odyssey*, which would redefine science fiction. After *2001*, the future would never be the same. Cartoonist Jun Miura savagely said "X From Outer Space *is the product of a society that lost World War II and* 2001 *the product of one that won it*". At the end of the day, Shochiku's stab at a giant monster epic is the worst such film produced in Japan during the 1960s. Even Nikkatsu's *Gappa*, released that same year, is superior. Yet *The X From Outer Space* is a lot of fun if you shut off your brain and take it in as an ironic comedy. Avoid the export English dub at all costs, however, it's one of the worst ever.

X was Shochiku's sole giant monster film, but a handful of sci-fi and horror films would follow. These would fare better, including *Goke, Body Snatcher From Hell*, *The Living Skeleton* and *Genocide* (all 1968). The latter was also directed by Nihonmatsu but boasts a better script. Guilala would be back, regardless, in a variety of media. First the suit made a brief appearance in Shochiku's rockabilly comedy *A Little Snack* (1968). Then stock footage from *The X From Outer Space* showed up in *Tora-San's Forbidden Love* (1984), an entry in the beloved Tora-San series. In 2008, director Minoru Kawasaki (*The Calamari Wrestler, The World Sinks Except Japan*) helmed *Monster X Strikes Back: Attack the G8 Summit*. In this farcical semi-sequel, Guilala attacks Japan in the middle of the G8 Summit in Yokohama. The suit in the film was later sent to the U.S. and used in a memorable 2009 commercial for the job site The Ladders.com.

GAMERA VS. ZIGRA (1971)
ガメラ対深海怪獣ジグラ
Daiei, *Director:* **Noriaki Yuasa**

The later *Showa* Gamera films don't do it for me. The first three are quite decent, but by *Gamera vs. Viras* those films get pretty tough to stomach. *Gamera vs. Zigra* is the worst of the batch and the last Gamera film for nine years. *Zigra* features a particularly annoying batch of kids including a Japanese-American girl (Arlene Zoellner) with a constant craving for Coca-Cola. Shot on location at Kamogawa Sea World, the film is flatly directed by Noriaki Yuasa, who seemed to be just going through the motions at this point. The special effects and miniature work is awful. The talking goblin-shark like Zigra is poorly executed. It features an especially shallow anti-pollution subtext. This was probably added late in scripting because Toho was making the far better *Godzilla vs. Hedorah* at the same time. *Gamera vs. Zigra* beat *Hedorah* to theaters in Japan by only one week. It is especially to be avoided in its English dub which amps up the obnoxiousness to 11.

Soon afterward, Daiei went bankrupt. This put the kibosh on another planned Gamera film which had already had its suits built. Gamera would be back in 1980's *Gamera: Supermonster* which is almost as awful. Yuasa returned as director. Yet it became a stock footage-filled "clipshow" with a very basic wraparound plot inspired by the hottest Hollywood films like *Superman* and *Star Wars*.

BYE BYE JUPITER (1984)
さよならジュピター

Toho, *Directors*: Sakyo Komatsu, Koji Hashimoto

It's ironic that *Bye Bye Jupiter* is a big space movie about scientists trying to solarize Jupiter to save Earth from an approaching black hole. The film is Toho's classic *Icarus* moment. *Bye Bye Jupiter* looked like it would be the film where the studio challenged Hollywood in the production of state-of-the-art special effects pictures. The film was almost a decade in planning. Produced the same year as *2010: The Year We Make Contact,* its release also coincided with Godzilla's 30th anniversary. Tomoyuki Tanaka wanted to make an ultimate tribute to Japan's *tokusatsu* legacy while beating Hollywood at its own game. On paper, everything seemed perfect. Sakyo Komatsu, the mind behind *Submersion of Japan* and *Virus*, was both the film's writer and co-director. The special effects director was Koichi Kawakita. Kawakita was a young successor to Tsuburaya who for this film pioneered Hollywood-style robotics never before used in Japanese cinema.

Yet what resulted was an unprecedented cinematic disaster. *Bye Bye Jupiter* is a sort of Japanese equivalent to Hollywood's *Xanadu* or *Ishtar*. The original co-director, Shiro Moritani (*Submersion of Japan),* dying before production did not help. His replacement was assistant Koji Hashimoto. Hashimoto, while he did good work in his following Godzilla reboot *The Return of Godzilla,* was inexperienced for such a large scale film. Komatsu's script is more cluttered and confusing than David Lynch's *Dune*. Its protagonist is named "Eiji Honda" (Tomokazu Miura) and there's a cult of hippie terrorists trying to sabotage the

Jupiter solarization project. There's a sequence of "space montage sex" between Miura's Honda and hippie Maria played by French actress Diane d'Angély. The "Jupiter Church" hippies, led by the enigmatic singer Peter (Paul Tagawa) are frequently shown partying. These lengthy scenes are as hilariously awesome as they are wrongheaded. Miyuki Ono, who would later play a Sigourney Weaver-like role in the brutal *Evil Dead Trap*, plays Peter's second-in-command. Sadly, it's also Akihiko Hirata's last film. He passed away shortly after release, keeping him from portraying Professor Hayashida in *The Return of Godzilla*.

Kawakita's FX scenes are beautiful and the film's saving grace. His images are impressive and near Hollywood quality, especially of Jupiter's surface. Hashimoto's direction however is pedestrian and the English actors are terrible. The wonky Hong Kong dub, recorded by Matt Oram and the gang, takes the camp value a step further. *Bye Bye Jupiter* would be a lot of fun ironically if it wasn't for a nearly two and a half hour runtime. Shinji Higuchi, who would one day direct another adaptation of Komatsu's *Japan Sinks*, was a PA for Kawakita's unit. It was his first professional *tokusatsu* job. When *Bye Bye Jupiter* came out, he took his girlfriend at the time to see it, exaggerating his role in it to impress her. She, unamused, soon dumped him. That's how bad *Bye Bye Jupiter* is.

SPACE WARRIORS 2000 (1985)
Chaiyo/Tsuburaya Productions/Spectacular International Films, *Directors:* **Sompote Sands (Oriental,** *sic***), Marc Smith (Accidental,** *sic***)**

Space Warriors 2000 is no doubt the worst English localization of an Asian film, indeed a film period, in cinema history. It's an abominable adaptation of the Thai re-release of *Hanuman vs. 7 Ultraman: Hanuman vs. 11 Ultraman*. That film consists of a lengthy first half pulled wholesale from the clipshow flick *Ultraman Zoffy*. The second half is an edited version of *Hanuman vs. 7 Ultraman*, the Thai-Japanese co-production between Sompote Saengduenchai's Chaiyo and Tsuburaya Pro. The distributor, Dick Randall, hired a director named Marc Smith to redub this footage. Wraparound scenes were also shot in England. This footage stars Nick Curror as a little boy who gets an Ultraman doll that transports him into the main shitshow. What resulted almost has to be seen to be believed, it's so fucking terrible.

The dubbing is beyond horrible. The battles between Ultraman and various kaiju from *Ultraman Zoffy* feature the parties taunting each other. This dialogue is so horribly written that it makes *Captain Planet* sound like Billy Wilder. The acoustics are echoey. The production values show such a lack of concern and care, they are on par with public access TV. They didn't even bother to properly pan and scan and format the footage. The distributors just left anamorphic 2.35 footage squeezed to 4:3. The early scenes, taken from the *Ultraman* TV show, are already cropped to 'scope. It's kind of like watching a film through a funhouse mirror.

Yet the most atrocious sin of *Space Warriors 2000* is that the tone taken in the adaptation is borderline racist. Sompote is called the "Oriental" director. The film is credited to a *"Whole cast of Japanese stuntmen whose names we could not read"*. Offensively, the film ends with a title card acknowledging *"the kamikaze pilots for clearing the runways during production"*. This was edgy in the '80s. By today's standards, such off color humor would not be considered fit for television airing. Honestly, the makers of *Space Warriors 2000* should feel ashamed. The film was sold to Cinema Shares. It briefly aired on television before lawsuits from Tsuburaya (thankfully) put an end to such shenanigans. *Space Warriors 2000* is macabrely amusing as an ironic comedy, but don't say I didn't warn you.

THE DRIFTING CLASSROOM (1987)
漂流教室
Toho, *Director:* **Nobuhiko Obayashi**

The Drifting Classroom is another unmitigated 1980s cinematic disaster. Once again, there seemed to be all the right elements for a successful film in place. The director of *House* and *The Little Girl Who Conquered Time* making an adaptation of Kazuo Umezu's popular manga seemed like a match made in cinematic heaven. Izo Hashimoto, who had penned the popular TV drama *Sukeban Deka* and was soon to help Katsuhiro Otomo write *Akira* was tapped as screenwriter. Sadly, it was not to be. The film even starts well with protagonist Sho (Yasufumi Hayashi) having a heated clash with his mother (Yoshiko Mita). Hashimoto's adaptation makes the dire mistake of setting the story at an international school instead of the manga's typical Japanese high school in what was a vain attempt to get an international audience. Hollywood B-lister Troy Donahue plays a teacher and the film's young amateur foreign actors are so terrible that parts of the movie are borderline unwatchable.

Once the time slip takes place and the school is thrust into a post-apocalyptic future, *The Drifting Classroom* becomes a world class cinematic abomination. At times painful to watch, the film deluges the audience with one bizarre, incoherent sequence after another. It's not a weirdness, ala *House*, that works either. The green screen effects are embarrassing. There's a handful of decent horror sequences that invoke Obayashi's *House*, but they are few and far between. There are some well puppeteered monsters and impressive matte paintings by Fuchimu Shimakura, but such tokusatsu ingenuity is wasted. It's too bad, because with better execution, *The Drifting Classroom* could have been a cult classic. At best, the film's wonky execution and awful performances make for a decent ironic comedy. Blink and you'll miss cameos by Ishiro and Kimi Honda.

PRINCESS FROM THE MOON (1987)
竹取物語
Toho, *Director:* Kon Ichikawa

Princess From the Moon is another project that seemed perfect on paper but wound up a trainwreck. It had one of Japan's greatest directors helming it: Kon Ichikawa (*The Burmese Harp, Fires on the Plain, Tokyo Olympiad*). It was also an adaptation of the beloved folk story *Tale of the Bamboo Cutter*. One of Eiji Tsuburaya's first films as cinematographer was a version of this folktale and he longed to do a remake until his death. *Princess From the Moon* features an all star cast headed by Toshiro Mifune. There are things to like about it: it's a pretty film. Teruyoshi Nakano shines in his swansong effort as special effects director. There are two especially impressive sequences. The first is a *Moby Dick*-style scene featuring a plesiosaur-like sea dragon attacking a ship. It's almost flawlessly executed. Rumors that it used a prop created for the shelved Toho-Hammer co-production *Nessie* are untrue. The film's finale is impressive too, featuring a *Close Encounters*-style alien spaceship showing up in ancient Japan.

Yet outside of Nakano's stunning FX work, it's a dull, pedestrian pop movie. *Princess From the Moon* has aged more like vinegar than wine since the 1980s. Yasuko Sawaguchi is bland and forgettable as the titular Kaguya. Perhaps taking a nod from *Legend of the Eight Samurai* by Kadokawa, the credits feature a corny love song by Chicago's Peter Cetera. *Princess From the Moon* flopped hard in Japan and got awful reviews. It was up for a surprising amount of Japanese Academy Awards, however. Nakano and his team won, a well deserved accolade. If you watch this, see it alongside Isao Takahata's *anime* re-adaptation *The Tale of the Princess Kaguya*. The two films could not be more different in their approaches and tones. Takahata's film is somber and minimalistic. Ichikawa's film is bombastic and unintentionally campy.

GODZILLA VS. SPACE GODZILLA (1994)
ゴジラVSスペースゴジラ
Toho, *Director:* Kensho Yamashita

I'm not high on the 1990s Godzilla films. A lot of fans see the '70s films as a sort of nadir of the series but I find them a lot of fun. The '90s films are really nothing special. *Godzilla vs. King Ghidorah* is the best thanks to Kazuki Omori's creative direction and its meditation on Godzilla's legacy. Takao Okawara's *Godzilla vs. Mothra* and *Godzilla vs. Mechagodzilla II* suffer from a dull, TV movie-like blandness. Kawakita's FX also became increasingly uninspired. *Godzilla vs. Space Godzilla,* however, is bottom of the barrel. *Space Godzilla* is something of the *Superman IV* or *Batman and Robin* of the Godzilla series.

The plot is ridiculous with a ludicrous monster spawned from (not making this up) *"Godzilla cells going into a black hole and exiting a white hole".* Minilla is sort of brought back as the embarrassing Little Godzilla. This character looks more like it belongs in an episode of *Hello Kitty* or *Pokemon* than a Godzilla movie. Kawakita's FX are at a low point. There are especially awful space scenes featuring styrofoam asteroids on strings. This is heartbreaking after his stupendous shots in *Bye Bye Jupiter*. One scene, of Godzilla doing battle with the navy at sea, was so lackluster Toho rejected it. They reused the similar scene from *Godzilla vs. Biollante* instead. The creative energy Kawakita brought to films like *Biollante* is now completely spent. The director, Kensho Yamashita, had little experience directing monster films, having helmed "teen idol flicks" up until this point. His direction is particularly pedestrian. The human sequences are barely distinguishable

from material made for Japanese television. Takayuki Hattori's score is bland and nondescript. He'd back to score several more entries including *Godzilla 2000* (1999) and the disastrous *anime* trilogy. *Space Godzilla*'s sole highlight is a better developed and humanized Miki Saegusa courtesy of Megumi Odaka. It isn't enough. The next Godzilla film, *Godzilla vs. Destoroyah,* is pretty bad too and a disappointing end to the *Heisei*/VS series.

REBIRTH OF MOTHRA II (1997)
モスラ2 海底の大決戦
Toho, *Director:* Kunio Miyoshi

Between 1995's *Godzilla vs. Destoroyah* and 1999's *Godzilla 2000*, Toho kept the ball rolling with three standalone Mothra pictures. These silly, child-oriented films are far from the best of Toho's monster oeuvre. The first film, *Rebirth of Mothra*, is tolerable, if nothing special. The second film, *Rebirth of Mothra II,* is one of the very worst *kaiju* flicks to come out of the studio. It features Mothra battling Dagahra, a pollution spawned monster that spits out toxic starfish beasties. *Rebirth of Mothra II* is pedestrian in execution, direction and cinematography. Its pace is meandering, its environmental message trite and its plot uninteresting and silly. *Rebirth of Mothra II* makes Takao Okawara's *Godzilla vs. Mothra* look like *Mothra '61.*

Rebirth of Mothra II isn't totally unwatchable. The Okinawan locales are pretty and Kawakita's FX work, his final job for a while, has some ethereal beauty. There's some nice miniature work and decent puppetry with a Muppety whatsit that can heal with its piss. *Rebirth of Mothra II*'s FX work isn't as bad as *Godzilla vs. Space Godzilla's.* The CGI VFX shots, of which there are far too many, have aged badly however. They're pretty embarrassing and some have that *Lawnmower Man* uncanny valley feel. Overall, *Rebirth of Mothra II* is recommended only as a minor distraction for your antsy children. Even they might not be very impressed. The third film, *Rebirth of Mothra III,* would be a marked improvement and bring back Okihiro Yoneda, the first film's director.

GODZILLA: FINAL WARS (2004)
ゴジラ ファイナルウォーズ
Toho, *Director:* **Ryuhei Kitamura**

Released on Godzilla's 50th anniversary, *Godzilla: Final Wars* was intended to be a special occasion. Toho and producer Shogo Tomiyama passed on Shusuke Kaneko's services and instead hired Ryuhei Kitamura. Kitamura (1969-) was a young hotshot director with Hollywood ambitions fresh off actioners *Versus* (2000) and *Azumi* (2003). Both made ripples overseas. Toho hoped that *Godzilla: Final Wars* could be extensively marketed abroad. It also had one of the biggest budgets in Japanese cinema history. Sadly, *Final Wars* would be a dismal flop and a cinematic catastrophe very much echoing *Bye Bye Jupiter.* Afterward, the series went into hibernation for its longest period yet.

Godzilla: Final Wars is outright an abrasive and obnoxious film. Kitamura was, overall, a terrible fit for the material. It features a handful of the old school *Showa* actors like Akira Takarada, Kenji Sahara and Kumi Mizuno. They are wasted on a film made by a director with outright contempt for old school Japanese cinema. The other performances range from the hammy but

endearing Kazuki Kitamura to Don Frye. Frye, a now MAGA-loving washed-up former wrestler, invokes *The Room* more than Nick Adams. This is a Godzilla movie by a director who doesn't like Godzilla. Kitamura has made his preference for Hollywood and Australian films clear in interviews. He directs the film like he'd much rather be making an action film ala *Versus* about super-powered mutants fighting aliens than a monster movie. Indeed, *Final Wars* has a feel almost akin to a Godfrey Ho flick in that it's like two different films edited together. It's like a *Matrix*-knockoff with characters in trenchcoats doing Yuen Woo Ping-style aunts featuring Godzilla sequences haphazardly cut in. To make matters worse, the film is awash in ugly, overbearing color grading. It looks like a first year film student with a Michael Bay fetish testing out LUTs.

Longtime FX assistant Eichi Asada actually does spirited special effects sequences. The monster designs by Shinji Nishikawa are also quite good. Too bad the monster scenes are cut to sound bytes and color graded hideously. Tragically, *Godzilla: Final Wars* would be a last hurrah for old school, *tokusatsu*-style filmmaking. It wound up being the final Godzilla film to use actors in monster suits. Even *Shin Godzilla*, made 11 years later, opted for an all-CGI portrayal of the creature. *Godzilla: Final Wars* also boasts an earsplitting soundtrack by Emerson, Lake and Palmer's Keith Emerson (1944-2016). It's even worse than his score for Dario Argento's *Inferno. Final Wars* does have a sizable cult following in the fandom. These fans argue that the film is a lot of fun ironically, almost as an anti-Godzilla movie. I once got behind that mindset but realized even on its own,

Godzilla: Final Wars is an awful film. If *Godzilla vs. Space Godzilla* is the series' *Superman IV: The Quest for Peace*, *Final Wars* is its *Batman v. Superman: Dawn of Justice*.

ATTACK ON TITAN (2015)
進撃の巨人
Toho, *Director:* **Shinji Higuchi**

Shinji Higuchi's *Attack on Titan* live action duology is another premiere cinematic dumpster fire. They are the most disappointing thing to come out of Japanese cinema since 2003's *Battle Royale II*. Hajime Isayama's *manga* and its *anime* adaptation are problematic as it is, boasting thinly-veiled neo-fascist elements. Yet they do boast quality storytelling and world-building with a strong, well developed cast of characters. *Attack on Titan* is a clever concept. In it, the post-apocalyptic remnants of humanity are driven to a medieval style society enclosed in a walled city as they fend off man-eating giants called Titans. Like previous Nippon pop mythologies, it's indicative of Japan's feelings of helplessness over its disaster prone status.

The live action adaptation of *Attack on Titan* was immediately controversial among the anime's fandom for using an all Japanese cast. The manga/anime features mostly Caucasian characters and is set in Europe. This change was quite forgivable given the limitations of the Japanese film industry. *Attack on Titan* seemed like a promising project in the lead-up. A Subaru commercial showing the Titans in action turned heads. A tokusatsu-style *Attack on Titan* channeling *The War of the Gargantuas* seemed like a fun angle.

It was not to be. Tomohiro Machiyama's script is utterly terrible with unlikeable, barely developed characters. Little actually entertaining about the anime is captured. All that's left is a narrative mess with characters you're so uninvested in you could care less who gets eaten by Titans next. The main character, Eren, had a strong *raison d'être* in the manga and anime, seeking to avenge his Titan-eaten mother. In the live action films, he (played by the tragically late Haruma Miura) has no such backstory and narrative drive. The Japanese-Korean-American Kiko Mizuhara looks the part of Mikasa, the manga's sole Japanese descended character. Yet the film's Mikasa lacks her intrigue and likability. As typical of director Higuchi at his worst, it's a beautiful looking film devoid of substance. When Higuchi and his associates like Katsuro Onoue get the chance to do what they do best, eye popping CGI-frosted tokusatsu sequences, the films are tolerable. These scenes , using a giant rod puppet for the arch villain Colossal Titan, are impressive. There's about 25 minutes towards the end of the first film where *Attack on Titan* almost comes alive. This segment is the most faithful to the anime and features an impressive melding of practical FX and CG. This includes a suitmation vision of Eren's Titan form reminiscent of Sanda from *Gargantuas*. Yet this all scuttled in the second part, *Attack on Titan: The End of the World*. *The End of the World* is even worse than the first part and veers into borderline nonsense.

In Stuart Galbraith's *Monsters Are Attacking Tokyo*, director Shue Matsubayashi claims that Eiji Tsuburaya once shot some footage with actors for him.

Upon viewing it, Matsubayashi said the actors behaved strangely, "like toys". In Japanese industry circles, there's a mean anonymous joke that the actors on a Shinji Higuchi set "look like they're at a wake". Higuchi, like Tsuburaya, is a master at creating stunning images. He is weaker at weaving a strong narrative story and directing actors. His work is better reinforced by other directors like Shusuke Kaneko or Hideaki Anno.

GODZILLA: KING OF THE MONSTERS (2019)
Warner Brothers/Legendary Pictures/Toho,
Director: **Michael Dougherty**

While it has vocal admirers, 2019's *Godzilla: King of the Monsters* is the worst thing to come out of the Godzilla brand. A sequel to Gareth Edwards' decent but unspectacular 2014 *Godzilla*, it is an unmitigated cinematic disaster. *Godzilla: King of the Monsters* is like a subversive Hollywood mockery of Japanese science fiction. I actually had high hopes, having enjoyed director Michael Dougherty's earlier *Trick or Treat* and *Krampus*. It seemed like he would make a more entertaining monster flick than Edwards' passable but dull film. I had also loved the previous film in the Legendary "Monsterverse": Jordan Vogt-Roberts' 2017 *Kong: Skull Island*. Despite being a Kong movie, Roberts' film better captures the exuberant feel of a classic Toho film than either Legendary Godzilla.

King of the Monsters, by contrast, is a film destined for a long life in the Walmart bargain bin. Yes, Dougherty likes these films and *Godzilla: King of the Monsters* does contain noticeable references to many kaiju classics. Yet all the fandom Easter eggs in the world can't save a soulless, joyless picture with a rancid screenplay and wrongheaded execution. It's like Dougherty and this film's surprisingly sizable fanbase enjoy these movies for a completely different reason. Dougherty captures everything Westerners see as bad about the *kaiju* genre rather than its good attributes. At the same time *Godzilla: King of the Monsters* plays into every negative modern corporate Hollywood film stereotype. The movie is riddled with dialogue about STDs and fortune cookies so embarrassing it wouldn't make the cut in an export dub. The film does offer a basic environmentalist subtext, but it's handled in a trite and shallow way. Talented actors like Ken Watanabe, Sally Hawkins, *The Departed*'s Vera Farmiga and *Game of Thrones*' Charles Dance are wasted. The characters, headed by *Stranger Things*' Millie Bobby Brown, are so uninteresting that one is indifferent to their fate. The film is sloppily shot and poorly edited, to boot.

Watching masses of CGI pixels do battle interests me far less than actors in handcrafted suits. Yet the monster sequences are terrible either way. They carry the obnoxious trend, started in *Pacific Rim*, of having the creatures fight in "atmospheric" stormy or snowy environments, never in broad daylight. Coupled with grading as dark as *Game of Thrones*' infamous *The Long Night*, you can barely tell what's happening even on an IMAX screen. The monster designs are visually pleasing, but good luck seeing through the film's glaucoma-like color timing. There's a slightly interesting take on the monsters, redubbed "Titans". They are depicted as Earth spirits restoring the balance of a dying planet like the classic *yonaoshi* gods. This is delved into only superficially, however. Skip this and watch *Ghidorah, the Three-Headed Monster* or *Invasion of Astro-Monster* again instead. The twice-delayed *Godzilla vs. Kong* directed by Adam Wingard is thankfully a major improvement.

SHIN GODZILLA

シン・ゴジラ

Shin Gojira "New Godzilla"
Toho/Cine Bazar/Khara, 7/29/2016 (*Heisei 28*), 119:43, Digital, ARRIRAW (2.7/3.4K)/UHD (4K)/GoPro/Redcode RAW (5K), 2K Digital Intermediate (2.39:1), color, 3.1 channel sound

Crew

Executive Producer: Akihiro Yamauchi
Chief Producer/Production Manager: Minami Ichikawa
Producer: Yoshihiro Sato
Producer: Masaya Shibusawa
Producer: Taichi Ueda
Producer: Kazutoshi Wadakura
Line Producer: Kensei Mori
Writer/Director: Hideaki Anno
Director/VFX Director: Shinji Higuchi
VFX Director: Katsuro Onoue
Director of Photography: Kosuke Yamada
Editors: Atsuki Sato, Hideaki Anno
Music: Shiro Sagisu
Production Designers: Yuji Hayashida. Eri Sakushima
Art Directors: Akira Sakamoto, Toshiaki Takahashi
Casting: Tsuyoshi Sugumo
Assistant Directors: Kimiyoshi Adachi, Kazuhiro Nakagawa
Supervising Assistant Director: Ikki Todoroki

Production Managers: Masato Inatsuki, Takashi Sato
Project Manager: Taiji Ueda
Monster Designs: Mahiro Maeda
Monster Modeling: Takayuki Takeya
Lighting: Takayuki Kawabe
Sound Recording: Jun Nakamura
Sound Design: Toru Noguchi
Sound Mix: Haru Yamada
Music Producer: Kyoko Kitahara
Music Arranger/Orchestrator: Masamichi Amano
Music Arranger: Chokkaku
Music Arranger: Teho
Conductor (London Symphony Orchestra): Nick Ingman
Music Recorder (London Symphony Orchestra): Jonathan Allen
Digital Colorist: Seiji Sato
Art Director (Miniatures): Toshio Miike
Miniatures: Yoshihiro Nishimura

Director of Photography (Miniatures): Keiichi Sakurai
VFX Supervisor: Atsushi Sato
VFX Producer: Tetsuo Oya
CG Producer: Hiromasa Inoue
CG Director: Akira Iwamoto
CG Supervisor: Tsuyoshi Fushimi
Composite Supervisor: Shingo Kobayashi
Modeling & Composites: Takuya Uenishi
Concept Animator: Shuhei Kumamoto
Planning: Kenji Kamiyama, Hideya Hamada, Kazuo Kawakami
Storyboards: Ikki Todoroki, Yuki Masago, Kazuya Tsurumaki, Mahiro Maeda, Shinji Higuchi, Hideaki Anno
Cinematographer (B-Camera): Sinya Kocho
Cinematographer (B-Unit): Keizo Suzuki
English Dialogue Coach: Sean Muramatsu
Stunt Performer: Mao Aso

Still Photographer: Akihiko Nawashima
Production Assistant: Yoko Higuchi

Cast
Hiroki Hasegawa (*Rando Yaguchi*)
Yutaka Takenouchi (*Hideki Akasaka*)
Satomi Ishihara (*Kayoco Ann Patterson*)
Ren Osugi (*Prime Minister Seiji Okochi*)
Akira Emoto (*Ryuta Azuma*)
Kengo Kora (*Yusuke Shimura, Deputy Chief Cabinet Secretary*)
Mikako Ichikawa (*Hiromi Ogashira, Deputy Director of Nature Conservation Bureau*)
Jun Kunimura (*Masao Zaizen, Integrated Chief of Staff*)
Pierre Taki (*Saigo, Combat Leader*)
Kyusaku Shimada (*Katayama, Minister of Foreign Affairs*)
Ken Mitsuishi (*Tokyo Governor Kozuka*)
Shingo Tsurumi (*Yajima, Joint Staff Deputy*)
Kimiko Yo (*Reiko Hanamori, Defense Minister*)
Takumi Saito (*Ikeda, Tank Captain*)
Takashi Fujiki (*Kawamata, Tokyo Lieutenant Governor*)
Yu Kamio (*Minister of Foreign Affairs*)
Tetsu Watanabe (*Hajime Koriyama, Deputy Chief Cabinet Secretary for Crisis Management*)
Shinya Tsukamoto (*Hazama, Biologist*)
Sei Hiraizumi (*Yusuke Satomi, Acting Prime Minister/Former Minister of Agriculture*)

Kenichi Yajima (*Kunihiko Yanagihara, Minister of Land, Infrastructure, Transport and Tourism*)
Akira Hamada (*Jun Kono, Minister of Internal Affairs and Communications*)
Toru Tezuka (*Goro Sekiguchi, Minister of Education, Culture, Sports, Science and Technology*)
Arata Furuta (*Sawaguchi, National Police Agency Commissioner-General*)
Moro Moroka (*Honbu, National Police Agency Criminal Investigation Bureau Director*)
Taro Suwa (*Disaster Prevention Division Director*)
Kanji Tsuda (*Fumiya Mori, Ministry of Health, Labor and Welfare Bureaucrat*)
Issey Takahashi (*Yasuda, Ministry of Education, Culture, Sports, Science and Technology Bureaucrat*)
Toru Nomaguchi (*Tachikawa, Ministry of Economy, Trade and Industry Official*)
Satoru Matsuo (*Shuichi Izumi, Vice Chairman of the Policy Affairs Research Council for the LDP*)
Kazuo Hara (*Biologist*)
Isshin Inudo (*Paleontologist*)
Akira Ogata (*Marine Biologist*)
Atsuko Maeda (*Refugee*)
Ren Mori (*Refugee*)
KREVA (*Murasaki, JSDF Official*)
Jun Hashimoto (*Miki, JSDF Official*)
Hairi Katagiri (*Prime Minister's Office Staffer*)
Matsuo Suzuki (*Journalist*)
Kawase Yota (*Journalist*)
Takahiro Miura (*Journalist*)

Ikuji Nakamura (*Koji Kanai, Cabinet Office Minister of State for Special Missions*)
Keisuke Koide (*Fire Brigade Captain*)
Kosei Kato (*National Police Agency in Charge of Crisis Management Personnel*)
Shohei Abe (*Fire and Disaster Management Agency in Charge of Crisis Management Personnel*)
Daisuke Kuroda (*Negishi, Nuclear Regulatory Agency Staffer*)
Bob Werley (*U.S. Embassy Staff*)
Ippei Osako (*Yuminari*)
Shota Taniguchi (*Taiji Sodehara*)
Sho Oyamada (*Akihisa Yanagi*)
Charles Glover (*Ambassador Lansing*)
ANI
Mark Chinnery
Toyotaka Hanazawa
Makoto Awane
Christiane Brew (*American Researcher*)
Mafia Kajita
Ko Maehara
Takeshi Obayashi
Seiko Seno
Koji Seki
Ichi Omiya
Mayumi Ogawa
Markus Müller (*German Scientist*)
Inge Murata (*German Scientist*)
Yasuko
Dennis Gunn
Don Johnson
Gil
Robert Z
Steven Smith
Tom Dolan

Charles Peck
Florian Geier
Maeva E
Mark Tanigawa

Alex Hormigo
Mansai Nomura *(Godzilla, motion capture)*

Alternate Titles
Godzilla: Resurgence (working English title)

"Japan lost the war to the Americans, since that time, the education we received is not one that creates adults."
-Hideaki Anno, Atlantic Magazine (2007)

A rare figure to go back and forth between *anime* and live action, Hideaki Anno has enjoyed both great commercial success and an unusual amount of creative freedom. Anno and Shinji Higuchi were announced as directors of Toho's new Godzilla film in early 2015. Those who knew Anno's prior work like the landmark *Neon Genesis Evangelion* were excited for him to bring his distinctive style to the Godzilla franchise. While overlong, *Shin Godzilla* is a successful reimagining of the series. It is everything Legendary Pictures' passable but dull *Godzilla* (2014) and abysmal *Godzilla: King of the Monsters* (2019) are not. Though darkened by a dubious political bent, *Shin Godzilla* presents the viewer with dynamic images courtesy of co-director Higuchi. It well translates Anno's anime aesthetic to live action. The first *Godzilla* brought its traumatized post-war audience back to the horrors of Hiroshima and Nagasaki. *Shin Godzilla*'s visuals bring similar memories to a Japan still reeling from the 3/11 tsunami and earthquake.

PLOT

A pleasure boat, the Glory Maru, is found drifting offshore near Tokyo Bay by the Japan Coast Guard. Moments later, the Tokyo Aqua Line springs a leak and floods.

Deputy Cabinet Secretary Rando Yaguchi (Hiroki Hasegawa) and his aide Shimura (Kengo Kora) are notified and disaster response begins. Yaguchi sees an internet video of the ongoing incident and is convinced that the flood is caused by a living creature. He warns Prime Minister Okochi (Ren Osugi) and his aide Akasaka (Yutaka Takenouchi) but is scoffed at by the bureaucracy, dead set that it's an underwater volcano. A cabinet meeting is interrupted by an on-air broadcast showing a giant creature's tail, proving Yaguchi correct. The Prime Minister and his flummoxed cabinet call on a panel of biologists for counsel. The men of science, fearing their academic careers are at stake, offer little in the way of answers. Shimura calls upon a school colleague, a conservation bureau member named Hiromi Ogashira (Mikako Ichikawa). Observing video footage, she speculates that it has legs and the ability to come on land to the incredulous cabinet.

Prime Minister Okochi gives a press conference to reassure the public, only to be interrupted by news that the creature has surfaced in Tokyo's Kamata ward. The salamander-like monster cuts a swath of destruction through the neighborhood as terrified citizens evacuate. For the first time since World War II, Okochi must authorize military action against the beast. The Self Defense Force sends a squadron of attack helicopters to take it out. As the monster reaches neighboring Shinagawa district, it evolves into a bipedal form. The helicopter squadron arrives on the scene and is about to fire on the monster. Okochi is forced to call off the attack due to the presence of civilians. The monster winds up retreating into the sea. As government officials survey the damage, Yaguchi laments at the inefficiency of bureaucracy. He is scoffed at by Akasaka.

The military hunts for the monster in the Uraga Channel. Meanwhile Yaguchi puts together a team of scientific outliers to research the creature without bureaucratic constraints. Ogashira theorizes that the monster could be radioactive. She is proven correct when radiation levels start to spike in the immediate path of the creature. The United States sends the aide to Japan's ambassador, Kayoco Ann Patterson (Satomi Ishihara), to gather intel on a missing scientist. This man, named Goro Maki, was said to have predicted the monster's appearance. He was expelled from Japanese academic circles, working at a U.S. energy firm before disappearing. His boat, the Glory Maru, was the ship found by the Japan Coast Guard before the monster's appearance. Found on board were only a few personal items, his research and a cryptic note. Patterson reveals that Maki had given the monster the name "Godzilla" after the ancient god of Maki's home Odo Island. Shimura tells

an investigative reporter to gather more intel on Maki. Ogashira and biologist Hazama (*Tetsuo*'s Shinya Tsukamoto) realize that Godzilla is powered by a biological nuclear reactor. They hypothesize "freezing" the reactor could halt the monster's advance. Yaguchi decides to go forward with a plan to administer coagulant to freeze the creature's blood. His colleagues dub it "the Yaguchi Plan".

As Yaguchi and his team work to develop this plan, Godzilla re-surfaces at Sagami Bay, mutating into a gigantic new form. The military mounts an attack in Kawasaki. Godzilla emerges completely unscathed and continues its advance. As Godzilla nears the heart of Tokyo, the U.S. sends bombers to attack the monster from Guam. The Americans' strike nearing, Okochi and his cabinet are urged to evacuate. After Godzilla is hit with the missiles, it begins to glow and projects an atomic beam. It vaporizes the American bombers, the helicopter carrying the Prime Minister and much of Tokyo. After emitting its beam, Godzilla freezes in place, having run out of energy.

With Godzilla temporarily halted, the government reconvenes in Tachikawa ward. An acting Prime Minister is selected: Yusuke Satomi (Sei Heraizumi), the Minister of Agriculture. Yaguchi brings his team back together and continues work on his plan. With Kayoco's help, a U.S./Japanese Godzilla research coalition forms. Field data reveals that Godzilla is planning to spread wings and propagate world wide. Kayoco is horrified as the U.S. decides to fire a nuclear warhead at Tokyo to kill it. Akasaka, who was at Yokota air base and so wasn't killed with the Prime Minister, tells Yaguchi to abandon his plan. Yaguchi refuses and after his team finds a coagulant that works on tissue samples of Godzilla, he orders it mass produced. The coalition finds that Godzilla is regenerating its energy and will start moving again in 15 days. The U.S. moves up their nuclear strike, withdrawing their ambassadors and giving Japan only two weeks to evacuate its citizens from Kanto.

BACKGROUND

Despite being known for his *anime* work, Hideaki Anno has had a love of *tokusatsu* since youth. A huge *Ultraman* buff, in college he produced a tribute to *Return of Ultraman*. His anime opuses *Gunbuster, Nadia* and *Evangelion* are filled with visual references to tokusatsu films and shows. In 2012 Anno curated a tokusatsu exhibit at Tokyo's Museum of Contemporary Art. Together with friend and frequent collaborator Shinji Higuchi, he produced a short film for it. Entitled *God Warrior Appears in Tokyo*, it was a co-production with Hayao Miyazaki's Studio Ghibli directed by Higuchi. An impressive mini-film made with practical means, it featured the God Warrior from *Nausicaa of the Valley of the Wind* obliterating Tokyo. The short was also shown before *Evangelion 3.0: You Can (Not) Redo* in Japanese theaters.

After the creative and financial failure of *Godzilla: Final Wars* in 2004, Toho would cease production on Godzilla entries for their longest period yet. A fun sequence in Takashi Yamazaki's *Always: Sunset on Third Street 2* (2007), would whet fans' appetites. Yet it was twelve years until another Japanese-produced Godzilla entry was released. Hideaki Anno and Shinji Higuchi signed on to *Shin Godzilla* in late 2014 and an announcement was made on April 1st, 2015. Some believed it to be an April Fools' joke as Higuchi was still deep in post-production for his *Attack on Titan* duology yet it was soon confirmed. Shooting on the movie would begin in September of 2015 with Higuchi's *Attack on Titan: The End of the World* barely picture locked.

PRINCIPAL PHOTOGRAPHY

Shin Godzilla's shoot would last three months. Hideaki Anno instructed the actors to speak quickly in the bureaucratic sequences, emulating the fast speech of Japanese politicians. Directors Anno and Higuchi co-directed the actor sequences on-set together. Anno and company brilliantly recreate his anime aesthetic in live action; the shot compositions and cuts invoking his *Evangelion* works. The military attack scenes resemble the final act of *Evangelion 1.0* in their staging, pacing, editing and imagery. The *"Operation Yashima"* sequences in that film were, incidentally, storyboarded by Shinji Higuchi.

Hideaki Anno, with Higuchi at his side giving the images polish, brings to life a unique depiction of Godzilla. It is far superior to Gareth Edwards' or Michael Dougherty's Hollywood takes. *Shin Godzilla* keeps reverence to Godzilla's history while presenting a dramatic reimagining of the creature some fans find heretical. Anno and Higuchi show off their diehard fandom from frame one. *Shin Godzilla* opens with the 1965 Toho logo and an exact replica of the opening shot of the 1954 film. They mix in Easter eggs like the Glory (*Eiko*) Maru, Goro Maki (named after *Son of Godzilla*'s protagonist), Odo Island and having Godzilla attack Shinagawa ward.

Shin Godzilla is a complex and multi-layered film. On its surface, it's a *Dr. Strangelove*-like political satire on the inefficiency of Japan's bureaucracy. Japanese science fiction has tackled this before. Even in Honda's original *Godzilla* there's a scene where opposing politicians in the Diet clash. *Shin Godzilla* takes Kaneko and Higuchi's notion of *"What if giant monsters really existed"* to a logical conclusion. It guts any past world building in the Godzilla series and assumes *"What would happen if Godzilla just showed up in Japan tomorrow?"*. The movie's view toward Japan's postwar bureaucracy is best summed up in one shot. As the Prime Minister prepares to have a public conference with his cabinet, the members must walk across the hall into a room reserved for official conferences. The image of a gaggle of politicians shambling from one room to another is one of the most comical in the film. It drives the concept of utter ridiculous inefficiency of Japan's government. Like Kubrick, Hideaki Anno is fond of using very wide focal lengths to create

a distorted and at times voyeuristic feel. The invention of the GoPro, a tiny consumer-grade camera that can be placed anywhere, allows Anno and DP Kosuke Yamada to go wild. If *Shin Godzilla* has any real flaws, the endless string of bureaucratic meetings get a little tedious. The picture could have used some cutting.

A major influence came not from Ishiro Honda, but from *Blood Type: Blue*'s Kihachi Okamoto, featured onscreen in a photograph. *Japan's Longest Day* (1967) and *Battle of Okinawa* (1971), two World War II-based docudramas Okamoto directed for Toho, are Anno's favorite films. Both feature a similar gaggle of politicians, bureaucrats and military officials, frequently named onscreen, coping with historical crises. *Japan's Longest Day*, with an all-star cast including Toshiro Mifune as War Minister Anami, focuses on the turmoil gripping Japan on the last day before its surrender. A faction of militarists believe the Emperor was coerced into capitulation. They try to stop Japan's bureaucrats from broadcasting his surrender speech. *Shin Godzilla* depicts a *kaiju* attack in a similar docudrama tone. Anno and his editor Atsuki Sato even copy Okamoto's cutting style verbatim. *Shin Godzilla* was cut on Adobe Premiere Pro, a popular and versatile video editing application.

Like Okamoto, Anno names every official who shows up on screen along with every piece of weaponry, showing off his military *otaku* roots. Covered in Gainax's OVA *Otaku no Video*, there's a subculture of *otaku* (a derogatory yet iconic term for "fanboy") obsessed with military history and hardware. They bear similarities to American militia and survivalists but are less politically active. Unable to play cowboy with real firearms like their American counterparts, instead they make do with airsoft replicas thanks to Japan's strict gun control. The character Aida in *Evangelion*, a nerdy kid with a military obsession, was based on Anno as a teenager. The film's trope of nerds coming together to save the world brings Studio Gainax's foundation to mind; when a group of *otaku* joined forces to break into the film industry.

ACTORS

The film's cast is fairly novel. With the exception of Akira Emoto (*Godzilla vs. Space Godzilla*) and Jun Kunimura (*Godzilla: Final Wars*), no Godzilla series veterans were cast. Kyusaku Shimada (1955-), who played the iconic black magician Yasunori Kato in *Tokyo, the Last Megalopolis* (1988) and its 1989 sequel *Tokyo, the Last War*, also plays a military official. Rumor had it that Akira Takarada expressed interest in appearing in *Shin Godzilla*, but Anno turned him down. Allegedly, the director wanted to avoid casting anyone strongly associated with the series, feeling it would distract from the narrative.

Of the players, Mikako Ichikawa makes an impression as Ogashira. Ichikawa (1978-) had previously appeared in Anno's *Cutie Honey* (2004). Her Ogashira has the "cool", even temperedness of a traditional Japanese woman with a modern outspokenness. She is the brilliant mind behind Yaguchi's plan.

Satomi Ishihara (1986-), however, is miscast as Kayoco Ann Paterson. She plays a supposed American character who speaks English with a thick Japanese accent. There are many pop stars in Japan with Western roots who speak perfect English, so the decision to cast someone who doesn't seems odd.

SFX/VFX

Shin Godzilla is often evaluated as something of an auteurist piece from Anno. In reality, it is just as much Shinji Higuchi's film and his end is impressive. The destruction scenes feature almost seamless composite shots, supervised by his right-hand man Katsuro Onoue. It can often be nearly impossible to tell what is computer generated, live action and miniatures. Anno and Higuchi's life-like images of mass destruction and civilians fleeing it are unsettling in the wake of the 3/11 earthquake. There was a surprising amount of miniature work done for the film, with models built by Higuchi's longtime associate Toshio Miike. One of the film's most impressive moments of an office building collapsing from the inside in the climax was created entirely with miniatures courtesy of Miike.

Like the monsters in the *Heisei Gamera* trilogy, Godzilla was designed by Mahiro Maeda. His Godzilla design was controversial but quite creative. It retains the Japanese aesthetic missing from American incarnations while taking its potential in a new direction. Godzilla's main form was to be brought to life through use of a CGI enhanced rod puppet like the Colossal Titan in Higuchi's *Attack on Titan*. In early 2016, images of the Godzilla puppet were leaked online to much fan speculation. It wound up scrapped after some test footage and Godzilla was rendered entirely with CGI. *Kyogen* performer Mansai Nomura did the motion capture for Godzilla. A sequence showing Godzilla's *"Shinagawa-kun"* form projectile vomiting a blood-like substance was cut. Anno's anime studio Khara, its staff idle between *Evangelion* movies, would handle a good chunk of the film's VFX.

MUSIC

Anno's usual composer, Shiro Sagisu, would create the lavish score. As with the *Evangelion* Rebuilds he makes heavy use of a choir chanting in English. *"Decisive Battle"*, a memorable piece from the *Evangelion* soundtrack, was reused in *Shin Godzilla* as well. The two standout tracks are *"Persecution of the Masses"* and *"Who Will Know Tragedy"*, both of which feature English choirs. *"Who Will Know Tragedy"* is particularly effective, it helps make Godzilla's destruction of Tokyo all the more stunning of a sequence.

Additionally, Anno, Sagisu and their sound designers sample Akira Ifukube tracks throughout and use Toho's stock effects library with glee. *Shin Godzilla* is even, oddly, mixed in 3.1 rather than typical 5.1 surround sound. This is perhaps a nod to Perspecta, a three to four track early surround sound system used in many of Toho's classic films from the late 1950s to early '60s.

REAL WORLD

Unlike classic entries which feature outlandish weaponry, *Shin Godzilla*'s military hardware is taken entirely from life. The Japanese Self Defense Force threw their full support behind this project. *Shin Godzilla* would even be used in SDF recruitment posters during its release. This provided fuel to the film's critics who accused it of neo-fascism. The helicopters that attack Godzilla's *"Shinagawa-kun"* form are AH-1S Cobras. Manufactured by Bell, these attack helicopters have a long history of use around the globe. The AH-1 was developed for use in the Vietnam War and first saw action in the Tet Offensive. The U.S. military phased them out in the '90s after Somalia and Haiti. There is still limited use of them in the Marine Corp where they are used for fighting forest fires. The AH-1S is an improved version developed for the Japanese Self Defense Force in the late '80s. The film's tanks are Type 90 models and upgraded Type 10s, created specifically for the JSDF in the early 2000s. The Boeing AH-64 Apache is later used against Godzilla's main form. These heavier duty attack helicopters were developed after the Vietnam War but their production did not begin until the early '80s. They did not see combat until 1989 with Operation Just Cause, the U.S. invasion of Panama. They have seen use in every conflict since and are still employed worldwide. The U.S. military deploys B-2 Spirit stealth bombers against Godzilla in Tokyo. These bombers are manned, though they resemble drones. Developed in the 1980s and introduced in 1997, they have been used in numerous conflicts since starting with Kosovo in 1999. They have seen heavy use in the invasions of Afghanistan, Iraq and Libya. Takanami-class destroyers developed for the SDF in the early 2000s are also seen. American Arleigh Burke-class destroyers are seen as well. These powerful U.S. Navy ships have dominated the seas since their introduction in the late '80s.

THEMES AND MOTIFS

Anno's script is spartan in character development as it deluges the audience with one bureaucrat, meeting and piece of military hardware after another. Yet Yaguchi, Shimura, Akasaka and Ogashira are given the largest focus. It is Yaguchi's unorthodox methods that drive the narrative. There are some shared tropes between *Shin Godzilla* and previous entries. Yaguchi, like Serizawa, defeats Godzilla with a chemical compound. U.S. forces attack Godzilla with missiles that have little effect like the scene used in the American version of *Mothra vs. Godzilla*. Like 1984's *The Return of Godzilla*, which Higuchi worked as an assistant on, the United States tries to bully Japan into letting them use a nuclear weapon on Godzilla. Yaguchi also plays into the trope, popular since *Submersion of Japan*, of the "sky is falling" scientist who is disbelieved by the establishment.

Japanese filmmakers have a knack for layering their themes and Anno is particularly fond of that storytelling style. Beneath the surface of *Shin Godzilla*'s satire on bureaucracy is a "Japan First" mentality. It's akin to Shintaro Ishihara and Sony founder Akio Morita's (in)famous book *The Japan That Can Say No*. Ishihara (1932-), brother of actor Yujiro Ishihara, was the conservative governor of Tokyo known for his denial of Japan's wartime atrocities. The book revolves around how an infantilized Japan needs to take back its autonomy on the world stage. This is *Shin Godzilla*'s hidden message. The film makes the case that, per the U.S. taking away Japan's military sovereignty, if a monster like Godzilla were to show up the Japanese would be woefully unprepared. Ren Osugi's ineffectual Prime Minister Okochi seems to represent Naoto Kan more than Shinzo Abe.

There are some unsettling fascistic elements to *Shin Godzilla*. The text of Article 9 of Japan's Constitution is flashed on the screen in a manner that seems almost mocking. A firm in Germany also helps Yaguchi's researchers analyze their data with a supercomputer, which could be interpreted as two old allies working together again. In *Neon Genesis Evangelion*, Germany is also a major ally (at first) of the Japanese NERV branch. Anno's work has had nationalistic tinges since his directorial debut, the OVA *Gunbuster*. *Gunbuster* uses World War II imagery in a manner that's nearly fetishistic in intensity. Anno, amusingly in Tomoo Haraguchi's *Death Kappa* (2010), portrayed the leader of a right wing terrorist group desperate to restore Japan's Imperial might. Higuchi is no stranger to right wing suspicions either, his second film was a controversial adaptation of Harutoshi Fukui's novel *Lorelei* (2005). In that novel a renegade submarine gifted by the Germans stops a third atomic bomb from being dropped on Tokyo.

RELEASE AND LEGACY

When it opened in Japan, followed by a small stateside run a few months later, *Shin Godzilla* got a controversial reception from some fans. Ryuji Honda, Ishiro's son, even spoke out against the film, claiming it went against his father's Pacifist intentions for Godzilla. Yet *Shin Godzilla* is a compelling and well produced update to the Godzilla mythos. It was released the same year that Donald Trump became U.S. President and populism was gaining traction in a chaotic world. Love it or hate it, as the original *Godzilla* is the perfect portrayal of Japan's postwar zeitgeist, *Shin Godzilla* is an accurate snapshot of current day Japan.

As the COVID-19 pandemic winds down, *Shin Godzilla* will no doubt take on even more relevance. Its themes of governments mishandling a catastrophe as science races to save the day already resonate. Its downbeat ending perfectly bookends both the Godzilla legacy and this volume. It is the essence of *shoganai*. These cataclysms are inevitable. Humanity and Japan's challenge is to learn how to adapt and live with them. As Anno returned to *Evangelion* for the final *Rebuild*, he and Higuchi collaborated again for an *Ultraman* reboot. This film, entitled *Shin Ultraman* (2021), was written by Anno and directed by Higuchi. Anno's next stop is the *Kamen Rider* franchise with *Shin Kamen Rider*, planned for release in 2023.

ALTERNATE VERSIONS

Anno has a penchant for doing touch-ups to his work on home video. The version released to Japanese DVD, Blu-ray and high dynamic range 4K Ultra HD in 2017 would be subtly different. Yet compared to the extensive alterations made to the home video versions of the first three *Evangelion* Rebuilds, *Shin Godzilla*'s changes are minor. They consist of only two redone CGI shots including a close up of Godzilla. There are no known editorial or sound design changes.

The film was exhibited the world over uncut, given a short-term subtitled U.S. release in October 2016. Its distributor, Funimation, gave *Shin Godzilla* an English dub written by Sean Whitley and directed by Cris George using voice actors who specialize in dubbing anime. It's an easier viewing experience for Anglophones in some ways, making reading the titles easier and smoothing over Satomi Ishihara's bad English. The voices are, however, a mixed bag. Main dubbing cast includes Todd Haberkorn (Rando Yaguchi), Trina Nishimura (Kayoco), J. Michael Tatum (Hideki Akasaka), Kent Williams (Prime Minister Okochi), Ian Sinclair (Yasuda), Micah Solusod (Yusuke Shimura) and Kate Oxley (Hiromi Ogashira). Supporting cast includes Christopher Bevins (Fumiya Mori), Ed Blaylock (Ryuta Azuma, Chief Cabinet Secretary, Jeremy Inman (Shuichi Izumi), Jeremy Schwartz (Professor Hazama), Charlie Campbell (Yusuke Satomi), R. Bruce Elliott (Kunihiko Yanagihara), Rachel Robinson (Reiko Hanamori), Barry Yandell (Koriyama), David Wald (Tanba) and John Burgmeier

(Goro Sekiguchi). Haberkorn and Tatum are effective and Trina Nishimura is fitting as Kayoco but other voices are less so. Overall the film is best viewed in Japanese with subtitles.

AMERICAN HOME VIDEO HISTORY

The film was released on DVD and Blu-ray in the U.S. on August 1, 2017. The main changes in Funimation's home video version are the deletion of the onscreen supers naming all the government officials, locales and hardware. English versions are mostly still included on the discs' subtitle tracks, however.

Further Viewing:

(2004)
キューティーハニー
Towani/Warner Brothers, *Director*: Hideaki Anno

Hideaki Anno's live action *Cutie Honey* is a fun adaptation of luminary Go Nagai's iconic *manga* and *anime* franchise. It is faithful to its source material without taking itself too seriously. Voluptuous, form-changing android Honey Kisaragi (Eriko Sato) battles the evil organization Panther Claw. Responsible for the death of her father, they are led by Sister Jill (Eisuke Sasai), reimagined from sadomasochistic nun to horticultural horror. Anno shows mastery of his craft by literally making an anime in live action form, quirks of the medium in all. He takes the concept verbatim, producing stylized anime imagery with flesh-and-blood actors instead of vinyl cels. Anno and crew filmed certain shots frame by frame to have the unique low frame rate look of an anime. The villains are hammy to the point that Sister Jill and big boss Black Claw get introductory musical numbers. There are even gags utilizing the "Itano circus" in live action. That was a stylistic flourish Anno learned from animation director Ichiro Itano (*Macross, Angel Cop*). Featuring a character dodging a flurry of missiles in fluid motion, it's instantly recognizable.

Cutie Honey's finale is where Anno's signature style takes hold and is a thrilling tour-de-force. It mixes *tokusatsu* destruction courtesy of Shinji Higuchi and Makoto Kamiya with showy Hong Kong-style fight scenes. The fight choreography was done by none other than Yukari Oshima. The Japanese-Chinese Oshima (1963-) was a prominent HK martial arts starlet and appeared on the *sentai* show *Bioman*. If *Cutie Honey* has any flaws, it's that the HD cinematography hasn't aged well and looks a bit "V-Cinema". Its production values are solid enough otherwise. When the film started principal photography, the Hollywood live action *Evangelion* project had been recently announced. Perhaps on some level *Cutie Honey* is Anno saying "*This* is how it's done". Amusingly enough, Anno and his associates at Gainax would produce a *Cutie Honey* anime series simultaneously. Titled *Re:*

Cutie Honey, it was released only two months after the live action film. More live action *Cutie Honey* followed, including a TV show called *Cutie Honey: The Live* in 2007 and another movie, *Cutie Honey: Tears,* in 2016.

DEEP-SEA MONSTER REIGO VS. THE BATTLESHIP YAMATO

(2005)
深海獣レイゴー
Shinkaiju Reigo Eiga , *Director*: Shinpei Hayashiya

Directed by fan filmmaker and *rakugoka* Shinpei Hayashiya, *Deep-Sea Monster Reigo vs. the Battleship Yamato* is an odd little movie. It features an ambitious, novel concept that, in better hands, could make a genre masterpiece. It's certainly a labor of love on Hayashiya's part. The problem is the execution is fairly poor with a general lack of polish. The production values are between an Asylum production and a "Syfy Original". The film, set during World War II in 1943, features the legendary *Yamato* going up against a proto-Godzilla of sorts, Reigo.

Reigo has some fun moments and a fairly thrilling climax. It is undone, however, by its low budget and many aesthetic problems. For every beautiful shot, there are about three genuinely embarrassing CGI effects. The practical FX fare best. Reigo is beautifully

designed by Keita Amemiya with the prop sculpted by Tomoo Haraguchi. According to Hayashiya, *Reigo* is a veiled origin story of a certain iconic Toho monster without arousing that company's legal ire. Reigo would survive its encounter with the Yamato and be exposed to American atomic bomb tests in 1954.

Sadly, *Reigo*'s production values and low budget can't keep up with its ambitious high concepts. The World War II feel is distractingly inauthentic. The young ensign protagonist (Taiyo Sugiura) even has blond highlights. The naval uniforms look cheap, not helped by dated HDV cinematography that screams "direct to video". Black and white scenes in the film fare better. One wishes Hayashiya had finished the whole film in monochrome as it would have better hidden the lack of polish. There's also a problematic romanticization of naval life aboard the *Yamato*. The use of a modern pop song in some bits is downright cringe-worthy. The film ends with the destruction of the *Yamato* two years later, which Hayashiya himself tells *kabuki*-style. In 2019, to cash on Legendary's *Godzilla: King of the Monsters* mockbuster-style, the film was finally released in the U.S. as *Reigo: King of the Sea Monsters*. Despite the film's flaws, it comes somewhat recommended for its unique concept. Hayashiya would be back for 2009's *Raiga* and 2019's *God Raiga vs. King Ohga*.

HIDEAKI ANNO
The Otaking

庵野秀明

5/22/1960-

"I honestly don't really like myself. I often hear that those with self esteem issues set their expectations of themselves too high. I don't think people who say that understand how painful it is."
-Hideaki Anno, *Extracurricular Lesson* TV Special (1998)

Hideaki Anno is one of Japanese pop culture's most influential luminaries. In the semi-autobiographical Gainax *anime Otaku no Video* (1991), the main character sets out to become the "Otaking". Though Anno himself is less than fond of modern *otaku* culture, "Otaking" is a fitting title for him. He's an auteur who has made his mark in both the anime and live action realms and enjoys unlimited artistic freedom. Like George Lucas or his mentor Hayao Miyazaki, Anno, now the CEO of his own animation company Khara Inc., is an institution into himself.

Hideaki Anno was born in Ube, Yamaguchi Prefecture. His father, who wore a prosthetic leg, was at times abusive to him. As a child, Anno loved watching *Ultraman* on TV. Visiting Expo '70 in Osaka was a particularly pivotal experience for him. As a teenager, he became interested in military history and *Space Battleship Yamato*. He even would put flyers advertising the show around his school. Anno was an honor student and realized that he could win the praise of others through academic achievement. Akin to his iconic character Rei Ayanami, he is a fervent vegetarian. During lunch, Anno would often subsist on only milk and bread when there were no

vegetarian options. He began making films and animation in high school on Super 8. Accepted into the Osaka University of the Arts, he was regarded as a prodigy. There, he would meet Gainax co-founders and friends Hiroyuki Yamaga, Takami Akai and Toshio Okada. His college years would later be documented in the humorous *manga* and TV show *Blue Blazes*. During this time, he worked as an animator on the iconic *Macross* (1982-83) and on Daicon Film (later Gainax)'s opening animations for the Nihon SF convention. He also produced a short fan film tribute to *Return of Ultraman*.

A game changer in Anno's career came when he was hired by Hayao Miyazaki. Miyazaki, impressed by Anno's art, was in need of more animators for *Nausicaa of the Valley of the Wind* (1984). Miyazaki was flummoxed by the disorganized state of Anno's workspace, but was extremely impressed with his output. Anno animated much of the film's stunning "God Warrior" sequence. When Gainax produced their first feature, *The Wings of Honneamise,* in 1987, Anno was animation director. At the age of only 28, he made his directorial debut, the original video animation *Gunbuster*. A mix of militarism, giant robots and fan service, it took the anime industry by storm. The TV show *Nadia: Secret of Blue Water* (1990-91) soon followed. Yoshiyuki Sadamoto designed the characters and Anno worked with composer Shiro Sagisu for the first time. Anno had trouble handling the show and fought creativity with his producers. The second half of the show was handled by friends such as Shinji Higuchi and animated mostly in Korea. The experience of *Nadia* was coupled with unrequited romantic affections. This plunged Anno into a terrible depression. In 1993 he began to develop his subsequent opus, one that would come to define his career.

A dark science fiction story based on his despair, *Neon Genesis Evangelion* started airing in October 1995. With its strong character development and compelling narrative, it won many admirers. Due to graphic violence in one episode, investor Sega withdrew their funding from the show. This resulted in Anno and his team being forced to work with a lower budget for the remaining episodes. The last two episodes, composed mostly of recycled animation, were the most controversial. He followed the show up with a pair of *Evangelion* movies intending to properly conclude the show. The second of them was the stunning *The End of Evangelion*. This ultra violent but beautifully animated film is either an alternative or proper ending depending on interpretation. *Evangelion* would be an international phenomenon. It spawned merchandise of every kind and, nearly, a Hollywood live action movie.

Anno's follow up to *Evangelion* was his first feature length live action work, *Love & Pop* (1998), based on a novel by *Tokyo Decadence*'s Ryu Murakumi. A voyeuristic portrait into the lives of high school girls involved in escort services, it was shot on consumer digital cameras. His next TV project was an anime romantic comedy entitled *His and Her Circumstances* (1998-99). Despite its eclectic subject matter, it was distinctively Anno. Due to creative differences with Masami Tsuda, who wrote the original *manga,* Anno departed midway through the show, leaving it in the hands of his assistant Kazuya Tsurumaki. The show was not renewed for a second season and its plot threads were left unfinished. Afterwards, he made another live action film in 2000: *Shiki-Jitsu (Ritual)*. It starred Shunji Iwai and Ayako Fujitani and was this time shot in 35mm Cinemascope.

Anno married *manga* artist Moyoco Anno in 2002 and the pair became inseparable. His next project was a live action adaptation of *Cutie Honey* in 2004. He also spearheaded the *Re: Cutie Honey* OVA. Around this time, he had a falling out with some of his former friends at Gainax and wound up resigning. Starting his own company, Khara, he began work on a new version of *Evangelion,* called the "Rebuilds". The first, a reanimated version of the opening six episodes with some plot changes, debuted in 2007 as *Evangelion 1.0: You Are (Not) Alone*. The second, which took more radical plot departures, came out in 2009 as *Evangelion 2.0: You Can (Not) Advance*. The third, *Evangelion 3.0: You Can (Not) Redo*, came out in 2012. By this time, the films had mutated into their own new story and the third film was not well received. Anno took that hard and fell back into depression to the point that his therapist advised him to stop making

Evangelion movies. During this time, he would also voice Zero plane designer Jiro Horikoshi in Miyazaki's *The Wind Rises* (2013).

In 2015, Shinji Higuchi talked him into signing on to Toho's upcoming Godzilla reboot, *Shin Godzilla*. *Shin Godzilla* was well received in Japan, though it was accused of nationalism by some aboard. Since then, he has been at work on the final *Evangelion Rebuild: 1.0+3.0*. Originally to be released summer of 2020, the film's date has been pushed back because of COVID-19. He has also scripted an upcoming reboot of Ultraman, *Shin Ultraman*, directed by Higuchi.

Selected Filmography

Super Dimension Fortress Macross (1982-83, TV) [animator]

Return of Ultraman (1983) [director, actor]

Nausicaa of the Valley of the Wind (1984) [animator]

Macross: Do You Remember Love? (1984) [animator]

Royal Space Force: The Wings of Honneamise (1987) [animation director]

Gunbuster (1988-89) [director/screenplay]

Nadia: Secret of Blue Water" (1990-91, TV) [director]

"Neon Genesis Evangelion" (1995-96, TV) [director/screenplay]

Neon Genesis Evangelion; Death and Rebirth (1997) [director/screenplay]

Neon Genesis Evangelion: The End of Evangelion (1997 [director/screenplay]

Love & Pop (1998) [director/screenplay]

"His and Her Circumstances" (1998-99, TV) [director/screenplay]

Shiki-Jitsu (2000) [director/screenplay]

Cutie Honey (2004) [director/screenplay]

Re: Cutie Honey (2004) [director]

Evangelion 1.0: You Are (Not) Alone (2007) [director/screenplay]

Evangelion 2.0: You Can (Not) Advance (2009) [director/screenplay]

Giant God Warrior Appears in Tokyo (2012) [screenplay]

Evangelion 3.0: You Can (Not) Redo (2012) [director/screenplay]

The Wind Rises (2013) [voice]

Shin Godzilla (2016) [director/screenplay]

Evangelion 1.0+3.0 (2021) [director/screenplay]

Shin Ultraman (2021) [screenplay]

REIWA

令和

May 1st, 2019 to current

On April 30th, 2019, something unprecedented happened. Emperor Akihito abdicated the Chrysanthemum Throne. This was something that had not happened within the royal family in nearly two hundred years. His son Naruhito succeeded him on May 1st, ushering in the new *Reiwa* era. Translating roughly to "beautiful harmony", the beginning of the *Reiwa* era has been far from harmonious. Japan enters this era in a perilous situation. A new nationalism is on the rise in Japan. Shinzo Abe, the longest serving Prime Minister in modern Japanese history, resigned in August 2020. Japan is also challenged by the novel SARS COV-2 coronavirus pandemic that originated in nearby China. Additionally, Japan faces particular peril from climate catastrophe in the coming years. Yet the Japanese, as they always have, will persevere. Even as the *tokusatsu* artform is supplanted by computer generated imagery, there will no doubt be many more science fiction films produced in Japan. They will continue to reflect the country's collective zeitgeist.

ANIME AND TOKUSATSU CONNECTIONS
(a complicated relationship)

アニメと特撮接続

by Kevin Derendorf

"Live action adaptations of anime all suck!"

I've heard this statement made so many times from so many *anime* fans that it's practically an aphorism. Each time it's generally based on a limited sample of high-profile examples, such as *Dragonball Evolution,* Netflix's *Death Note* and *Ghost in the Shell* with Scarlett Johansson. I won't argue that those particular examples are worth defending but trashing an entire medium seems short-sighted. I often make the rounds at conventions, encouraging folks to check out works like the *Rurouni Kenshin, Cromartie High School* and *Cutie Honey* live-action films. I point out that a ton of elements in anime draw from live-action entertainment. I sometimes get into pedantic arguments about how *anime* and *manga* seem to get lumped into one bucket while other media such as Japanese video games, *tokusatsu* and light novels are segregated for some reason. Perhaps that's why I was tasked with writing about the relationship between *anime* and *tokusatsu.* It's a daunting prospect because it's so heavily ingrained. It's like writing about the

relationship between Japanese and Chinese entertainment: there's a lot to unpack!

Let's start at what's considered "the beginning", the year 1963. *Astro Boy* was not the first animation created in Japan by a long shot. Yet it was the first weekly half-hour animated program and its production techniques codified what "*anime*" would become synonymous with. The show was produced by Mushi Production, a studio founded by Osamu Tezuka. Tezuka is regarded as the God of Manga in the same way that Eiji Tsuburaya is considered the God of Special Effects in the Japanese cultural lexicon. *Astro Boy* was based on Tezuka's 1952 manga series. Believe it or not, it had already been adapted for television as a *tokusatsu* show in 1959. Later in 1963 another major anime hit the airwaves, *Gigantor*. *Gigantor* also had previously been adapted into *tokusatsu* in 1960. That series is credited as the first giant robot show on Japanese television and is based on Mitsuteru Yokoyama's *manga* from 1956. That was a year before *The Mysterians* had the first giant robot show up on Japanese cinema screens.

Gigantor would go on to be an influence on works like *Akira* and *20th Century Boys*, which was adapted into a very expensive live-action trilogy by Toho. Yokoyama's other works like *Giant Robo* (aka *Johnny Sokko*), *Princess Comet* and *Red Shadow* would thrive in both animated and live-action media. Tezuka meanwhile, in addition to many *manga* and *anime* projects, flirted with *tokusatsu*. He helped create the live-action/anime hybrid *Vampires*, a knock-off of *Ultraman* titled *Thunder Mask* and Ultraman's direct competitor *Ambassador Magma (The Space Giants)*. *Magma* would later be made into an anime as well. Tezuka was also a mentor to one of his assistants on *Astro Boy*, Shotaro Ishinomori. Ishinomori, a *manga* legend in his own right, is the person credited with the Guinness World Record for most comic pages drawn by one person.

Ishinomori got his big break in 1963 with his popular superhero *manga Cyborg 009*. The name was taken from the popularity of James Bond 007 and Japan's first cyborg superhero, *8-Man*. *8-Man*, in addition to allegedly inspiring the creation of *RoboCop*, was also adapted into its own live-action movie. *Cyborg 009* has never been directly adapted into *tokusatsu*, but it got *anime* movies in 1966 and 1967. The latter film heavily owes to the *kaiju* boom going on in Japanese media at the time, leading to a TV series and pop culture immortality. In 1971, Toei was looking to create a competitor to Tsuburaya's *Return of Ultraman*. Ishinomori recycled *Cyborg 009*'s premise of a person kidnapped by an evil organization and turned into a cyborg, only to escape and fight them. This concept became *Kamen Rider*, one of the most prolific *tokusatsu* franchises in history. From there he created dozens of other *tokusatsu* heroes such as *Kikaider, Inazuman* and *Robot Detective*. The other most notable one is *Himitsu Sentai Goranger*. It also used elements of the *Cyborg 009* formula along with the Tatsunoko anime series *Gatchaman*, which was kind of a *Kamen Rider* knock-off. It led to the Super Sentai franchise, Toei's other *tokusatsu* titan. On top of all this, Ishinomori had his own set of students, including one Go Nagai. Nagai revolutionized the *anime* world with piloted super robots (*Mazinger Z*), the future Sentai staple of combining robots (*Getter Robo*) and magical girls (*Cutie Honey*). This was on top of rocking *manga* audiences with new levels of lewd and crass humor. Much of Nagai's work has been adapted into live-action such as *Cutie Honey, Devilman, Kekko Kamen* and *Sukeban Boy*. Nagai was also involved with many *tokusatsu* productions, however. These included *Star Fleet, Battle Hawk, Aztekaiser* and more. He even took a crack at directing with *The Ninja Dragon*! Nagai's most seminal work is *Devilman*. While a mediocre anime, it was a fantastic *manga* that proved influential. *Devilman* went on to inspire manga like Clamp's *X*, anime like *Evangelion* and live action films like *Tokyo Gore Police*.

I could keep going, but this should be a representative sample of the Gordian knot that *manga, anime* and *tokusatsu* all form with each other. This permeates each of the industries to every degree. This applies on several levels: properties themselves, creators and influence. Let's start with the properties. Whether it's *Godzilla, Ultraman, Kamen Rider, Kikaider, Barom 1, Red Baron, Garo, Gridman, Atragon, Moonlight Mask, Sukeban Deka, Rainbowman, Tomie, Wolf Guy* or *School in the Crosshairs*. It seems that if you name a *tokusatsu* property, odds are it has at least one *anime* entry. What's astounding, though, is that you'll run into fans of *anime* based on live-action works with no clue about their origins. Whether it's *Iria* (a prequel to *Zeiram*), *Jin-roh* (a prequel to *The Red Spectacles*), *Night Head Genesis* (based on *Night Head*), *Doomed Megalopolis* (which draws from the same novel as *Tokyo: The Last Megalopolis*), *Giant Robo* or even *Ghost Stories* (from *School of Ghosts*, though most people just like that for the parody dub). You sometimes see the opposite of this with cult movie fans and Japanese live-action cinema (e.g. *Ichi the Killer* or *Spook Warfare*). There's usually a better understanding that lots of movies are based on *manga* or *anime*, sometimes even assuming it's based on a *manga* when it's not.

Recently, it's become a bit of a cross-promotional practice to develop anime TV series in tandem with live-action movie versions for manga. This is why films like *Parasyte, Inuyashiki, Assassination Classroom, Gatchaman Crowds, Yattermen, Erased, Usagi Drop, Another, Mushishi* and Shusuke Kaneko's version of *Death Note* came out closely to the series. This was also the plan for *Attack on Titan*, but the live-action version was delayed even as the *anime* continued. One of the biggest hits of the last decade owes a debt to this corporate synergy. That's to say nothing of adaptations where live-action versions of evergreen titles come out of the blue for nostalgia's sake. These include *Space Battleship Yamato, Casshern, Dororo, Patlabor, Lupin III* and the recent *Video Girl Ai* TV drama. Or just hit a few years after their prime like *Terra Formars, Tokyo Ghoul, Gantz, Saikano*, etc. There's a whole other conversation to be had about international live-action attempts. These have been made in Hong Kong with titles like *Story of Ricky, Wicked City* and *Peacock King*. The US made the *Guyver* movies, *Speed Racer, Ghost in the Shell* and *Alita: Battle Angel*. France produced *Nicky Larson, Lady Oscar, Crying Freeman* and South Korea with *Blood the Last Vampire, Dragon Ball, Illang* and so forth.

It's not obscure filmmakers that take on the task of bringing these new adaptations to light. Auteur industry bigwigs like Takashi Miike, Sion Sono and Sabu have been known to bring animated works into live-action. Many anime fans are surprised to know that, say, Mamoru Hosoda's *The Girl Who Leapt Through Time* or Masaaki Yuasa's *Japan Sinks* draw on prior live-action works and not just their source novels. There are also plenty of talented creative folks who keep a foot planted in both mediums, making movies in both animation and live-action. The foremost champion in this regard is Mamoru Oshii. He is known to anime fans for directing surreal and psychological opi like *Ghost in the Shell, The Angel's Egg* and *Sky Crawlers*. He's often lamented for focusing his recent career on live-action works like *Avalon, Garm Wars* and *Assault Girls*. For those who know what to look for, Oshii's worn his appreciation for live-action effects shows on his sleeve from the beginning. *Twilight Q* was named after *Ultra Q* and

The Twilight Zone, after all. He has strong support for cross-media adaptations of his work as well as decades of insistence on creating a live-action version of *Patlabor*. Oshii has also surrounded himself with similarly-minded individuals. These include Kazunori Ito who wrote *Ghost in the Shell* and *Gamera: Guardian of the Universe* the same year. Gamera trilogy director Shusuke Kaneko also began his career working on Oshii's *anime* series *Urusei Yatsura*. Another *Urusei Yatsura* alumnus is Hideaki Anno. Anno has made a name for himself in *anime* and *tokusatsu* circles via astounding work championing both. He has been dedicated to working both mediums since his college short films. Anno is a textbook case for the cross-pollination of tokusatsu and anime influences. His animated works such as *Neon Genesis Evangelion* and *Nadia: The Secret of Blue Water* are full of *tokusatsu* aesthetic and allusions. By contrast, his live-action titles like *Cutie Honey* and *Shin Godzilla* go into some very *anime*-esque territory. His main creative partner, Shinji Higuchi, is likewise prolific in both special effects and cartoons. He's deservedly lauded for his masterful handling of the Gamera trilogy's effects. Yet it's seldom brought up how he did storyboarding and direction on seminal *anime* of the 80s and 90s simultaneously with his effects career.

I could rattle off more famous anime directors. One of Katsuhiro Otomo's live-action movies was written by Satoshi Kon. Yet they're far from the only ones who straddle the *anime/tokusatsu* divide. Chiaki J Konaka was one of the hottest anime screenwriters of the 90s and 2000s. Konaka penned *Serial Experiments Lain, The Big O, Digimon Tamers, Hellsing* and *Armitage*

III. He also channeled that Lovecraftian horror sensibility into the likes of *Ultraman Tiga, Ultraman Gaia, Marebito* and other live-action works. Konaka's frequent collaborator Keiichi Hasegawa has also made a name for himself with *SSSS.Gridman, Zoids* and the 2006 *Gegege no Kitaro*. He's also the man responsible for *Ultraman Nexus* and *Ultraman Dyna*. *Madoka Magica* and *Psycho Pass* creator Gen Urobuchi is known in the *anime* world for his nihilism and philosophy. This extends a bit into his scripts for *Kamen Rider Gaim*, but less so for *Thunderbolt Fantasy*. Urobuchi has further straddled the *toku-anime* divide by writing the too-thematically-heavy Godzilla anime trilogy. Yasuko Kobayashi has two of the biggest anime hits of the 2010s under her anime screenwriting belt: *Attack on Titan* and *Jojo's Bizarre Adventure*. Yet she could also be lauded for the excellent *Kamen Rider OOO, Mirai Sentai Timeranger* or the perennial *Kamen Rider DenOh*. Sho Aikawa blew minds by writing violent anime like *Urotsukidoji* and *Violence Jack* along the fantastic *Martian Successor Nadesico*. Aikawa also wrote some quite tame entries in the Super Sentai franchise. Aikawa's *Garo* collaborator Toshiki Inoue penned the anime megahits *Ranma ½* and *Death Note*. He is better known for creating *Chojin Sentai Jetman* and *Kamen Rider 555*.

Creature and mechanical designers also cross over frequently. You find the likes of Shoji Kawamori, Yasushi Nirasawa, Keita Amemiya, Keiichi Sato, Masakazu Katsura, Mahiro Maeda, Takayuki Takeya and Kia Asamiya have anime and tokusatsu gigs on their resumes. As CGI becomes integral to the special effects landscape, animation directors have found work in the live-action industry. Even Ichiro Itano, whom the spiraling missile *"Itano circus"* is named, has orchestrated Ultraman flight sequences. Music composers are another field with significant overlap between media. While a *tokusatsu* fan may recognize, say, Shunsuke Kikuchi for doing the jazzy *Showa* Gamera scores, anime fans will jump at his memorable soundtrack to *Dragon Ball*. Akira Ifukube, Shiro Sagisu, Riichiro Manabe, Masaru Sato, Kow Otani, Kenji Kawai, Michiaki Watanabe, Michiru Oshima, Godiego, even Keith Emerson; if there's a *tokusatsu* composer you can think of, odds are they've worked on an *anime* soundtrack.

The logical endpoint of so much gray area between production crews is that the works invariably influence each other. This is why you wind up with anime like *Concrete Revolutio* or *Tiger & Bunny* that feel so "*tokusatsu*". Tokusatsu like *Gunhed*, *Akibaranger* or *Sh15uya* also can come across as very "*anime*". Creators need not actually work on projects to be influenced by them. Both forms of entertainment are ubiquitous in Japanese culture. These influences are not always obvious, though, so even in the case of something like *Neon Genesis Evangelion*. Evangelion transparently lifts elements whole cloth from numerous influences, chiefly *Ultraman* and Gerry Anderson's *UFO*. Fans often do not recognize the allusion. This can also be felt in western media; one only has to look at the cinematic melting pots that Quentin Tarantino and George Lucas purvey. Thus it's interesting to note that *Attack on Titan*, a mega hit of the *anime* world, was only lukewarmly embraced by occidental *kaiju* fandom. *Attack on Titan* is a *kaiju* opus, as the creator makes clear his

inspirations in *War of the Gargantuas*, *Godzilla vs. Biollante* and *Gamera: Guardian of the Universe*. Of course, Gamera effects guru Shinji Higuchi would later adapt *Attack on Titan* to live-action to universal resentment. Even the titles that are themselves synonymous with the stereotype of "*anime*" echo traces of *tokusatsu*. Let's consider some tentpoles:

•Pokemon: The idea of capsule monsters, on which the entire Pokemon franchise is based, was introduced in *Ultraseven*, to creator Satoshi Tajiri's admission.

•Dragon Ball: Akira Toriyama is a massive *kaiju* fan, even taking part in *The Return of Godzilla* as an extra in a crowd scene. The same year that that movie came out, he began publishing *Dragon Ball*. It has proved one of the most successful franchises of all time. The series has some transparent shout-outs to Toriyama's fandom, such as the heroic Saiyaman and the petite Baby Gamera. Even its core elements of flashy beam battles and heroes that transform to gain more power are reminiscent of Tsuburaya's creations. In fact, the first time Godzilla was adapted to *anime* with 1994's *Godzilland*, the opening theme to *Dragon Ball Z* played as an intro.

•Naruto: Like every popular series for juvenile males to follow in its footsteps, *Naruto* emulates *Dragon Ball*'s template to some extent. Since its author Masashi Kishimoto is also a *kaiju* fan, the series is populated with giant powerful creatures. While three of the main characters (Jiraiya, Orochimaru and Tsunade) are straight out of *kabuki* theater, they draw most inspiration from the versions in 1966's *The Magic Serpent*, It draws from other imagery from the 1960s "ninja boom" as well, which spanned television, film and comics. Don't tell fans that the much-memed *"Naruto run"* was due to *Shinobi no Mono*!

•*Sailor Moon*: The modern concept of superheroine magical girls goes back to *Cutie Honey*, in turn inspired by *Rainbowman*. The clever twist that *Sailor Moon* brought to the formula was introducing a color-coded team in true Super Sentai fashion. The series has a handful of other tokusatsu influences such as *Moonlight Mask*. This meant that Toei's live-action adaptation of the show (sadly never brought to the west) was particularly apt.

Of course, *tokusatsu* owes a lot to *anime* as well. Along with *Gatchaman* and *Getter Robo*, there was the late 1960s yokai boom ignited by the first television adaptation of *Gegege no Kitaro*. There was also the fixation on "realistic" military mecha in the 80s after the success of *Mobile Suit Gundam* and the introspective science fiction of the late 1990s that arose with *Evangelion*. One can even feel it today. Recent series like *Garo: Versus Road* are embracing the fantasy cyberpunk format of the pervasive *isekai* genre. The point is that the Japanese entertainment industry is a complex ecosystem rather than an array of disconnected silos. It's worth having an eye on animation and special effects shows in tandem for a more complete view of Japan's pop culture. Even if your tastes are more inclined towards one at first, you might find more to appreciate in the other.

BIBLIOGRAPHY

書誌

BOOKS
The Dinosaur Scrapbook (1980) by Donald F. Glut
The Japanese Film: Art and Industry (1982) by Joseph L. Anderson and Donald Richie
The Psychotronic Encyclopedia of Film (1983) by Michael Weldon
The Psychotronic Video Guide (1995) by Michael Weldon
Stanley Kubrick: A Biography (1997) by John Baxter
A Critical History and Filmography of Toho's Godzilla Series (1997, 2nd edition 2010) by David Kalat
Japan's Favorite Mon-Star: The Unauthorized Biography of "The Big G" (1998) by Steve Ryfle

Monsters Are Attacking Tokyo (1998) by Stuart Galbraith IV
Movie Director, Naval Officer, Jodo-Shinshu Buddhist Minister (1999) by Shue Matsubayashi
Tokyoscope: The Japanese Cult Film Companion (2001) by Patrick Macias
The Emperor and the Wolf: The Lives and Films of Akira Kurosawa and Toshiro Mifune (2002) by Stuart Galbraith IV
Eiji Tsuburaya: Master of Monsters (2007) by August Ragone
The Toho Studios Story: A History and Complete Filmography (2008) by Stuart Galbraith IV
Ishiro Honda : A Life in Film, from Godzilla to Kurosawa

(2017) by Steve Ryfle and Ed Godziszewswki
The Big Book of Japanese Giant Monster Movies: The Lost Films (2017) by John LeMay
Kaiju for Hipsters: 101 "Alternative" Giant Monster Movies (2018) by Kevin Derendorf
Agents of World Renewal: The Rise of Yonaoshi Gods in Japan (2019) by Takashi Miura

DOCUMENTARIES
Behind the Scenes of The Last Dinosaur (1977)
Virus TV Special (1980)
The Making of The Return of Godzilla (1984)

The Making of The Eight-Headed Serpent Strikes Back (1985)
Toho Special Effects Outtake Collection (1986)
The Making of Godzilla vs. Biollante (1989)
The Making of Gamera: Guardian of the Universe (1995)
The Making of Gamera 2 (1996)
Extracurricular Lesson TV Special with Hideaki Anno (1998)
Gamera 1999 (1999)
The Making of Godzilla, Mothra and King Ghidorah: Giant Monsters All-Out Attack (2001)
Toho HiVision Restoration Documentary (2007)
Teshigahara and Abe: A Collaboration (2007)
Bringing Godzilla Down to Size (2008)
Space Battleship Yamato VFX (2011)
Behind the Scenes of Shin Godzilla (2016)
Making of Alita: Battle Angel (2019)

VIDEO INTERVIEWS
Ishiro Honda (1990), Director's Guild of Japan
Keita Amemiya and Yuko Moriyama (1992) on *Zeiram* (1991), GAGA
Shinji Higuchi (2002), Tokuma
Kinji Fukasaku (2002) on *Virus* (1980), Kadokawa
Sakyo Komatsu (2002) on *Virus* (1980), Kadokawa
Teruyoshi Nakano (2003) on *Matango* (1963), Toho Video
Teruyoshi Nakano (2003) on *The War in Space* (1977), Toho Video
Richard Taylor and Ben Wooten on *Live Action Evangelion* (2004), ADV Films

James Quandt, *The Face of Another* video essay (2007), Criterion
Akira Takarada (2011) on *Godzilla* (1954), Criterion
Akira Takarada (2011) on *Godzilla* (1954), Criterion
Haruo Nakajima (2011) on *Godzilla* (1954), Criterion
Yoshio Irie (2011) on *Godzilla* (1954), Criterion
Eizo Kaimai (2011) on *Godzilla* (1954), Criterion
Shinya Tsukamoto (2012) on *The Adventure of Denchu Kozo* (1987) and *Tetsuo: The Iron Man,* Kaijyu Theater
Kaiju Masterclass Interviews with Allyson Adams, Pat Saperstein, Shusuke Kaneko and Tab Murphy (2020)

COMMENTARY TRACKS
Godzilla (1954) with David Kalat, Criterion
The Mysterians (1957) with Koichi Kawakita and Shinji Higuchi, Toho Video
Mothra (1961) with Steve Ryfle and Ed Godziszewswki, Sony
The Last War (1961) with Shue Matsubayashi, Toho Video
Matango (1963) with Akira Kubo, Toho Video
Atragon (1963) with Koji Kajita, Toho Video
Mothra vs. Godzilla (1964) with Steve Ryfle and Ed Godziszewswki, Classic Media
Gamera: The Giant Monster (1965) with August Ragone, Shout! Factory
Invasion of Astro-Monster (1965) with Stuart Galbraith IV, Classic Media
The War of the Gargantuas (1966) with Kumi Mizuno, Toho Video

Goke, Body Snatcher from Hell (1968) with Shinji Higuchi and Jun Miura, Shochiku Video
All Monsters Attack (1969) with Richard Pusateri, Classic Media
Godzilla vs. Hedorah (1971) with Teruyoshi Nakano, Toho Video
Under the Flag of the Rising Sun (1972) with Linda Hoaglund, Home Vision Entertainment
Submersion of Japan (1973) with Sakyo Komatsu, Koji Hashimoto and Teruyoshi Nakano, Toho Video
The Return of Godzilla (1984) with Koji Hashimoto and Teruyoshi Nakano, Toho Video
Tetsuo: The Iron Man (1989) with Tom Mes, Arrow Video

MAGAZINES AND OTHER
Freedom of Information Act: *Masters of Deceit,* J. Edgar Hoover (1959)
G-FAN
South China Morning Post
Famous Monsters of Filmland
Variety
Fangoria
Newtype
The Super Infra-Man liner notes by August Ragone and Damon Foster, Image Entertainment

WEBSITES AND BLOGS
Kaiju Conversations (http://www.davmil.org/www.kaijuconversations.com)
Henshin Online (Archived)
Sci-Fi Japan
Vantage Point Interviews
Shusuke Kaneko Information Website
Maser Patrol
Toho Kingdom
Reuters

CHRONOLOGY

年代記

1892: Kinescope invented by Thomas Edison.

5.1.1893-10.30.1893: The World's Fair held in Chicago, Illinois, U.S.

7.25.1894-4.17.1895: First Sino-Japanese War; ends in Japanese victory. Taiwan, the Liaodong Peninsula and other territories ceded to Japan.

12.28.1895: Lumiere Brothers hold the first commercial film screening in Paris, France.

1897: First Japanese film screened of Tokyo urban life.

4.21.1898-8.13.1898: Spanish-American War; ends in U.S. victory.

2.4.1899-7.2.1902: Phillipine-American War; ends in U.S. victory.

11.2.1899-9.7.1901: Boxer Rebellion in China.

7.10.1901: Eiji Tsuburaya born.

9.14.1901: U.S. President William McKinley is assassinated.

9.10.1902: A Trip to the Moon released in France; one of the first science fiction films.

12.17.1903: The Wright Brothers execute the first manned flight in a motorized airplane.

2.8.1904-9.5.1905: Russo Japanese War; ends in Japanese victory.

11.17.1905: Japan-Korea treaty signed.

1.21.1906: Masaichi Nagata born.

1906: Kinemacolor, the first color motion picture film process, invented by George Albert Smith.

10.26.1909: Hirobumi Ito assassinated.

3.23.1910: Akira Kurosawa born.

4.26.1910: Tomoyuki Tanaka born.

8.22.1910: Greater Korea is annexed by Japan.

5.7.1911: Ishiro Honda born.

10.10.1911-2.12.1912: The 1911 Revolution takes place in China. Manchu Emperor Puyi abdicates, ending the Qing Dynasty. The Republic of China is established.

7.30.1912: Emperor Mutsuhito dies and the Meiji era ends. His son Yoshihito succeeds him, beginning the Taisho era.

9.10.1912: Nikkatsu founded.

2.18.1914: Gertie the Dinosaur released in the U.S., one of the very first fully animated films.

6.28.1914: Archduke Franz Ferdinand is assassinated, leading to the start of World War I.

8.23.1914: Japan sides with England, joining the Allied Powers in the coming World War I.

3.8-3.16.1917: February Revolution in Russia. Tsar Nicholas II abdicates.

11.7.1917: The October Bolshevik Revolution takes place, beginning the Russian Civil War.

3.1918: Spanish flu pandemic begins.

11.11.1918: Kaiser Wilhelm II abdicates and Germany signs an armistice. World War I ends.

6.28.1919: Germany signs the Treaty of Versailles.

4.1920: Spanish flu pandemic ends.

8.26.1920: Nineteenth Amendment certified in U.S., granting women the right to vote.

11.8.1920: Shochiku's film production arm founded.

12.30.1922: Soviet Union established.

2.17.1923: Jun Fukuda born.

9.1.1923: Great Kanto earthquake strikes the Tokyo area.

2.17.1924: Kihachi Okamoto born.

3.7.1924: Kobo Abe born.

12.25.1926: Emperor Yoshihito dies and the Taisho era ends. His son Hirohito succeeds him, beginning the Showa era.

8.1.1927: Chinese Civil War between the Republic of China and the Communist Party of China begins.

10.5.1927: Toshio Masuda born.

10.6.1927: The Jazz Singer released in the U.S; the first feature length sound film.
7.2.1928: First television broadcast transmitted in the United States.
11.3.1928: Osamu Tezuka born.
10.24-10.29.1929: U.S. stock market crashes, beginning the Great Depression.
7.3.1930: Kinji Fukasaku born.
1.28.1931: Sakyo Komatsu born.
9.18.1931: The Mukden incident takes place and Japan invades Manchuria.
3.1.1932: The puppet state of Manchukuo is established by Japan in Northeast China.
1.30.1933: Adolf Hitler becomes chancellor of Germany.
3.27.1933: Japan withdraws from the League of Nations.
4.7.1933: King Kong released in the U.S.
9.28.1933: Noriaki Yuasa born.
10.16.1934-10.22.1935: Mao Zedong's Long March.
10.9.1935: Teruyoshi Nakano born.
2.26-28.1936: February 26th Incident.
1937: PCL, J.O and other companies merge to form Toho.
7.7.1937: Marco Polo Bridge Incident. Japan begins full scale invasion of Mainland China.
8.13-11.26.1937: Battle of Shanghai; ends in Japanese victory.

12.1-12.13.1937: Battle of Nanjing; ends in Japanese victory.
12.13.1937-1.1938: Nanjing Massacre.
1.9.1938: Nobuhiko Obayashi born.
1.25.1938: Shotaro Ishinomori born.
3.24-4.7.1938: Battle of Tai'erzhuang; ends in Chinese victory.
6.8.1938: Toei founded as Toyoko Eiga.
6.11-10.27.1938: Battle of Wuhan; ends in Japanese victory.
12.17.1938: Nuclear fission discovered in Germany by Otto Hahn and Fritz Strassman.
1939: First television broadcasts take placed in Japan.
4.20-5.24.1939: Battle of Suixian-Zaoyang; ends in Chinese victory.
9.1.1939: Germany invades Poland, leading to the start of World War II.
9.17-10.6.1939: First Battle of Changsha; ends in Chinese victory.
11.15.1939-11.30.1940: Battle of South Guangxi; ends in stalemate.
5.1-6.18.1940: Battle of Zaoyi; ends in Japanese victory.
8.8.1940: The Yamato, the largest battleship ever built, is launched by the Japanese Imperial Navy.
9.22-9.26.1940: Japan invades and conquers French Indochina.
9.27.1940: Japan signs the Tripartite Pact and joins

Germany and Italy in the Axis Powers.
12.7.1941: Japan attacks Pearl Harbor in Hawaii.
12.8.1941: The United States declares war on Japan, entering World War II. Japan invades Thailand, who then allies with them.
12.8-12.10.1941: First Battle of Guam; ends in Japanese victory.
12.8-12.23.1941: Battle of Wake Island; ends in Japanese victory.
12.8-12.25.1941: Battle of Hong Kong; ends in Japanese victory.
1942: Daiei founded as Dai Nippon Films.
1.7-4.9.1942: Battle of Bataan; ends in Japanese victory.
2.8-2.15.1942: Battle of Singapore; ends in Japanese victory. Nearby Malaya also falls to the Japanese.
2.19.1942: Bombing of Darwin, Australia by the Japanese.
2.27.1942: Battle of the Java Sea; ends in Japanese victory.
3.31-4.10.1942: Battle of Ceylon; ends in Japanese victory.
4.11-4.19.1942: Battle of Yenangyaung; ends in Allied victory.
5.4-5.8.1942: Battle of the Coral Sea; ends in stalemate tending toward Allied victory.
5.9.1942: The Philippines fall to Japan.
5.31-6.8.1942: Attack on Sydney Harbor, Australia by Japanese submarines.
6.4-6.7.1942: Battle of Midway; ends in U.S. victory.

8.7.1942-2.9.1943: Battle of Guadalcanal; ends in Allied victory.

12.5.1942: Koichi Kawakita born.

3.2-3.5.1943: Battle of the Bismark Sea; ends in Allied victory.

6.30.1943: Woodlark Island, Kiriwina, New Georgia and Rendova all captured from Japanese control by Allied forces.

8.15-10.6.1943: Battle of Vella Lavella; ends in Allied victory.

9.3.1943: Axis power Italy surrenders to the Allies in the Armistice of Cassibile.

9.5.1943: Lae, New Guinea captured from Japanese control by Allied forces.

10.27-11.12.1943: Battle of the Treasury Islands; ends in Allied victory.

11.1.1943: Allied forces land at Bouganville.

11.20-11.23.1943: Battle of Tarawa; ends in U.S. victory.

11.20-11.24.1943: Battle of Makin; ends in U.S. victory.

12.15.1943-2.24.1944: Battle of Arawe; ends in Allied victory.

12.26.1943-1.16.1944: Battle of Cape Gloucester; ends in Allied victory.

1.2-2.10.1944: Battle of Saidor; ends in Allied victory.

1.2-2.10.1944: Battle of Saidor; ends in Allied victory.

1.31-2.3.1944: Battle of Kwajalein; ends in U.S. victory.

2.17-2.23.1944: Battle of Eniwetok; ends in U.S. victory.

6.15-7.9.1944: Battle of Saipan; ends in U.S. victory.

6.19-6.20.1944: Battle of the Philippine Sea; ends in U.S. victory.

7.21-8.10.1944: Battle of Guam; ends in U.S. victory.

7.24-8.1.1944: Battle of Tinian; ends in U.S. victory.

9.15-11.27.1944: Battle of Peleliu; ends in U.S. victory.

9.17-10.22.1944: Battle of Angaur; ends in U.S. victory.

10.23-10.26.1944: Battle of Leyte Gulf; ends in U.S. victory.

2.19-3.26.1945: Battle of Iwo Jima; ends in U.S. victory.

3.26-7.2.1945: Battle of Okinawa; ends in Allied victory.

4.6-6.9.1945: Battle of West Hunan; ends in Allied victory.

4.12.1945: U.S. President Franklin Delano Roosevelt dies. *Momotaro: Sacred Sailors* released in Japan; the first feature length anime film.

4.30.1945: During the Battle of Berlin, Adolf Hitler commits sucide.

5.2.1945: Berlin, Germany falls to the Soviets; puting an end to the Nazi regime.

7.16.1945: First nuclear test in New Mexico, U.S.

7.26.1945: Potsdam Declaration issued by the Allies to Japan, urging its surrender.

8.6.1945: U.S. airship Enola Gay drops atomic bomb "Little Boy" on Hiroshima, Japan.

8.9.1945: The U.S. airship Bockscar drops atomic bomb "Fat Man' on Nagasaki, Japan. The Soviet Union

declares war on Japan and mounts an invasion of Manchuria.

8.15.1945: Emperor Hirohito announces his decision to surrender to the Allies. His voice, urging capitulation, is heard for the first time on Japanese radio.

8.28.1945: U.S. Occupation of Japan begins.

9.2.1945: Japan formally surrenders to the Allies.

10.24.1945: United Nations formally established.

4.10.1946: Japan holds its first post-war election; Shigeru Yoshida is elected Prime Minister.

4.26.1946: International Military Tribunal for the Far East is convened in Tokyo.

7.1946: U.S. conducts multiple nuclear tests at the Bikini Atoll in Operation Crossroads.

3.1947; Shin Toho founded by disgruntled former Toho employees after union disputes.

8.29.1949: The Soviet Union conducts their first nuclear test in Kazakhstan.

9.25.1949: The Invisible Man Appears released in Japan; technically the first live action and feature length Japanese science fiction film.

10.1.1949: Mao Zedong's People's Liberation Army drives out Chiang Kai-shek's Kuomintang from mainland China. Mao proclaims China, now under communist control, as the People's Republic.

12.1949: Chiang Kai-shek makes Taipei, Taiwan the

capital of the Republic of China.

1950: Eastman color, the first single strip motion picture color process, developed by Eastman Kodak.

6.25.1950: North Korea invades South Korea as the Korean War begins.

8.8.1951: Mamoru Oshii born.

9.8.1951: Treaty of San Francisco signed; beginning the end of the U.S. Occupation of Japan.

4.28.1952: U.S. Occupation of Japan formally ends.

7.27.1953: Korean Armistice Agreement signed; largely ending the Korean War.

9.17.1953: *The Robe* released in the U.S.; the first film shot in an anamorphic widescreen format.

3.1.1954: U.S. Castle Bravo nuclear bomb test. Japanese fishing boat the Lucky Dragon No. 5 is exposed to contamination from the blast.

11.3.1954: *Godzilla* released in Japan.

12.29.1954: *The Invisible Avenger* released in Japan.

4.24.1955: *Godzilla Raids Again* released in Japan.

6.8.1955: Shusuke Kaneko born.

8.14.1955: *Half Human* released in Japan.

1.29.1956: *Warning From Space* released in Japan.

4.27.1956: *Godzilla, King of the Monsters!* released in the U.S..

11.7.1956: *Fearful Invasion of Flying Saucers* released in Japan.

12.18.1956: Japan joins the United Nations.

12.26.1956: *Rodan* released in Japan.

7.30.1957: *Super Giant* released in Japan.

8.13.1957: *Super Giant Continues* released in Japan.

8.25.1957: *The Invisible Man vs. the Human Fly* released in Japan.

10.1.1957: *Super Giant: The Mysterious Spacemen's Demonic Castle* released in Japan.

10.4.1957: Sputnik 1 launched into Earth's atmosphere by the Soviet Union.

10.8.1957: *Super Giant: Earth on the Verge of Destruction* released in Japan.

12.28.1957: *The Mysterians* and *Super Giant: The Artificial Satellite and the Destruction of Humanity* released in Japan.

1.3.1958: *Super Giant: The Spaceship and the Clash of the Artificial Satellite* released in Japan.

4.29.1958: *Super Giant: The Space Mutant Appears* released in Japan.

5.28.1958: *The H-Man* released in Japan.

10.14.1958: *Varan* released in Japan.

11.4.1958: *Planet Prince* begins airing on Japanese television; one of the first Japanese science fiction TV shows.

3.27.1959: *Super Giant: The Devil's Incarnation* released in Japan.

4.24.1959: *Super Giant: Kingdom of the Poison Moth* released in Japan.

5.19.1959: *Planet Prince* released in Japan.

5.25.1959: *Planet Prince: The Terrifying Spaceship* released in Japan.

12.26.1959: *Battle in Outer Space* released in Japan.

1.1.1960: Shinya Tsukamoto born.

1.19.1960: Treaty of Mutual Cooperation and Security between the United States and Japan, also known as the ANPO Treaty, signed.

2.13.1960: France detonates its first nuclear bomb in the Gerboise Bleue test.

4.10.1960: *The Secret of the Telegian* released in Japan.

5.22.1960: Hideaki Anno born.

10.19.1960: *World War III Breaks Out* released in Japan.

12.11.1960: *The Human Vapor* released in Japan.

1961: Shin Toho goes bankrupt.

4.12.1961: The Soviets send the first man into space, Yuri Gagarin, in the Vostok 1 mission.

7.19.1961: *Iron Sharp* released in Japan.

7.30.1961: *Mothra* released in Japan.

10.8.1961: *The Last War* released in Japan.

10.30.1961: Tsar Bomba, the most powerful nuclear weapon in history, tested by the Soviet Union.

3.21.1962: *Gorath* released in Japan.

8.11.1962: *King Kong vs. Godzilla* released in Japan.

10.16-10.28.1962: Cuban Missile Crisis.

1963: Tsuburaya Pro established.

1.1.1963: Astro Boy begins airing on Japanese television.

7.13.1963: Wind Velocity 75 Meters released in Japan.

8.11.1963: Matango released in Japan.

10.20.1963: Gigantor begins airing on Japanese television.

11.22.1963: U.S. President John F. Kennedy is assassinated.

12.22.1963: Atragon released in Japan.

4.29.1964: Mothra vs. Godzilla released in Japan.

8.2.1964: Gulf of Tonkin incident; Vietnam War escalates.

8.11.1964: Dogora released in Japan.

10.10-10.24.1964: Summer Olympics held in Tokyo, Japan.

10.16.1964: China tests its first nuclear weapon in Project 596.

12.20.1964: Ghidorah, the Three-Headed Monster released in Japan.

3.8.1965: U.S. Marines land near Da Nang, Vietnam as the ground war begins.

3.20.1965: Gulliver's Travels Beyond the Moon released in Japan.

8.8.1965: Frankenstein Conquers the World released in Japan.

9.22.1965: Shinji Higuchi born.

11.27.1965: Gamera, the Giant Monsters released in Japan.

12.19.1965: Invasion of Astro-Monster released in Japan.

1.2.1966: Ultra Q begins airing on Japanese television.

4.17.1966: Gamera vs. Barugon released in Japan.

5.1966: Cultural Revolution begins in China.

7.1.1966: Water Cyborg released in Japan.

7.15.1966: The Face of Another released in Japan.

7.16.1966: Ultraman begins airing on Japanese television.

7.21.1966: Cyborg 009 released in Japan.

7.31.1966: The War of the Gargantuas released in Japan.

12.17.1966: Ebirah, Horror of the Deep released in Japan.

12.21.1966: The Golden Bat released in Japan.

3.15.1967: Gamera vs. Gyaos released in Japan.

3.25.1967: The X From Outer Space released in Japan.

4.22.1967: Gappa, the Triphibian Monster released in Japan.

7.22.1967: King Kong Escapes released in Japan.

10.11.1967: Giant Robo begins airing on Japanese television.

12.16.1967: Son of Godzilla released in Japan.

1.30.1968: Tet Offensive launched by Viet Cong forces in Vietnam, escalating the war further.

3.20.1968: Gamera vs. Viras released in Japan.

4.4.1968: Martin Luther King Jr. is assassinated.

6.26.1968: Iwo Jima returned to Japan.

8.1.1968: Destroy All Monsters released in Japan.

8.14.1968: Goke, Body Snatcher From Hell released in Japan.

11.9.1968: Genocide released in Japan.

12.19.1968: The Green Slime released in Japan.

3.21.1969: Gamera vs. Guiron released in Japan.

6.28-7.3.1969: Stonewall riots in New York City, U.S.

7.20.1969: U.S. spacecraft Apollo 11 lands on the moon and Neil Armstrong takes humanity's first steps off world. *Flying Phantom Ship* released in Japan.

7.26.1969: Latitude Zero released in Japan.

12.20.1969: All Monsters Attack and *Konto 55: Grand Space Adventure* released in Japan.

1.25.1970: Eiji Tsuburaya dies.

3.15-9.13.1970: Expo '70 held in Osaka, Japan.

3.21.1970: Gamera vs. Jiger released in Japan.

8.1.1970: Space Amoeba released in Japan.

1.2.1971: Spectreman begins airing on Japanese television.

4.3.1971: Kamen Rider begins airing on Japanese television.

7.17.1971: Gamera vs. Zigra released in Japan.

7.24.1971: Godzilla vs. Hedorah released in Japan.

12.1971: Daiei goes bankrupt.

3.12.1972: Godzilla vs. Gigan released in Japan.

5.15.1972: Okinawa returned to Japanese administrative control.

12.3.1972: Mazinger Z begins airing on Japanese television.

12.17.1972: Daigoro vs. Goliath released in Japan.
3.17.1973: Godzilla vs. Megalon released in Japan.
10.6.1973: Oil crisis begins with the Arab-Israeli Yom Kippur War as the Organization of Arab Petroleum Exporting Countries places an embargo on countries supportive of Israel.
10.13.1973: Cutie Honey begins airing on Japanese television.
12.29.1973: Submersion of Japan released in Japan.
3.21.1974: Godzilla vs. Mechagodzilla released in Japan.
8.3.1974: Prophecies of Nostradamus released in Japan.
8.9.1974: U.S. President Richard Nixon resigns while facing impeachment charges for the Watergate scandal.
10.6.1974: Space Battleship Yamato begins airing on Japanese television.
3.15.1975: Terror of Mechagodzilla released in Japan.
4.5.1975: Go Ranger begins airing on Japanese television.
4.17.1975: Khmer Rouge captures Phnom Penh, Cambodia.
4.30.1975: Vietnam War ends with the fall of Saigon and surrender of South Vietnam.
5.15.1975: Getter Robo G begins airing on Japanese television.
6.20.1975: Jaws released in the U.S.
7.12.1975: Conflagration released in Japan.

1976: Kadokawa Films founded.
9.9.1976: Chinese Cultural Revolution ends with the death of Mao Zedong.
4.29.1977: Legend of the Dinosaur and Monster Bird released in Japan.
5.25.1977: Star Wars released in the U.S.
9.10.1977: The Last Dinosaur released in Japan.
12.17.1977: The War in Space released in Japan.
4.29.1978: Message From Space released in Japan.
7.14.1978: Farewell to Space Battleship Yamato released in Japan.
11.23.1978: Blood Type: Blue released in Japan.
4.7.1979: Mobile Suit Gundam begins airing on Japanese television.
5.25.1979: Alien released in the U.S.
7.20.1979: The Bermuda Depths released in Japan.
8.4.1979: Galaxy Express 999 released in Japan.
10.6.1979: The Man Who Stole the Sun released in Japan.
12.15.1979: Time Slip released in Japan.
3.20.1980: Gamera: Supermonster released in Japan.
6.28.1980: Virus released in Japan.
8.2.1980: Be Forever Yamato released in Japan.
8.30.1980: Deathquake released in Japan.
10.4.1980: X-Bomber starts airing on Japanese television.
3.14.1981: Mobile Suit Gundam: The Movie released in Japan.

5.18.1981: First known cases of HIV/AIDS reported.
7.11.1981: The Aimed School and *Mobile Suit Gundam II: Soldiers of Sorrow* released in Japan.
8.1.1981: Adieu Galaxy Express 999 released in Japan.
8.12.1981: First personal computer released by IBM.
3.14.1982: Mobile Suit Gundam III: Encounters in Space released in Japan.
7.3.1982: Space Adventure Cobra released in Japan.
10.3.1982: Super Dimension Fortress Macross starts airing on Japanese television.
10.30.1982: Future War 198X released in Japan.
2.11.1983: Urusei Yatsura: Only You released in Japan.
3.12.1983: Crusher Joe and *Harmageddon: Genma Taisen* released in Japan.
3.19.1983: Final Yamato released in Japan.
7.16.1983: The Little Girl Who Conquered Time released in Japan.
9.26.1983: The Soviet nuclear early warning system detects the launch of multiple American missiles; it is determined to be a false alarm.
2.11.1984: Urusei Yatsura 2: Beautiful Dreamer released in Japan.
3.11.1984: Nausicaa of the Valley of the Wind released in Japan.
3.17.1984: Bye Bye Jupiter released in Japan.
7.21.1984: Macross: Do You Remember Love? released in Japan.

12.15.1984: The Return of Godzilla released in Japan.
1.26.1985: Urusei Yatsura 3: Remember My Love released in Japan.
8.10.1985: Odin: Photon Sailer Starlight released in Japan.
10.24.1985: Masaichi Nagata dies.
12.15.1985: The Angel's Egg released in Japan.
12.21.1985: Vampire Hunter D released in Japan.
2.22.1986: Urusei Yatsura 4: Lum the Forever released in Japan.
3.8.1986: Fist of the North Star released in Japan.
4.26.1986: Chernobyl nuclear accident takes place in the Ukraine.
6.21.1986: Project A-ko released in Japan.
1.17.1987: Tokyo Blackout released in Japan.
2.7.1987: The Red Spectacles released in Japan.
3.14.1987: Royal Space Force: The Wings of Honneamise released in Japan.
7.11.1987: The Drifting Classroom released in Japan.
7.21.1987: Robot Carnival released in Japan.
8.1.1987: Nineteen is released in Japan.
9.14.1987: Princess From the Moon released in Japan.
11.21.1987: Twilight of the Cockroaches released in Japan.
2.6.1988: Legend of the Galactic Heroes: My Conquest is the Sea of Stars and *Urusei Yatsura: The Final Chapter* released in Japan.
3.12.1988: Mobile Suit Gundam: Char's Counterattack released in Japan.

7.16.1988: Akira released in Japan.
1.7.1989: Emperor Hirohito dies and the Showa era ends. His son Akihito succeeds him, beginning the Heisei era.
2.9.1989: Osamu Tezuka dies.
3.11.1989: Venus Wars released in Japan.
4.15-6.4.1989: Tiananmen Square protests in Beijing, China.
7.1.1989: Tetsuo: The Iron Man released in Japan.
7.15.1989: Patlabor: The Movie released in Japan.
7.22.1989: Gunhed released in Japan.
7.23.1989: "Otaku Murderer" Tsutomu Miyazaki arrested.
11.9.1989: The Fall of the Berlin Wall takes place as the Cold War draws to a close.
12.16.1989: Godzilla vs. Biollante released in Japan.
5.11.1990: Dreams released in Japan.
12.22.1990: A Wind Named Amnesia released in Japan.
1.17.1991: U.S. led Operation Desert Storm begins in Kuwait.
3.16.1991: Mobile Suit Gundam F91 released in Japan.
3.24.1991: Stray Dog: Kerberos Panzer Cops released in Japan.
8.1991: The internet becomes available to the general public.
8.18.1991: Urusei Yatsura: Always My Darling released in Japan.
9.14.1991: Roujin Z released in Japan.

11.8.1991: Mikadroid released in Japan.
12.14.1991: Godzilla vs. King Ghidorah released in Japan.
12.21.1991: Zeiram released in Japan.
12.26.1991: The Soviet Union is officially dissolved.
3.7.1992: Sailor Moon begins airing on Japanese television.
12.12.1992: Godzilla vs. Mothra and *Legend of the Galactic Heroes: Golden Wings* released in Japan.
1.22.1993: Kobo Abe dies.
2.28.1993: Ishiro Honda dies.
7.17.1993: Samurai Kids released in Japan.
8.7.1993: Patlabor 2: The Movie released in Japan.
8.28.1993: Mighty Morphin' Power Rangers begins airing on U.S. television.
9.25.1993: Big Wars released in Japan.
12.11.1993: Godzilla vs. Mechagodzilla II released in Japan.
11.3.1994: Night Head released in Japan.
12.10.1994: Godzilla vs. Space Godzilla released in Japan.
12.17.1994: Zeiram 2 released in Japan.
1.17.1995: Hanshin earthquake strikes the Kobe area.
3.11.1995: Gamera: Guardian of the Universe released in Japan.
3.20.1995: Tokyo subway sarin gas attack by members of the Aum Shinrikyo cult.
10.4.1995: Neon Genesis Evangelion begins airing on Japanese television.
11.18.1995: Ghost in the Shell released in Japan.

12.9.1995: Godzilla vs. Destoroyah released in Japan.
12.23.1995: Memories released in Japan.
4.20.1996: Armitage III: Poly Matrix released in Japan.
12.14.1996: Rebirth of Mothra released in Japan.
2.1.1997: Parasite Eve released in Japan.
3.16-5.27.1997: Kobe child murders.
4.2.1997: Tomoyuki Tanaka dies.
7.1.1997: Mainland handover of Hong Kong from British rule.
7.19.1997: The End of Evangelion released in Japan.
11.8.1997: The Little Girl Who Conquered Time released in Japan.
11.29.1997: Moon Over Tao released in Japan.
12.13.1997: Rebirth of Mothra II released in Japan.
1.28.1998: Shotaro Ishinomori dies.
10.4.1998: Cowboy Bebop begins airing on Japanese television.
5.20.1998: Godzilla released in the U.S.
9.6.1998: Akira Kurosawa dies.
12.12.1998: Rebirth of Mothra III released in Japan.
3.6.1999: Gamera 3: Revenge of Iris released in Japan.
4.20.1999: Columbine school massacre in Colorado, U.S.
6.3.2000: Jin-Roh: The Wolf Brigade released in Japan.
12.3.2000: Jun Fukuda dies.
12.11.1999: Godzilla 2000 released in Japan.
6.10.2000: Pyrokinesis released in Japan.

12.16.2000: Godzilla vs. Megaguirus released in Japan.
4.21.2001: Vampire Hunter D: Bloodlust released in Japan.
5.26.2001: Metropolis released in Japan.
9.1.2001: Cowboy Bebop: The Movie released in Japan.
9.11.2001: September 11th terrorist attacks in U.S.
10.7.2001: The United States invades Afghanistan.
12.15.2001: Godzilla, Mothra and King Ghidorah: Giant Monsters All-Out Attack released in Japan.
8.31.2002: Returner released in Japan.
11.2002: Daiei's holdings acquired by Kadokawa.
12.14.2002: Godzilla Against Mechagodzilla released in Japan.
1.12.2003: Kinji Fukasaku dies.
3.19.2003: The United States invades Iraq.
6.14.2003: Noriaki Yuasa dies.
8.30.2003: Dragonhead released in Japan.
12.13.2003: Godzilla: Tokyo S.O.S released in Japan.
2.14.2004: Zebraman released in Japan.
3.5.2004: Ghost in the Shell 2: Innocence released in Japan.
4.18.2004: Appleseed released in Japan.
4.24.2004: Casshern released in Japan.
5.29.2004: Cutie Honey released in Japan.
7.17.2004: Steamboy released in Japan.
7.30.2004: The Calamari Wrestler released in Japan.

12.4.2004: Godzilla: Final Wars released in Japan.
2.19.2005: Kihachi Okamoto dies.
3.5.2005: Lorelei released in Japan.
3.19.2005: Tetsujin 28: The Movie released in Japan.
6.11.2005: Samurai Commando: Mission 1549 released in Japan.
9.1.2005: Astro Boy: Mighty Atom – Visitor of 100,000 Light Years, IGZA released in Japan.
9.14.2005: Final Fantasy VII: Advent Children released in Japan.
1.7.2006: Origin: Spirits of the Past released in Japan.
4.29.2006: Gamera the Brave released in Japan.
7.15.2006: Sinking of Japan and *The Girl Who Leapt Through Time* released in Japan.
9.2.2006: The World Sinks Except Japan released in Japan.
11.25.2006: Paprika released in Japan.
9.1.2007: Evangelion: 1.0 You Are (Not) Alone released in Japan.
10.20.2007: Appleseed Ex Machina released in Japan.
7.26.2008: Monster X Strikes Back: Attack the G8 Summit released in Japan.
8.2.2008: The Sky Crawlers released in Japan.
8.8-8.24.2008: Summer Olympics held in Beijing, China.
8.30.2008: 20th Century Boys released in Japan.
9.2008: Global financial crisis worsens.

1.31.2009: 20th Century Boys 2: The Last Hope released in Japan.

6.29.2009: Evangelion: 2.0 You Can (Not) Advance released in Japan.

8.1.2009: Summer Wars released in Japan.

8.29.2009: 20th Century Boys 3: Redemption released in Japan.

12.12.2009: Space Battleship Yamato: Resurrection released in Japan.

3.13.2010: Time Traveller: The Girl Who Leapt Through Time released in Japan.

5.1.2010: Zebraman 2: Attack on Zebra City released in Japan.

11.27.2010: Death Kappa released in Japan.

12.1.2010: Space Battleship Yamato released in Japan.

1.29.2011: GANTZ released in Japan.

3.11.2011: Tohoku earthquake and tsunami hits Japan, Fukushima Daiichi nuclear disaster.

4.23.2011: GANTZ 2: Perfect Answer released in Japan.

7.26.2011: Sakyo Komatsu dies.

10.14.2011: Steins;Gate begins airing on Japanese television.

10.27.2012: 009 Re:Cyborg released in Japan.

11.17.2012: Evangelion 3.0: You Can (Not) Redo released in Japan.

4.7.2013: Attack on Titan begins airing on Japanese television.

4.20.2013: Steins;Gate: The Movie – Load Region of Déjà Vu released in Japan.

11.23.2013: The Tale of the Princess Kaguya released in Japan.

5.16.2014: Godzilla released in the U.S.

10.25.2014: Garm Wars: The Last Druid released.

11.29.2014: Parasyte released in Japan.

12.5.2014: Koichi Kawakita dies.

4.25.2015: Parasyte: Part 2 released in Japan.

6.26.2015: Same-sex marriage legalized in the United States.

8.1.2015: Attack on Titan released in Japan.

9.19.2015: Attack on Titan Part 2: The End of the World released in Japan.

6.23.2016: United Kingdom votes to leave the European Union.

7.29.2016: Shin Godzilla released in Japan.

8.26.2016: Your Name released in Japan.

3.10.2017: Kong: Skull Island released in the U.S.

9.17.2017: North Korea fires ballistic missile over Japan.

11.17.2017: Godzilla: Planet of the Monsters released in Japan.

5.18.2018: Godzilla: City on the Edge of Battle released in Japan.

11.9.2018: Godzilla: The Planet Eater released in Japan.

2.14.2019: Alita: Battle Angel released in the U.S.

4.30.2019: Emperor Akihito abdicates and the Heisei era ends.

5.1.2019: Akihito's son Yoshihito succeeds him as Emperor, beginning the Reiwa era.

5.10.2019: Pokemon: Detective Pikachu released in the U.S.

6.3.2019: Godzilla: King of the Monster released in the U.S.

6.9.2019: Protests begin in Hong Kong.

12.31.2019: Outbreak of novel coronavirus COVID-19 first reported in Wuhan, China.

3.2020: 2020 Summer Olympics in Tokyo postponed due to COVID-19 pandemic.

4.10.2020: Nobuhiko Obayashi dies.

7.9.2020: Japan Sinks 2020 released worldwide.

8.28.2020: Shinzo Abe announces his resignation as Prime Minister.

9.16.2020: Yoshihide Suga succeeds Abe as Prime Minister.

12.11.2020: First COVID-19 vaccine approved.

3.8.2021: Evangelion: 3.0+1.0 Thrice Upon a Time released in Japan.

ABOUT THE AUTHOR

Jules L. Carrozza (1986-) is a movie and commercial director, copywriter, video editor, graphic designer, wine connoisseur and crazy person. He's had a passion for these films much of his life. As a boy, he wore out his dubbed VHS copies of the *Showa* Godzilla films. In school, he was more interested in learning about Ishiro Honda and Eiji Tsuburaya than reading, writing and arithmetic.

Carrozza is also keen on *anime* and Hong Kong cinema. He has written for websites and publications such as *Animerica, Toho Kingdom, Asian Cult Cinema, Monster Attack Team* and *Otaku USA*. This is his first book. His most recent films, the apocalyptic horror short *Fungus* (2019) and the sci-fi filmette *Visit* (2021), were influenced by Japanese science fiction. Carrozza also directed *Little Red Riding Hood* (2006) and *Eater* (2017). He conducted an in-depth video interview with late and controversial Chinese filmmaker and propagandist T.F. Mou in 2009. It is partially available on Massacre Video's Blu-ray of Mou's *Men Behind the Sun*.

His favorite non-Japanese genre films include *2001: A Space Odyssey, Alien, Blade Runner, Star Wars, A Clockwork Orange, Dawn of the Dead '78, The Lord of the Rings: The Fellowship of the Ring, Suspiria '77, King Kong '33, One Million Years B.C., Planet of the Apes '68* and *The Matrix*. He lives in Boston, Massachusetts with his cats but plans a move to Taiwan soon. He spends many nights listening to David Bowie and Pink Floyd. He also maintains his own website at *www.jlcarrozza.com*. His video editing arm is on Facebook, Instagram and YouTube as *"Goliath Post"*.

His upcoming books include *Japanese Special Effects Cinema: Godfathers of Tokusatsu, Tempestuous Showa: Japan's World War II Films, Commonwealth Chronicles: The People's History of Massachusetts, Hong Kong Pulp Cinema* and *SF 2: Classic Sci-Fi Anime*.

COMING SOON FROM OROCHI BOOKS

Tokusatsu is the art of Japanese cinematic special effects. From the dawn of cinema to the digital age, delve into the history of an underappreciated national art form. Find out the techniques used to bring *tokusatsu* films and television shows to life such as miniature sets, pyrotechnics, monster suit construction and innovative cinematography. Discover how each generation of artisans mentored the next. Get a candid look at the making of the effects sequences in monster classics like *Godzilla, Rodan, Mothra* and *Gamera*, along with iconic television franchises such as *Ultraman, Kamen Rider* and *Super Sentai*. Yet the medium of tokusatsu is not all monsters and heroes, it

also encompasses wartime propaganda, disaster films and even the Japanese equivalent to Biblical epics. **Japanese Special Effects Cinema: Godfathers of Tokusatsu** promises to take you on a thrilling historical journey through Japan's film industry.

Anime is one of Japan's iconic art forms and exports, an industry worth billions. It closely cohabitates with Japan's sci-fi legacy informed by wartime and disaster trauma. **SF 2** delves into decades of animated Japanese science fiction works from Osamu Tezuka to *Your Name*. Covered in deep analysis are classics such as *Nausicaa of the Valley of the Wind*, *Akira* and *Ghost in the Shell*. Iconic franchises like *Space Battleship Yamato*, *Gundam*, *Legend of the Galactic Heroes* and *Evangelion* are featured; alongside deeper cuts such as *Flying Phantom Ship*, *Future War 198X*, *Twilight of the Cockroaches* and *Robot Carnival*. **SF 2** will appeal to casual fans looking to delve deeper and diehard *otaku* alike.

This book also features informative articles and insider information.

Find out the secrets of Japan's anime industry. Read about luminaries of the genre: Leiji Matsumoto, Katsuhiro Otomo, Yoshiyuki Tomino, Mamoru Oshii, Yoshiaki Kawajiri, Go Nagai and many more. **SF 2: Classic Sci-Fi Anime** covers Japan's anime culture, science fiction history and the geniuses who put it in motion.